Child Sexual Abuse in Civil Cases

Child Sexual Abuse in Civil Cases

A Guide to Custody and Tort Actions

Ann M. Haralambie

Section of Family Law
American Bar Association

Cover design by Kathy Karrys.

This book has built on (and sometimes used verbatim parts from) ANN M. HARALAMBIE, HANDLING CHILD CUSTODY, ABUSE, AND ADOPTION CASES (2nd ed., Clark Boardman Callaghan 1993, West Group 1997). Such parts of that work are reprinted with permission of West Group. I appreciate the West Group's permission to reprint those portions without specific reference to each use.

Pages 220–228, Reprinted by Permission of Sage Publications, Inc.

03 02 01 00 99   5 4 3 2 1

Haralambie, Ann M.
Civil aspects of child sexual abuse / by Ann M. Haralambie.
p. cm.
Includes bibliographical references and index.
ISBN 1-57073-662-6
1. Incest—United States. 2. Child sexual abuse—United States.
3. Actions and defenses—United States. 4. Evidence, Expert—United States. I. Title.
KF9323.H34 1999
345.73'02536—dc21   99-12691
CIP

Discounts are available for books ordered in bulk. Special consideration is given to state bars, CLE programs, and other bar-related organizations. Inquire at Book Publishing, ABA Publishing, American Bar Association, 750 North Lake Shore Drive, Chicago, Illinois 60611.

www.abanet.org/abapubs

In loving memory of
Sonia J. Young, R.N.,
who always kept me centered on God
and let me focus on the good I could do
rather than on the despair in my clients' lives

until we meet again, my friend

Slán agus beannacht

CONTENTS

CHAPTER 7
MEDICAL AND PHYSICAL EVALUATIONS OF SEXUAL ABUSE ALLEGATIONS 199

CHAPTER 8
REPRESENTING THE PROTECTIVE PARENT OR INTERVENOR 231

ACKNOWLEDGMENTS

This book has been a difficult one for me to complete because my best friend and mentor died in the middle of its preparation. To those who helped me through the grief, you have my undying thanks and respect: Jean Baker, Anna Binkiewicz, Irene and Louis Bracke, John and Maura Campbell, John and Marguerite Casteel, Deborah Glaser Chagal, Rich Cozzola, Howard Davidson, Barbara Hassel, Carla Hinton, Mike Keyes, Michael Kroack, Kee MacFarlane, Joan Mendelson, Jean Koh Peters, Velma Perez, Marcia and Jennifer Purcell, Donna Rosenberg, Eileen Schrader, Anastasia Smith, Maria Vindiola, Jean Wortman. Thanks for listening. And my greatest joy, who prophetically answered my sorrow, my undying love to Dominic Galen Fernie, my first grandchild, born a month before my friend's death.

I appreciate the patience and understanding of Barbara Stark and the rest of the American Bar Association Family Law Section Publications Board for allowing a two-year delay in the delivery of my manuscript.

Child sexual abuse is one of the most difficult types of legal cases to try. What passes as expert testimony is too often personal opinion that cannot properly be called science. The failure of experts to police themselves, or even to know how many of their conclusions are based on "junk science," and the inability of lawyers and judges to scrutinize that testimony has resulted in too many incorrect results. Incorrect decisions can improperly rupture parent-child relationships or fail to protect a child, sometimes throwing the child into his or her molester's arms. A lawyer trying a child sexual abuse case needs the help of good, multidisciplinary expertise. I have been fortunate to have had many experts educate me, answer my ongoing questions, and provide me with their research studies pending publication.

Pediatrician Donna Rosenberg, M.D., has reminded me of the importance of distinguishing good science from "junk science" and has eloquently expressed what science is and how to put it to the test in the courtroom. Researchers Judith Becker, Ph.D., Gail Goodman, Ph.D., and Karen J. Saywitz, Ph.D., have been generous in keeping me informed and supplied with the latest research, and in answering my questions. Researcher and clinician Kathleen Coulbourne Faller, Ph.D., has been ready to answer my questions and point me in the right direction. Pediatrician Anna I. S. Binkiewicz, M.D., and psychologists Jean M. Baker, Ph.D., and Rachel B. Burkholder, Ph.D., continue to educate and challenge me. Howard Davidson and the rest of his colleagues at the ABA Center on Children and the Law are willing and consistent resources. My numerous interdisciplinary colleagues from the National Association of Counsel for Children and the American Professional Society on the Abuse of Children continue to provide me with information, fellowship, and a platform.

I appreciate the general reprint permission for my adaptation of two articles from the American Bar Association, Ann M. Haralambie, *Child Sexual Abuse: Defending the Alleged Abuser* 17/3 FAMILY ADVOCATE 52 (winter 1995) and Ann M. Haralambie, *Child Sexual Abuse: Representing the Accuser* 17/3 FAMILY ADVOCATE 61 (winter 1995).

Sonia, I have appreciated your help and support before and during my work on this book, even while you were dying of cancer. You taught me that abused children must still be responsible for their lives, getting past their earlier experiences. You taught me not to wallow in their circumstances but to help them move on. You taught me most of what I have needed to know about what is important for life and godliness. You were a living witness of God's love. You planted and watered, and you gave me my wings.

Finally, thank you, Lord, for sticking with me whether I've been aware of it or not. You have enabled me to do what You have called me to do. May it be to Your glory.

FOREWORD

As I write this I streak across the sky at more than 500 miles an hour, seated comfortably (well, maybe not comfortably) in a middle seat in the coach section of a Boeing 737. The electronic marvel that translates my finger strokes into words on a computer screen hums quietly on my lap. What a far cry is this modern jet from the Wright brothers' humble biplane. And what a marvel is this laptop computer compared to the first typewriter. Yet, the first airplane and the earliest typewriter were state-of-the-art in their time. It is only from the vantage point of the late twentieth century that early prototypes seem primitive. Breakthroughs, whether technological, scientific, or social, often look clumsy in time's rear-view mirror.

But what has this to do with Ann Haralambie's new book on child sexual abuse? As it turns out, quite a bit. This book is the literary equivalent of the modern jet plane. The past twenty years witnessed remarkable improvements in the investigation and litigation of allegations of child sexual abuse. Although the American legal and social services systems never ignored sexual abuse, few would disagree that sexual abuse was largely hidden until the late 1970s and early 1980s. Only during the past twenty years did child sexual abuse emerge from relative obscurity. Indeed, examine the *Index to Legal Periodicals and Books* and you will find that the topic "child sexual abuse" did not appear until 1991! Thus, the recognition of child sexual abuse twenty years ago was a major breakthrough. Given the relatively recent recognition of child sexual abuse, it should come as no surprise that some of the investigative and courtroom methods used during the early 1980s seem clumsy compared to today's techniques. In particular, early investigative interviewing was primitive compared to interviewing today. During the early '80s, little was known about children's suggestibility, and interviewers paid little heed to the risks of suggestive and leading questions during interviews. Today, by contrast, interviewers are trained about suggestibility, and are taught to minimize the use of suggestive and leading questions. Turning from investigative interviewing to the courtroom, the 1990s witnessed significantly improved understanding of the uses and abuses of expert testimony in child sexual abuse cases. Additionally, important steps were taken to alter time-honored courtroom practices in order to accommodate child witnesses. Thus, we have come a long way toward greater understanding of child sexual abuse and of how to respond to this serious sociolegal problem. The techniques of 1980 resemble the Wright brothers' biplane when we stack them up against today's more sophisticated approach.

The beauty of this book—written by the person I believe to be America's leading practitioner-scholar on child abuse—is its comprehensive yet accessible synthesis of twenty years of experience and learning about child sexual abuse. Whether you are a novice in these matters or a veteran, you will find this book a *tour de force* of useful knowledge, insight, and information. As I mention above, Ann has written the literary equivalent of the modern jet plane. So, fasten your seat belt, return your tray table to the upright and locked position, sit back, and enjoy the flight as you glean from these pages the most up-to-date information on child sexual abuse.

John E. B. Myers
Professor of Law
University of the Pacific
McGeorge School of Law
Sacramento, California

About the Author

Ann M. Haralambie is an attorney in private practice in Tucson, Arizona, where she limits her practice to juvenile and domestic relations cases. She is a certified family law specialist, fellow of the American Academy of Matrimonial Lawyers, president of the Arizona Association of Counsel for Children, past president of the National Association of Counsel for Children, and life charter member of the American Professional Society on the Abuse of Children. She was a member of the Advisory Committee for the National Judicial Education Program, Adjudicating Allegations of Child Sexual Abuse When Custody Is in Dispute: A Model Curriculum for Judges and Court Personnel (1995–1996). In 1986, she received the Child Advocacy Award from the Arizona Council of Attorneys for Children. In 1995 she was a Child Advocacy National Certificate of Recognition recipient from the Young Lawyers Division of the American Bar Association. In 1993 she was a Harrison Tweed Special Merit Award recipient from the American Law Institute-American Bar Association Committee on Continuing Legal Education.

1 Understanding Child Sexual Abuse

How Big Is the Problem?

The most recent statistics[1] available show an increase in the number of child sexual abuse cases both reported and substantiated. The Third National Incidence Study of Child Abuse and Neglect (NIS-3)[2] found that the number of children whose sexual abuse was substantiated and resulted in harm to the child (their more restrictive definition) had more than doubled between 1986 and 1993. It is likely that increased reporting is more a function of professional and public awareness than of a real increase in sexual abuse.[3] Further, much

1. In reviewing statistical reports, it is important to note that "incidence" refers to the number of new cases in a defined population over a specific period of time, and "prevalence" refers to the total number of cases existing in a defined population at a specific period or point of time.

2. National Center on Child Abuse and Neglect, Third National Incidence Study of Child Abuse and Neglect (1996).

3. *See, e.g.*, David Finkelhor, *Current Information on the Scope and Nature of Child Sexual Abuse*, 4 The Future of Children 31 (1994); William Feldman, Eva Feldman, John T. Goodman, Patrick McGrath, Robert P. Pless, Linda Corsini & Susan Bennett, *Is Childhood Sexual Abuse Really Increasing in Prevalence?: An Analysis of the Evidence*, 88/1 Pediatrics 29 (1991).

sexual abuse is never reported, and therefore is not reflected in any of the statistics.[4] There has been a recent decline in the rate of reporting child abuse, which the reporting states attribute to a change in data system, increased public awareness, more community involvement, definitional changes, and caseworker workloads.[5] There was also a decline in the proportion of reported cases involving sexual abuse allegations.[6] It is estimated that over 200,000 children were reported as victims of sexual abuse in 1996, with 87,210 new cases of child sexual abuse being accepted for service.[7] While various studies employ differing methodologies and use of terminology,[8] all of the available incidence studies document that child sexual abuse remains a significant problem in our society, affecting both male and female victims from infancy through adolescence.[9]

WHAT CONSTITUTES CHILD SEXUAL ABUSE?

As used in this book, intrafamilial child sexual abuse involves sexual contact or activity with a member of one's family or household, including sexual activity with one's natural or adopted children, stepchildren, or children of one's "significant other." It is often referred to as incest. Such sexual abuse does not require that there be intercourse, or even that there be actual contact. Having a child watch one masturbate or taking pornographic pictures of a child con-

---

4. *See, e.g.*, David Finkelhor, *Current Information on the Scope and Nature of Child Sexual Abuse*, 4 THE FUTURE OF CHILDREN 31 (1994); Jessie Anderson, Judy Martin, Paul Mullen, Sarah Romans & Peter Herbison, *Prevalence of Childhood Sexual Abuse Experiences in a Community Sample of Women*, 32 J. AM. ACADEMY OF CHILD & ADOLESCENT PSYCHIATRY 911 (1993).

5. Ching-Tung Wang & Deborah Daro, *Current Trends in Child Abuse Reporting and Fatalities: The Results of the 1996 Annual Fifty State Survey* 6 (National Committee to Prevent Child Abuse 1997). The annual reports of the National Center on Child Abuse Prevention Research, a program of the NCPCA, are available from the organization at 332 S. Michigan Avenue, Suite 1600, Chicago, Ill. 60604, (312) 663-3520, fax (312) 939-8962, web site http://www.childabuse.org.

6. *Id.* at 7. In 1986 sexual abuse constituted 16 percent of all reports. By 1996 it constituted only 7 percent of all reports and 9 percent of substantiated reports. *Id.*

7. *Id.* at 9-10.

8. *See generally*, Sharon G. Portwood, *Coming to Terms with a Consensual Definition of Child Maltreatment*, 4/1 CHILD MALTREATMENT 56 (1999); Ching-Tung Wang & Deborah Daro, CURRENT TRENDS IN CHILD ABUSE REPORTING AND FATALITIES: THE RESULTS OF THE 1996 ANNUAL FIFTY STATE SURVEY (National Committee to Prevent Child Abuse 1997); Timothy F. Wynkoop, Steven C. Capps & Bobby J. Priest, *Incidence and Prevalence of Child Sexual Abuse: A Critical Review of Data Collection Procedures*, 4/2 J. CHILD SEXUAL ABUSE 49 (1995); Michael E. Lamb, *The Investigation of Child Sexual Abuse: An International, Interdisciplinary Consensus Statement*, 28/1 FAM. L. Q. 151 (1994); John Briere, *Methodological Issues in the Study of Sexual Abuse Effects*, 60/2 J. CONSULTING & CLINICAL PSYCHOL. 196 (1992).

9. *See, e.g.*, David M. Greenberg, John Bradford & Susan Curry, *Infantophilia—A New Subcategory of Pedophilia?: A Preliminary Study*, 23 BULL. AM. ACADEMY OF PSYCHIATRY AND LAW 63 (1995); David Finkelhor, *Current Information on the Scope and Nature of Child Sexual Abuse*, 4 THE FUTURE OF CHILDREN 31 (1994).

stitutes sexual abuse even when the adult never touches the child. Similarly, having children engage in sexual contact with one another while the adult watches constitutes sexual abuse. Fondling over clothing can also be sexual abuse.[10] Fondling, oral-genital contact, romantic kissing, inserting objects in a child's vagina or anus, digital penetration, and penile penetration are other forms of sexual abuse.[11]

The Child Abuse Prevention and Treatment and Adoption Reform Act[12] defines sexual abuse for the purposes of that Act as including:

> (A) the employment, use, persuasion, inducement, enticement, or coercion of any child to engage in, or assist any other person to engage in, any sexually explicit conduct or simulation of such conduct for the purpose of producing a visual depiction of such conduct; or
>
> (B) the rape, and in cases of caretaker or inter-familial relationships, statutory rape, molestation, prostitution, or other form of sexual exploitation of children, or incest with children.

A more conceptual definition was provided by Drs. Ruth and C. Henry Kempe, who saw sexual abuse as "the involvement of dependent, developmentally immature children and adolescents in sexual activities that they do not fully comprehend, to which they are unable to give informed consent, or that violate the social taboos of family roles."[13]

The DIAGNOSTIC AND STATISTICAL MANUAL OF MENTAL DISORDERS[14] (DSM-IV), referring specifically to the disorder of pedophilia, 302.2, states that:

---

10. *See, e.g.*, Matter of Jennifer M., 229 A.D.2d 940, 645 N.Y.S.2d 231 (1996).

11. Psychiatrist David Jones divides "child sexual abuse" into direct sexual acts (contacting child's genital or anal area; anal, vaginal, or oral penetration; and other acts in which the child is the object of the adult's gratification, such as bondage, frotteurism, ejaculation onto the child, and fondling of a postpubertal child's breasts) and indirect sexual acts (genital exposure, production of pornographic material, encouraging children to have sex together, and exposing children to pornographic material). He defines "child sexual abuse" as "the actual or likely occurrence of a sexual act (or acts) perpetrated on a child by another person." *See* David P. H. Jones, *Assessment of Suspected Child Sexual Abuse*, in THE BATTERED CHILD 296, 296-297 (Mary Edna Helfer, Ruth S. Kempe & Richard D. Krugman, eds., 5th ed. 1997).

12. 42 U.S.C.A. § 5106g(4).

13. *See* RUTH S. KEMPE & C. HENRY KEMPE, CHILD ABUSE 43 (1978).

14. AMERICAN PSYCHIATRIC ASSOCIATION, DIAGNOSTIC AND STATISTICAL MANUAL OF MENTAL DISORDERS (4th ed. 1994).

> Individuals with pedophilia who act on their urges with children may limit their activity to undressing the child and looking, exposing themselves, masturbating in the presence of the child, or gentle touching or fondling of the child. Others, however, perform fellatio or cunnilingus on the child or penetrate the child's vagina, mouth, or anus with their fingers, foreign objects, or penis and use varying degrees of force to do so. These activities are commonly explained with excuses or rationalizations that they have "educational value" for the child, that the child derives "sexual pleasure" from them, or that the child was "sexually provocative"—themes that are also common in pedophiliac pornography.[15]

In addition to the actual abuse, a person who molests a child may bribe or threaten the child to secure his or her acquiescence.[16] This "complicity" by the child in the act of abuse may make the child feel responsible or guilty, especially if the child derived some pleasure from the molestation. This may contribute to the child's reluctance or unwillingness to disclose the abuse. The child may also be directly threatened not to disclose.[17]

Prentky, Knight, and Lee report that while the DSM-IV diagnostic criteria "may succeed in isolating the 'pedophilic' child molester, it fails to capture those incest and extrafamilial offenders without known 6-month histories of sexualized interest in children . . . [which will] inevitably screen out a large number of child molesters."[18] Therefore, Prentky believes that the DSM-IV will fail to provide adequate coverage in classifying most child molesters.[19]

WHO COMMITS CHILD SEXUAL ABUSE?

The stereotypical picture of a child molester is the "dirty old man" in a trench coat hanging around playgrounds and elementary-school

---

15. *Id.* at 527-528.

16. *See, e.g.*, Thomas Lyon, *The Effect of Threats on Children's Disclosure of Sexual Abuse*, 9 THE APSAC ADVISOR 9 (1996); Gail S. Goodman & Beth M. Schwartz-Kenney, *Why Knowing a Child's Age Is Not Enough: Influences of Cognitive, Social, and Emotional Factors on Children's Testimony*, in CHILDREN AS WITNESSES (Helen Dent & Rhona Flin, eds. 1992).

17. AMERICAN PSYCHIATRIC ASSOCIATION, DIAGNOSTIC AND STATISTICAL MANUAL OF MENTAL DISORDERS 527-528 (4th ed. 1994).

18. *See* Robert A. Prentky, Raymond A. Knight & Austin F.S. Lee, *Child Sexual Molestation: Research Issues* 4 (National Institute of Justice 1997).

19. *See* Robert A. Prentky, *Child Sexual Molestation*, in HANDBOOK OF PSYCHOLOGICAL APPROACHES WITH VIOLENT OFFENDERS: CONTEMPORARY STRATEGIES AND ISSUES 267 (M. Hersen & V. van Hasselt, eds., 1999).

fences. Such a person is typically a predatory pedophile, whose primary or only sexual attraction is to children. Most incestuous offenders do not fit this stereotype. In fact, most predatory pedophiles do not fit the stereotype either. Some people are sexually attracted to children in general and may seek out opportunities to be with children, often in socially accepted positions such as scout leader, coach, or Sunday School teacher. The DSM-IV points out that except where pedophilia is associated with sexual sadism, "the person may be attentive to the child's needs in order to gain the child's affection, interest, and loyalty and to prevent the child from reporting the sexual activity."[20]

Other persons do not have primary sexual attraction to children but end up molesting children in their own household out of their improper responses to various stressful situations.[21] The DSM-IV classifies pedophilia, 302.2, as either Exclusive Type, where the sexual attraction is only towards children, or Nonexclusive Type, where the sexual attraction may also be to adults.[22]

The DSM-IV states that some pedophiles,

> particularly those who frequently victimize children, develop complicated techniques for obtaining access to children which may include winning the trust of the child's mother, marrying a woman with an attractive child, trading children with other individuals with Pedophilia, or in rare instances, taking in foster children from nonindustrialized countries or abducting children from strangers.[23]

Further, the person may be attracted just to males, just to females, or to both.[24] While the disorder generally begins in adolescence, some pedophiles report that they did not become aroused by children until middle age.[25] The frequency of the sexual activity "often fluctuates

---

20. AMERICAN PSYCHIATRIC ASSOCIATION, DIAGNOSTIC AND STATISTICAL MANUAL OF MENTAL DISORDERS 528 (4th ed. 1994).

21. The DSM-IV states that "[i]ndividuals may limit their activities to their own children, stepchildren, or relatives or may victimize children outside their families." *Id.*

22. *Id.* at 527-528.

23. *Id.* at 528.

24. *Id.*

25. *Id.*

with psychosocial stress."[26] Marital discord, divorce, moving out of the family home, and the tension that often accompanies visitation and other communications during domestic-relations litigation certainly constitute psychosocial stress, which may exacerbate such inappropriate sexual behavior.[27]

The perpetrator does not have to be an adult for the activity to constitute child sexual abuse. Any time there is a great disparity in power and authority, such as between a teenage child and a young sibling or step-sibling, sexual contact takes on the characterization of abuse.[28] The type of sexual abuse being discussed in this book is that committed by or with the knowledge of family members or de facto members of one's household, or the failure of a family member to protect the child from sexual abuse once it is revealed.

While the great majority of child sexual abuse is committed by males, females may also molest children.[29] It is likely that the number of female perpetrators is under-reported and underestimated.[30] The few studies available indicate that females may be more likely to molest females than males,[31] but it is widely believed that sexual abuse of males, especially by females, is greatly under-reported.[32] Therefore, those statistics may be particularly unreliable. Societal stereotypes often support the idea that a male molested by a female

---

26. *Id.*

27. The psychodynamics of sexual abuse surrounding divorce or post-divorce litigation are dealt with more fully in Chapter 2.

28. For example, the DSM-IV diagnostic criteria for pedophilia require for that particular diagnosis that the perpetrator be at least sixteen years old and at least five years older than the victim. *Id.* at 528.

29. *See generally*, FEMALE SEXUAL ABUSE OF CHILDREN (Michele Elliott, ed., 1993); C.M. ALLEN, WOMEN AND MEN WHO SEXUALLY ABUSE CHILDREN: A COMPARATIVE ANALYSIS (1991); Anne Banning, *Mother-Son Incest: Confronting a Prejudice*, 13/4 CHILD ABUSE & NEGLECT 563 (1989); Kathleen Faller, *Women Who Sexually Abuse Children*, 2 VIOLENCE & VICTIMS 263 (1987).

30. *See, e.g.*, C. ALLEN, A COMPARISON OF SEXUAL ABUSE PERPETRATED AND EXPERIENCED BY FEMALE AND MALE CHILD SEXUAL OFFENDERS (1991); C. Allen, *Women as Perpetrators of Child Sexual Abuse: Recognition Barriers*, in THE INCEST PERPETRATOR 108 (A. Horton, B. Johnson, L. Roundy & D. Williams, eds. 1990).

31. *See, e.g.*, Peter Fehrenbach & Caren Monastersky, *Characteristics of Female Adolescent Sexual Offenders*, 58/1 AM. J. ORTHOPSYCHIATRY 148 (1988) (57.1 percent of sample abused females, 35.7 percent abused males); Kathleen C. Faller, *Women Who Sexually Abuse Children*, 2 VIOLENCE AND VICTIMS 263 (1987). *Cf.* Kathleen C. Faller, *A Clinical Sample of Women Who Have Sexually Abused Children*, 4/3 J. CHILD SEXUAL ABUSE 13 (1995) (48.6 percent of sample abused both males and females, 40.3 percent abused only females, 11.1 percent abused only males).

32. *See, e.g.*, CHRISTIANE SANDERSON, COUNSELLING ADULT SURVIVORS OF CHILD SEXUAL ABUSE (1990); Anthony J. Urquiza & L.M. Keating, *The Prevalence of Sexual Victimization of Males* in 1 THE SEXUALLY ABUSED MALE: PREVALENCE, IMPACT, AND TREATMENT (Mic Hunter, ed. 1990); FRANK G. BOLTON, LARRY A. MORRIS & ANN E. MACEACHRON, MALES AT RISK: THE OTHER SIDE OF CHILD SEXUAL ABUSE (1989); E. PORTER, TREATING THE YOUNG MALE VICTIM OF SEXUAL ASSAULT: ISSUES AND INTERVENTION STRATEGIES (1986); David Finkelhor, *Sexual Abuse of Boys* in RAPE AND SEXUAL ASSAULT 97 (Ann W. Burgess, ed. 1985).

is "lucky" rather than victimized.[33] Further, a male may be particularly embarrassed to admit being abused by a female, who is supposed to be weaker. Females may molest children either accompanied or coerced by males,[34] which differs from male perpetrators, who are far less likely to molest with a cohort.

Females may also observe abuse by males but fail to intervene to protect the child, sometimes out of fear or excessive dependence on the male perpetrator. The author once represented a male molester[35] whose wife sat on the bed holding the child's hand while the father molested her. The mother said she objected to the abuse, felt helpless to stop it, and wanted to "be supportive" to her daughter.

WHAT ARE THE EFFECTS OF INTRAFAMILIAL CHILD SEXUAL ABUSE?

In many ways intrafamilial sexual abuse is more devastating to children than molestation by a stranger.[36] When a stranger molests a child, the family usually pulls together to support the child in a protective fashion. Where can the child run for help and protection when it is a household member who is doing the molesting? Lack of family support is the worst post-abuse environment for the sexual

---

33. *See, e.g.*, Deloris T. Roys & Robert J. Timms, *Personality Profiles of Adult Males Sexually Molested by Their Maternal Caregivers: Preliminary Findings*, 4/4 J. CHILD SEXUAL ABUSE 63 (1995).

34. *See, e.g.*, Kathleen C. Faller, *A Clinical Sample of Women Who Have Sexually Abused Children*, 4/3 J. CHILD SEXUAL ABUSE 13 (1995); Keith L. Kaufman, Anne M. Wallace, Charles Felzen Johnson & Mark Lesley Reeder, *Comparing Female and Male Perpetrators' Modus Operandi: Victims' Reports of Sexual Abuse*, 10/3 J. INTERPERSONAL VIOLENCE 322 (1995); E. Rowan, J. Rowan & P. Langelier, *Women Who Molest Children*, 18/1 BULL. AM. ACAD. PSYCHIATRY & L. (1990); RUTH MATHEWS, J. MATHEWS & K. SPELTZ, FEMALE SEXUAL OFFENDERS: AN EXPLORATORY STUDY (1989); L. M. McCarty, *Mother-Child Incest: Characteristics of the Offender*, 65/5 CHILD WELFARE 447 (1986); Florence A. Wolf, *Twelve Female Sexual Offenders* (1985), *cited in* Peter Fehrenbach & Caren Monastersky, *Characteristics of Female Adolescent Sexual Offenders*, 58/1 AM. J. ORTHOPSYCHIATRY 148 (1988); David Finkelhor & Diana Russell, *Women as Perpetrators: Review of the Evidence* in DAVID FINKELHOR, CHILD SEXUAL ABUSE: NEW THEORY AND RESEARCH 171 (1984).

35. In the mid-1980s the author represented a number of men who had admitted to molesting their children or stepchildren, who were criminally prosecuted, and who retained the author in order to get a "therapeutic" sentence, usually requiring jail time with work-release. This benefitted the children because the perpetrators admitted their guilt, took full responsibility for it, apologized to the children, and continued to earn a living to support the children and their mothers. The men were never permitted to return home sooner than one to two years after conviction and intensive therapy. Most families divorced and did not ever return to living together.

36. *See, e.g.*, Clare Davenport, Kevin Browne & Robert Palmer, *Opinions on the Traumatizing Effects of Child Sexual Abuse: Evidence for Consensus*, 18/9 CHILD ABUSE & NEGLECT 725 (1994).

abuse victim.[37] Further, the important bond of trust that is established between children and the adult authorities in their homes is betrayed and broken when one of those adults misuses that authority and power over the child to sexualize the child.[38] The scars from that betrayal can run very deep, affecting the molested children into adulthood and complicating their relationships with future sexual partners. Psychiatrist and child-abuse expert Brandt Steele has written that "[s]exual abuse is more complex in its origin, expression, and impact than other forms of child maltreatment."[39]

Some offenders feel that their molestations were relatively minor because there was "no penetration." But the wounds of intrafamilial child sexual abuse are as much about the betrayal of innocence and trust and the shattering of the family as a place of safety, as about the sexual acts themselves. It may be as devastating for a child to be fondled repeatedly as it is to be penetrated. The sense of shame and the loss of self-esteem, as well as the impediments to trusting people in the future, are the same, whether there was penetration or not.

Male victims of sexual abuse tend to be particularly angry.[40] They may externalize that anger through aggressive and antisocial behavior.[41] They may become depressed, remaining depressed even

---

37. *See, e.g.*, Delores D. Stroud, *Familial Support as Perceived by Adult Victims of Childhood Sexual Abuse* 11/2 SEXUAL ABUSE: A JOURNAL OF RESEARCH & TREATMENT 159 (1999); Esther Deblinger, Robert Steer & Julie Lippmann, *Maternal Factors Associated with Sexually Abused Children's Psychosocial Adjustment*, 4/1 CHILD MALTREATMENT 13 (1999); Nancy C. Morrison & Jeanine Clavenna-Valleroy, *Perceptions of Maternal Support as Related to Self-Concept and Self-Report of Depression in Sexually Abused Female Adolescents*, 7/1 J. CHILD SEXUAL ABUSE 23 (1998); Clare Davenport, Kevin Browne & Robert Palmer, *Opinions on the Traumatizing Effects of Child Sexual Abuse: Evidence for Consensus*, 18/9 CHILD ABUSE & NEGLECT 725 (1994); C. Bagley & R. Ramsey, *Sexual Abuse in Childhood: Psychological Outcomes and Implications for Social Work Practice* in SOCIAL WORK PRACTICE IN SEXUAL PROBLEMS (J. Gripton & M. Valentich, eds., 1986).

38. Child psychologist Elizabeth Seagull describes a related problem as follows:

> Sexually abusive parents distort the nurturant function by using physical closeness with the child to meet the adult's needs. When sexual abuse has been intertwined with nurturance, children are quite confused about the difference between nurturance and sexuality. In some families the sexualized relationship will have been the child's only significant experience of warmth. Replacing such experiences with healthy loving relationships in the family must be carefully considered in the treatment of the incestuous family. Simply removing the offender does not solve this problem.

Elizabeth A.W. Seagull, *Family Assessment*, in THE BATTERED CHILD 150, 165 (Mary Edna Helfer, Ruth S. Kempe & Richard D. Krugman, eds., 5th ed. 1997).

39. *See* Brandt F. Steele, *Psychodynamic and Biological Factors in Child Maltreatment* in THE BATTERED CHILD 73, 83 (Mary Edna Helfer, Ruth S. Kempe & Richard D. Krugman, eds., 5th ed. 1997).

40. *See, e.g.*, John Briere, Diane Evans, Marsha Runtz & Timothy Wall, *Symptomatology in Men Who Were Abused as Children: A Comparison Study*, 58/3 AM. J. OF ORTHOPSYCHIATRY 457 (1988).

41. *See, e.g.*, Joseph M. Chandy, Robert W. Blum & Michael D. Resnick, *Sexually Abused Male Adolescents: How Vulnerable Are They?*, 6/2 J. CHILD SEXUAL ABUSE 1 (1997); James M. Hepburn, *The Implications of Contemporary Feminist Theories of Development for the Treatment of Male Victims of Sexual Abuse*, 3/4 J. CHILD SEXUAL ABUSE 1 (1994); A. J. Urquiza & M. Capra, *The Impact of Sexual Abuse: Initial and Long-Term Effects* in 1 THE SEXUALLY ABUSED MALE: PREVALENCE, IMPACT, AND TREATMENT (M. Hunter, ed. 1990).

as adults.[42] If they were molested by another male, they may question their sexual identity.[43] They are more likely to become perpetrators themselves.[44]

While there may not be a profile or syndrome diagnostic of child sexual abuse, experts may testify that various behaviors, symptoms, and disorders are consistent with sexual abuse.[45] Explicit sexualized play in the absence of a history explaining the child's knowledge (such as exposure to watching people engaged in sexual activity or exposure to sexually explicit pornographic material) is a frequently discussed behavior that may be indicative of sexual abuse.[46] It is important to remember, however, that not all molested children engage in sexualized play.

Sexually molested children may have immediate behavior changes, such as depression, aggression, somatic complaints, nightmares and other sleep problems, eating problems, regressed behaviors (such as toilet-trained children who lose bowel and bladder control, thumb-sucking, reversion to a bottle, and so on), clinging behaviors, sexual acting out or promiscuity, seductive behaviors, self-mutilation, substance abuse, and suicide gestures and attempts, with some of these behaviors persisting over time.[47] Children may suffer

---

42. *See, e.g.*, Joseph M. Chandy, Robert W. Blum & Michael D. Resnick, *Sexually Abused Male Adolescents: How Vulnerable Are They?*, 6/2 J. CHILD SEXUAL ABUSE 1 (1997); Deloris T. Roys & Robert J. Timms, *Personality Profiles of Adult Males Sexually Molested by Their Maternal Caregivers: Preliminary Findings*, 4/4 J. CHILD SEXUAL ABUSE 63 (1995).

43. *See, e.g.*, Deloris T. Roys & Robert J. Timms, *Personality Profiles of Adult Males Sexually Molested by Their Maternal Caregivers: Preliminary Findings*, 4/4 J. CHILD SEXUAL ABUSE 63 (1995); James M. Hepburn, *The Implications of Contemporary Feminist Theories of Development for the Treatment of Male Victims of Sexual Abuse*, 3/4 J. CHILD SEXUAL ABUSE 1 (1994).

44. *See, e.g.*, James M. Hepburn, *The Implications of Contemporary Feminist Theories of Development for the Treatment of Male Victims of Sexual Abuse*, 3/4 J. CHILD SEXUAL ABUSE 1 (1994).

45. *See, e.g.*, Broderick v. King's Way Assembly of God Church, 808 P2.d 1211 (Alaska 1991); Ward v. State, 519 So.2d 1082 (Fla. Dist. Ct. App. 1988); State v. Reser, 244 Kan. 306, 767 P.2d 1277 (1989); State v. Alberico, 116 N.M. 156, 861 P.2d 192 (1993); State v. Speller, 102 N.C. App. 697, 404 S.E.2d 15 (1991); State v. Schumpert, 435 S.E.2d 859 (S.C. 1993).

46. *See generally* W. Friedrich, *Sexual Victimization and Sexual Behavior in Children: A Review of Recent Literature*, 17/1 CHILD ABUSE & NEGLECT 59 (1993).

47. *See, e.g.*, Kelli L. Korte, Connie Burrows Horton & Daniel Graybill, *Child Sexual Abuse and Bulimic Behaviors: An Exploratory Investigation of the Frequency and Nature of a Relationship*, 7/1 J. CHILD SEXUAL ABUSE 53 (1998); 1 JOHN E. B. MYERS, EVIDENCE IN CHILD ABUSE AND NEGLECT CASES § 5.3 (3rd ed. 1997); David M. Fergusson, L. John Horwood & Michael T. Lynskey, *Childhood Sexual Abuse, Adolescent Sexual Behaviors and Sexual Revictimization* 21/8 CHILD ABUSE & NEGLECT 789 (1997); David B. Sarwer, Isiaah Crawford & Joseph A. Durlak, *The Relationship Between Childhood Sexual Abuse and Adult Male Sexual Dysfunction*, 21/7 CHILD ABUSE & NEGLECT 649 (1997); Patricia A. Harrison, Jayne A. Fulkerson & Timothy J. Beebe, *Multiple Substance Abuse Among Adolescent Physical and Sexual Abuse Victims*, 21/6 CHILD ABUSE & NEGLECT 529 (1997); Jan Morrow, Catherine A. Yeager & Dorothy Otnow Lewis, *Encopresis and Sexual Abuse in a Sample of Boys in Residential Treatment*, 21/1 CHILD ABUSE & NEGLECT 11 (1997); Joseph M. Chandy, Robert W. Blum & Michael D. Resnick, *Gender-Specific Outcomes for Sexually Abused Adolescents*, 20/12 CHILD ABUSE & NEGLECT 1219 (1996); David B. Sarwer & Joseph A. Durlak, *Childhood Sexual Abuse as a Predictor of Adult Female Sexual Dysfunction: A Study of Couples Seeking Sex Therapy*, 20/10 CHILD ABUSE & NEGLECT 963 (1996); Marcellina Mian, Peter Marton & Deborah LeBaron, *The Effects of Sexual Abuse on 3- to 5-Year-Old Girls*, 20/8 CHILD ABUSE & NEGLECT 731 (1996); Amy B. Silverman, Helen Z. Reinherz & Rose M. Giaco-

from post-traumatic stress disorder[48] (PTSD) as a result of the molestation.[49] Post-traumatic stress disorder may help to explain why child sexual abuse victims may bury memories that surface at different times in the victims' lives.[50] Children may suffer from acute stress disorder (ASD), the essential feature of which is "the development of characteristic anxiety, dissociative, and other symptoms that

---

nia, *The Long-Term Sequelae of Child Abuse and Adolescent Abuse: Longitudinal Community Study*, 20/8 Child Abuse & Neglect 709 (1996); Patricia Coffey, Harold Leitenberg, Kris Henning, Tonia Turner & Robert T. Bennett, *Mediators of the Long-Term Impact of Child Sexual Abuse: Perceived Stigma, Betrayal, Powerlessness, and Self-Blame*, 20/5 CHILD ABUSE & NEGLECT 447 (1996); Sandra T. Sigmon, Melodie P. Greene, Kelly J. Rohan & Jennifer E. Nichols, *Coping and Adjustment in Male and Female Survivors of Childhood Sexual Abuse*, 5/3 J. CHILD SEXUAL ABUSE 57 (1996); P. E. Mullen, J. L. Martin, J. C. Anderson, S. E. Romans & G. P. Herbison, *The Long-Term Impact of Physical, Emotional, and Sexual Abuse of Children: A Community Study*, 20/1 CHILD ABUSE & NEGLECT 7 (1996); Cathy S. Widom & Joseph B. Kuhns, *Childhood Victimization and Subsequent Risk for Promiscuity, Prostitution, and Teenage Pregnancy: A Prospective Study*, 86/11 AM. J. OF PUBLIC HEALTH 1607 (1996); Myra Leifer & Jeremy P. Shapiro, *Longitudinal Study of the Psychological Effects of Sexual Abuse in African American Girls in Foster Care and Those Who Remain Home*, 4/4 J. CHILD SEXUAL ABUSE 27 (1995); Shan A. Jumper, *A Meta-Analysis of the Relationship of Child Sexual Abuse to Adult Psychological Adjustment*, 19/6 CHILD ABUSE & NEGLECT 715 (1995); Ann Hazzard, Marianne Celano, Jenny Gould, Suzanne Lawry & Carol Webb, *Predicting Symptomatology and Self-Blame Among Child Sex Abuse Victims* 19/6 CHILD ABUSE & NEGLECT 707 (1995); Ronald W. Thompson, Karen Authier & Penney Ruma, *Behavior Problems of Sexually Abused Children in Foster Care: A Preliminary Study*, 3/4 J. CHILD SEXUAL ABUSE 79 (1994); William N. Friedrich, *Sexual Victimization and Sexual Behavior in Children: A Review of Recent Literature*, 17/1 CHILD ABUSE & NEGLECT 59 (1993); Pamela C. Alexander, *The Differential Effects of Abuse Characteristics and Attachment in the Prediction of Long-Term Effects of Sexual Abuse*, 8 J. INTERPERSONAL VIOLENCE 346 (1993); Kathleen A. Kendall-Tackett, Linda Meyer Williams & David Finkelhor, *Impact of Sexual Abuse on Children: A Review and Synthesis of Recent Empirical Studies*, 113/1 PSYCHOLOGICAL BULLETIN 164 (1993); John Briere & Marsha Runtz, *Childhood Sexual Abuse: Long-Term Sequelae & Implications for Psychological Assessment*, 8 J. INTERPERSONAL VIOLENCE 312 (1993); H. Inderbitzen-Pisaruk, C. R. Shawchuck & T. S. Hoier, *Behavioral Characteristics of Child Victims of Sexual Abuse: A Comparison Study*, 21 J. CLINICAL CHILD PSYCHOLOGY 14 (1992); Angela Browne & David Finkelhor, *Impact of Child Sexual Abuse: A Review of the Research*, 99 PSYCHOLOGICAL BULLETIN 66 (1986); Angela Browne & David Finkelhor, *Initial and Long-Term Effects: A Review of the Research*, in A SOURCEBOOK ON CHILD SEXUAL ABUSE 143 (David Finkelhor, ed. 1986).

48. AMERICAN PSYCHIATRIC ASSOCIATION, DIAGNOSTIC AND STATISTICAL MANUAL OF MENTAL DISORDERS 424 (4th edition 1994). The DSM-IV states that "[f]or children, sexually traumatic events may include developmentally inappropriate sexual experiences without threatened or actual violence or injury." *Id.*

49. *See generally* Jane Timmons-Mitchell, Dawn Chandler-Holtz & William E. Semple, *Post Traumatic Stress Disorder Symptoms in Child Sexual Abuse Victims and Their Mothers*, 6/4 J. CHILD SEXUAL ABUSE 1 (1997); Lynne Briggs, *What Determines Post-Traumatic Stress Disorder Symptomatology for Survivors of Childhood Sexual Abuse?*, 21/6 CHILD ABUSE & NEGLECT 575 (1997); Ned Rodriguez, Susan W. Ryan, Anderson B. Rowan & David W. Foy, *Posttraumatic Stress Disorder in a Clinical Sample of Adult Survivors of Childhood Sexual Abuse*, 20/10 CHILD ABUSE & NEGLECT 943 (1996); Anderson B. Rowan *et al.*, *Posttraumatic Stress Disorder in a Clinical Sample of Adults Sexually Abused as Children*, 18/1 CHILD ABUSE & NEGLECT 51 (1994); David A. Wolfe *et al.*, *Factors Associated with the Development of Posttraumatic Stress Disorder among Child Victims of Sexual Abuse*, 18/1 CHILD ABUSE & NEGLECT 37 (1994); Benjamin E. Saunders, Lorenz A. Villeponteaux, Julie A. Lipovsky, Dean G. Kilpatrick & Lois J. Veronen, *Child Sexual Assaults as a Risk Factor for Mental Disorders Among Women*, 7/2 J. INTERPERSONAL VIOLENCE 189 (1992); E. Deblinger, S. McLeer, M. Atkins, D. Ralphe & E. Foa, *Post-Traumatic Stress in Sexually Abused, Physically Abused, and Nonabused Children*, 13/3 CHILD ABUSE & NEGLECT 403 (1989); S. McLeer, E. Deblinger, M. Atkins, E. Foa & D. Ralphe, *Post-Traumatic Stress Disorder in Sexually Abused Children*, J. AM. ACAD. CHILD AND ADOLESCENT PSYCHIATRY 651 (1988); POST-TRAUMATIC STRESS DISORDER IN CHILDREN (S. Eth & R. Pynoos, eds. 1985).

Experts have been permitted to testify that PTSD in a child is consistent with a history of sexual abuse. *See, e.g.*, Broderick v. King's Way Assembly of God Church, 808 P.2d 1211 (Alaska 1991); Brady v. State, 540 N.E.2d 59 (Ind. Ct. App. 1989); Commonwealth v. Dockham, 405 Mass. 618, 542 N.E.2d 591 (1989); State v. Alberico, 116 N.M. 156, 861 P.2d 192 (1993).

50. *See, e.g.*, Lenore E. Walker, *PTSD and Child Sexual Abuse: Commentary*, 2/4 J. CHILD SEXUAL ABUSE 129 (1993).

occurs within one month after exposure to an extreme traumatic stressor," referring to the same types of stressors as can lead to PTSD.[51] Some children may experience periods of dissociation, even warranting a diagnosis of dissociative identity disorder[52] (formerly called multiple personality disorder).[53] Children who experience more shame and self-blaming attributions are more likely to suffer depression, poor self-esteem, PTSD symptoms, and sexual eroticism.[54] Some sexually abused children will have additional periods of difficulty at later stages of development, such as at puberty, when they first become voluntarily sexually active or involved in romantic relationships, and when they become parents. Intrafamilial child sexual abuse may also make it more likely that a girl will engage in early teenage sex with an older man[55] or that she may become engaged in prostitution.[56] Some molested children do not exhibit any short-term symptoms of the abuse;[57] however, children are more likely to exhibit symptoms where there was a close relationship between the child and abuser, high frequency of sexual contact, long duration of the molestation, use of force, or oral, anal, or vaginal penetration.[58]

51. *See* AMERICAN PSYCHIATRIC ASSOCIATION, DIAGNOSTIC AND STATISTICAL MANUAL OF MENTAL DISORDERS 429 (4th ed. 1994). *See generally*, Cheryl Koopman, Cheryl Gore-Felton & David Spiegel, *Acute Stress Disorder Symptoms Among Female Sexual Abuse Survivors Seeking Treatment*, 6/3 J. CHILD SEXUAL ABUSE 65 (1997).

52. AMERICAN PSYCHIATRIC ASSOCIATION, DIAGNOSTIC AND STATISTICAL MANUAL OF MENTAL DISORDERS 484 (4th ed. 1994). The DSM-IV states that persons with this disorder "frequently report having experienced severe physical and sexual abuse, especially during childhood." *Id.* at 485.

53. *See generally* F. Putnam, *Dissociative Disorders in Children: Behavioral Profiles and Problems*, 17/1 CHILD ABUSE & NEGLECT 39 (1993); JOHN N. BRIERE, CHILD ABUSE TRAUMA: THEORY AND TREATMENT OF THE LASTING EFFECTS (1992); J. Chu & D. Dill, *Dissociative Symptoms in Relation to Childhood Physical and Sexual Abuse*, 147 J. PSYCHIATRY 887 (1990); CHILDHOOD ANTECEDENTS OF MULTIPLE PERSONALITY (R. Kluft, ed., 1985); Vicki Saltman & Robert S. Solomon, *Incest and Multiple Personality*, 50 PSYCHOLOGICAL REPORTS 1127 (1982).

54. *See, e.g.* Candice Feiring, Lynn Taska & Michael Lewis, *The Role of Shame and Attributional Style in Children's and Adolescents' Adaptation to Sexual Abuse*, 3/2 CHILD MALTREATMENT 129 (1998).

55. *See, e.g.*, E. J. RUBIN, M. A. WALLER & B. SEAGRAVE-WHITTLE, CONSENTING VICTIMS: YOUNG TEENS IMPREGNATED BY ADULT MEN (in press), *cited in* SHAROL G. ELSTEIN & NOY DAVIS, SEXUAL RELATIONSHIPS BETWEEN ADULT MALES AND YOUNG TEEN GIRLS: EXPLORING THE LEGAL AND SOCIAL RESPONSES (ABA Center on Children and the Law 1997); J. S. USICK, YOUNG, POOR AND PREGNANT: THE PSYCHOLOGY OF TEENAGE MOTHERHOOD (1993).

56. *See, e.g.*, C. S. Widom & J. B. Kuhns, *Childhood Victimization and Subsequent Risk for Promiscuity, Prostitution, and Teenage Pregnancy*, 86/11 AM. J. PUB. HEALTH 1607 (1996).

57. *See, e.g.*, Robert D. Wells, John McCann, Joyce Adams, Joan Voris & John Ensign, *Emotional, Behavioral, and Physical Symptoms Reported by Parents of Sexually Abused, Nonabused, and Allegedly Abused Prepubescent Females*, 19/2 CHILD ABUSE & NEGLECT 155 (1995); Kathleen A. Kendall-Tackett, Linda Meyer Williams & David Finkelhor, *Impact of Sexual Abuse on Children: A Review and Synthesis of Recent Empirical Studies*, 113 PSYCHOLOGICAL BULLETIN 164 (1993).

58. *See, e.g.*, Kathleen A. Kendall-Tackett, Linda Meyer Williams & David Finkelhor, *Impact of Sexual Abuse on Children: A Review and Synthesis of Recent Empirical Studies*, 113 PSYCHOLOGICAL BULLETIN 164 (1993).

In many cases of intrafamilial child sexual abuse there are multiple forms of maltreatment in the home, which add to the short- and long-term problems the child may experience.[59] The investigation of every sexual abuse case should include inquiry into possible physical and emotional abuse and neglect.

In handling an intrafamilial child sexual abuse case, it is important for the lawyer to present expert evidence on the mechanics of the harm to the child, including how far-reaching the effects of incest are. Judges cannot take adequate steps to safeguard children until they realize the danger. Nobody expects date-rape victims to go through therapy to reestablish a relationship with their rapists merely because they were once close. But it is the norm to "rehabilitate" the relationship between a child and his or her molester if that person is the parent. Many judges believe that if the child is safe from remolestation (such as in a supervised visit), there is no harm to the child in continuing contact between the child and molester. Such a view trivializes the child's pain and vulnerability. That view also embodies a policy of parental entitlement to power and control over a child even when that power has been badly abused in the past, assuming that the fact of parenthood entitles one to a continued relationship.[60]

On the other hand, children often have ambivalent feelings about parents who abuse them, whether the abuse is physical, sexual, or emotional. The child usually has positive feelings about some aspects of the parent-child relationship. Further, the child often does not want to bear the guilt of tearing the family apart, sending the molester to jail, or diminishing the family's economic resources. A

---

59. *See generally* Brandt F. Steele, *Psychodynamic and Biological Factors in Child Maltreatment* in THE BATTERED CHILD 73, 84 (Mary Edna Helfer, Ruth S. Kempe & Richard D. Krugman, eds., 5th ed. 1997); Elizabeth A. W. Seagull, *Family Assessment* in THE BATTERED CHILD 150, 153 (Mary Edna Helfer, Ruth S. Kempe & Richard D. Krugman, eds., 5th ed. 1997); Donna Andrea Rosenberg, *Unusual Forms of Child Abuse* in THE BATTERED CHILD 431, 443 (Mary Edna Helfer, Ruth S. Kempe & Richard D. Krugman, eds., 5th ed. 1997); L. A. McClosky, A. J. Figueredo & M. P. Koss, *The Effects of Systemic Family Violence on Children's Mental Health*, 66 CHILD DEVELOPMENT 1239 (1995); Tamerra P. Moeller, Gloria A. Bachman & James R. Moeller, *The Combined Effects of Physical, Sexual, and Emotional Abuse During Childhood: Long-Term Health Consequences for Women*, 17/5 CHILD ABUSE & NEGLECT 623 (1993).

60. *See, e.g.*, *Sherry L.H. v Hey*, 419 S.E.2d 17 (W. Va. 1992) (reversing trial court's order for supervised visitation following master's finding that the two children had been molested by the father and recommendation that there be no visitation; trial court failed to weigh the risk of harm to the children; the court remanded the case and directed the trial court that if supervised visitation were ordered, the supervisor should be a person the children trust and are familiar with in order to protect them from emotional and psychological trauma).

child who is denied all contact with a parent, even if that parent has molested him or her, may feel doubly punished. There is much yet to be learned about incest and its aftermath, and the needs of the child are very individual. Therefore, lawyers, judges, social workers, and mental-health professionals should not adopt positions based on generalizations and hypotheses. Rather, it is essential to make a particularized determination about the individual child's needs and desires.

Lawyers must present sufficient compelling expert testimony about the particular child's needs to enable the judge to weigh appropriately the dangers and benefits of contact. Before contact is reestablished—if it ever is—a great deal of therapeutic work needs to be done with the child. If possible, both parents should also have therapy. It is the author's strong belief that the therapist for the child should be the person whose opinion is given the greatest weight in controlling when and if contact takes place, and if so, under what circumstances. The judge should issue clear orders regarding the implementation of contact.

Parents can do things that forfeit their right to have the deciding vote concerning their children. What we know about the effects of incest make it clear that child sexual abuse constitutes one of those forfeiting circumstances. Contact should be resumed if it is safe for the child and will serve the child's need for a reestablished relationship. The author does not believe that contact should be resumed merely to meet the need of the molesting parent for reestablishing contact if such a course of action would be detrimental to the child.

Many statutes provide that noncustodial parents are entitled to unrestricted visitation unless visitation would seriously endanger the child's physical or emotional health.[61] Some states explicitly provide

---

61. *See, e.g.*, ARIZ. REV. STAT. ANN. § 25-408(A) (Supp. 1998); COLO. REV. STAT. § 14-10-129(1) (1997); DEL. CODE ANN. tit. 13, § 728(a) (1997); 750 ILL. COMP. STAT. ANN. § 5/607(a) (1993); MO. ANN. STAT. § 452.400(a) (1997); WIS. STAT. ANN. § 767.24(4)(b) (1993); U.M.D.A. § 407, 9A U.L.A. 207-208 (Master ed. 1979). *See also*, *French v. French*, 452 So.2d 647 (Fla. App. 1984) (reversing total ban on visitation based on father's seeming insensitivity to his children's reaction to his extramarital affair); Fontaine v. Hoffman, 359 N.W.2d 692 (Minn. Ct. App. 1984) (reversing termination of visitation where father had neglected to exercise his visitation rights); Cox v. Moulds, 490 So. 2d 866 (Miss. 1986) (overnight visitation permitted despite lack of private sleeping accommodation for adolescent girl); *In re* D.F.D., 261 Mont. 186, 862 P.2d 368 (1993) (reversing restrictions on cross-dressing father's visitation and denial of his request for joint custody; father did not meet diagnostic criteria for transvestism, his cross-dressing was done in private, and there was no showing of harm to the child); Eichelberger v. Eichelberger, 345 S.E.2d 10 (Va. Ct. App. 1986) (noncustodial parent not be prevented from allowing child to ride mini-trail bike absent a finding of danger).

that child abuse warrants restrictions on visitation.[62] Lawyers should present sufficient expert evidence to allow the judge to make an informed decision on endangerment, particularly emotional endangerment.

Sometimes there is evidence of sexual abuse with respect to only one child in the home. The question becomes whether only the abused child or the other children need to be protected. Similarly, a person may have molested a child from another relationship, and the question of protection for other children and step-children arises. Courts have held that evidence of sexual abuse of one child is relevant to the issue of molestation of a sibling.[63] Where one child has been molested, other children in the home may also be removed from the home or otherwise given protection by the court.[64] A person who molests a child presents a role-model problem. For this reason, that person may be an inappropriate custodian of male children, for example, even if only a female child has been molested and there is little danger that the male children will be molested themselves.

Child molestation represents, at the very least, a demonstration of poor impulse control, bad judgment, and the inability to place the child's needs and protection before the molester's needs. Substance abuse may contribute to the lack of impulse control.[65] Even if that person never molests again, the psychological condition of the person that allowed the previous molestation to occur is a significant factor against that person's claim to custody, and perhaps, unre-

---

62. *See, e.g.*, MD. CODE ANN. FAM. LAW § 9-101(b) (Repl. Vol. 1991) (unless the court specifically finds that there is no likelihood of further child abuse or neglect, the court shall deny visitation, except the court may approve a supervised visitation arrangement that assures the safety and the physiological, psychological, and emotional well-being of the child); 23 PA. CONS. STAT. ANN. § 5303(b) and (c) (1998) (if a parent has been convicted of child sexual abuse or endangerment, the court shall determine that the parent does not pose a threat of harm to the child before making an order of partial custody or visitation to that parent; the convicted parent shall receive counseling which addresses, but is not limited to, issues regarding physical and sexual abuse, domestic violence, the psychology of the offender, and the effects of abuse on the victim); WASH. REV. CODE ANN. § 26.09.191(2)(a)(ii) and (iii) (1997) (court shall limit parent's residential time if the parent has engaged in physical, sexual, or a pattern of emotional abuse of a child); WIS. STAT. ANN. § 767.24(5)(h) (1993) (the court shall consider evidence of child abuse). *See also* Cooper v. Cooper, 158 So. 2d 248 (La. Ct. App. 1963); Porges v. Porges, 63 A.D.2d 712, 405 N.Y.S.2d 115 (1978); Jakab v. Jakab, 664 A.2d 261 (Vt. 1995) (affirming limited, supervised visitation for father who physically abused his children).

63. *See, e.g.*, Morgan v. Foretich, 846 F.2d 941 (4th Cir. 1988).

64. *See, e.g.*, *In re* S.G., 581 A.2d 771 (DC Ct. App. 1990) (upholding neglect finding concerning younger half-siblings of seven-year-old molested by her stepfather); *In re* Katherine C., 471 N.Y.S.2d 216 (1984) (upholding neglect finding concerning brothers of girl molested by her father since age ten, despite lack of showing specific harm to them).

65. *See, e.g.*, Elizabeth A. W. Seagull, *Family Assessment* in THE BATTERED CHILD 150, 163 (Mary Edna Helfer, Ruth S. Kempe & Richard D. Krugman, eds., 5th ed. 1997); R. Famularo, R. Kinscherff & T. Fenton, *Parental Substance Abuse and the Nature of Child Maltreatment*, 16/4 CHILD ABUSE & NEGLECT 475 (1992).

stricted visitation. The lawyer should introduce expert testimony concerning the molester's underlying psychological problems and their effect on custody and visitation. If the court has the jurisdictional authority to do so, or the molester agrees, competent therapy for the molester, and demonstrated improvement in therapy, should be prerequisites to any type of custody or unrestricted access to that person's children.

It makes everyone uneasy not to know the truth about a molestation allegation, but we do not have a litmus test or magic bullet at this time, and the legal profession must work to ensure that children are safe. One of the best ways to do this is to appoint a trained lawyer for the child in every case in which there are allegations of child sexual abuse and provide properly qualified expert resources to that lawyer.[66]

WHAT ARE THE LEGAL INTERVENTIONS IN CHILD SEXUAL ABUSE CASES?

Despite the general consensus that child sexual abuse is wrong, only a small proportion of substantiated abuse cases result in any kind of legal intervention.[67] When the number of unreported cases, cases with inconclusive findings, cases of inaccurate investigation and conclusions, and cases of informal settlement is counted, it is clear that most children who are molested never have their cases adjudicated in a court proceeding. Of those cases that do result in legal intervention, most involve civil child protection cases.[68] Child sexual abuse is raised as an allegation in some domestic-relations custody and abuse cases.[69] A relatively few cases involve criminal prosecution, most often where the abuser is a stranger to the child.[70] Even fewer cases

---

66. For a more complete discussion of how the child's lawyer can best represent the child under such circumstances, *see* ANN M. HARALAMBIE, THE CHILD'S ATTORNEY: A GUIDE TO REPRESENTING CHILDREN IN CUSTODY, ADOPTION, AND PROTECTION Cases (American Bar Association 1993).

67. *See, generally*, Patricia G. Tjaden & Nancy Thoennes, *Predictors of Legal Intervention in Child Maltreatment Cases*, 16/6 CHILD ABUSE & NEGLECT 807 (1992) (study of substantiated abuse cases, including sexual abuse, in one county each in California, Colorado, and Delaware, showed that only 4 percent of the cases resulted in criminal prosecution, and only 21 percent of the cases resulted in a civil protection case being filed).

68. See Chapter 3.

69. See Chapter 2.

70. This book does not address any of the criminal aspects of child sexual abuse cases. For an excellent collection and analysis of such cases *see*, JOHN E. B. MYERS, EVIDENCE IN CHILD ABUSE AND NEGLECT CASES (3rd ed. 1997).

involve termination of parental rights.[71] Finally, victims of child sexual abuse, usually after they reach adulthood, may file tort actions against the abuser or third parties otherwise deemed liable.[72]

This book will deal with the civil legal interventions and the various strategies that may be employed in them. Although the percentage of abuse cases resulting in legal intervention is small, the numbers are large enough to be significant, and most family-law practitioners who deal with child custody will come across intrafamilial child sexual abuse allegations at some point. It is important for the health and safety of the child and family for there to be a legal intervention in many cases; a court order may be necessary to ensure that the abuser, nonprotective or nonsupportive family members, and the child begin and remain in treatment long enough to make meaningful changes.[73]

TREATMENT

Once there is a legal intervention, it is particularly helpful for the child to be involved in ongoing treatment to deal with the inherent uncertainties and stresses of litigation as well as with the direct results of the intervention, such as a change of placement, change in the constellation of family members living together, participation in evaluations and interviews, and the possibility of testifying. The child often feels responsible for adverse consequences to the family, including the "trouble" the abuser is in, removal of the abuser from the home, decline in the family's economic circumstances, exposure of the family to public scrutiny, and blame from family members and friends. Concurrent treatment is an important buffer from such reactions. Treatment for the child can also assist the child in reporting and resisting the threats and bribes that often accompany sexual abuse and its disclosure.

Aside from the assistance to the child victim, treatment and therapeutic interview techniques can assist the legal system by

---

71. See Chapter 4.
72. See Chapter 5.
73. *See generally* Anna Maria Irueste-Montes & Francisco Montes, *Court-Ordered vs. Voluntary Treatment of Abusive and Neglectful Parents*, 12/1 CHILD ABUSE & NEGLECT 33 (1988); David A. Wolfe, *et al.*, *The Importance of Adjudication in the Treatment of Child Abusers: Some Preliminary Findings*, 4/1 CHILD ABUSE & NEGLECT 127 (1980).

encouraging full disclosure and by supporting the child in his or her cooperation with the investigation.[74] When young children do not understand the questions they are asked, they may nevertheless attempt to answer, resulting in inaccurate and inconsistent information.[75] Children are often overwhelmed by the legal process and stop talking rather than continue to endure multiple interviews and evaluations. Worse yet for the fact-finding process, some children just answer whatever the questioner of the moment appears to want to hear, or they just answer randomly. It is important for the investigation and court process that the most accurate information possible be made available. The appropriate support can help to maximize the acquisition of such information.[76]

---

74. *See, e.g., Preparing Child Witnesses—An Interview with Dr. Karen J. Saywitz*, 16/11 CHILD LAW PRACTICE 161 (1998); Julie Lipovsky & Paul Stern, *Preparing Children for Court: An Interdisciplinary View*, 2/2 CHILD MALTREATMENT 150 (1997); John E. B. Myers, Karen J. Saywitz & Gail S. Goodman, *Psychological Research on Children as Witnesses: Practical Implications for Forensic Interviews and Courtroom Testimony*, 28/1 PACIFIC L.J. 3 (1996); Karen J. Saywitz, Lynn Snyder & Vivian Lamphear, *Helping Children Tell What Happened: A Follow-Up Study of the Narrative Elaboration Procedure* 1/3 CHILD MALTREATMENT 200 (1996); Karen J. Saywitz & Lynn Snyder, *Narrative Elaboration: Test of a New Procedure for Questioning Children*, 64 J. CONSULTING & CLINICAL PSYCHOLOGY 1347 (1996); Michelle R. McCauley & Ronald P. Fisher, *Facilitating Children's Eyewitness Recall with the Revised Cognitive Interview*, 80 J. APPLIED PSYCHOLOGY 510 (1995); Ronald P. Fisher & Michelle R. McCauley, *Improving Eyewitness Testimony With the Cognitive Interview*, in MEMORY AND TESTIMONY IN THE CHILD WITNESS 141 (Maria S. Zaragoza, John R. Graham, Gordon C. N. Hall, Richard Hirschman & Yossef S. Ben-Porath, eds., 1995); R. Edward Geiselman, Karen J. Saywitz & Gail K. Bornstein, *Effects of Cognitive Questioning Techniques on Children's Recall Performance*, in CHILD VICTIMS, CHILD WITNESSES: UNDERSTANDING AND IMPROVING TESTIMONY 77 (Gail S. Goodman & Bette L. Bottoms, eds., 1993); A. Memon, O. Cronin, R. Eaves & R. Bull, *The Cognitive Interview and Child Witnesses*, in 20 CHILDREN, EVIDENCE AND PROCEDURE: ISSUES IN CRIMINOLOGICAL AND LEGAL PSYCHOLOGY 3 (N. K. Clark & G. M. Stephenson, eds., 1993); John C. Yuille, Robin Hunter, Risha Joffe & Judy Zaparniuk, *Interviewing Children in Sexual Abuse Cases*, in CHILD VICTIMS, CHILD WITNESSES: UNDERSTANDING AND IMPROVING CHILDREN'S TESTIMONY 95 (Gail S. Goodman & Bette L. Bottoms, eds., 1993). Because of their developmental limitations, the cognitive interview (CI) may not be helpful with very young children. *See, e.g.*, D. A. Bekerian & J. L. Dennett, *An Introduction to the Cognitive Interview Technique*, in TRUE AND FALSE ALLEGATIONS OF CHILD SEXUAL ABUSE: ASSESSMENT AND CASE MANAGEMENT 192 (T. Ney, ed., 1995); Karen J. Saywitz, R. Edward Geiselman, & Gail K. Bornstein, *Effects of Cognitive Interviewing and Practice on Children's Recall Performance*, 77 J. APPLIED PSYCHOLOGY 744 (1992).

75. *See, e.g.*, Karen J. Saywitz, *Improving Children's Testimony: The Question, The Answer, and the Environment*, in MEMORY AND TESTIMONY IN THE CHILD WITNESS 113 (Maria S. Zaragoza, John R. Graham, Gordon C.N. Hall, Richard Hirschman & Yossef S. Ben-Porath, eds., 1995).

76. *See generally* Chapter 13.

1-1

Appendix

The Investigation of Child Sexual Abuse: An International, Interdisciplinary Consensus Statement*

Michael E. Lamb**

A group of experts from Europe, North America, and the Middle East met at a conference center in Satra Bruk, Sweden from September 26-29, 1993, under the joint sponsorship of the U.S. National Institute of Child Health and Human Development, the Swedish Allmanna Barnhuset Foundation, and the Socialvetenskapliga Forsknings Radet (Swedish Social Science Research Council). The group's mandate was to evaluate existing knowledge regarding the ways in which child sexual abuse allegations could be investigated most productively. This document represents a statement co-signed by twenty of the participants summarizing areas of agreement regarding the current status of knowledge in this area. It concludes with a statement regarding the areas in which further research remains necessary before greater

* The names of the participants at this conference are listed in the appendix.

** Head, Section on Social and Emotional Development, National Institute of Child Health and Human Development, 9190 Rockville Pike, Bethesda, Maryland 20814; (301) 496-0420; fax: (301) 480-5775.

clarity can be achieved. The report is designed to guide state and local officials, professionals, and advocates seeking to investigate child sexual abuse. A preliminary draft of this consensus document was prepared by Michael E. Lamb following the three-day consensus-building conference. The draft was reviewed and revised by all the participants over the ensuing months. This report, revised in accordance with the participants' comments, is the culmination of this consensus-building process.

I. THE PROBLEM

Although the final section of this article underscores how much remains to be learned about child sexual abuse, the participants agreed that a great deal has already been learned and that the magnitude of the problem makes it necessary and timely to synthesize this knowledge. Over the last two decades, all of the countries represented (Finland, Germany, Israel, Norway, Sweden, the United Kingdom, and the United States), like most of the other Western industrialized nations, have witnessed substantial increases in the number of reported incidents of child sexual maltreatment. It is unclear whether these increases in the number of reported cases reflect real increases in the incidence of child sexual abuse, increasing awareness of the problem, increased willingness to report such recognized incidents to authorities, or a combination of these factors. Whatever the reason, the numbers of reported cases are quite startling. In the United States, for example, the most recent available statistics show nearly a half million reported cases of sexual maltreatment in 1992, compared with 325,000 in 1985. Since there are approximately 70 million U.S. residents under the age of eighteen, this suggests that approximately 0.7 percent of the children in the United States were reported as victims of sexual abuse in 1992 (0.46 percent in 1985). Approximately 40 percent of all child abuse reports are substantiated by social welfare authorities.

The incidence of reported cases is lower in most other countries. Recent statistics from the United Kingdom show increases from 3,700 new substantiated cases (.034 percent) in 1991 to 4,200 new substantiated cases (.037 percent in 1992. In Oslo, Norway, 200 of the 91,000 children in the city were reported as victims in 1992, for an incidence rate of 0.22 percent. In Israel, there were 1,438 reported cases in 1992, an increase from 1,260 in 1991, with steady annual increases of about 10 percent over the seven years that these statistics have been kept.

Evidently, child sexual abuse is an all-too-frequent phenomenon that is both a crime and a form of child maltreatment that may seriously and deleteriously affect children's development. Furthermore, the high rate of nonsubstantiation highlights the difficulty that may arise when attempting to validate allegations. These factors alone underscore the importance of developing reliable and valid means of investigating reports of child sexual maltreatment.

Unfortunately, because of its very nature, child sexual abuse usually occurs in private with no witnesses other than the perpetrator and the victim. Even when confronted with compelling evidence, many perpetrators remain unwilling to admit their misconduct. In the fact of their denials, investigators typically must depend on children's accounts or physical and material evidence in order to determine whether or not allegations of sexual maltreatment are valid. Much of the physical evidence available to investigators is obtained from the medical examination of young victims. Considerable progress has been made in the last decade in the evaluation of genital and perianal injuries. This evidence can help determine whether or not some form of sexual abuse had occurred. Medical evidence is seldom sufficient to identify a specific perpetrator, however, and many forms of sexual abuse do not leave any physical signs. Such information can typically be obtained only from alleged victims and the difficulties of obtaining information from children are considerable. These difficulties have also increased dramatically in the last several years as the number of younger alleged victims has increased

Considerable controversy has long existed concerning the credibility of child witnesses. Countries whose legal system was derived from the British common law traditionally precluded testimony from young children, particularly those under seven years of age. Over the last several years, however, procedural changes have taken place such that the testimony of children is now widely admissible unless the court rules that it should be excluded. In most parts of Continental Europe, children under fourteen are interviewed outside the court. In Israel, "youth investigators" interview children under fourteen years of age, decide whether the children should testify, and may represent and evaluate the children's testimony in court.

Questions concerning the reliability and credibility of children's accounts are often raised in adversarial legal proceedings and these have fostered a highly contentious debate concerning the value and limitations of children's testimony. Unfortunately, this contentiousness has often spread into the relevant scholarly literatures, creating considerable confusion and doubt. As we show in this document, there is actually much greater agreement concerning the value, validity, and reliability of children's evidence than is widely recognized.

A primary purpose of this document is to summarize the relevant empirical data and clear away much of the contention which obscures substantial areas of agreement and consensus concerning both children's testimony and medical findings. Because it represents the consensus of a number of scholars and practitioners from a variety of backgrounds, this document focuses on broad areas of agreement rather than on narrow areas of contention. In order to facilitate our presentation, we have avoided explicit references to the scholarly literature in this document.

II. BEHAVIORAL INDICATORS

Reports to investigative and child protection authorities are often precipitated by adults' reports of sexualized behaviors on the part of young children. Behaviors that appear to mimic sexual activity and sexualized behaviors such as touching an adult's genitals or breasts are more commonly evinced by children who have been sexually abused than by non-abused children. Such behaviors are also displayed by children who have not been abused, however, and thus their occurrence cannot be used to conclude that sexual abuse has taken place. Instead, this behavior may signal the need for further evaluation using the investigative techniques described below.

As in the case of sexualized play with anatomically detailed dolls (see below), sexualized behavior by young children must be viewed in historical, cultural, and family contexts. Cultures (and families within them) vary widely in their attitudes and behavioral responses to both nudity and sexuality and these differences are known to affect children's behavior. Because we know too little about the meaning of sexualized behavior and the knowledge of sex on the part of children in various cultural and subcultural contexts, it is not yet possible to define developmentally appropriate or inappropriate knowledge and behavior conclusively.

No specific behavioral syndromes characterize victims of sexual abuse. Sexual abuse involves a wide range of possible behaviors which appear to have widely varying effects on its victims. The absence of any sexualized behavior does not confirm that sexual abuse did not take place any more than the presence of sexualized behavior conclusively demonstrates that sexual abuse occurred; rather, both pieces of information affect the level of suspicion concerning the child's possible experiences and should serve to promote careful and nonsuggestive investigation.

III. INTERVIEWING CHILD VICTIMS

As stated earlier, most of the information regarding possible child sexual abuse must be obtained from alleged victims. Despite frequent objections to the reliability and legal admissibility of children's testimony, it is clear that young victims are able to provide reliable and accurate accounts of events they have witnessed or experienced. Furthermore, despite frequent claims that children are uniquely susceptible to external influence, it is clear that when children are encouraged to describe their experiences without manipulation by interviewers, their accounts can be extremely informative and accurate. Such interviewing is difficult, however, and is best conducted by well-trained and experienced interviewers.

The most complete and reliable information can be elicited from children who are interviewed skillfully as soon as possible after the alleged incidents have taken place, although some children may be hesitant to disclose sensitive information. Central elements of salient events can be remembered for long periods of time, whereas more peripheral details tend to be forgotten when long delays occur. Accounts that contain peripheral details and are logically embedded in a rich context appear to be more likely when the events described have actually been experienced. Peripheral details may often be missing from accounts of repeated abusive incidents, however, and thus the failure to mention peripheral details or embed the account in a spatio-temporal context cannot be used to infer that the events did not take place. Furthermore, children's accounts, like those of adults, are at times susceptible to "post-event contamination," in which the report of an incident is distorted by the inclusion of details that were not part of the incident or of the original account. This may raise problems when children are interviewed on multiple occasions by unskilled interviewers (including parents, teachers, and friends) who ask highly suggestive questions that may unwittingly lead children to alter their accounts.

The most reliable and accurate information is obtained from children who are responding to open-ended questions designed to elicit free narrative accounts of events that they have experienced. Most children are capable of providing such accounts of their experiences, but younger children (especially those under five years of age) are unlikely to provide lengthy narratives or as much information as older children. Direct or focusing questions are usually needed to access further information and are especially necessary when the alleged victims are young. When direct questions are asked, they should be formulated as nonsuggestively as possible using developmentally and individually appropriate vocabulary and sentence construction, although different interviewing techniques may be needed in certain circumstances. Whenever possible, direct questions should be followed by attempts to elicit free narratives. Repeated, highly leading, or suggestive questions asked in an accusatory manner are ill-advised because they are most likely to promote distortion on the part of the child and may introduce details that are incorporated into and contaminate subsequent accounts. Preschool-aged children and those with developmental and/or communicative disabilities pose special problems and challenges because their cognitive, communicative, and interpretive capacities are less developed. The emotional responses of younger children may also be quite idiosyncratic.

In order to reduce the number of interviews, which may be stressful for young children and may also lead to a change in some aspects of children's accounts, it is desirable to tape record—preferably in video format—all primary investigative interviews. These records permit review of the child's statement by a variety of investigators who would otherwise have to conduct separate interviews. In addition, video recordings allow a careful and dispassionate evaluation of the extent to which the quality of the interview may have distorted the information obtained. A video recording provides a means of evaluating what information, if any, is likely to have been affected by leading or suggestive questions and what aspects of the account seem unaffected by such questions.

IV. Using Dolls and Other Props

Especially when interviewing children under five years of age, but also when interviewing older children who are reticent and uncommunicative, additional tools may assist interviewers in eliciting information from children. These tools or props include play materials, dolls, human figure drawings, or anatomically detailed dolls, all of which must be used with special care to avoid distracting children from their account or suggesting forms of information that the interviewers may expect or wish to hear. Props such as anatomically detailed dolls are widely used in some countries and the risks and benefits of their use vary depending upon the purposes for which they are employed and the skillfulness and experience of the adults using them.

In the context of investigation, these dolls may be helpful when used early in an interview to determine children's labels for certain body parts. Similarly, puppets or dolls may be used by children as media through which to make verbal statements regarding events they have experienced. These uses are unlikely to pose any serious investigative difficulties, provided the interviewers avoid overly suggestive questions.

Dolls can also be used later in investigative interviews to reenact events children have experienced and for which their expressive vocabulary appears inadequate. Such reenactments impose a burden of interpretation on adult interpreters, however, and thus should be attempted only by skillful and well-trained investigators who avoid nonverbal suggestion just as all interviewers avoid verbally suggestive questions. The potential problem is exacerbated by the fact that some children who have not been abused may initiate sexualized play when they are offered anantomically detailed dolls, although such play is more common in abused children. Nevertheless, the mere appearance of sexualized play with dolls should not ordinarily be used in and of itself to conclude that a child has been sexually abused. Instead, sexualized play with dolls may prompt a skillful interviewer to obtain more information, ideally using nonsuggestive verbal inquiries to supplement and clarify whatever nonverbal information was suggested by the child during his or her play with the props. Because defense attorneys frequently allege that dolls, especially anatomically detailed dolls, have been misused suggestively, we reiterate our recommendation that interviews should be video recorded whenever possible. Courts and other potential users of investigative interviews should understand that there is no anatomically detailed doll "test" yielding conclusive scores quantifying the probability that a child has been sexually abused.

V. MEDICAL EXAMINATIONS

Although many forms of sexual abuse may leave no physical signs on young victims, medical examinations are still indicated in most cases. Over the last fifteen years, there have been dramatic changes in the evaluation of medical evidence suggestive of child sexual abuse. Initial claims regarding the conclusiveness of medical exams were unfortunately overstated in light of professional ignorance regarding both normative ano-genital development and the effects of trauma on tissues in the ano-genital region. Recent and ongoing research designed to provide a clearer understanding of these issues is yielding a firmer and growing database that helps medical examiners better understand the significance of their findings and more correctly interpret unusual ano-genital signs.

Contrary to popular belief, sexual abuse may leave few, if any, physical effects. Fondling, oral copulation, and other forms of sexual molestation that do not cause tissue damage may leave no signs other than a slight amount of redness which rapidly disappears. Likewise, gentle penetration of the rectum, even by relatively large objects, may cause no permanent tissue damage, especially when a lubricant is employed. Thus, signs of trauma or injury are more likely to be found when the alleged incident appears to have involved forceful penetration of the vaginal or anal areas leading to both pain and bleeding.

When they are appropriate, medical examinations should be performed only by trained and experienced examiners as soon as possible after the alleged incidents. Successful and atraumatic examinations are much more easily accomplished when alleged victims and their families are adequately informed regarding the purposes and non-invasive nature of the examination. Anxiety levels can be decreased and the need for anesthesia or sedation greatly reduced when the ano-genital portion of the examination is incorporated into a comprehensive evaluation of a relaxed child.

Professionals in many medical centers throughout the world employ a multimethod ano-genital examination procedure in which magnifying devices are used to visualize the tissues and cameras are used to record the findings. In some centers, both the interview with the child and the ano-genital examination are videotaped for subsequent review. Even when such records are available, however, medical examiners need to prepare detailed reports of their findings, written in a form that is comprehensible to non-medical personnel in the legal and social welfare communities, yet sufficiently detailed to permit independent evaluation by other medical experts.

When vaginal penetration is alleged or suspected, female patients should be examined in more than one position to maximize certainty about the presence or absence of physical signs. Two commonly used methods of examination are performed while the child is lying on her back (supine position), while the other involves turning the child over into a knee-chest (prone) position. The two supine methods of labial separation and labial traction afford an excellent view of the tissues surrounding the vagina. Labial traction is particularly successful in separating the edges of the hymen so that the margins may be seen and the interior of the vagina visualized. The knee-chest position affords a superior view of the hymen, as it stretches out under its own weight, and of the vaginal canal as the anterior wall falls forward. Even the cervix may be visualized about two-thirds of the time during the knee-chest portion of the examination without the need for a speculum.

Penetration of a prepubertal girl's vagina by a penis or other large object usually results in a tear of her hymen and, at times, of the surrounding tissues as well. Recent hymenal tears are usually sharp edged and "V" shaped. They are most commonly found on the posterior rim of the hymen between the three and nine o'clock positions, resulting in a narrow rim at the point of injury and exposure of the underlying intravaginal structures. Any bleeding or redness resulting from the abuse usually disappears within forty-eight hours. The tears themselves heal within five to ten days and the sharp edges of the wounds smooth out and round off over a period of three to six months. Over time, these injuries become increasingly difficult to detect and may only be evident by multimethod examination, if at all. As a result, the absence of physical signs does not prove that no abuse occurred.

If the child has been penetrated by a "skillful" perpetrator who has carefully avoided hurting the child or injuring the tissues by gradually stretching the hymen, an examiner may observe only a smooth-edged hymen with a narrow rim. In such cases, there may be no reports of pain. The reduced width of the hymenal rim and exposure of the intravaginal contents may thus represent the only indications that sexual abuse with penetration had occurred. Deformations of the hymen remain visible from the time of penetration until the onset of puberty and may provide the clearest indication that penetration occurred. Such deformations of the posterior hymenal rim do not occur naturally and are unlikely to be caused by any other known trauma, including "straddle injuries."

The size of the hymenal orifice is no longer viewed as a reliable indicator of abuse; even children who have received significant hymenal injuries as the result of sexual abuse may have relatively small openings. In fact, the size of the hymenal orifice varies so widely from child to child in both abused and non-abused children that the width of the hymenal rim has replaced the size of the vaginal opening as a marker of sexual molestation.

At the onset of puberty, the hymenal membrane becomes thick and redundant. If molestation has ceased, the width of the hymen increases significantly and thus, without special examination techniques, a previous injury to the hymen may appear to be no more than a fold in the tissues.

Perianal injuries caused by sexual abuse occur relatively infrequently and are more difficult to detect. Although severe physical injuries can result from a violent act of sodomy, it is less clear what tissue changes should be expected following ongoing, relatively gentle penetration of the anal orifice when a lubricant is used. As a result, considerable controversy persists concerning the evaluation of perianal signs (including anal dilation reflexes) in children who may have experienced anal penetration. Other perianal soft tissue damage is similarly difficult to interpret when the history is unclear or the child is very young. As with genital trauma, perianal injuries heal rapidly, leaving little evidence of previous tissue damage.

Even in the absence of physical signs, examiners cannot conclude that anal or vaginal penetration did not take place. Healing is extremely rapid, visible injury is not inevitable, and it is difficult to perform examinations on young children, making it more likely that minor damage will go unrecognized. In addition, children, like adults, are often poor reporters of whether or not penetration has taken place. A child may report sharp pain in either the anal or vaginal area and report that something was placed "in there" when in fact the penetration was attempted rather than achieved.

VI. Areas in Need of Further Investigation

In the last decade, researchers have made considerable progress in their efforts to develop and validate the diverse techniques that must be used to investigate child sexual abuse. In this document, we have highlighted those areas of consensus and progress that are often obscured by the disagreements that continue to exist in areas that are the focus of continuing and/or more recent scholarship. In this section, we briefly identify those areas in which controversy persists and where further research is especially necessary.

As noted earlier, considerable ignorance exists concerning developmental, subcultural, and cultural variations in sexual knowledge and sexualized behavior. Certainly, the widespread exposure to soft- and hard-core pornography, particularly on video media, appears to have increased many children's knowledge of sexual behavior beyond that recognized by most parents and professionals. As a result, it is often difficult for professionals to attribute "age-inappropriate knowledge" to specific sexual experiences.

Considerable work remains to be conducted on the degrees to which accusatory, suggestive, or leading interviews distort children's accounts. It is also unclear when and which children can be expected to reveal details of sexual abuse in response to open-ended questions and when children may require more intensive interviewing. This ignorance precludes firm conclusions regarding the potential merits of open-ended questions. Likewise, little is known about the most effective strategies for interviewing children with communicative difficulties. It is not yet known how frequently children make false allegations and what circumstances affect the likelihood that these allegations may be offered.

Few systematic attempts have been made to evaluate the amount of detail and the accuracy of information yielded by children in responses to different types of questions (open-ended, leading, directive, suggestive, etc.) Considerable controversy now exists concerning "the repressed memory syndrome" (and its corollary "the false memory syndrome") and the validity of claims offered by alleged victims years after incidents may have taken place. Research on the empirical verification of these memories is only now beginning.

As far as anatomically detailed dolls are concerned, considerably more information is needed regarding the appropriate interpretation of various sexualized behaviors and little is known about the effects of dolls and other props on the quality and richness of children's verbal reports of their abusive experiences. Within the medical community, it is now widely recognized that physical examinations may not yield conclusive evidence that sexual abuse either did or did not occur. Further research is needed on the immediate physical consequences of specific sexual acts as well as on the developmental changes in these physical signs in the succeeding years. Such research will complement a growing but still inadequate understanding of normative ano-genital development and variability, particularly in diverse ethnic and racial subgroups.

In sum, many questions remain concerning the investigation and validation of child maltreatment reports. These questions are currently the focus of considerable research around the world. However, our lack of knowledge about these topics should not obscure the remarkable progress that has been made, especially over the last two decades. This brief consensus statement summarizes these recent solid gains in our knowledge and understanding, and augurs well for comparable progress in the years ahead.

SELECTED BIBLIOGRAPHY

The position represented in the consensus statement summarizes the areas of agreement among the participants based on their own research, professional experience, and synthesis of the scholarly literature. Although the participants do not necessarily agree with the conclusions of the authors cited below, they consider the following articles and books to be useful resources for readers interested in exploring more fully the issues discussed in the consensus statement.

Jan Bays & David Chadwick, *Medical Diagnosis of the Sexually Abused Child*, 17 CHILD ABUSE AND NEGLECT 91 (1993).

DOUGLAS J. BESHAROV, RECOGNIZING CHILD ABUSE (1990).

Stephen J. Ceci & Maggie Bruck, *The Suggestibility of the Child Witness*, 113 PSYCHOLOGICAL BULLETIN 403 (1993).

JOHN DORIS, THE SUGGESTIBILITY OF CHILDREN'S RECOLLECTIONS: IMPLICATIONS FOR EYEWITNESS TESTIMONY, AMERICAN PSYCHOLOGICAL ASSOCIATION (Washington, D.C. 1991).

Mark D. Everson & Barbara W. Boat, *Putting the Anatomical Doll Controversy in Perspective: An Examination of the Major Uses and Criticisms of the Dolls in Child Sexual Abuse Evaluations*, 18 CHILD ABUSE AND NEGLECT 113-129 (1994).

William N. Friedrich, *Sexual Victimization and Sexual Behavior in Children: A Review of Recent Literature*, 17 CHILD ABUSE AND NEGLECT 59 (1993).

GAIL S. GOODMAN & BETTE L. BOTTOMS, CHILD VICTIMS, CHILD WITNESSES: UNDERSTANDING AND IMPROVING CHILDREN'S TESTIMONY (1993).

Michael E. Lamb, et al., *Factors Influencing the Reliability and Validity of Statements Made by Young Victims of Sexual Maltreatment*, J. APPLIED DEVELOPMENTAL PSYCHOL. (forthcoming).

Memorandum of Good Practice (on video-recorded interviews with child witnesses for criminal proceedings) (London, Her Majesty's Stationery Office 1992).

APPENDIX

The foregoing statement was drafted by Michael E. Lamb on behalf of the group, and later revised by him in light of the others' comments. The statement represents the consensus of the following professionals:

Arnon Bentovim, Consultant Child Psychiatrist, Hospital for Sick Children, Great Ormond Street, London;
Douglas J. Besharov, Resident Scholar, American Enterprise Institute, Washington, D.C.;
Barbara W. Boat, Associate Professor of Psychiatry, University of Cincinnati;
Ray Bull, Professor of Psychology, University of Portsmouth, England;
Anita Cederstrom, Assistant Professor of Education, University of Stockholm;
Sven-Ake Christiansson, Associate Professor of Psychology, University of Stockholm;
Phillip W. Esplin (*Co-Organizer*), Forensic Psychologist, Phoenix, Arizona;
Lena Feuk, Children's Rights Attorney, Stockholm;
William N. Friedrich, Professor of Psychology and Psychiatry, Mayo Clinic, Rochester, Minnesota;
Gail S. Goodman, Professor of Psychology, University of California at Davis;
Irit Hershkowitz, Visiting Fellow, Section on Social and Emotional Development, National Institute of Child Health and Human Development, Bethesda, Maryland;
Philip Hwang (*Co-Organizer*), Professor of Child Studies, University of Linkoping, Sweden;
Charles D. Jamieson, Attorney in private practice, West Palm Beach, Florida;
Michael E. Lamb (*Co-Organizer and Rapporteur*), Head, Section on Social and Emotional Development, National Institute of Child Health and Human Development, Bethesda, Maryland;
John McCann, Associate Professor of Clinical Pediatrics, University of California, Davis;
Willard Mollerstrom, Researcher, Family Advocacy Program Office, San Antonio, Texas;
Erik Kreyberg Normann, Chief, Unit on Child Sexual Abuse and Neglect, Aker University Hospital, Oslo;
Heikki Sariola, Research, Central Union for Child Welfare, Helsinki;
Kathleen J. Sternberg (*Co-Organizer*), Research Psychologist, Section on Social and Emotional Development, National Institute of Child Health and Human Development, Bethesda, Maryland; and
Udo Undeutsch, Professor of Psychology, University of Cologne, Germany.

2 Sexual Abuse Allegations in Custody/Visitation Cases

The Climate

One of the most difficult types of civil child sexual abuse litigation involves allegations of molestation during the course of domestic-relations litigation. These cases are often more difficult to diagnose by medical and mental-health experts and more difficult to prove for lawyers because of questions about motivation and the already heightened emotional tensions between the parties. They are often subject to particular scrutiny.[1]

Domestic-relations judges may tend to be more skeptical about sexual abuse allegations than juvenile or criminal-court judges, who daily see parties who have committed violence or other abusive acts. Domestic-relations judges are used to hearing litigants exaggerate trivial events that were accepted during the marriage

1. For example, an appellate court wrote in dictum: "Given the fact that the allegations against respondent arose in tandem with a custody dispute, we carefully examined the record for indications that the victim was being manipulated or prevaricating, and found none." *See*, In the Matter of Robert "H," 681 N.Y.S.2d 887, 889 (App. Div. 1998).

but that take on the characterization of grievous abuse during the divorce trial. In addition to exaggerations, some domestic-relations litigants lie in order to gain an advantage or punish the other parent. It is within this context that many domestic-relations judges view allegations of sexual abuse.

Further, a number of people have spoken and written publicly about the "epidemic" of false allegations in custody cases and the "tactic" of alleging sexual abuse to gain an advantage in a custody or visitation case.[2] For example, child psychiatrist Richard Gardner writes:

> We are living in dangerous times. Sex-abuse hysteria is omnipresent. Open any newspaper or magazine and the likelihood of seeing an article on sex abuse is extremely high. Hardly a day goes by when there are not at least some television or radio programs devoted to the subject of sex abuse. There is no question that many accusations of child sex abuse are true, and this is especially so in settings such as homes and boarding schools (where the potential abuser has the opportunity for ongoing contact with the children). However, there is no question, as well, that many of the accusations are false, especially in child-custody disputes (where the vengeance element and the opportunity for exclusion of a hated spouse is operative) and day-care centers and nursery schools (where the potential abuser has little opportunity for ongoing contact alone with the child).[3]

Frequently it is the mother who raises allegations against the father, in which case she may be perceived as a "vindictive bitch," or the father who raises the allegations against the mother's boyfriend or new husband, in which case he may be perceived as jealous and controlling. These charges of epidemics and witch hunts have been made with very little empirical evidence, even though they may have been published by professionals in articles and books that purport to

---

2. *See, e.g.*, RICHARD A. GARDNER, PSYCHOTHERAPY WITH SEX-ABUSE VICTIMS: TRUE, FALSE, AND HYSTERICAL (1996); EDWARD NICHOLS, FALSE ALLEGATIONS OF CHILD SEXUAL ABUSE: THE ATTORNEY'S DESK REFERENCE (1994); RICHARD A. GARDNER, SEX ABUSE HYSETERIA: SALEM WITCH TRIALS REVISITED (1991); HOLLIDA WAKEFIELD & RALPH UNDERWAGER, ACCUSATIONS OF CHILD SEXUAL ABUSE (1988).

3. *See*, RICHARD A. GARDNER, PSYCHOTHERAPY WITH SEX-ABUSE VICTIMS: TRUE, FALSE, AND HYSTERICAL 420 (1996). For an excellent critical analysis of Dr. Gardner's writings on Parental Alienation Syndrome and the Sexual Abuse Legitimacy Scale, *see, e.g.*, Kathleen Coulborn Faller, *The Parental Alienation Syndrome: What Is It and What Data Support It?*, 3/2 CHILD MALTREATMENT 100 (1998).

be scientific. Some of the authors admit that 95 percent of the allegations are true, but they spend their energy and media savvy on the 5 percent that they label an epidemic.[4] While it is certainly true that there are instances of deliberately fabricated allegations, one has to question who is displaying the hysteria and witch-hunt mentality. There is no empirical basis cited for the dramatic claims of witch hunts and hysteria, but they have become absorbed into the "common knowledge" of many members of the public, including judges and other professionals who sometimes deal with sexual abuse allegations. What the media choose to report or exploit is not scientific evidence for the frequency of events, and it is important to avoid the influence of extraneous issues in determining whether a *particular* child in a *particular* family was molested or needs protection.[5]

The publicity has affected professionals in the field, as well as members of the public in general. When that publicity is combined with the heightened emotions associated with divorce litigation, it is

4. Even Dr. Gardner has written:

> [I]t would be an error for the reader to conclude that children whose parents are litigating for their custody are not likely to be sexually abused. It would also be an error to conclude that children who are suffering with parental alienation syndromes are immune from such abuse. This is not so. My main point here was to demonstrate that the fabricated sex-abuse allegation is likely to take place within the context of a custody dispute, especially when the child has developed manifestations of the parental alienation syndrome. One must still consider the possibility that bona fide abuse may still occur in the context of such a custody dispute. . . . The abuse may have taken place prior to the separation, and the child may have been fearful of divulging it because of the omnipresence of the father. A custody dispute may increase a child's animosity and thereby increase the likelihood that the abuse will be revealed, especially if the child has developed a parental alienation syndrome. Here the child is using the abuse allegation as another form of *real* ammunition rather than as a fantasized one.
>
> Just as the divorce situation is **likely to precipitate the child's divulgence of a pre-existing pattern of abuse,** the divorce situation **may actually precipitate sex abuse** on the part of a parent when it did not exist previously. Divorce is one of the most important and severe stresses of life. Under this stress some parents may regress and involve themselves in pedophilia. Contested divorces are even more stressful, and custody litigation adds even further to that stress. The child offers innocent and unconditional acceptance of a potential abuser. There is little chance of rejection. Rejected by a spouse, the parent may then turn to a child. In the context of weekend visitation, in a one-bedroom apartment with an adoring child, the parent may be unable to resist the pedophilic urges. RICHARD A. GARDNER, THE PARENTAL ALIENATION SYNDROME AND THE DIFFERENTIATION BETWEEN FABRICATED AND GENUINE SEX ABUSE 168-169 (1987). [Italics in original, bold added.]

Psychiatrists Arthur Green and Diane Schetky write that "[a] **small number** of parents caught up in custody battles or visitation disputes have exploited the epidemic of sexual abuse by using such allegations to promote their own interests at the expense of their child and their former spouse." Arthur H. Green and Diane H. Schetky, *True and False Allegations of Child Sexual Abuse*, in DIANE H. SCHETKY & ARTHUR H. GREEN, CHILD SEXUAL ABUSE: A HANDBOOK FOR HEALTH CARE AND LEGAL PROFESSIONALS (1988). [Emphasis added.]

5. *See generally*, THE BACKLASH: CHILD PROTECTION UNDER FIRE (John E. B. Myers, ed., 1994); BILLIE WRIGHT DZIECH & CHARLES B. SCHUDSON, ON TRIAL: AMERICA'S COURTS AND THEIR TREATMENT OF SEXUALLY ABUSED CHILDREN (1989); DAVID HECHLER, THE BATTLE AND THE BACKLASH: THE CHILD SEXUAL ABUSE WAR (1988).

not difficult to understand how Child Protective Services workers often develop a bias against believing allegations made in the context of domestic-relations cases.

THE STUDIES

Allegations of intrafamilial sexual abuse have increased in *all* contexts in the last decade.[6] This increase may be attributable to an actual increase in the incidence of sexual abuse, a greater willingness to report abuse,[7] or a combination of the two factors. One study that has reviewed allegations of sexual abuse in litigated domestic-relations cases has found that the rate of allegations is no higher than in the general population.[8] In the largest study to date, of the more than 9,000 contested custody cases in twelve states that were reviewed, fewer than 2 percent involved allegations of sexual molestation. Of that 2 percent, 50 percent were considered to be valid, in 33 percent (0.66 percent of all contested custody cases reviewed) no abuse was believed to have occurred, and in 17 percent it was unclear whether or not there had been abuse. Of the 33 percent where no abuse was believed to have occurred, in only 25 percent (8 percent of all allegations, 0.16 percent of all contested custody cases) was the good faith of the reporter questioned.[9]

Another study was done looking at all of the custody and visitation cases (603) that were finalized in one South Carolina county during 1987.[10] Of those cases 85 were contested. Only 2 percent of the contested cases (0.16 percent of all custody/visitation cases reviewed) involved allegations of sexual molestation.[11] The study did not attempt to determine whether the allegations were true.

---

6. *See, e.g.*, NATIONAL CENTER ON CHILD ABUSE AND NEGLECT, THIRD NATIONAL INCIDENCE STUDY OF CHILD ABUSE AND NEGLECT (1996).

7. *See, e.g.*, Feldman, Feldman, Goodman, McGrath, Rless, Corsini & Bennett, *Is Childhood Sexual Abuse Really Increasing in Prevalence? An Analysis of the Evidence*, 88 PEDIATRICS 29 (1991).

8. *See, e.g.*, Nancy Thoennes & Patricia G. Tjaden, *The Extent, Nature, and Validity of Sexual Abuse Allegations in Custody/Visitation Disputes*, 14/2 CHILD ABUSE & NEGLECT 151 (1990); Thoennes, *Child Sexual Abuse: Whom Should a Judge Believe? What Should a Judge Believe*, 27 JUDGES J. 14 (Summer 1988).

9. *Id.*

10. *See also*, McIntosh & Prinz, *The Incidence of Alleged Sexual Abuse in 603 Family Court Cases*, 17 L. & HUMAN BEHAVIOR 95 (Feb 1993).

11. *Id.* The numbers were small: five cases involved allegations, of which three cases were contested and two cases were uncontested.

What is telling about these two studies is that sexual abuse allegations are not common in domestic-relations cases, despite the widespread public perception of a flood of allegations, let alone a flood of false allegations. These numbers hardly reflect an "epidemic" or "witch hunt."[12] The fact is that reports of sexual abuse are increasing in general, and it should come as no surprise that greater numbers of allegations would be dealt with in that arena as well.

Two other studies not limited to custody/visitation cases also found that fabricated allegations were infrequent. All of the reports of sexual abuse referred to the Denver, Colorado, Department of Social Services in 1983 were reviewed. Of the 576 reports, 8 percent were deemed to be deliberate fabrications, misperceptions, or confused interpretations of nonsexual events.[13] All 551 reports to the same agency in 1995 were reviewed, with only 1.5 percent deemed to be fictitious.[14]

Part of the reason for the increase in allegations has probably been the greater public awareness of the problem and encouragement of victims to report their abuse. The incest taboo used to be so strong in our culture that victims felt alone and ashamed with their secret. They were often threatened that they would not be believed, and when they did tell, they were too infrequently believed or helped. When they were believed, *they*, not the offender, were removed from the home, further punishment and estrangement for a child who had already been violated.

In the past fifteen years mental-health and social-science professionals have dramatically changed the way child sexual abuse victims are treated. Even preschools have presented prevention and awareness programs, teaching the difference between good and bad touches, and encouraging children to report bad touches. Often children who did report their experiences were believed and given

12. The author's practice is concentrated in the area of custody and child abuse, and she handles a disproportionate number of sexual abuse cases in her community. Nevertheless, even in such a highly specialized practice, fewer than 10 percent of the litigated divorce and post-divorce custody cases involve allegations of sexual abuse.

13. See David P. H. Jones & C. Melbourne McGraw, *Reliable and Fictitious Accounts of Sexual Abuse to Children*, 2 J. Interpersonal Violence 27 (1986). No distinction was made between cases of deliberate fabrication or good faith but erroneous reports. Therefore, the rate of actually fabricated allegations was something less than the eight percent figure.

14. This study is reported in 1 John E. B. Myers, Evidence in Child Abuse and Neglect Cases 438 (3rd ed. 1997).

therapeutic support, and the abuser was removed from the home, leaving the child with a greater semblance of stability than foster care offers. An increasing number of offenders admitted to the abuse and were given therapeutic sentences rather than long prison time. Some families were even reunited within one or two years.

In this climate, it was not as difficult for children to report their abuse, for nonabusing parents to believe the child's reports, or for all family members to talk about incest. In the 1980s and 1990s more and more celebrities, from Oprah Winfrey to Marilyn Van Derbur Atler to Roseanne Barr, revealed their previously secret childhood sexual abuse.

It is not surprising that with this new atmosphere of openness and compassion more sexual abuse victims would come forward or even that some children who were not abused might make false allegations. It is also not surprising that many parents, given lists of "warning signs" and "red flags" would erroneously, but in good faith, misinterpret signs of anxiety and depression in their children as signs of sexual abuse. In fact, with the exception of acting out sexual conduct, most of the child-sexual-abuse warning signs are general symptoms of anxiety and depression, which could be caused by things other than sexual abuse—including the child's reaction to the breakup of the parents' marriage.

WHY TRUE ALLEGATIONS MAY FIRST COME TO LIGHT DURING DOMESTIC LITIGATION

There are many psychodynamic explanations for why molestation may not begin or may not be revealed until a separation, divorce, or custody/visitation modification action is brought.[15] Lawyers must

---

15. *See, e.g.*, DONNA PENCE & CHARLES WILSON, TEAM INVESTIGATION OF CHILD SEXUAL ABUSE: THE UNEASY ALLIANCE ch. 11 (1994); Elizabeth A. Sirles & Colleen E. Lofberg, *Factors Associated With Divorce in Intrafamily Child Sexual Abuse Cases*, 14/2 CHILD ABUSE & NEGLECT 165 (1990); KATHLEEN C. FALLER, UNDERSTANDING CHILD SEXUAL MISTREATMENT (1990); David L. Corwin, Lucy Berliner, Gail Goodman, Jean Goodwin, & Sue White, *Child Sexual Abuse and Custody Disputes*, 2/1 J. INTERPERSONAL VIOLENCE 91 (1987); Kee MacFarlane, *Child Sexual Abuse Allegations in Divorce Proceedings*, in SEXUAL ABUSE OF YOUNG CHILDREN: EVALUATION AND TREATMENT 121 (Kee MacFarlane & Jill Waterman, eds. 1986); Patricia Bresee, Geoffrey B. Stearnes, Bruce H. Bess & Leslie S. Packer, *Allegations of Child Sexual Abuse in Child Custody Disputes: A Therapeutic Assessment Model*, 56/4 AM. J. OF ORTHOPSYCHIATRY 560 (1986); Mary de Young, *A Conceptual Model for Judging the Truthfulness of a Young Child's Allegation of Sexual Abuse*, 56/4 AM. J. OF ORTHOPSYCHIATRY 550 (1986).

not merely dismiss allegations arising in such contexts as too suspicious. The lawyer and the judge need to understand why a child not previously molested might first be molested during his or her parents' separation or domestic-relations litigation and why a child previously molested might first reveal the molestation during those time periods.

Incestuous offenders who are not generally sexually attracted to children might first begin to molest their own children following the deterioration of the marital relationship. The offender may be lonely and in a great deal of emotional distress. Under stress many people have greater difficulty with impulse control. A child who gives the parent unconditional, unquestioning love and affection and who looks up to the parent as a powerful and worthy person may provide a great deal of solace to a parent in pain. Such a parent may be "carried away" during normal affection and begin to sexualize the contact, leading to some forms of molestation. The offending parent may have moved into a smaller residence, requiring the sharing of bathroom or bedroom facilities with the child, setting up circumstances that may make molestation more likely to happen.

Judges often view with suspicion allegations based on the child's statements only to one of the litigating parents, especially where those statements have not been repeated to third-party investigators. But it is not unusual for children, particularly young children, to disclose abuse first to the nonoffending parent. Children are used to telling their parents about their hurts and fears. Young children may not have much contact with the world outside their families, greatly limiting the range of potential people to whom to disclose abuse. Further, disclosure about such a private thing as sexual molestation is much more difficult when the child does not have an established relationship of trust and confidence with the other person. This explains why children who may consistently describe abuse to their mothers may not disclose anything to the police, social worker, or psychologist.

The existence of threats from the perpetrator make disclosure to these other people even more risky for the child. While Child Protective Services workers and judges may prefer cases where the child first discloses to an unbiased third party, it is unrealistic to expect that children, particularly young children, will accommodate that preference. Their disclosures should not be ignored merely because they come through the adult reports of one parent. A competent assessment by a properly trained professional is necessary, even though it may take more time than the legal system would like. However, it is important to know what, if anything, happened, even if the disclosures to the professional come slowly and piecemeal.

A child who has been molested during the marriage may have been threatened should the child tell. Some common threats are that the family will break up, the offender will go to jail, the family will lose their house and have to live on the street, or the offender will kill the child, the other parent, himself, or the family pet. Once the family is already split by separation or divorce, some of those threats may lose much of their power. The child may become emotionally closer to the nonoffending parent during separation or divorce, leading both to share more confidences with each other. Those circumstances make it more likely that the child will reveal the molestation.

A child who was willing to tolerate a certain level of molestation might become more afraid or unwilling enough to overcome the reluctance to disclose the abuse if the child now faces the prospect of spending longer times alone with the offender. This may cause the child to disclose abuse for the first time when facing the possibility of visitation or increases in visitation. It is essential that the lawyer trying to prove sexual abuse in these circumstances present competent expert testimony explaining why the "suspicious circumstances" of the allegations are not indicative of a vindictive fabrication.

Sometimes, as has been mentioned, the child is exhibiting signs of depression or anxiety that are not caused by sexual abuse. Too often parents who are trying to protect their children are punished by a judicial backlash against what is perceived as a vindictive charge.[16] An erroneous, good faith belief that a child has been molested should not be grounds for losing custody. After all, Child Protective Services routinely removes children from the homes of parents who refuse to believe that their children have been molested and, therefore, are unable to protect them from further abuse. Public policy demands

---

16. For more information on the backlash in general as it pertains to allegations of child sexual abuse, *see, e.g.*, THE BACKLASH: CHILD PROTECTION UNDER FIRE (John E. B. Myers, ed. 1994); Jon R. Conte, *Child Sexual Abuse: Awareness and Backlash*, 4/2 THE FUTURE OF CHILDREN 224 (1994); BILLIE WRIGHT DZIECH & CHARLES B. SCHUDSON, ON TRIAL: AMERICA'S COURTS AND THEIR TREATMENT OF SEXUALLY ABUSED CHILDREN (1989).

that parents who believe their children have been abused take steps to protect those children. Mandatory reporting laws require that action be taken based on reasonable suspicion. The alarming increase in judicial "punishment" of such parents in domestic-relations actions is contrary to the best interests of children.

FALSE ALLEGATIONS, FALSE DENIALS, AND FALSE RECANTATIONS

It is clear that some parents *do* make knowingly false allegations of sexual abuse. Such false allegations constitute emotional abuse of the child, as well as of the falsely accused adult. Children who are told that they have been molested, when in fact they were not, are psychologically damaged. Whether out of desperation or vindictiveness, such false allegations not only improperly interfere with the child's right to a good relationship with both parents, but also contribute to a negative self-view as a victim whose body was not respected.

Such deliberately false allegations may be relatively easy to detect, and psychiatrist Jean Goodwin and her colleagues have written that "thorough investigation will reveal precipitants of the hoax, psychodynamic explanations for this behavior, and the step-by-step development of the hoax."[17] In most cases the child is unable to give a detailed description of what happened. When it is the child, not the parent, who makes a false accusation, the accusation is likely to be opportunistic, with the child admitting the hoax upon detailed questioning.[18]

A parent who makes false allegations of sexual abuse risks losing custody himself or herself.[19] However, it is contrary to the public

---

17. *See*, Jean Goodwin, Doris Sahd & Richard T. Rada, *False Accusations and False Denials of Incest: Clinical Myths and Clinical Realities* in SEXUAL ABUSE: INCEST VICTIMS AND THEIR FAMILIES 17, 24 (Jean Goodwin, ed. 1982); Jean Goodwin, Doris Sahd & Richard T. Rada, *Incest Hoax: False Accusations, False Denials*, 6 BULL. AM. ACAD. PSYCHIATRY & LAW 269 (1979).

18. *See*, Goodwin, Sahd & Rada, *False Accusations and False Denials of Incest: Clinical Myths and Clinical Realities* in SEXUAL ABUSE: INCEST VICTIMS AND THEIR FAMILIES 18 (J. Goodwin, ed. 1982).

19. *See, e.g.*, Routh v. Routh, 492 S.E.2d 415 (S.C. Ct. App. 1997) (mother made false allegations of sexual abuse; mother was diagnosed as having a personality disorder, and father was happily remarried to a wife who loved the child); Williams v. Hinckle, 1997 WL 565969 (Ohio Ct. App. 9/11/1997) (mother's false sexual abuse allegations, relocation, and interference with father's visitation among factors warranting change of custody); Hanson v. Spolnik, 685 N.E. 71 (Ind. Ct. App. 1997) (mother made numerous false allegations of sexual abuse by father and engaged in a pattern of parental alienation); Hall v. Hubbard, 697 So.2d 486 (Ala. Civ. App. 1997) (mother made malicious false allegations of sexual abuse against father); Bruggeman v. Bruggeman, 1997 WL 202436 (Neb. Ct. App. 1997) (father made false allegations of sexual and physical abuse by mother and interfered with her visitation); Krywanczyk v. Krywanczyk, 236 A.D. 2d 746, 653 N.Y.S. 2d 970 (1997) (mother's allegations of sexual abuse entirely unfounded); Chance v. Chance, 911

policy favoring parental action to protect children and contrary to the child's best interests for custody to be changed merely as punishment for a parent's erroneous but good faith belief that the child has been molested by the other parent or stepparent.

To further complicate matters, it is well documented that there are often *false denials* of incest or *false recantations* of true allegations. A normal reaction of a normal victim is to say nothing about the ongoing molestation and to retract any reports after they are made. This subjects the victims to impeachment unless sufficient expert testimony is presented. This phenomenon of false denial and false recantation has been called the child sexual abuse accommodation syndrome.[20]

Assuming that the expert is properly qualified, testimony may be allowed to show that retraction is part of a pattern of intrafamilial sexual abuse.[21] Experts may be hard to find, however, and the lawyer

S.W.2d 40 (Tex. Ct. App. 1995) (mother made false allegations of sexual abuse and interfered with father's visitation); Young v. Young, 212 A.D.2d 114, 628 N.Y.S.2d 957 (1995) (court reversed trial court's *failure* to change custody based on mother's unfounded allegations of sexual abuse and interference with father's visitation where both the court appointed psychiatrist and law guardian recommended that the father be awarded custody); Beekman v. Beekman, 96 Ohio App. 3d 783, 645 N.E.2d 1332 (1994) (mother's allegations of sexual abuse by father were unsubstantiated; she attempted to poison the relationship between the children and their father); Beyer v. Tranelli-Ashe, 195 A.D.2d 972, 600 N.Y.S. 598 (1993) (mother repeatedly filed false allegations of physical and sexual abuse by the father and interfered with his visitation); Becker v. Becker, 613 So.2d 275 (La. Ct. App. 1993) (mother fabricated allegations of abuse and planted the notion in the children's minds to alienate them from their father); Pallay v. Pallay, 605 So.2d 582 (Fla. Dist. Ct. App. 1992) (mother consistently interfered with father's visitation, coached children to make false allegations and filed abuse charges prior to custody and visitation hearings); *In re* Interest of D.A., 475 N.W.2d 511 (Neb. 1991) (mother's continued unfounded allegations of sexual abuse and coaching the child resulted in state dependency action); Peterson v. Peterson, 818 P.2d 1305 (Utah Ct. App. 1991) (father's false allegations and coaching the child resulted in awarding mother custody and restricting father's visitations). *Cf.*, *In re* Morgan L., 716 A.2d 658 (Pa. Super. 1998) (affirming dependency adjudication and award of custody to unwed father based on mother's continual accusations that father molested child and her subjecting the child to numerous sexual abuse examinations despite evidence of no abuse; psychologist testified that mother had mental illness, Factitious Disorder by Proxy; child at risk of sexual exploitation through mother's continued actions).

20. *See, e.g.*, Roland Summit, *The Child Sexual Abuse Accommodation Syndrome*, 7 CHILD ABUSE & NEGLECT 177 (1983).

21. *See, e.g.*, State v. Lindsay, 149 Ariz. 472, 720 P.2d 73 (1986); People v. Sanchez, 256 Cal. Rptr. 446 (1989) (testimony concerning the child sexual abuse accommodation syndrome admissible to rehabilitate victim's credibility); *In re* Cheryl H., 153 Cal. App. 3d 1098, 200 Cal. Rptr. 789 (1984); Ward v. Florida (Fla. Dist. Ct. App., Feb 1, 1988) (psychologist permitted to testify that child's symptoms were consistent with child sexual abuse syndrome); State v. Kim, 647 Haw. 598, 645 P.2d 1330 (1982); State v. Myers, 359 N.W.2d 604 (Minn. 1984); Smith v. State, 100 Nev. 570, 688 P.2d 326 (1984); State v. J.Q., 599 A.2d 172 (N.J. Super. Ct. App. Div. 1991) (allowing testimony about the syndrome to explain children's secrecy and delayed disclosure not to prove affirmatively that children had been sexually abused); *In re* Nicole V., 510 N.Y.S.2d 567 (App. Div. 1987) (social worker who was child's therapist permitted to offer corroborating testimony that in her opinion child had been molested by father based on child's statements and physical manifestations); State v. Middleton, 294 Or. 427, 657 P.2d 1215 (1983); State v. Haseltine, 120 Wis. 2d 92, 353 N.W.2d 673 (1984). *But see, e.g.*, Lantrip v. Commonwealth, 713 S.W.2d 816 (Ky. 1986) (disallowing testimony on child sexual abuse accommodation syndrome as not having achieved scientific acceptance); Michigan v. Beckley, 456 N.W.2d 391 (Mich. 1990) (disallowing testimony in criminal cases on child sexual abuse accommodation syndrome, but permitting testimony explaining the individual behaviors at issue in the victim). *See generally* John E. B. Myers, Jan Bays, Judith Becker, Lucy Berliner, David L. Corwin & Karen J.

should question prospective experts carefully concerning their knowledge of and experience with intrafamilial sexual abuse. The child sexual abuse accommodation syndrome is a descriptive explanation of why many incest victims falsely deny and recant. It is important to realize that the syndrome is not diagnostic. In other words, the fact that a child does *not* deny or recant is *not* evidence that the child was not molested. Similarly, the mere fact that the child denies or recants is not evidence that the child *has* been molested. Unfortunately, some experts have attempted to use the syndrome diagnostically, a use which is neither supported by empirical evidence nor intended or defended by Dr. Roland Summit, who identified the syndrome.[22] If there is other evidence that a child has been molested, the syndrome is properly used to explain why a truly molested child would deny or recant allegations of molestation. The lawyer should make sure that any syndrome evidence is being used appropriately.

STRATEGIES

The most important strategy in representing parties in domestic cases involving allegations of abuse is to make a good faith attempt to determine the truth. The lawyer should refer parents who believe their children are being molested to qualified experts, who will try to determine whether the child's symptoms are indicative of molestation or other stress. Properly qualified experts can assist the parent and the court in devising safe visitation arrangements in situations where the facts are not clear[23] and can reassure parents who have interpreted certain behaviors as abuse-related when, in fact, the child is just having difficulty accepting the changes in his or her life.

The client's willingness to accept expert advice is essential and will benefit the client at every step of the process. Of course, this is

---

Saywitz, *Expert Testimony in Child Sexual Abuse Litigation*, 68 NEB. L. REV. 1 (1989); Berliner, Blick & Bulkley, *Expert Testimony on the Dynamics of Intra Familial Child Sexual Abuse and the Principles of Child Development*, in CHILD SEXUAL ABUSE AND THE LAW 166 (J. Bulkley ed. 3d ed 1982). For an excellent discussion of evidence concerning all types of syndromes, *see* John E. B. Myers, *Expert Testimony Describing Psychological Syndromes*, 24/3 PACIFIC L. J. 1449 (1993).

22. *See, e.g.*, Roland Summit, *Abuse of the Child Sexual Abuse Accommodation Syndrome*, 1/4 J. CHILD SEXUAL ABUSE 153 (1992).

23. One modality that strikes a sensible balance between the need of the child for protection and the rights of an accused parent who may have done nothing wrong is found at Appendix 14-1.

one reason why selection of a well-qualified and experienced expert is particularly important. The client probably comes to the lawyer with a strong opinion that the child has or has not been molested. It is the lawyer's job to ensure that the client has confidence that the expert will do a good evaluation and will do his or her best to act in the best interest of the child. If the expert is not objective and well-qualified, there is little reason for the client to accept his or her advice.

The client's willingness to have an open mind, to discover the real truth, is the best defense against charges of fabrication. The best *reality* for the child would be that he or she was not, in fact, molested. An evaluator or judge would find it strange that a parent would not be relieved to learn that his or her child had not been molested. A parent so convinced that the child was molested that he or she is unwilling to accept any contrary opinion, no matter how skilled the evaluator, will lose credibility. This same strategy applies to the accused parent, who must be willing to be open to the fact that the child has been molested, albeit by someone else. Even though the client may know that he or she did not molest the child, the best *reality* for a child who has been molested is to be believed and supported. A parent whose investment in denying any abuse at all is so strong that he or she will not consider that the child has been molested is likely to be viewed as insensitive to the child's needs and unable to provide appropriate protection and support for the child.

The client can certainly express an opinion, even a very strong opinion, that the child was or was not molested based on articulated reasons, but it is important for the client also to express a willingness to consider the expert's findings, whatever the final conclusion is. Otherwise the client will be perceived as expert-shopping, rejecting any opinion that is not consistent with what he or she wants to hear. Again, this will severely reduce the client's credibility and position in the litigation.

Another strategy designed to demonstrate that the client really is attempting to serve the child's best interests is to ask for appointment of a qualified lawyer for the child. The child's lawyer has no loyalty except to the child and is, therefore, at least theoretically free from the taint of having a personal agenda to be served in making or denying the allegations. The lawyer should be experienced in both sexual abuse and domestic relations cases if at all possible.[24] If the child's lawyer is properly qualified and experienced, the parent's lawyer should consider deferring the lead in the case to that lawyer. This will make it easier for the court to look at the child's best interests without being biased by the presumed self-interested motivation of the parents.

Specific strategies will differ based on whom the lawyer is representing. These strategies are discussed in detail in Chapters 8 through 11.

GOING UNDERGROUND

As mentioned above, domestic-relations judges may be more likely than juvenile or criminal judges to disbelieve a sexual abuse allegation. The failure to believe a true allegation may result in failure to protect the child, or even worse, a change in custody from the protective parent to the abusive parent. The rationale for this response is that a falsely accused parent may have no ability to reestablish or maintain a healthy relationship with the child if the child remains with a custodial parent who continues to maintain that the child was abused, especially if that parent continues to take the child to a series of evaluators in an effort to prove the nonexistent abuse.[25] The protective parent sometimes responds to this order changing custody by disappearing with the child—going underground. This self-help remedy may be taken for the best of motives, to protect the child from further abuse. However, it can result in placing the child in even greater danger.

The media have given a great deal of attention to this child-abuse "underground," whether done alone, with the help of friends

24. *See generally*, JEAN KOH PETERS, REPRESENTING CHILDREN IN CHILD PROTECTIVE PROCEEDINGS: ETHICAL AND PRACTICAL DIMENSIONS (1997); AMERICAN BAR ASSOCIATION, STANDARDS OF PRACTICE FOR LAWYERS WHO REPRESENT CHILDREN IN ABUSE AND NEGLECT CASES Standard I-2 (1996); *Recommendations of the Conference on Ethical Issues in the Legal Representation of Children*, 64/4 FORDHAM L. REV. 1302, 1306, Recommendation I(B)(1) (1996); ANN M. HARALAMBIE, THE CHILD'S ATTORNEY: REPRESENTING CHILDREN IN CUSTODY, ADOPTION, AND PROTECTION CASES (American Bar Association 1993).

25. *See, e.g.*, Beekman v. Beekman, 96 Ohio App. 3d 783, 645 N.E.2d 1332 (1994) (mother's false allegations that father molested child sufficiently changed circumstances to warrant change of custody); Pallay v. Pallay, 605 So.2d 582 (Fla. Dist. Ct. App. 1992) (mother consistently interfered with father's visitation, coached children to make false allegations and filed abuse charges prior to custody and visitation hearings); *In re* Interest of D.A., 239 Neb. 264, 475 N.W.2d 511 (1991) (mother's continued unfounded allegations of sexual abuse and coaching the child resulted in state dependency action); Peterson v. Peterson, 818 P.2d 1305 (Utah Ct. App. 1991) (father's false allegations and coaching the child resulted in awarding mother custody and restricting father's visitations).

and family members, or with the involvement of an organized system. The most well-known organized "underground" is Faye Yager's Children of the Underground in Atlanta, Ga. Faye Yager is one of the few participants in the child-abuse underground who has spoken to the press and appeared on numerous talk shows.[26]

Perhaps the most widely publicized underground case involved physician Elizabeth Morgan, who sent her daughter Hillary Foretich underground in response to the failure of a Washington, D.C., court to protect the child from alleged sexual abuse by her father, dentist Eric Foretich. The trial judge had found the evidence regarding sexual abuse to be "in equipoise," ruling, therefore, that Dr. Morgan had failed to meet her burden of proof.[27] Dr. Morgan was jailed for contempt until Congress passed special legislation to have her released. She joined her daughter in New Zealand, where she had been living with Dr. Morgan's parents. The New Zealand courts have supported Dr. Morgan's position.

I have never advised a client dissatisfied with the court's handling of the sexual-abuse case to go underground with the child. When I have been retained to represent clients who were underground, I have advised them to return voluntarily. It is difficult to imagine being in the position of a parent who believes that his or her child has been molested and who has sought help from the court system, only to have that system turn the child over to his or her molester. It is understandable that in the face of such circumstances a parent would lose faith in the system. However, while going underground may prevent remolestation, at least in the short-term, it is more likely to compound the child's problems.[28]

Living as a fugitive is not a healthy upbringing for a child. Not only is the child cut off from most or all friends and family, but he or she may have to change identity, lie about his or her past, move frequently, and become hypervigilant. The protective parent unwit-

---

26. For two views of Faye Yager's organization from the popular press, *see, e.g.*, Steve Lopez, *Hide and Seek*, TIME (May 11, 1998, page 56); Mackenzie Carpenter, *Children of the Underground*, series in PITTSBURGH POST-GAZETTE (December 14-18, 1997).

27. *See* Morgan v. Foretich, 546 A.2d 407, 410 (D.C. Ct. App. 1988), *cert. denied* 488 U.S. 1007, 109 S.Ct. 790, 102 L.Ed.2d 781.

28. *See generally*, JOHN E. B. MYERS, A MOTHER'S NIGHTMARE—INCEST: A PRACTICAL LEGAL GUIDE FOR PARENTS AND PROFESSIONALS (1997); Sheila Brogna, *Notes from the Underground: A Dialogue Among Attorneys Who Have Been There*, 17/2 FAMILY ADVOCATE 67 (1995).

tingly may be exchanging one form of abuse for another. If custody was given to the alleged abuser, the absconding parent is likely to be violating the state laws against custodial interference, which becomes a federal offense if the parent crosses state lines or leaves the country.[29] Therefore, law-enforcement officers are likely to be on the trail of the parent, and he or she risks arrest and incarceration if found. Aside from the possible criminal ramifications, the domestic-relations court is likely to be especially harsh with a parent who has gone underground. Visitation, if permitted at all, may be restricted to carefully supervised only. The parent who set out to protect the child might find himself or herself even more unable to protect the child.

A better strategy is to manage the legal case well, and if the judge makes a devastatingly wrong decision, to continue to work within the system, even if immediate protection is not possible. The lawyer must keep the client focused on the long-term interests of the child, even if that means accepting a short-term setback. It is not that continued molestation for the short term is acceptable. It is that the alternative may be much worse for the child and the parent who desires to be protective.

---

29. *See* Parental Kidnapping Prevention Act of 1980, Pub. L. No. 96-611, 94 Stat. 3566 § 10(a), declaring the intent of Congress "that section 1073 of title 18, United States Code, apply to cases involving parental kidnapping and interstate or international flight to avoid prosecution under applicable State felony statutes." For a more complete discussion of custodial interference, *See* 2 ANN M. HARALAMBIE, HANDLING CHILD CUSTODY, ABUSE AND ADOPTION CASES ch. 19 (2nd ed. Clark Boardman Callaghan 1993, West Group 1998).

Sexual Abuse Allegations in Protection Cases

3

Sexual Abuse in Protection Cases

Probably the most common forum in which to litigate child sexual abuse is in protection cases. These are the proceedings filed by Child Protective Services (CPS) and sometimes other agencies or private individuals, often in juvenile, family, or probate courts, depending on state law.[1] States refer to such cases by different names, such as children in need of assistance (CINA), children in need of care (CINC), children in need of protective services (CHIPS), child in need of services (CHINS), child protective proceeding, dependency, or dependency and neglect (D & N). For purposes of this book, all such cases will be referred to as protection cases, and the status of an adjudicated case will be referred to as a status of dependency. In 1996 sexual abuse cases constituted approximately 7 percent of all reports to CPS and 9 percent of all substantiated

1. For further information on dependency cases, *See generally*, 1 Ann M. Haralambie, Handling Child Custody, Abuse, and Adoption Cases ch. 11 (2nd ed, Clark Boardman Callaghan 1993, West Group 1998); 1 Thomas A. Jacobs, Children and the Law: Rights and Obligations ch. 2 (Clark Boardman Callaghan 1993, West Group 1997).

reports to CPS.[2] The proportion of sexual-abuse reports has declined during the past ten years[3] but continues to constitute a significant problem.

Protection actions involve the court directly in the supervision of children under its jurisdiction. This differs, for example, from domestic-relations cases where the court adjudicates the rights between the two parents but does not generally continue to monitor their behavior unless one party brings a subsequent modification or enforcement action before the court. In a protection case CPS or another petitioning party asks for court supervision because the child has no parent able to care properly for him or her. CPS may intervene in cases where both parents commit or allow the abuse or where the nonoffending parent fails to protect the child from the abuse.[4] If one parent is willing to protect the abused child, such as by divorcing the abuser and obtaining appropriate orders regulating the abuser's contact with the child, CPS may decide not to file a protection action. Such a decision is not an indication that the agency did not believe that abuse had occurred, but rather, an indication only that state intervention was not necessary to protect the child.[5]

Sexual abuse is explicitly listed as a ground for intervention in most states[6] and is implicitly included in the definition of interven-

---

2. *See* Ching-Tung Wang & Deborah Daro, *Current Trends in Child Abuse Reporting and Fatalities: The Results of the 1996 Annual Fifty State Survey* 7 (National Committee to Prevent Child Abuse 1997), based on data from 25 states for all reports and from 31 states for substantiated reports. The annual reports of the National Center on Child Abuse Prevention research, a program of the NCPCA, are available from the organization at 332 S. Michigan Avenue, Suite 1600, Chicago, IL 60604, (312) 663-3520, fax (312) 939-8962, web site http://www.childabuse.org.

3. *Id.*

4. *See, e.g.*, Matter of Elizabeth G., 680 N.Y.S.2d 32 (App. Div. 1998).

5. The failure of counsel and courts to appreciate the basis for such a CPS decision creates havoc in many domestic relations cases where a CPS report has been made but no action has been taken. The often inaccurate inference is drawn that CPS found the allegation of abuse to be spurious. This situation is dealt with in Chapter 2. A related problem, also dealt with in Chapter 2, is the heightened skepticism CPS workers may have where allegations are reported in the context of a separating family or parents involved in post-decree litigation.

6. *See* ALASKA STAT. § 47.17.290(2) and (16); ARIZ. REV. STAT. § 8-201(2); ARK. CODE ANN. § 9-27-303(4)(A); CAL. WELF. & INST. CODE § 300(d); CONN. GEN. STAT. ANN. § 46b-120(3)(C); D.C. CODE ANN. § 16-2301(23) and (25); FLA. STAT. ANN. § 39.01(2); HAW. REV. STAT. § 587-2; IDAHO CODE § 16-1602(a)(2); IND. CODE ANN. § 31-6-4-3(a)(3); IOWA CODE ANN. § 232.2(6)(d) and (i) and (49); KAN. STAT. ANN. § 38-1502(a)(3) and (c); KY. REV. STAT. ANN. § 600.020(1), (49), and (50); LA. REV. STAT. ANN. art. 603(1)(c) and (9); ME. REV. STAT. ANN. tit. 22, § 4002(1) and 10(C); MD. CODE ANN. FAM. LAW § 5-701(b)(2); MINN. STAT. ANN. § 260.015 subd. 2a(2)(i); MISS. CODE ANN. § 43-21-105(m); MO. ANN. STAT. § 210.110(1); MONT. CODE ANN. § 41-3-102(7)(b), (12)(a) and (13); NEV. REV. STAT. ANN. § 432B.020(1)(b); N.H. REV. STAT. ANN. § 169-C:3(II)(a) and (XXVII-a); N.J. REV. STAT. ANN. § 9:6-89(c) and 9:6-8.21(c)(3); N.M. STAT. ANN. § 32A-4-2(B)(2), (E), and (F); N.C. GEN. STAT. § 7A-517(1)(c); OHIO REV. CODE ANN. § 2151.031(A); S.D. CODIFIED LAWS ANN. § 26-8A-2(8); TENN. CODE ANN. § 37-1-102(10)(I) (this section refers specifically to what would be considered sexual exploitation, rather than to direct sexual abuse); UTAH CODE ANN. § 78-3a-103(a); VA.

tion in the remaining states. Failure to protect from sexual abuse is explicitly listed as a form of neglect in several states[7] and constitutes a basis for intervention in other states as well.[8] Allowing one's child to commit a sex offense may also constitute a ground for intervention.[9] A protection case may be based on the parent's acquiescence in a consensual but inappropriate sexual relationship between the child and another person.[10] Molestation of one child in the home may be sufficient to constitute a protection case as to the other children in the home.[11] Further, molestation of another child by the same alleged perpetrator is relevant to whether the sibling in question was molested.[12]

INVESTIGATION AND EVALUATION

Because sexual abuse typically occurs without witnesses and is often cloaked in secrecy, most reports of sexual abuse arise from disclosures made by the child, often to a parent or other close relative, caretaker, or teacher. CPS workers investigating allegations of abuse often attempt to interview the child without prior notice to the parents, often by talking to the child at school or preschool. While this procedure generally angers parents, it is an understandable and justifiable act in light of the secrecy with which sexual abuse generally takes place and the pressures placed on children not to tell. If the parents were given advance notice of the interview, they could more easily threaten or bribe the child to deny the abuse. In almost all protection-case contexts, the parent's anger at CPS or the "system" is counterproductive. The lawyer for either parent, therefore, should attempt to keep the client child-focused rather than agency-blaming.

CODE ANN. § 16.1-228(4); WASH. REV. CODE ANN. § 26.44.020(12) and (15); W. VA. CODE § 49-1-3(a)(2), (c), (e), and (i)-(m); WIS. STAT. ANN. § 48.02(1)(b); WYO. STAT. § 14-3-202(a)(ii).

7. *See, e.g.*, ARK. CODE ANN. § 9-27-303(23)(C); ME. REV. STAT. ANN. tit. 22, § 4002(1); N.M. STAT ANN. § 32A-4-2(C)(3).

8. *See, e.g.*, *In re* Appeal in Pima County Juvenile Dependency Action No. 97247, 158 Ariz. 55, 760 P.2d 1104 (Ct. App. 1988).

9. *See, e.g.*, IND. CODE ANN. § 31-6-4-3(a)(5).

10. *See, e.g.*, New Jersey Division of Youth & Family Services v. R.W., 273 N.J. Super. 365, 641 A.2d 1124 (Ch. Div. 1994) (dependency may be based on parent's acquiescence in 13-year-old daughter's sexual relationship with 19-year-old man allowed to share her bedroom).

11. *See, e.g.*, *In re* S.G., 581 A.2d 771 (D.C. Ct. App. 1990) (upholding neglect finding concerning younger half-siblings of 7-year-old molested by her stepfather); *In re* Katherine C., 471 N.Y.S.2d 216 (1984) (upholding neglect finding concerning brothers of girl molested by her father since age 10, despite lack of showing specific harm to them).

12. *See, e.g.*, Morgan v. Foretich, 846 F.2d 941 (4th Cir 1988).

Prior to the 1980s the most common CPS response to credible evidence of sexual abuse was to remove the abused child from the home. However, this served to penalize the child victim rather than the abuser. Therefore, the practice now is usually to keep the child in the home if there is a supportive parent willing to protect the child, and the perpetrator leaves the home. This more fairly requires the heaviest consequences to be paid by the party at fault. In most cases the lawyer for any of the involved parties should encourage cooperation with this policy. The lawyer for the child will seek to minimize disruption to the child's life, the lawyer for the protective parent will strengthen the perception of the client as a fit, protective parent, and the lawyer for the accused will show that the client is willing to be sensitive and defer to the child's comfort and continuity of placement. A request that the alleged perpetrator leave the house at least during the investigative stage should be complied with, except where there is no basis whatsoever for a suspicion that the child may be in danger if left in the home with the alleged perpetrator.[13] Even then, the lawyer should consider the benefits of being gracious and cooperative even under an unfair attack.

The CPS investigator has a difficult task in investigating sexual abuse cases, even with competent help from medical and psychological experts. Most incestuous sexual abuse does not involve violent or traumatic injury to the child. Usually there are no physical signs accompanying the abuse,[14] and none would be expected from the fondling and oral-genital contact frequently employed. There are no definitive psychological tests or batteries of tests to identify abused children or their abusers.[15] Therefore, the investigation of a sexual abuse allegation relies largely on history and nonexclusive behavioral or emotional symptoms.

Children's responses to sexual abuse vary considerably.[16] Responded to with parental support, nonviolent, isolated incidents

---

13. *See, e.g.*, Croft v. Westmoreland County, Children and Youth Services, 103 F.3d 1123 (3rd Cir. 1997) (parents may sue agency for interfering with their 14th Amendment liberty interest in their companionship with their child where the agency investigator told the father he must immediately leave the house or the child would be placed in foster care, based only on an anonymous report that the child was being molested; there was no reasonable ground to believe that the child was in imminent danger under the circumstances).

14. See Chapter 7.

15. See Chapter 6.

16. *See, e.g.*, Robert A. Prentky, *Child Sexual Molestation*, in HANDBOOK OF PSYCHOLOGICAL APPROACHES WITH VIOLENT OFFENDERS: CONTEMPORARY STRATEGIES AND ISSUES 267 (M. Hersen & V. Van Hasselt, eds., 1999); David P. H. Jones, *Assessment of Suspected Child Sexual Abuse*, in THE BATTERED CHILD 296 (Mary Edna

of sexual abuse by a stranger may leave little or no lasting ill effects. At the other extreme, chronic, sadistic sexual abuse by a caretaker may leave permanent damage throughout the child's life. In general, the negative effect of the abuse will be greater the closer relationship the abuser has with the child, the more frequent the abuse is, and the more violent or degrading the abuse is. However, children will respond very differently even to the same level of abuse by a similarly situated abuser. This variability is important, not only to appreciate the treatment needs of sexually abused children, but also to understand the wide continuum of observable symptoms in children. The fact that a child does not demonstrate anxiety, depression, regressed behaviors, or somatic complaints, for example, is not evidence that the child was not abused or that state intervention is not necessary to protect the child. Similarly, the fact that a child is severely disturbed does not mean that the child must have been molested.

CPS investigators generally have a limited number of boxes to check in order to determine whether or not there is a basis to believe that a child has been sexually molested and CPS intervention is warranted. Some workers are restricted to only two choices, such as "founded" or "unfounded," "substantiated" or "unsubstantiated," or "valid" or "invalid." These all-or-nothing choices are wholly inadequate for several reasons. First, use of these terms connotes a positive finding that the abuse did occur or that the abuse did not occur. In many cases, however, a third category, "insufficient information" or "I don't know," is more accurate.[17] Better yet, and a more honest reflection of the limits of our current assessment capabilities, would be a continuum, such as the one used by the Kempe Children's Cen-

---

Helfer, Ruth S. Kempe & Richard D. Krugman, eds. 1997); Anthony P. Mannarino & Judith A. Cohen, *A Follow-Up Study of Factors That Mediate the Development of Psychological Symptomatology in Sexually Abused Girls*, 1/3 CHILD MALTREATMENT 246 (1996).

17. Use of the option "unable to substantiate" has been discouraged by the National Association of Public Child Welfare Administrators. *See* GUIDELINES FOR A MODEL SYSTEM OF PROTECTIVE SERVICES FOR ABUSED AND NEGLECTED CHILDREN AND THEIR FAMILIES (National Association of Public Child Welfare Administrators, ed. 1988). However the organization did emphasize that a finding of "unsubstantiated" should not be taken as a positive finding of no abuse, but rather, as a negative finding of insufficient evidence. Despite the NAPCWA recommendation, ten years later other professionals and members of the public continue to view "unsubstantiated," "unfounded," and their other synonyms as an indication that the child was not likely to have been abused.

ter (Kempe Center) in Denver, Colorado. The categories of choice on the Kempe Center continuum are:[18]

- Reliable or substantiated accounts: Reports considered by the caseworkers after applying a systematic process of validation to be likely accounts of child sexual abuse.
- Recantations: Cases that were felt to be likely accounts of child sexual abuse that were subsequently retracted by the child. Their retraction was considered to be falsely made under duress (Summit, 1983).
- Unsubstantiated suspicions: Reports by an adult about a child. The adult reported his/her suspicion without malice. The individual making the report accepted the conclusion of [the agency] that child sexual abuse had not occurred.
- Insufficient information reports: Those for which [the agency] did not have enough data to conclude whether or not child sexual abuse had occurred.
- Fictitious reports by adults: Those made about children, yet considered by [the agency] to have not occurred. Deliberate falsifications, misperceptions, and confused interpretations of nonsexual events were all potentially included in this category.[19]
- Fictitious reports by children: Those in which the child provided an account of sexual abuse that was considered falsely made. As in the previous category, falsifications and misperceptions were included, as well as situations where the child had been coached by an adult to make a false account.

CPS workers possess a wide range of formal and informal training and experience in recognizing and dealing with child sexual

18. As stated in J. Melbourne McGraw & Holly A. Smith, *Child Sexual Abuse Allegations Amidst Divorce and Custody Proceedings: Refining the Validation Process*, 1/1 J. CHILD SEXUAL ABUSE 49, 53 (1992).

19. This last sentence reflects a troubling ambiguity in this category. I believe strongly that misperceptions and confused interpretations warrant their own category, which I have called "good faith but erroneous" allegations.

abuse. Particularly where case workers are overloaded with cases, there may be an inordinate deference given to various quick screening instruments or clinical rules of thumb in deciding whether or not to intervene. Because inappropriate intervention or the failure to intervene appropriately both disserve children and their families, it is essential that the investigation and evaluation of sexual abuse cases be undertaken by the best-qualified, most-experienced people possible, using state-of-the art knowledge and techniques. Because these are changing rapidly, a lawyer involved in a protection case should find out the qualifications and ongoing training of the people making the decisions about the case.

PRE-ADJUDICATION OPTIONS AND STRATEGIES

The most important strategy for the parent's lawyer is to adopt a sincere, child-focused position in the case. In the earliest stages of the case the parent is most likely to be angry and resentful of the process. The parent is also likely to be defensive. Because the rest of the participants in "the system" consider themselves to be at least partially child-focused, one of the lawyer's first tasks is to deal with the parent's emotional perspective. The parent who is thinking about the effect of the proceedings on the child, including the reactions of everyone involved, is in the best position to work with the lawyer to formulate a reasonable approach to the case.

Cooperation is usually my preferred approach to protection cases. CPS workers make many subjective determinations in cases, which then get memorialized in progress notes, case reports, and referral letters to subsequent evaluators and therapists. A case file takes on a life of its own, which may or may not be an accurate account of the facts in the case. Information and opinions of one person become part of the basis for subsequent professionals' opinions and reports. It is not unheard of for blatant errors to be repeated in many different reports and charts, with each repetition in an "independent" document taken as corroboration for the truth of the statement. Therefore, offending or creating problems for a CPS worker may trigger a long series of unflattering interpretations that will be passed on to others and to the court. Parents in protection cases need the best face possible when they get to court, and how they will appear at the adjudicatory trial is related in large part to how they have comported themselves from the beginning of the investigation.

CPS has dual goals: to protect children and to rehabilitate families. The best strategy for parents is to head in the same direction. Since CPS investigators are regularly greeted with animosity and hostility by the parents they investigate, most develop a thick skin. They generally understand that parents resent the intrusion and the upheaval in their lives. However, they appreciate a parent who expresses (and acts on) genuine concern for the child and a willingness to discover the truth. Of course, this applies primarily to the parent who is not directly abusing or aiding the abuse of the child. The desired response from the abuser is admission, contrition, and rehabilitation.

There is a caveat with respect to admitting abuse. While it is my opinion[20] that it is always in the child's best interests for the abuser to admit the abuse, take full responsibility, apologize to the child, get therapy to address the underlying problems, and base the rehabilitation of the relationship on the child's readiness, admission carries a potential risk of criminal prosecution. The alleged abuser should be advised of this potential criminal exposure. Parents are less likely than other persons to be prosecuted for sexually abusing their children.[21] Many prosecutors will not file a case of sexual abuse if the matter is being addressed in a protection case, believing that the child victim is being adequately protected and that the abusive parent is being held responsible. Therefore, if it is unlikely that criminal action will be taken in a particular case, it is generally best to advise a client who has, in fact, molested the child to cooperate in repairing the damage done to the child. The prosecutor may be will-

---

20. I am first and foremost a child advocate. While I do represent parents, including guilty parents, in protection cases the court is going to be concerned with the child's best interests, and the best representation of most parents' positions is to show that what the parent is requesting would serve the child's best interests. This is something more than a shallow invocation of a magic phrase. It must be based on the parent's ability to focus on being a good parent, on doing the right thing for the child.

21. *See, e.g.*, J. R. Chapman & B. Smith, *Response of Social Service and Criminal Justice Agencies to Child Sexual Abuse Complaints*, 10/3 RESPONSE TO THE VICTIMIZATION OF WOMEN AND CHILDREN (1987); David Finkelhor, *Removing the Child—Prosecuting the Offender in Cases of Sexual Abuse: Evidence from the National Reporting System for Child Abuse and Neglect*, 7/2 CHILD ABUSE & NEGLECT 195 (1983).

ing to sign an agreement not to use any admissions made in the course of the protection case and related therapy. The lawyer for the abuser should point out to the prosecutor how this approach will facilitate the child victim's healing. Usually a prosecutor will want to limit this agreement to past abuse or allegations already disclosed. Admissions to ongoing abuse will not be protected.

Placement pending the adjudicatory trial is an important issue to consider and plan for at the earliest possible time. It is better for children to be with safe caretakers they know rather than with strangers. If the allegation runs only to one parent, the best strategy is to have that parent leave the home, at least until the adjudicatory trial is complete. It is important for the parent's lawyer to emphasize the importance of following the CPS rules and expectations for continued placement at home. For example, the other parent should agree to follow all CPS or court rules regarding limitations on contact with the alleged perpetrator. The parent with whom the child is placed should not initiate discussions of the case with the child and should not try to talk the child into recanting any allegations which he or she has made. The parent should ensure that the child makes all evaluation or therapy sessions and should not interrogate the child about what was said during those sessions. The parent should not make the child feel guilty about disclosing the allegations or causing the family to come under CPS and court scrutiny. In other words, the parent should be supportive of the child and demonstrate an ability to protect the child. This is true even if the parent is not convinced that the allegations are true.

Sometimes the child tells the protective parent that the allegations were false. There are false recantations and false denials as well as false allegations. False recantations may reflect the child's fear about the consequences of the disclosure, concern for the parents' well-being, or guilt, among other possible explanations. The best advice to give a parent under such circumstances is simply to encourage the child to tell the truth, regardless of the perceived ramifications. The parent should tell the evaluator, therapist, or CPS worker about the child's statement and repeat that the parent's advice to the child was to tell the truth. The parent should express the hope that *either way*, the truth will be able to be determined. This is an important strategy because if the parent is unwilling to believe and act on the truth, his or her credibility[22] and ability to protect the child will be diminished. It is in the child's best interests for the truth to be known and dealt with, and the protective parent's ultimate response to the situation will differ based on whether or not the child was molested. Even if the child was not molested, there is usually a problem in the child, parent, or family, which led to the false allegation. That problem will need to be dealt with.

If the CPS worker or the court is unwilling to allow the child to remain with one or both parents, the lawyer for the child or for a parent should consider which other family members or friends might be available to take the child. These third persons should have at least an open mind about the allegations. The court is unlikely to approve placement with people who are convinced that the child was not abused, because at best they are unlikely to be supportive of the child, and at worst they might try to persuade the child to recant. Friends or family members are more likely to be flexible about scheduling visits and maintaining the child's normal school, social, and extracurricular activities than agency-sponsored foster parents might be. It is essential, however, that such third parties scrupulously abide by the court orders and CPS instructions.

Unless the case against the parents is weak, a full-fledged adjudicatory trial generally will not help the parents. If the court adjudicates the child, the judge will have heard the most damaging information about the parents. If adjudication is a foregone conclusion, it is generally preferable to stipulate to an adjudication and concentrate on the dispositional hearing. The judge will appreciate the parents' willingness to accept responsibility for the abuse, and he or she will not have heard all of the possible damaging evidence.

It may be possible to negotiate a revision in the language of the original petition to be more palatable for the parents to admit. Sometimes the most egregious allegations may be omitted. Parents may object primarily to inaccuracies in peripheral facts, which are almost always able to be corrected through an amended petition. It may be possible to add an allegation that the parent now realizes

22. Credibility is diminished to the extent that the court sees a bias, including a predetermined view which may not be swayed despite evidence to the contrary.

that the conduct alleged was inappropriate and has begun counseling to more clearly define appropriate boundaries. A formerly nonprotective parent may now believe the allegations and be willing to support and protect the child. The lawyer should consider what the parent's negotiable and non-negotiable positions are with respect to the language in the petition, and attempt to negotiate an amendment that will fulfill the statutory requirements as well as meet the parent's objections.

In negotiating, the lawyer must remember the larger context of the case. Amended petitions do more than merely resolve the adjudicatory issues in the case. They may form the baseline against which the parent's rehabilitation efforts are measured. They may form the basis for a subsequent petition to terminate parental rights. Admissions may constitute res judicata or collateral estoppel in a subsequent tort action based on the abuse or failure to protect. The lawyer may be able to negotiate for a "no contest" plea rather than an admission where there is a credible possibility of criminal or tort actions being filed. However, the parent needs to understand that the court will be making a finding that the abuse occurred. While agencies are sometimes willing to agree to an amendment that essentially says that the child will be adjudicated based on the child's allegations, the parent's denial, and the untenable situation of having the child reside at home under those circumstances, such a settlement may create more problems than it resolves. Future visitation and therapeutic services should be based on whether or not the abuse occurred, not merely that there is a parent-child dispute.[23]

It may be possible to defer adjudication if it is likely that the child can be protected fairly quickly. For example, a protective parent may divorce the abuser and obtain a domestic-relations order prohibiting visitation or requiring supervised visitation for the abuser. CPS may be willing to defer the adjudication in contemplation of dismissing the case once the divorce is final.

If it appears that the case is not well-founded, or if the parties refuse to work out a reasonable settlement, then the lawyer must prepare for trial. The investigation may have been performed by a

---

23. For example, some of the problems that flow from such an adjudication are discussed in *In re* Iris M., 118 Md. App. 636, 703 A.2d 1279 (1998).

CPS investigator, law-enforcement officer, or both. All of the available records must be gathered and reviewed. Discrepancies may exist in comparing various accounts. Timelines, side-by-side charts comparing witness statements, and other litigation tools should be employed to organize the case.

In most cases, the expert evidence will be crucial. Therefore, the lawyer must carefully assess the data, the expert's qualifications and experience, the expert's analysis, and the conclusions.[24] The lawyer should consider retaining the use of expert consultants to assist in understanding the opposing views and the weaknesses of those experts' credentials, methods, and conclusions. If possible, the lawyer should determine the detailed basis for the opposing expert's opinion. Funds may be unavailable to conduct depositions, especially in court-appointed cases. However, the opposing expert may be available for informal interview. Any studies or other literature that form a basis for the expert's position should be obtained and reviewed.

Because protection cases are civil, the parents may be compelled to testify. While they are entitled to claim the Fifth Amendment privilege against self-incrimination, local evidence law may permit the court to draw an adverse inference from invocation of the privilege or may permit the court to strike the rest of their testimony.[25] The parent should be carefully prepared for the anticipated testimony, keeping in mind the strategic advantages of being genuinely child-focused. Anger, hostility, sarcasm, blaming everybody else, and vilifying the child are tactics that rarely persuade judges hearing protection cases.

THE ADJUDICATORY TRIAL

In most jurisdictions the adjudicatory trial must determine whether the child was molested or otherwise improperly parented *and* that the child cannot be adequately protected without state intervention.

---

24. For more detailed information see Chapter 6, Behavioral Health Evaluations of Sexual Abuse Allegations, and Chapter 7, Medical and Physical Evaluations of Sexual Abuse Allegations. See also, ANN M. HARALAMBIE, HANDLING CHILD CUSTODY, ABUSE AND ADOPTION CASES ch. 22 (2nd ed. Clark Boardman Callaghan 1993, West Group 1998).

25. *See, e.g.*, Baxter v. Palmigiano, 425 U.S. 308 (1976) (permissible for court in a civil case to draw an adverse inference from invocation of Fifth Amendment privilege against self-incrimination).

Protection cases are almost always bench trials, and a civil burden of proof is used unless the case is being tried under the Indian Child Welfare Act.[26] Further, special evidentiary rules may apply to permit the child's hearsay statements about the abuse.[27] The lawyer must be aware of the substantive and procedural rules which will apply to the case.

Strategies for the various parties are discussed more specifically in Chapters 8 through 11. In general, it is not necessary to prove that the parent molested the child if the court finds that the child was molested while under the parent's care. Therefore, inadequate supervision and other forms of failure to protect the child may suffice for adjudication. An unrebutted prima facie case may also support an adjudication.[28] If the child was abused by a third party, the central question is whether the parent is able to protect the child from further abuse and to support the child in dealing with the aftermath of abuse.

DISPOSITIONAL ALTERNATIVES

Once the child has been adjudicated as dependent, the court must enter dispositional orders. In some cases the parties stipulate to the

---

26. 25 U.S.C. § 1901 *et seq.* This Act is dealt with in more detail in 2 ANN M. HARALAMBIE, HANDLING CHILD CUSTODY, ABUSE AND ADOPTION CASES ch. 15 (2nd ed. Clark Boardman Callaghan 1993, West Group 1998); 1 THOMAS A. JACOBS, CHILDREN AND THE LAW: RIGHTS AND OBLIGATIONS ch. 5 (Clark Boardman Callaghan 1995, West Group 1997); B. J. JONES, THE INDIAN CHILD WELFARE ACT HANDBOOK: A LEGAL GUIDE TO THE CUSTODY AND ADOPTION OF NATIVE AMERICAN CHILDREN (American Bar Association 1995).

27. *See, e.g.*, FED. R. EVID. 803(25); ALA. CODE § 15-25-31 through -37 (1997); ARIZ. REV. STAT. § 8-238 (1989); CAL. EVID. CODE § 1360 (1998); COLO. REV. STAT. § 13-25-129 (1997); DEL. CODE ANN. tit. 11, § 3513 (1997); FLA. STAT ANN. § 90.803(23) (1997); GA. CODE ANN. § 24-3-16 (1998); IDAHO CODE § 19-3024 (1997); IND. CODE ANN. § 35-37-4-6 (1998); KAN. STAT. ANN. § 60-460(dd) (1997); ME. REV. STAT. ANN. tit. 15, § 1205 (1997); MD. CODE 1957 Art. 27, § 775 (1997); MASS. GEN LAWS ANN. ch. 233, § 81 (1998); MICH. R. EVID. 803A; MINN. STAT. ANN. § 595.02(3) (1997); MISS. R. EVID. 803(25); MO. ANN. STAT. § 491.075 (1996); NEV. REV. STAT. ANN. § 51.385 (1997); N.J. R. EVID. 803(27); OHIO R. EVID. 807; OKLA. STAT. ANN. tit. 12, § 2803.1 (1993); OR. REV. STAT. § 40.460 (1997); PA. STAT. ANN. tit.42, § 5985.1 (1998); S.D. CODIFIED LAWS ANN. § 19-16-38 (1998); TEX. CRIM. P. CODE ANN. Art. 38.072 (1998); UTAH CODE ANN. § 76-5-411 (1997); VT. R. EVID. 804a. *See generally*, 2 JOHN E. B. MYERS, EVIDENCE IN CHILD ABUSE AND NEGLECT CASES § 7.53 (3rd ed. 1997); 2 ANN M. HARALAMBIE, HANDLING CHILD CUSTODY, ABUSE AND ADOPTION CASES § 21.12 (2nd ed. Clark Boardman Callaghan 1993, West Group 1998); Robert G. Marks, *Should We Believe the People Who Believe the Children? The Need for a New Sexual Abuse Tender Years Hearsay Exception Statute*, 32 HARVARD J. LEGISLATION 207 (1995); Michelle M. Zehnder, *A Step Forward: Rule 803(25), A New Approach to Child Hearsay Statements*, 20 WILLIAM MITCHELL L. REV. 875 (1994).

28. *See, e.g.*, *In re* Najam M., 232 A.D.2d 281, 648 N.Y.S.2d 559 (1996) (reversing trial court's dismissal of petition based on sexual abuse of four-year-old child). The Court stated that a prima facie case of abuse may be established by showing an injury to the child which would not ordinarily occur absent an act or omission of the parents and that the parents were the caretakers of the child at the time the injury occurred. Once the prima facie showing is made, the burden shifts to the parent to offer a satisfactory explanation to rebut the evidence of abuse.

status of dependency, and the major contested hearing is the dispositional hearing. Where the entire case is contested, the court may combine the dispositional hearing with the adjudicatory trial. This section deals with dispositional issues regardless of what the hearing at which they are addressed is called. The dispositional issues include legal and physical custody, visitation, therapy, and other services. The dispositional hearing may also determine what the case plan will be.

The court's first decision is whether to place the child in the legal custody of a parent, third party, or governmental agency. If the court is concerned about providing services to the family or close monitoring, legal custody will most likely be placed with a state or county agency. The agency is then charged with attempting to rehabilitate and reunite the family if possible. In most cases, the court awards legal custody of the child to the agency. The court is more likely to award legal custody to a third party when the third party has filed the protection case.[29] Grandparents, aunts, and uncles are the most likely to fit in this category. The court is most likely to award legal custody to a parent in situations where the parents are not currently married to each other and there is an impediment to the nonoffending parent's obtaining immediate custody in another proceeding. For example, the offending parent may have custody from a divorce action, and the nonoffending parent may not have been able to obtain a modification of custody yet. Another example is the situation of unmarried parents where legal paternity has not yet been established and custody determined. In such cases, the protection case may be a short-term solution pending the nonoffending parent's obtaining custody in a domestic-relations action.[30]

The physical-placement issues at the dispositional hearing are similar to the pre-adjudicatory placement issues. An effort should be made to place the child in the most familiar, most comfortable environment that will provide adequate support and nurturance for the

29. In some states only an agency can file a protection action. In others, third parties may also file. *See generally* ANN M. HARALAMBIE, HANDLING CHILD CUSTODY, ABUSE AND ADOPTION CASES § 11.04 (2nd ed. Clark Boardman Callaghan 1993, West Group 1998).

30. Because protection cases may preempt domestic relations custody actions, it may make sense to consolidate the two actions to allow for a permanent custody order to be made. In some states, such as California, the juvenile court is permitted to enter exit orders, terminating the protection case under orders which bridge the time until a domestic relations order is obtained.

child. Ideally, this will be in the child's own home, in the physical custody of a protective parent. It is more equitable to remove the abuser from the home than to remove the child. However, where the child cannot be safe at home, a relative or friend should be sought as a placement. It is essential that a privately located placement be willing to comply with the court's orders. While agency foster homes are familiar with restrictions on the child's contact with family members, restrictions on taking the child out of the jurisdiction on vacation without prior agency approval, and other rules limiting the custodian's authority, private parties may not be used to living their lives with such governmental oversight.

Whoever had physical custody pending adjudication has a tremendous advantage in seeking to continue that custody at the dispositional hearing. This is especially true if the child has been placed with a parent, relative, or friend. Courts do not want to disrupt children's lives any more than is necessary. Unless there is a problem with the current placement, there should be a substantial reason to warrant a change. Such a reason may be found more easily where the child is in a foster home.

The case plan provides a starting point for placement decisions. If the plan is to return the child to a parent, then the placement should facilitate that goal. If the parent can be a safe custodian pending final termination of the case, then the child should be placed with that parent (usually the nonoffending parent). If the parent is not yet able to provide adequate safety and nurturance, then the child should be placed in a safe home under circumstances that permit ongoing contact with the intended future custodian. Placement with a relative or friend often allows the child to have more flexible contact with the parent(s) and continuation of his or her ordinary life. Such third parties may be more willing to transport the child to the neighborhood school, continue extracurricular activities, facilitate contacts with friends, and otherwise provide less disruption than placement in a foster home. On the other hand, if the case plan is termination of parental rights or long-term foster care or guardianship, then the child should be placed in a home likely to adopt the child or keep the child long-term. A succession of placements rarely benefits the child. If the child must be placed in a foster home, every effort should be made to find a foster home that can best accommodate the child's regular routine and activities.

In my opinion, whether or not there is visitation should be based solely on the child's needs. The question goes far beyond the ability to protect the child's physical safety, such as by providing supervised visits. The circumstances warranting adjudication show a failure of the parents to provide a safe environment for the child. In addition to the sexual abuse itself, the child is likely to have suffered emotional damage as well. Some children need ongoing contact, even with the abuser, as part of their healing. Others need the refuge of no contact. The lawyer for any party should present mental-health testimony concerning how the *child* will benefit from a particular visitation schedule. The court's desire to punish a parent should not deprive the child of needed contact. Similarly, the court's desire to reunify the family should not prematurely force a child to visit a parent contrary to the child's well-being. The parents' lawyers should also present evidence concerning how the visitation schedule fits into the case plan.

Services should be offered to the child regardless of whether the case plan is to reunify the child or place the child in another permanent placement. Those services should be based on what the child's individual needs are. Services to the family will depend on whether a termination petition will be filed immediately. If not, then reunification services will be necessary. One problem that often occurs with reunification services is that the offender is not motivated to engage in therapy. In such cases, it is an unnecessary burden on the child welfare agency and inappropriate task for the mental health community to order treatment. Donna Moore and her colleagues state:

> Meaningful sex offender treatment requires voluntary participation on the part of the offender, since successful treatment requires acknowledgment of personal responsibility for sex offending prior to developing coping strategies that will aid offenders in controlling and inhibiting their sex offending patterns of behavior. The motivation for participation in treatment must be self generated by the offender and cannot be imposed by external agents. . . .
>
> Sex offending behavior is a complex, multi-determined pattern of destructive behavior. Effective treatment of such complex behavior cannot be accomplished by simple, superficial, or rapid means. . . . Sex offenders who are not amenable to treatment or who are at high risk for noncompletion of treatment are not legitimately the purview of

> mental health professionals. . . . Solutions to the problem of untreatable sex offenders will most appropriately come from other sectors.[31]

The dispositional hearing should result in meaningful orders setting forth what services will be provided to each member of the family and what objectives the services are designed to meet. Parents who have molested their children clearly need therapy.[32] Similarly, nonabusing parents require therapy to learn to be more protective and to learn how to support the abused child. Nonoffending parents are often clinically depressed and feel guilty for not knowing about or preventing the abuse. Such parents will need their own supportive therapy. Each party's compliance with the case plan will be an issue at subsequent review hearings, and the parents' failure to comply might result in grounds for termination of their parental rights.[33] Therefore, the lawyer should insist on a specific case plan, with behavioral objectives clearly set forth.

The case plan should indicate not only what services will be provided and what the parents will be expected to attend, but also, what the parents will be expected to *accomplish*. Behavioral objectives should set forth measurable changes. The parties, court, and lawyers should be able to know whether or not the objectives have been met. Vague case-plan requirements such as "stable housing and employment" and "effective parenting" are of little use, and there may be considerable dispute as to whether or not the terms have been met. Further, the behavioral objectives should relate to the reasons underlying the protection action. State intervention should not be used to force families to change every conceivable weakness that might be discovered. Rather, the intervention should be limited to what is necessary to address the grounds for the action and any additional matters that the family voluntarily chooses to address.

REUNIFICATION EFFORTS

Protection cases are temporary proceedings. The court expects to return the child home or to find another permanent home for the

31. Donna L. Moore, Barbra A. Bergman & Pamela L. Knox, *Predictors of Sex Offender Treatment Completion*, 7/3 J. CHILD SEXUAL ABUSE 73, 84–85 (1999).
32. See, e.g., In re Patrick H., 229 A.D.2d 682, 645 N.Y.S.2d 166 (1996).
33. See Chapter 4.

child. The federal Adoption Assistance and Child Welfare Act of 1980[34] mandates that state agencies that receive certain federal funds must make reasonable efforts to prevent removal of the child whenever possible and to facilitate speedy reunification once the child has been removed.[35] Each child in federally funded or state-supervised foster care must have a case plan specifying the services to be offered to prevent out-of-home placement or facilitate return to the family.[36] The Adoption and Safe Families Act of 1997 clarified that these reasonable efforts to reunify the family are not mandatory "if a court of competent jurisdiction has determined that—(i) the parent has subjected the child to aggravated circumstances (as defined in State law, which definition may include but need not be limited to . . . sexual abuse)."[37] State law should be consulted to determine whether or not the agency is required to provide rehabilitative services. If not, the court still has the discretion to order rehabilitative services. Such a determination should be made if that is in the child's best interests.[38]

If the case plan is to return the child to a parent, services need to be provided to all members of the family. The key is to have a good understanding of what the particular family members' problems are, what strengths they can build on, and what resources can be put together to reunify the family. Too often agencies put family through their series of "standard" services. This scattershot approach is an inefficient use of time and resources. The lawyers for all parties should insist on services tailored to meet the specific needs of each family member. As discussed above, behavioral objectives should be articulated, together with a description of the measures to be used to determine whether each objective has been met. Clear, specific behavioral objectives will allow the parties and their service providers to know exactly what is expected. Such specificity

34. 42 U.S.C. §§ 620 *et seq.*
35. *See* 42 U.S.C. § 671(a)(15).
36. *See* 45 C.F.R. § 1356.21(d)(4).11.
37. 42 U.S.C. § 671(a)(15)(D).
38. The Adoption and Safe Families Act also clarified the Adoption Assistance and Child Welfare Act by providing that "in determining reasonable efforts to be made with respect to a child . . . and in making such reasonable efforts, the child's health and safety shall be the paramount concern." 42 U.S.C. § 671(a)(15)(A).

will also enable the court to know when and if the parties have satisfied the case plan.

REVIEW HEARINGS

As a prerequisite to receiving federal funding, federal law mandates that each foster child's status be reviewed administratively or judicially at least every six months.[39] In addition, a court or administrative body must review the case of each child in foster care within eighteen months of the initial placement and at least every twelve months thereafter.[40] With court review hearings, the court is required to make a finding as to whether or not the grounds for dependency continue to exist. If not, the case is terminated. Most states require more frequent review hearings, typically every six months.[41] If the status of dependency continues to exist, the court will check on provision of services, the family's progress towards reunification, the child's well-being, and any necessary changes in

39. See 42 U.S.C. § 675(5)(B) ("to determine the continuing necessity for and appropriateness of the placement, the extent of compliance with the case plan, and the extent of progress which has been made toward alleviating or mitigating the causes necessitating placement in foster care, and to project a likely date by which the child may be returned to the home or placed for or adoption or legal guardianship").

40. See 42 U.S.C. § 675(C) (to "determine the future status of the child" and applying procedural safeguards to "parental rights pertaining to the removal of the child from the home of his parents, to a change in the child's placement, and to any determination affecting visitation privileges of parents").

41. For states requiring reviews at least every six months *see, e.g.*, ARIZ. REV. STAT. ANN. § 8-847 (1998); CAL. WELF. & INST. CODE § 366 (1984); COLO. REV. STAT. § 19-1-115(4)(c) (1997); CONN. GEN. STAT ANN. § 17a-15(b) (1992) (every six months); D.C. CODE ANN. § 16-2323(a) (1997) (every 6 months for children under 6 or in placement for under 2 years; every year for other children); FLA. STAT. ANN. § 39.453(3) (19) (every 6 months for children under 13, and at least every year for children 13 and older who have been in foster care for more than 18 months) (1988); GA. CODE ANN. § 15-11-41(j) (1997) (within 90 days of the dispositional order, but no later than 6 months after placement, then every 6 months thereafter); HAW. REV. STAT. ANN. § 587-71(m)(2) (1997); 705 ILL. COMP. STAT. ANN. § 405/2-28.01(c) (1997) (every 6 months, in counties over 3,000,000 population); IND. CODE ANN. § 31-34-21-2(a); IOWA CODE ANN. § 232.102(8) (1994) (initial dispositional review hearing may not be waived or continued beyond 6 months after dispositional hearing; subsequent reviews may not be waived or continued beyond twelve months after the most recent review); LA. REV. STAT ANN. art. 692 (1995); MD. CODE ANN., Cts. & Jud. Proc. § 3-826.1(g) (1997) (every six months only where the child is in long term foster care); MICH. COMP. LAWS ANN. § 712A.19(2) and (3) (1993) (every 91 days for the first year after disposition, then every 182 days); MINN. STAT. ANN. § 257.071 subd. 2 (1992); MO. ANN. STAT. §§ 210.710 and 210.720 (1996); NEB. REV. STAT. § 43-1313 (1996); N.M. STAT ANN. §§ 32A-3B-19 and 32A-4-25 (1997); N.C. GEN. STAT. § 7A-657(a) (1997) (first two reviews every six months, every twelve months thereafter); OHIO REV. CODE ANN. § 2151.416(A) (1997) (administrative review every six months); OKLA. STAT ANN. §§ 7003-5.4(A) and 7303-5.6(A) (1997); 42 PA. CONS. STAT. ANN. § 6351(e) (1997) (first two reviews every six months, every twelve months thereafter); S.C. CODE ANN. § 20-7-766 (G) (1997); S.D. CODIFIED LAWS ANN. § 26-8A-24 (1997); TEX. FAM. CODE ANN. § 263.501(a) and (b) (1997); UTAH CODE ANN. § 78-3a-313(1) (1997); VT. STAT. ANN. tit. 33, § 5531(a) (every six months for children under three, every twelve months for children between three and six) (1997); VA. CODE ANN. §§ 16.1-281(F) and -282(E) (1997); WASH. REV. CODE ANN. § 13.32A.130(5) (1993); WASH. REV. CODE ANN. § 13.32A.190(1) (1993) (initial review within 3 months of dispositional order). *Cf.* IDAHO CODE § 16-1623(i) (1997) (reports must be made to court at least every six months).

the case plan. At each review hearing the court is required to make a finding as to whether the social-services agency has made reasonable efforts to prevent removal of the child or to rehabilitate the family[42] and whether it would be contrary to the welfare of the child to be maintained in or returned to the home.[43]

In many jurisdictions, especially those with large caseloads, review hearings are perfunctory five-minute hearings, with no real opportunity for evidence to be taken. Social-work reports are substituted for testimony, and lawyer argument for examination and cross-examination. A better practice is to allow a real evidentiary hearing, with the opportunity for the judge to critically review how the case is being handled and whether there is real progress being made. Most of the work in a protection case occurs between hearings, and review hearings often represent an impetus for people to act. If the judge does not take a firm hand at review hearings, holding all parties accountable for their respective parts in the case plan, it is less likely that timely progress will be made. Overburdened caseworkers may be slow to put services in place, follow up when providers leave the system, and forward referrals to necessary services. The parents may have been referred to a "standard" series of services that are not specifically designed to meet their particular problems. There may be personality clashes between the parents and the assigned therapist that interfere with their progress. Appropriate services may have long waiting lists, or the parents may have logistical barriers to attending the selected services, such as transportation difficulties or inflexible work schedules. A court order may resolve some of these problems, keeping the case moving.

On the other hand, the parents may not be motivated to follow through with the case plan. Perfunctory review hearings may provide little incentive for them to acknowledge and work on their problems. Further, cases that merely plod from review hearing to review hearing may attenuate the parents' interest in working on their problems. They may become discouraged with the lack of movement in the case and give up altogether. Without active work

42. See 42 U.S.C. § 671(a)(15).
43. See 42 U.S.C. § 672(a)(1).

going on with all of the parties, the child's temporary status is needlessly prolonged.

Finally, the child's day-to-day needs may be overshadowed in a perfunctory hearing. In addition to placement considerations (whether the child can be returned home or placed with a relative or friend), the court should consider whether changes should be made to the visitation orders and whether the child is receiving appropriate services.

The lawyer should prepare carefully for a review hearing, having specific issues in mind to address, whether through presentation of evidence or argument. If evidence is not permitted, the lawyer should consider filing a written memorandum, attaching any pertinent exhibits. The lawyer should go to the review hearing prepared to ask for specific relief and prepared to justify the legal basis and need for that relief. If there is a particular problem, the lawyer should consider filing a motion well in advance of the scheduled date, asking for more than the allotted amount of time.

The client's interest should not be preempted by the need for judicial efficiency. For the parties involved in a protection case, if not for the professionals, the case is a central matter of their lives, and the failure to provide timely and appropriate services or to make timely permanent decisions may irrevocably destroy the fabric of the family and alter the life of the child victim.

PERMANENCY PLANNING

In November 1997 President Clinton signed the Adoption and Safe Families Act of 1997, which was designed, in part, to free children for adoption more quickly. The Act clarified existing federal law to provide that reunification efforts do not need to be made under certain circumstances, including cases where the child was sexually abused.[44] This does not necessarily mean that a state *cannot* provide rehabilitative efforts, but only that it need not do so. Lawyers will need to monitor their own state laws to see whether or not rehabili-

44. 42 U.S.C. § 671(a)(15)(D)(i).

tative efforts are necessary. Further, the lawyer should determine whether reunification services are appropriate to the facts of the case, whether or not they are legally required.

In the past decade or so state legislatures began to require permanency-planning hearings, now required by federal law. The Adoption and Safe Families Act of 1997, which sets requirements for states to qualify for certain federal funds, has reduced the time by which the court must hold a permanency-planning hearing from eighteen to twelve months from the time the child enters foster care.[45] These are special review hearings designed to force a decision on the child's permanent placement, rather than to allow a child to remain in foster care for an indeterminate time. It is expected that a decision will be made at the permanency-planning hearing as to whether the child should be returned home or freed for adoption. Under some circumstances a middle-ground alternative, such as permanent relative guardianship or long-term foster care, is appropriate. The Adoption and Safe Families Act requires that the permanency plan include:

> whether, and if applicable when, the child will be returned to the parent, placed for adoption and the State will file a petition for termination of parental rights, or referred for legal guardianship, or (in cases where the State agency has documented to the State court a compelling reason for determining that it would not be in the best interests of the child to return home, be referred for termination of parental rights, or be placed for adoption, with a fit and willing relative, or with a legal guardian) placed in another planned permanent living arrangement.[46]

If the parents have not made significant progress by the time of the permanency-planning hearing, or if it does not appear that the child will able to return home within the reasonably near future, the agency is typically relieved of its responsibility to provide further rehabilitative efforts, and the case plan is changed to a goal other than to return the child home.

45. 42 U.S.C. § 475(5)(C)(2).
46. 42 U.S.C. § 675(5)(C)(4).

4 Sexual Abuse Allegations in Termination Cases

Sexual Abuse as a Legal Basis for Termination

Sexual abuse sometimes forms the basis for the termination of parental rights.[1] In many cases, sexual abuse is coupled with physical abuse, neglect, or other forms of maltreatment, which together form the basis for termination. Termination is especially likely where the abuse was severe or chronic, and the abuser does not get appropriate therapy. Some states explicitly provide that sexual abuse is a statutory ground for termination.[2] Sexual abuse may be included by inference in the catch-all category of "abuse" or "maltreatment" warranting

1. For further information on termination cases, *see generally*, 1 Ann M. Haralambie, Handling Child Custody, Abuse, and Adoption Cases ch. 13 (2nd ed, Clark Boardman Callaghan 1993, West Group 1998); 1 Thomas A. Jacobs, Children and the Law: Rights and Obligations ch. 3 (Clark Boardman Callaghan 1995, West Group 1997).

2. *See, e.g.*, Alaska Stat. § 25.23.180(c)(3) (1997) (sexual abuse resulting in conception of the child); Colo. Rev. Stat. § 19-5-105(3.1)(a)(III) (1997) (sexually abusive conduct); Ga. Code Ann. § 15-11-81(b)(4)((B)(iv) (1997) (egregious sexually cruel or abusive conduct); Kan. Stat. Ann. § 38-1583(b)(2) (1993) (sexually cruel or abusive conduct); Ky. Rev. Stat. Ann. § 625.090(1)(e) (1997) (sexual abuse or exploitation); Mass. Gen. Laws ch. 210, § 3(c)(ix) (1997) (severe or repetitive sexual abuse basis for not requiring consent to adoption); Mo. Ann. Stat. § 211.447(2)(2)(c) (1996) (severe or recurrent sexual abuse or any act of incest); N.H. Rev. Stat. Ann. § 170-C:5(V) (1997) (severe sexual abuse); Or. Rev. Stat. § 419B.502(1) (1997) (rape, sodomy, or sex abuse); Or. Rev. Stat. § 419B.504(2) (1997) (sexual conduct); Wis. Stat. Ann. § 48.415(1)(g), (7), (9)(1996) (incestuous parenthood, parenthood as a result of sexual assault).

termination.[3] Further, if the sexual abuse has caused the child to be in an out-of-home placement for a particular length of time,[4] or if the sexual abuse resulted in certain felony criminal convictions, those grounds for termination may be employed.[5] However, conviction is not necessary to warrant termination, and the civil court can find termination appropriate even if the abuser has been acquitted of the criminal charge based on the same alleged conduct.[6] Sexual abuse of another child or sibling may also constitute grounds for termination.[7] Some state statutes provide that conception through

3. *See, e.g., In re* S.H., D.H. & J.H., 284 Ill. App.3d 392, 672 N.E.2d 403 (1996) (father's conviction for vaginally and orally penetrating his 5-year old child with his penis constitutes overwhelming evidence of "depravity," warranting termination); *In re* Interest of N.H., 383 N.W.2d 570 (Iowa 1986) (sexual and emotional abuse); *In re* Adoption of Diane, 400 Mass. 196, 508 N.E.2d 837 (1987) (physical and sexual abuse and neglect); *In re* Interest of Gooden, 208 Neb. 256, 303 N.W.2d 278 (1981) (physical and sexual abuse). *See generally,* Donald C. Bross, *Terminating the Parent-Child Legal Relationship as a Response to Child Sexual Abuse,* 26 LOY. U. CHI. L. J. 287 (1995); Annot, *Sexual Abuse of Child by Parent as Ground for Termination of Parental Right to Child,* 58 ALR 3d 1974 (1974).

4. *See, e.g.,* ARIZ. REV. STAT. § 8-533(B)(7) (1997); ARK. CODE ANN. § 9-27-341(b)(2)(A); DEL. CODE ANN. tit. 13, § 1103(5)(a); GA. CODE ANN. § 15-11-81(b)(4)(c); 750 ILL. COMP. STAT. ANN. § 50/1(D)(m); IND. CODE ANN. § 313-6-5-4(c); LA. REV. STAT. ANN. art. 1015(5)-(7); ME. REV. STAT. ANN. tit. 22, § 4055(1)(C)-(E); MD. CODE ANN. FAM. LAW § 5-313(a)(3); MASS. GEN. LAWS ch. 210, § 3(c)(iii)-(v); MINN. STAT. ANN. § 260.221 subdivision 1(b)(5); MISS. CODE ANN. § 93-15-103(3)(c); MO. ANN. STAT. § 211.447(2)(3); N.C. GEN. STAT. § 7A-289.32(3) and (4); OKLA. STAT. ANN. tit. 10, § 7006-1.1(A)(6) and (7); 23 PA. CONS. STAT. ANN. § 2511(a)(5) and (8); R.I. GEN. LAWS § 15-7-7(1)(b)(iii) and (c); S.C. CODE ANN. § 20-7-1572(2) and (3); TENN. CODE ANN. § 36-1-113(g)(3)(A); WASH. REV. CODE ANN. § 13.34.180; WIS. STAT. ANN. § 48.415(2)(c) and (4).

5. *See, e.g.,* ARIZ. REV. STAT. § 8-533(B)(4) (1989) (felony must be of such a nature as to prove unfitness of the parent); DEL. CODE ANN. tit. 13, § 1103(a)(4) (1997) (child is victim or crime involves harm to child); GA. CODE ANN. § 15-11-81(b)(4)(B)(iii) (1998) (felony and imprisonment therefor must have demonstrable negative effect on quality of parent-child relationship); KAN. STAT. ANN. § 38-1583(b)(5) (1993); LA. REV. STAT. ANN. CHILDRENS CODE art. 1015(1) and (3)(a) (1995) (conviction for murdering child's other parent or any conviction for murder); ME. REV. STAT. ANN. tit. 22, § 4055(1)(B) (1997) (criminal conviction need not be a felony; designated crimes where the victim was a child in the household or a child who frequented the defendant's household); MASS. GEN. LAWS ch. 210, § 3(c)(xiii) (1997) (conviction of a felony of such a nature that the child will be deprived of a stable home for a period of years; however, incarceration alone insufficient); MISS. CODE ANN. § 93-15-103(3)(f) (1998) (designated crimes where the defendant's child or child of a cohabiting partner); MISS. CODE ANN. § 93-15-103(5) (1998) (criminal conviction need not be a felony; must be a designated crime against a child); MO. ANN. STAT. § 211.447(3)(6) (1996) (conviction of a felony of such a nature that the child will be deprived of a stable home for a period of years); N.H. REV. STAT. ANN. § 170-C:5(VI) (1994) (conviction of a felony of such a nature and a period of incarceration for such duration that the child would be deprived of proper parental care and protection and left in an unstable or impermanent environment for a longer time than would be prudent); OKLA. STAT. tit. 10, § 7006-1.1(A)(6) and (7) (1998) (criminal conviction need not be a felony; must be a crime relating to child abuse or neglect); TEX. FAM. CODE ANN. § 161.001(a)(1)(L) (1996) (criminal conviction need not be a felony; must constitute responsibility for death or serious injury of a child); VT. STAT. ANN. tit. 15A, § 3-504(a)(3) (Supp. 1998) (criminal conviction need not be a felony; must be a crime of violence); WIS. STAT. ANN. § 48.415(8) and (9m) (1996) (designated crime against child or homicide of child's parent).

6. *See, e.g., In re* J.N., 492 So.2d 1118 (Fla. Dist. Ct. App. 1986).

7. *See, e.g., In re* S.H., D.H. & J.H., 284 Ill. App.3d 392, 672 N.E.2d 403 (1996) (father's conviction for sexually assaulting his 5-year old daughter supported termination also with respect to his two sons); Cabinet for Human Resources v. Rogeski, 909 S.W.2d 660 (Ky. 1990) (termination upheld based on father's imprisonment for raping the children's half-sister); *In re* L., 888 S.W.2d 337 (Mo. Ct. App. 1994) (upholding termination of father's parental rights based on his having raped his two sisters, ages seven and nine, holding that the sisters were members of his family within the meaning of the statute including incest as a ground for termination, noting that such ground focuses on a parent's propensity for abuse); *In re* Patrick "H.," 226 A.D.2d 921, 640 N.Y.S.2d 690 (1996) (father's exposure of his son to his sexual molestation of two of his paramour's children and his failure to complete sex offender program justified termination); *In re* Christina, 194 W. Va. 446, 460 S.E. 2d 692 (1995) (sexual abuse of one child justifies termination with

an act of sexual assault[8] or incest[9] may also constitute grounds for termination.

Because termination statutes are remedial, parental rights may be terminated based on a prospective showing of harm to the child in question.[10] This may be shown by the failure of the abusive parent to successfully complete therapy,[11] take responsibility for the

---

respect to another child living in the home at the time of the abuse if that child's health or welfare is harmed or threatened).

8. *See, e.g.*, IDAHO STAT. § 16-2005(j)(1) (1997) (statute presumes that termination under such circumstances are in the child's best interests); MO. ANN. STAT. § 211.447(5) (1997) (conception as a result of an act of forcible rape is a ground for termination; father's plea of guilty or conviction of the forcible rape is conclusive evidence supporting termination of his parental rights); WIS. STAT. § 48.415(9) (1996) (parenthood as a result of sexual assault is a ground for termination). *Cf.* Pena v. Mattox, 84 F.3d 894 (7th Cir. 1996) (father whose child was conceived as a result of his criminal intercourse with a minor has no constitutionally protected interest in the child); MINN. STAT. ANN. § 259.47(b)(1) (1997) (mother exempt from making efforts to identify and locate the natural father where the child was conceived as the result of incest or rape); N.M. STAT. ANN. § 32A-5-19(C) (1997) (consent to adoption not required from father whose child was conceived as a result of rape or incest); N.Y. DOM. REL. LAW § 111-a(1) (1997) (consent to adoption not required from father whose child was conceived as a result of rape if the father was convicted of forcible rape); N.Y. SOC. SERV. LAW § 384-c(1) (1992) (consent to adoption not required from father whose child was conceived as a result of rape if the father was convicted of forcible rape); OHIO REV. CODE ANN. § 3107.07(F) (1997) (consent to adoption not required from father whose child was conceived as a result of rape if the father was convicted of or pled guilty to rape); 23 PA. CONS. STAT. ANN. § 20-7-1734(C) (1997) (consent to adoption not required from father whose child was conceived as a result of criminal sexual or incest). *But see, e.g.*, Doe v. Brown, 489 S.E.2d 917 (S.C. 1997) (despite adoption statute's waiver of notice to fathers of children conceived through criminal sexual conduct or incest, S.C. CODE ANN. § 20-7-1734(C), court erred in finding that such fathers have no parental rights; such fathers must be treated as other out-of-wedlock parents for purposes of requiring parental consent to adoption, relinquishment, or termination of parental rights).

9. *See, e.g.*, IDAHO STAT. § 16-2005(j)(1) (1997) (statute presumes that termination under such circumstances are in the child's best interests); WIS. STAT. ANN. § 48.415(7) (1996) (incestuous parenthood is ground for termination); Wisconsin v. Allen M., 214 Wis.2d 302, 571 N.W.2d 872 (1997) (holding WIS. STAT. ANN. § 48.415(7) to be constitutional, affirming termination of parental rights of siblings who continue to maintain their incestuous relationship). *Cf.* MINN. STAT. ANN. § 259.47(b)(1) (mother exempt from making efforts to identify and locate the natural father where the child was conceived as the result of incest or rape); N.M. STAT. ANN. § 32A-5-19(C) (1997) (consent to adoption not required from father whose child was conceived as a result of rape or incest); 23 PA. CONS. STAT. ANN. § 20-7-1734(C) (1997) (consent to adoption not required from father whose child was conceived as a result of criminal sexual or incest).

10. *See, e.g.*, Crawford v. Arkansas Department of Human Services, 951 SW2d 310 (Ark. 1997) (termination warranted where father denied sexual abuse, refused to attend counseling for sexual offenders, and was in prison); *In re* L., 888 S.W.2d 337 (Mo. Ct. App. 1994) (upholding termination of father's parental rights based on his having raped his two sisters, ages seven and nine, holding that the sisters were members of his family within the meaning of the statute including incest as a ground for termination, noting that such ground focuses on a parent's propensity for abuse); *In re* L.B., 416 N.W.2d 598 (S.D. 1987) (sexual abuse of one child relevant to termination of parental rights with respect to siblings); *In re* R.M., 150 Vt. 59, 549 A.2d 1050 (1988) (mother's denial of father's sexual abuse and failure to protect her older children from such abuse warrants termination of parental rights with respect to sibling). *Cf. In re* Joseph A., 199 W. Va. 438, 485 S.E.2d 176 (1997) (expert testimony not required to support conclusion that watching pornography has harmful effects upon children; exposure to adult sexual activities can have far reaching effects on the personality and behavior of child victims; sexually explicit videos remain in the home; where the daughter was sexually abused and her brothers physically abused, the father has denied abusive behavior, family secrecy abounds, and the father has threatened the children to lie about the abuse, court cannot assume that the boys are not at risk for sexual abuse because of their gender).

11. *See, e.g.*, Adams v. Marion County Office of Family and Children, 659 N.E.2d 202 (Ind. Ct. App. 1995) (parents' failure to successfully complete treatment a factor warranting termination); *In re* Interest of Tabitha J., 5 Neb. App. 609, 561 N.W.2d 252 (1997) (termination where father did not complete his sexual offender program; his incarceration was of his own making and does not insulate him from termination); *In re* Patrick "H.," 226 A.D.2d 921, 640 N.Y.S.2d 690 (1996) (father's exposure of his son to his sexual molestation of two of his paramour's children and his failure to complete sex offender program justified termination); *In re* Kayte "M.," 201 A.D.2d 835, 608 N.Y.S.2d 711 (1994) (mother's failure to attend and successfully complete a program for adjudicated sex offenders warrants termination); *In re* Interest of R.W., 2 Neb.

molestation,[12] or demonstrate the ability to be a safe custodian for the child[13] within a reasonable period of time.[14]

FAILURE TO PROTECT FROM SEXUAL ABUSE AS A LEGAL BASIS FOR TERMINATION

A custodial parent's responsibility includes the duty to take reasonable efforts to protect the child from sexual abuse.[15] Failure to protect one's child from sexual abuse may also constitute a ground for termination. This is particularly likely to happen where the nonprotecting parent does not believe that the child was molested,[16] does

---

App. 297, 509 N.W. 2d 237 (1993) (father's failure to participate in sexual abuse therapy willful despite his incarceration). Sexual offenders who do not complete treatment have higher recidivism rates than those who do, *see, e.g.*, R. Karl Hanson & Monique T. Bussière, *Predicting Relapse: A Meta-Analysis of Sexual Offender Recidivism Studies*, 66/2 J. CONSULTING & CLINICAL PSYCHOLOGY 348 (1998); therefore, there is an empirical justification for weighing such lack of treatment against the abuser.

12. *See, e.g.*, *In re* A.P., 1999 WL 194696 (Pa. Super 1999) (affirming permanency plan of adoption based in part on mother's failure to admit her sexual abuse of child); *In re* Interest of H.R.K., 433 N.W.2d 46 (Iowa 1988) (parents' failure to admit sexual abuse could be considered in termination action); *In re* Jesus J.J., 232 A.D.2d 752, 649 N.Y.S.2d 61 (1996) (finding that child was molested while in the father's custody was sufficient to make the father's acknowledgment of the abuse a realistic goal, and his failure to do so was sufficient basis for termination); *In re* Tammy B., 587 N.Y.S.2d 377 (App. Div. 1992) (affirming termination when father's refusal to admit sexual abuse prevented his therapeutic progress, thereby constituting a failure to plan for the child's future). *Cf. In re* Interest of S.M.L., 228 Ga. App. 81, 491 S.E.2d 186 (1997) (termination upheld based on sexual molestation, abandonment, and failure to support by father who expressed no remorse or culpability and was "in a state of denial rarely observed" by the court); *In re* Michelle "F.," 222 A.D.2d 747, 635 N.Y.S.2d 709 (1995) (parent's refusal to admit that father molested the children warrants termination).

13. *See, e.g.*, *In re* Interest of W.S., 899 S.2d 772 (Tex. Ct. App. 1995) (termination warranted where, *inter alia*, parents performed sexual acts on each other in the presence of the some of the children, all four children showed evidence of sexual abuse, father admitted fondling stepdaughter several times, and mother left children alone with father after observing an incident of abuse).

14. *See, e.g.*, *In re* A.W., K.W. & A.T., 708 A.2d 910 (Vt. 1998) (sufficient evidence to support court's findings that the abused children should not have to be subjected to further delay or uncertainty because of the mother's "stagnation").

15. *See, e.g.*, *In re* Jesus "J.J.," 232 A.D. 2d 752, 649 N.Y.S.2d 61 (1996).

16. *See, e.g.*, *In re* Lauren R., 49 Conn. App. 763, 715 A.2d 822 (1998) (termination affirmed where mother never acknowledged the sexual abuse and the child was aware that the mother did not believe her); State v. N.A.A., 1998 WL 726639 (Tenn. App. 1998) (termination affirmed where parents refuse to acknowledge possibility of sexual abuse or discuss the allegations in counseling); *In re* C.C. 299 Ill. App. 3d 827, 702 N.E.2d 598 (1998) (failure to acknowledge child's sexual abuse, which precludes taking adequate steps to protect child in future, justifies termination based on failure to make reasonable progress toward return of child); *In re* Interest of M.E.C., 228 Ga. App. 9, 491 S.E.2d 107 (1997) (mother's failure to believe that her son was molested by his uncle was one factor justifying termination); *In re* A.B., 492 N.W.2d 446 (Iowa Ct. App. 1992) (termination affirmed where mother's failure to believe that stepfather had molested child made her not amenable to treatment); *In re* Lisa C., 684 A.2d 801 (Me. 1996) (termination affirmed where mother did not believe father had molested the child, she did not develop empathy for the child, and she was inconsistent in attending group therapy); *In re* Jesus "J.J.," 232 A.D. 2d 752, 649 N.Y.S.2d 61 (1996) (father's acknowledgment that his daughter was molested while in his care was necessary for him to gain any insight into responsibility for the abuse, and his failure to acknowledge the abuse supported termination based on his failure to adequately plan for his children's future).

not appreciate the impact of the abuse on the child,[17] continues the relationship with the abuser or other abusive persons,[18] or cannot demonstrate an ability to safeguard the child from further abuse.[19]

STANDARD OF PROOF

The standard of proof in most dependency cases[20] that involve a temporary deprivation of parental rights, is the general civil standard of proof by a preponderance of the evidence. Because parents have a fundamental constitutional right to the care, custody, and control of their children, the United States Supreme Court held in *Santosky v. Kramer*[21] that parental rights may not permanently be terminated absent due process and proof by clear and convincing evidence. This heightened standard of proof reflects the permanence of the interference with the constitutionally protected right. For children covered by the Indian Child Welfare Act,[22] proof must be beyond reasonable doubt and must include evidence, including testimony from a qualified expert witness, that custody by the parent would be likely to result in serious emotional or physical damage to the child.[23]

---

17. *See, e.g., In re* J.S. & P.S., 269 Mont. 170, 887 P.2d 719 (1994) (termination upheld where mother failed to appreciate destruction the father's molestation had done and failed to demonstrate the ability to protect the children); *In re* Interest of Joshua M., 251 Neb. 614, 558 N.W. 2d 548 (1997) (mother's failure to appreciate impact of the abuse on her children one factor supporting termination); *In re* Cheyenne "Q.," 657 N.Y.S.2d 224 (App. Div. 1997) (termination upheld based, in part, on mother's refusal to meaningfully discuss or acknowledge her involvement in the abuse or to meaningfully address the problem); *In re* B.W., 162 Vt. 287, 648 A.2d 652 (1994) (father's parental rights terminated where he did not appreciate the trauma to his daughter of her molestation by her brothers, rejected treatment services, and blamed the child for the abuse).

18. *See, e.g., In re* Adoption of Kimberly, 414 Mass. 526, 609 N.E.2d 73 (1993) (termination warranted where mother continued her relationship with abusive father); *In re* Interest of D.B., D.T. & S.L.B., 916 S.W.2d 430 (Mo. Ct. App. 1996) (termination warranted where mother knew or should have known that her boyfriend had physically and sexually abused her sons, but she continued to live with and eventually married him); *In re* Interest of Joshua M., 251 Neb. 614, 558 N.W. 2d 548 (1997) (parent's unwillingness to comply with rehabilitation program warrants termination; mother repeatedly violated order forbidding contact with man convicted of sexual assault, including against one of her children); *In re* John "F.," 221 A.D.2d 858, 634 N.Y.S.2d 256 (1995) (mother's continued cohabitation with father who molested their children and with other sex offenders warrants termination based on failure to plan for children's future).

19. *See, e.g., In re* Tabitha T., 51 Conn. App. 595, 722 A.2d 1232 (1999) (mother failed to protect children from sexual abuse by their older brothers and told one child not to disclose the abuse to her therapist); In the Interest of D.A., 506 N.W.2d 478 (Iowa Ct. App. 1993).

20. See Chapter 3.

21. 455 U.S. 745, 102 S. Ct. 1388, 71 L.Ed. 2d 599 (1982).

22. 25 U.S.C. § 1901 *et seq.*

23. 25 U.S.C. § 1912(f). For additional information on handling cases under the Indian Child Welfare Act, *see generally*, 2 ANN M. HARALAMBIE, HANDLING CHILD CUSTODY, ABUSE, AND ADOPTION CASES ch. 15 (2nd ed, Clark Boardman Callaghan 1993, West Group 1998); 1 THOMAS A. JACOBS, CHILDREN AND THE LAW: RIGHTS AND OBLIGATIONS ch. 5 (Clark Boardman Callaghan 1995, West Group 1997); B. J. JONES, THE INDIAN CHILD WELFARE ACT HANDBOOK: A LEGAL GUIDE TO THE CUSTODY AND ADOPTION OF NATIVE AMERICAN CHILDREN (American Bar Association 1995).

IS TERMINATION IN THE CHILD'S BEST INTERESTS?

In addition to proving the substantive grounds for termination, the petitioner must also prove that termination is in the child's best interests.[24] This determination must be made on a case-by-case basis, considering the circumstances of the abuse, the reaction of the nonabusing parent, progress in rehabilitation, the child's desires, and the available alternatives. Where the parent is not likely to be rehabilitated to the extent that the child may be returned home within a reasonable time, the child's need for a permanent home may require termination.

If one parent is supportive of the child and willing to provide protection, the child may prefer to continue supervised visits or even to terminate all visits, without terminating the abuser's parental rights. The child's right to filiation may outweigh the need for termination, using alternatives to protect the child from further abuse short of termination. This is particularly true if it is likely to be difficult to find an adoptive home for the child or the child has a strong attachment to the abuser and desire to maintain ongoing contact with him or her. However, the quality, as well as the strength of the attachment is important, because some abused children form traumatic bonds or other pathological, although strong, attachments to their abusers.

Children who have been molested have a variety of feelings about the abuser and about a nonprotecting parent. Some children are afraid of the abuser and want to end permanently the possibility of further contact with him or her. Some do not want to lose contact, but want only to be protected from further incidents of abuse. Some do not see anything wrong with an incestuous lifestyle and want to continue things the way they have always been. In some cases there is a protective stepparent, other family member, or friend by whom the child wishes to be adopted.

It is important that lawyers not react with an automatic desire to punish the parent for the abuse by terminating his or her rights.

---

24. *See, e.g., In re* Appeal in Maricopa County Juvenile Action No. JA 33794, 171 Ariz. 90, 828 P.2d 1231 (Ct. App. 1991); *In re* J.L.P., 416 So.2d 1250 (Fla. Dist. Ct. App. 1982); *In re* Interest of M.E.C., 228 Ga. App. 9, 491 SE2d 107 (1997); *In re* Welfare of M.P., 542 N.W.2d 71 (Minn. Ct. App. 1996); *In re* B.W., 162 Vt. 287, 648 A.2d 652 (1994).

Such an action is almost always extremely traumatic for the child, who often feels that he or she is being punished and further abused by the loss of a parent. On the other hand, a child's desire to remain with an abuser should not always be determinative. The importance of a careful, case-by-case analysis by counsel and the court cannot be overemphasized.

REHABILITATION AND REUNIFICATION EFFORTS

In most child-welfare cases the agency has an affirmative obligation to make reasonable efforts to prevent removal of the child from the home, to rehabilitate the abuser, and to reunify the family if removal of the child was not able to be prevented. The federal Adoption Assistance and Child Welfare Act of 1980[25] mandates that state agencies that receive certain federal funds must make reasonable efforts to prevent removal of the child whenever possible and to facility speedy reunification once the child has been removed.[26] Each child in federally funded or state-supervised foster care must have a case plan specifying the services to be offered to prevent out-of-home placement or facilitate return to the family.[27] When a child is in an out-of-home placement, the court is required to make findings that continuation in the home would be contrary to the child's welfare and that the agency had made reasonable efforts to prevent removal or facilitate return.[28] All states and the District of Columbia have accepted the terms of such federal funding.[29] They have often amended their protection statutes to include such requirements. A frequent defense to termination is that the agency has failed to make the required reasonable efforts to reunify the family.

However, the agency is not required to exhaust all possible efforts or to provide futile efforts. In the sexual abuse context, the abuser's failure to admit the abuse has relieved the agency of the obligation to provide further rehabilitative efforts. For example, a

25. 42 U.S.C. § 620 *et seq.* and § 679 *et seq.*
26. *See* 42 U.S.C. § 671(a)(15).
27. *See* 45 C.F.R. § 1356.21(d)(4).
28. *See* 42 U.S.C. § 672(a)(1).
29. A good discussion of the Act is found in MAKING REASONABLE EFFORTS: STEPS FOR KEEPING FAMILIES TOGETHER (L. Lange, ed., n.d.) (available through the Edna McConnell Clark Foundation, 250 Park Avenue, New York, NY 10177-0026).

New York appellate court pointed out that once there has been a judicial determination that a person has molested a child, the child-welfare agency is not required to offer an alternate plan for reunification that would not require the parent to admit the abuse.[30] The Rhode Island Supreme Court has indicated that a molester's failure to admit the molestation and obtain therapy for two years while awaiting trial, and his admission only after he had been incarcerated for numerous sex offenses against children, absolved the child-welfare agency of the obligation to offer reunification services.[31]

There has been a great deal of concern about the consequences of an accused parent to refuse admitting the abuse. A California Court of Appeal addressed what it called the "confession dilemma" of a parent improperly accused of molestation who, therefore, does not admit the molestation, and the failure to admit is subsequently used as evidence that return of the child to that parent would be detrimental.[32] The court pointed out the importance of a correct initial determination of whether or not the child was abused, because the consequences of a wrong determination in either direction are too great.

Some parents will not or cannot change, even if they attend all required treatment.[33] Therefore, the provision of rehabilitative efforts should be viewed in the context of the parent's demonstrated commitment and ability to change his or her attitudes and behaviors.[34] British psychiatrist David Jones lists the following categories of families that do not respond to treatment:

1. There are some families who simply will not change. They do not intend or want to change.
2. Some parents persistently deny abusive behavior in the face of clear evidence to the contrary.

---

30. *See In re* Michelle "F.," 222 A.D.2d 747, 635 N.Y.S.2d 709 (1995).
31. *See In re* Alan W., 665 A.2d 877 (R.I. 1995).
32. *See* Blanca P. v. Superior Court, 45 Cal. App. 4th 1738, 53 Cal. Rptr. 2d 687 (1996).
33. *See, e.g.*, David P. H. Jones, *The Untreatable Family*, 11/3 CHILD ABUSE AND NEGLECT 409 (1987); *Cf.*, Donna L. Moore, Barbra A. Bergman & Pamela L. Knox, *Predictors of Sex Offender Treatment Completion*, 7/3 J. CHILD SEXUAL ABUSE 73 (1999).
34. For a more detailed discussion of assessing offenders for the risk of reabuse see Chapter 6.

3. Some families cannot change in spite of a will to do so. There may be a subgroup here of families who are willing to change but resources to help them are not available.
4. Some parents can change, but not "in time" for their child's developmental needs. For example, a six-month-old baby's abusive parent, who after two years becomes less impulsive and dangerous, but in the meantime whose baby has developed a strong attachment to a surrogate parent.
5. Similarly, other parents may change in time for their next child but not for the index one.
6. Finally there is the category of untreatable parents who fail to respond to one treatment approach but who may be amenable to another agency or approach.[35]

Even if the parent is unable to timely change through no fault of the parent, the child should not be held hostage to a temporary placement, and the federal law does not require that extraordinary efforts be made at such a cost to the child. The Adoption and Safe Families Act of 1997 clarified that reasonable efforts to reunify the family are not mandatory "if a court of competent jurisdiction has determined that—(i) the parent has subjected the child to aggravated circumstances (as defined in State law, which definition may include but need not be limited to . . . sexual abuse)."[36] Further, compliance with the reasonable efforts requirement is not an independent constitutional prerequisite to termination.[37]

CONCLUSION

Lawyer Donald C. Bross, founder of the National Association of Counsel for Children and legal counsel to the Kempe Children's Center, has noted the following factors as raising the possibility of termination based on child sexual abuse: "a criminal conviction of

35. *See* David P. H. Jones, *The Untreatable Family*, 11/3 CHILD ABUSE AND NEGLECT 409, 410 (1987).
36. 42 U.S.C. § 671(a)(15)(D).
37. *See, e.g.*, *In re* A.C., 597 A.2d 920 (D.C. 1991) (agency's failure to make reasonable efforts at reunification only one factor in termination decision; District of Columbia's statute did not provide that reasonable efforts were a prerequisite to termination).

the child's caretaker for sexually abusing the child, prolonged abuse, severe abuse, a failure to protect, other maltreatment, and failure to keep siblings from sexually abusing each other or other children."[38] Termination of parental rights is a serious remedy for both the parents and the child. Sexual abuse is also a serious matter and can properly form the legal basis for termination. It is crucial that the lawyer look at the specific facts of the case, particularly the child's long- and short-term needs and desires.

---

38. *See*, Donald C. Bross, *Terminating the Parent-Child Legal Relationship As a Response to Child Sexual Abuse*, 26/2 LOYOLA U. CHICAGO L.J. 287, 303 (1995).

CHILD SEXUAL ABUSE TORT CASES

5

INTRODUCTION

Child sexual abuse constitutes a tort, and the abused child may seek civil damages based on that abuse. It is important for the lawyer involved in any case involving abuse, whether in a domestic relations, child protection, or other context, to recognize, preserve, and inform the client of the possible tort cause of action, even if the lawyer does not intend to initiate the action. Failure to do so may expose the lawyer to malpractice liability.[1] If the abused child is still a child, any malpractice claim against the lawyer will be tolled during the child's minority, creating a long tail for the exposure.

Tort actions can secure advantages for the child not available in other actions. For example, courts in protection actions can order counseling and medical services for the child, but those services typically end with the court's involvement. At the latest, the services may be provided until the child reaches majority. A domestic-relations court can apportion the costs of counseling and related medical services for the child to be paid entirely by the parent who molested the child, but the

1. *See generally* LEONARD KARP & CHERYL KARP, DOMESTIC TORTS § 8.17B (Clark Boardman Callaghan, West Group 1998).

court's jurisdiction to enter such a continuing order ends when the child reaches majority or is otherwise ineligible to receive child support. Similarly, where the molester was convicted of the abuse the criminal court can order the defendant to pay restitution for similar services to the child. But the dollar amount of that restitution is either determined at the time of the sentencing, or the obligation to continue to pay for services may end upon completion of probation. The child is not a party to the criminal action, and even if a victim-impact statement is filed on behalf of the child, it is unlikely to explore in depth the future monetary needs of the child related to the abuse. Finally, none of the other available actions provides an adequate forum in which to obtain punitive damages in addition to full compensatory damages.

The consequences of the abuse may follow the child well into adulthood, and some psychological sequelae may surface only during adulthood. Those long-term consequences are generally addressed only in the tort context. There are strategic considerations involved in the decision to file the tort action during the child's minority, when the evidence is fresher and the plaintiff most appealing but the extent of the damages is incomplete, or later, when the evidence may be stale but the extent of the damage to the abuse victim is more fully evident. If the child waits until adulthood, he or she may forget to pursue the action or may be barred by the statute of limitations. The lawyer involved during the child's minority must carefully weigh the pros and cons of proceeding immediately or waiting. This should result in a deliberate choice, not merely the inadvertent failure to file a tort action because there is no immediate statute of limitations date driving the process. If the decision is made to wait, the lawyer should do everything possible to preserve evidence in an form which will be admissible in a subsequent tort trial, such as by sworn depositions, requests for admission, interrogatories, or trial testimony. Videotaped interviews of the child demonstrating his or her distress should be preserved for possible future use.

Child sexual abuse torts may be brought many years after the underlying actions. There may or may not have been other legal proceedings concerning the same factual circumstances, and there may or may not be records or other evidence collected near the time of the actions. Further, the molestation may have spanned a long period of time. All of these circumstances may present challenges for the lawyers trying either side of a child sexual abuse tort case brought when the plaintiff is an adult. Ideally the evidence will have been preserved in a compelling and admissible fashion. If not, the lawyer will need to gather and reconstruct the necessary evidence.

Most custody and child-abuse lawyers are not experienced in handling tort cases as well, and they may be professionally and financially ill-equipped to handle the tort action. In such a case, the lawyer should either refer the client to competent tort lawyer or recommend that he or she seek such counsel, emphasizing that a statute of limitations is involved. Associating tort counsel can be an excellent way to handle these cases, with one lawyer having the expertise in tort litigation (and the finances to carry the litigation) while the other has the expertise in child abuse.

JURISDICTION

While most sexual abuse torts are brought in state courts—where there is diversity of jurisdiction and the dollar limit is met (which it should be in all child sexual abuse cases)—they may be brought in federal court, even though the abuse may have occurred within the family. Some federal courts previously had refused to hear such cases based on the domestic-relations exception. However, in *Ankenbrandt v. Richards*, the United States Supreme Court has now resolved that question, holding that even though the case arises in a family context, the domestic-relations exception to diversity jurisdiction does not apply, reversing the dismissal of children's tort action against their father based on his abuse of them.[2] The Court saw no reason to deny the children a federal forum merely because the tort occurred between family members.

Bringing the action in federal court may permit a wider range of prior acts evidence to be introduced than state evidence rules allow. The Violent Crime Control and Law Enforcement Act of 1994[3] included amendments to the Federal Rules of Evidence to permit admission of evidence of the defendant's prior similar offense in civil

2. 504 U.S. 689, 112 S. Ct. 2206, 119 L.Ed.2d 468 (1992).
3. Pub. Law 103-322, 108 Stat. 1796 (1994).

cases involving sexual assault or child molestation.[4] The purpose of permitting such prior acts to be considered is, in part, to help victims of sexual offenses prevail in swearing contests between themselves and defendants where there are no other witnesses and to allow them to rebut the defendant's claim of consent or lack of intent.[5]

STATUTES OF REPOSE AND LIMITATION

The statute of limitations generally begins to run at the time a cause of action accrues. However, statutes of limitation are generally tolled during a plaintiff's minority, at least to allow some period of time after reaching majority within which to file the action, and during periods of the plaintiff's disability.[6] Some of the statutes have specific

4. *See* FED. R. EVID. 415(a), which provides: "In a civil case in which a claim for damages or other relief is predicated on a party's alleged commission of conduct constituting an offense of sexual assault or child molestation, evidence of that party's commission of another offense or offenses of sexual assault or child molestation is admissible and may be considered as provided in Rule 413 and Rule 414 of these rules."

The Act also permitted such evidence to be admitted in criminal cases. *See* FED. R. EVID. 414. Rule 414(a) permits prior act evidence to be "considered for its bearing on any matter to which it is relevant."

5. *See, e.g.*, Frank v. County of Hudson, 924 F. Supp. 620, 626-627 (D.N.J. 1996) (court did not permit evidence of alleged molestation of stepdaughter to be introduced in sexual harassment action against employer; the court noted that "[c]hild sexual abuse deservedly carries a unique stigma in our society; such highly prejudicial evidence should therefor carry a very high degree of probative value if it is to be admitted").

6. *See, e.g.*, ALA. CODE § 6-2-8 (1996) (3 years after reaching majority or after disability terminates, but not longer than 20 years after claim accrued); ALASKA STAT. § 09.10.140 (1997) (child sexual abuse claim may be brought within 3 years after the plaintiff reaches majority or discovered or should have discovered through due diligence that the act caused the injury or condition or discovered the effect of the injury or condition); ARIZ. REV. STAT. ANN. § 12-502 (1992) (limitations period begins to run upon reaching majority or upon removal of disability); ARK. CODE ANN. § 16-56-116 (1997) (3 years after the disability is removed); CAL. CIV. PROC. CODE § 340.1 (1994) (child sexual abuse claim may be brought within 8 years of reaching majority or within 3 years of the date the plaintiff discovers or reasonably should have discovered that psychological injury or illness occurring after the age of majority was caused by the sexual abuse, whichever expires later); CAL. CIV. PROC. CODE § 340.5 (1982) (action against a health care provider for professional negligence shall be commenced by a minor within three years, or by a minor under 6 within 3 years or prior to his eighth birthday, whichever provides a longer period); COLO. REV. STAT. § 13-80-103.7(1) (1997) (child sexual abuse claim shall be brought within 6 years after disability removed or cause of action accrues, whichever is later); DEL. CODE ANN. tit. 10, § 8116 (1997) (3 years after removal of disability of infancy or incompetency); D.C. CODE ANN. § 12-302 (1996) (limitations period begins to run upon reaching majority or upon removal of disability); GA. CODE ANN. § 9-3-90 (1997) (limitations period begins to run upon reaching majority or upon removal of disability); HAW. REV. STAT. § 657-13 (1997) (limitations period begins to run upon reaching majority or upon removal of disability); 735 ILL. COMP. STAT. ANN. § 5/13-202.2(b) (1997) (child sexual abuse claim may be brought within 2 years of the date the plaintiff discovers or through reasonable diligence should discover that the abusive act or the last act in a series of abusive acts occurred and that the injury was caused by the child sexual abuse); 735 ILL. COMP. STAT. ANN. § 5/13-202.2(d) (1997) (limitations period begins to run upon reaching majority or upon removal of disability); IND. CODE ANN. § 34-1-2-5 (1983) (2 years after legal disability terminates); IOWA CODE ANN. § 614.8 (1996) (1 year after reaching majority or after disability terminates); IOWA CODE ANN. § 614.8A (1996) (child sexual abuse claim not discovered until after the plaintiff is an adult may be brought within 4 years from the time of discovery by the plaintiff of both the injury and the causal relationship between the injury and the sexual abuse); KAN. STAT. ANN. § 60-515 (1996) (1 year after reaching majority or after disability terminates, but not longer than 8 years after the cause of action accrues); KY. REV. STAT. ANN. § 413.170(1) (1997) (limitations period begins to run upon reaching majority or upon removal of disability); ME. REV. STAT. ANN. tit. 14, § 853 (1980) (limitations period begins to run upon reaching majority or upon removal of disability); MD. CTS. & JUD. PROC. CODE ANN. § 5-201 (1997) (action may be brought within the lesser of three years or the applicable period

rules for child abuse or child sexual abuse torts.[7] Commentators,[8] courts, and legislatures increasingly have addressed statute of limitations issues with respect to various child-abuse torts; therefore, a lawyer determining whether or not an action may be filed should be sure to consult the current state law in the relevant state or states.

---

of limitations after the disability is removed); MASS. GEN. LAWS ch. 260, § 7 (1992) (limitations period begins to run upon reaching majority or upon removal of disability); MICH. COMP. LAWS ANN. § 600.5851 (1997) (1 year after the disability is removed); MINN. STAT. ANN. § 541.073 (1997) (cause of action against a person who sexually molested plaintiff or negligently permitted the sexual abuse may be brought within 6 years of the time the plaintiff knew or had reason to know that the injury was caused by the sexual abuse); MINN. STAT. ANN. § 541.15(a)(1) (1997) (minority not counted within limitations period); MISS. CODE ANN. § 15-1-59 (1995) (limitations period begins to run upon reaching majority or upon removal of disability, but never longer than 21 years); MO. ANN. STAT. § 516.105 (1997) (medical malpractice may be brought on behalf of a minor under the full age of 10 years by his twelfth birthday); MO. ANN. STAT. § 516.170 (1997) (limitations period begins to run upon reaching majority or upon removal of disability); MONT. CODE ANN. § 27-2-401 (1997) (limitations period begins to run upon reaching majority or upon removal of disability); MONT. CODE ANN. § 27-2-216 (1997) (child sexual abuse claim may be brought within 3 years after the plaintiff discovered or reasonably should have discovered that the injury was caused by the act); NEB. REV. STAT. § 25-213 (1996) (limitations period begins to run upon reaching majority or upon removal of disability); NEV. REV. STAT. ANN. § 11.215 (1997) (action for child sexual abuse may be brought within 10 years after reaching majority or after plaintiff discovers or reasonably should have discovered that his injury was caused by the sexual abuse); NEV. REV. STAT. ANN. § 11.250 (1997) (limitations period begins to run upon reaching majority or upon removal of disability); N.H. REV. STAT. ANN. § 508:8 (1996) (2 years after disability is removed); N.J. STAT. ANN. § 2A:14-21 (1987) (limitations period begins to run upon reaching majority or upon removal of disability); N.Y. CIV. PRACT. L. & R. LAW § 208 (1997) (if the time otherwise limited for commencing the action is three years or more and expires no later than three years after the disability ceases, the action may be brought within three years after the disability; if the time otherwise limited is less than three years, the time shall be extended by the period of disability, but not more than 10 years for medical malpractice); N.C. GEN. STAT. § 1-17 (1997) (limitations period begins to run upon reaching majority or upon removal of disability); N.D. CENT. CODE § 28-01-25 (1997) (time of disability not a part of the period of limitation, but time cannot be tolled more than 12 years for infancy or five years for disability other than infancy, nor longer than one year after the disability ceases); OHIO REV. CODE ANN. § 2305.16 (1997) (limitations period begins to run upon reaching majority or upon removal of disability); OR. REV. STAT. § 12.117 (1996) (limitations period begins to run upon reaching majority or upon removal of disability, but not more than five years or more than one year after disability ends); OR. REV. STAT. § 12.117 (1996) (child abuse action may be brought 6 years after reaching majority or within 3 years of the date the plaintiff discovers or reasonably should have discovered the injury or the causal connection between the child abuse and the injury, whichever period is longer); OR. REV. STAT. § 12.160 (1996) (limitations period begins to run upon reaching majority or upon removal of disability, but not more than five years or more than one year after disability ends); 42 PA. CONS. STAT. ANN. § 5533 (1981) (limitations period begins to run upon reaching majority); R.I. GEN. LAWS § 9-1-19 (1997) (limitations period begins to run upon reaching majority or upon removal of disability); S.C. CODE ANN. § 15-3-40 (1997) (limitations period begins to run upon reaching majority or upon removal of disability, but not more than five years for a disability other than infancy or more than one year after disability ends); S.D. COD. LAWS ANN. § 15-2-22 (1997) (limitations period begins to run upon reaching majority or upon removal of disability, but not more than five years for a disability other than infancy or more than one year after disability ends); S.D. COD. LAWS ANN. § 26-10-25 (1997) (action for child sexual abuse may be brought within three years of the act or of the time the plaintiff discovers or reasonably should have discovered that his injury was caused by the sexual abuse); TENN. CODE ANN. § 28-1-106 (1997) (3 years after the disability is removed); TEX. CIV. PRAC. & REM. CODE ANN. § 16.001 (1997) (limitations period begins to run upon reaching majority or upon removal of disability); UTAH CODE ANN. § 78-12-25.1 (1997) (child sexual abuse action may be brought within 4 years after the plaintiff reaches majority or discovers the sexual abuse, whichever occurs later); UTAH CODE ANN. § 78-12-36 (1997) (limitations period begins to run upon reaching majority or upon removal of disability); VT. STAT. ANN. tit. 12, § 522 (1997) (child sexual abuse action may be brought within 6 years after the plaintiff reaches majority or discovers that his injury was caused by the sexual abuse, whichever period expires later); VT. STAT. ANN. tit. 12, § 551 (1997) (limitations period begins to run upon reaching majority or upon removal of disability); VA. CODE ANN. § 8.01-229(A) (1998) (limitations period begins to run upon reaching majority or upon removal of disability); VA. CODE ANN. § 8.01-243.1 (1997) (minor's cause of action against a health care provider accruing after July 1, 1987 shall be commenced within 2 years or until the plaintiff's tenth birthday if the plaintiff was under the age of 8 when the cause of action accrued); VA. CODE ANN. § 8.01-249(6) (1998) (child sexual abuse action accrues when the disability of infancy or incompetency is removed, or, if the fact of the injury and its causal connection to the sexual abuse is not then known, when the fact of the injury and its causal connection to the sexual abuse is first communicated to the person by a licensed

The California legislature has amended its child sexual abuse statute of limitations several times, most recently in 1998. The current statute permits actions to be brought within eight years of the plaintiff's reaching the age of majority or within three years of "the date the plaintiff discovers or reasonably should have discovered that psychological injury or illness occurring after the age of majority was caused by the sexual abuse, whichever period expires later."[9] The 1998 amendments provided that actions against third parties, as distinct from actions against the person committing the abuse, may not be commenced "on or after the plaintiff's 26th birthday."[10] The California Court of Appeals held that the 1990 amendments, however, did not revive claims that had lapsed prior to the January 1, 1991, effective date.[11] The Court of Appeals subsequently held that

---

physician, psychologist, or clinical psychologist); WASH. REV. CODE ANN. § 4.16.190 (1997) (limitations period begins to run upon reaching majority or upon removal of disability); WASH. REV. CODE ANN. § 4.16.340 (1997) (child sexual abuse action may be brought within 3 years of the act, within 3 years of the time the plaintiff discovered or reasonably should have discovered that the injury or condition was caused by the act, within 3 years of the time the plaintiff discovered the act; limitations period tolled until plaintiff reaches the age of 18 years); W. VA. CODE § 55-2-15 (1997) (limitations period begins to run upon reaching majority or upon removal of disability, but not more than 20 years after the right accrues); WIS. STAT. ANN. § 893.16 (1997) (3 years after reaching majority or after disability terminates, but not longer than 5 years where the disability is due to insanity); WYO. STAT. § 1-3-114 (1997) (3 years after the disability is removed). *Cf.* CONN. GEN. STAT. ANN. § 52-577d (1991) (child sexual abuse action tolled for maximum of 17 years); FLA. STAT. ANN. § 95.051 (1997) (tolled for maximum of 7 years except for medical malpractice); IDAHO CODE § 5-230 (1997) (tolled for maximum of 6 years); OKLA. STAT. ANN. tit. 12, § 96 (1988) (tolled for maximum of 7 years for medical malpractice when child was under 12 years old); S.D. COD. LAWS ANN. § 15-2-22.1 (1997) (tolled for maximum of 3 years for medical malpractice when child was over 6 years old and until age 8 if child was under 6 years old). *But see, e.g.*, Harden v State, 434 N.W.2d 881 (Iowa 1989) (not tolled for tort actions against the state).

7. *See, e.g.*, ALASKA STAT. § 09.10.140 (1997); CAL. CIV. PROC. CODE § 340.1 (1994); COLO. REV. STAT. § 13-80-103.7(1) (1997); CONN. GEN. STAT. ANN. § 52-577d (1991); 735 ILL. COMP. STAT. ANN. § 5/13-202.2(b) (1997); IOWA CODE ANN. § 614.8A (1996); MINN. STAT. ANN. § 541.073 (1997); MONT. CODE ANN. § 27-2-216 (1997); NEV. REV. STAT. ANN. § 11.215 (1997); OR. REV. STAT. § 12.117 (1996); S.D. COD. LAWS ANN. § 26-10-25 (1997); UTAH CODE ANN. § 78-12-25.1 (1997); VT. STAT. ANN. tit. 12, § 522 (1997); VA. CODE ANN. § 8.01-249(6) (1998); WASH. REV. CODE ANN. § 4.16.340 (1997).

8. *See, e.g.*, J. S. Dorado, *Remembering Incest: The Complexities of this Process and Implications for Civil Statutes of Limitations*, in TRAUMA AND MEMORY 93 (Linda Meyer Williams & Victoria L. Banyard, eds., 1998); Annotation, *Posttraumatic Syndrome As Tolling Running of Statute of Limitations*, 12 A.L.R.5th 546 (1993); Annotation, *Emotional or Psychological "Blocking" or Repression As Tolling Running of Statute of Limitations*, 11 A.L.R.5th 588 (1993); Annotation, *Running of Limitations Against Action for Civil Damages for Sexual Abuse of Child*, 9 ALR5th 321 (1993); Comment, *Adult Survivors of Childhood Sexual Abuse and the Statute of Limitations: The Need for Consistent Application of the Delayed Discovery Rule*, 20 PEPPERDINE L. REV. 1359 (1993); Lisa Bickel, *Tolling the Statute of Limitations in Actions Brought by Adult Survivors of Childhood Sexual Abuse*, 33 ARIZ. L. REV. 427 (1991); Ann M. Hagen, *Tolling the Statute of Limitations for Adult Survivors of Childhood Sexual Abuse*, 76 IOWA L. REV. 355 (1991); Jocelyn B. Lamm, *Easing Access to the Courts for Incest Victims: Toward an Equitable Application of the Delayed Discovery Rule*, 100 YALE L.J. 2189 (1991); Rosenfeld, *The Statute of Limitations Barriers in Childhood Sexual Abuse Cases: The Equitable Estoppel Remedy*, 12 HARVARD WOMEN'S L.J. 206 (1988-89); Handler, *Civil Claims of Adults Molested as Children: Maturation of Harm and the Statute of Limitations Hurdle*, 15 FORDHAM URB. L.J. 722 (1987). For an up-to-date listing of state statutes and case law dealing with tolling the statute of limitations during minority, *see* LEONARD KARP & CHERYL L. KARP, DOMESTIC TORTS: FAMILY VIOLENCE, CONFLICT AND SEXUAL ABUSE app. G (West Group Supp. 1998).

9. CAL. CODE CIV. PROC. § 340.1 (1998).

10. CAL CODE CIV. PROC. § 340.1(b) (1998).

11. *See* David A. v. Superior Court of the City and County of San Francisco, 20 Cal. App. 4th 281, 24 Cal. Rptr. 2d 537 (1993).

the 1994 amendments did revive causes of action which had lapsed or expired under the law existing prior to January 1, 1991.[12] However, this retroactive revival of lapsed claims applies only to claims against the perpetrator of the abuse, not to related, ancillary actions against third parties.[13]

The Supreme Court of Nevada made some interesting statements concerning the uniqueness of child sexual abuse, finding that adult survivors of child sexual abuse (CSA):

> present unique circumstances and injuries that do not readily conform to the usual constructs upon which periods of limitations are imposed. In a sense, such survivors are analogous to victims of false imprisonment, where each new day of confinement creates a new cause of action. Unfortunately, however, CSA survivors are hostage to their own thought processes, implanted by their abusers, and from which they may never be totally released. Indeed the mental and emotional dysfunction suffered by such victims may virtually prevent them from seeking relief against their tormentors until the period of limitations has long since expired. To place the passage of time in a position of priority and importance over the plight of CSA victims would seem to be the ultimate exaltation of form over substance, convenience over principle.
>
> Based upon the foregoing, we hold that no existing statute of limitations applies to bar the action of an adult survivor of CSA when it is shown by clear and convincing evidence that the plaintiff has in fact been sexually abused during minority by the named defendant. Absent such evidence, a cause of action based upon allegations of child sexual abuse will be subject to the regular two-year period of limitation.[14]

The Supreme Court of Virginia has held that the retroactive extension of the statute of limitations for child sexual abuse, with the cause of action not accruing until the victim first learned of the causal connection between the victim's injuries and the abuse, did not revive causes of action that were already barred by the statute of limitations, stating that the statute of limitations defense is a vested

12. *See* Lent v. Doe, 40 Cal. App. 4th 1177, 47 Cal. Rptr. 2d 389 (1995).

13. *See, e.g.*, Chaney v. Superior Court of Los Angeles County, 39 Cal. App. 4th, 46 Cal. Rptr. 2d 73 (1995) (claim against perpetrator's wife for negligent supervision barred); Debbie Reynolds Professional Rehearsal Studios v. Superior Court of Los Angeles County, 25 Cal. App. 4th 222, 30 Cal. Rptr. 2d 514 (1994) (claim against perpetrator's employer for negligent hiring, training, and retaining barred).

14. Peterson v. Bruney, 106 Nev. 781, 792 P.2d 18, 24-25 (1990).

right.[15] The Pennsylvania Supreme Court has also held that the statute tolling the statute of limitations during the plaintiff's minority[16] cannot be applied retroactively to revive previously barred claims.[17]

A defendant's fraudulent concealment of material facts, preventing the plaintiff from discovering the cause of action, may constitute an equitable basis for tolling or postponing commencement of the statute of limitations.[18] This fraudulent concealment may arise from deception or violation of a duty, such as a parent or legal guardian's duty to inform a child of significant childhood events, including the child's molestation.[19] However, the mere fact that the defendant had control over the child does not constitute fraudulent concealment.[20] The estoppel effect of the bar for fraudulent concealment ends at the time the plaintiff learns of facts, conditions, and circumstances that would cause a reasonable person to make an inquiry which would lead to discovery of the cause of action.[21]

Sometimes the effects of the sexual abuse are severe enough to place the plaintiff under a disability that tolls the statute during the period of disability. Some courts will toll the statute of limitations only for disability or "insanity" that is so severe that it renders the plaintiff unable to function in society in general.[22] Others toll the statute if the disability or "insanity" rendered the plaintiff unable to understand and assert the relevant legal rights.[23] Courts are divided over whether repressed memory of the abuse can be considered a disability sufficient to toll the statute of limitations.[24]

---

15. Starnes v Cayouette, 244 Va. 202, 419 S.E.2d 669 (1992).
16. 42 PA. CONS. STAT. ANN. § 5533 (1984).
17. *See* Dalrymple v. Brown, 701 A.2d 164 (Pa. 1997).
18. *See, e.g.*, S.A.P. v. State Department of Health & Rehabilitative Services, 704 So.2d 583 (Fla. App. 1997); Fager v. Hundt, 610 N.E.2d 246. (Ind. 1993).
19. *See, e.g.*, Fager v. Hundt, 610 N.E.2d 246. (Ind. 1993).
20. *See, e.g.*, State v. Henry, 834 S.W.2d 273 (Tenn. 1992) (parental control was not concealment to toll criminal statute of limitations for incest prosecution).
21. *See, e.g.*, Marshall v. First Baptist Church of Houston, 949 S.W.2d 504 (Tex. App. 1997).
22. *See, e.g.*, Overall v. Estate of Klotz, 52 F.3d 398 (2d. Cir. 1995); Strata v. Patin, 545 So.2d 1180 (La. App. 1989); O'Neal v. Division of Family Services, State of Utah, 821 P.2d 1139 (Utah 1991), *reh'g denied* (1992).
23. *See, e.g.*, Doe v. Roe, 955 P.2d 951 (Ariz. 1998); Jones v. Jones, 242 N.J. Super. 195, 576 A.2d 316 (1990).
24. *Compare* Lemmerman v. Fealk, 449 Mich. 56, 534 N.W.2d 695 (1995) (repressed memory does not trigger insanity grace period as a matter of balancing public policies); Olsen v. Hooley, 865 P.2d 1345 (Utah 1993) (alleged complete repression of memory of sexual abuse did not render plaintiff mentally incompetent so as to toll statute of limitations), *with* Doe v. Coffee County Board of Education, 852 S.W.2d 899 (Tenn. App. 1992) (dicta that in some cases repressed memory may constitute unsound mind for purposes of tolling the statute of limitations).

DELAYED DISCOVERY

Most courts have permitted tort actions to be brought beyond the usual period of limitations based on the delayed-discovery rule, which delays the time that the cause of action accrues to the time of discovery or the time when discovery reasonably should have occurred.[25] However, some state's statutes of repose may bar some delayed-discovery cases.[26] Unlike minority or disability, which tolls the statute of limitations even though the cause of action has accrued, delayed discovery affects the date on which the cause of action accrues. The delayed discovery in child sexual abuse cases is often based on delayed memory, which is a phenomenon by which certain very traumatic incidents are not remembered during some periods of time.[27] One of the most well-publicized examples of such delayed memory involves Marilyn Van Derbur Atler, the 1958 Miss America who revealed her childhood sexual abuse in 1989.[28] She said she had a "day child," the one who excelled, appeared well-adjusted, and had no memory of being abused, and a "night child," the one who was sexually molested by her father. The day child had no memory of the night child, and she had blocked out all memory of the abuse until she was an adult. Mental-health professionals con-

---

25. *See, e.g.*, Doe v. Roe, 191 Ariz. 313, 955 P.2d 951 (1998); Sellery v. Cressey, 48 Cal. App. 4th 538, 55 Cal. Rptr.2d 706 (1996); Farris v. Compton, 652 A.2d 49 (D.C. 1994); Dunlea v. Dappen, 83 Hawaii 28, 924 P.2d 196 (1996); Phillips v. Johnson, 231 Ill. App. 3d 890, 599 N.E.2d 4 (1992); Doe v. Cherwitz, 518 N.W.2d 362 (Iowa 1994); Doe v. Roman Catholic Church, 656 So.2d 5 (La. App.), *cert. denied*, 662 So.2d 478 (La. 1995); Nuccio v. Nuccio, 673 A.2d 1331 (Me. 1996); Phinney v. Morgan, 39 Mass. App. Ct. 202, 654 N.E.2d 77, *rev. denied*, 421 Mass. 1104, 656 N.E.1258 (1995); Sheehan v. Sheehan, 901 S.W.2d 57 (Mo. 1995); Petersen v. Bruen, 106 Nev. 271, 792 P.2d 18 (1990); McCollum v. D'Arcy, 138 N.H. 285, 638 A.2d 797 (1994); Jones v. Jones, 242 N.J. Super. 195, 576 A.2d 316, *cert. denied*, 122 N.J. 418, 585 A.2d 412 (1990); Peterson v. Huso, 552 N.W.2d 83 (N.D. 1996); Ault v. Jasko, 70 Ohio St. 3d 114, 637 N.E.2d 870 (1994); Lovelace v. Keohane, 831 P.2d 624 (Okla. 1992); Olsen v. Hooley, 865 P.2d 1345 (Utah 1993); Hammer v. Hammer, 142 Wis.2d 257, 418 N.W.2d 23 (Wis. App. 1987), *rev. denied*, 144 Wis.2d 953, 428 N.W.2d 552 (1988). *But see, e.g.*, Travis v. Ziter, 681 So.2d 1348 (Ala. 1996); Doe v. Maskell, 342 Md. 684, 679 A.2d 1087 (1996); Lemmerman v. Fealk, 449 Mich. 56, 534 N.W.2d 695 (1995); Dalrymple v. Brown, 701 A.2d 164 (Pa. 1997); Tyson v. Tyson, 107 Wash. 2d 72, 727 P.2d 226 (1986) (this case now has been superseded by statute); Smith v. Smith, 830 F.2d 11 (2d Cir. 1987).

26. *See, e.g.*, MISS. CODE ANN. § 15-1-59 (1995) (limitations period begins to run upon reaching majority or upon removal of disability, but never longer than 21 years); N.C. GEN. STAT. § 1-52(16) (1997) (no cause of action shall accrue more than 10 years from the last act or omission of the defendant giving rise to the cause of action).

27. *See, e.g.*, Bessel van der Kolk & W. Kadish, *Amnesia, Dissociation, and the Return of the Repressed* in B. VAN DER KOLK, PSYCHOLOGICAL TRAUMA (1987). For additional discussion of delayed memories, see Chapter 6.

28. *See*, M. Van Derbur Atler, *The Darkest Secret*, 35/2 PEOPLE MAGAZINE 88 (June 10, 1991).

tinue to debate the issues of delayed memory, whether it exists, and what mechanisms account for it.[29]

The discovery rule is an equitable rule that is based on a balancing of the public policies preventing stale claims from being litigated and allowing plaintiffs to have a fair opportunity to pursue just claims. Courts are divided as to whether to apply the discovery rule to cases of repressed memory of child sexual abuse.[30] The Arizona Supreme Court has stated:

> The policy behind the discovery rule is . . . served by application to repressed memory cases involving childhood sexual abuse and is, we believe, logically appropriate given that the intentional act of the tortfeasor caused both the damage and the repression of memory. To hold otherwise would be to effectively reward the perpetrator for the egregious nature of his conduct and the severity of the resulting emotional injury.[31]

Some courts divide delayed-discovery cases into two categories: those in which the plaintiff was aware of the abuse but not that various other problems were caused by the abuse ("type 1"), and those in which the plaintiff was unaware of the underlying abuse itself ("type 2").[32] Courts are more likely to allow actions to be brought where

---

29. *See, e.g.*, David H. Gleaves, *The Evidence for "Repression": An Examination of Holmes (1990) and the Implications for the Recovered Memory Controversy*, 5/1 J. CHILD SEXUAL ABUSE 1 (1996); Constance J. Dalenberg, *Making and Finding Memories: A Commentary on the Repressed Memory Controversy*, 3/3 J. CHILD SEXUAL ABUSE 109 (1994); Sandra L. Elvik, *Professionals under Fire: Delayed Memories vs. the False Memory Syndrome*, 3/3 J. CHILD SEXUAL ABUSE 123 (1994); Richard Ofshe, *Making Grossly Damaging But Avoidable Errors: The Pitfalls of the Olio/Cornell Thesis*, 3/3 J. CHILD SEXUAL ABUSE 95 (1994); Karen A. Olio & William F. Cornell, *Making Meaning Not Monsters: Reflections on the Delayed Memory Syndrome*, 3/3 J. CHILD SEXUAL ABUSE 77 (1994); Robert M. Reece, *Making Meaning—A Pediatrician's View*, 3/3 J. CHILD SEXUAL ABUSE 119 (1994); H.G. Pope, *"Recovered Memories": Recent Events and Review of Evidence*, 13/7 CURRENTS IN AFFECTIVE ILLNESS (1994). For a discussion of the legal implications of the debate, *see generally*, 1 JOHN E. B. MYERS, EVIDENCE IN CHILD ABUSE AND NEGLECT CASES § 1.7 (3rd ed. 1997); Cynthia Grant Bowman & Elizabeth Mertz, *A Dangerous Direction: Legal Intervention in Sexual Abuse Survivor Therapy*, 109 HARV. L. REV. 549 (1996).

30. *Compare* cases which permit use of discovery rule: Moriarty v. Garden Sanctuary Church of God, 1999 WL 21235 (S.C. App. 1999); Doe v. Roe, 191 Ariz. 313, 955 P.2d 951 (Ariz. 1998); Farris v. Compton, 652 A.2d 49 (D.C. App. 1994); Phillips v. Johnson, 231 Ill. App. 3d 890, 599 N.E.2d 4 (1992); Callahan v. State, 464 N.W.2d 268 (Iowa 1990); McCollum v. D'Arcy, 138 N.H. 285, 638 A.2d 797 (1994); Osland v. Osland, 442 N.W.2d 907 (N.D. 1989); Ault v. Jakso, 70 Ohio St. 3d 114, 637 N.E.2d 870 (1994); Olsen v. Hooley, 865 P.2d 1345 (Utah 1993), *with* cases which do not permit use of discovery rule: Lemmerman v. Fealk, 449 Mich. 56, 534 N.W.2d 695 (1995); Bailey v. Lewis, 763 F. Supp. 802 (E.D. Pa. , *aff'd.* 950 F.2d 721 (3d Cir. 1991); S.V. v. R.V., 39 Tex. Sup. Ct. J. 386, 933 S.W.2d 1 (1996); Joseph W. v. Catholic Diocese of Madison, 212 Wis.2d 925, 569 N.W.2d 795 (1997).

31. Doe v. Roe, 191 Ariz. 313, 955 P.2d 951, 960 (Ariz. 1998) (citation omitted).

32. *See, e.g.*, Mary Doe v. John Doe, 216 Cal. App. 3d 285, 264 Cal. Rptr. 633 (1989). For a more complete discussion of these two categories and how courts treat them, *see* LEONARD KARP & CHERYL KARP, DOMESTIC TORTS § 4.23 (Clark Boardman Callaghan 1989, West Group 1998).

the abuse itself was not remembered[33] rather than where the consequences of the abuse were not fully appreciated, but the abuse was known.[34] The Pennsylvania Supreme Court has held that the discovery rule "applies only to those situations where the nature of the injury itself is such that no amount of vigilance will enable the plaintiff to detect an injury."[35] Because sexual abuse constitutes a battery, the Pennsylvania Supreme Court declined to extend the discovery rule to cases of repressed memory.[36]

When discovery occurs is generally a fact question. Therefore, a motion for summary judgment or to dismiss should not be granted in favor of a defendant where there is a genuine issue of fact concerning when the plaintiff discovered sufficient facts for the cause of action to accrue.[37] A plaintiff is charged with the duty to investigate with due diligence to discover the necessary facts that underlie the cause of action.[38] The Arizona Supreme Court has stated that this reasonable diligence component of the discovery rule "does not impose a rigid investigate and discover standard that ignores the psychology of repressed memory. . . . To impose such a standard to memories that may be physiologically inaccessible to the conscious mind is antithetical to the policy behind the discovery rule."[39] Some courts hold that the test for whether the plaintiff reasonably should

---

33. *See, e.g.*, Meiers-Post v. Schafer, 170 Mich. 174, 427 N.W.2d 606 (1988). *But see, e.g.*, Tyson v. Tyson, 107 Wash. 2d 72, 727 P.2d 226 (1986) (rejecting delayed discovery rule because there was no independent means of verifying the allegations; this case was superseded by statute).

34. For cases refusing to apply the delayed discovery rule to such cases *see, e.g.*, Marsha V. v. Gardner, 231 Cal. App. 3d 265, 281 Cal. Rptr. 473 (1991); E.W. v. D.C.H., 231 Mont. 481, 754 P.2d 817 (1988); Hildebrand v. Hildebrand, 736 F. Supp. 1512 (S.D. Ind. 1990). *But see, e.g.*, J.L. v. J.F., 317 N.J. Super. 418, 722 A.2d 558 (1999) (delayed discovery rule applies from date plaintiff reasonably discovers the injury and the causal connection between the alleged abuse and the injury); Franke v. Geyer, 209 Ill. App. 3d 1009, 568 N.E.2d 931 (1991) (delayed discovery rule applied where the plaintiff did not realize that her problems had been caused by the sexual abuse); Callahan v. State, 464 N.W.2d 268 (Iowa 1990) (discovery or reasonably expected discovery of both the abuse and the resulting injury required); Osland v. Osland, 442 N.W.2d 907 (N.D. 1989) (delayed discovery rule applied where the plaintiff's severe emotional trauma resulted in her being unable to fully understand or discover her cause of action during the applicable statutory limitations period); Hammer v. Hammer, 142 Wis. 2d 257, 418 N.W.2d 23 (Ct. App. 1987) *review denied*, 142 Wis. 2d 257, 428 N.W.2d 552 (1988) (allowing the action based on delayed discovery of the extent and cause of psychological problems).

35. *See* Dalrymple v. Brown, 701 A.2d 164 (Pa. 1997).

36. *Id.*

37. *See, e.g.*, J.L. v. J.F., 317 N.J. Super. 418, 722 A.2d 558 (1999); Moriarty v. Garden Sanctuary Church of God, 1999 WL 21235 (S.C. App. 1999); Doe v. Roe, 191 Ariz. 313, 955 P.2d 951 (1998); Hildebrand v. Hildebrand, 736 F. Supp. 1512 (S.D. Ind. 1990); Peterson v. Huso, 552 N.W.2d 83 (N.D. 1996); Olsen v. Hooley, 865 P.2d 1345 (Utah 1993); Hammer v. Hammer, 142 Wis.2d 257, 418 N.W.2d 23 (App. 1987). *Cf.* Livingston v. Diocese of Cleveland, 1998 WL 45345 (Ohio App. 1998) (agreeing with rule, but in this case facts showed that no memories were repressed).

38. *See, e.g.*, Doe v. Roe, 191 Ariz. 313, 955 P.2d 951 (1998).

39. *Id.*

have discovered the cause of action is subjective,[40] while others apply an objective person standard.[41] This is an evolving area of the law for courts and legislatures, and lawyers should research the applicable rules before an action is filed.

One defense being raised against delayed discovery of sexual abuse is the "false memory syndrome," (FMS), which purports to explain the delayed memory syndrome. FMS is a theory that states that false "memories" of child sexual abuse that never occurred are implanted in the minds of people, generally women, and generally during therapy with master's level female therapists. Dr. Roland Summit, an expert in intrafamilial child sexual abuse, recounts that the Institute for Psychological Therapies "spun off a new illness, *false memory syndrome*,"[42] to describe what was felt to be delayed "memories" of nonexistent childhood sexual abuse, often during the course of therapy.[43]

COLLATERAL ESTOPPEL

Where there has been a finding of abuse in a domestic relations, child protection, or criminal action, that finding collaterally estops the abuser from denying the abuse in a subsequent tort action, provided that the abuser was a party to the previous action and actually litigated the abuse issue. A finding that there was no abuse may not collaterally estop the plaintiff, however.

If the action involved a higher standard of proof, such as a termination of parental rights or criminal action, the plaintiff should be permitted to relitigate the abuse in an action requiring proof only by

40. *Id.*

41. *See, e.g.*, W.J.L. v. Bugge, 573 N.W.2d 677 (Minn. 1998).

42. *See*, Roland Summit, *Misplaced Attention to Delayed Memory*, 5/3 THE ADVISOR 21 at 24 (Summer 1992) (emphasis in original).

43. An organization called the False Memory Syndrome Foundation was spun off from the Institute for Psychological Therapies to respond to the allegations on behalf of people who claim to be falsely accused of perpetrating such abuse. *See generally*, H. Wakefield & R. Underwager, *Magic, Mischief, and Memories: Remembering Repressed Abuse* (n.d.). For a discussion of the work of Underwager and Wakefield in the sexual abuse area, *see, e.g.*, ANNA SALTER, ACCURACY OF EXPERT TESTIMONY IN CHILD SEXUAL ABUSE CASES: A CASE STUDY OF RALPH UNDERWAGER AND HOLINDA WAKEFIELD (1991). Lawyers who are faced with information on the false memory syndrome from the False Memory Foundation also should be aware of an interview published concerning two of the foundation's founders, Ralph Underwager and Hollida Wakefield, in a Dutch publication, *Paidika, The Journal of Paedophilia*, J. Geraci, *Interview: Hollida Wakefield and Ralph Underwager*, 3/2 PAIDIKA, J. OF PAEDOPHILIA 2 (Winter 1993).

a preponderance of the evidence. If the child was not represented by counsel in the previous action, collateral estoppel may not apply to preclude the tort action. In a protection action,[44] the state may be required to prove that the child has no parent willing and able to provide proper care and protection. Where one parent is protective, the dismissal of the dependency action may not necessarily involve a finding that there was no abuse, but only that the child has one parent able to provide proper care. Further, the tort action may be pled in a way to involve different legal issues, such as the negligent infliction of emotional distress or negligent supervision.

THEORIES AGAINST THE ABUSER OR NONPROTECTIVE PARENT

Child sexual abuse can result in causes of action for both intentional and negligent torts. Sexual abuse clearly falls under the tort of assault and battery.[45] Restatement (Second) of Torts § 13 requires a harmful or offensive contact resulting from an act intended to cause the contact or apprehension that such contact is imminent.

The child may have a claim for intentional infliction of emotional distress for emotional abuse or as an emotional injury accompanying physical or sexual abuse.[46] Further, some courts have allowed claims for intentional infliction of emotional distress for children who watched the physical abuse of a parent.[47] Restatement (Second) of Torts § 46 requires that the conduct causing the emotional distress be "so outrageous in character, and so extreme in degree, as to go beyond all possible bounds of decency, and to be

---

44. See Chapter 3.

45. *See, e.g.*, Wilson v. Wilson, 742 F.2d 1004 (6th Cir. 1984) (reversing dismissal of child's action against her adoptive father for three years of molestation); Doe v. Durtschi, 110 Idaho 466, 716 P.2d 1238 (1986) (student may sue teacher for molestation); Connolly *ex rel* Connolly v. Holt, 323 N.C. 90, 418 S.E.2d 511 (1992) (children molested by father during ten-year period); Osland v. Osland, 442 N.W.2d 907 (N.D. 1989) (child molested by father from ages 10 to 15); Elkington v. Foust, 618 P.2d 37 (Utah 1980) (child recovered $42,000 against stepfather for nine years of molestation).

46. *See, e.g.*, Petersen v. Bruen, 106 Nev. 271, 792 P.2d 19 (1990); Laurie Marie M. v. Jeffrey T.M., 77 N.Y.2d 803, 569 N.E.2d 874, 568 N.Y.S.2d 15 (1991); Connolly *ex rel* Connolly v. Holt, 323 N.C. 90, 418 S.E.2d 511 (1992); Hammer v. Hammer, 142 Wis. 2d 257, 418 N.W. 2d 23 (Ct. App. 1987), *review denied*, 142 Wis. 2d 257, 428 N.W.2d 552 (1988). *But see, e.g.*, Anthony H. v. John G., 415 Mass. 196, 612 N.E.2d 663 (1993) (boy who was molested by his older brother may not recover against man who molested older brother, because he was not present during the brother's molestation and did not have a severe emotional reaction when he learned of his brother's molestation).

47. *See, e.g.*, Courtney v. Courtney, 186 W. Va. 597, 413 S.E.2d 418 (1991) (stepfather assaulted mother in child's presence).

regarded as atrocious, and utterly intolerable in a civilized community." A parent may be able to recover for intentional infliction of emotional distress based on the abuse of the parent's child.[48]

In some states there is an implied tort arising out of the tortfeasor's violation of a criminal statute.[49] All states have criminal statutes involving child abuse and neglect. Therefore, the lawyer should determine whether an action may be plead based on violation of one of those statutes.[50]

Most physical and sexual abuse results in emotional injury, even if the abuser was not aware of that consequence. It is the abuser's lack of awareness of foreseeable emotional injury that constitutes the gravamen of the tort of negligent infliction of emotional distress. Some courts will not allow a negligence claim when it is based on abusive conduct that is clearly intentional.[51] However, a claim may lie for the negligent infliction of emotional distress to the abused child's parents.[52]

ACTIONS AGAINST PARENTS

Traditionally children could not sue their parents for torts committed against them based on the doctrine of parental immunity. This doctrine frequently has been abrogated completely or in part. In most jurisdictions there is no parental immunity for intentional child

---

48. *See, e.g.*, Morgan v. Foretich, 846 F.2d 941 (4th Cir. 1988).

49. *See generally* Restatement (Second) of Torts § 875A (1979).

50. *See generally* LEONARD KARP & CHERYL KARP, DOMESTIC TORTS: FAMILY VIOLENCE, CONFLICT, AND SEXUAL ABUSE § 4.20 (Clark Boardman Callaghan 1989, West Supp. 1998).

51. *See, e.g.*, Landis v. Allstate Insurance Co., 546 So.2d 1051 (Fla. 1989) (day care provider's subjective intent to gain sexual satisfaction rather than to inflict harm was irrelevant; it is presumed that harm inherently flows from molestation, which is an intentional act, and therefore, excluded by the homeowner policy's intentional acts exclusion); Allstate Insurance Co. v. Mugavero, 589 N.E.2d 365 (N.Y. 1992) (injury is inherent in child sexual abuse, and since the abuse was intentional, the injuries were intentionally caused as a matter of law); St. Michelle v. Robinson, 52 Wash. App. 309, 759 P.2d 467 (1988) (father's sexual abuse of his daughter was clearly intentional; therefore, the facts did not support the claim of negligent infliction of emotional distress); Allstate Insurance Company v. Bailey, 723 F. Supp. 665 (M.D. Fla 1989) (specific intent to harm child is not required; the intentional act of sexual molestation was sufficient to come within the exclusion for intentional acts).

52. *See, e.g.*, Marlene F. v. Psychiatric Medical Clinic, 48 Cal. 3d 583, 770 P.2d 278, 257 Cal. Rptr. 98 (1989) (mothers could maintain action against therapist who molested their sons during the course of family counseling); Doe v. Cuomo, 43 Conn. Supp. 222, 649 A.2d 266 (1994) (parents could maintain action against man who molested their daughter, who had been entrusted to his care); Haselhorst v. State, 240 Neb. 891, 485 N.W.2d 180 (1992) (parents could maintain action against state for placing foster child, who molested their children, in their home).

sexual abuse torts.[53] Parents may also have liability for failure to protect children in their care or to protect other children from foreseeable abuse by their child or spouse.[54]

Where insurance coverage is not available,[55] filing a suit against the parents may result in an uncollectible judgment. The lawyer will need to weigh the benefits of obtaining such a judgment against the possibly pyrrhic victory. Any legal action between family members is likely to cause loyalty divisions within the nuclear and extended family. The child may want a forum in which to address the wrong done to him or her or may want validation that he or she was abused. A tort case may not be the best way to achieve those psychological needs, and the lawyer should discuss other alternatives with the client. It may assist the client to have him or her discuss the ramifications with a mental-health professional in therapy or as part of a consultation through the lawyer. If the lawyer hires the mental-health professional for this purpose, the resulting discussions should fall within the lawyer work product privilege.

HOME OWNER'S INSURANCE

Early cases used to be able to obtain recoveries from the molester's homeowner's insurance policy by pleading at least one negligence

53. *See, e.g.*, Herzfeld v. Herzfeld, 1999 WL 68794 (Fla. Dist. Ct. App., Dist. 3, 1999) (no parental immunity for child sexual abuse); Henderson v. Woolley, 230 Conn. 472, 644 A.2d 1303 (1994) (no parental immunity for child sexual abuse); Swartz v. Swartz, 887 S.W.2d 644 (Mo. Ct. App. 1994) (no parental immunity for child sexual abuse; parental immunity for failure to protect based on factual determination of the impact of the litigation on the harmony of the family unit); Barnes v. Barnes, 603 N.E.2d 1337 (Ind. 1992) (immunity abrogated as to intentional sexual abuse of 15-year-old child); Connolly *ex rel* Connolly v. Holt, 323 N.C. 90, 418 S.E.2d 511 (1992) (no immunity for parent's sexual abuse over a ten-year period); Hurst v. Capitell, 539 So.2d 264 (Ala. 1989) (mother and stepfather have no parental immunity for sexual abuse of child because the abuse had already disrupted the family harmony; however, allegations must be proven by clear and convincing evidence). *But see*, Richards v. Richards, 599 So.2d 135 (Fla. Dist. Ct. App., Dist. 5, 1992) (parental immunity barred child's action against her father for sexual abuse). *See generally* 2 ANN M. HARALAMBIE, HANDLING CHILD CUSTODY, ABUSE AND ADOPTION CASES §§ 20.03-20.04 (2nd ed. Clark Boardman Callaghan 1993, West Group 1998); LEONARD KARP & CHERYL KARP, DOMESTIC TORTS: FAMILY VIOLENCE, CONFLICT, AND SEXUAL ABUSE § 3.16 (Clark Boardman Callaghan 1989, West Group 1998).

54. *See, e.g.*, National Union Fire Insurance Co. v. Lynette C., 228 Cal. App. 3d 1073, 279 Cal. Rptr. 394 (1991) ($1.25 million judgment against foster mother who negligently failed to protect foster child from molestation by her husband for two and one-half years and failed to tell the child welfare agency that the placement was inappropriate because of her husband); Doe v. Roe, No 88-CV-384 (Kenosha County, Wisconsin Cir Ct 9/21/91) ($983,000 jury verdict against neighbor to each of two girls molested by the neighbor's spouse based on her negligent failure to warn them of his prior molestations, failure to report, and failure to seek psychiatric help for her husband). *See generally*, LEONARD KARP & CHERYL KARP, DOMESTIC TORTS: FAMILY VIOLENCE, CONFLICT, AND SEXUAL ABUSE § 8.18A (Clark Boardman Callaghan 1989, West Group 1998). *But see, e.g.*, Colley v. Hosier, 659 N.E.2d 1127 (Ind. Ct. App. 1996) (parental immunity survives to bar negligent supervision suit to be filed against a custodial parent).

55. See *infra*.

count. In response to those cases, many homeowner's policies now explicitly exclude coverage for the homeowner's abuse of a child. Most courts that have considered the matter have determined that insurers may exclude coverage for child sexual abuse committed by the insured under exclusions for intentional misconduct, inferring intent as a matter of law from the nature of the act committed, regardless of whether the perpetrator actually intended harm.[56] Further, most recent decisions have gone behind the negligence label to view the molestation as an intentional act.[57]

THEORIES AGAINST THIRD PARTIES AS DEFENDANTS

The most obvious defendant in a child abuse or neglect tort is the parent or other person who abused or neglected the child, often a parent or stepparent. However, many such tortfeasors do not have the financial resources to pay a judgment rendered against them. For that reason, many plaintiffs' lawyers plead the case to include causes of action that may be covered under the defendant's home-owner's insurance[58] or may name third-party defendants who are more likely to have the resources or insurance coverage to pay a judgment or settlement. Spouses of molesters may be held liable if the molesta-

---

56. *See, e.g.*, Fittanto v. Klein, 788 F. Supp. 1454 (N.D. Ill. 1992) (applying Alabama substantive law); State Farm Fire & Cas. Co. v. Davis, 612 So.2d 458 (Ala. 1993) (exception applies only to cases of child sexual abuse); J.C. Penney Cas. Ins. Co. v. M.K., 52 Cal. 3d 1009, 804 P.2d 689, 278 Cal. Rptr. 64 (1991). *Cf.* K.B. v. State Farm Fire and Casualty Co., 941 P.2d 1288 Ct. App. 1997) (attempted molestation excluded as an intentional act; guilty plea precluded use of voluntary intoxication to deny intention).

57. *See, e.g.*, Metropolitan Property & Casualty Ins. Co. v. Miller, 1999 WL 93090 (Minn. 1999) (in case filed against parents' friend for allegedly negligent failure to prevent repeated sexual abuse of child by friend's husband, policy exclusion for bodily injury barred recovery regardless of whether the insured perpetrated the abuse or negligently failed to prevent it); Tara N. by Kummer v. Economy Fire & Casualty Ins. Co, 197 Wis. 2d 77, 540 N.W.2d 26 (Ct. App. 1995) (in case filed against grandparents who negligently supervised visitation between the child and her father, policy exclusion for bodily injury arising out of an expected, anticipated, or foreseeable sexual act bars recovery for psychological and bodily injuries to the child, mother's loss of consortium, child's medical expenses and loss of earning capacity); Allstate Insurance Co v. Mugavero, 589 N.E.2d 365 (N.Y. 1992) (injury is inherent in child sexual abuse, and since the abuse was intentional, the injuries were intentionally caused as a matter of law); Allstate Insurance Company v. Bailey, 723 F. Supp. 665 (M.D. Fla 1989) (specific intent to harm child is not required; the intentional act of sexual molestation was sufficient to come within the exclusion for intentional acts); Landis v. Allstate Insurance Co, 546 So.2d 1051 (Fla 1989) (day care provider's subjective intent to gain sexual satisfaction rather than to inflict harm was irrelevant; it is presumed that harm inherently flows from molestation, which is an intentional act, and therefore, excluded by the homeowner policy's intentional acts exclusion); St. Michelle v Robinson, 52 Wash. App. 309, 759 P.2d 467 (1988) (father's sexual abuse of his daughter was clearly intentional; therefore, the facts did not support the claim of negligent infliction of emotional distress).

58. See the discussion of insurance *infra*.

tion was foreseeable.[59] The New Jersey Supreme Court listed several factors that it found to be relevant in determining whether a molestation by a spouse is foreseeable:

> whether the husband had previously committed sexual offenses against children; the number, date, and nature of those prior offenses; the gender of prior victims; the age of prior victims; where the prior offenses occurred; whether the prior offense was against a stranger or a victim known to the husband; the husband's therapeutic history and regimen; the extent to which the wife encouraged or facilitated her husband's unsupervised contact with the current victim; the presence of physical evidence such as pornographic materials depicting children and the unexplained appearance of children's apparel in the marital home; and the extent to which the victims made inappropriate sexual comments or engaged in age-inappropriate behavior in the husband and wife's presence.[60]

The court pointed out that a "wife may well be the only person with the kind of knowledge or opportunity to know that a particular person or particular class of persons is being sexually abused or is likely to be abused by her husband."[61]

Similarly, parents of molesters may have a duty to warn the parents of children who come in contact with the molester under certain circumstances.[62]

Torts related to child sexual abuse may be brought against a wide variety of third parties, such as child-welfare agencies, schools, churches, professionals who evaluated or treated the child, and oth-

---

59. *See, e.g.*, J.S. v. R.G.H., 155 N.J. 330, 714 A.2d 924 (1998) ("particularized foreseeability" test applied; wife knew or had reason to know of her husband's proclivities, knew that her husband was spending daily time alone with the girls who lived next door, and never confronted her husband about the unsupervised time they were spending together); Doe v. Franklin, 930 S.W.2d 921 (Tex. Ct. App. 1996) (molestation foreseeable where wife knew that her husband was a pedophile, she invited the child victim into her home, she left the child unsupervised with her husband, and the child tried to tell her about the molestation); Phillips v. Deihm, 213 Mich. App. 389, 541 N.W.2d 566 (1995) (cause of action against molester's spouse exists where she allegedly was aware of but failed to prevent abuse which occurred in the marital home and vehicle); Pamela L. v. Farmer, 112 Cal. App. 3d 206, 169 Cal. Rptr 282 (1980) (molestation foreseeable where wife knew that her husband had molested other children, she invited the child victim into her home, and she left the children unsupervised with her husband).

60. J.S. v. R.G.H., 155 N.J. 330, 714 A.2d 924 (1998).

61. *Id.*

62. *See, e.g.*, Isbell v. Ryan, 983 S.W.2d 335 (Tex. App. 1998) (mother of minor child who was accused of molesting his young cousin may have duty to warn stepdaughters' mother of child's possible danger under some circumstances; summary judgment reversed).

ers with a duty to have intervened to protect the child.[63] The lawyer should determine who the child might have told about the abuse or who might have been in a position to discover the abuse. Such people are potential defendants. For example, the child may have been seen by a physician for abuse- or neglect-related injuries. The physician may have failed to diagnose or report the abuse, breaching a duty to the child.

Failure to comply with mandatory child-abuse reporting laws is a frequent negligent tort,[64] especially because most of the defendants can pay settlements or judgments. Some states provide expressly for civil actions.[65] Violation of a statutory duty constitutes negligence per se under common law, but some courts have held that violation of penal mandatory reporting laws does not give rise to a negligence claim.[66] In some states even the attorney-client privilege may not apply to prevent a lawyer from reporting current or anticipated

---

63. There is also a trend toward permitting suits to be filed against therapists who are alleged to have implanted false memories of sexual abuse or otherwise improperly diagnosed sexual abuse. *See, e.g.*, Wilkinson v. Balsam, 885 F. Supp. 651 (D. Vt. 1995) (factual issues existed, precluding summary judgment for physician and social workers sued by father allegedly falsely accused of molesting his son and stepson); Sullivan v. Chesier, 846 F. Supp. 654 (E.D. Ill. 1994) (factual issues existed, precluding summary judgment for psychologist who allegedly implanted false memories of sexual abuse of plaintiffs' daughter); L.A.R. v Ludwig, 170 Ariz. 24, 821 P.2d 291 (Ct. App. 1991) (factual issues existed, precluding summary judgment for counselor who allegedly negligently treated a child she found to have been molested by plaintiff); Montoya v. Bebensee, 761 P.2d 285 (Colo. Ct. App. 1988) (factual issues existed, precluding summary judgment for supervising psychologist and associate who allegedly made a bad faith report that plaintiff molested his daughter). *But see, e.g.*, Trear v. Sills, 69 Cal. App. 4th 1341, 82 Cal. Rptr. 2d 281 (1999) (father may not sue therapist for adult daughter based on "recovered memory" of child sexual abuse); Bird v. W.C.W., 868 S.W.2d 767 (Tex. 1994) (father may not sue psychologist who allegedly falsely accused him of molesting his son). *See generally*, Cynthia Grant Bowman & Elizabeth Mertz, *A Dangerous Direction: Legal Intervention in Sexual Abuse Survivor Therapy*, 109 HARV. L. REV. 549 (1996); John G. Watkins, *Dealing with the Problem of "False Memory" in Clinic and Court*, 21 J. PSYCHIATRY & L. 297 (1993). The California Court of Appeals, Fourth District, wrote a thoughtful opinion explaining the policy reasons why alleged abusers should not be permitted to sue the therapists for their adult children who allegedly "recover" false memories of childhood abuse. *See* Trear v. Sills, 69 Cal. App. 4th 1341, 82 Cal. Rptr. 2d 281 (1999).

64. *See generally* 1 ANN M. HARALAMBIE, HANDLING CHILD CUSTODY, ABUSE AND ADOPTION CASES § 11.21, apps. 11-1 and 11-2 (2nd ed. Clark Boardman Callaghan 1993, West Group 1998); LEONARD KARP & CHERYL KARP, DOMESTIC TORTS: FAMILY VIOLENCE, CONFLICT, AND SEXUAL ABUSE apps. C and D (West Group Supp. 1998); SETH C. KALICHMAN, MANDATED REPORTING OF SUSPECTED CHILD ABUSE: ETHICS LAW AND POLICY (1993); Annotation, *Civil Liability of Physician for Failure to Diagnose or Report Child Abuse*, 73 ALR 4th 782 (1989 & Supp 1997).

65. *See, e.g.*, ARK. CODE ANN. § 12-12-504(b) (1997) (civil liability for willful failure to report); COLO. REV. STAT. § 19-3-304(4)(b) (1997) (civil liability for willful failure to report); IOWA Code ANN. § 232.75(2) (1994) (civil liability for knowing failure to report); MICH. COMP. LAWS ANN. § 722.633(1) (1993) (civil liability for failure to report); MONT. CODE ANN. § 41-3-207(1) (1997) (civil liability for failure to report or preventing another from reasonably doing so); N.Y. SOC. SERV. LAW § 420(2) (1992) (civil liability for knowing and willful failure to report); R.I. GEN. LAWS § 40-11-6.1 (1990) (civil liability for knowing failure to report or knowingly preventing another from reasonably doing so).

66. *Compare* Lienteries v. Flood, 17 Cal. 3d 399, 131 Cal. Rptr. 69, 551 P.2d 389 (1976) (finding civil cause of action) *with* Fischer v Metcalf, 543 So.2d 85 (Fla. Ct. App. 1989); Cechman v. Travis, 202 Ga. App. 255, 414 S.E.2d 282 (1991); Kansas State Bank & Trust Company v. Specialized Transportation Services, Inc., 249 Kan. 348, 819 P.2d 587 (1991) (reporting statutes do not create an implied civil cause of action).

future child abuse committed by the lawyer's client.[67] Failure to make a mandatory report of abuse also may be considered professional malpractice.[68] Similarly, professionals who have knowledge that a person is likely to abuse children or a particular child may have a duty to warn the child or those who have care of the child. The breach of such duty may give rise to liability for failure to warn.[69]

Negligent failure to diagnose child abuse is a fairly common child-abuse tort theory.[70] However, in the child sexual abuse context, the diagnostic state of the art has developed slowly, and it may be difficult to establish that the physician or mental-health professional fell below the applicable standard of care. Given the more recent professional attention to diagnosis of sexual abuse,[71] with standards and consensus in a number of areas, this tort is likely to become more successful in the future.

Child-welfare agencies have been found to be liable for failure to investigate reported abuse,[72] negligent failure to remove a child

---

67. *See, e.g.*, N.J. Supreme Court Advisory Committee on Professional Ethics, Op. 280 Supp., 97 N.J.L.J. (1974) (the attorney may not report past abuse but must report the client's propensity for continuing abuse); State Bar of Wisconsin, Committee on Professional Ethics, Op. E-88-11 (1988) (the attorney must if he or she reasonably believes that the abuse will continue despite the attorney's efforts to encourage the client to stop and to get counseling). *Cf.* Indiana State Bar Association, Legal Ethics Committee, Op. 1-1986 (1986) (the attorney may not report past abuse but whether or not the attorney may report suspected future abuse is too complex and unsettled to describe the ethical obligation with any certainty). *See generally*, Stuart, *Child Abuse Reporting: A Challenge to Attorney-Client Confidentiality*, 1 GEORGETOWN J. LEGAL ETHICS 243 (Summer 1987); Sands, *The Attorney's Affirmative Duty to Warn Foreseeable Victims of a Client's Intended Violent Assault*, 21/2 TORT & INS. L. J. 355 (1986); R. THURMAN, CLIENT INCEST AND THE LAWYER'S DUTY OF CONFIDENTIALITY (ABA Center for Professional Responsibility 1986).

68. *See, e.g.*, Lienteries v. Flood, 17 Cal. 3d 399, 131 Cal. Rptr. 69, 551 P.2d 389 (1976).

69. The classic failure-to-warn case is Tarasoff v. Regents of the University of California, 17 Cal 3d 425, 551 P.2d 334, 131 Cal. Rptr. 14 (1976) (therapist employed by university clinic had duty to warn identified victim of patient's death threat), giving rise to the term "*Tarasoff* duty" to describe this type of liability.

70. *See generally* Annotation, *Civil Liability of Physician for Failure to Diagnose or Report Child Abuse*, 73 ALR 4th 782 (1989 & Supp. 1997).

71. See Chapters 6 and 7 and corresponding appendices.

72. *See, e.g.*, Mammo v. State, 138 Ariz. 528, 675 P.2d 1347 (Ct. App. 1983) ($300,000 jury verdict remitted from $1,000,000 to noncustodial father for beating death of child after child protective services failed to investigate a report of abuse); Turner v. District of Columbia, 532 A.2d 662 (D.C. Ct. App. 1987) (mother could maintain action as child's personal representation against police and agency which failed to remove children from the abusive father and failed to follow up on mother's repeated complaints to CPS); Florida First National Bank v. City of Jacksonville, 339 So.2d 632 (Fla. 1976) (police failed to adequately investigate several reports of abuse in accordance with accepted procedures); Estate of Bailey v. County of York, 768 F.2d 503 (3rd Cir. 1985) (failure to investigate reports of abuse adequately may form the basis of tort or civil rights causes of action). *See also* Gilliam v. Dept. of Social and Health Services, Child Protective Services, 89 Wash. App. 569, 950 P.2d 20 (1998) (caseworkers investigating child sexual abuse allegations are not entitled to absolute immunity from negligent investigation claim; dismissal reversed; father sued CPS, claiming that caseworker's inadequate investigation of his ex-wife's claim inordinately prolonged the dependency proceedings and his separation from his children; dependency was eventually dismissed and he was awarded custody).

from an abusive home,[73] and negligent placement or negligent supervision of a child in its custody if the child is later abused in placement.[74] However, the U.S. Supreme Court held in *DeShaney v. Winnebago County Department of Social Services*[75] that no 42 U.S.C. § 1983 civil-rights action would lie against a state agency for failure to protect a child who was no longer in its legal custody. Joshua DeShaney had been in state custody, but was returned to his father, who beat him to death. The Court held that the state had a no federal duty to protect the child, despite having investigated the home many times over more than one year. In a 6-3 decision Chief Justice Rehnquist stated that the due process clause confers "no affirmative right to governmental aid, even where such aid may be necessary to secure life, liberty or property interest of which the government itself may not deprive the individual,"[76] unless there is a "special relationship" between the child and the agency, arising where the "state takes a person into its custody and holds him there against his will."[77] Dicta in the majority opinion did indicate that there may be liability based on state tort law.[78]

Cases prior to *DeShaney* had often found a special relationship or duty between child protective-services agencies and abused children, finding liability under state tort law for failing to protect children from abuse.[79] A number of cases since *DeShaney* have failed to find liability when state agencies did not promptly or thoroughly investi-

73. *See generally* Annotation, *Tort Liability of Public Authority for Failure to Remove Parentally Abused or Neglected Children from Parents' Custody*, 60 ALR 4th 942 (1988 & Supp. 1992).

74. *See, e.g.*, Vonner v. State, 275 So. 2d 252 (La. 1973) (state could be held liable for child beaten to death by foster mother more than three months after the child's older siblings had run away and reported that they were being beaten in the foster home; the agency placed the children in detention without investigating their report); Bradford v. Davis, 290 Or. 855, 626 P.2d 1376 (1981) ($90,000 settlement against state for failure of agency to screen foster home, supervise the child's placement, and investigate reports that the child was being beaten in the foster home); Babcock v. Washington, 116 Wash.2d 596, 809 P.2d 143 (1991) (social workers had only qualified immunity for placing children with an uncle who molested them; if they did not comply with statutory and regulatory procedures and their placement decision was not reasonable, they could be found liable).

75. 489 US 189 (1989).

76. *Id.* at 196.

77. *Id.* at 199-200.

78. *Id.* at 201-202.

79. *See, e.g.*, Turner v. District of Columbia, 532 A.2d 622 (DC 1987); Florida Department of Health and Rehabilitative Services v. Yamuni, 529 So. 2d 258 (Fla. 1988); Coleman v. Cooper, 89 N.C. App. 188, 366 S.E.2d 2 (1988).

gate allegations of abuse,[80] inadequately supervised,[81] or improvidently returned a child home to receive further abuse.[82]

However, where the child is in the custody of the state agency, a special relationship may exist between the agency and the child, giving rise to a duty to protect the foster child. *DeShaney* distinguished the duty that had been found in prisoner and involuntarily committed mental-patient cases by stating that the state's "affirmative act of restraining the individual's freedom to act on his own behalf—through incarceration or other similar restraint of personal liberty"—was the deprivation of liberty that triggered the substantive due process clause protection, "not its failure to act to protect his liberty interests against harms inflicted by other means."[83] The Supreme Court specifically stated that if the state had removed Joshua DeShaney from his home and placed him in a state foster home, "we might have a situation sufficiently analogous to incarceration or institutionalization to give rise to an affirmative duty to protect."[84] The Court pointed out that several circuit courts of appeals had found state liability for failure to protect children in state foster homes who were abused by their foster parents.[85]

Following *DeShaney* several courts have recognized that the state may have a duty to protect children who are in foster care.[86] There-

80. *See, e.g.*, Doe v. District of Columbia, 74 F.3d 1164 (D.C. Cir. 1996) (violation of Child Abuse Prevention and Treatment Act requirement of promptly investigating reports of child abuse does not give rise to § 1983 private cause of action; CAPTA is a funding act creating only generalized duties similar to those in the Adoption Assistance and Child Welfare Act for which a private right of action was rejected by Suter v. Artist M., 503 US 347 (1992)); S.L.D. v. Krane, 498 N.W.2d (Minn. Ct. App. 1993) (social workers had immunity for decision not to investigate out-of-state father's allegations of sexual abuse). *But see, e.g.*, Chrissy F. v. Mississippi Dept. of Public Welfare, 925 F.2d 844 (5th Cir. 1991) (sexually abused child may maintain action against prosecutor and social workers for their failure to act on reports of abuse or to transfer the case as required by statute).

81. *See, e.g.*, Williams v. Horton, 175 Mich. App. 25, 437 N.W.2d 18 (1989) (reversing judgment against social workers for negligent placement and supervision of child who was murdered after leaving a group home).

82. *See, e.g.*, Powell v. Georgia Dept. of Human Resources, 114 F.3d 1074 (11th Cir. 1997) (no liability against welfare agency and its employees for infant killed after being returned to mother's abusive home); McComb v. Wambaugh, 934 F.2d 474 (3rd Cir. 1991).

83. DeShaney v. Winnebago County Department of Social Services, 489 U.S. 189, 199-200 (1989).

84. *Id.* at 201, n.9.

85. *Id.*, citing Doe v. New York City Dept. of Social Services, 649 F.2d 134 (2d Cir. 1981), *after remand*, 709 F.2d 782, *cert. denied sub nom* Catholic Home Bureau v. Doe, 464 U.S. 864 (1983); Taylor *ex rel* Walker v. Ledbetter, 818 F.2d 791 (11th Cir. 1987) (*en banc*), *cert denied sub nom* Ledbetter v. Taylor, 489 U.S. 1065 (1989).

86. *See, e.g.*, Kara B. by Albert v. Dane County, 205 Wis.2d 140, 555 N.W.2d 630 (1996) (construing *DeShaney* and several other cases, when read together, as recognizing a clearly established constitutional right to a reasonably safe and secure foster home placement, county officials not entitled to qualified immu-

fore, a child who is injured while in state custody may not be barred from suing the state, especially where liability is based on a reckless or intentional tort theory.[87] In *Camp v. Gregory* the Seventh Circuit Court of Appeals set forth some nonexclusive factors for agency liability in placement decisions where the child is injured based on lack of proper supervision: the case worker must have failed to exercise bona fide professional judgment; a caretaker can be expected only to provide a reasonable degree of supervision; the injury must be reasonably foreseeable to the official; and there must be a sufficient causal link between the failure to provide reasonable supervision and the injury.[88]

Sometimes the abuse or neglect itself occurs while the child is in the care of a third party or institution that may become a defendant. Persons, schools, or agencies who negligently hire convicted child abusers who are allowed to be around children may be liable for negligent hiring, failure to screen, or negligent supervision of the employee who later abuses a child.[89] Similarly, state agencies may be liable for negligent licensing or supervision of day-care centers[90] or

---

nity in 42 U.S.C. § 1983 action filed by children physically and sexually abused in their foster home; professional judgment to be applied); Meador v. Cabinet for Human Resources, 902 F.2d 474 (6th Cir. 1990) (foster child in state foster care has due process right to personal safety); Norfleet v. Arkansas Dept. of Human Services, 796 F. Supp. 1194 (E.D. Ark. 1992). *Cf.* K.H. *ex rel* Murphy v. Morgan, 914 F.2d 846 (7th Cir 1990) (child in state custody has right "not to be handed over by state officers to a foster parent or other custodian, private or public, **whom the state knows or suspects to be a child abuser**"). *See generally* Chou, *Renewing the Good Intentions of Foster Care: Enforcement of the Adoption Assistance and Child Welfare Act of 1980 and the Substantive Due Process Rights to Safety*, 46 VAND. L. REV. 683 (1993).

87. *See, e.g.*, Norfleet v. Arkansas Dept. of Human Services, 796 F. Supp. 1194 (E.D. Ark. 1992) (although negligence is insufficient to constitute a deprivation of due process, "deliberate or conscious indifference to the plaintiffs' constitutional rights are sufficient").

88. 67 F.3d 1286 (7th Cir. 1995). The Court held, however, that a caseworker was entitled to qualified immunity where prior case law did not make it clear that he could not knowingly place a child over whom the state has been made guardian with a caretaker who cannot provide a reasonable degree of supervision, following which the child was killed by third parties.

89. *See, e.g.*, Ward v. Forrester Day Care, Inc., 547 So.2d 410 (Ala. 1989) (*res ipsa loquitur* could be used to maintain action against a day care center who had the care of an 11-week-old child when the child's arm was broken); Doe v. MCLO Enterprises, No. 74028 (Cuyahoga County, Ohio, 9/28/89), 33 ATLA L. Rep. 1 (2/27/90) ($1.75 million jury verdict against owners of an apartment complex for hiring a convicted sex offender, who molested a 7-year-old boy living at the complex, as custodian).

90. *See, e.g.*, Doe v. State, No. 16-90-02157 (Lane County, Oregon Cir. Ct., 1/9/91), 33 ATLA L. Rep. 222 (Aug. 1991) ($654,570 jury verdict against state agency for negligent licensing of day care center where six-year-old girl was molested daily for one year; the agency did not contest liability). *But see, e.g.*, P.W. v. Kansas Dept. of Social & Rehabilitative Services, 255 Kan. 827, 877 P.2d 430 (1994) (licensing/regulatory agency lacked special relationship with abused children, therefore, owing them no duty).

foster homes. However, there must be a reasonable basis for imposing a duty on the third party. For example, a fifteen-year-old girl alleged that she was sexually molested by her parish priest and sued the church based on negligent hiring, retention, and supervision of the priest because it should have known of his dangerous propensities as a sexual exploiter of children. However, the California Court of Appeals held that the church was entitled to summary judgment in its favor because the church had "neither prior notice of the priest's unfitness nor a duty in the employment context to investigate the priest's sexual conduct."[91] The court noted that the priest had been ordained in the Philippines prior to coming to San Diego; therefore, the church had no duty "to screen or test him for matters relating to sexuality, unless and until a sexual problem manifested itself." The court also pointed out that an employer who questions employees on sexual behavior is subject to claims for invasion of privacy. The court also found that there is no "special relationship" created by the priest/parishioner relationship so as to create a heightened duty of care. However, the Washington Court of Appeals found that church workers may in fact have a "special relationship" with children in their care, stating:

> we believe that churches and the adult church workers who assume responsibility for the spiritual well being of children of the congregation, whether as paid clergy or as volunteers, have a special relationship with those children that gives rise to a duty to protect them from reasonably foreseeable risk of harm from those members of the congregation whom the church places in positions of responsibility and authority over them.[92]

---

91. Roman Catholic Bishop of San Diego v. Superior Court of San Diego County, 42 Cal. App. 4th 1556, 50 Cal. Rptr. 2d 399 (1996).

92. W.J.L. v. Bugge, 950 P.2d 501, 509 (Minn. 1998) (reversing summary judgment dismissal against child plaintiffs).

Schools,[93] day-care centers,[94] or other entities who have the part-time care of children may be liable for negligent supervision if they fail to prevent a child under their care from being abused. The lawyer should consider all of the persons and agencies who have been involved with the child to determine whether any are potential defendants.

93. *See, e.g.*, Mirand v. City of New York, 84 N.Y.2d 44, 637 N.E.2d 263, 637 N.Y.S.2d 372 (1994) (affirming judgment against school for negligent supervision of student who assaulted two sisters since it had done nothing following first sister's complaint of prior assault and death threat); Doe v. Taylor Independent School District, 15 F.3d 443 (5th Cir. 1994) (affirming judgment against high-school principal for deliberate indifference to student's constitutional rights by failing to take action to protect child from sexual abuse by teacher after receiving numerous complaints about the teacher in question); Doe v. Paukstat, 863 F. Supp. 884 (E.D. Wis. 1994) (school had no duty to protect student from sexual abuse by teacher but may be liable based on policies that "allowed sexual abuse to flourish"); Haley v. McManus, 593 So.2d 1339 (La. Ct. App. 1991) (affirming $10,000 jury verdict for each parent for child's petit mal seizures and aggravation of Attention Deficit Disorder following teacher's beating of first grade student with a belt); Dixon v. Board of Education of the City of New York, No. 15626/87 (N.Y. Sup. Ct. 6/19/91), 11 Verdicts, Settlements & Tactics 433 (Dec 1991) ($350,000 jury verdict against Board of Education for negligent supervision of 9-year-old girl who was sexually molested in a school restroom by two other school children after her teacher allowed her to go to the restroom down the hall without a pass instead of an unoccupied restroom adjacent to her class); Pagano v. Massapequa Public Schools, 714 F. Supp. 641 (E.D.N.Y. 1989) (child could maintain civil rights action against school district and school officials for failure to protect him on at least 17 occasions from abuse by other students on the school property); Woodell v. Marion School District One, 414 S.E.2d 795 (S.C. Ct. App. 1992) (fact question existed concerning whether school district was grossly negligent in failing to supervise where a student was assaulted by another student); Stoneking v. Bradford Area School District, 882 F.2d 720 (3rd Cir. 1988), *cert. denied sub nom* Smith v. Stoneking, 493 U.S. 1044 (1990) (school authorities liable for maintaining inadequate customs and policies which resulted in student being sexually molested by band director); Doe v. Taylor Independent School District, 975 F.2d 137 (5th Cir. 1992), *cert. denied sub nom* Caplinger v. Doe, 113 S.Ct. 1066 (1993) (state had affirmative duty to protect student from sexual abuse by teacher). *But see, e.g.*, Godar v. Edwards, 588 N.W.2d 701 (Iowa 1999) (school not liable for sexual abuse of boy by school employee because such abuse was not expected, foreseeable, or sanctioned by the school); Walton v. Alexander, 44 F.3d 1297 (5th Cir. 1995) (school has no constitutional duty to protect student at residential public school for the deaf from sexual assault on child by fellow student); L.K. v. Reed, 631 So. 2d 604 (La. Ct. App. 1994) (school board not liable for failing to protect seventh-grade student from sexual assault by high school student on school grounds during school hours; no duty of constant individual supervision exists); Kimberly M. v. Los Angeles Unified School District, 215 Cal. App. 3d 545, 263 Cal. Rptr. 612 (1989) (school district not liable for teacher's molestation of 5-year-old student); Russell *ex rel* Russell v. Fannin County School District, 784 F. Supp. 1576 (ND Ga 1992) (school had no duty to protect high school student from assault by another student; therefore civil rights action dismissed); Robbins v. Maine School Administrative District No. 56, 807 F. Supp. 11 (D. Me. 1992) (school district's special education placement policies did not create a known danger making it liable for students' injuries from other students); Elliott v. New Miami Board of Education, 799 F. Supp. 818 (S.D. Ohio 1992) (school district had no duty to protect high school student from assaults by other students); D.R. v. Middle Bucks Area Vocational School, 972 F.2d 1364 (3rd Cir. 1992), *cert. denied* 113 S.Ct. 1045 (1993) (school district had no duty to protect students from sexual assaults by several other students). *See, generally*, Richard Fossey & Todd A. Demitchell, *"Let the Master Answer:" Holding Schools Vicariously Liable When Employees Sexually Abuse Children*, 25 J. L. & EDUC. 575 (1996).

94. *See, e.g.*, Ward v. Forrester Day Care, Inc., 547 So.2d 410 (Ala. 1989) (*res ipsa loquitur* could be used to maintain action against a day care center who had the care of an 11-week-old child when the child's arm was broken).

6 Behavioral-Health Evaluations of Sexual Abuse Allegations

Background

The lawyer should have a good working knowledge of the field in order most effectively to present and cross-examine mental-health testimony about child sexual abuse. A number of books and articles have been published that provide the results of the important clinical research findings concerning child sexual abuse and otherwise explain the dynamics and effects of child sexual abuse.[1] Experts who claim to rely on Freud for their

---

1. *See, e.g.*, LANE J. VELTKAMP & THOMAS W. MILLER, CLINICAL HANDBOOK OF CHILD ABUSE & NEGLECT (1995); David A. Wolfe, Louise Sas & Christine Wekerke, *Factors Associated with the Development of Posttraumatic Stress Disorder Among Child Victims of Sexual Abuse*, 18/1 CHILD ABUSE & NEGLECT 37 (1994); A. Mannarino, J. Cohen & S. Berman, *The Relationship Between Preabuse Factors and Psychological Symptomatology* in SEXUALLY ABUSED GIRLS 63 (1994); John Briere & Marsha Runtz, *Childhood Sexual Abuse, Long-Term Sequelae and Implications for Psychological Assessment*, 3 J. INTERPERSONAL VIOLENCE 312 (1993); Beitchman, Zucker, Hood, daCosta, Akman & Cassavia, *A Review of the Long-Term Effects of Child Sexual Abuse*, 16/1 CHILD ABUSE & NEGLECT 101 (1992); Pribor & Dinwiddie, *Psychiatric Correlates of Incest in Childhood*, 149 AM. J. PSYCHIATRY 52 (1992); Jacobson & Herald, *The Relevance of Childhood Sexual Abuse to Adult Psychiatric Inpatient Care*, 41 HOSP. & COMMUNITY PSYCHIATRY 154 (1990); Chu & Dill, *Dissociative Symptoms in Relation to Childhood Physical and Sexual Abuse*, 147 AM. J. PSYCHIATRY 887 (1990); Deblinger, McLeer, Atkins, Ralphe & Foa, *Post-Traumatic Stress in Sexually Abused, Physically Abused, and Non-Abused Children*, 13 CHILD ABUSE & NEGLECT 403 (1989); J. HAUGAARD & N. REPPUCCI, THE SEXUAL ABUSE OF CHILDREN (1988); Briere & Runtz, *Symptomatology Associated with Childhood Sexual Victimization in a Non-Clinical Sample*, 12 CHILD ABUSE & NEGLECT 51 (1988); SEXUAL ABUSE OF YOUNG CHILDREN (Kee MacFarlane & Jill Waterman eds. 1986).

understanding of child sexual abuse are generally not up to date on their sources. Freud's fantasy-neurosis theory has been credited with discounting most reports of actual incest as being merely the fantasies of the victim.[2] Only recently are well-conceived studies being conducted to assist in the detection of child sexual abuse and to differentiate between molested and nonmolested children.[3]

OFFENDER EVALUATIONS

Risk assessments are sometimes performed and used in civil cases as part of an opinion concerning whether a person is likely to have molested a child or whether someone who has molested a child is likely to remolest. Such assessments do not yet have very good predictive ability. In looking at predictive correlations, a correlation (expressed as "r = x") of 1.0 means perfect predictive accuracy. Correlations of .05 or greater are considered to be "statistically significant;" however, mere statistical significance does not mean good predictive accuracy. One report, looking at ten different studies, found that the average accuracy of clinical assessments to predict sexual offender recidivism was only r = .10, a very poor prediction rate.[4] That same report found that many of the "standard" clinical risk factors, such as a history of child sexual abuse or denial, do not predict sexual-offense recidivism.[5]

Most risk-assessment measures have been developed with incarcerated sex offenders, including child molesters. It is likely that this population constitutes the most pathological group of offenders and the most serious offenders. They do not include those who have been convicted but not incarcerated, who have not been criminally

---

2. For further discussion of the problems with Freud's analysis *see, e.g.*, GEOFFEREY MASSON, ASSAULT ON THE TRUTH: FREUD'S SUPPRESSION OF THE SEDUCTION THEORY (1984). *See also* KATHLEEN COULBORN FALLER, CHILD SEXUAL ABUSE: AN INTERDISCIPLINARY MANUAL FOR DIAGNOSIS, CASE MANAGEMENT, AND TREATMENT, (1988); E. Ward, FATHER-DAUGHTER RAPE (1985); A. MILLER, THOU SHALT NOT BE AWARE: SOCIETY'S BETRAYAL OF THE CHILD (1984); J. HERMAN, FATHER-Daughter INCEST (1982); F. Rush, *The Freudian Cover-up*, 1 CHRYSALIS 31 (1977).

3. *See, e.g.*, William N. Friedrich, *Sexual Victimization and Sexual Behavior in Children: A Review of the Recent Literature*, 17/1 CHILD ABUSE & NEGLECT 59 (1993); Gail Goodman & C. Aman, *Children's Use of Anatomically Detailed Dolls to Recount an Event in Child Development* 61 CHILD DEVELOPMENT 1859 (1990); Abigail B. Sivan, David P. Schor, Gina K. Koeppl & Linn D. Noble, *Interaction of Normal Children with Anatomical Dolls*, 12/3 CHILD ABUSE & NEGLECT 295 (1988).

4. *See* R. Karl Hanson & Monique T. Bussière, *Predictors of Sexual Offender Recidivism: A Meta-Analysis*, User Report No. 1996-04, Department of the Solicitor General of Canada (1996).

5. *Id.*

convicted, or whose abuse has not been reported. The official recidivism rates must be considered as underestimates, especially because many sexual offenses are not reported.[6]

The Multiphasic Sex Inventory II[7] (MSI II), which is sometimes used as a part of an evaluation of offenders, is not able to tell whether a person *who does not admit to the abuse* has molested the child.[8] The instrument may assist in determining which paraphilias an offender has, but a person denying the abuse would know immediately what the "correct" answer to give would be. Most lawyers and judges do not realize what the true-false questions are, and therefore, may assume that the "results" from the MSI-II can be relied on as evidence that an alleged offender did not molest the child. An effective method of cross-examining an expert witness who used the instrument is to point out the manual's limiting language[9] and to read some of the questions from the instrument, such as:

11. I have felt sexual when I have been around a child.
21. I have molested a child who was too young to start school.
53. I have looked for ways or chances to be able to molest a child.
151. I have molested several children.
181. I have molested a girl.
221. I have molested a boy.
272. A child has put my penis in their [*sic*] mouth.
313. I have molested 20 or more children.
381. I have put my mouth on the privates of a child.[10]

It is readily apparent that a person denying the molestation would know the "correct" answers to give to the MSI-II to appear to be innocent of the alleged conduct.

---

6. *See, e.g.*, J. Bonta & R. K. Hanson, *Gauging the Risk for Violence: Measurement, Impact and Strategies for Change*, User Report No. 1994-09, Department of the Solicitor General of Canada (1994).

7. NICHOLS & MOLINDER, MULTIPHASIC SEX INVENTORY II (1990).

8. *See*, H. Nichols & I. Molinder, MULTIPHASIC SEX INVENTORY MANUAL (1984) at page 39: "Finally, it is important to remember that the MSI is not appropriate for use in the legal pursuit of guilt or innocence. The alledged [*sic*] offender must acknowledge culpability in order for the inventory to be used."

9. *Id.*

10. NICHOLS & MOLINDER, MULTIPHASIC SEX INVENTORY II (1990). The MSI-II has 560 true-false questions covering all types of paraphilia (such as rape, child molestation, exhibitionism, etc.). At least 34 questions are obviously related to child molestation, as represented by the few questions included here.

There is no Minnesota Multiphasic Personality Inventory (MMPI)[11] scale or profile which can identify an incestuous offender[12] or a molested child.[13] Similarly, there is no item or cluster of items on the Child Sexual Behavior Inventory (CSBI) that can determine that a child has or has not been sexually abused.[14] A recent National Institute of Justice Research report says:

> The sexual abusers of children are highly dissimilar in terms of personal characteristics, life experiences, and criminal histories. No single "molester profile" exists. Child molesters arrive at deviancy via multiple pathways and engage in many different sexual and nonsexual "acting out" behaviors.[15]

Numerous cases, mostly in the criminal context, have made it clear that experts are not permitted to express an opinion that the child is telling the truth about the abuse allegations.[16] A somewhat related issue involves mental-health professionals' use of polygraph

---

11. S. R. HATHAWAY & J. C. MCKINLEY, MINNESOTA MULTIPHASIC PERSONALITY INVENTORY-2, now revised and known as the MMPI-2 (1989).

12. However, some studies have noted that elevations on the 4, 8, and 9 scales of the MMPI were the most frequent elevations in child sexual abusers' profiles. *See, e.g.*, John A. Hunter, Jr., Susan E. Childers, Roque Gerald & Hayden Esmalaili, *An Examination of Variables Differentiating Clinical Subtypes of Incestuous Child Molesters*, 34/2 INT'L J. OFFENDER THERAPY & COMPARATIVE CRIMINOLOGY 95 (1990); Evelyn Yanagida & June W.J. Chin, *MMPI Profiles of Child Abusers*, 49 J. CLINICAL PSYCHOLOGY 569 (1993); BYRON EGELAND ET AL., MMPI-2 PROFILES OF WOMEN AT RISK (1991); Ronald Scott & David Stone, *MMPI Measures of Psychological Disturbance in Adolescent and Adult Victims of Father-Daughter Incest*, 42 J. CLINICAL PSYCHOLOGY 257 (1986); Gordon Hall *et al*, *The Utility of the MMPI with Men Who Have Sexually Assaulted Children*, 54 J. CONSULTING & CLINICAL PSYCHOLOGY 493 (1986).

13. *See, e.g.*, LEONARD KARP & CHERYL L. KARP, DOMESTIC TORTS: FAMILY VIOLENCE, CONFLICT AND SEXUAL ABUSE § 4.03 (Cum. Supp. 1998); J. A. Hunter, S. E. Childers, & H. Esmalaili, 34 J. OFFENDER THERAPY & COMPARATIVE CRIMINOLOGY 94 (1990); Judith V. Becker & Vernon L. Quinsey, *Assessing Suspected Child Molesters*, 17/1 CHILD ABUSE & NEGLECT 169 (1993); S. Lewin & L. Stava, *Personality Characteristics of Re-Offenders: A Review*, 16 ARCHIVES OF SEXUAL BEHAVIOR 57 (1987); Hall, Marino, Vitaliano & Proctor, *The Utility of the MMPI with Men Who Have Sexually Assaulted Children*, 54 J. CONSULTING & CLINICAL PSYCHOLOGY 493 (1986).

14. *See, e.g.* W. N. Friedrich, *The Clinical Use of the Child Sexual Behavior Inventory: Commonly Asked Questions*, 8/1 APSAC ADVISOR 1 (1995).

15. Robert A. Prentky, Raymond A. Knight & Austin F. S. Lee, *Child Sexual Molestation: Research Issues* 2 (National Institute of Justice 1997).

16. *See, e.g.*, Plate v. State, 925 P.2d 1057 (Alaska Ct. App. 1996); Campbell v. State, 221 Ga. App. 135, 470 S.E.2d 524 (1996); Taylor v. Commonwealth, 21 Va. App. 557, 466 S.E.2d 118 (1996); Hoult v. Hoult, 57 F.3d 1 (1st Cir. 1995); United States v. Rivera, 43 F.3d 1291 (9th Cir. 1995); State v. Butler, 36 Conn. App. 525, 651 A.2d 1306 (1995); People v. Peterson, 450 Mich. 349, 537 N.W.2d 857 (1995); *In re* Thompson, 893 P.2d 301 (Mont. 1995); Feller v. State, 637 So.2d 911 (Fla. 1994); Yount v. State, 99 Md. App. 207, 636 A.2d 50 (1994); United States v. Whitted, 11 F.3d 782 (8th Cir. 1993); Felix v. State, 109 Nev. 151, 849 P.2d 220 (1993); State v. J.Q., 599 A.2d 172 (N.J. Super. Ct. App. Div. 1991); State v. Lindsay, 149 Ariz. 472, 720 P.2d 73 (1986). *See generally* 1 JOHN E.B. MYERS, EVIDENCE IN CHILD ABUSE AND NEGLECT CASES § 5.50 (3rd ed. 1997).

results from the alleged perpetrator as a part of an assessment of that person. A mental-health professional who bases an opinion that a person did not molest the child in part on the basis of polygraph results is, in effect, expressing an opinion that the alleged perpetrator is telling the truth in denying the allegations.

Courts have consistently ruled that the results of polygraph examinations are inadmissible absent a stipulation of the parties.[17] There is no known physiological response that is specific to deception; polygraph examiners interpret certain physiological responses as indicators of fear, and interpret the fear as a fear of being caught lying.[18] Such evidence is inadmissible because it is not sufficiently reliable. If polygraph evidence is not admissible on its own merit because it is unreliable, then it should not be admissible as part of a psychological evaluation. In fact, there is reason to believe that polygraph examinations are *particularly unreliable* in the case of intra-familial child sexual abuse.[19] Cross and Saxe point out that the theoretical basis for using the polygraph has two logical problems:

> First, it demands that subjects, whether guilty or innocent, must have a sufficient degree of belief in the polygraph to fear telling a lie more than they fear telling the truth. Second, it requires that control questions inspire more fear in innocent subjects than questions about the crime itself; innocent subjects must have a greater physiological response to a question about a misdeed that is not under investigation, nor is necessarily a crime, than to a question about the crime of which they are suspected.[20]

If the person being examined does not have a clear memory of the event or rationalizes the event, the subject may not believe that he or she is lying and, therefore, may not become anxious during the

---

17. *See, e.g.*, Frye v. United States, 293 F.2d 1013 (D.C. Cir. 1923). *Cf.* Boling v. Boling, 887 S.W.2d 437 (Mo. Ct. App. 1994) (reversing change of custody from mother to father based on polygraph evidence showing that the mother was untruthful in alleging emotional and physical abuse by father and stepmother).

18. *See, e.g.*, Saxe, Dougherty & Cross, *The Validity of Polygraph Testing: Scientific Analysis and Public Controversy*, 40 AMERICAN PSYCHOLOGIST 355 (1985); D. T. LYKKEN, A TREMOR IN THE BLOOD: USES AND ABUSES OF THE LIE DETECTOR (1981).

19. *See, e.g.*, T. Cross & L. Saxe, *A Critique of the Validity of Polygraph Testing in Child Sexual Abuse Cases*, 1/4 J. CHILD SEXUAL ABUSE 19 (1992).

20. *See* T. Cross & L. Saxe, *A Critique of the Validity of Polygraph Testing in Child Sexual Abuse Cases*, 1/4 J. CHILD SEXUAL ABUSE 19 at 23-24 (1992).

relevant questioning.[21] Distortion of the offender's perception of the child sexual abuse and denial are both common in sexual abuse cases.[22]

The Violence Risk Appraisal Guide (VRAG) was developed to assess risk of recidivism of mentally disordered offenders, but it has been suggested that it may be used with other populations of sexual offenders.[23] However, the VRAG predicts violent recidivism better than sexual recidivism and requires professionally trained interviewers and careful file review.[24] The VRAG's predictions of sexual recidivism have a correlation of .20 ($r = .20$). Therefore, this assessment instrument cannot be relied on by courts to accurately predict recidivism, much less to discriminate between offenders and nonoffenders.

A new brief actuarial risk assessment instrument was developed in Canada, the Rapid Risk Assessment for Sexual Offense Recidivism (RRASOR).[25] It added together the four best predictor variables: prior sexual offenses, offender age under 25, any male victims, and any extrafamilial victims. The RRASOR correlates .27 with sexual recidivism, as good as or better than other risk-assessment instruments,[26] but still not adequate for judicial use in determining whether an alleged offender is likely to have molested a child or is at risk to remolest.

Profiles of incestuous offenders, incest victims, and incestuous families have come and gone. None has proven definitive because there is no one stereotype that fits all situations. There are some

---

21. *Id.* at 26.

22. *See, e.g.*, T. W. Haywood & L. S. Grossman, *Denial of Deviant Sexual Arousal and Psychopathology in Child Molesters*, 25 BEHAVIOR THERAPY 327 (1994); Bruce Laflen & William R. Sturm, Jr., *Understanding and Working with Denial in Sexual Offenders*, 3/4 J. CHILD SEXUAL ABUSE (1994); ANNA C. SALTER, TREATING CHILD SEX OFFENDERS AND THEIR VICTIMS: A PRACTICAL GUIDE (1988); Jon Conte, *Clinical Dimensions of Adult Sexual Abuse of* CHILDREN, 3 BEHAVIORAL SCIENCES & THE LAW 341 (1985); Gene Abel, Judith Becker & Cunningham-Rathner, *Complications, Consent and Cognitions in Sex Between Children and Adults*, 7 INTERNATIONAL J. LAW & PSYCHIATRY 89 (1984); JUDITH L. HERMAN, FATHER-DAUGHTER INCEST (1982). *Cf.* Mary McGrath, Steven Cann & Robert Konopasky, *New Measures of Defensiveness, Empathy and Cognitive Distortions for Sexual Offenders Against Children*, 10/1 SEXUAL ABUSE: A JOURNAL OF RESEARCH & TREATMENT 25 (1998).

23. *See, e.g.*, M. E. Rice & G. T. Harris, *Cross-Validation and Extension of the Violence Risk Appraisal Guide for Child Molesters and Rapists*, 21 L. & HUMAN BEHAVIOR 231 (1997).

24. *See* R. Karl Hanson & Monique T. Bussère, *Predicting Relapse: A Meta-Analysis of Sexual Offender Recidivism Studies*, 66/2 J. CONSULTING & CLINICAL PSYCHOLOGY 348 (1998).

25. *See* R. Karl Hanson & Monique T. Bussère, *Predicting Relapse: A Meta-Analysis of Sexual Offender Recidivism Studies*, 66/2 J. CONSULTING & CLINICAL PSYCHOLOGY 348 (1998). *See also* R. Karl Hanson, *The Development of a Brief Actuarial Risk Scale for Sexual Offense Recidivism*, User Report No. 1997-04, Department of the Solicitor General of Canada (1997).

26. *Id.*

characteristics and loose profiles, but witnesses relying on the presence or absence of certain results on a psychological test are not using acceptable standards.[27] Courts have been reluctant to permit offender profile or syndrome testimony for failure to show admissibility under either the *Frye*[28] or *Daubert*[29] foundational tests for scientific evidence.[30]

VICTIM EVALUATIONS

In the fall of 1993 a group of experts from Europe, North America, and the Middle East met "to evaluate existing knowledge regarding the ways in which child sexual abuse allegations could be investigated most productively."[31] The twenty co-signatories to the consensus statement agreed that "[n]o specific behavioral syndromes characterize victims of sexual abuse," and that the presence or absence of certain behavior affects only the level of suspicion.[32] The victim's report of the abuse is particularly important in sexual abuse cases, where often there are no physical findings to corroborate the account.[33]

While there may not be a profile or syndrome that is diagnostic of child sexual abuse, experts may testify that various behaviors,

27. *See, e.g.*, State v. Tlamka, 3 Neb. 28, 511 N.W.2d 135 (1993) (upholding ruling that psychologist's testimony that his psychological testing, review of police reports, and interview with the defendant showed that the defendant was a normal heterosexual incapable of sexually molesting a child was inadmissible because his methodology was not generally accepted in the scientific community; no evidence showed that the tests, while generally accepted in the scientific community, could actually determine whether a person was a "normal heterosexual" or that a "normal heterosexual" was incapable of child molesting); Michael E. Lamb, *The Investigation of Child Sexual Abuse: An International, Interdisciplinary Consensus Statement*, 28/1 FAM. L. Q. 151 (1994) [this statement was also published at 18/12 CHILD ABUSE & NEGLECT 1021 (1994) and 3/4 J. CHILD SEXUAL ABUSE 93 (1994)]. *See generally*, Judith V. Becker, *Offenders: Characteristics and Treatment*, 4/2 THE FUTURE OF CHILDREN 176 (1994).

28. Frye v. United States, 293 F.2d 1013 (D.C. Cir. 1923).

29. Daubert v. Merrell Dow Pharmaceuticals, Inc., 509 U.S. 579 (1993).

30. *See, e.g.*, United States v. Powers, 59 F.3d 1460 (4th Cir. 1995) (psychologist's proposed testimony that defendant did not fit profile a fixated sexual offender properly excluded as irrelevant); Flanagan v. State, 625 So. 2d 827 (Fla. 1993) (sex offender profile evidence not admissible because it fails the *Frye* test); Tungate v. Commonwealth, 901 S.W.2d 41 (Ky. 1995) (testimony by psychiatrist Dr. Richard Gardener concerning 24 indicators for pedophilia properly excluded for failure to meet *Frye* or *Daubert* tests); State v. Cavaliere, 140 N.H. 108, 663 A.2d 96 (1995) (psychologist's proposed testimony that defendant's profile was not consistent with that of a sexual offender properly excluded for failure to meet the *Daubert* test; court noted that there is no test or group of tests that can determine if a person is likely to be a sexual offender).

31. *See*, Michael E. Lamb, *The Investigation of Child Sexual Abuse: An International, Interdisciplinary Consensus Statement*, 28/1 FAM. L. Q. 151 (1994) [this statement was also published at 18/12 CHILD ABUSE & NEGLECT 1021 (1994) and 3/4 J. CHILD SEXUAL ABUSE 93 (1994)].

32. *Id.* at 154.

33. *See, e.g.*, Elizabeth A. W. Seagull, *Family Assessment* in THE BATTERED CHILD 150, 156 (Mary Edna Helfer, Ruth S. Kempe & Richard D. Krugman, eds., 5th ed. 1997); Jan Bays & David Chadwick, *Medical Diagnosis of the Sexually Abused Child*, 17/1 CHILD ABUSE & NEGLECT 91 (1993).

symptoms, and disorders are consistent with sexual abuse.[34] Testimony about any such patterns or profiles, however, must be based on the foundational showing of reliability and acceptance in the mental-health field of the pattern or profile.[35] Explicit sexualized play in the absence of a history explaining the child's knowledge (such as exposure to watching people engaged in sexual activity or exposure to sexually explicit pornographic material) is a frequently discussed behavior that may be indicative of sexual abuse.[36] It is important to remember, however, that not all molested children engage in sexualized play.

A certain group of sexually abused children exhibit symptoms of post-traumatic stress disorder (PTSD), particularly if the sexual abuse was violent. *The American Psychiatric Association's Diagnostic and Statistical Manual of Mental Disorders* (4th ed., 1994) (DSM-IV) lists childhood sexual or physical abuse as among the stressors that can lead to post-traumatic stress disorder.[37] Experts may testify that PTSD in a child is consistent with a history of sexual abuse.[38] The DSM-IV also describes a disorder called acute stress disorder (ASD), the essential feature of which is "the development of characteristic anxiety, dissociative, and other symptoms that occurs within 1 month after exposure to an extreme traumatic stressor," referring to the same types of stressors as can lead to PTSD.[39]

---

34. *See, e.g.*, State v. Reser, 767 P.2d 1277 (Kan. 1989).

35. *See, e.g.*, State v. Rimmasch, 775 P.2d 388 (Utah 1989).

36. *See generally* W. Friedrich, *Sexual Victimization and Sexual Behavior in Children: A Review of Recent Literature*, 17/1 CHILD ABUSE & NEGLECT 59 (1993).

37. *See* AMERICAN PSYCHIATRIC ASSOCIATION, DIAGNOSTIC AND STATISTICAL MANUAL OF MENTAL DISORDERS 424 (4th edition 1994). The DSM-IV states that "[f]or children, sexually traumatic events may include developmentally inappropriate sexual experiences without threatened or actual violence or injury." *Id. See generally*, LEONARD KARP & CHERYL L. KARP, DOMESTIC TORTS: FAMILY VIOLENCE, CONFLICT AND SEXUAL ABUSE § 4.11A (Cum. Supp. 1998); Jane Timmons-Mitchell, Dawn Chandler-Holtz & William E. Semple, *Post Traumatic Stress Disorder Symptoms in Child Sexual Abuse Victims and Their Mothers*, 6/4 J. CHILD SEXUAL ABUSE 11 (1997); Diana M. Elliot & John N. Briere, *Posttraumatic Stress Associated with Delayed Recall of Sexual Abuse: A General Population Study*, 8/4 J. TRAUMATIC STRESS 629 (1995); E. Deblinger, S. McLeer, M. Atkins, D. Ralphe & E. Foa, *Post-Traumatic Stress in Sexually Abused, Physically Abused, and Nonabused Children*, 13/3 CHILD ABUSE & NEGLECT 403 (1989); POST-TRAUMATIC STRESS DISORDER IN CHILDREN (S. Eth & R. Pynoos eds. 1985).

38. *See, e.g.*, Broderick v. King's Way Assembly of God Church, 808 P.2d 1211 (Alaska 1991); Brady v. State, 540 N.E.2d 59 (Ind. Ct. App. 1989); Commonwealth v. Dockham, 405 Mass. 618, 542 N.E.2d 591 (1989); State v. Alberico, 116 N.M. 156, 861 P.2d 192 (N.M. 1993).

39. *See* AMERICAN PSYCHIATRIC ASSOCIATION, DIAGNOSTIC AND STATISTICAL MANUAL OF MENTAL DISORDERS 429 (4th edition 1994). *See generally*, Cheryl Koopman, Cheryl Gore-Felton & David Spiegel, *Acute Stress Disorder Symptoms Among Female Sexual Abuse Survivors Seeking Treatment*, 6/3 J. CHILD SEXUAL ABUSE 65 (1997).

Some sexually molested children, particularly those whose victimization was violent, terrorizing, and prolonged, develop various dissociative disorders, the most extreme of which is dissociative identity disorder (formerly called multiple personality disorder).[40] It is important to realize that while experts may testify that a child's symptoms are consistent with having been sexually abused,[41] not all molested children will exhibit symptoms, and the inference may not be drawn that the absence of symptoms indicates the absence of abuse.[42]

ANATOMICALLY DETAILED DOLLS

Contrary to what some people believe, there is no "anatomical-doll test."[43] Experts cannot observe a child's play and, without more, diagnose child sexual abuse. When they are properly used during a sexual abuse evaluation, anatomically detailed dolls do not appear to be suggestive or misleading.[44] The diagnostic use of anatomically detailed dolls is discussed primarily as a red herring and is specifically disapproved by all of the protocols and guidelines that mention the issue. It has been demonstrated that children may be as able to demonstrate sexual abuse with nondetailed dolls as with anatomically detailed dolls;[45] however, many experts prefer to use anatomically detailed dolls. An expert can allow a child to demonstrate what

---

40. *See generally* FRANK W. PUTNAM, DISSOCIATION IN CHILDREN AND ADOLESCENTS: A DEVELOPMENTAL PERSPECTIVE (1997); J. Chu & D. Dill, *Dissociative Symptoms in Relation to Childhood Physical and* SEXUAL ABUSE, 147 J. PSYCHIATRY 887 (1990); Childhood Antecedents of Multiple Personality (R. Kluft ed. 1985).

41. *See, e.g.*, Broderick v. King's Way Assembly of God Church, 808 P.2d 1211 (Alaska 1991); Ward v. State, 519 So. 2d 1082 (Fla. Dist. Ct. App. 1988); State v. Reser, 244 Kan. 306, 767 P.2d 1277 (1989); State v. Alberico, 116 N.M. 156, 861 P.2d 192 (1993); State v. Speller, 102 N.C. App. 697, 404 S.E.2d 15 (1991); State v. Schumpert, 435 S.E.2d 859 (S.C. 1993).

42. *See, e.g.*, State v. Scheffelman, 250 Mont. 334, 820 P.2d 1293 (1991).

43. *See, e.g.*, Michael E. Lamb, *The Investigation of Child Sexual Abuse: An International, Interdisciplinary Consensus Statement*, 28/1 FAM. L. Q. 151,157 (1994).

44. *See, e.g.*, G. Goodman & C. Aman, *Children's Use of Anatomically Detailed Dolls to Recount an Event*, 61 CHILD DEVELOPMENT 1859 (1990); Goodman, Rudy, Bottoms & Aman, *Children's Concerns and Memory: Issues of Ecological Validity in the Study of Children's Eyewitness Testimony*, in KNOWING AND REMEMBERING IN YOUNG CHILDREN 249 (R. Fivush & J. Hudson eds. 1990); Glaser & Collins, *The Response of Young, Non-Sexually Abused Children to Anatomically Correct Dolls*, 30 J. CHILD PSYCHOLOGY & PSYCHIATRY 547 (1989); Leventhal, Hamilton, Rekedal, Tebano-Micci & Eyster, *Anatomically Correct Dolls Used in Interviews of Young Children Suspected of Having Been Sexually Abused*, 84 PEDIATRICS 900 (1989).

45. *See* H. Britton & M. O'Keefe, *Use of Nonanatomical Dolls in the Sexual Abuse Interview*, 15/4 CHILD ABUSE & NEGLECT 567 (1991).

occurred during the abuse with the aid of anatomically detailed dolls. Experts are generally permitted to testify about a child's anatomical-doll play.[46]

Two researchers, Mark Everson and Barbara Boat, have identified seven potential functional uses of anatomically detailed dolls in sexual abuse evaluations: comforter, icebreaker, anatomical model, demonstration aid, memory stimulus/diagnostic screen, and diagnostic test.[47] Only two of the twenty sets of written guidelines and protocols reviewed described the "comforter" use of anatomically detailed dolls to create a more relaxed atmosphere for the evaluation.[48] Five guidelines mentioned the "icebreaker" role, but Everson and Boat find such a use to be potentially highly valuable in introducing the conversation on the topic of sexuality.[49] Sixteen of the guidelines referred to the use of anatomically detailed dolls as a model for labelling body parts in the child's own words.[50] Eighteen of the guidelines discussed using dolls as demonstration aids, the mostly widely accepted function of anatomically detailed dolls.[51] Nine of the guidelines referred to the use of dolls as a stimulus for memory (to trigger the child's recall of specific sexual events) or diagnostic screen (providing a nonthreatening environment for the child to spontaneously reveal sexual interest, knowledge, or concerns).[52] As mentioned earlier, there is no accepted use of anatomically detailed dolls as a diagnostic test, which would assume that sexually molested children interact with dolls in different ways than nonabused children do. Several of the guidelines explicitly warn against such a use of the dolls.[53]

---

46. *See, e.g.*, *People v. Barger*, 251 Ill. App. 3d 448, 624 N.E.2d 405 (Ill. Ct. App. 1993), *cert. denied*, 633 N.E.2d 7 (Ill. 1994) (expert's testimony about child's demonstration admitted under statutory hearsay exception for child sexual abuse victim's statement); *In re* Rinesmith, 144 Mich. App. 475, 376 N.W.2d 139 (1985); *In re* M.E., 715 S.W.2d 572 (Mo. Ct. App. 1986); State v. Speller, 102 N.C. App. 697, 404 S.E.2d 15 (1991); *In re* C.L., 397 N.W.2d 81 (S.D. 1986). *But see, e.g.*, United States v. Gillespie, 852 F.2d 475 (9th Cir. 1988) (use of anatomically detailed dolls must meet the *Frye* test of scientific acceptance); *In re* Amber B., 191 Cal. App. 3d 682, 236 Cal. Rptr. 623 (1987) (use of anatomically detailed dolls must meet the *Frye* test of scientific acceptance); *State v. Mayfield*, 302 Or. 631, 733 P.2d 438 (1987) (assertive play with anatomically detailed dolls inadmissible as hearsay). *See generally* 1 JOHN E. B. MYERS, EVIDENCE IN CHILD ABUSE AND NEGLECT CASES § 1.17 (3d. ed. 1997).

47. *See* M. Everson & B. Boat, *Putting the Anatomical Doll Controversy in Perspective: An Examination of the Major Uses and Criticisms of the Dolls in Child Sexual Abuse Evaluations*, 18/2 CHILD ABUSE & NEGLECT 113 (1994).

48. *Id.* at 115.

49. *Id.*

50. *Id.* at 116.

51. *Id.*

52. *Id.* at 117.

53. *Id.* at 118.

Touching and exploration of anatomically detailed dolls is generally viewed as fairly typical behavior. However, explicit sexual demonstrations with the dolls during free play is considered to be quite rare, and sexually abused children are generally more likely to play and interact with the dolls in a sexual way than their nonabused peers.[54] The studies suggest that anatomically detailed dolls "do not induce young, nonabused, sexually naive children to engage in explicit sexual play" but "may provide sexually knowledgeable children with at least implicit permission as well as an easy vehicle for demonstrating their sexual knowledge."[55] There does not appear to be any empirical basis for distrusting evaluations that used anatomically detailed dolls as a part of the process.[56] It is important, however, for the lawyer to determine how the dolls were used. Where anatomically detailed dolls have been used, the lawyer should determine whether they were used in a professionally accepted way.[57]

Lawyers sometimes use anatomically detailed dolls to assist a child victim to describe and demonstrate the abuse during interviews and/or testimony. Some state statutes specifically provide for the use of anatomically detailed dolls and/or drawings to assist in the presentation of a child victim's testimony.[58]

CRITERIA-BASED CONTENT ANALYSIS/STATEMENT VALIDITY ANALYSIS

Criteria-Based Content Analysis (CBCA)[59] is a technique of reviewing children's statements as part of an evaluation format called State-

---

54. *Id.* at 120.

55. *Id.* at 123.

56. *Id.* at 126. *See generally*, M. Everson & B. Boat, *Sexualized Play Among Young Children: Implications for the Use of Anatomical Dolls in Sexual Abuse Evaluations*, 29 J. ACAD. CHILD & ADOLESCENT PSYCHIATRY 736 (1990).

57. For guidance on what is accepted, *see, e.g.*, G. P. Koocher, G. S. Goodman, S. White, W. N. Friedrich, A. B. Sivan & C. R. Reynolds, *Psychological Science and the Use of Anatomically Detailed Dolls in Child Sexual Abuse Assessments. Final Report of the American Psychological Association Anatomical Doll Task Force*, 118 PSYCHOLOGICAL BULLETIN 199; American Professional Society on the Abuse of Children Practice Guidelines for the Use of Anatomical Dolls in Child Sexual Abuse Assessments (reprinted at Appendix 6-3).

58. *See, e.g.*, ALA. CODE § 15-25-5 (1997) (child under 10 may use anatomically correct dolls to assist testimony in criminal and juvenile cases); N.J. STAT. ANN. § 2A:84A 16.1 (1994) (child under 16 may use anatomically correct dolls or drawings to assist testimony in certain criminal cases); N.Y. CRIM. PROC. LAW § 60.44 (1992) (in court's discretion child under 16 may use anatomically correct dolls to assist testimony in certain criminal cases); N.Y. EXEC. LAW § 642-a (7) (1996) (in discretion of court child witness should be permitted to use anatomically correct dolls or drawings); W. VA. CODE § 61-8B-11(d) (1997) (child under 11 may use anatomically correct dolls to assist testimony in criminal incest cases).

59. *See generally*, David C. Raskin & Phillip W. Esplin, *Assessment of Children's Statements of Sexual Abuse*, in THE SUGGESTIBILITY OF CHILDREN'S RECOLLECTIONS: IMPLICATIONS FOR EYEWITNESS TESTIMONY 153 (John Doris, ed., 1991); Max Steller & G. Keohnken, *Criteria-Based Statement Analysis*, in PSYCHOLOGICAL METHODS IN CRIMINAL INVESTIGATION AND EVIDENCE 217 (David C. Raskin, ed. 1989).

ment Validity Analysis (SVA).[60] CBCA and SVA assume that statements concerning actually experienced events are qualitatively different from fabricated or imagined statements. As of early 1998 there is not yet a scientific basis to support the use of CBCA and SVA as a valid and reliable way of distinguishing between true and false allegations of sexual abuse.[61] Further, CBCA and SVA are not generally accepted within the relevant scientific community,[62] and therefore, a lawyer faced with evidence based on this technique should object on the basis of a lack of foundation. Law professor and expert on the evidence of child abuse and neglect cases John E. B. Myers has written that "expert testimony describing CBCA would constitute a direct opinion on a child's credibility—something which courts have heretofore uniformly rejected."[63]

THE SEXUAL ABUSE LEGITIMACY SCALE

One "test" sometimes still used in child sexual abuse cases arising in the divorce or post-divorce context is psychiatrist Richard Gardner's Sexual Abuse Legitimacy (SAL) Scale, self-published in Richard Gardner, *The Parental Alienation Syndrome and the Differentiation Between Fabricated and Genuine Child Sex Abuse.*[64] The SAL scale was widely criticized for lacking an empirical basis for the weightings and for requiring as much clinical judgment to score it as to render an opinion about the abuse in the first place. It has now been disavowed by Dr. Gardner himself.[65] However, some clinicians con-

---

60. *See generally* Charles R. Honts, *Assessing Children's Credibility: Scientific and Legal Issues in 1994*, 70 N.D. L. REV. 879 (1994); David A. Anson, Stephen L. Golding & Kevin J. Gully, *Child Sexual Abuse Allegations: Reliability of Criteria-Based Content Analysis*, 17 L. & HUMAN BEHAVIOR 331 (1993); David C. Raskin & Phillip W. Esplin, *Assessment of Children's Statements of Sexual Abuse*, in THE SUGGESTIBILITY OF CHILDREN'S RECOLLECTIONS 153 (John Doris, ed. 1991); David C. Raskin & Phillip W. Esplin, *Statement Validity Assessment: Interview Procedures and Content Analysis of Children's Statements of Sexual Abuse*, 13 BEHAVIORAL ASSESSMENT 265 (1991); David C. Raskin & Max Steller, *Assessing the Credibility of Allegations of Child Sexual Abuse: Polygraph Examinations and Statement Analysis*, in CRIMINAL BEHAVIOR AND THE JUSTICE SYSTEM 290 (H. Wegener, F. Loesel & J. Haisch, eds. 1989); U. Undeutsch, *The Development of Statement Reality Analysis*, in CREDIBILITY ASSESSMENT 101 (J. C. Yuille, ed., 1989).

61. *See, e.g.*, Michael E. Lamb, Kathleen J. Sternberg, Phillip W. Esplin, Irit Hershkowitz, Yael Orbach & Meir Hovav, *Criterion-Based Content Analysis: A Field Validation Study*, 21/3 CHILD ABUSE & NEGLECT 255 (1997).

62. *See, e.g.*, Lucy Berliner & Jon R. Conte, *Sexual Abuse Evaluations: Conceptual and Empirical Obstacles*, 17/1 CHILD ABUSE & NEGLECT 111 (1993); Gary L. Wells & Elizabeth F. Loftus, *Commentary: Is the Child Fabricating? Reactions to a New Assessment Technique*, in SUGGESTIBILITY OF CHILDREN'S RECOLLECTIONS 168 (John Doris, ed. 1991).

63. *See* 1 JOHN E. B. Myers, EVIDENCE IN CHILD ABUSE AND NEGLECT CASES 102 (3rd ed. 1997).

64. (Creative Therapeutics 1987).

65. *See, e.g.*, RICHARD A. GARDNER, TRUE AND FALSE ACCUSATIONS OF CHILD SEXUAL ABUSE (1992).

tinue to use it. Scholarly criticism of Gardner's theories and the SAL Scale shows the lack of empirical support for his conclusions and his underlying assumptions and biases.[66]

The SAL Scale can be cross-examined effectively by referring to Gardner's own admissions and caveats. The Scale itself contains on its cover page, "**WARNING**: In order to be used in a meaningful way, this instrument *must* be used in association with the information provided in . . . chapters 3, 4, and 5. . . . The book explains how best to evaluate and score each of the items in the scale. Failure to use these guidelines may result in misleading or erroneous conclusions." The lawyer should go through the book carefully to pull out useful impeachment information. This section addresses only the highlights.

The SAL Scale has never been standardized, validated, or accepted in a peer-reviewed journal, the means accepted in the mental-health community for determining that psychological instruments are accepted in the field. Gardner recognizes that some might criticize his lack of scientific evidence to support his conclusion, saying "I agree that I have no such studies to support my hypothesis and that my conclusions are based on my own experiences as well as colleagues in the mental health professions. . . ."[67] He says that examiners "are advised that the cutoff levels and their significance should be viewed as preliminary and tentative."[68] He also warns that evaluators "should not use this scale independently of other data."[69]

With respect to his criteria for mothers, Gardner states, "What I present below are tentative conclusions, held by many who examine such mothers. We must recognize, however, that these conclusions will probably have to be modified as we gain more experience in this area."[70] Gardner states that "it is dangerous for an examiner to conclude that there are typical personality patterns of the parents of sexually abused children and/or the parents of fabricators."[71] He con-

66. *See, e.g.*, Kathleen Coulborn Faller, *The Parental Alienation Syndrome: What Is It and What Data Support It?*, 3/2 CHILD MALTREATMENT 100 (1998).

67. Richard Gardner, THE PARENTAL ALIENATION SYNDROME AND THE DIFFERENTIATION BETWEEN FABRICATED AND GENUINE CHILD SEX ABUSE 106 (Creative Therapeutics 1987).

68. *Id.* at 176.

69. *Id.*

70. *Id.* at 124.

71. *Id.* at 131.

tinues, "The fathers who are bona fide abusers are often said to fall into certain personality categories. I believe such generalizations are dangerous."[72] Nevertheless, his scoring depends on these very generalizations and patterns.

When dealing specifically with allegations in the divorce-related arena, Gardner says that "it would be an error for the reader to conclude that children whose parents are litigating for their custody are not likely to be sexually abused. It would also be an error to conclude that children who are suffering with parental alienation syndromes are immune from such abuse. This is not so."[73] He points out: "The abuse may have taken place prior to the separation, and the child may have been fearful of divulging it because of the omnipresence of the father. A custody dispute may increase a child's animosity and thereby increase the likelihood that the abuse will be revealed. . . . Just as the divorce situation is likely to precipitate the child's divulgence of a pre-existing pattern of abuse, the divorce situation may actually precipitate sex abuse on the part of a parent when it did not exist previously. Divorce is one of the more important and severe stresses of life. Under this stress some parents may regress and involve themselves in pedophilia. Contested divorces are even more stressful, and custody litigation adds even further to that stress. The child offers innocent and unconditional acceptance of a potential abuser. There is little chance of rejection. Rejected by a spouse, the parent may then turn to a child. In the context of a weekend visitation, in a one-bedroom apartment with an adoring child, the parent may be unable to resist the pedophilic urges."[74]

The scale itself says "face validity only is claimed for these items."[75] The scale also says that the "cutoff levels and their significance should be viewed as preliminary and tentative."[76] The criteria and scoring for the SAL Scale were based on Gardner's review of about thirty cases in his own practice for which he had made a determination that there was or was not abuse. In his review of those

72. *Id.* at 132.
73. *Id.* at 168.
74. *Id.* at 168-69.
75. *Id.* at 301. (*Sexual Abuse Legitimacy Scale* p. 3).
76. *Id.* at 176.

cases, he decided that some bona fide abusers obtained scores in the vicinity of 30 to 40 percent of the maximum range, but in "order to diminish the likelihood that innocents might be falsely considered bona fide offenders, I decided to use the 50 percent level as the cut-off point. This conservative approach to the setting of the cutoff point for bona fide sex abuse is based on the American legal principle that it is better to let 100 guilty men go free than to convict one innocent man. . . . I have chosen to recommend a cutoff point at a level that *might* indeed exonerate bona fide perpetrators in order to protect innocents who might be falsely considered guilty."[77] Unfortunately for children, application of the criminal presumption of innocence for an accused provides no protection for the molested child. It may be conservative in the criminal arena, but it is certainly not conservative for the best interests of the child, the applicable legal touchstone in the divorce and post-divorce context.

By Gardner's own writing, he is deliberately slanting his scoring system to favor the accused. A review of the weighted criteria also show Gardner's admitted bias. Despite requiring a 50 percent or better showing to determine that the allegations are true, he admits that over half of the available points may tend to miss actual abuse. Gardner states in the sections on each question containing direct cautions that he hopes other criteria will accurately distinguish between true and false allegations. However, with 47 percent, 81 percent, and 93 percent of the points for the three categories (child, accuser, and accused, respectively) risking missing true allegations and 10 percent, 4 percent, and 20 percent of the points risking false allegation, the usefulness of a weighted instrument, especially with its "tentative" conclusions, to the trier of fact is highly suspect.

By using Gardner's own admissions and caveats, the lawyer may be able to preclude testimony about the results of the SAL Scale during voir dire as not meeting the foundational requirements of *Frye v. United States*.[78] If an expert is permitted to testify about the SAL Scale, the book should be used to impeach the instrument during cross-examination.

77. *Id.* at 175–76.
78. 293 F.2d 1013 (D.C. Cir. 1923).

SYNDROMES

The term "syndrome" has been used very loosely, with a great deal of confusion in the legal arena.[79] The syndromes used in sexual abuse cases are generally not really syndromes in the diagnostic sense. The most prominent syndrome used is the child sexual abuse accommodation syndrome (CSAAS).[80] Dr. Roland Summit, who identified the CSAAS, identified various factors in a pattern of response to molestation that many children shared: 1) secrecy; 2) helplessness; 3) entrapment and accommodation; 4) delayed, conflicted, and unconvincing disclosure; and 5) retraction.[81] The CSAAS does not *diagnose* sexual abuse. Rather, it is a clinical opinion that *explains* why a child who has been molested might exhibit certain behaviors that appear to be inconsistent with having been sexually abused.[82]

Summit states that the "proper foundation for relevance of CSAAS testimony is the inference raised by the defense that an inconsistent pattern of disclosures by the child is indicative of deceit."[83] Those behaviors include delayed reporting, false denial, recantation of true allegations. Summit says that CSAAS is "meaningless" in court if there is no disputed disclosure.[84] Misapplication of the CSAAS has resulted in expert testimony that a given child had not been molested because he or she did not evidence the symptoms of CSAAS.[85] Similarly, criminal convictions have been reversed based on admission of CSAAS testimony to prove that abuse had occurred.[86] However, the proper use of the CSAAS to explain why

---

79. For an excellent discussion of syndromes, *see*, John E. B. Myers, *Expert Testimony Describing Psychological Syndromes*, 24/3 PACIFIC L. J. 1449 (1993).

80. *See, e.g.*, Roland Summit, *The Child Sexual Abuse Accommodation Syndrome*, 7 CHILD ABUSE & NEGLECT 177 (1983).

81. *Id.*

82. *See*, Roland Summit, *Abuse of the Child Sexual Abuse Accommodation Syndrome*, 1/4 J. CHILD SEXUAL ABUSE 153 at 156 (1992).

83. *See, e.g.*, Roland Summit, *The Rehabilitation of the Child Sexual Abuse Accommodation Syndrome in Trial Courts in Kentucky: Commentary*, 1/4 J. CHILD SEXUAL ABUSE 147 at 148 (1992).

84. *See* Roland Summit, *Abuse of the Child Sexual Abuse Accommodation Syndrome*, 1/4 J. CHILD SEXUAL ABUSE 153 at 158 (1992).

85. Dr. Summit has lamented the misuse of the syndrome he identified and has repeatedly pointed out that it is not meant to be used diagnostically. *See, e.g.*, Roland Summit, *Abuse of the Child Sexual Abuse Accommodation Syndrome*, 1/4 J. CHILD SEXUAL ABUSE 153 (1992); Meinig, *Profile of Roland Summit*, 1 VIOLENCE UPDATE 6 (May 1991).

86. *See, e.g.*, People v. Duell, 163 A.D.2d 866, 558 N.Y.S.2d 395 (1990).

the child's paradoxical behaviors are not inconsistent with sexual abuse, should be admissible through competent expert testimony.[87]

One of the newest "syndromes" to be used in the sexual-abuse area is the "false memory syndrome" (FMS), a theory that states that false "memories" of child sexual abuse that never occurred are implanted in the minds of people, generally women, and generally during therapy with master's-level female therapists. Dr. Summit recounts that the Institute for Psychological Therapies "spun off a new illness, *false memory syndrome*,"[88] to describe what was felt to be delayed "memories" of nonexistent childhood sexual abuse, often during the course of therapy.[89] FMS purports to explain what has been called "delayed memory syndrome," which itself is explanatory and not diagnostic.

DELAYED MEMORY

Delayed memory is a phenomenon by which certain very traumatic incidents are not remembered during some periods of time.[90] Mental-health professionals theorize that to defend against the trauma the mind either represses the memory or, through some dissociative

87. *See, e.g.*, Steward v. State, 652 N.E.2d 490 (Ind. 1995) (CSAAS testimony not admissible to prove that child was abused, but once child's credibility is questioned, it may be admitted to explain unexpected behavior patterns seemingly inconsistent with abuse); People v. Gray, 187 Cal. App. 3d 213, 231 Cal. Rptr. 658 (1986); State v. Payton, 481 N.W.2d 325 (Iowa 1992); State v. J.Q., 599 A.2d 172 (N.J. Super. 1991); People v. Lopez, 589 N.Y.S.2d 920 (App. Div. 1992). For a line of cases which misconstrues the use of the syndrome as improper "bolstering," *see, e.g.*, Hellstrom v. Commonwealth, 825 S.W.2d 612 (Ky. 1992) (this case is particularly strange because inasmuch as it denies CSAAS evidence as bolstering seen though CSAAS was not mentioned, but only the behavioral characteristics explained); Commonwealth v. Evans, 603 A.2d 608 (Pa. Super. Ct. 1992); State v. W.L., 278 N.J. Super. 295, 650 A.2d 1035 (1995).

88. *See* Roland Summit, *Misplaced Attention to Delayed Memory*, 5/3 THE ADVISOR 21 at 24 (Summer 1992) (emphasis in original).

89. An organization called the False Memory Syndrome Foundation was spun off from the Institute for Psychological Therapies to respond to the allegations on behalf of people who claim to be falsely accused of perpetrating such abuse. *See generally*, H. Wakefield & R. Underwager, *Magic, Mischief, and Memories: Remembering Repressed Abuse* (n.d.). The director, Pamela Freyd, is the mother of psychologist Jennifer Freyd, whose "recovered" memories of sexual abuse were denied by her parents. *See generally*, Jennifer Freyd, *Personal Perspectives on the Delayed Memory Debate*, 9/3 FAMILY VIOLENCE & SEXUAL ASSAULT BULLETIN 28 (1993).

For a discussion of the work of Underwager and Wakefield, among the founders of the False Memory Syndrome Foundation, in the sexual abuse area, *see, e.g.*, ANNA SALTER, ACCURACY OF EXPERT TESTIMONY IN CHILD SEXUAL ABUSE CASES: A CASE STUDY OF RALPH UNDERWAGER AND HOLINDA WAKEFIELD (1991). Lawyers who are faced with information on the false memory syndrome from the False Memory Foundation also should be aware of an interview published concerning two of the foundation's founders, Ralph Underwager and Hollida Wakefield, in a Dutch publication, *Paidika, The Journal of Paedophilia*, J. Geraci, *Interview: Hollida Wakefield and Ralph Underwager*, 3/2 PAIDIKA, J. PAEDOPHILIA 2 (Winter 1993).

90. *See, e.g.*, Susan Roth & Matthew J. Friedman, *Childhood Trauma Remembered: A Report on the Current Scientific Knowledge Base and Its Applications*, 7/1 J. CHILD SEXUAL ABUSE 83 (1998); B. van der Kolk & W. Kadish, *Amnesia, Dissociation, and the Return of the Repressed* in B. VAN DER KOLK, PSYCHOLOGICAL TRAUMA (1987).

mechanism, splits off that memory from the person's accessible memory. At a later time, the memory may surface, resulting in reports by adults of childhood sexual abuse that they had not remembered during at least some periods of their lives. The International Society for Traumatic Stress Studies (ISTSS) summarizes the various explanatory mechanisms proposed to account for "forgetting" as follows:

- *Failure to encode:* a failure to create a memory at time of the event.
- *Dissociation:* an altered cognitive state that sometimes occurs during a traumatic event and that may interfere with the normal porcesses for remembering (encoding, consolidation, or retrieval) of such events.
- *Simple forgetting:* the fading of memory over time (a normal phenomenon with nontraumatic memories).
- *Repression:* an active psychological process that prevents conscious retrieval of memories.
- *Conditioned extinction:* a laboratory phenomenon by which certain conditions can activate inhibition (or reduce the availability) of previously learned behavior.
- *State dependent learning:* a mechanism that would explain why traumatic memories can only be retrieved when the individual is in the same emotional, environmental, and neurobiological state that was present during the original traumatic event.
- *Long-term depression:* a cellular mechanism that suppresses the transmission of data from certain nerve cells to others; this could theoretically impair the retrieval of previously accessible information.[91]

ISTSS states:

> Research findings suggest that age at the time of the childhood trauma is associated with forgetting, and that those who were younger are

91. *See* Susan Roth & Matthew J. Friedman. *Childhood Trauma Remembered: A Report on the Current Scientific Knowledge Base and Its Applications*, 7/1 J. CHILD SEXUAL ABUSE 83, 95 (1998).

more likely to have forgotten and to report recovered memories. A wide variety of triggers seem to be associated with the recovery of memory for childhood trauma, including watching a television program or reading some materials about trauma, undergoing a similar experience at a later time, and discussions with family and friends. It is likely that situations that have some characteristics that are similar to the original event are associated with recovered memories. Interestingly, a majority of recovered memories are reported to occur outside of therapy.[92]

There continues to be debate within the mental-health field concerning delayed memory.[93] ISTSS indicates that there is general agreement that "(1) traumatic events are usually remembered in part or in whole; (2) traumatic memories may be forgotten, then remembered at some later time; (3) illusory memories can also occur."[94] Because there is not a standard procedure for establishing the accuracy of a particular person's memories absent evidence or corroboration, there may be differences of opinion concerning the validity of individual reports.[95]

Repressive, amnesic, and/or dissociative responses to major trauma are well-documented.[96] The traumatic stress responses associated with child sexual abuse are also well-documented and under-

---

92. *Id.* at 88 (citation omitted).

93. For a series of articles which debates the issues of delayed memories, pseudomemories, and false memories, see, Constance J. Dalenberg, Making and Finding Memories: A Commentary on the "Repressed Memory" Controversy, 3/3 J. Child Sexual Abuse 109 (1994); Sandra L. Elvik, Professionals Under Fire—Delayed Memories vs. the False Memory Syndrome, 3/3 J. Child Sexual Abuse 123 (1994); Richard Ofshe, Making Grossly Damaging But Avoidable Errors: The Pitfalls of the Olio/Cornell Thesis, 3/3 J. Child Sexual Abuse 95 (1994); Karen A. Olio & William F. Cornell, Making Meaning Not Monsters: Reflections on the Delayed Memory Syndrome, 3/3 J. Child Sexual Abuse 77 (1994); Robert M. Reece, Making Meaning—A Pediatrician's View, 3/3 J. Child Sexual Abuse 119 (1994). See also Elizabeth Loftus & Katherine Ketchum, *The Myth of Memory Repression* (1994); D. Stephen Lindsay & J. Don Read, Psychotherapy and Memories of Childhood Sexual Abuse: A Cognitive Perspective, Applied Cognitive Psychology 281 (1994); J. Don Read & D. Stephen Lindsay, Moving Toward a Middle Ground in the "False Memory" Debate: Reply to Commentaries on Lindsay and Read, 8 Applied Psychology 407 (1994); Donald Barstow, Critical Examination of the "False Memory Syndrome," 9/1 Family Violence and Sexual Assault Bulletin 21 (1993); John G. Watkins, Dealing with the Problem of "False Memory" in Clinic and Court, J. Psychiatry & Law 297 (Fall 1993); Gary M. Ernsdorff & Elizabeth F. Loftus, Let the Sleeping Memories Lie? Words of Caution About Tolling the Statute of Limitations, 84 J. Crim. L. & Criminology 129 (1993).

94. *Id.* at 97.

95. *Id.*.

96. *See, e.g.*, Bessel van der Kolk & R. Fisler, *Dissociation and the Fragmentary Nature of Traumatic Memories: Overview and Exploratory Study*, 8 J. TRAUMATIC STRESS 505 (1995); Bessel van der Kolk & W. Kadish, *Amnesia, Dissociation, and the Return of the Repressed*, in B. VAN DER KOLK, PSYCHOLOGICAL TRAUMA (1987); M. Horowitz, STRESS RESPONSE SYNDROMES (2d ed. 1986).

stood by mental-health professionals.[97] The common diagnosis of post-traumatic stress disorder may help to explain why child sexual abuse victims may bury memories that surface at different times in the victims' lives.[98] The secrecy that almost always accompanies intrafamilial child sexual abuse may further contribute to the blocking or forgetting of memories of the abuse.[99]

Application of repression, amnesia, or dissociation of traumatic memories, with delayed memories and false memory syndrome, to the child sexual abuse context is currently being studied and documented through research.[100] The studies which have addressed the issue appear to find a significant number of people sexually abused as children who report periods of having no memory of their abuse.[101] There are still many questions that remain to be answered. ISTSS summarizes the current state of knowledge as follows:

1. Memory is not a simple unitary process.
2. Memories are not stored as complete and separate "packets" of information.
3. Memory is not a perfect representation like a photograph.

---

97. *See, e.g.*, M. Donaldson & R. Gardner, *Diagnosis and Treatment of Traumatic Stress Among Women After Childhood Incest*, in TRAUMA AND ITS WAKE: THE STUDY OF POST TRAUMATIC STRESS DISORDER (C. Figley ed., 1985); F. Lindberg & L. Distad, *Post-Traumatic Stress Disorders in Women Who Experienced Childhood Incest*, 9 CHILD ABUSE & NEGLECT 521 (1985).

98. *See, e.g.* Lenore E. Walker, *PTSD and Child Sexual Abuse: Commentary*, 2/4 J. CHILD SEXUAL ABUSE 129 (1993).

99. *See, e.g.*, Christine A. Courtois, *The Memory Retrieval Process in Incest Survivor Therapy*, 1/1 J. CHILD SEXUAL ABUSE 15 at 18 (1992).

100. In addition to the study discussed in the text, *see, e.g.*, John Briere & Jon Conte, *Self-Reported Amnesia for Abuse in Adults Molested as Children*, 6/1 J. TRAUMATIC STRESS 21 (1993); Judith Herman & Emily Schatzow, *Recovery and Verification of Memories of Childhood Sexual Trauma*, 4 PSYCHOANALYTIC PSYCHOLOGY 1 (1987). These studies involving clinical samples found 60 percent and 64 percent, respectively, had some degree of amnesia or severe memory deficits concerning their childhood sexual abuse.

101. *See, e.g.*, John Briere & Jon Conte, *Self-Reported Amnesia for Abuse in Adults Molested as Children*, 6/1 J. TRAUMATIC STRESS 21 (1993) (59.3 percent of the 450 men and women studied reported having had some period of amnesia for their abuse in the past); Linda Williams, *Adult Memories of Childhood Abuse: Preliminary Findings from a Longitudinal Study*, 5/3 THE ADVISOR 19 (Summer 1992) (as discussed in the text, 38 percent of the 200 women studied had or reported no memory of the abuse which had reported at a hospital 17 years earlier); Judith Herman & Emily Schatzow, *Recovery and Verification of Memories of Childhood Sexual Trauma*, 4 PSYCHOANALYTIC PSYCHOLOGY 1 (1987) (64 percent of the 53 women studied reported having had some period of amnesia for their abuse in the past). Widom and Morris found that 32 percent of women and 58 percent of men whose child sexual abuse had been substantiated by a court did not report their abuse twenty years later upon re-interview. *See*, C. S. Widom & S. Morris, *Accuracy of Adult Recollections of Childhood Victimization: Part 2: Childhood Sexual Abuse*, 9 PSYCHOLOGICAL ASSESSMENT 34 (1997). Elliot's random national sample of 505 people found 116 child sexual abuse victims, of whom 20 percent reported that there was a period of time when they had no memory of their abuse. *See*, D. M. Elliot, *Traumatic Events: Prevalence and Delayed Recall in the General Population*, 65 J. CONSULTING & CLINICAL PSYCHOLOGY 810 (1997).

4. There are two basic forms of memory: explicit and implicit memory.
5. Traumatic memories may be different than ordinary memories.
6. There are a number of, as yet, unproven mechanisms that might explain how memories are "forgotten."
7. There is currently no scientific consensus regarding how a "forgotten" memory can later be "recovered."[102]

One particularly interesting study looked at women who had been seen as children, from infancy to age twelve, at a city hospital based on allegations of child sexual abuse.[103] The details of the sexual abuse allegations had been recorded earlier, shortly after the abuse was reported, as a part of a study of the immediate consequences of abuse. The current study contacted the child victims seventeen years later, with 200 participating in the study. The subjects of the study were told that the researchers were following up on the lives and health of women who had received medical care at the hospital, without any mention of the reasons for their treatment at the hospital. Questions about childhood sexual experiences with sex and screening questions about child sexual abuse were asked, including whether or not reports of sexual abuse that did not actually occur had been made by them or others. The interviewers did not know the circumstances involved in any of the subjects' hospital visits. Thirty-eight percent of the women did not remember or would not disclose the abuse that was revealed in the medical records, despite the fact that they did disclose numerous other very personal matters, and 53 percent of the women who did not disclose the abuse in the medical records did report other childhood sexual victimizations. One illustration indicating that the subjects really did not remember the abuse involved a woman who revealed hearing from her mother that before she was born an uncle had been killed by a woman whose

102. *See* Susan Roth & Matthew J. Friedman. *Childhood Trauma Remembered: A Report on the Current Scientific Knowledge Base and Its Applications*, 7/1 J. CHILD SEXUAL ABUSE 83, 91 (1998).

103. *See* Linda M. Williams, *Recovered Memories of Abuse in Women with Documented Child Sexual Victimization Histories*, 8 J. TRAUMATIC STRESS 649 (1995); Linda M. Williams, *Adult Memories of Childhood Abuse: Preliminary Findings from a Longitudinal Study*, 5/3 THE ADVISOR 19 (Summer 1992).

little girl he had molested. A comparison of the medical record showed that the uncle had molested the subject (who was four at the time she was seen at the hospital), her seven-year-old sister, and a playmate, and that the playmate's mother had murdered the uncle. The sister also reported no sexual victimization during the interview.

While it is certainly possible to induce people to believe that they have experienced something that they have not, there is insufficient data to support any finding of widespread false memories or the existence of a false memory syndrome.

EXPERT WITNESSES

It is almost impossible to present a sexual abuse case without appropriate expert testimony. Not every physician or mental-health professional is an expert in intrafamilial child sexual abuse, an extremely specialized field. Especially in light of the growing judicial skepticism of sexual abuse allegations in domestic-relations litigation, it is essential that a properly qualified expert evaluate the allegations.

It is particularly important for the lawyer to be familiar with the current literature in the field. There are some dangerous "experts" speaking, writing, and testifying in the field. The only way to discredit their testimony or the experts who rely on their writings is to know how to tell the good research and theories from the bad. The ABA Center on Children and the Law (formerly known as the ABA National Legal Resource Center for Child Advocacy and Protection) has published some good books that review the psychological literature as well as provide legal assistance.[104] A number of other books and articles also provide good background and assistance in recognizing poor research and reasoning in sexual abuse cases, as well as the dynamics of intrafamilial child sexual abuse.[105] Because so

---

104. *See, e.g.*, SEXUAL ABUSE ALLEGATIONS IN CUSTODY AND VISITATION CASES (E. Nicholson, ed. 1988).

105. *See, e.g.*, John E. B. Myers, Karen J. Saywitz & Gail S. Goodman, *Psychological Research on Children as Witnesses: Practical Implications for Forensic Interviews and Courtroom Testimony*, 28/1 PACIFIC L.J. 3 (1996); KATHRYN KUEHNLE, ASSESSING ALLEGATIONS OF CHILD SEXUAL ABUSE (1996); ANNA C. SALTER, TRANSFORMING TRAUMA: A GUIDE TO UNDERSTANDING AND TREATING ADULT SURVIVORS OF CHILD SEXUAL ABUSE (1995); David Finkelhor, *Current Information on the Scope and Nature of Child Sexual Abuse*, 4/2 THE FUTURE OF CHILDREN 31 (1994); John N. Briere & Diana M. Elliott, *Immediate and Long-Term Impacts of Child Sexual Abuse*, 4/2 THE FUTURE OF CHILDREN 54 (1994); John E. B. Myers, Jan Bays, Judith Becker, Lucy Berliner, David L. Corwin & Karen J. Saywitz, *Expert Testimony in Child Sexual Abuse Litigation*, 68 NEB. L. REV. 1 (1989); Jon Conte & Lucy Berliner, *The Impact of Sexual Abuse on Children: Empirical Findings*, in HANDBOOK ON SEXUAL

much research is just now being done with respect to intrafamilial child sexual abuse, it is essential that the lawyer not rely on the articles and books cited here but also look at the updated writings of the same authors and others who are respected in the child-welfare community.

Unfortunately, these cases create great polarization among medical and mental-health professionals and lawyers working in the area. Experts relied on by one "side" may disapprove of the experts on the "other side" of the issue. It is essential for the lawyer to determine whether the experts being used or referred to in the case are people actually working in the field or paid experts who may have little or no actual experience.

In evaluating the credentials of the experts involved in the case, the lawyer should consider their general education, any specialized training, particularly regular attendance at ongoing conferences and seminars on the topic, publication in *peer-reviewed* journals, membership in professional organizations dealing with child abuse,[106] and research or practical experience in evaluating and treating victims or perpetrators of intrafamilial child sexual abuse. Many such experts are regularly requested to do evaluations or treatment for child protective services and, therefore, have the volume of cases that develops real expertise.

It is helpful to know an expert's views about child sexual abuse, because those views may reveal a bias that affects the expert's opinion. One example of views that may color an expert's assessment of a child sexual abuse allegation will be discussed in this section for illustrative purposes. Ralph Underwager and his wife, Hollida Wakefield,[107] were interviewed in a Dutch publication, *Paidika, The*

Abuse of Children 72 (Lenore Walker, ed. 1988); David L. Corwin, Lucy Berliner, Gail S. Goodman, Jean Goodwin & Sue White, *Child Sexual Abuse and Custody Disputes*, 2 J. Interpersonal Violence 91 (1987); Investigation and Prosecution of Child Abuse (P. Toth & M. Whalen, eds. 1987); Sexual Abuse of Young Children (K. MacFarlane & J. Waterman eds. 1986). *See, generally*, 1 John E. B. Myers, Evidence in Child Abuse and Neglect Cases ch. 5 (3rd ed. 1997); Leonard Karp & Cheryl Karp, Domestic Torts: Family Violence, Conflict and Sexual Abuse § 4.06-4.14 (Clark Boardman Callaghan 1989, West Group 1998).

106. Such as the American Professional Society on the Abuse of Children (APSAC), Association for the Treatment of Sexual Abusers (ATSA), or the International Society for Prevention of Child Abuse and Neglect (ISPCAN).

107. Underwager and Wakefield have written, lectured, and testified in the area of child sexual abuse, founded the Institute for Psychological Therapies, are the publishers of the journal Issues in Child Abuse Accusations, and primary authors of H. Wakefield and R. Underwager, *Accusations of Child Sexual Abuse* (1988).

Journal of Paedophilia.[108] In that article Dr. Underwager is quoted as making the following statements:

> [Q] *Is choosing paedophilia for you a responsible choice for the individual?*
>
> RU: Certainly it is responsible. . . . Paedophiles can boldly and courageously affirm what they choose. They can say that what they want is to find the best way to love. I am also a theologian and as a theologian I believe it is God's will that there be closeness and intimacy, unity of the flesh, between people. A paedophile can say: "This closeness is possible for me within the choices that I've made."
>
> Paedophiles are too defensive. They go around saying, "You people out there are saying that what I choose is bad, that it's no good. . . ." What I think is that paedophiles can make the assertion that the pursuit of intimacy and love is what they choose. With boldness they can say, "I believe this is in fact part of God's will." They have the right to make these statements for themselves as personal choices. Now whether or not they can persuade other people they are right is another matter (laughs).
>
> . . . I do believe that God's will is that we have absolute freedom. No conditions. No contingencies.[109]

Dr. Underwager was also quoted as saying, "I was urging earlier that you make the loving image clearer to the outside world. What appears to the public is not the picture of a loving man but rather the picture of the dirty old man lurking in alleys. . . ."[110] He continues later in the interview: "The solution that I'm suggesting is that paedophiles become much more positive. They should directly attack the concept, the image, the picture of the paedophile as an evil, wicked, and reprehensible exploiter of children."[111]

In answering a question about how he would "describe a spirituality for paedophiles," Dr. Underwager stated that he did not see the issue as one between right and wrong, but rather as between good and evil:

> Good and evil only pays attention to outcomes. You can never know the outcomes until you have already acted. . . .

---

108. J. Geraci, *Interview: Hollida Wakefield and Ralph Underwager*, 3/2 PAIDIKA, THE J. OF PAEDOPHILIA 2 (Winter 1993).

109. *Id.* at 3-4.

110. *Id.* at 5.

111. *Id.* at 6.

> As with all human behavior, I would suggest that paedophiles can say, "I have chosen; I choose; I will act in this fashion. I believe that the outcome will be good. I will pay the price for that act, whatever the price may be."[112]

As synopsized (and disagreed with "100 percent") by Ms. Wakefield, Dr. Underwager views radical feminist opposition to pedophilia as coming "out of women's jealousy because men can have meaningful paedophile relationships, and they wish they could. . . ."[113]

Dr. Underwager points out certain difficulties in talking freely about the issue, stating that "[t]he climate is such in the United States that the discussion would have to be carefully sanitized, completely abstract. There couldn't be any reference whatsoever to somebody who might be in an ongoing relationship because we would have to call the police and say, 'That person has been sexual with minors,' and if we didn't do that, we would lose our licenses as psychologists, face a fine of $5,000, and six months in jail."[114]

The advice Dr. Underwager gave the interviewer was:

> Take the risk, the consequences of the risk, and make the claim: This is something good. Paedophiles need to become more positive and make the claim that paedophilia is an acceptable expression of God's will for love and unity among human beings. This is the only way the question is going to be answered, of whether or not it is possible. . . . You need to get involved in discourse, and to do so while acting.[115]

Ms. Wakefield raised a disturbing suggestion for a research study:

> It would be nice if someone could get some kind of big research grant to do a longitudinal study of, let's say, a hundred twelve-year-old boys in relationships with loving paedophiles. Whoever was doing the study would have to follow them at five year intervals for twenty years. This is impossible in the U.S. right now. We're talking a long time in the future.[116]

---

112. *Id.* at 11.
113. *Id.* at 9.
114. *Id.* at 7.
115. *Id.* at 12.
116. Id.

In addition to looking at the expert's qualifications, experience, and personal views, the lawyer should also carefully review the procedures and instruments used in the evaluation to determine whether they are generally accepted in the field of child sexual abuse evaluation.

A number of witnesses use as primary authority for their conclusions published instruments that have never been peer-reviewed and have not been established as valid or reliable by the mental-health community. Despite the crying need for a magic bullet to distinguish true from false allegations of sexual abuse, there is no instrument that proves or disproves molestation.

RESOURCES

Self-help groups for incestuous families, such as Parents United and Daughters and Sons United, may provide not only a great deal of current research information and referrals to local experts, but also a treatment program that can assist the family in getting beyond the molestation, perhaps to a safe reunion. In addition to providing direct services to clients, they can often refer lawyers to local experts and current literature in the field.

The National Judicial Education Program and the ABA Center on Children and the Law have produced a curriculum for judges, including helpful interdisciplinary readings, ADJUDICATING ALLEGATIONS OF CHILD SEXUAL ABUSE WHEN CUSTODY IS IN DISPUTE (1996). This training curriculum is designed to educate and sensitize judges to the complex issues involved in sexual abuse cases. The materials contain many mental-health resources that should be useful to judges and lawyers.

Until the time that a definitive test or battery of tests exists to diagnose child sexual abuse, risk of offending, or risk of recidivism, experts and the lawyers who examine and cross-examine them in court must be scrupulous in pointing out the weaknesses and limitations of the objective measures used. Training, experience, and clinical judgment are currently the best diagnostic tools available.[117]

---

117. *See, e.g.*, Carolyn J. Levitt, *The Medical Examination in Child Sexual Abuse: A Balance Between History and Exam*, 1/4 J. CHILD SEXUAL ABUSE 113 at 115 (1992); Roland Summit, *The Rehabilitation of the Child Sexual Abuse Accommodation Syndrome in Trial Courts in Kentucky: Commentary*, 1/4 J. CHILD SEXUAL ABUSE 147 at 149 (1992).

Appendix 6-1

Practice Parameters for the Forensic Evaluation of Children and Adolescents Who May Have Been Physically or Sexually Abused

ABSTRACT

These practice parameters describe the forensic evaluation of children and adolescents who may have been physically or sexually abused. The recommendations are drawn from guidelines that have been published by various professional organizations and authors and are based on available scientific research and the current state of clinical practice. These parameters consider the clinical presentation of abused children, normative sexual behavior of children, interview techniques, the possibility of false statements, the assessment of credibility, and important forensic issues. These parameters were approved by Council of the American Academy of Child and Adolescent Psychiatry in September 1996. *J. Am. Acad. Child Adolesc. Psychiatry*, 1997, 36(3):423-442. **Key Words:** child abuse, sexual abuse, forensic, evaluation, practice parameters.

Individuals in private practice, as well as those employed by courts or other agencies, see children who may have been mentally, physically, or sexually abused. There are three distinct roles for them: forensic evaluator; clinician, who is conducting mental health assessments and providing treatment; and consultant regarding public policy.

Working as a forensic evaluator, the practitioner may evaluate children in a private practice for a forensic purpose, evaluate children and collaborate with other mental health professionals in a government agency such as protective services, or work with an interdisciplinary team at a pediatric medical center. He or she may assist the court in determining what happened to the child, make recommendations regarding placement or treatment, or offer an opinion on the termination of parental rights. A forensic evaluation may involve critiquing the work that was previously done by another mental health professional or by a protective services investigator. The forensic evaluation may be used in a civil suit in which the child is a plaintiff seeking remuneration for damages related to the abuse. The evaluator may be asked to testify in a juvenile court (regarding the issue of abuse and neglect), in a civil court (if a civil suit is being pursued), or in a criminal court (if the alleged perpetrator comes to trial).

Working as clinicians, mental health professionals may provide assessments and treatment for abused children and their families in both outpatient and inpatient settings. Many psychiatric hospitals and residential treatment centers have specialized programs for abused children and adolescents. There are also programs for adolescent perpetrators of sexual abuse, many of whom were also victims of sexual abuse.

Mental health professionals may deal with these issues on the level of public policy by sharing information with and educating attorneys and judges about the psychiatric aspects of abuse and the developmental needs of children (Goldstein et al., 1973, 1979). In some states, clinicians have helped shape the laws that control how the legal system deals with abused children, including the criteria for reporting abuse and the methods of evaluation and procedures for hearing the child's testimony.

There are some differences in the method of evaluating children who may have been abused, depending on whether the evaluator is conducting a forensic or a clinical assessment. These parameters pertain to the process for forensic evaluation, i.e., evaluations that are intended to address a legal issue or question. Practice parameters regarding the clinical assessment and treatment of abused children will be provided in a separate document. Also, these parameters should be considered in the light of the more general guidelines for how diagnostic evaluations should be conducted, which are presented in "Practice Parameters for the Psychiatric Assessment of Children and Adolescents" (American Academy of Child and Adolescent Psychiatry, 1995) and "Practice Parameters for the Psychiatric Assessment of Infants and Toddlers" (American Academy of Child and Adolescent Psychiatry, in press).

Practice parameters provide guidelines for patterns of practice, not for the care of the particular individual being evaluated and/or treated. This document is not intended to be construed or to serve as a standard of medical care. Standards of medical care are determined on all facts and circumstances involved in an individual case and are subject to change as scientific knowledge and technology advance. Parameters of practice should not be construed as including all proper methods of care or excluding other acceptable methods of care reasonably expected to obtain the same results. Adherence to these parameters will not ensure a successful outcome in every case. The ultimate judgment regarding any specific clinical procedure or treatment must be made by the physician in light of all the circumstances presented by the patient and family and the resources available. These practice parameters were approved as of the date indicated, and they should not be applied to clinical situations occurring before that date.

In this paper, the term "child" refers to both adolescents and younger children unless explicitly noted. Unless otherwise noted, "parents" refers to the child's primary caretakers, regardless of whether they are the biological or adoptive parents or legal guardians.

REVIEW OF THE LITERATURE

The list of references for this paper was developed by *Medline* and *Psychological Abstracts* literature searches, by reviewing the bibliographies of book chapters and review articles, and by asking colleagues for suggestions. The *Medline* search, conducted in August 1994, used the following text words in various combinations: child abuse, sexual abuse, forensic, and evaluation. The search covered 1990 to 1994 and yielded about 175 articles. These were reviewed and the most relevant were included in this list of references.

These practice parameters pertain to the evaluation of children who may have been physically and/or sexually abused. Child and adolescent psychiatrists are more likely to be involved in a forensic evaluation in instances of possible sexual abuse, so these parameters include more material related to sexual abuse than physical abuse. Although the focus of this set of practice parameters is on the forensic evaluation of children who may have been abused, the following general and related works may be of interest.

General works regarding forensic child psychiatry have been written or edited by Benedek (1986), Herman (1990), Nurcombe and Partlett (1994), and Schetky and Benedek (1985, 1992).

General works regarding the identification, evaluation, and treatment of abused children have been written by Besharov (1990), Helfer and Kempe (1976, 1987), Kempe and Helfer (1972), Kempe and Kempe (1978), Pelton (1981), Schmitt (1978), and Wasserman and Rosenfeld (1985). The history of child maltreatment from ancient to contemporary time was described by deMause (1991) and Kahr (1991).

General works regarding sexual abuse of children have been published by Abright (1986), Bulkley (1981), Corwin and Olafson (1993), Faller (1988a), Finkelhor (1979, 1984, 1986), Friedrich (1990), Glaser and Frosh (1988), Haugaard and Reppucci (1988), Hunter (1990), MacFarlane and Waterman (1986), Nurcombe and Unützer (1991), Olafson et al. (1993), Rosenfeld et al. (1977), Rush (1980), Schetky and Green (1988), and Sgroi et al. (1982). In its Debate Forum (Terr, 1989), the *Journal of the American Academy of Child and Adolescent Psychiatry* published a discussion by four experts of whether child sex abuse is overdiagnosed.

DEFINITIONS

The legal definitions of terms related to the maltreatment of children vary from state to state. Clinicians should be aware of the definitions used in their own locale. Broadly speaking:

Neglect is the willful failure to provide adequate care and protection for children. Physical neglect may involve failure to feed the child adequately, failure to provide medical care, or failure to protect the child from danger.

Physical abuse is the infliction of injury by a caretaker. It may take the form of beating, punching, kicking, biting, or other methods. The abuse can result in injuries such as broken bones, internal hemorrhages, bruises, burns, and poisoning. It is important to consider cultural factors in assessing whether the discipline of a child is abusive.

Sexual abuse of children refers to sexual behavior between a child and an adult or between two children when one of them is significantly older or uses coercion. The perpetrator and the victim may be of the same sex or the opposite sex. The sexual behaviors include touching breasts, buttocks, and genitals, whether the victim is dressed or undressed; exhibitionism; fellatio; cunnilingus; and penetration of the vagina or anus with sexual organs or with objects. Pornographic photography is usually included in the definition of sexual abuse. It is important to consider developmental factors in assessing whether sexual behaviors between two children are abusive or normative.

Psychological abuse occurs when a person conveys to a child that he or she is worthless, flawed, unloved, unwanted, or endangered. The perpetrator may spurn, terrorize, isolate, or berate the child. Psychological abuse may also be caused by repeatedly taking a child for unnecessary medical treatment. When psychological abuse is severe, it is often accompanied by neglect, physical abuse, and/or sexual abuse.

The maltreatment of children occurs in a wide range of circumstances. It may have happened only once or twice, or it may have constituted severe torture over a period of years. It may have been perpetrated by parents or other family members, by nonrelated caretakers, or by total strangers.

In American society there are wide variations in parenting practices. These variations are partly determined by the cultural heritage and religious beliefs of the family. The cultural context of the alleged act should be taken into consideration when one is evaluating suspected neglect and abuse.

BRIEF HISTORY OF CHILD MALTREATMENT

In the 1860s, a French forensic pathologist described severe child abuse after performing autopsies on children who had been beaten to death (Tardieu, 1860, 1868). In the United States, child abuse came to public attention through the case of Mary Ellen, an 8-year-old girl who was severely maltreated (Ross, 1977). She was discovered by church workers in New York City in 1874, but they found that the only agency that was available to help was the Society for the Prevention of Cruelty to Animals. Thus, they founded the Society for the Prevention of Cruelty to Children. In 1875, New York was the first state to adopt a child protection law, which became the model for other states.

In the 20th century, the rediscovery of child abuse was signaled by a radiologist in a hospital emergency room. Caffey (1946) noticed a syndrome of children with multiple skeletal injuries and chronic subdural hematomas. Until the 1960s, it was thought that physical abuse of children was rare—partly because physical discipline of children was generally more acceptable and partly because of societal denial concerning violence toward children. In an important article in the *Journal of the American Medical Association*, Kempe et al. (1962) described the battered-child syndrome. In 1974 the federal government passed the Child Abuse Prevention and Treatment Act, which resulted in every state passing laws in which designated persons were required to report child abuse.

It took a separate societal realization during the 1970s to acknowledge the extent of sexual abuse. It was known that incest occurred, but most people believed that it must be very unusual and that it happened primarily among very deviant families. We now know that incest and other forms of sexual abuse are not rare.

EPIDEMIOLOGY

The National Committee to Prevent Child Abuse (1995) collects data each year on the incidence of child maltreatment. The Committee estimated that in 1994 more than 3 million alleged victims were reported to child protective services. Of those reports about 1 million were found to be substantiated. The reported cases were distributed in the following manner: neglect, 45 percent; physical abuse, 26 percent; sexual abuse, 11 percent; emotional abuse, 3 percent; and other or unspecified cases, 16 percent. The Committee reported that in 1994 almost 1,300 children died as the result of maltreatment. The National Center on Child Abuse and Neglect (U.S. Department of Health and Human Services, 1995) also collects data each year on child maltreatment. The Center estimated that in 1993 the median age of the victim of child maltreatment was 7 years. Of the victims, about 53 percent were girls and 47 percent were boys. It was reported that 77 percent of the victims were abused by parents, 12 percent by other relatives, 5 percent by noncaretakers, and 2 percent by foster parents, facility staff, or child care staff. These figures are approximations because the actual amount of abuse is unclear. It is known that the reporting of abuse has increased in recent years.

Thompson (1994) reviewed the epidemiology and sociology of child maltreatment. Although child abuse occurs at all socioeconomic levels, it is highly associated with poverty and financial stress. Child maltreatment is strongly correlated with less parental education, underemployment, poor housing, welfare reliance, and single parenting. Child abuse tends to occur in multiproblem families, i.e., families characterized by domestic violence, social isolation, parental mental illness, and parental substance abuse, especially alcoholism.

Cicchetti and Toth (1995) emphasized that child maltreatment should be understood within a developmental psychopathology perspective. The probability of maltreatment may be increased by transient or enduring risk factors, such as the child's prematurity, mental retardation, and physical handicap. The probability of maltreatment may be reduced by transient or enduring protective factors, such as adequate parental support. These factors may relate to the perpetrator, victim, family, community, or culture.

BRIEF REVIEW OF CLINICAL PRESENTATIONS

Abused children manifest diverse symptoms, including a variety of emotional, behavioral, and somatic reactions. These symptoms are neither specific nor pathognomonic, in that the same symptoms may occur without any history of abuse. The symptoms manifested by abused children can be organized into clinical patterns. Although it may be helpful to note whether a particular case falls into one of these patterns, that is not in itself diagnostic of child abuse. The following studies are often cited as examples of clinical patterns associated with abuse. Since this is an evolving and developing area, these studies are not definitive. In general, the research on child maltreatment has been limited because of the wide variance in definitions of abuse and because of the absence of adequate control groups.

Schmitt (1987) described the characteristics of physically abused children and their parents: the parents have delayed seeking help for the injuries; the history given by the parents is implausible or incompatible with the physical findings; there is evidence of repeated suspicious injuries; the parents blame a sibling or claim the child injured himself or herself; and the parent has unrealistic expectations of the child.

DeAngelis (1992) described a number of behaviors associated with abuse that should arouse the suspicions of the health professional. For example: the child is unusually fearful or docile, distrustful, and guarded; shows no expectation of being comforted; is wary of physical contact; is on the alert for danger, continually sizing up the environment; attempts to meet parents' needs by role reversal and superficial relationships with adults; and is afraid to go home.

Cicchetti and Toth (1995) reviewed the literature regarding the psychological effects of physical abuse and neglect. They noted a wide range of effects: affect dysregulation; disruptive and aggressive behaviors; insecure and atypical attachment patterns; impaired peer relationships, involving either increased aggression or social withdrawal; academic underachievement; and psychopathology, including depression, conduct disorder, attention-deficit/hyperactivity disorder, oppositional disorder, and posttraumatic stress disorder.

Sgroi (1982, 1988) described a pattern that is typical of intrafamilial sexual abuse and other sexual abuse that occurs over a period of time. The process evolves through five phases: (1) the engagement phase, when the perpetrator induces the child into a special relationship; (2) the sexual interaction phase, in which the sexual behaviors progress from less intimate to more intimate forms of abuse; (3) the secrecy phase; (4) the disclosure phase, when the abuse is discovered; and (5) the suppression phase, when the family pressures the child to retract his or her statements.

Summit (1983) described the child sexual abuse accommodation syndrome. He characterized the sexual abuse of girls by men as having five characteristics: secrecy; helplessness; entrapment and accommodation; delayed, conflicted, and unconvincing disclosure; and retraction. The process of accommodation occurs because the child learns that she "must be available without complaint to the parent's sexual demands." The child may find various ways to accommodate: by maintaining secrecy in order to keep the family together, by turning to imaginary companions, and by employing altered states of consciousness. Others may become aggressive, demanding, and hyperactive. This "syndrome" is intended to help clinicians understand the dynamics of abuse, not to diagnose abuse. There is no such thing as a "child sexual abuse syndrome," that is, a specific cluster of symptoms that are diagnostic of sexual abuse.

Browne and Finkelhor (1986) reviewed and summarized almost 30 empirical studies that described the emotional and behavioral effects of child sexual abuse. They concluded that some sexually abused children show initial reactions of fear, anxiety, depression, anger, hostility, and inappropriate sexual behavior. The inappropriate sexual behavior included open masturbation, excessive sexual curiosity, and frequent exposure of the genitals.

Friedrich et al. (1987) and Friedrich and Grambsch (1992) found that the child who has been sexually abused is more likely than the normal child to manifest inappropriate sexual behaviors, such as trying to undress other people, talking excessively about sexual acts, masturbating with an object, imitating intercourse, inserting objects into the vagina or anus, and rubbing his or her body against other people. It is possible for a normal child who has never been abused to exhibit these behaviors. For the behaviors to suggest sexual abuse, they would need to be numerous and persistent. Friedrich and colleagues' studies were notable in that they compared abused children with normal controls.

Beitchman et al. (1991) reviewed the short-term effects of child sexual abuse. They found that victims of child sexual abuse are more likely than nonvictims to develop some type of inappropriate sexual behavior. In children this preoccupation with sexuality was manifested by sexual play, masturbation, seductive or sexually aggressive behavior, and age-inappropriate sexual knowledge. In adolescents, there was evidence of sexually acting out, such as promiscuity and possibly a higher rate of homosexual contact. They also found that the following factors were associated with more severe symptoms in the victims of sexual abuse: greater frequency and duration, sexual abuse that involved force or penetration, and sexual abuse perpetrated by the child's father or stepfather. Beitchman et al. (1992) also reviewed the long-term effects of child sexual abuse.

Green (1993) reviewed the immediate and long-term effects of child sexual abuse. He found that the major psychological problems found in sexually abused children were the following: anxiety disorders, such as fearfulness, nightmares, phobias, somatic complaints, and posttraumatic stress disorder; dissociative reactions and hysterical symptoms, such as periods of amnesia, trance-like states, and multiple personality disorder; depression, low self-esteem and suicidal behavior; and disturbance of sexual behavior including sexual hyperarousal and aggressive sexual behavior as well as avoiding sexual stimuli through phobias and inhibitions. Green did not believe that there is a specific child sexual abuse syndrome with predictable sequelae.

Kendall-Tackett et al. (1993) reviewed 45 studies regarding the impact of sexual abuse on children. They found that sexually abused children have more symptoms than nonabused children. The symptoms included fears, posttraumatic stress disorder, behavior problems, sexualized behaviors, and poor self-esteem. No one symptom characterized a majority of sexually abused children. Approximately one third of victims had no symptoms.

Terr (1990, 1991) described the psychological sequelae of children who have experienced acute and chronic trauma. Her work may be relevant in some cases of physical and sexual abuse. Terr listed four characteristics that occur after both types of trauma: (1) visualized or repeatedly perceived memories of the event; (2) repetitive behaviors; (3) fears specifically related to the trauma; and (4) changed attitudes about people, life, and the future. Children who sustained single, acute traumas manifested full, detailed memories of the event; a sense for "omens," such as looking for reasons why the event occurred; and misperceptions, including visual hallucinations and peculiar time distortions. On the other hand, many children who experienced severe, chronic trauma, such as repeated sexual abuse, manifested massive denial and psychic numbing, self-hypnosis and dissociation, and rage. In some of her work, Terr compared traumatized children (the children of Chowchilla who were kidnaped from their school bus) with normal controls (children from other towns).

THE FORENSIC EVALUATION

Normative Sexual Behaviors of Children. It is important to be aware of normative sexual behaviors of children for two reasons. First, normal sexual play activities between children should not be taken to be sexual abuse. In assessing this issue, the evaluator should consider the age difference between the children, the developmental level of the children, whether one child was coercing the other child, and whether the act itself was intrusive, forceful, or dangerous. The second reason to be aware of normative sexual behaviors of children is that sexually abused children manifest more sexual behaviors than normal, so it is important to know what the baseline is. For a more detailed discussion, the reader is referred to Green (1988) and Johnson and Friend (1995). Rosenfeld et al. (1986) studied a nonclinical population and found that it is not uncommon for children, aged 2 to 10, to sometimes touch a parent's genitals. Rosenfeld et al. (1987) also studied bathing practices for children of various ages. Friedrich et al (1991) studied the normative sexual behavior of children by asking parents whether specific behaviors had occurred in the last 6 months. For example, they reported that at least 15% of the boys in the sample, aged 2 to 6, manifested the following behaviors: shows sex parts to children and adults, masturbates with hand, touches sex parts in public and at home. They reported that at least 15% of the girls in the sample, aged 2 to 6, manifested the following behaviors: talks flirtatiously, masturbates with hand, shows sex parts to adults, touches sex parts in public and at home.

Guidelines for the Forensic Evaluation of Children Who May Have Been Abused. Guidelines for the forensic evaluation of children who may have been abused have been published by several individuals and organizations. The American Academy of Child and Adolescent Psychiatry (1988) published "Guidelines for the Clinical Evaluation of Child and Adolescent Sexual Abuse," which had been formulated by the AACAP Committee on Rights and Legal Matters. These parameters are based, in part, on the AACAP position paper. The American Professional Society on the Abuse of Children (APSAC) (1990) developed guidelines for the psychosocial evaluation of suspected sexual abuse in young children, with a view that "the results of such evaluations may be used to assist in legal decisionmaking and in directing treatment planning." APSAC (1995a,b) has also published guidelines on the use of anatomical dolls and on the psychosocial evaluation of suspected psychological maltreatment. Jenkins and Howell (1994), proposing guidelines for child sexual abuse examinations, noted that "the position of the examiner is not to be a therapist or child advocate, but one to arrive at objective conclusions based on unbiased data." Gardner (1995), Ney (1995), Sgroi et al. (1982), Terr (1989), Walker (1988, 1990), Weissman (1991), and Wideman (1989, 1990) have contributed to the literature on this topic.

Interview Techniques. Daly (1991), Goodman and Saywitz (1994), Jones and McQuiston (1985), Lamb et al. (1995), Raskin and Yuille (1989), Sgroi et al. (1982), and Yuille et al. (1993) have proposed interview techniques for evaluating children who may have been abused. Dent and Stephenson (1979) studied the effectiveness of different techniques of questioning child witnesses. White and Quinn (1988) and Quinn and White (1989) described how statements and behaviors of the interviewer affect the outcome of the interview and may cause distortion of the data. Hibbard and Hartman (1993) showed that individuals from different professional groups (physicians and nurses; child protective service workers; lawyers, judges, and law enforcement officers; and psychologists) emphasize different topics when they investigate these cases.

In general, the professional who conducts forensic evaluations of children who may have been abused is faced with several important tasks: finding out what happened, evaluating the child for emotional disorders, considering other possible explanations for these disorders, being aware of developmental issues, avoiding biasing the outcome with one's own preconceptions, pursuing these objectives in a sensitive manner and taking care not to retraumatize the child, being supportive to family members, and keeping an accurate record that will be useful in future court proceedings.

The Step-Wise Interview described by Yuille et al. (1993) presents a systematic approach to achieve these goals. It is not known scientifically or empirically whether the Step-Wise Interview is preferable to other interview methods in eliciting accurate reports. This method is presented here as an illustration, since individual evaluators may develop their own ways to achieve the goals of the interview. The Step-Wise Interview consists of the following components:

1. Rapport Building. During this time the interviewer makes informal observations of the child's behavior, social skills, and cognitive abilities.

2. Describing Two Specific Events. The interviewer asks the child to describe two specific past experiences, such as a birthday party or a school outing. In doing so, the interviewer models the form of the interview for the child by asking nonleading, open-ended questions, a pattern that will hold through the rest of the interview.

3. Telling the Truth. The interviewer establishes the need to tell the truth, in a stepwise fashion. Start with asking general questions and proceed, if necessary, to more specific questions. Reach an agreement that in this interview only the truth will be discussed, not "pretend" or imagination.

4. Introducing the Topic of Concern. Start with more general questions, such as "Do you know why you are talking with me today?" Proceed, if necessary, to more specific questions, such as, "Has anything happened to you?" or "Has anyone done something to you?" Drawings may be helpful in initiating disclosure. That is, either the child or the interviewer makes an outline of a person. Then the child is asked to add and name each body part and describe its function. If sexual abuse is suspected, when the genitals are

described the interviewer could ask whether the child has seen or touched that part on another person and who has seen or touched that part on the child. If physical abuse is suspected, the interviewer could ask whether particular parts have been hurt in some way.

5. Free Narrative. Once the topic of abuse has been introduced, the interviewer encourages the child to describe each event from the beginning without leaving out any details. The child is allowed to proceed at his or her pace, without correction or interruption. If abuse had occurred over a period of time, the interviewer may ask for a description of the general pattern and then for an account of specific episodes.

6. General Questions. The interviewer may ask general questions in order to elicit further details. These questions should not be leading or suggestive and should be phrased in such a way that an inability to recall or lack of knowledge is acceptable. A leading question is: "Uncle Joe touched your bottom, didn't he?" A suggestive question is: "Did Uncle Joe touch your bottom?"

7. Specific Questions, if Necessary. It may be helpful to obtain clarification by asking more specific questions. For example, the interviewer may follow up on inconsistencies in a gentle, nonthreatening manner. If the child has used a term that seems inappropriate for a child, the interviewer may ask where he or she learned that word. In asking specific questions, one should avoid repetitive questions. Also, one should avoid rewarding answers in any way, particularly with praise.

8. Interview Aids, if Necessary. Anatomical dolls (with representation of genitals) may be useful in understanding exactly what sort of abusive activity occurred. The dolls are not used to establish a diagnosis, but they may be used to clarify what happened. A more detailed discussion of anatomical dolls is in a subsequent section.

9. Concluding the Interview. Toward the end of the interview, the interviewer may ask a few leading questions about irrelevant issues, such as "You came here by taxi, didn't you?" If the child demonstrates susceptibility to the suggestions, the interviewer would need to verify that the information obtained earlier did not come about through contamination. At the end, the child is thanked for participating, regardless of the outcome of the interview. The interviewer should not make any promises he or she cannot keep.

Use of Drawing in Interviews. Children's drawings are useful as an associative tool for assessing and accessing traumatic memories (Burgess and Hartman, 1993). Drawings are helpful in forensic assessments, including spontaneous drawings, asking the child to draw a male and female, kinetic family drawings, self-portraits, what happened and where it happened, or even a picture of the alleged offender. The usefulness of drawings lies in the affect and information they elicit and certain findings that may be suggestive of sexual abuse such as depiction of genitalia or avoidance of sexual features altogether. They should be interpreted in the context of the overall clinical picture.

Use of Anatomical Dolls in Interviews. It is not necessary to use anatomical dolls in the assessment of sexual abuse. They may be useful for eliciting a young child's terminology for anatomical parts and for allowing the child, who cannot tell or draw what happened, to demonstrate what happened. The dolls may also trigger memories of sexual events. Care should be taken not to use these dolls in a way to instruct, coach, or lead the child. They should not be used as a short cut to a more comprehensive evaluation of the child and the child's family.

Boat and Everson (1988a,b), Leventhal et al. (1989), and Skinner and Berry (1993) described how anatomical dolls may be used in these evaluations. Everson and Boat (1994) described how these dolls might be used in specific ways: as a comforter, as an icebreaker in the interview, as an anatomical model, as a demonstration aid, as a memory stimulus, as a diagnostic screen (in which the child's sexualized behavior is taken as a possible indicator of abuse that warrants further evaluation), and as a diagnostic test (from which an evaluator can draw definitive conclusions about the likelihood of abuse). These authors noted that no authority in this field has advocated the use of anatomical dolls as a diagnostic test. Realmuto et al. (1990) also concluded that anatomical dolls were a poor source of information to rely on in deciding whether a young child had been abused, in the absence of other pertinent history.

Several small studies (August and Forman, 1989; Cohn, 1991; Jampole and Weber, 1987; White et al., 1986) have compared sexually abused and presumably nonabused children as to their play with anatomical dolls. In general, these studies found that both abused and nonabused children explored these dolls in a sexual way (such as inserting their fingers into doll openings), but that abused children were more likely to demonstrate sexually related behavior.

Several authors have reported normative data, i.e., descriptions of anatomical doll play by normal children. Everson and Boat (1990) found that about 6% of 223 normal children, aged 2 to 5, manifested explicit sexualized play. It occurred more often when the interviewer was absent from the room than when he was present and was more likely to occur among poor African-American males. On the other hand, Sivan et al. (1988) observed 144 presumably nonabused children in a playroom with anatomical dolls. They reported that "nonreferred children found these dolls no more interesting than other toys" and that "no explicit sexual activity was observed."

Britton and O'Keefe (1991) showed that children manifest sexually explicit behavior with nonanatomical dolls as frequently as when they are interviewed with anatomical dolls. They concluded that either type of doll provides similar information in the interview setting.

Interviewing Young Children. The evaluation of an infant (aged less than 12 months), toddler (aged 12 to 36 months), or preschool child requires more specialized techniques. It is important to collect a developmental history from the parents or other caregivers. This includes the parents' perceptions and attitudes toward the child and the child's role in the family. The evaluator may want to see the child alone and in a joint meeting with one or both parents. This allows the evaluator to conduct an age-appropriate mental status examination and to assess the style of the parents and the relationship between the parent and the child. For further information, see "Practice Parameters for the Psychiatric Assessment of Infants and Toddlers" (American Academy of Child and Adolescent Psychiatry, in press).

Other Interviews. It is usually important to interview, separately, the individual making the allegation and the alleged perpetrator. In some cases, such as divorce-related allegations of sexual abuse, these interviews are the best way to reach an understanding of the case.

It is not appropriate to interview the child jointly with the alleged perpetrator to assess the validity or nature of the accusation. A joint interview is indicated only in helping to assess the possibility of reunification of the child and accused parent when the initial assessment reasonably suggests that the allegation of sexual abuse is false. The evaluator should consider the potential impact of such an interview on the child before proceeding. This issue has been addressed by Faller et al. (1991), Corwin et al. (1987), and Ehrenberg and Elterman (1995).

Psychological Testing. Psychological testing does not diagnose child abuse, but testing may be useful as part of the evaluation process. Waterman and Lusk (1993) reviewed the topic of testing in the evaluation of child sexual abuse and concluded that there are systematic and significant differences between sexually abused and nonabused children in many research studies. They thought that these differences in most tests are not the result of sexual abuse per se, but are the result of more generalized psychological distress or trauma. Leifer et al. (1991) described the Rorschach assessment of sexually abused girls. They found that sexually abused female subjects showed more disturbed thinking and experienced a higher level of stress relative to their adaptive abilities than did nonabused females.

Behavior Checklists. Testing that involves an assessment of sexual behavior may indicate the possibility of sexual abuse. For example, Friedrich et al. (1987, 1988) found that sexually abused children had higher scores than normative controls on the Sexual Problems scale of the Child Behavior Checklist. Kolko et al. (1988) used the Sexual Abuse Symptoms Checklist to discriminate children who were sexually abused from those who were physically abused. Friedrich and colleagues (Friedrich and Grambsch, 1992; Friedrich et al., 1991) used the Child Sexual Behavior Inventory to discriminate sexually abused children from nonabused children. Chantler et al. (1993) used the Louisville Behavior Checklist and the Emotional Indicator Scoring System for Human Figure Drawings to discriminate sexually abused children, clinic patients who were not abused, and community controls. Although the group scores were clearly different, some individual patients would have been misclassified by these measures. In using checklists, it is important to differentiate between sexual behaviors that were manifested during the time frame of the alleged abuse and the time frame since disclosure. That is, children who were not abused and were subjected to repeated interrogations may develop sexual symptoms that resemble the symptoms of children who were actually abused.

False Statements and the Possible Explanations of Abuse Allegations. Children may make false statements in psychiatric evaluations. Sometimes they make false denials regarding abuse (Sgroi, 1982; Sorenson and Snow, 1991; Summit, 1983). Children may make a false denial or recant a previous disclosure for many reasons, including pressure from the perpetrator or the family and fear of the judicial process. The child may "forget" what happened, may minimize the abuse, or may defend against bad feelings by empowering himself or herself ("He used to touch me but I hit him and ran away."). The child may deny the abuse because of fear of having done something wrong ("I was afraid you wouldn't love me if you knew what I did.").

Children may also make false allegations. Berner (1993) reviewed this topic and developed a differential diagnosis of abuse allegations. Benedek and Schetky (1985), Everson and Boat (1989), Gardner (1992, 1995), Goodwin et al. (1978, 1980), Quinn (1991), Schuman (1986, 1987), and Yates and Musty (1988) have contributed to the literature on this issue. The evaluation of these children is complex because there are a number of distinct mental processes, both conscious and unconscious, that may result in false allegations. Long before the current interest in false allegations, Healy and Healy (1915) described how some of the children they evaluated in the first juvenile court clinic manifested pathological lying in making allegations of abuse. Green (1986) described how a delusional mother, who believed that her ex-husband had been molesting their daughter, induced the girl to state that the father had rubbed against her in bed. Clawar and Rivlin (1991) presented many examples of "programming" of children, especially in custody disputes. In some cases inept interviewers, by repeatedly asking leading or suggestive questions, have induced children to make false allegations of abuse. Bernet (1993) described how children may knowingly lie about abuse. Young children may tell "tall tales," and these innocent lies may result in false allegations of abuse. Older children may lie about abuse for revenge or for some personal advantage. For example, an adolescent girl, who became pregnant by her boyfriend, tried to accuse her stepfather of molesting her. In some cases, multiple allegations of abuse may have been generated through group contagion or epidemic hysteria (Ceci and Bruck, 1995; Kenner, 1989).

Sexual abuse allegations that occur in the context of a child custody dispute may be particularly complex. Faller (1991) identified four scenarios that result in allegations during or after divorce: abuse leading to divorce, abuse revealed during the divorce, abuse precipitated by the divorce, and improbable allegations during custody and access disputes. In these cases, Derdeyn (1994) has said that there should be serious consideration of alternative explanations for phenomena reported by a parent as indicative of abuse.

Research on Memory and Suggestibility of Children. Several research studies have examined the suggestibility of children. For example, Cohen and Harnick (1980) compared how well younger children (grade 3), older children (grade 6), and college students remembered the events in a film and how resistant they were to suggestive questions. They found that the younger children were less accurate in their memory and much more likely to be influenced by misleading suggestions. Goodman and Reed (1986) compared how well very young children (3-year-olds), young children (6-year-olds), and adults recalled their interaction with an unfamiliar adult and how well they resisted suggestive questioning. They found that the very young children were less accurate on answering objective questions and were more likely to be misled by suggestive questions. They also found that on free recall the number of correct recollections increased with age. Johnson and Foley (1984) found that young children (under age 8) had more difficulty than did older children and adults in distinguishing between imagined events and those that actually occurred. Tobey and Goodman (1992) studied 4-year-olds who interacted with a "baby-sitter" and, in some cases, with a "policeman," who suggested that the "baby-sitter" may have done something wrong. In a subsequent interview the children who were exposed to the "policeman" were more likely to make incorrect comments after misleading questions. Loftus and Ketcham (1994) related an experiment in which a 14-year-old boy came to believe that he had been lost in a shopping mall as a child when actually he had not. Ceci et al. (1994)

showed how some children who repeatedly thought about a "non-event" (for example, that the child's fingers had been caught in a mousetrap) came to believe that the fictitious event actually happened. Surveys of the research in this area were presented by Ross et al. (1987, 1989), Doris (1991), Goodman et al. (1986), and Goodman and Helgeson (1988). Ceci and Bruck (1993, 1995) presented a historical review of this issue.

The Child's Competency. Competency refers to the child's ability to testify in court in a reliable, meaningful manner. Benedek and Schetky (1987a), Goodman and Bottoms (1993), Goodman et al. (1986), Melton (1981), Nurcombe (1986), Quinn (1986), Ross et al. (1989), and Zaragoza et al. (1995) have addressed this issue. Weissman (1991) summarized the four criteria that are generally required to establish competency: "the capacity to perceive facts accurately (e.g., mental capacity at the time of instant occurrence to observe or receive accurate impressions of the occurrence), the capacity to recollect and recall (e.g., memory sufficient to retain an independent recollection of the observation); the capacity to understand the oath (e.g., capacity to differentiate truth from falsehood, to comprehend the duty to tell the truth, and to understand the consequences of not fulfilling the duty); and the capacity to communicate based on personal knowledge of the facts (e.g., capacity to communicate the memory of such observation, and to understand simple questions about the occurrence)."

The Child's Credibility. Credibility refers to the child's truthfulness and accuracy. The child's credibility is ultimately determined by the jury or the judge, not by the forensic evaluator. Benedek and Schetky (1987b), Faller (1988b), Faller and Corwin (1995), Green (1986), Nurcombe (1986), Quinn (1988), Raskin and Esplin (1991, 1992), Rogers (1990a,b), and Steller (1989) have addressed how mental health professionals can assess credibility. For example, Benedek and Schetky (1987b) listed factors in the child that they thought enhanced credibility: the child uses his or her own vocabulary rather than adult terms and tells the story from his or her own point of view; the child reenacts the trauma in spontaneous play; sexual themes are present in play and drawings: the affect is consonant with the accusations; the child's behavior is seductive, precocious, or regressive; there is good recall of details, including sensory motor and idiosyncratic details; and the child has a history of telling the truth. Rogers (1990a) described the application of statement validity analysis and criteria-based content analysis to the evaluation of children who allege sexual molestation. She said that the following characteristics occur on unreliable or fictitious allegations: the child's statements become increasingly inconsistent over time; the statement is often dramatic or implausible, such as relating the presence of multiple perpetrators or situations in which the perpetrator has not taken ordinary steps against discovery; and statements progress from relatively innocuous behavior to increasingly intrusive, abusive, aggressive activities. These criteria for assessing credibility have been based on clinical experience and on limited preliminary research. They should not be taken to be infallible and could be misunderstood or misused. Finally, it should be noted that a child's spontaneous statement made while he or she was emotionally upset may have substantial value later in court (White v. Illinois, 1992).

Physical Examination of Children Who May Have Been Abused. The physical findings in children who were physically and/or sexually abused were described and illustrated by Reece (1994), Monteleone (1994), and Monteleone and Brodeur (1994). The pattern and significance of physical findings in children who were sexually abused were described by Durfee et al. (1986), Finkel (1988), McCann et al. (1988, 1989, 1990a,b), Muram (1986, 1989a-c), and Muram and Elias (1989). The American Academy of Pediatrics (1991) has published guidelines for the evaluation of sexual abuse of children. In most cases of sexual abuse there are no abnormal physical findings. In Adams et al. (1994) the genital examination in sexually abused girls was clearly abnormal in only 14% of cases. Dubowitz et al. (1992) emphasized the importance of the interdisciplinary team approach in the assessment of child sexual abuse, which includes both psychological evaluation and medical examination. They found that "both a disclosure by the child and abnormal physical findings were significantly and independently associated with the team's diagnosis of sexual abuse, whereas the presence of sexualized behavior, somatic problems, and the child's response to the [physical] examination did not make an additional contribution to the diagnosis."

Testimony by Children. In some instances when allegations of child abuse have been made, a criminal trial occurs and the child may need to testify. Child advocates have been concerned that the trial procedures may retraumatize the child, especially have to relate the abuse experience and being in the courtroom with the alleged perpetrator. Although testifying may be traumatic for some children, it is helpful for others. Kermani (1991, 1993) explained how the Supreme Court has tried to balance the constitutional rights of the defendant (to have a face-to-face confrontation with the child witness) with the best interests of the child (to avoid being retraumatized by the process). In Maryland v. Craig (1990), a slim majority of five justices decided that the Sixth Amendment indicates a "preference," but not an "absolute" right, for the defendant to have a face-to-face meeting with the accuser. As a result, the Supreme Court said it was acceptable in that particular trial to use closed-circuit television, which allowed the defendant to see the child, but protected the child from seeing the defendant. Another way to deal with the issue of the child's testimony is to make a videotape of the child early in the investigation. The videotape protects the child from repeated questioning and, in some states, may substitute for testimony in court.

IMPORTANT FORENSIC ISSUES

Role Definition. The evaluator needs to know whether he or she is conducting a forensic evaluation intended to be read by attorneys and used at court or a clinical assessment for treatment purposes. These practice parameters pertain to the forensic evaluation of children who may have been abused. The child's therapist should not be the person who is conducting the forensic evaluation. However, the child's therapist should be available to share information with the independent evaluator.

The evaluator also needs to know who has hired him or her and to whom he or she owes professional responsibility. This is the issue of agency. That is, in most clinical situations the evaluator is serving as the agent of the patient. In most forensic situations, the evaluator is serving as the agent for someone or some institution other than the individual being examined. Regardless of who has hired the evaluator, the process remains the same and the conclusions remain the same; what changes is who receives the report. The evaluator should have a clear understanding of what is expected, such as the preparation of a report and a willingness to testify in court.

Clear Communication. The forensic evaluator should make sure that the child who is being assessed and the parent understand the reason for the evaluation and the role of the evaluator. The child should understand, consistent with his or her level of development, that this is an evaluation and is not therapy, that this evaluation is being done at the request of a particular person or agency, and that the results will be sent to the appropriate people.

Confidentiality. Forensic evaluations are frequently performed on behalf of some person or agency other than the child and parents. It is important for the parent and child to know that the evaluation will not be confidential. If a clinician has reason to believe that physical or sexual abuse has occurred, the federal government and all states require that the circumstances be reported to the agency that is legally authorized to investigate the matter. Finlayson and Koocher (1991) have studied how professional judgment affects the decision to report child abuse. Since there are so many exceptions to the doctrine of confidentiality, the clinician should be aware that any written record may be read in the future by the individual being evaluated and by many other people.

Privilege. Privilege is a form of confidentiality that may arise in a judicial setting. A person has the right of testimonial privilege when he or she has the right to refuse to testify or to prevent another person from testifying about specific information. For instance, a person may claim that his or her therapy is covered by clinician-patient privilege, preventing the clinician from testifying about him or her. The person may waive the right to clinician-patient privilege and allow the clinician to testify. The clinician ordinarily should testify only if the patient has waived his or her right to privilege. In some circumstances, however, the court can order the clinician to testify in spite of the patient's objections.

The Problem of Bias. It is important for the clinician to be aware of his or her own motivations, as well as the agendas of the other professionals involved in the case. Despite all that is known about countertransference, therapists sometimes base conclusions on their own preconceived assumptions rather than on the data that have been presented. Bias is important in forensic cases in two ways. First, bias creates a distorted filter through which the evaluator views the situation. Second, a clinician who enters a case with a particular bias is likely to change the situation that should be studied objectively. For example, mental health professionals often see themselves as healers and caretakers; this perspective may affect their ability to consider a case completely objectively.

To guard against bias, clinicians should be aware of their own motivations. Another way for the clinician to safeguard against bias is to indicate in detail the reasons for the conclusions in the written report, so that the court will fully understand the basis for the opinion. The clinician should also preserve a record, the raw data, that another person can review. If in doubt about the possible role of bias in an evaluation, the clinician should discuss the case with a colleague.

Awareness of Limitations. It is important for mental health professional to recognize the limits of scientific knowledge in this area. Horner et al. (1993a,b) questioned the reliability of clinical opinions in cases of alleged child sexual abuse. They found that experienced clinicians arrived at widely different conclusions after considering the same case. Divergent opinions may be the result of subtle biases, different emphases that clinicians attach to components of the evaluation, and the withholding of crucial information from the evaluators. Another factor to recognize is the influence of the many participants in these cases. The individuals involved may be extremely opinionated and may try to influence the evaluator through comments or behaviors that may be either subtle or blatant.

Degrees of Certainty. There are several standards of proof or levels of certainty that must be established in order for a judicial decision to go a particular way. (1) The least exacting level of certainty is "probable cause."

In clinical practice, that may be a sufficient level of certainty to report a suspected instance of child abuse. (2) In civil cases, the side prevails that establishes a "preponderance of the evidence." This can be expressed quantitatively as being 51% certain. (3) In some cases that involve psychiatric evidence, the level of certainty is "clear and convincing proof," which is proof necessary to persuade by a substantial margin, which is more than a bare preponderance. For example, the proof that child abuse has occurred or the basis for terminating parental rights must be clear and convincing. (4) Criminal cases require proof that is "beyond a reasonable doubt," or beyond question. To convict a specific person of child abuse would require proof beyond a reasonable doubt. (5) When physicians testify in court, they frequently are asked whether their opinions are given with "a reasonable degree of medical certainty." Rappeport (1985) has proposed that reasonable medical certainty is a level of certainty equivalent to what a physician uses when making a diagnosis and starting treatment. The implication is that the degree of certainty would depend on the clinical situation.

Knowledge of the Law. In performing a forensic evaluation it is important to know the legal issue that is the original basis for the dispute and the evaluation. The attorney involved in the case can provide the relevant legal information. The pertinent legal issue may be defined in an actual law that the federal or state legislature has passed, or it may be embodied in case law. For example, the concept of the best interests of the child was enunciated by Justice Benjamin Cardozo in Finlay v. Finlay (1925). The requirement that physicians report suspected abuse was reinforced in Landeros v Flood (1976). The creation of false recollections of abuse through suggestive interviews was criticized in State v. Michaels (1994). The reader may wish to consult *Legal Issues in Child Abuse and Neglect* (Myers, 1992).

SCIENTIFIC AND CLINICAL RATINGS

Decisions regarding the appropriateness of either diagnostic or treatment recommendations in these parameters were made by considering both the available scientific literature as well as the general clinical consensus of child and adolescent psychiatry practitioners. The validity assigned to any particular scientific finding was judged using the routine criteria by which research is assessed, that is the appropriateness of design, sample selection and size, inclusion of comparison groups, generalizability, and agreement with other studies. The limitations in the available research literature as well as the relative indications for specific interventions are noted in both the literature review and the specific parameters.

The recommendations regarding specific diagnostic evaluations and treatment interventions reflect those methods of practice that are either supported by methodologically sound empirical studies and/or are considered a standard of care by competent clinicians. However, the general paucity of sound scientific data regarding childhood psychiatric disorders and their treatment necessitated that most of the recommendations set forth in these parameters were based on clinical consensus. Those practices that are described as having limited or no research data and also lack clinical consensus regarding their efficacy may still be used in some selected cases, but the clinician should be aware of the limitations and document the rationale for their use.

Clinical consensus was initially derived by the members of the Work Group on Quality Issues in preparation of these parameters. A preliminary draft was sent to experts for review and their comments were incorporated. A draft was distributed to the entire membership of the American Academy of Child and Adolescent Psychiatry for review. In addition, the proposed recommendations were discussed at an open forum held at the Academy's 1995 annual meeting. The Work Group incorporated suggested revisions into the final version of the parameters, which then was sent to the Academy's Council for review and approval.

Those practices that are not recommended represent areas in which there is neither sound empirical data nor high clinical consensus that such practices are effective, or their potential risks are not justified. If such practices are to be used, the clinician should clearly document the justification for that decision.

OUTLINE OF PRACTICE PARAMETERS FOR THE FORENSIC EVALUATION OF CHILDREN AND ADOLESCENTS WHO MAY HAVE BEEN PHYSICALLY OR SEXUALLY ABUSED

The evaluator of a possible victim of abuse should adhere to the same basic principles as those employed in any thorough psychiatric evaluation. That is, the examiner should take a history and strive to collect data that are as complete and accurate as possible. The interview of the child should lead to observations about both conscious and unconscious processes and should address both form (the way the child communicates and how he or she relates to the interviewer) and content (what he or she actually says), and the examiner should keep an open mind regarding the differential diagnosis and the possible explanations for the data that have been collected. The forensic evaluation differs from the usual psychiatric evaluation in that it relies more heavily on collateral data, such as police reports, statements from witnesses, medial reports, and assessments of other family members.

I. Role definition and clarification.
   A. Explain evaluator's role to the parents, to the other adults and systems, and to the child in an age-appropriate manner.
   B. Explain who has requested the evaluation, the purpose of the evaluation, and confidentiality issues, such as who gets the report.
   C. Clarify that the forensic evaluator and the child's therapist should be separate individuals.
   D. Be prepared to testify in court.
   E. Clarify payment issues prior to performing the evaluation.

II. Diagnostic assessment.
   A. Obtain a history from parents, child, and other pertinent informants. Refer to the "Practice Parameters for the Psychiatric Assessment of Children and Adolescents" with added emphasis on:
      1. How the allegation originally arose and subsequent statements that were made. Determine the emotional tone of the first disclosure, such as whether the disclosure arose in the context of a high level of suspicion of abuse.
      2. Sequence of previous examinations, techniques employed, and what was reported. Try to determine whether the previous interviews were likely to have distorted the child's recollections. For instance, review transcripts, audiotapes, and videotapes of earlier interviews.
      3. Symptoms and behavioral changes that sometimes occur in physically abused children, such as depression, aggressive behaviors, and dissociate symptoms.
      4. Symptoms and behavioral changes that sometimes occur in sexually abused children.
         a. Anxiety symptoms, such as fearfulness, phobias, insomnia, nightmares that directly portray the abuse, somatic complaints, posttraumatic stress disorder.
         b. Dissociative reactions and hysterical symptoms, such as periods of amnesia, day-dreaming, trance-like states, hysterical seizures, and multiple personality disorder.

   c. Depression, manifested by low self-esteem, suicidal and self-mutilative behaviors.
   d. Disturbances in sexual behaviors, including sexual hyperarousal manifested by frequent or open masturbation, excessive sexual curiosity, imitating intercourse, inserting objects into vagina or anus, sexual promiscuity, and sexually aggressive behavior toward others. Age-inappropriate sexual knowledge. May also avoid sexual stimuli through phobias and inhibitions.
   e. Somatic complaints, such as enuresis, encopresis, anal and vaginal itching, anorexia, obesity, headache, and stomachache.
   f. Nonabused children may exhibit any of these symptoms and behaviors.
5. History of overstimulation, prior abuse, or other traumas. Consider other stresses besides abuse that could account for the child's symptoms.
6. Exposure to other possible male and female perpetrators.
7. Confounding variables, such as psychiatric disorder or cognitive impairment, that may need to be considered.
8. Family's attitude toward discipline, sex, and modesty.
9. Developmental history, from birth through periods of possible trauma to the present.
10. Family history, such as earlier abuse of the parents; substance abuse by the parents; spouse abuse; psychiatric disorder in the parents.
11. Underlying motivation and possible psychopathology of adults involved.
12. History from the perspective of each parent.

B. Consider requesting collateral information from the following, after obtaining authorizations:
   1. Protective services.
   2. School personnel and past school records.
   3. Other caretakers, such as baby-sitters.
   4. Other family members, such as siblings.
   5. Pediatrician.
   6. Police reports.

C. Process of the interview with the child, including mental status examination.
   1. Choose a relaxed and neutral location.
   2. If possible, audiotape or videotape the interview.
   3. Establish rapport, which may require two or three interviews. Keep the number of interviews to a minimum, as multiple interviews may encourage confabulation.
   4. Test the child's ability to describe historical events accurately.
   5. Assess the child's understanding of telling the truth, as opposed to pretending.
   6. Encourage spontaneous narrative.
   7. Proceed from more general statements to more specific questions.
   8. Avoid repetitive questions, either/or questions, multiple questions. As much as possible, avoid leading and suggestive questions.
   9. Use restatement, i.e., repeating the child's account back to the child. This allows the interviewer to determine whether the child is consistent and to make sure the interviewer understands the child's account.
   10. In general, the examination should take place without the parent present.
   11. If child is very young, consider having a family member in room. Utilize observations of the child's language and behavior rather than direct questioning.
   12. The examination technique used should be appropriate to the child's age and developmental level.
   13. Determine the child's terms for body parts and sexual acts. Do not educate or provide new terms.

D. Content of the interview with the child. The following areas should be explored during the interview, but not in the form of an interrogation. Note the child's affect while discussing these topics and be tactful in helping the child manage anxiety. Young children may not be able to report all of the relevant information.
   1. Whether the child was told to report or not to report anything.

2. Who the alleged perpetrator was.
3. What the alleged perpetrator did.
4. Where it happened.
5. When it started and when it ended.
6. The number of times the abuse occurred.
7. The method of initially engaging the child and how the abuse progressed over time.
8. How the alleged perpetrator induced the child to maintain secrecy.
9. Whether the child is aware of specific injuries or physical symptoms associated with the abuse.
10. Whether photography or videotaping was involved.

E. Other precedures.
1. Consider the risks and benefits of drawing pictures to identify body parts, to show what happened. This should be considered only one part of the entire forensic evaluation.
2. Consider the risks and benefits of using anatomical dolls to identify body parts, to show what happened. This should be considered only one part of the entire forensic evaluation.
3. The following are contraindicated in forensic evaluations of children who may have been abused: hypnosis, Amytal interviews, facilitated communication, guided imagery to enhance memory, and either rewards or negative reinforcement that are used to encourage openness or communication. It should be possible to be generally supportive without rewarding the child's statements.

F. Psychological testing.
1. Consider culturally appropriate intelligence testing and educational testing if the child has manifested academic problems or if retardation may be a factor in assessing competency.
2. Consider personality testing if it might be helpful in clarifying diagnostic issues.
3. Consider parent questionnaires that assess sexual behaviors, such as the Child Behavior Checklist, the

Sexual Abuse Symptom Checklist, and the Child Sexual Behavior Inventory. If these checklists are used, it is essential to differentiate between sexual behaviors during the time frame of the alleged abuse and sexual behaviors after disclosure.

4. The results of psychological testing should be considered as only one part of the entire forensic evaluation. Do not rely on testing by itself to make conclusions regarding abuse. Psychological testing does not by itself distinguish true and false allegations.

G. Physical examination of the physically abused child. Ordinarily the mental health professional would review the examination that has been done by a pediatrician. Photographic documentation may be useful. Among the potential signs of abuse:
   1. Injuries commonly seen after physical punishment, such as bruises on the buttocks and lower back, perhaps at different stages of healing.
   2. Bruises with the configuration of hand marks, pinch marks, and strap marks.
   3. Certain types of burns, such as multiple cigarette burns and scalding of the hands, feet, perineum, and buttocks.
   4. Subdural hematoma.
   5. Abdominal trauma, leading to ruptured liver or spleen.
   6. Fractures, when there is no plausible explanation for how the injury occurred.
   7. Radiological signs of multiple broken bones.
   8. Retinal hemorrhages, which occur in shaken baby syndrome.

H. Physical examination of the sexually abused child. Ordinarily the mental health professional would review the examination by a pediatrician or by another qualified clinician. It is important to take precautions to preserve evidence.
   1. Most sexually abused children do not have any corroborating physical findings.
   2. Findings that are consistent with sexual abuse but are nonspecific: inflammation, scratching, purulent dis-

charge, small skin fissures or lacerations in the area of the posterior fourchette, or foreign bodies in genital, anal, or urethral openings.

3. Findings that strongly suggest sexual abuse: recent or healed lacerations of the hymen, vaginal mucosa, or anal mucosa; enlarged hymenal opening; teeth marks; laboratory reports of sexually transmitted disease that was not acquired perinatally, including gonorrhea, syphilis, human immunodeficiency virus, *Chlamydia*, *Trichomonas vaginalis*, condylomata acuminatum, and herpes.
4. Findings that are definitive that sexual activity occurred: presence of sperm or of acid phosphatase; pregnancy.

I. Other interviews
   1. If possible, interview the person who is raising the concern about the possibility of abuse.
   2. If possible, interview the alleged perpetrator, to elicit his or her version and explanation for what has happened.
   3. A joint interview of the child and alleged perpetrator is not appropriate to assess the validity or nature of the accusation. It may be useful, however, for assessing the possibility of reunification when the initial evaluation reasonably suggests the allegation of sexual abuse is false. Keep in mind the effect of such an interview on the child.

J. Consider an in-home evaluation by the evaluator or a child protection team member.

III. Possible explanations of denials of abuse. Sometimes children may deny or retract allegations of abuse. This may occur for several reasons, including the following:
   A. The alleged abuse did not occur.
   B. The child was pressured by the perpetrator or by family members to recant the allegation. The pressure may consist of bribery, mockery, or threats of injury.
   C. The child may be protecting a parent or other family member, even without external coercion. That is, the child may be taking on this responsibility through role reversal.

D. The child was frightened or distressed by the investigation process and decided to withdraw his or her participation. For instance, an interviewer could have induced a false denial by asking overly challenging questions.
E. The child did not want to testify because of shame or guilt.
F. The child may have mistakenly assumed that he or she may be responsible for what happened.
G. The child consciously or unconsciously took the role of "accommodating" to the abuse rather than objecting to it.
H. The interviewer could have triggered a false denial by questioning the child in the room with the alleged perpetrator.

IV. Possible explanations of allegations of abuse. Sometimes children make false allegations. Although most allegations made by children are true, the evaluator should consider the ways in which false allegations might come about. An allegation may be partly true (that the child actually was abused), but partly false (as to who was the perpetrator). An allegation may have a nidus of truth, but may have been inaccurately elaborated in response to repetitive questioning.

A. A false allegation arises in the mind of a parent or other adults and is imposed on the child.
1. Parental misinterpretation and suggestion. The parent has misinterpreted an innocent remark or neutral piece of behavior as evidence of abuse and induced the child to endorse this interpretation. This happens sometimes in child custody disputes as well as other settings.
2. Misinterpreted physical condition. The parent has assumed that an unremarkable rash or insect bite, for instance, is a sign of abuse.
3. Parental delusion. The parent and child may share a *foliè a deux* or the child may simply give in and agree with the delusional parent.
4. Parental indoctrination. The parent fabricated the story and induced the child to collude in presenting it to the authorities.
5. Interviewer's suggestion. Previous interviewers have asked leading or suggestive questions.

6. Misinterpreted parental behavior. The parent's behavior, though not abusive in itself, becomes problematic and perhaps overstimulating in the context of parental separation and divorce (for example, sleeping in the same bed with an older child).
7. Group contagion. In epidemic hysteria people modify what they have heard in a way that meets their own emotional needs. The rumor may become more convincing as it is retold.

B. The allegation is produced by mental mechanisms in the child that are not conscious or not purposeful.
   1. Fantasy. A younger child may confuse fantasy with reality.
   2. Delusion. Although rare, delusions about sexual activities may occur in older children and adolescents in the context of a psychotic illness.
   3. Misinterpretation. The child may have misunderstood what happened, so he or she later reported it inaccurately.
   4. Miscommunication. The child may misunderstand an adult's question; the adult may misinterpret or take the child's statement out of context.
   5. Confabulation. The child fills gaps in his or her memory with whatever information makes sense to him or her and others at the time.

C. The allegation is produced by mental mechanisms in the child that are usually considered conscious and purposeful.
   1. Fantasy lying. Children who understand the significance of lying may nonetheless fabricate because of frustration or disappointment.
   2. Innocent lying. Children make false statements because that seems to be the best way to handle the situation. Developmentally, this happens more with younger children.
   3. Deliberate lying. Children may choose to avoid or distort the truth for some personal advantage. This happens more with older children.

D. Perpetrator substitution. The child actually may have been sexually abused and manifests symptoms consistent with abuse, but identifies the wrong person as the perpetrator, resulting in a false allegation. The child may do this to protect the actual offender or the child may displace the memories and accompanying affects onto another individual.

V. Issues regarding the child's testimony.

A. Competency refers to the child's ability to testify in court in a reliable, meaningful manner. The following factors should be considered in evaluating competency.

1. Child's capacity to perceive facts accurately.
2. Child's capacity to recollect and recall.
3. Child's capacity to distinguish truth from falsehood, fantasy from reality; to comprehend duty to tell the truth.
4. Child's capacity to communicate based on personal knowledge of the facts.

B. Credibility refers to the child's truthfulness and accuracy, the assessment of which is ultimately the province of the judge or jury. The following factors may indicate that the child is more credible, but none is definitive. It has not been shown scientifically that these factors distinguish true from false allegations.

1. Spontaneity, in that the child volunteers information spontaneously rather than after the parent admonishes him or her to tell the story.
2. Detailed descriptions in the child's own language and from the child's point of view, using age-appropriate terminology.
3. Realistic account, in that the story is plausible and physically possible.
4. Idiosyncratic sensory detail, such as a verbatim conversation and specific memories that are peripheral to the main event.
5. Generally consistent account, but having slight variations with retelling.
6. Relating story bit by bit, rather than all at once. This means that the credible child may relate the story piecemeal over several interviews, until the account is complete. However, the child who endlessly adds more and more information (more perpetrators, more acts,

increasingly bizarre information) may be engaging in confabulation or fantasy lying.

7. Appropriate affect, although there may be many reasons why the child is anxious, fearful, or defensive or manifests isolation of affect.
8. Candid style, such as making spontaneous corrections, admitting there are details he or she cannot recall.
9. Favorable comparison of the history of the child's symptoms and behaviors with the content of the interview.

C. Whether the child should testify.
   1. Consider making a statement as to whether the child should testify, weighing the psychological risks and benefits to the child.
   2. Consider alternatives to face-to-face testimony, such as taping the evaluation and using closed-circuit television, consistent with local law.

VI. Recommendations regarding placement and treatment.
   A. The clinician should follow state law in determining whether the case should be reported to protective services. If in doubt, call protective services and discuss the case without giving the patient's name. Keep a record of any contact with protective services.
   B. If the child is considered at risk, the decision regarding placement of the child is usually made by protective services or by the court. The clinician may be asked to make recommendations. A variety of options should be considered, such as:
      1. Remove the alleged perpetrator from the home. The court may specify that the alleged perpetrator undergo treatment and/or incarceration before returning to the home.
      2. Remove the child from the home. When rehabilitation of the abuser is under way, the court may allow the child to return home under the supervision by a child protection agency. If efforts at rehabilitation are unsuccessful, the court may decide to terminate parental rights.

3. It might be possible to keep the family together if the parents are highly motivated and appear responsible, if active treatment is under say, and if the perpetrator accepts responsibility for his or her actions and is capable of controlling his or her behavior.

C. If asked, the clinician may make general recommendations regarding referral for further assessment and treatment. This may involve a multidisciplinary treatment plan, including crisis intervention, individual therapy, group therapy, family therapy, inpatient treatment, residential treatment, and pharmacotherapy. Consider further evaluation, especially if there is comorbidity with other psychiatric conditions.

D. Consider whether other children, such as siblings and close friends, are at risk. If so, recommend evaluations of these children by protective services.

VII. Written report.

A. Identifying information, such as names and birth dates.

B. Referral information.

1. Name, agency of referral source.
2. Circumstances of the referral.
3. Current status of the case.
4. Statement of specific purpose of evaluation.

C. Procedure for this evaluation. Document:

1. The discussion of the evaluator's role and the lack of confidentiality.
2. The various meetings and interviews that were held. Mention special circumstances, such as who was present and whether the evaluation was electronically recorded.
3. Psychological testing utilized.
4. Outside information that was considered.

D. Current situation. In the context of a chronological account, address:

1. Circumstances of the alleged abuse (who, what, when, where, how).
2. Symptoms that might be related to the alleged abuse.
3. How disclosure came about.

4. What happened then, including a statement regarding previous evaluations and interviews of the child. Comment on whether the previous evaluations employed appropriate techniques.

E. Past history, especially prior level of functioning and information that might be related to the possible abuse or alternative explanations for the symptoms.

F. Family history, especially information that might be related to the possible abuse.

G. Developmental history.

H. Medical history, including the findings from the forensic pediatric examination.

I. Mental status examination, including comments regarding competency and credibility.

J. Psychological testing.
   1. Performed when, where, and by whom, and which tests were administered.
   2. Summary of testing results.

K. Diagnoses.
   1. DSM-IV. Abused children do not necessarily have posttraumatic stress disorder or any other mental disorder. Use the diagnoses, if any, that most accurately reflect the condition of this individual.
   2. If a false denial or false allegation is likely, discussion of the possible explanations.

L. Conclusions.
   1. A list of specific statements that are supported by the data in the report.
   2. Express an opinion about whether abuse occurred and the degree of certainty. The evaluator should keep in mind that in some cases it is not possible to arrive at conclusions that are certain enough to be helpful to a court.
   3. Use language that will be understandable in court. Avoid professional jargon.

M. Recommendations that are realistic and follow logically from the conclusions.

CONFLICT OF INTEREST

In keeping with the requirement that practice parameters be developed by experienced clinicians and researchers, some of the contributors to these practice parameters are in active clinical practice. Through their practices, it is likely that some of these child and adolescent psychiatrists have received income related to services discussed in these parameters. Some contributors are primarily involved in research or other academic endeavors; it is possible that through such activities, many of them have also received income related to services discussed in these parameters. A number of mechanisms are in place to minimize the potential for producing biased recommendations due to conflicts of interest: First, the development process calls for extensive review of the document before it is finalized. All members of the Academy have the opportunity to comment on the parameters before they are approved. Comments have been solicited and received from a broad group of reviewers from child and adolescent psychiatry, psychology, and the legal profession. Second, the contributors and reviewers have all been asked to base their recommendations on an objective evaluation of the available evidence. Third, we ask that any contributor or reviewer who believes that he or she has a conflict of interest that may bias or appear to bias his or her work should notify the Academy.

REFERENCES

Abright, A. R. (1986), Psychiatric aspects of sexual abuse. *Bull Am Acad Psychiatry* Law 14:331-343.

Adams, J. A.; Harper, K.; Knudson, S.; Revilla, J. (1994), Examination findings in legally confirmed child sexual abuse: it's normal to be normal. *Pediatrics* 94:310-317.

American Academy of Child and Adolescent Psychiatry (1988), Guidelines for the clinical evaluation of child and adolescent sexual abuse. *J Am Acad Child Adolesc Psychiatry* 27:655-657.

American Academy of Child and Adolescent Psychiatry (1995), Practice parameters for the psychiatric assessment of children and adolescents. *J Am Acad Child Adolesc Psychiatry* 34:1386-1402.

American Academy of Child and Adolescent Psychiatry (in press), Practice parameters for the psychiatric assessment of infants and toddlers (0-36 months). *J Am Acad Child Adolesc Psychiatry.*

American Academy of Pediatrics (1991), Guidelines for the evaluation of sexual abuse of children. *Pediatrics* 87:254-260.

American Professional Society on the Abuse of Children (1990), Guidelines for psychosocial evaluation of suspected sexual abuse in young children. (Available from APSAC, 407 South Dearborn Avenue, Suite 1300, Chicago IL 60605).

American Professional Society on the Abuse of Children (1995a), Guidelines for psychosocial evaluation of suspected sexual abuse in young children. (Available from APSAC, 407 South Dearborn Avenue, Suite 1300, Chicago IL 60605).

American Professional Society on the Abuse of Children (1995b). Guidelines for psychosocial evaluation of suspected sexual abuse in young children. (Available from APSAC, 407 South Dearborn Avenue, Suite 1300, Chicago IL 60605).

August, R. I.; Forman, B. D. (1989), A comparison of sexually abused and nonsexually abused children's behavioral responses to anatomically correct dolls. *Child Psychiatry Hum Dev* 20:39-47.

Beitchman, J. H.; Zucker, K. J.; Hood, J. E.; daCosta, G. A.; Akman, D. (1991), A review of the short-term effects of child sexual abuse. *Child Abuse Negl* 15:537-556.

Beitchman, J. H.; Zucker, K. J.; Hood, J. E.; daCosta, G. A.; Akman, D.; Cassavia, E. (1992), A review of the long-term effects of child sexual abuse. *Child Abuse Negl* 16:101-118.

Benedek, E. P. (1986), Forensic child psychiatry: an emerging subspecialty. *Bull Am Acad Psychiatry Law* 14:295-300.

Benedek, E. P.; Schetky, D. H. (1985), Allegations of sexual abuse in child custody and visitation disputes. In: *Emerging Issues in Child Psychiatry and the Law*, Schetky, D. H. & Benedek, E. P., eds. New York: Brunner/Mazel.

Benedek, E. P.; Schetky, D. H. (1987a), Problems in validating allegations of sexual abuse. Part I. Factors affecting perception and recall of events. *J Am Acad Child Adolesc Psychiatry* 26:912-915.

Benedek, E. P.; Schetky, D. H. (1987b), Problems in validating allegations of sexual abuse. Part II. Clinical evaluation. *J Am Acad Child Adolesc Psychiatry* 26:916-921.

Bernet, W. (1993), False statements and the differential diagnosis of abuse allegations. *J Am Acad Child Adolesc Psychiatry* 32:903-910.

Besharov, D. J. (1990), *Recognizing Child Abuse.* New York: Free Press.

Boat, B. W.; Everson, M. D. (1988a), Interviewing young children with anatomical dolls. *Child Welfare* 67:337-352.

Boat, B. W.; Everson, M. D. (1988b), Use of anatomical dolls among professionals in sexual abuse evaluations. *Child Abuse Negl* 12:171-179.

Britton, H. L.; O'Keefe, M. A. (1991), Use of nonanatomical dolls in the sexual abuse interview. *Child Abuse Negl* 15:567-573.

Browne, A.; Finkelhor, D. (1986), Impact of child sexual abuse: a review of the research. *Psychol Bull* 99:66-77.

Bulkley, J.; ed. (1981), *Child Sexual Abuse and the Law.* Washington DC: American Bar Association.

Burgess, A. W.; Hartman, C. R. (1993), Children's drawings. *Child Abuse Negl* 17:161-168 (special issue: Clinical Recognition of Sexually Abused Children).

Caffey, J. (1946), Multiple fractures in the long bones of infants suffering from chronic subdural hematoma. *AJR Am J Rventgenol* 56:163-173.

Ceci, S.; Bruck, M. (1993), Suggestibility of the child witness: a historical review and synthesis. *Psychol Bull* 113:403-439.

Ceci, S.; Bruck, M. (1995), *Jeopardy in the Courtroom: A Scientific Analysis of Children's Testimony*. Washington, DC: American Psychological Association.

Ceci, S. J.; Huffman, M. L. C.; Smith, E. (1994), Repeatedly thinking about a non-event: source misattributions among preschoolers. *Consciousness and Cognition* 3:388-407.

Chantler, L.; Pelco, L.; Mertin, P. (1993), The psychological evaluation of child sexual abuse using the Louisville behavior checklist and human figure drawing. *Child Abuse Negl* 17:271-279.

Cicchetti, D.; Toth, S. L. (1995), A developmental psychopathology perspective on child abuse and neglect. *J Am Acad Child Adolesc Psychiatry* 34:541-565.

Clawar, S. S.; Rivlin, B. V. (1991), *Children Held Hostage: Dealing With Programmed and Brainwashed Children*. Chicago: American Bar Association.

Cohen, R. L.; Harnick, M. A. (1980), The susceptibility of child witnesses to suggestion: an empirical study. *Law Hum Behav* 4:201-210.

Cohn, D. S. (1991), Anatomical doll play of preschoolers referred for sexual abuse and those not referred. *Child Abuse Negl* 15:455-466.

Corwin, D. L.; Berliner, L.; Goodman, G.; Goodwin, J.; White, S. (1987), Child sexual abuse and custody disputes: no easy answers. *J Interpersonal Violence* 2:91-105.

Corwin, D. L. & Olafson, E., eds. (1993), Special issue: clinical recognition of sexually abused children. *Child Abuse Negl* 17:1-185.

Daly, L. W. (1991), The essentials of child abuse investigation and child interviews. *Issues Child Abuse Accusations* 3:90-98.

DeAngelis, C. (1992), Clinical indicators of child abuse. In: *Clinical Handbook of Child Psychiatry and the Law*. Schetky, D. H., Benedek, E. P., eds. Baltimore: Williams & Wilkins.

deMause, L. (1991), The universality of incest. *J Psychohist* 19:123-164.

Dent, H.; Stephenson, G. (1979), An experimental study of the effectiveness of different techniques of questioning child witnesses. *Br J Soc Clin Psychol* 18:41-51.

Derdeyn, A. (1994), Adequate evaluation of divorce-related child sexual abuse allegations. *Bull Am Acad Psychiatry Law* 22:279-287.

Doris, J., ed (1991), *The Suggestibility of Children's Recollections*. Washington, DC: American Psychological Association.

Dubowitz, H.; Black, M.; Harrington, D. (1992), The diagnosis of child sexual abuse. *Am J Dis Child* 146:688-693.

Durfee, M.; Heger, A. H.; Woodling, B. (1986), Medical evaluation. In: *Sexual Abuse of Young Children*. Waterman, J., MacFarlane, K., eds. New York: Guilford.

Ehrenberg, M. F.; Elterman, M. F. (1995), Evaluating allegations of sexual abuse in the context of divorce, child custody, and access disputes. In: *True and False Allegations of Child Sexual Abuse: Assessment and Case Management*. Ney T ed. New York: Brunner/Mazel.

Everson, M. D.; Boat B. W. (1989), False allegations of sexual abuse by children and adolescents. *J Am Acad Child Adolesc Psychiatry* 28:230-235.

Everson, M. D.; Boat B. W. (1990), Sexualized doll play among young children: implications for the use of anatomical dolls in sexual abuse evaluations. *J Am Acad Child Adolesc Psychiatry* 29:736-742.
Everson, M. D.; Boat, B. W. (1994), Putting the anatomical doll controversy in perspective: an examination of the major uses and criticisms of the dolls in child sexual abuse evaluations. *Child Abuse Negl* 18:113-129.
Faller, K. C. (1988a), *Child Sexual Abuse.* New York: Columbia University Press.
Faller, K. C. (1988b), Criteria for judging the credibility of children's statements about their sexual abuse. *Child Welfare* 67:389-401.
Faller, K. C. (1991), Possible explanations for child sexual abuse allegations in divorce. *Am J Orthopsychiatry* 61:86-91.
Faller, K. C.; Corwin, D. L. (1995), Children's interview statements and behaviors: role in identifying sexually abused children. *Child Abuse Negl* 19:71-82.
Faller, K. C.; Froning, M. L.; Lipovsky, J. (1991), The parent-child interview: use in evaluating child allegations of sexual abuse by the parent. *Am J. Orthopsychiatry* 61:552-537.
Finkel, M. (1988), The medical evaluation of child sexual abuse. In: *Child Sexual Abuse: A Handbook for Health Care and Legal Professionals.* Schetky, D., Green, A., eds. New York: Brunner/Mazel.
Finkelhor, D. (1979), *Sexually Victimized Children.* New York: Free Press.
Finkelhor, D. (1984), *Child Sexual Abuse: New Theory and Research*, New York: Free Press.
Finkelhor, D., ed. (1986), *A Sourcebook on Child Sexual Abuse.* Beverly Hills, CA: Sage.
Finlay v. Finlay (1925), 240 NY 429.
Finlayson, L. M.; Koocher, G. P. (1991), Professional judgment and child abuse reporting in sexual abuse cases. *Prof Psychol Res Pract* 22:464-472.
Friedrich, W. N. (1990), *Psychotherapy of Sexually Abused Children and Their Families.* New York: Norton.
Friedrich, W. N.; Beilke, R. L.; Urquiza, A. J. (1987), Children from sexually abusive families: a behavioral comparison. *J Interpersonal Violence* 2:391-402.
Friedrich, W. N.; Beilke, R. L.; Urquiza, A .J. (1988), Behavioral problems in young sexually abused boys: a comparison study. *J Interpersonal Violence* 3:21-28.
Friedrich, W. N.; Grambsch, P. (1992), Child sexual behavior inventory: normative and clinical comparisons. *Psychol Assess* 4:303-311.
Friedrich, W. N.; Grambsch, P.; Broughton, D.; Kuiper, J.; Beilke, R. L. (1991), Normative sexual behavior in children. *Pediatrics* 88:456-464.
Gardner, R. A. (1992), *True and False Accusations of Child Sex Abuse.* Cresskill, NJ: Creative Therapeutics.
Gardner, R. A. (1995), *Protocols for the Sex-Abuse Evaluation.* Cresskill, NJ: Creative Therapeutics.
Glaser, D.; Frosh, S. (1988), *Child Sexual Abuse.* Chicago: Dorsey Press.
Goldstein, J.; Freud, A.; Solnit, A. (1973), *Beyond the Best Interests of the Child.* New York: Free Press.
Goldstein, J.; Freud, A.; Solnit, A. (1979), *Before the Best Interests of the Child.* New York: Free Press.

Goodman, G.; Helgeson, V. (1988), Children as witnesses: what do they remember? In: *Handbook on Sexual Abuse of Children: Assessment and Treatment Issues.* Walker, L., ed. New York: Springer.

Goodman, G.; Hepps, D.; Reed, R. (1986), The child victim's testimony. In: *New Issues for Child Advocates.* Haralambie A, ed. Tucson: Council of Attorneys for Children.

Goodman, G. S.; Bottoms, B. L. (1993), *Child Victims, Child Witnesses: Understanding and Improving Testimony.* New York: Guilford.

Goodman, G. S.; Reed, R. S. (1986), Age differences in eyewitness testimony. *Law Hum Behav* 10:317-332.

Goodman, G. S.; Saywitz, K. J. (1994), Memories of abuse: interviewing children when sexual victimization is suspected. *Child Adolesc Psychiatr Clin North Am* 3:645-661.

Goodwin, J.; Cauthorne, C. G.; Rada, R. T. (1980), Cinderella syndrome: children who simulate neglect. *Am J Psychiatry* 137:1223-1225.

Goodwin, J.; Sahd, D.; Rada, R. T. (1978), Incest hoax: false accusations, false denials. *Bull Am Acad Psychiatry Law* 6:269-276.

Green, A. H. (1986), True and false allegations of sexual abuse in child custody disputes. *J Am Acad Child Psychiatry* 25:449-456.

Green, A. H. (1988), Overview of normal psychosexual development. In: *Child Sexual Abuse: A Handbook for Health Care and Legal Professionals.* Schetky, D. & Green, A. H., eds. New York: Brunner/Mazel.

Green, A. H. (1993), Child sexual abuse: immediate and long-term effects and intervention. *J Am Acad Child Adolesc Psychiatry* 32:890-902.

Haugaard, J.; Reppucci, N. (1988), *The Sexual Abuse of Children: A Comprehensive Guide to Current Knowledge and Intervention Strategies.* San Francisco: Jossey-Bass.

Healy, W.; Healy, M. T. (1915), *Pathological Lying, Accusation, and Swindling: A Study in Forensic Psychology.* Boston: Little Brown.

Helfer, R. E.; Kempe, C. H., eds. (1976), *Child Abuse and Neglect: The Family and the Community.* Cambridge, MA: Ballinger Publishing.

Helfer, R. E.; Kempe, C. H., eds. (1987), *The Battered Child,* 4th ed. Chicago: University of Chicago Press.

Herman, S. P. (1990), Forensic child psychiatry. *J Am Acad Child Adolesc Psychiatry* 29:955-957.

Hibbard, R. A.; Hartman, G. L. (1993), Components of child and parent interviews in cases of alleged sexual abuse. *Child Abuse Negl* 17:495-500.

Horner, T. M.; Guyer, M. J.; Kalter, N. M. (1993a), The biases of child sexual abuse experts: believing is seeing. *Bull Am Acad Psychiatry Law* 21:281-292.

Horner, T. M.; Guyer, M. J.; Kalter, N. M. (1993b), Clinical expertise and the assessment of child sexual abuse. *J Am Acad Child Adolesc Psychiatry* 32:925-931.

Hunter, M. (1990), *The Sexually Abused Male.* Lexington, MA: Lexington Books.

Jampole, L.; Weber, M. K. (1987), An assessment of the behavior of sexually abused and nonsexually abused children with anatomically correct dolls. *Child Abuse Negl* 11:187-192.

Jenkins, P. H.; Howell, R. J. (1994), Child sexual abuse examinations: proposed guidelines for a standard of care. *Bull Am Acad Psychiatry Law* 22:5-17.

Johnson, M. K.; Foley, M. A. (1984), Differentiating fact from fantasy: the reliability of children's memory. *J Soc. Issues* 40:33-50 (special issue: The Child Witness).

Johnson, T. C.; Friend, C. (1995), Assessing young children's sexual behaviors in the context of child sexual abuse evaluations. In: *True and False Allegations of Child Sexual Abuse: Assessment and Case Management.* Ney, T. ed. New York: Brunner/Mazel.

Jones, D.; McQuiston, M, (1985), *Interviewing the Sexually Abused Child.* Denver: C. Henry Kempe National Center for the Prevention and Treatment of Child Abuse and Neglect.

Kahr, B. (1991), The sexual molestation of children: historical perspectives, *J Psychohist* 19:191-214.

Kempe, C. H.; Helfer, R. E., eds. (1972), *Helping the Buttered Child and His Family.* Philadelphia: Lippincott.

Kempe, C. H.; Silverman, F. N.; Steele, B. F.; Droegmueller, W.; Silver, H. (1962), The battered child syndrome. *JAMA* 181:17-24.

Kempe, R. S.; Kempe, C. H. (1978), *Child Abuse.* Cambridge, MA: Harvard University Press.

Kendall-Tackett, K. A.; Williams, L. M.; Finkelhor, D. (1993), Impact of sexual abuse on children: a review and synthesis of recent empirical studies. *Psychol Bull* 113:164-180.

Kenner, W. D. (1989), The sex abuse controversy (letter). *J Am Acad Child Adolesc Psychiatry* 28:800.

Kermani, E. J. (1991), The US Supreme Court on victimized children: the constitutional rights of the defendant versus the best interests of the child. *J Am Acad Child Adolesc Psychiatry* 30:839-844.

Kermani, E. J. (1993), Child sexual abuse revisited by the US Supreme Court. *J Am Acad Child Adolesc Psychiatry* 32:971-974.

Kolko, D. J.; Moser, J. T.; Weldy, S. R. (1988), Behavioral/emotional indicator of sexual abuse in child psychiatric inpatients: a controlled comparison with physical abuse. *Child Abuse Negl* 12:529-541.

Lamb, M. E.; Sternberg, K. J.; Esplin, P. W. (1995), Making children into competent witnesses. *Psychol Public Policy Law* 1:438-449.

Landeros v. Flood (1976), 17 Cal 3d 399.

Leifer, M.; Shapiro, J. P.; Martone, M. W.; Kassem, L. (1991), Rorschach assessment of psychological functioning in sexually abused girls *J Pers Assoc* 46:14-28.

Leventhal, J. M.; Hamilton, J.; Rekedal, S.; Tebano Micci, A.; Eyster, C. (1989) Anatomically correct dolls used in interviews of young children suspected of having been sexually abused. *Pediatrics* 84:900-906.

Loftus, E.; Ketcham, K. (1994), *The Myth of Repressed Memory.* New York: St. Martin's Press.

MacFarlane, K. & Waterman, J., eds. (1986), *Sexual Abuse of Young Children.* New York: Guilford.

Maryland v. Craig (1990), 110 S Ct 3157.

McCann, J.; Voris, J.; Simon, M. (1988), Labial adhesions and posterior fourchette injuries in childhood sexual abuse. *Am J Dis Child* 142:659-663.

McCann, J.; Voris, J.; Simon, M. (1989), Perianal findings in prepuberty children selected for nonabuse: a descriptive study. *Child Abuse Negl* 13:179-193.

McCann, J.; Voris, J.; Simon, M.; Wells, R. (1990a), Comparison of genital examination techniques in peripubertal girls. *Pediatrics* 85:182-187.

McCann, J.; Wells, R.; Simon, M.; Voris, J. (1990b), Genital findings in prepubertal girls selected for nonabuse: a descriptive study. *Pediatrics* 86:428-439.

Melton, G. (1981), Children's competency to testify. *Law Hum Behav* 5:73-85.

Monteleone, J. A. (1994), *Child Maltreatment: A Comprehensive Photographic Reference Identifying Potential Child Abuse.* St. Louis: G W Publishing.

Monteleone, J. A.; Brodeur, A. E. (1994), *Child Maltreatment: A Clinical Guide and Reference,* St. Louis: G W Publishing.

Muram, D. (1986), Genital tract injuries in the prepubertal child. *Pediatr Ann* 15:616-620.

Muram, D. (1989a), Anal and Perianal abnormalities in prepubertal victims of sexual abuse. *Am J Obstet Gynecol* 161:278-281.

Muram, D. (1989b), Child sexual abuse: relationship between sexual acts and genital findings. *Child Abuse Negl* 13:211-216.

Muram, D. (1989c), Child sexual abuse: genital tract findings in prepubertal girls. I. The unaided medical examination. *Am J Obstet Gynecol* 160:328-333.

Muram, D.; Elias S (1989), Child sexual abuse: genital tract findings in prepubertal girls. II. Comparison of colposcopic and unaided examinations. *Am J Obstet Gynecol* 160:333-335.

Myers, J. E. B. (1992), *Legal Issues in Child Abuse and Neglect.* Newbury Park, CA: Sage.

National Committee to Prevent Child Abuse (1995). *Current Trends in Child Abuse Reporting and Fatalities: The Results of the 1994 Annual Fifty State Survey.* (Available from NCPCA, 332 S. Michigan Avenue, Suite 1600, Chicago, IL 60604).

Ney, T., ed. (1995), *True and False Allegations of Child Sexual Abuse: Assessment and Case Management.* New York: Brunner/Mazel.

Nurcombe, B. (1986), The child as witness: competency and credibility. *J Am Acad Child Psychiatry* 25:453-480.

Nurcombe, B.; Partlett, D. J. (1994), *Child Mental Health and the Law.* New York: Free Press.

Nurcombe, B.; Unützer, U. (1991), The ritual abuse of children: clinical features and diagnostic reasoning. *J Am Acad Child Adolesc Psychiatry* 30:272-276.

Olafson, E.; Corwin, D. L.; Summit, R. C. (1993), Modern history of child sexual abuse awareness: cycles of discovery and suppression. *Child Abuse Negl* 17:7-24.

Pelton, L., ed. (1981), *The Social Context of Child Abuse and Neglect.* New York: Human Sciences Press.

Quinn, K. M. (1986), Competency to be a witness: a major child forensic issue. *Bull Am Acad Psychiatry Law* 14:311-321.

Quinn, K. M. (1988), The credibility of children's allegations of sexual abuse. *Behav Sci Law* 6:181-199.

Quinn, K. M. (1991), False and unsubstantiated sexual abuse allegations: clinical issues. *Child Youth Serv* 15:145-157.

Quinn, K. M.; White, S.; Santilli, G. (1989), Influences of an interviewer's behaviors in child sexual abuse investigations. *Bull Am Acad Psychiatry Law* 17:45-52.

Rappeport, J. (1985), Reasonable medical certainty. *Bull Am Acad Psychiatry Law* 13:5-15.

Raskin, D. C.; Esplin, P. W. (1991), Assessment of children's statements of sexual abuse. In: *The Suggestibility of Children's Recollections.* Doris J, ed. Washington DC: American Psychological Association.

Raskin, D. C.; Esplin, P. W. (1992), Statement validity assessment: interview procedures and content analysis of children's statements of sexual abuse. *Behav Assess* 13:265-291.

Raskin, D. C.; Yuille, J. C. (1989), Problems in evaluation interviews of children in sexual abuse cases. In: *Perspectives on Children's Testimony,* Ceci, S. J.; Ross, D. F.; Toglia, M. P., eds. New York: Springer-Verlag.

Realmuto, G. M.; Jensen, J. B.; Wescoe, S. (1990), Specificity and sensitivity of sexually anatomically correct dolls in substantiating abuse: a pilot study, *J Am Acad Child Adolesc Psychiatry* 29:743-746.

Reece, R. M. (1994), *Child Abuse: Medical Diagnosis and Management.* Philadelphia: Lea & Febiger.

Rogers, M. L. (1990a), Coping with alleged false sexual molestation: examination and statement analysis procedures. *Issues Child Abuse Accusations* 2:57-68.

Rogers, M. I. (1990b), Review of the current status of the use of statement validity analysis procedures in sex abuse cases in the United States. *Issues Child Abuse Accusations* 2:69-75.

Rosenfeld, A.; Bailey, R.; Siegel, B.; Bailey, G. (1986), Determining incestuous contact between parent and child: frequency of children touching parents' genitals in a nonclinical population. *J Am Acad Child Psychiatry* 25:481-484.

Rosenfeld, A. A.; Nadelson, C. C.; Krieger, M. J.; Backman, J. (1977), Incest and sexual abuse of children. *J Am Acad Child Psychiatry* 16:327-339.

Rosenfeld, A. A.; Siegel, B.; Bailey, R. (1987), Familial bathing patterns: implications for cases of alleged molestation and for pediatric practice. *Pediatrics* 79:224-229.

Ross, C. J. (1977) Society's children: the case of indigent youngsters in New York City, 1875-1903. Dissertation, Yale University, New Haven, CT.

Ross, D. F.; Toglia, M. P.; Ceci, S. J., eds. (1987), *Children's Eyewitness Memory.* New York: Springer-Verlag.

Ross, D. F.; Toglia, M. P.; Ceci, S. J., eds. (1989), *Perspectives on Children's Testimony.* New York: Springer-Verlag.

Rush, F. (1980), *The Best Kept Secret: Sexual Abuse of Children.* New York: McGraw Hill.

Schetky, D. H.; Benedek, E. P., eds. (1985), *Emerging Issues in Child Psychiatry and the Law.* New York: Brunner/Mazel.

Schetky, D. H.; Benedek, E .P., eds. (1992), *Clinical Handbook of Child Psychiatry and the Law.* Baltimore: Williams & Wilkins.

Schetky, D. H.; Green, A. M. (1988), *Child Sexual Abuse: A Handbook for Health Care and Legal Professionals.* New York: Brunner/Mazel.

Schmitt, B., ed. (1978), *The Child Protection Team Handbook.* New York: Garland STPM Press.

Schmitt, B. (1987), The child with nonaccidental trauma. In: *The Battered Child.* 4th ed. Helfer R. E. & Kempe C. H., eds. Chicago: University of Chicago Press.

Schuman, D. C. (1986), False accusations of physical and sexual abuse. *Bull Am Acad Psychiatry Law* 14:5-21.

Schuman, D. C. (1987), Psychodynamics of exaggerated accusations: positive feedback in family systems. *Psychiatr Ann* 17:242-247.

Sgroi, S. M., ed. (1982), *Handbook of Clinical Intervention in Child Sexual Abuse.* Lexington, MA: Lexington Books.

Sgroi, S. M. (1988), *Vulnerable Populations: Evaluation and Treatment of Sexually Abused Children and Adult Survivors,* Vol 1. New York: Free Press.

Sgroi, S. M.; Porter, F.; Blick, L. (1982), Validation of child sexual abuse. In: *Handbook of Clinical Intervention in Child Sexual Abuse.* Sgroi SM, ed. Lexington, MA: Lexington Books.

Sivan, A. B.; Schor, D. P.; Koeppl, G. K.; Noble, L. D. (1988), Interaction of normal children with anatomical dolls. *Child Abuse Negl* 12:295-304.

Skinner, L.; Berry, K. (1993), Anatomically detailed dolls and the evaluation of child sexual abuse allegations: psychometric considerations. *Law Hum Behav* 17:399-421.

Sorenson, T.; Snow, B. (1991), How children tell: the process of disclosure in child sexual abuse. *Child Welfare* 70:3-15.

State v. Michaels (1994), 136 NJ 299.

Steller, M. (1989), Recent developments in statement analysis. In: *Credibility Assessment.* Yuille J, ed. Dordrecht, Netherlands: Kluwer.

Summit, R. C. (1983), The child sexual abuse accommodation syndrome. *Child Abuse Negl* 7:177-193.

Tardieu, A. (1860), Etude medico-legale sur les services et mauvais traitments exerces sur des enfants. *Ann Hyg Publ Med Leg* 13:361-398.

Tardieu, A. (1868), *Etude Medico-Legale sur L'infanticide.* Paris.

Terr, L. C. (1989), Resolved: child sexual abuse is overdiagnosed. *J Am Acad Child Adolesc Psychiatry* 28:788-797.

Terr, L. C. (1990), *Too Scared to Cry: Psychic Trauma in Childhood.* New York: Harper & Row.

Terr, L. C. (1991), Childhood traumas: an outline and overview. *Am J Psychiatry* 148:10-20.

Thompson, R. A. (1994), Social support and the prevention of child maltreatment. In: *Protecting Children from Abuse and Neglect.* Melton GB, Barry FD, eds. New York: Guilford.

Tobey, A.; Goodman, G. (1992), Children's eyewitness memory: effects of participation and forensic context. *Child Abuse Negl* 16:779-796.

U.S. Department of Health and Human Services, National Center on Child Abuse and Neglect (1995), *Child Maltreatment 1993: Reports from the States to the*

National Center on Child Abuse and Neglect. Washington, DC: US Government Printing Office.

Walker, L., ed. (1988), *Handbook on Sexual Abuse of Children: Assessment and Treatment Issues.* New York: Springer.

Walker, L. E. A. (1990), Psychological assessment of sexually abused children for legal evaluation and expert witness testimony. *Prof Psychol Res Prac* 21:344-353.

Wasserman, S.; Rosenfield, A, (1985), Decision-making in child abuse and neglect. *Bull Am Acad Psychiatry Law* 13:259-271.

Waterman, J.; Lusk, R. (1993), Psychological testing in evaluation of child sexual abuse. *Child Abuse Negl* 17:145-159.

Weissman, H. N. (1991), Forensic psychological examination of the child witness in cases of alleged sexual abuse. *Am J Orthopsychiatry* 61:48-58.

White, S.; Quinn, K. M. (1988), Investigatory independence in child sexual abuse evaluations: conceptual considerations. *Bull Am Acad Psychiatry Law* 16:269-278.

White, S.; Strom, G. A.; Santilli, G.; Halpin, B. M. (1986), Interviewing young sexual abuse victims with anatomically correct dolls. *Child Abuse Negl* 10:518-529.

White v. Illinois (1992), 112 S Ct 736.

Wideman, J. C. (1989), Investigative procedures in allegations of child sexual abuse. Part I. The initial criminal investigation. *Issues Child Abuse Accusations* 1:35-43.

Wideman, J. C. (1990), Investigative procedures in allegations of child sexual abuse. Part II. Victim and subject interviews. *Issues Child Abuse Accusations* 2:7-14.

Yates, A.; Musty, T. (1988), Preschool children's erroneous allegations of sexual molestation. *Am J Psychiatry* 145:989-992.

Yuille, J. C.; Hunter, R.; Joffe, R.; Zaparniuk, J. (1993), Interviewing children in sexual abuse cases. In: *Child Victims, Child Witnesses: Understanding and Improving Testimony.* Goodman G. S., Bottoms B. L., eds. New York: Guilford.

Zaragoza, M. S.; Graham, J. R.; Hall, G. C. N.; Hirschman, R.; Ben-Porath, Y. S. (1995), *Memory and Testimony in the Child Witness.* Thousand Oaks, CA: Sage.

Appendix 6-2

Psychosocial Evaluation of Suspected Sexual Abuse in Children. Second Edition

Statement of Purpose

These Guidelines for mental health professionals reflect current knowledge and an emerging consensus about the psychosocial evaluation of suspected sexual abuse in children. They are not intended as a standard of practice to which practitioners are expected to adhere in all cases. Evaluators must have the flexibility to exercise clinical judgment in individual cases. Laws and local customs may also influence the accepted method in a given community. Practitioners must be prepared to justify their decisions about particular practices in specific cases. As experience and scientific knowledge expand, further refinement and revision of these Guidelines are expected.

These Guidelines are specific to psychosocial evaluations. Psychosocial evaluations are a systematic process of gathering information and forming professional opinions about the source and meaning of statements, behavior, and other evidence that are the basis of concern about possible sexual abuse. The results of such evaluations may be used to direct treatment planning and to assist in legal decision making.

Psychosocial evaluators should first establish the purpose of the evaluation and their role in the evaluation process.

Psychosocial evaluations may be conducted for purely clinical reasons or be forensic in nature. These guidelines pertain to both situations.

Clinical evaluations may be requested by parents, guardians or other professionals to determine whether there is reason to be concerned about possible abuse. It is also customary for clinicians to precede treatment for the effects of sexual abuse with an assessment of the sexual abuse history. Forensic evaluations have the explicit purpose of contributing to legal decision making or legal proceedings. Such evaluations may be requested by parents or guardians, public child protective services (CPS) agencies, attorneys, guardians ad litem (or court appointed special advocates), or other professionals. The results may be used in civil or criminal proceedings. As noted in these guidelines, forensic evaluations are different from clinical evaluations in generally requiring a different professional stance and additional components.

In all cases, evaluators should be aware that any interview with a child regarding possible sexual abuse may be subject to scrutiny and have significant implications for legal decision making and the child's safety and well-being.

GUIDELINES

I. THE EVALUATOR

A. CHARACTERISTICS

1. The evaluator should possess a graduate level mental health degree in a recognized discipline (e.g. psychiatry, psychology, social work, nursing, child development) or be supervised by a professional with a graduate level degree.
2. The evaluator should have professional experience assessing and treating children and families, and professional experience with sexually abused children. A minimum of two years of professional experience with sexually abused children is expected; three to five years is preferred for forensic evaluators. If the evaluator does not possess such experience, supervision is essential.
3. The evaluator must have had specialized training in child development and child sexual abuse. This training should be documented in terms of formal course work,

supervision, or attendance at conferences, seminars, and workshops.

4. The evaluator should be knowledgeable about the dynamics and the emotional and behavioral consequences of sexual abuse experiences. The evaluator should be familiar with the professional literature and with current issues relevant to understanding and evaluating sexual abuse experiences.
5. The evaluator should be familiar with different cultural values and practices that may affect definitions of sexual abuse, child and/or family comfort with the evaluation process, child and/or family willingness to provide complete and accurate information, and the evaluator's own interpretation of responses.
6. If the purpose of the evaluation is forensic, the evaluator should have experience in conducting forensic evaluations and providing expert testimony. If the evaluator does not possess such experience, supervision is essential.
7. The evaluator should approach the evaluation with an open mind to all possible responses from the child and all possible explanations for the concern about sexual abuse. The evaluator should recognize that all sources of information have limitations and may contain inaccuracies. in forming an opinion, the evaluator should consider plausible alternative hypotheses.

II. COMPONENTS OF THE EVALUATION

A. PROTOCOL

1. A written protocol is not necessary: however, evaluations should ordinarily involve reviewing those materials considered relevant for the type of evaluation; conducting collateral interviews when necessary; establishing rapport; assessing the child's developmental status, cognitive capacity, level of functioning and level of distress; and specifically evaluating the possibility of abuse. The evaluator may use discretion in the order and method of assessment. Forensic evaluations differ from evaluations conducted for purely clinical reasons

in that they generally involve reviewing relevant materials and conducting collateral interviews.

2. If information is available prior to the evaluation that meets the respective state's definition of reasonable suspicion for a CPS report, but no CPS report has yet been made, the evaluator should make the report and may choose to defer the evaluation until the CPS investigation has been conducted.
3. When possible, unsupervised contact between the child and the suspected offender should be strongly discouraged during the evaluation process.

B. EMPLOYER OF THE EVALUATOR

1. Evaluation of the child may be conducted at the request of a legal guardian prior to court involvement. When only one parent has requested the evaluation, evaluators should give careful consideration to informing the other parent about the evaluation whether or not that parent is the focus of concern. When the other parent is the focus of concern, that parent is likely to request another evaluation; evaluators should consider whether it would be in the child's best interest to have a mutually agreed upon or court appointed evaluator to avoid unnecessary evaluations.
2. If the evaluation is specifically requested or intended for use in a legal proceeding or a court is already involved, the preferred practice is a court-appointed or mutually agreed upon evaluator of the child. In some circumstances exceptions to this practice are acceptable or are customary practice (e.g., contractual arrangements with child protective services, civil damage suits, when one party refuses to cooperate).
3. Discretion should be used in agreeing to conduct an evaluation of a child when the child has already been evaluated. Additional evaluations should be conducted only if they clearly further the best interests of the child. When a second opinion is required, review of the records may eliminate the need for re-interviewing the child.

C. NUMBER OF EVALUATORS

1. The evaluation may be conducted by a single evaluator or by a team of professionals.

D. COLLATERAL INFORMATION GATHERED AS PART OF THE EVALUATION

1. Evaluators may seek and review background materials or conduct interviews as part of the evaluation process. The amount and nature of information reviewed depends on the purpose of the evaluation and the extent to which such information will be helpful in addressing the referral question and understanding the child's presenting problems or concerns. For clinical evaluations, clinical judgment should determine the necessity for additional records, materials, or interviews. Evaluators should request that background material be made available and collateral interviews be permitted for forensic evaluations.
2. The evaluation report should reflect an objective review of collateral information relied upon in the evaluation or opinion forming process.

E. INTERVIEWING THE ACCUSED OR SUSPECTED INDIVIDUAL

1. It is not necessary to interview the accused or suspected individual in order to form an opinion about possible sexual abuse of the child.
2. An interview with or review of the statements from a suspected or accused individual may provide additional relevant information (e.g., alternative explanations, admissions, insight into relationship between child and accused individual).
3. If the accused or suspected individual is a parent who seeks to participate in the evaluation and there are no contraindications (e.g., criminal investigation or charges pending, civil suit), interviewing of the accused or suspected parent should be given strong consideration.

F. RELEASING INFORMATION

1. Suspected abuse should always be reported to authorities as dictated by state law. Except as specified by law, clinical evaluators have no affirmative duty to disclose confidential clinical information.

2. Permission should be obtained from legal guardian(s) to request collateral materials and for release of information about the evaluation to relevant medical or mental health professionals, other professionals (e.g., schoolteachers), and involved legal systems (e.g., CPS, law enforcement, lawyers, courts). Discretion should be used in releasing sensitive individual and family history that does not directly relate to the purpose of the assessment.
3. Feedback about the results of the evaluation should usually be offered to parent(s) or legal guardian(s) and may be offered to the child, except where doing so would not be in the best interests of the child.

III. INTERVIEWING

A. RECORDING OF INTERVIEWS

1. Written documentation is the minimum requirement. Verbatim quotation of significant questions and answers is desirable. Forensic evaluations should contain specific documentation of questions and responses (verbal and nonverbal) regarding possible sexual abuse.
2. Audio or video recording may be preferred practice in some communities. Professional preference, logistics, or clinical considerations may contraindicate recording interviews. Professional discretion is permitted in recording policies and practices.
3. When audio and video recordings are used, the child and legal guardian should be informed. It is desirable to obtain assent from the child (when age appropriate) and consent from legal guardian(s).

B. OBSERVATION OF THE INTERVIEW

1. Professional discretion is permitted in observation policies and practices. Observation of interviews by involved professionals (CPS, law enforcement, etc.), may be indicated if it reduces the need for additional interviews and will not compromise the evaluation process.
2. Observation by non-accused and non-suspected primary caregiver(s) may be indicated for particular clini-

cal reasons; however, great care should be taken that the observation is clinically appropriate, does not unduly distress the child, and does not affect the validity of the evaluation process.

3. If interviews are observed, the child must be informed. It is desirable to obtain assent from the child (when age appropriate) and consent from legal guardian(s).

C. NUMBER OF INTERVIEWS

1. The evaluator determines the number of interviews necessary to address the referral question and assess the child's presenting problems or concerns. This does not imply that all sessions must include specific questioning of possible sexual abuse. The evaluator may decide, based on the individual case circumstances, to adopt a less direct approach and reserve questioning about possible sexual abuse for subsequent interviews. Repeated direct questioning of the child regarding sexual abuse when the child is not reporting or is denying abuse is usually contraindicated.
2. If the child does not report abuse and further direct questioning is judged to be counterproductive, but the evaluators has continuing concerns about the possibility of abuse, the child may be referred for an extended evaluation or therapy that is less directive, but diagnostically focused. Recommendations regarding conditions necessary to insure the child's protection from possible abuse should be made.

D. FORMAT OF INTERVIEW

1. When possible, interviewing the primary caregiver and reviewing other collateral data first to gather background information may facilitate the evaluation process.
2. The child should be seen individually, except when the child refuses to separate from a parent/guardian. Discussion of possible abuse with the child in the presence of the caregiver during evaluation interviews should be avoided except when necessary to elicit information from the child. In such cases, the interview setting

should be structured to reduce the possibility of improper influence by the caregiver on the child's behavior or statements.

3. In some cases, joint sessions with the child and the non-accused caregiver or accused or suspected individual might be helpful to obtain information regarding the overall quality of the relationships. Such joint sessions should not be conducted for the purpose of determining whether abuse occurred based on the child's reactions to the participating adult. Joint sessions should not be conducted if they will cause significant distress for the child.
4. Joint sessions with a child and an accused or suspected individual should only be considered when the individual is a parent or primary caregiver. In making a decision about conducting a joint session with a child and the accused or suspected parent, the evaluator should carefully weigh the possibility of gaining valuable information against the significant potential for negative consequences for an abused child and for the evaluation process. A child should never be asked to discuss the possible abuse in front of an accused or suspected parent.

IV. CHILD INTERVIEW

A. GENERAL PRINCIPLES

1. The evaluator should create an atmosphere that enables the child to talk freely, including providing physical surroundings and a climate that facilitates the child's comfort and communication.
2. The evaluator should convey to all parties that no assumptions have been made about whether abuse has occurred.
3. Language and interviewing approach should be developmentally and culturally appropriate.
4. The evaluator should take the time necessary to perform a complete evaluation and should avoid any coercive quality to the interview.
5. Interview procedures may be modified in cases involving very young, minimally verbal children or children

with special problems (e.g., developmentally delayed, electively mute, non-native speakers).

6. The difference between the evaluation phase and a treatment phase should be articulated. Under certain circumstances (e.g., disputed custody cases) it may be preferable to obtain agreement from the parties before proceeding with treatment following evaluation.

B. QUESTIONING

1. It may be helpful to preface questioning with specific statements designed to reduce misunderstandings during the interview(s), and promote accuracy and completeness.
2. It may be helpful to begin the interview with open-ended questions about neutral topics (e.g. family, school, recent events) so that the child has an opportunity to practice providing free recall responses.
3. Initial substantive questioning should be open-ended and as non-directive as possible to elicit free recall responses. More focused or specific questioning should follow. Once information is provided in response to a specific question, open-ended prompts should again be used.
4. The child should be questioned directly about possible sexual abuse at some point in the evaluation if less directive approaches have not yielded adequate information to answer the referral question.
5. The evaluator may use the form of questioning deemed necessary and justified to elicit information on which to base an opinion. Highly specific questioning should only be used when other methods of questioning have failed, when previous information warrants substantial concern, or when the child's developmental level precludes more non-directive approaches. However, responses to these questions should be carefully evaluated and weighed accordingly. Coercive or intimidating questioning is never justified.

C. USE OF DOLLS AND OTHER DEVICES

1. A variety of non-verbal tools may be used to assist young children in communication, including drawings,

toys, doll-houses, dolls, puppets, etc. Since such materials have the potential to be distracting or misleading they should be used with care. They are discretionary for older children.

2. Anatomical dolls are accepted interview aids. Evaluators using anatomical dolls should be knowledgeable about the functions they may serve and should conform to accepted practice. (Refer to the APSAC Guidelines on the Use of Anatomical Dolls in Child Sexual Abuse Assessments).
3. Anatomical dolls should not be used as a diagnostic test for sexual abuse. Definitive conclusions about a history of sexual abuse should not be based solely on interpretation of behavior with the dolls. Unusual behavior with the dolls may suggest further lines of inquiry that should be pursued. The unusual behavior and the responses to further questioning should be noted in the evaluation report.
4. Story books, coloring books or videos that contain explicit descriptions of abuse situations are potentially suggestive and are primarily teaching tools. They are typically not appropriate for evaluation purposes.

D. PSYCHOLOGICAL TESTING

1. Formal psychological testing of the child is not necessary for the purpose of proving or disproving a history of sexual abuse.
2. Psychological testing may be useful when the clinician has questions about the child's intellectual or developmental level. Psychological tests can also provide helpful information regarding a child's emotional status and general functioning.
3. Psychological testing of parents is not a routine component of child evaluations. An evaluation that includes assessment of parents may involve psychological tests.

V. CONCLUSIONS/REPORT

A. GENERAL PRINCIPLES

1. The evaluation report should document the sources of information and/or data relied on in forming an opinion and making recommendations.

2. The evaluator may state an opinion that abuse did or did not occur, an opinion about the likelihood of the occurrence of abuse or simply provide a description and analysis of the gathered information.
3. Opinions should include supporting information (e.g., the child, parent(s)/guardian(s) and/or the accused individual's statements, behavior, psychological symptoms). Possible alternative explanations should have been considered. The evaluator should not suggest that mental health professionals have any special ability to detect whether an individual is telling the truth.
4. The evaluation may be inconclusive. If so, the evaluator should cite the information that causes continuing concern but does not enable confirmation or disconfirmation of abuse. If inconclusiveness is due to such problems as missing information or an untimely or poorly-conducted investigation, these obstacles should be clearly noted in the report.
5. Recommendations should be made regarding therapeutic or environmental interventions to address the child's emotional and behavioral functioning and to ensure the child's safety.

ACKNOWLEDGMENTS

These Guidelines are the product of APSAC's Task Force on the Psychosocial Evaluation of Suspected Sexual Abuse in Children, chaired by Lucy Berliner, M.S.W. The initial version was the result of a lengthy, iterative process. These revisions are the result of a similar process conducted in 1996. Appreciation goes to the many APSAC members who contributed their time and expertise to produce these Guidelines. The Guidelines will be updated periodically. Any comments or suggestions about them should be directed to Lucy Berliner through APSAC, 332 South Michigan Avenue, Suite 1600, Chicago, Illinois, 60604.

6-3 Appendix

Use of Anatomical Dolls in Child Sexual Abuse Assessments

I. Uses and Limitations of Guidelines

These Guidelines have been developed to reflect current knowledge and generally accepted practice concerning the use of anatomical dolls in interviewing children during assessments of suspected child sexual abuse. The Guidelines are offered to encourage appropriate use of anatomical dolls and to provide direction in the development of training for professionals. The Guidelines are not intended to establish a legal standard of care or a rigid standard of practice to which professionals are expected to adhere. Interviewers must have the flexibility to exercise judgment in individual cases. Laws and local customs may influence accepted methods in a given community. Professionals should be knowledgeable about various constraints on practice and prepared to justify their decisions about particular practices in specific cases. As experience and scientific knowledge expand, further revision of these Guidelines is expected.

These Guidelines apply to the use of anatomical dolls in investigative and diagnostic interviews of children in case of alleged or suspected child sexual abuse. Such interviews are designed to determine whether an allegation is likely true, and if so, the nature of the abuse. Investigative interviews are typically conducted by child protective services and law enforcement professionals and by child interview specialists in specialized child abuse programs. Diagnostic interviews are typically conducted by mental health or health care professionals as a part of psychological or medical evaluations (American Medical Association, 1985). Diagnostic interviews often go beyond the focus of investigative interviews in also assessing the child's psychological status and the possible need for psychological treatment.

These Guidelines are not designed to address the use of anatomical dolls in psychotherapy. Furthermore, these Guidelines do not address the broad issue of questioning techniques during investigative or diagnostic interviews. These Guidelines have the narrower purpose of providing direction on the use of dolls as an adjunct to the questioning process. It is also not the purpose of these Guidelines to provide a comprehensive discussion of the clinical and empirical rationale for the use of anatomical dolls in child sexual abuse assessments.[1]

II. INTRODUCTION

Anatomical dolls are widely used as interview aids by professionals involved in the investigation and evaluation of child sexual abuse (Boat & Everson, 1988a; Conte, Sorenson, Fogarty & Dalla Rosa, 1991; Kendall-Tackett & Watson, 1992). Nevertheless, concern has been expressed about possible harm through the use of anatomical dolls in this context. One concern is that anatomical dolls may suggest sexual material, encouraging false reports from non-abused children. Another is that the dolls may be overstimulating or even traumatizing to non-abused children by introducing them prematurely to sexual ideas and body parts. A final concern is that interviewers using the dolls may be poorly trained and overzealous in their search for sexual abuse, eliciting unreliable, if not erroneous, evidence of abuse.

Research does not support the concern that anatomical dolls are inherently too suggestive or sexually stimulating (Everson & Boat, 1994). Follow-up interviews of parents whose young children had

1. For such a discussion, the reader is referred to the final report of the American Psychological Association's Task Force on Anatomical Dolls (Keecher, G.P. *et al.* 1995).

previously been exposed to anatomical dolls do not support the concern that the dolls are traumatizing to non-abused children or may induce them to become preoccupied with sexual issues (Boat, Everson & Holland, 1990; Bruck, Ceci, Francoeur & Renick, 1995; Dawson, Vaughn & Wagner, 1992). Research suggests that the level of training among interviewers using the dolls has increased substantially over the last several years (Boat & Everson 1988a; Kendall-Tackett & Watson, 1992). The actual skill level of interviewers, however, has only recently become the focus of systematic study and empirical findings on this topic are still limited (Boat & Everson, 1995).

When used by a knowledgeable and experienced professional, anatomical dolls can be an effective tool to aid in interviewing children to determine (1) whether an allegation of sexual abuse is likely true, and (2) if so, the nature of the abuse. Anatomical dolls are, however, only one of many useful interview tools (e.g. drawing materials, puppets, anatomical drawings) and cannot take the place of sound, child-sensitive interview skills and reasoned clinical judgment. Professionals should be able to describe how the dolls were used in the particular case and how this use conforms to accepted practice (Myers & White, 1989). Professionals should also be familiar with current research on the dolls.

III. SUMMARY OF RESEARCH FINDINGS

A. SUGGESTIBILITY

1. The majority of available research does not support the position that the dolls are inherently too suggestive and overly stimulating to be useful in sexual abuse investigations and evaluations (see review by Everson & Boat, 1994; Everson & Boat, 1990). Specifically, there is little empirical evidence that exposure to the dolls induces non-abused, sexually naive children to have sexual fantasies and to engage in sex play that is likely to be misinterpreted as evidence of sexual abuse.
2. Although analogue studies of children's memory and suggestibility find children four and younger more suggestible than older ones (see review by Ceci & Bruck, 1993), anatomical dolls have not generally been found to be a significant source of increased suggestibility and recall error. Three studies using anatomical dolls as interview aids with children in the 3- to 7-year old range have found that the dolls increased recall accuracy with little or no increase in false reports of genital touching (Katz, Schonfeld, Carter, Leven-

thal & Cicchetti, 1995; Saywitz, Goodman, Nicholas & Moan, 1991; Steward & Steward, in press). In contrast, one study reported high rates of false assertions and false denials of genital touching among children under age 3-1/2 years when the dolls were used as interview aids in conjunction with direct, leading and misleading questions (Bruck et al, 1995).

B. INTERPRETING BEHAVIOR WITH DOLLS

Young children suspected or known to be sexually abused are statistically more likely than presumably non-abused children to engage in explicit sexualized interactions with dolls. However, many victims of sexual abuse do not display such behavior, and some non-abused children may display such behavior (White, Strom, Santilli & Halpin, 1986; Jampole & Weber, 1987; August & Forman, 1989). Following are empirical findings that provide some guidance for interpreting sexual behavior with the dolls:

Explicit sexual positioning of dolls (e.g., penile insertion in vaginal, oral, and anal openings) is uncommon among non-referred, presumably non-abused young children (see review by Everson & Boat, 1990). When allowed to manipulate the dolls, especially in the absence of adults, a small percentage of presumably non-abused children demonstrate explicit sexual intercourse between dolls or, more rarely, attempt to enact apparent sexual acts between themselves and a doll. Such behavior with the dolls appears to be related to prior sexual exposure (Glaser & Collins, 1989; Everson & Boat, 1990) and to age, gender, socioeconomic status, and possibly race, with four- and five-year-old boys from lower socioeconomic status families somewhat more likely to enact explicit sexual acts with dolls than younger children, girls, or children from higher socioeconomic status families (Boat & Everson, 1994; Everson & Boat, 1990). Therefore, while explicit demonstrations of sexual intercourse with anatomical dolls always deserve further exploration, such activities among younger children and children without known prior sexual exposure are of particular concern.

Among non-referred, presumably non-abused children, mouthing or sucking a doll's penis is very rare prior to about age four and infrequent after age four (Sivan, Schor, Koeppl & Noble, 1988; Glaser & Collins, 1989; Everson & Boat, 1990). This finding suggests that penises on dolls do not encourage most young children to seek oral gratification by sucking them. Sucking a doll's penis therefore should raise serious concerns about possible prior sexual exposure.

When a young child's positioning of the dolls indicates detailed knowledge of the mechanics of sexual acts, the probability of sexual abuse is increased, and further investigation of the source of the child's sexual knowledge is warranted. This is especially true for children under approximately four years of age and for children displaying knowledge of oral and anal intercourse (Everson & Boat, 1990).

Manual exploration of a doll's genitals, including inserting a finger in the doll's vaginal or anal openings, is fairly common behavior among young, presumably non-abused children (Boat & Everson, 1994; Glaser & Collins, 1989). Such behavior is likely to be more concerning if it is accompanied by distress reactions (e.g. anxiety, fear), behavioral regression, or displays of anger and aggression (Gordon, Schroeder, & Abrams, 1990a, 1990b), or by obsessive repetition (Terr, 1981).

C. THE EFFICACY OF ANATOMICAL DOLLS

1. When compared to reliance solely on verbal communication, the use of anatomical dolls has been shown to enhance children's ability to recall and describe events (Katz et al., 1995; Leventhal, Hamilton, Rekedal, Tebanao-Micci & Eyster, 1989; Saywitz et al., 1991; Steward & Steward, 1995). However, the dolls may not necessarily be superior to other interview aids such as anatomical drawings or regular dolls (Britton & O'Keefe, 1991; Goodman & Aman, 1990; Steward & Steward, in press). Additional research is needed, especially examining the various functions anatomical dolls can serve in the assessment process among children of different developmental levels.

IV. APPROPRIATE USES

A. No predetermined amount of time must expire before dolls are introduced, nor must a predetermined number or type of questions be asked before using dolls. Every child is unique and interviewers should use their judgment to determine when, and if, dolls may be useful.

B. If possible, the interviewer should be aware of the extent and nature of the child's possible prior exposure to anatomical dolls. This information is important for assessing the likely usefulness of the dolls in the current interview and for better understanding the child's reaction to and behavior with the dolls. Such information is especially important in cases in which children may have had multiple, prior doll interviews or may have been exposed to the dolls in a play therapy format in which fantasy play was encouraged.

C. The number of dolls presented (e.g., individual dolls vs. set of two, three, or four) depends upon their specific use in the interview.

D. When sexual abuse is suspected, dolls can be used as part of the assessment process in the following ways (Everson & Boat, 1994):

   1. Anatomical Model: The dolls can function as anatomical models for assessing a child's labels for parts of the body, understanding of bodily functions, and possible precocious knowledge of the mechanics of sexual acts. The interviewer may point to sexual and non-sexual body parts and ask questions like, "What do you call this part?," "What is it for?," and "Is it for anything else?"

      The dolls can also serve as visual aids for direct inquiries about the child's personal experiences with private parts. This may include questions such as, "Do you have one (vagina)?," "Has anything ever happened to yours?," and "Has it ever been hurt?"

      If the child uses a non-standard term, such as "kitty cat," to refer to a body part, the dolls can be used to clarify the child's meaning. It is appropriate to use the child's terms for body parts.

   2. Demonstration Aid: The dolls can serve as props to enable children to "show" rather than "tell" what happened, especially when limited verbal skills or emotional issues, such as fear of telling or embarrassment about discussing sexual activities, interfere with direct verbal description. This function of the dolls also includes their use to clarify a child's statement after a disclosure of abuse has been made. Whether or not a child experiences difficulty communicating about sexual abuse, dolls are sometimes useful to confirm an interviewer's understanding of a child's description of abuse and to reduce the likelihood of miscommunication between the child and the interviewer.

      Interviewers should be cautious in using anatomical dolls as demonstration aids with children under approximately age 3-1/2 years. This caution is based on questions about the cognitive ability of young preschoolers to use dolls to represent themselves in behavioral reenactments (DeLoache, 1995) and on concerns about the potential of the dolls to distract very young children (e.g., Goodman & Aman, 1990). These concerns do not preclude other uses of the dolls with young children. Furthermore, young children may use an anatomical doll to represent someone other than themselves and may, for example, demonstrate with a doll on their own bodies what they experienced.

3. Memory Stimulus: Exposure to the dolls, and especially to such features as secondary sexual characteristics, genitalia, and articles of clothing, may be useful in stimulating or triggering a child's recall of specific events of a sexual nature. Supporting this use is research suggesting that props and concrete cues may be more effective in prompting memories in young children than are verbal cues or questions (e.g., Nelson & Ross, 1980). To encourage recall, it may be appropriate for the interviewer to ask questions such as, "Have you seen one (penis)?" or "Do the dolls help you remember anything else that happened?"
4. Screening Tool: This function, which sometimes overlaps with the Memory Stimulus use, is based on the premise that exposure to the dolls in a non-threatening setting may provide an opportunity for the child to spontaneously reveal his/her sexual interests, concerns, or knowledge. Typically, the child is given the opportunity freely to examine and manipulate the dolls while the interviewer observes the child's play, reaction, and remarks. The interviewer can be either present or absent (observing through a one-way mirror) during this time, although children are likely to be less inhibited in their manipulations of the dolls without an adult present. After a period of uninterrupted manipulation and exploration of the dolls, the interviewer asks follow-up questions about the child's behavior with, or reaction to, the dolls (e.g., "What were the dolls doing?" "Where did you learn about that?"). Graphic sexual behavior, unusual emotional responses, as well as spontaneous "suspicious" statements made by the child (e.g. "Daddy's pee-pee gets big sometimes") should be the focus of follow-up questions to the child.

5. Icebreaker: The dolls can serve as a conversation starter on the topic of sexuality by focusing the child's attention in a non-threatening, non-leading manner on sexual issues and sexual body parts. This may be especially important in the case of younger children and children with less well developed language skills who may require very direct cueing to understand what, from the universe of possibilities, the interviewer wants the child to talk about (Steward & Steward, in press). Dolls can also be useful in helping a child feel comfortable about talking about body parts, sexuality, etc., and in conveying tacit permission for the child to describe or demonstrate sexual knowledge and experience.

D. Sexually abused children are not always able to give a coherent verbal account of sexual abuse for a variety of reasons, including developmental level, language limitations, fear, embarrassment, and guilt. When a child's characteristics allow it, however, interviewers should generally attempt to obtain a verbal description from the child before asking the child to demonstrate with the dolls.

E. Generally accepted practice is to present the dolls clothed, but exceptions exist. For example, it may be appropriate to present the dolls unclothed when they are being used as a demonstration aid with a child who has already indicated that the individuals in his/her account were naked.

F. Depending upon individual child characteristics, anatomical dolls can be appropriately used in interviews with children from a wide age range, including with some adolescents. Some uses, however, such as screening tool and icebreaker, are less common among older children (Boat & Everson, 1995; Kendall-Tackett & Watson, 1992).

V. INAPPROPRIATE USES

A. The use of anatomical dolls as a diagnostic test for child sexual abuse is not supported by the empirical evidence (Everson & Boat, 1994). Specifically, it is not appropriate to draw definitive conclusions about the likelihood of abuse based solely upon interpretations of a child's behavior with the dolls. There is no known behavior with the dolls that can be considered a definitive marker of sexual abuse in the absence of other factors, such as the child's verbal account or medical evidence (Everson & Boat, 1990; Realmuto, Jensen & Wescoe, 1990; Boat & Everson, 1994).

B. Interviewers should refrain from making statements that might encourage the child to view the dolls as toys or objects for fantasy play. This includes the use of words such as "play," "pretend," or "make believe." Interviewers should also be cautious in the use of conjecture in questioning with the dolls because of the possibility of encouraging fantasy (e.g., "If someone were to touch a girl in a way she didn't like, show me how they would do it."). The interviewer should consider giving the child the clear admonition that the dolls are used to help talk about and show "things that really happened."

C. The practice of the interviewer placing the dolls in sexually explicit positions and asking the child to relate the depiction to the child's experience (e.g., "Did this ever happen to you?") is leading and should be avoided.

D. Like any interview tool or technique, anatomical dolls can be misused. For example, dolls can be used in conjunction with inappropriately suggestive questions. Interviewers should monitor themselves to avoid improperly suggestive use of dolls (White & Quinn, 1988; Quinn, White & Santilli, 1989).

VI. DOLL SPECIFICATIONS

A. The utility of dolls in the interview process depends in large measure on the presence of certain physical features of the dolls. The following are considered to be important features:

1. Genitalia and breasts that are proportional to body size and appropriate to the gender and age of the given doll.
2. Oral, vaginal, and anal openings that will accommodate the adult male doll's penis.
3. Facial expressions that are at least reasonably attractive and devoid of negative emotions, such as fear or anxiety.
4. A size that can reasonably be manipulated by young children.
5. Sturdy construction that can withstand rough handling.
6. Clothes that can be easily removed.
7. Clothes, including underwear, that are appropriate to the doll's represented age and gender.

B. The impact of the racial features and skin color of the dolls on the child's response has not been empirically examined. Preferred practice is to match the dolls with the race of the child. If it is likely that the alleged perpetrator is a different race from the child, the interviewer should consider presenting dolls of both races or a set of race non-specific dolls with neutral skin tones.

VII. TRAINING AND SKILL LEVEL OF INTERVIEWERS

A. Professionals using dolls should possess the training and/or knowledge and experience required to conduct forensic investigative or diagnostic interviews with children suspected of having been sexually abused. Refer to the APSAC Guidelines for Psychosocial Evaluation of Suspected Sexual Abuse in Young Children for general requirements regarding training, skill level, and supervision for interviewers.

B. Before using the dolls, the interviewer should acquire the requisite skills through familiarity with the research literature and applicable guidelines, consultation with colleagues, and/or clinical supervision. The interviewer should be familiar with developmental issues in the use of the dolls, appropriate and inappropriate uses of the dolls, and potential problems caused by using leading questions or other suggestive techniques with the dolls.

C. A formal, structured protocol detailing the use of dolls in interviews is not required and, given the state of our knowledge and the need for flexibility in individual cases, rigid protocols are probably not advisable. However, these guidelines and other general guidelines on the use of anatomical dolls in sexual abuse evaluations are available and may be helpful (e.g., Boat and Everson, 1986, 1988b; Levy, Kalinowski, Markovic, Pittman & Ahart, 1991; Morgan, 1995; White, 1991).

VIII. DOCUMENTATION

A. Detailed documentation of the interview process should be provided. Because of the potential subtlety and richness of the child's behavior with anatomical dolls, videotape recording of the interview may offer advantages. If videotaping is impracticable or contraindicated, the interviewer's questions and the child's verbal, non-verbal, and affective responses regarding sexual abuse allegations or concerns should be documented. This can be done in writing or using a combination of audiotape and written notes.

B. It is desirable to prepare a verbatim record of all portions of the interview specifically relating to the issue of possible sexual abuse. This includes a description of the child's behavior with dolls, including the child's positioning of the dolls, critical verbal statements, and any verbal, non-verbal, or affective behavior with the dolls, such as avoidance, anxiety, fear, anger, or regression.

IX. CONCLUSIONS

A. Anatomical dolls are a useful and accepted tool for investigative and diagnostic interviews of children in cases of possible sexual abuse.

B. Professionals using anatomical dolls in child sexual abuse assessments should be knowledgeable and experienced in conducting forensically sound interviews with children and in the specific use of anatomical dolls.

C. Interviewers should be prepared to describe how they used anatomical dolls in each specific case and how this use conforms to accepted practice.

D. Interviewers should be aware of the limitations in the use of anatomical dolls. Specifically, anatomical dolls should not be considered to be a diagnostic test of sexual abuse, nor be overemphasized in the assessment process to the exclusion of broader interview techniques and sound clinical reasoning.

REFERENCES

American Medical Association (1985). AMA diagnostic and treatment guidelines concerning child abuse and neglect. *Journal of the American Medical Association, 254*, 796-803.

American Professional Society on the Abuse of Children (1990). Guidelines for psychosocial evaluation of suspected sexual abuse in young children. Chicago: Author.

August, R. L. & Forman, B. D. (1989). A comparison of sexually and nonsexually abused children's behavioral responses to anatomically correct dolls. *Child Psychiatry and Human Development, 20*, 39-47.

Boat, B. W. & Everson, M. D. (1995). Interview errors in the use of anatomical dolls in child protective services investigations. Paper presented at the Biennial Conference of the Society for Research in Child Development. April.

Boat, B. W. & Everson, M. D. (1994). Anatomical doll exploration among nonreferred children: Comparisons by age, gender, race, and socioeconomic status, *Child Abuse and Neglect, 18*, 139-153.

Boat, B. W. & Everson, M. D. (1988a). Use of anatomical dolls among professionals in sexual abuse evaluations. *Child Abuse and Neglect, 12*, 171-179.

Boat, B. W. & Everson, M. D. (1988b). Interviewing young children with anatomical dolls. *Child Welfare, 67*, 337-351.

Boat, B. W. & Everson, M. D. (1986). Using anatomical dolls: Guidelines for interviewing young children in sexual abuse investigations. Chapel Hill, NC: University of North Carolina.

Britton, H. & O'Keefe, W. A. (1991). Use of anatomical dolls in the sexual abuse interview. *Child Abuse and Neglect, 15*, 567-573.

Bruck, M.; Ceci, S.; Francoeur, D.; & Renick, A. (1995). Anatomical detailed dolls do not facilitate preschoolers' reports of a pediatric examination involving genital touching. *Journal of Experimental Psychology: Applied, 1*, 95-109.

Ceci, S. J. & Bruck, M. (1993). Suggestibility of the child witness: A historical review and synthesis. *Psychological Bulletin*, 113, 403-439.

Conte, J. R.; Sorenson, E.; Fogarty, L.; & Dalla Rosa, J. (1991). Evaluating children's reports of sexual abuse: Results from a survey of professionals. *American Journal of Orthopsychiatry, 61*, 3:428-437.

DeLoache, J. (1995). The use of dolls in interviewing young children. In Zaragoza, M. S., Graham, J. R., Hall, G. H., Hirschman, R. & Ben-Porath, Y.S. (eds.). *Memory and testimony in the child witness*. Newbury Park, CA: Sage Publications.

Everson, M. D. & Boat, B. W. (1990). Sexualized doll play among young children: Implications for the use of anatomical dolls in sexual abuse evaluations. *Journal of the American Academy of Child & Adolescent Psychiatry, 29*, 736-742.

Everson, M. D. & Boat, B. W. (1994). Putting the anatomical dolls controversy in perspective: An examination of the major uses and criticisms of the dolls in child sexual abuse evaluations. *Child Abuse and Neglect, 18*, 113-129.

Glaser, D. & Collins, C. (1989). The response of young, non-sexually abused children to anatomically correct dolls. *Journal of Child Psychology & Psychiatry, 30*, 547-560.

Goodman, G. & Aman, C. (1990). Children's use of anatomically correct dolls to report an event. *Child Development, 61*, 1859-1871.

Gordon, B. N.; Schroeder, C.; & Abrams, J. M. (1990a). Children's knowledge of sexuality: A comparison of sexually abused and nonabused children. *American Journal of Orthopsychiatry, 60*, 250-257.

Gordon, B. N.; Schroeder, C.; & Abrams, J. M. (1990b). Age and social class differences in children's knowledge of sexuality. *Journal of Clinical Child Physiology, 19*, 33-43.

Jampole, L. & Weber, M. K. (1987). An assessment of the behavior of sexually abused and non-sexually abused children with anatomically correct dolls. *Child Abuse and Neglect, 11*, 187-192.

Katz, S.; Schonfeld, D. J.; Carter, A. S.; Leventhal, J. M.; & Cicchetti, D. V. (1995). The accuracy of children's reports with anatomically correct dolls. *Developmental and Behavioral Pediatrics, 16(2)*, 71-76.

Kendall-Tackett, K. A. & Watson, M. W. (1992). Use of anatomical dolls by Boston-area professionals. *Child Abuse and Neglect, 16*, 423-428.

Koocher, G. P.; Goodman, G. S.; White, S.; Friedrich, W. N.; Sivan, A. B.; & Reynolds, C. R. (1995). Psychological science and the use of anatomically detailed dolls in child sexual abuse assessments. Final report of the American Psychological Association Anatomical Doll Task Force. *Psychological Bulletin, 118*, 2.

Leventhal, J. M.; Hamilton, J.; Rekedal, S.; Tebano-Micci, A.; & Eyster, C. (1989). Anatomically correct dolls used in interviews of young children suspected of having been sexually abused. *Pediatrics, 84*, 900-906.

Levy, J.; Kalinowski, N.; Markovic, J.; Pittman, M.; & Ahart, S. (1991). Victim-sensitive interviewing in child sexual abuse. Chicago, IL: Mount Sinai Hospital Medical Center.

Morgan, M. (1995). *How to interview sexual abuse victims.* Newbury Park, CA: Sage Publications.

Myers, J. E. B. & White, S. (1989). Dolls in court? *The APSAC Advisor, 2(3)*, 5-6.

Nelson, K. & Ross, G. (1980). The generalities and specifics of long-term memory in infants and young children. In M. Perlmutter (ed.), *New directions for child development, 10, Children's memory*, 87-101. San Francisco: Jossey-Bass.

Realmuto, G. M.; Jensen, J. B.; & Wescoe, S. (1990). Specificity and sensitivity of sexually anatomically correct dolls in substantiating abuse: A pilot study. *Journal of the American Academy of Child and Adolescent Psychiatry, 29(5)*, 743-746.

Sivan, A.; Schor, D.; Koeppl, G. K.; & Noble, L. D. (1988). Interactions of normal children with anatomically correct dolls. *Child Abuse and Neglect, 12*, 295-304.

Steward, M. & Steward, D. (in press). Interviewing young children about body touch and handling. *Monograph Series for the Society for Research in Child Development.*

Terr, L. (1981). Forbidden games: Post-traumatic child's play. *Journal of the American Academy of Child Psychiatry, 20*, 740-759.

White, S. (1991). Using anatomically detailed dolls in interviewing preschoolers. In C. Schaefer, K. Gitlund, & D. Sandgrund (eds.). *Play diagnosis and assessment*, 317-330, New York: Wiley & Sons.

White, S. & Quinn, K. (1988). Investigatory independence in child sexual abuse evaluations: Conceptual considerations. *Bulletin of the American Academy of Psychiatry Law, 16*, 269-278.

White, S.; Strom, G.; Santilli, G.; & Halpin, B. (1986). Interviewing young children with anatomically correct dolls. *Child Abuse and Neglect, 19*, 519-529.

APPENDIX A: ADDITIONAL RESOURCES ON INTERVIEWING

American Professional Society on the Abuse of Children. (1990). *The APSAC Advisor, 3*, 2. (Special issue dedicated to child interviewing).

Faller, K. C. (1995). *APSAC Study Guide: Interviewing children suspected of having been sexually abused.* Newbury Park, CA: Sage Publications.

Faller, K. C., (1990). *Understanding child sexual maltreatment.* Newbury Park, CA: Sage Publications.

Garbarino, J. & Stott, F. M. (1990). *What children can tell us.* San Francisco: Jossey-Bass.

Jones, D. P. H. & McQuiston, M. (1985). *Interviewing the sexually abused child.* Denver: C. Henry Kempe National Center for the Prevention and Treatment of Child Abuse and Neglect.

MacFarlane, K. & Waterman, J. (1986) *Sexual abuse of young children.* New York: Guilford Press.

Myers, J. E. B. (1992). *Legal issues in child abuse and neglect practice.* Newbury Park, CA: Sage Publications.

Perry, N. W. & Wrightsman, L. S. (1991). *The child witness.* Newbury Park, CA: Sage Publications.

ACKNOWLEDGMENTS

These Guidelines are the product of APSAC's Task Force on the Use of Anatomical Dolls in Child Sexual Abuse Assessments chaired by Mark D. Everson, Ph.D., John E. B. Myers, J.D., and Sue White, Ph.D. The first draft was published for comment in *The APSAC Advisor* in Spring, 1993. In addition, four open Task Force meetings were held to request input on early drafts of the Guidelines: at the San Diego Conference on Responding to Child Maltreatment in January 1993; at the First National APSAC Colloquium in Chicago, June 1993; at the Second National APSAC Colloquium in Cambridge, Massachusetts, May 1994; and at the San Diego Conference on Responding to Child Maltreatment in January, 1995. The current version of the Guidelines reflects the experience and expertise of a large number of APSAC members as well as the APSAC Board of Directors. We gratefully acknowledge the many individuals who contributed their time and expertise to make these Guidelines possible and especially to Kathleen Coulborn Faller, Ph.D., A.C.S.W.

These Guidelines will be updated periodically. Any comments or suggestions should be directed to Mark D. Everson, Ph.D. through APSAC, 407 South Dearborn, Suite 1300, Chicago, IL 60605.

Medical and Physical Evaluations of Sexual Abuse Allegations

7

Introduction

In many sexual abuse cases there are medical examinations or requests for such examinations. It is important to understand the value and limitations of such examinations. For example, where the allegations concern forms of sexual abuse not expected to leave physical findings, it may be unduly traumatic to require the child to submit to a potentially embarrassing physical examination. Similarly, requests for physical examinations long after the alleged abusive acts may be unlikely to yield meaningful information. Where there is a history of sexual assault within the past seventy-two hours or symptoms of genital discharge, bleeding, or pain, a physical examination may be warranted.[1] In determin-

1. *See, e.g.*, S. Jean Emans, *Physical Examination of the Child and Adolescent*, in EVALUATION OF THE SEXUALLY ABUSED CHILD: A MEDICAL TEXTBOOK AND PHOTOGRAPHIC ATLAS 40 (Astrid Heger & S. Jean Emans, eds., 1992); Carole Jenny, *Forensic Examination: The Role of the Physician as "Medical Detective,"* in EVALUATION OF THE SEXUALLY ABUSED CHILD: A MEDICAL TEXTBOOK AND PHOTOGRAPHIC ATLAS 52 (Astrid Heger & S. Jean Emans, eds., 1992) (stating that while sperm may persist in the vagina for up to 17 days, and acid phosphatase has been recovered for up to 5 days, evidence is unlikely to be recovered after a few days; therefore, a reasonable compromise is to perform a forensic examination if the patient is seen within 72 hours of the assault).

ing whether or not to request or agree to such an examination, the realistic possibility of obtaining useful information must be weighed against the effect on the child of the examination itself.

NEGATIVE PHYSICAL FINDINGS

It is important to understand that while the presence of physical (medical) evidence is probative of sexual abuse, negative findings *are not* probative. Positive physical findings are the exception with sexually abused children.[2] History is probably the most important criterion in diagnosing child sexual abuse.[3]

It is not uncommon for sexually abused children to have normal physical examinations, including normal genital examinations.[4] Because the vagina is very vascular, injuries heal quickly, often without leaving behind any medical evidence, even under magnification,[5]

---

2. *See, e.g.*, Jan Bays & David Chadwick, *Medical Diagnosis of the Sexually Abused Child*, 17/1 CHILD ABUSE & NEGLECT 91 (1993).

3. *See, e.g.*, Elizabeth A. W. Seagull, *Family Assessment* in THE BATTERED CHILD 150, 156 (Mary Edna Helfer, Ruth S. Kempe & Richard D. Krugman, eds., 5th ed. 1997); C. Levitt, *The Medical Examination in Child Sexual Abuse: A Balance Between History and Exam*, 1/4 J. CHILD SEXUAL ABUSE 113 (1992); J. Adams, *Significance of Medical Findings in Suspected Sexual Abuse: Moving Towards Consensus*, 1/3 J. CHILD SEXUAL ABUSE 91 at 97 (1992); D. Chadwick, *Commentary: The Medical Examination in Child Sexual Abuse: A Balance Between History and Exam*, 1/4 J. CHILD SEXUAL ABUSE 123 (1992); D. Runyan, *Commentary: The Medical Examination in Child Sexual Abuse: A Balance Between History and Exam*, 1/4 J. CHILD SEXUAL ABUSE 127 (1992); A. DeJong & M. Rose, *Legal Proof of Child Sexual Abuse in Girls Under Thirteen*, 88 PEDIATRICS 506 (1991); David Muram, *Child Sexual Abuse: Relationship Between Sexual Acts and Genital Findings*, 13 CHILD ABUSE & NEGLECT 211 (1989); J. Myers, *Role of the Physician in Preserving Verbal Evidence of Child Abuse*, 109 J. PEDIATRICS 409 (1986).

4. *See, e.g.*, CAROLE JENNY, MEDICAL EVALUATION OF PHYSICALLY AND SEXUALLY ABUSED CHILDREN 77 (1996); C. Levitt, *The Medical Examination in Child Sexual Abuse: A Balance Between History and Exam*, 1/4 J. CHILD SEXUAL ABUSE 113 at 114 (1992); J. Adams, *Significance of Medical Findings in Suspected Sexual Abuse: Moving Towards Consensus*, 1/3 J. CHILD SEXUAL ABUSE 91 at 95-98 (1992); American Academy of Pediatrics, Committee on Child Abuse and Neglect, *Guidelines for the Evaluation of Sexual Abuse of Children*, 87 PEDIATRICS 254 (1991) [reprinted in app 7-1]; A. DeJong & M. Rose, *Legal Proof of Child Sexual Abuse in the Absence of Physical Findings*, 88 PEDIATRICS 506 (1991); David Muram, *Child Sexual Abuse: Relationship Between Sexual Acts and Genital Findings*, 12 CHILD ABUSE & NEGLECT 211 (1989); DAVID CHADWICK, CAROL BERKOWITZ, D. KERNS, JOHN MCCANN, M. REINHART & S. STRICKLAND, COLOR ATLAS OF CHILD SEXUAL ABUSE 80 (1989).

5. *See, e.g.*, Michael E. Lamb, *The Investigation of Child Sexual Abuse: An International, Interdisciplinary Consensus Statement*, 28/1 FAM. L. Q. 151, 158-159 (1994) (bleeding or redness from hymenal tears usually disappears within 48 hours; the tears heal within 5 to 10 days; the sharp edges of the wounds smooth out and round off over a period of 3 to 6 months; over time the injuries may be difficult, if not impossible, to detect; perianal injuries also heal rapidly, leaving little evidence of previous tissue damage) (this statement is reproduced in its entirety in Appendix 1-1); J. Adams, *Significance of Medical Findings in Suspected Sexual Abuse: Moving Towards Consensus*, 1/3 J. CHILD SEXUAL ABUSE 91 at 97 (1992); John McCann, J. Voris & M. Simon, *Genital Injuries Resulting from Sexual Abuse: A Longitudinal Study*, 89 PEDIATRICS 307 (1989). *Cf.* Martin A. Finkel, *Anogenital Trauma in Sexually Abused Children*, 84 PEDIATRICS 317 (1989) (signs of past abuse may be masked by changes that occur during child's normal sexual development).

and even anal tears from violent abuse can heal completely, without leaving any residual scarring.[6] Therefore, negative medical findings may not be inconsistent with a history of trauma that is not very recent. Pediatrician Jean Emans has written that reports of physical examinations should make this clear, stating:

> . . . when the finding is that of a "normal genital examination," the examiner should note that this "does not rule out a prior history of sexual abuse." A report of nonspecific findings, such as erythema, vaginal discharge, or labial fusion, should note that these are abnormalities that may occur in a number of conditions, including sexual abuse.[7]

Most acts of child molestation would not be expected to leave evidence: fondling, oral-genital contact, digital penetration, exhibitionism, and nude photography. Many children are not injured in any way during the molestation. Young children might not have any sense that the contact is "wrong," and would not be expected, therefore, to exhibit signs of psychological trauma from the abuse. The lawyer must keep in mind the entire context of the molestation and make sure that expert testimony is presented that will focus the judge on what is really relevant information.

POSITIVE PHYSICAL FINDINGS

Positive findings, when they occur, can be powerful evidence of sexual abuse. Some findings in children, including absent hymen, lacerated hymen, notching in the posterior half of the hymen, and scarring, have been considered to be diagnostic of penetrating vaginal injury.[8] However, there are a variety of conditions that can mimic

---

6. *See, e.g.*, David Muram, *Anal and Perianal Abnormalities in Prepubertal Victims of Sexual Abuse*, 1619 AM. J. OBSTETRICS & GYNECOLOGY 278 (1989).

7. *See* S. Jean Emans, *Physical Examination of the Child and Adolescent*, in EVALUATION OF THE SEXUALLY ABUSED CHILD: A MEDICAL TEXTBOOK AND PHOTOGRAPHIC ATLAS 49 (Astrid Heger & S. Jean Emans, eds., 1992).

8. *See, e.g.*, D. L. Kerns, M. L. Ritter & R. G. Thomas, *Concave Hymenal Variations in Suspected Child Sexual Abuse Victims*, 90 PEDIATRICS 458 (1992); S. J. Emans, E. R. Woods, N. T. Flagg & A. Freeman, *Genital Findings in Sexually Abused, Symptomatic, and Asymptomatic Girls*, 79 PEDIATRICS 778 (1987).

abuse,[9] so it is important for the physician performing the examination to rule out these other conditions.

There is sometimes medical evidence of vaginal or anal penetration in a child. Very recent traumatic penetration may be revealed by lacerations or bruising. Because the hymen is an elastic tissue, it is possible for there to have been penetration without tearing the hymen or leaving an enlarged opening.[10] There has been some discussion in the medical literature concerning the significance of the size of the hymenal opening in a girl examined for sexual abuse. Differences in degree of the child's relaxation and in the techniques of examination among physicians may be significant, making it difficult to get an accurate size of the hymenal opening. It has been suggested that the only reliable findings are those based on an examination with the child fully relaxed and with the hymenal opening completely open.[11] A number of articles and books have discussed what range of sizes is normal.[12] However, most experts in the field now believe that the size of hymenal opening is not diagnostic of abuse, but rather, must be evaluated in relation to other findings.[13]

---

9. *See, e.g.*, Jan Bays & Carole Jenny, *Genital and Anal Conditions Confused with Child Sexual Abuse*, 144 AM. J. DISEASES OF CHILDREN 1319 (1990); John McCann, R. Wells, M. Simon & J. Voris, *Genital Findings in Prepubertal Girls Selected for Nonabuse: A Descriptive Study*, 86 PEDIATRICS 428 (1990); J.A. Adams & M. Horton, *Is it Sexual Abuse? Confusion Caused by a Congenital Anomaly of the Genitalia*, 28 CLINICAL PEDIATRICS 146 (1989); John McCann, J. Voris & M. Simon, *Labial Adhesions and Posterior Fourchette Injuries in Childhood Sexual Abuse*, 142 AM. J. DISEASES OF CHILDREN 659 (1988).

10. *See, e.g.*, C. Levitt, *The Medical Examination in Child Sexual Abuse: A Balance Between History and Exam*, 1/4 J. CHILD SEXUAL ABUSE 113 at 116 (1992); J. Adams, *Significance of Medical Findings in Suspected Sexual Abuse: Moving Towards Consensus*, 1/3 J. CHILD SEXUAL ABUSE 91 (1992); A. Heger & S. Emans, *Introital Diameter as the Criterion for Sexual Abuse*, 85 PEDIATRICS 222 (1990).

11. *See*, C. Levitt, *The Medical Examination in Child Sexual Abuse: A Balance Between History and Exam*, 1/4 J. CHILD SEXUAL ABUSE 113 at 116 (1992).

12. *See, e.g.*, S. Jean Emans, *Physical Examination of the Child and Adolescent*, in EVALUATION OF THE SEXUALLY ABUSED CHILD: A MEDICAL TEXTBOOK AND PHOTOGRAPHIC ATLAS 44 (Astrid Heger & S. Jean Emans, eds., 1992); A. Berenson, A. H. Heger, J. M. Hayes, R. K. Bailey & S. J. Emans, *Appearance of the Hymen in Prepubertal Girls*, 89 PEDIATRICS 387 (1992); C. Levitt, *The Medical Examination in Child Sexual Abuse: A Balance Between History and Exam*, 1/4 J. CHILD SEXUAL ABUSE 113 at 116-117 (1992); A. Berenson, A. Heger & S. Andrews, *Appearance of the Hymen in Newborns*, 87 PEDIATRICS 458 (1991); John McCann, R. Wells, M. Simon & J. Voris, *Genital Findings in Prepubertal Girls Selected for Nonabuse: A Descriptive Study*, 86 PEDIATRICS 428 (1990); A. Heger & S. J. Emans, *Introital Diameter as the Criterion for Sexual Abuse*, 85 PEDIATRICS 222 (1990); DAVID CHADWICK, CAROL BERKOWITZ, D. KERNS, JOHN MCCANN, M. REINHART & S. STRICKLAND, COLOR ATLAS OF CHILD SEXUAL ABUSE 2 (1989); David Muram, *Child Sexual Abuse: Relationship Between Sexual Acts and Genital Findings*, 13 CHILD ABUSE & NEGLECT 211 (1989); Adams, Ahmand & Phillips, *Anogenital Findings and Hymenal Diameter in Children Referred for Sexual Abuse Examination*, 1 ADOLESCENT & PEDIATRIC GYNECOLOGY 123 (1988); H. B. Cantwell, *Update on Vaginal Inspection as it Relates to Child Sexual Abuse in Girls Under Thirteen*, 11/4 CHILD ABUSE & NEGLECT 545 (1987); H. B. Cantwell, *Vaginal Inspection as it Relates to Child Sexual Abuse in Girls Under Thirteen*, 7 CHILD ABUSE & NEGLECT 171 (1983).

13. *See, e.g.*, Susan K. Reichert, *Medical Evaluation of the Sexually Abused Child* in THE BATTERED CHILD (Mary Edna Helfer, Ruth S. Kempe & Richard D. Krugman, eds., 5th ed. 1997); CAROLE JENNY, MEDICAL EVALUATION OF PHYSICALLY AND SEXUALLY ABUSED CHILDREN 76 (1996); Martin A. Finkel & Allan R. DeJong, *Medical Findings in Child Sexual Abuse*, in CHILD ABUSE: MEDICAL DIAGNOSIS AND MANAGEMENT 185 (Robert M. Reece, ed. 1994); James A. Monteleone, John R. Brewer & Timothy J. Fete, *Physical Examination in Sexual Abuse*, in CHILD MALTREATMENT: A CLINICAL GUIDE AND REFERENCE 133 (Armand E. Brodeur & James A.

Medical findings that have been called suggestive of sexual abuse include abrasions, lacerations, swelling, and bruising (only if the abuse was very recent), a significantly enlarged hymenal opening, scarring or tearing of the hymen, absent hymenal tissue, scars, the presence of semen or sperm, bite marks, and the presence of sexually transmitted diseases.[14] A child who has been forcibly sexually abused may have grab mark bruises on the thighs. One physician has listed symptoms that may be diagnostic of penetration as follows:

> new or healed lacerations of the hymen, which are rarely caused by accidental penetration; chlamydia and gonorrhea, which have not been shown to be transmitted in vivo by non-human contact; absent or scarred hymens, hymens that have synechia that are not due to chronic infection; teeth marks; a proctoepisiotomy; and a horizontal hymenal diameter of two standard deviations above the norm for age. . . . [T]he presence of sperm in the vagina or vestibule is diagnostic of sexual abuse.[15]

Unexplained sexually transmitted diseases in children may form the basis for a finding of sexual abuse[16] and consequent state intervention.[17]

Montleone, eds. 1994); Allan R. DeJong, *Genital and Anal Trauma*, in CHILD ABUSE: A MEDICAL REFERENCE 231 (Stephen Ludwig & Allan E. Kornberg, eds. 1992); J. McCann, R. Wells, M. Simon & J. Voris, *Genital Findings in Prepubertal Girls Selected for Nonabuse: A Descriptive Study*, 85 PEDIATRICS 428 (1990).

14. *See, generally*, Deborah Stewart, *Sexually Transmitted Diseases*, in EVALUATION OF THE SEXUALLY ABUSED CHILD: A MEDICAL TEXTBOOK AND PHOTOGRAPHIC ATLAS 145 (Astrid Heger & S. Jean Emans, eds., 1992); C. Levitt, *The Medical Examination in Child Sexual Abuse: A Balance Between History and Exam*, 1/4 J. CHILD SEXUAL ABUSE 113 (1992); American Academy of Pediatrics, Committee on Child Abuse and Neglect, *Guidelines for the Evaluation of Sexual Abuse of Children*, 87 PEDIATRICS 254 (1991) (reprinted at Appendix 7-1); David Muram & S. Elias, *Child Sexual Abuse-Genital Tract Findings in Pre-pubertal Girls-II: Comparison of Colposcopic and Unaided Examinations*, 160 J. OBSTETRICS & GYNECOLOGY 333 (1989); DAVID CHADWICK, CAROL BERKOWITZ, D. KERNS, JOHN MCCANN, M. REINHART & S. STRICKLAND, COLOR ATLAS OF CHILD SEXUAL ABUSE ch. 4 (1989); John McCann, J. Voris & M. Simon, *Labial Adhesions and Posterior Fourchette Injuries in Childhood Sexual Abuse*, 142 AM. J. DIS. CHILD 659 (1988); J. Siedel, *Presentation and Evaluation of Sexual Misuse in the Emergency Department*, 2 PEDIATRIC EMERGENCY CARE 157 (1986); S.M. Sgroi, *Pediatric Gonorrhea and Child Sexual Abuse: The Venereal Disease Connection*, 9 SEX TRANSM. DIS. 154 (1982).

15. *See* Charles F. Johnson, *Use of an M.D.-Social Worker Team in the Evaluation of Child Sexual Abuse: A Response*, 2/2 J. CHILD SEXUAL ABUSE 99, 100 (1993).

16. *See generally* CAROLE JENNY, MEDICAL EVALUATION OF PHYSICALLY AND SEXUALLY ABUSED CHILDREN 89 (1996); *Sexually Transmitted Diseases*, 23 PEDIATRIC ANNALS 329 (Carole Jenny, issue ed.); M. Hammerschlag & S. Rawstron, *Sexually Transmitted Diseases*, in CHILD ABUSE: A MEDICAL REFERENCE 249-63 (S. Ludwig & A. Kornberg, eds. 1992); American Academy of Pediatrics, *Guidelines for the Evaluation of Sexual Abuse of Children*, 87 PEDIATRICS 254 (1991) (reprinted at Appendix 7-1); K. K. HOLMES, P. A. MARDH, P. E. SPARLING, P. J. WIESNER, W. CATES, Jr., S. M. LEMON & W. E. STAMM, SEXUALLY TRANSMITTED DISEASES (2d ed. 1990).

17. *See, e.g.*, *In re* Philip M., 82 N.Y.2d 238, 624 N.E.2d 168, 604 N.Y.S.2d 40 (1993) (unexplained presence of chlamydia in children established prima facie showing of sexual abuse; parents did not seek treatment or show how future injury could be prevented).

DIFFERENTIATING PHYSICAL FINDINGS NOT CAUSED BY ABUSE

Sometimes medical findings have causes other than abuse.[18] For example, children may sustain straddle injuries from falling on playground equipment or bicycle bars. The abrasions and bruises resulting from such accidental injuries, however, tend to appear on the more exposed, superficial parts of the body, with areas such as the hymen and vagina not receiving the blunt trauma.[19] Accidental penetrating injuries are much rarer.[20]

Infections may also create genital inflammations, rashes, and even bleeding.[21] Foreign objects in the vagina, such as pieces of toilet paper or feces, may cause vaginal discharge, which may be blood-tinged.[22] Passage of large, hard stools may result in fairly superficial, straight, and narrow anal fissures.[23] However, if the fissures are deep, irregular, extending beyond the rugal folds, or are accompanied by swelling, bleeding, or hematomas, there is some suspicion of an abusive etiology.[24]

COLPOSCOPY

A useful tool for a sexual abuse examination is the colposcope, which provides a greatly magnified and intensely lighted view during a genital examination.[25] Further, the colposcope provides the ability to document the findings photographically. There is now even a video colposcope available. Colposcopic photographs can show minute fis-

---

18. *See generally*, J. Adams, *Significance of Medical Findings in Suspected Sexual Abuse: Moving Towards Consensus*, 1/3 J. CHILD SEXUAL ABUSE 91 (1992); DAVID CHADWICK, CAROL BERKOWITZ, D. KERNS, JOHN MCCANN, M. REINHART & S. STRICKLAND, COLOR ATLAS OF CHILD SEXUAL ABUSE ch. 3 (1989). Adams, cited in this note, lists the following findings as nonspecific: irregular vascularity, erythema of the vestibule, labial adhesions, urethral dilatation with labial traction, friability of the posterior fourchette, hymenal septa, transverse measurements of the hymenal orifice over 5 mm, using labial separation (supine), and vaginal discharge. *Op. cit.* at 93.

19. *See, e.g.*, DAVID CHADWICK, CAROL BERKOWITZ, D. KERNS, JOHN MCCANN, M. REINHART & S. STRICKLAND, COLOR ATLAS OF CHILD SEXUAL ABUSE 57 (1989).

20. *Id.*

21. *See, e.g.*, DAVID CHADWICK, CAROL BERKOWITZ, D. KERNS, JOHN MCCANN, M. REINHART & S. STRICKLAND, COLOR ATLAS OF CHILD SEXUAL ABUSE 58-59 (1989) (listing vulvovaginitis, streptococcal perianal disease, diaper dermatitis, lichen sclerosis et atrophicus, and postinflammatory labial adhesions).

22. *Id.*

23. *Id.*

24. *Id.*

25. *See generally* John McCann, *Use of the Colposcope in Childhood Sexual Abuse Examinations*, 37 PEDIATRIC CLINIC, NORTH AMERICA 863 (1990); L.R. Ricci, *Medical Forensic Photography of the Sexually Abused Child*, 12/3 CHILD ABUSE & NEGLECT 305 (1988).

sures and scars.[26] Testimony based on colposcopic examinations is properly admissible.[27] It is important to make sure that a physician whose testimony is based on colposcopic examination is properly trained, however.[28] Not many pediatricians have extensive experience in interpreting findings to distinguish between normal variations, congenital abnormalities, and evidence of trauma.[29] If the physician is not properly experienced, it is better not to use colposcopic evidence.

PENILE PLETHYSMOGRAPHY

Some experts, often in the context of therapy groups for incarcerated sex offenders, use a penile plethysmograph, a device that measures arousal by measuring penile tumescence. It is used in treatment to determine what sexually arouses the offender and to measure decreases in arousal during the treatment process. Some experts have attempted to use the plethysmograph as a kind of genital polygraph to determine whether a person is a pedophile or whether a man has molested a particular child. However, there is no strong evidence to suggest that arousal is a good predictor of sexual acting out, and the penile plethysmograph has not been shown to accu-

---

26. *See, e.g.*, David Muram & S. Elias, *Child Sexual Abuse-Genital Tract Findings in Pre-pubertal Girls-II: Comparison of Colposcopic and Unaided Examinations*, 160 J. OBSTETRICS & GYNECOLOGY 333 (1989); B. A. Woodling, *The Use of the Colposcope in the Diagnosis of Sexual Abuse in the Pediatric Age Group*, 10 CHILD ABUSE & NEGLECT 111 (1986); W. R. Teixeira, *Hymenal Colposcopic Examination in Sexual Offenses*, 2 AM. J. FORENSIC MED PATHOLOGY 209 (1981). For a color atlas showing photographs taken with a colposcope, *see*, DAVID CHADWICK, CAROL BERKOWITZ, D. KERNS, JOHN MCCANN, M. REINHART & S. STRICKLAND, COLOR ATLAS OF CHILD SEXUAL ABUSE (1989).

27. *See, e.g.*, People v. Mendibles, 245 Cal. Rptr. 553, 199 Cal. App. 3d 1277 (1988); State v. Noltie, 786 P.2d 332 (Wash. Ct. App. 1990).

28. *See, e.g.*, C. Levitt, *The Medical Examination in Child Sexual Abuse: A Balance Between History and Exam*, 1/4 J. CHILD SEXUAL ABUSE 113 at 116 (1992).

29. *See, e.g.*, C. Levitt, *The Medical Examination in Child Sexual Abuse: A Balance Between History and Exam*, 1/4 J. CHILD SEXUAL ABUSE 113 (1992); D. Runyan, *Commentary: The Medical Examination in Child Sexual Abuse: A Balance Between History and Exam*, 1/4 J. CHILD SEXUAL ABUSE 127 at 131 (1992); J. Adams, *Significance of Medical Findings in Suspected Sexual Abuse: Moving Towards Consensus*, 1/3 J. CHILD SEXUAL ABUSE 91 at 92 (1992); J. Gardner, *Descriptive Study of Genital Variation in Healthy, Non-abused Premenarchal Girls*, 120 J. PEDIATRICS 251 (1992); N. Kellogg & J. Para, *Linea Vestibularis: A Previously Undescribed Normal Genital Structure in Female Neonates*, 87 PEDIATRICS 926 (1991); J. Paradise, *The Medical Evaluation of Sexually Abused Children*, 37 PEDIATRIC CLINICS OF NORTH AMERICA 839 (1990); DAVID CHADWICK, CAROL BERKOWITZ, D. KERNS, JOHN MCCANN, M. REINHART & S. STRICKLAND, COLOR ATLAS OF CHILD SEXUAL ABUSE chs. 2-4 (1989). Adams, cited in this note, lists the following findings as normal: periurethral bands, external hymenal ridges, longitudinal intravaginal ridges, clefts in the ventral 180° of hymenal ring (on or above the 9 o'clock–3 o'clock line in supine position), hymenal tags, hymenal bumps, hymenal cysts, and linea vestibularis. *Op. cit.* at 93.

rately discriminate between incestuous molesters and nonmolesters.[30] The American Professional Society on the Abuse of Children (APSAC) has circulated "Proposed Guidelines for Penile Plethysmography,"[31] in which psychologist Dr. Judith Becker states:

> Historically, the penile plethysmograph has been used in research settings and with individuals who admitted paraphilic behavior. Murphy and Barbaree (1988) note in their current extensive review of the use of the plethysmograph, "The currently available evidence on validity and reliability does not provide strong support for the use of this procedure with populations where there are questions regarding whether the individual has engaged in deviant behavior." That is, there is no evidence to support the use of erection measures as a means of determining guilt or innocence in an alleged sex crime. Therefore, *since reliability and validity have not been established to date with non-admitters, there is no empirical data to justify its use in diagnosis, or prediction of treatment outcome or recidivism. . . .*
>
> Especially problematic has been the appearance of penile plethysmography results in the courtroom setting. *The use of penile plethysmography results in the courtroom is strongly discouraged until the validity and reliability of its use in that setting have been established.* [Emphasis added].[32]

There is not yet any standardization in testing or interpretation of plethysmographic assessments, which further limits the usefulness of penile plethysmography as part of a forensic sexual-abuse evalua-

30. However, Prentky, Knight, and Lee recently have stated that plethysmographic assessment "has demonstrated an ability to discriminate between child molesters and comparison groups of nonmolesters, as well as among subgroups of child molesters defined by victim gender preference (same sex vs. opposite sex) and by relationship to victim (incest vs. nonincest)." Robert A. Prentky, Raymond A. Knight & Austin F. S. Lee, *Child Sexual Molestation: Research Issues* 2 (National Institute of Justice 1997) (footnote omitted). *See generally*, Martin L. Lalumiere & Grant T. Harris, *Common Questions Regarding the Use of Phallometric Testing with Sexual Offenders*, 10/3 SEXUAL ABUSE: A JOURNAL OF RESEARCH & TREATMENT 227 (1998). The July 1998 issue of the journal published by the Association for the Treatment of Sexual Abusers, SEXUAL ABUSE: A JOURNAL OF RESEARCH & TREATMENT (volume 10, number 3), has a number of articles dealing with penile plethysmography.

31. *See* 1 THE ADVISOR 7 (Aug. 1988).

32. Quoted in J. E. B. Myers, J. Bays, J. Becker, L. Berliner, D. Corwin & K. Saywitz, *Expert Testimony in Child Sexual Abuse Litigation*, 68 NEBRASKA L. REV. 134-135 n.593 (1989).

tion.[33] Courts have excluded evidence from penile plethysmography for lack of proof that such evidence is scientifically reliable.[34]

Researcher David Finkelhor has reported findings that in the examination of "the penile responses of a matched sample of sixteen incestuous and sixteen nonincestuous child offenders, they found "that incestuous child molesters have more appropriate sexual age preferences (adults) than those who are nonincestuous."[35] Finkelhor also reports that there is clear experimental evidence of heightened arousal to children among child molesters *except* for incest offenders.[36] Prentky, Knight, and Lee report that "exclusive incest offenders demonstrate far less sexual arousal in response to children than do extrafamilial child molesters."[37] Another problem with using plethysmography results is that some men give a "flat line" response, essentially showing no arousal to any sexual stimuli, including to erotic material most men would find stimulating. Such repressed responses do not provide any meaningful data.[38]

---

33. *See, e.g.* Richard J. Howes, *A Survey of Plethysmographic Assessment in North America*, 7/1 SEXUAL ABUSE: A J. OF RESEARCH AND TREATMENT 9 (1995).

34. *See, e.g.*, R.D. v. State, 706 So.2d 770 (Ala. Crim. App. 1997) (citing expert testimony that "a plethysmograph is an instrument we use basically to understand the arousal pattern of an individual. A plethysmograph is not an instrument for making judgment about what a person has done"); Garren v. State, 220 Ga. App. 66, 467 S.E.2d 365 (1996); State v. Spencer, 119 N.C. App. 662, 459 S.E.2d 812 (1995); United States v. Powers, 59 F.3d 1460 (4th Cir. 1995) (inadmissible under *Daubert* test); Gentry v. State, 213 Ga. App. 24, 443 S.E.2d 667 (1994); In the Interest of A.V., 849 S.W.2d 393 (Tex. App. 1993), *In re* Mark C., 7 Cal. App.4th 433, 8 Cal. Rptr. 2d 856 (1992); Cooke v. Naylor, 573 A.2d 376 (Me. 1990); Nelson v. Jones, 781 P.2d 964 (Alas. 1989), *cert. denied* 498 U.S. 810, 111 S.Ct. 44, 112 L.Ed.2d 20 (1990); Dutchess County Dept. of Social Services v. Mr. G., 534 N.Y.S.2d 64, 141 Misc.2d 641 (Fam. Ct., Dutchess Cty, 1988); People v. John W., 185 Cal. App.3d 801, 229 Cal. Rptr. 783 (1986). The court in *John W.* pointed out that "it is the proponent of the testimony who has the burden of showing the reliability of the new technique" and that despite the penile plethysmograph's wide use "in many diagnostic and treatment centers which involve sexual offenders . . . such a statement does not satisfy the 'general acceptance' standard. . . ." 229 Cal. Rptr. at 785. The court disallowed the entire report because of its reliance on plethysmography results.

35. *See, e.g.*, DAVID FINKELHOR, A SOURCEBOOK ON CHILD SEXUAL ABUSE at 102 (1986), quoting V. L. Quinsey, T. C. Chaplin & W. F. Carrigan, *Sexual Preferences Among Incestuous and Non-incestuous Child Molesters*, 10 BEHAVIOR THERAPY 562-565 (1979).

36. *Id.* at 93.

37. *See* Robert A. Prentky, Raymond A. Knight & Austin F. S. Lee, *Child Sexual Molestation: Research Issues* 2 (National Institute of Justice 1997).

38. *See generally*, Jan Looman, Jeffrey Abracen, Greg Maillet & R. Difazio, *Phallometric Nonresponding in Sexual Offenders*, 10/4 SEXUAL ABUSE: A JOURNAL OF RESEARCH & TREATMENT 325 (1998). *Cf.* Robin J. Wilson, *Psychophysiological Signs of Faking in the Phallometric Test*, 10/2 SEXUAL ABUSE: A JOURNAL OF RESEARCH & TREATMENT 113 (1998); Judith V. Becker & Vernon L. Quinsey, *Assessing Suspected Child Molesters*, 17/1 CHILD ABUSE & NEGLECT 169 (1993); V. Quinsey & D. Laws, *Validity of Physiological Measures of Pedophilic Sexual Arousal in a Sex Offender Population: A Critique of Hall, Proctor & Nelson*, 58 J. CONSULTING & CLINICAL PSYCHOLOGY 886 (1990); K. Freund, R. Watson & D. Rienzo, *Signs of Feigning in the Phallometric Test*, 26 BEHAV. RESEARCH & THERAPY 105 (1988).

EVALUATING THE EVALUATION

The lawyer should carefully investigate the evaluating physician's experience and training in the specific area of child sexual abuse. Pediatrician Astrid Heger has written:

> The diagnosis of sexual abuse is difficult for medical professionals because their training has traditionally been inadequate with regard to the recognition of sexual abuse or even the evaluation of normal genital anatomy. Pediatric and adolescent patients who present with behavioral changes are diagnosed as going through a "stage," and genital complaints are attributed to poor hygiene or type of underwear worn by the child. This general ignorance is then compounded by fear and an unwillingness to interact with the legal system.[39]

The most useful examinations are forensic examinations that are undertaken with the expectation that legally relevant evidence must be collected. Most physicians are not trained to do forensic examinations. Even physicians trained to do forensic rape examinations may not have particular expertise with child sexual abuse examinations. Therefore, it is important for the lawyer to understand who has done or will do the examination and whether that person has experience with forensic child sexual abuse examinations. Such examinations should proceed according to an established protocol.[40]

Some procedures differ if the sexual abuse victim is an adult or child. For instance, direct fluorescent antibody (DFA) and enzyme immunoassay (EAI) tests for sexually transmitted diseases are not recommended for use with children or adolescents.[41] Prepubertal children generally do not need an internal examination in the

39. *See* Astrid Heger, *Helping the Medical Professional Make the Diagnosis of Sexual Abuse*, in EVALUATION OF THE SEXUALLY ABUSED CHILD: A MEDICAL TEXTBOOK AND PHOTOGRAPHIC ATLAS 3 (Astrid Heger & S. Jean Emans, eds., 1992) (footnote omitted).

40. *See* CAROLE JENNY, MEDICAL EVALUATION OF PHYSICALLY AND SEXUALLY ABUSED CHILDREN 83 (1996); Carole Jenny, *Forensic Examination: The Role of the Physician as "Medical Detective,"* in EVALUATION OF THE SEXUALLY ABUSED CHILD: A MEDICAL TEXTBOOK AND PHOTOGRAPHIC ATLAS 51-61 (Astrid Heger & S. Jean Emans, eds., 1992). Several child sexual abuse protocols are reprinted in EVALUATION OF THE SEXUALLY ABUSED CHILD: A MEDICAL TEXTBOOK AND PHOTOGRAPHIC ATLAS appendices A-D (Astrid Heger & S. Jean Emans, eds., 1992).

41. *See, e.g.*, Deborah Stewart, *Sexually Transmitted Diseases*, in EVALUATION OF THE SEXUALLY ABUSED CHILD: A MEDICAL TEXTBOOK AND PHOTOGRAPHIC ATLAS 147-148 (Astrid Heger & S. Jean Emans, eds., 1992).

absence of upper-tract bleeding, a foreign body in the vagina, or vaginal pathology.[42] Some children will need to be sedated or anesthetized in order to tolerate a physical examination.[43]

Medical records contain differing degrees of detail. It is important to determine which entries in the record are objective descriptions of what the physician observed or the results of laboratory testing. Statements attributed to the child or third persons may be direct quotations or may be paraphrases. A paraphrase may actually reflect a misunderstanding of what was said, which may be crucial to an accurate assessment of the abuse allegations. Therefore, the lawyer should interview the author of the medical records in question to learn as much as possible about the context of the statements, whether the statements were direct quotations, how much time passed between the statement and its recording, and whether anybody else was present when the statement was made. Any person present should be interviewed individually.

CONCLUSION

Medical evaluations may or may not be useful to a court case. They may be forensically dangerous if conducted by physicians who are not experienced with child sexual abuse cases or with lawyers who do not understand the limitations of such evaluations. In almost all cases, the lawyer should consult an expert in child sexual abuse to review any medical evaluations and to prepare to meet or offer medical testimony. If other professionals, such as mental-health professionals or social workers, are basing their opinions in part on the medical evidence (or lack of evidence), it is also important to ensure that they properly understand it.

---

42. *See, e.g.*, A. S. Botash, *What the Office-Based Pediatricians Need to Know About Child Sexual Abuse*, 34 CONTEMPORARY PEDIATRICS 275 (1994).

43. *See, e.g.*, CAROLE JENNY, MEDICAL EVALUATION OF PHYSICALLY AND SEXUALLY ABUSED CHILDREN 75 (1996).

7-1 APPENDIX

AMERICAN ACADEMY OF PEDIATRICS, COMMITTEE ON CHILD ABUSE AND NEGLECT

GUIDELINES FOR THE EVALUATION OF SEXUAL ABUSE OF CHILDREN

There are few areas of pediatrics that have so rapidly expanded in clinical importance in recent years as sexual abuse of children. What Kempe referred to in 1977 as a "hidden pediatric problem"[1] is certainly less hidden. Recent incidence studies, while imperfect, suggest approximately 1% of children will experience some form of sexual abuse each year.[2] Children may be sexually abused either in intrafamilial or extrafamilial settings and are more frequently abused by males. Boys may be victimized nearly as often as girls. Adolescents are perpetrators in at least 20% of reported cases,[2] and women may be perpetrators, especially in day-care settings.[3] Pediatricians will encounter these cases in their practices and will be asked by parents and other professionals for their opinions. These guidelines are prepared for use by the primary care pediatrician. Pediatricians who "specialize" in the area of child abuse or child sexual abuse have generally developed their own protocols for their referral practices. In addition, specific American Academy of Pediatrics guidelines for the evaluation of rape of the adolescent are published and should be used for this age-group.[4]

Because a pediatrician has unique skills and a trusted relationship with patients and families, he or she will often be in a position to provide essential support and gain information not readily available to others involved in the investigative, evaluative, or treatment processes. By the same token, the pediatrician may feel inadequately prepared to perform a medical examination of a sexually abused child. The pediatrician should think about these issues when determining how best to utilize his or her skills while avoiding actions that may obstruct the collection of essential evidence. The pediatrician should know what resources are available in the community and should identify these in advance, including a consultant with special expertise in evaluating sexually abused children.

DEFINITION

Sexual abuse can be defined as the engaging of a child in sexual activities that the child cannot comprehend, for which the child is developmentally unprepared and cannot give informed consent, and/or that violate the social and legal taboos of society. The sexual activities may include all forms of oral-genital, genital, or anal contact by or to the child, or non-touching abuses, such as exhibitionism, voyeurism, or using the child in the production of pornography.[1] Sexual abuse includes a spectrum of activities ranging from violent rape to a gentle seduction.

Criminal statutes define and classify sexual abuse as misdemeanors or felonies, depending on whether varying degrees of penetration of body orifices occurred or whether physical or psychological force was used.

Sexual abuse can be differentiated from "sexual play" by assessing the frequency and coercive nature of the behavior and by determining whether there is developmental asymmetry among the participants. Thus, when young children are mutually looking at or touching each other's genitalia, and they are at the same developmental stage, no coercion is used, and there is no intrusion of the body, this should be considered normal (i.e., nonabusive) behavior. However, when a 6-year-old coercively tries to have anal intercourse with a 3-year-old, this is not normal behavior, and the health and child protective systems should respond to it whether or not it is legally considered an assault.

PRESENTATION

Sexually abused children will be seen by pediatricians in a variety of circumstances: (1) They may be brought in for a routine physical examination or for care of a medical illness, behavioral condition, or physical finding that would include child sexual abuse as part of the differential diagnosis. (2) They have been or are thought to have been sexually abused and are brought by a parent to the pediatrician for evaluation. (3) They are brought to the pediatrician by social service or law enforcement professionals for a "medical evaluation" as part of an investigation.

In the first instance, the diagnosis of sexual abuse and the protection of the child from further harm will depend on the pediatrician's willingness to consider abuse as a possibility. There are many ways sexual abuse can be present,[5] and because children who are sexually abused are generally coerced into secrecy, a high index of suspicion is required to recognize the problem. On the other hand, the presenting symptoms are often so general in nature (e.g., sleep disturbances, enuresis, encopresis, phobias) that caution must be exercised because these behaviors may be indicators of physical or emotional abuse or other nonabuse-related stressors. Among the more specific signs and symptoms of sexual abuse are rectal or genital pain, bleeding, or infection; sexually transmitted diseases; and developmentally precocious sexual behavior. Pediatricians evaluating children who have these signs and symptoms should at least consider the possibility of abuse and, therefore, should complete a report (see below).

Pediatricians who suspect sexual abuse as a possibility are urged to inform the parents of their concerns in a neutral and calm manner. It is critical to realize that the individual who brought the child to the pediatrician may have no knowledge of, or involvement in, the sexual abuse of the child. The physician may need to reinforce this point with office, clinic, or hospital staff. Children spend many hours in the care of people, other than the parents, who may be potential abusers. A complete history, including behavioral symptoms and associated signs of sexual abuse, should ensue. In some instances, the pediatrician may need to protect the child and, therefore, may delay informing the parent(s) until a report is made and an expedited interview with law enforcement and child protective services agencies can be conducted.

TAKING A HISTORY/INTERVIEWING THE CHILD

In many states, the suspicion of child sexual abuse as a possible diagnosis requires a report to the appropriate law enforcement or child protective services agency. All physicians should know what their state law requires and where and when to file a written report. The diagnosis of sexual abuse has both civil (protective) and criminal ramifications. Investigative interviews should be conducted by the designated agency or individual in the community to minimize repetitive questioning of the child. This does not preclude physicians asking relevant questions needed for a detailed pediatric history, including a review of systems. Occasionally children will spontaneously describe their abuse and indicate who it was who abused them. When asking 3- to 6-year-old children about abuse, the use of line drawings,[6] dolls,[7] or other aids[8] may be helpful. The American Academy of Child and Adolescent Psychiatry has guidelines for interviewing sexually abused children.[9] Children may also describe their abuse during the physical examination. It is desirable for those conducting the interview to use nonleading questions; avoid demonstrations of shock, disbelief, or other emotions; and maintain a "tell me more" or "and then what happened" approach. If possible, the child should be interviewed alone.

A behavioral review of systems may reveal events or behaviors relevant to sexual abuse, even in the absence of a clear history of abuse in the child.[5]The parent may be defensive or unwilling to accept the possibility of sexual abuse. This unwillingness is not of itself diagnostic, but it also does not negate the need for investigation.

In the second situation, where children are brought to physicians by parents who suspect abuse, the same behavioral history and approach is warranted.

In the third instance, when children are brought by protective personnel, little or no history may be available, other than that provided by the child. The pediatrician should try to obtain an appropriate history in all cases before performing a medical examination. The child may spontaneously give additional history during the physical examination as the mouth, genitalia, and anus are examined. When children are brought in by professionals, the history should focus on whether the symptoms are explained by sexual abuse, physical abuse to the genital area as a response to toileting accidents, or other medical conditions.

PHYSICAL EXAMINATION

The physical examination of sexually abused children should not lead to additional emotional trauma for the child. The examination should be explained to the child and conducted in the presence of a supportive adult not suspected of being party to the abuse. Many children are anxious about giving a history, being examined, or having procedures performed. Enough time must be allotted to relieve a child's anxiety.

When the alleged sexual abuse has occurred within 72 hours, and the child provides a history of sexual abuse including ejaculation, the examination should be performed immediately. In this acute situation, rape kit protocols modified for child sexual assault victims should be followed to maintain a "chain of evidence." Adult rape kits have been adapted and standardized in some states (Florida, Indiana). These are available in emergency rooms, rape treatment centers, or law enforcement agencies. When more than 72 hours has elapsed, the examination usually is not an emergency, and therefore, the evaluation should be scheduled at the earliest convenient time for the child, physician, and investigative team.

The child should have a thorough pediatric examination, including assessments of developmental, behavioral, and emotional status. Special attention should be paid to the growth parameters and sexual development of the child. In the rare instance when the child is unable to cooperate and the examination must be performed because of the likelihood of trauma, infection, and/or the need to collect forensic samples, consideration should be given to performing the examination with the child under general anesthesia. Instruments that can magnify and illuminate the genital and rectal areas may be used if available, but they are not required. Any signs of trauma should be carefully documented. Specific attention should be given to the areas involved in sexual activity—the mouth, breasts, genitals, perineal region, buttocks, and anus. Any abnormalities should be noted.

In female children, the genital examination should include inspection of the medical aspects of the thighs, labia majora and minora, clitoris, urethra, periurethral tissue, hymen, hymenal opening, fossa navicularis, and posterior fourchette. Findings that are consistent with, but not diagnostic of, sexual abuse include (1) chafing, abrasions, or bruising of the inner thighs and genitalia; (2) scarring, tears, or distortion of the hymen; (3) a decreased amount of or absent hymenal tissue; (4) scarring of the fossa navicularis; (5) injury to or scarring of the posterior fourchette; (6) scarring or tears of the labia minora; and (7) enlargement of the hymenal opening. The volume of published literature is expanding quickly in this area.[10-15]

Various methods for visualizing the hymenal opening in prepubertal children have been described. Published studies are not uniform in their approach. The degree of relaxation of the child; the degree of separation, traction (gentle, moderate) on the labia majora, and the position of the child (supine, lateral, knee-chest); and the time taken will all influence the size of the orifice and the exposure of the hymen and the internal structures.[16] The technique used is less important than maximizing the view and recording the method and results (see below for discussion of significance of findings). Invasive procedures (e.g., speculum or digital) are generally not necessary in the prepubertal child.

In male children, the thighs, penis, and scrotum should be examined for bruises, scars, chafing, bite marks, and discharge.

In both sexes, the anus can be examined in the supine, lateral, or knee-chest position. As with the vaginal examination, position may influence the anatomy. The presence of bruises around the anus, scars, anal tears (especially those that extend into the surrounding perianal skin), and anal dilation are important to note. Laxity of the sphincter, if present, should be noted, but digital examination is not always necessary. (See below for discussion of significance of findings.) Note the child's behavior and demeanor during the examination, and ask the child to demonstrate what, if anything, happened. Care should be taken not to suggest answers to questions.

LABORATORY DATA

In the examination occurring within 72 hours of acute sexual assault or sexual abuse with ejaculation, forensic studies should be performed. Routine cultures and screening of all sexually abused children for gonorrhea, syphilis, human immunodeficiency virus, or other sexually transmitted diseases are not recommended. The yield of positive cultures is very low in asymptomatic prepubertal children, especially those whose history indicates fondling only. When epidemiologically indicated, or when the history and/or physical findings suggest the possibility of oral, genital, or rectal contact, appropriate cultures and serologic tests should be obtained. The Centers for Disease Control and American Academy of Pediatrics Committee on Infectious Diseases also provide recommendations on laboratory evaluation.[17] [18] The implications of the diagnosis of a sexually transmitted disease for the reporting of child sexual abuse are listed in Table 1.

Pregnancy prevention guidelines have been published by the Committee on Adolescence,[4] and the American Academy of Pediatrics Task Force on Pediatric AIDS has developed guidelines for human immunodeficiency virus testing for assailants.

DIAGNOSTIC CONSIDERATIONS

The diagnosis of child sexual abuse is made on the basis of a child's history. Physical examination alone is infrequently diagnostic in the absence of a history and/or specific laboratory findings. The physician, the multidisciplinary team evaluating the child, and the courts must establish a level of certainty about whether a child has been sexually abused. Table 2 as prepared by the AAP Committee on Child Abuse and Neglect provides suggested guidelines for making the decision to report sexual abuse of children based on currently (November 1990) available information.

TABLE 1. Implications of Commonly Encountered Sexually Transmitted Diseases (STDs) for the Diagnosis and Reporting of Sexual Abuse of Prepubertal Infants and Children

STD Confirmed	Sexual Abuse	Suggested Action
Gonorrhea·	Certain	Report[†]
Syphilis·	Certain	Report
Chlamydia·	Probable[‡]	Report
Condylomata acuminatum·	Probable	Report
Trichomonas vaginalis	Probable	Report
Herpes 1 (genital)	Possible	Report[§]
Herpes 2	Probable	Report
Bacterial vaginosis	Uncertain	Medical follow-up
Candida albicans	Unlikely	Medical follow-up

· If not perinatally acquired.
† To agency mandated in community to receive reports of suspected sexual abuse.
‡ Culture only reliable diagnostic method.
§ Unless there is a clear history of autoinoculation.
Prepared by the American Academy of Pediatrics Committee on Child Abuse and Neglect (November 1990).

As indicated in Table 2, the presence of semen/sperm/acid phosphatase, a positive culture for gonorrhea, or a positive serologic test for syphilis makes the diagnosis of sexual abuse medical certainty, even in the absence of a positive history (congenital forms of gonorrhea and syphilis excluded).

Other physical signs or laboratory findings may be "suggestive of" or "consistent with" a child's history of sexual abuse. In the absence of a positive history, these findings are, at the least, worrisome or suspicious and require a complete history. If the history is negative, the physician may wish to observe the child closely to monitor changes in behavior or physical findings. If the history is positive, sexual abuse is more than worry, and a report should be made to the agency authorized to receive reports of sexual abuse.

The differential diagnosis of genital trauma also includes accidental injury and physical abuse. This differentiation may be difficult and may require a careful history and multidisciplinary approach. There are many congenital malformations and infectious or other causes of anal-genital abnormalities that may be confused with abuse. Familiarity with these is important.[19]

After the examination, the physician should provide appropriate feedback and reassurance to the child and family.

TABLE 2. Guidelines for Making the Decision to Report Sexual Abuse of Children

Data Available			Response	
History	**Physical**	**Laboratory**	**Level of Concern About Sexual Abuse**	**Action**
None	Normal examination	None	None	None
Behavioral changes	Normal examination	None	Low (worry)	Report*; follow closely (possible mental health referral)
None	Nonspecific findings	None	Low (worry)	Report*; follow closely
Nonspecific history by child or history by parent only	Nonspecific findings	None	Possible (suspect)	Report*; follow closely
None	Specific findings	None	Probable	Report
Clear statement	Normal examination	None	Probable	Report
Clear statement	Specific findings	None	Probable	Report
None	Normal examination, nonspecific or specific findings	Positive culture for gonorrhea; positive serologic test for syphilis; presence of semen, sperm, acid phosphatase	Definite	Report
Behavioral changes	Nonspecific changes	Other sexually transmitted diseases	Probable	Report

*A report may or may not be indicated. The decision to report should be based on discussion with local or regional experts and/or child protective services agencies.
Prepared by the American Academy of Pediatrics Committee on Child Abuse and Neglect (November 1990).

RECORDS

Because the likelihood of civil or criminal court action is high, detailed records, drawings, and/or photographs should be kept. The submission of written reports to county agencies and law enforcement departments is encouraged. The more detailed the reports and the more explicit the physician's opinion, the less likely the physician may need to testify in civil (juvenile) court proceedings. Testimony will be likely, however, in criminal court where records alone are not a substitute for personal appearance. In general, the ability to protect a child may often depend on the quality of the physician's records.[20]

TREATMENT

All children who have been sexually abused should be evaluated by competent mental health providers to assess the need for treatment. Unfortunately, treatment services for sexually abused children are not universally available. The need for treatment will vary with the type of sexual molestation (intrafamilial vs extra familial), the length of time the molestation has gone on, and the age and symptoms of the child. In general, the more intrusive the abuse, the more violent the assault, the longer the sexual molestation has occurred, and the closer the relationship of the perpetrator to the victim, the worse the prognosis and the greater the need for long-term treatment. Whether or not the parents are directly involved, the parents may also need treatment and support in order to cope with the emotional trauma of the child's abuse (as in the instance when the child has been the victim of extrafamilial molestation).

LEGAL ISSUES

The legal issues confronting pediatricians in evaluating sexually abused children include mandatory reporting with penalties for failure to report; involvement in the civil, juvenile, or family court systems; involvement in divorce/custody proceedings in divorce courts; and involvement in criminal prosecution of defendants in criminal court. In addition, there are medical liability risks for pediatricians.

All pediatricians in the United States are required under the laws of each state to report suspected as well as known cases of child sexual abuse. These guidelines do not suggest that a pediatrician who sees a child with an isolated behavioral finding (nightmares, enuresis, phobias, etc.) or an isolated physical finding (e.g., the hymenal diameter of 5 mm) must feel obliged to report these cases as suspicious. If additional historical, physical, or laboratory findings suggestive of sexual abuse are present, the physician may have an increased level of suspicion and then should report. Pediatricians are encouraged to discuss cases with their local or regional child abuse consultants as well as with their local child protective services agency. In this way, agencies may be protected from being overburdened with large numbers of vague reports, and physicians may be protected from potential prosecution for failure to report.

Civil courts in most states will intervene protectively if it is more likely than not that child abuse or neglect has occurred. The court should be acting in the best interest of the child to try to determine the safety of the child's environment and should be less concerned with "who did it" than with how recurrence can be prevented. These courts should order evaluations and/or treatment, appoint a guardian ad litem and/or therapist for the child, and monitor the family during a treatment plan.

Pediatricians and children are faced with increasing numbers of cases in which parents who are in the process of separation or divorce are alleging that one or the other (or both) is sexually abusing the child during custodial visits. These cases are generally more difficult for the pediatrician, the child protective services system, and law enforcement agencies. They require more time and should not be unsubstantiated or dismissed simply because a custody dispute exists. Allegations of abuse that occur in the context of divorce proceedings should be reported to the child protective services agency. A juvenile court proceeding may ensue to determine whether the child needs protection. The pediatrician should act as an advocate for the child in these situations and should encourage the appointment of a guardian ad litem by the court to represent the child's best interests. It should be noted that the American Bar Association indicates that the majority of divorces do not involve custody disputes, and relatively few custody disputes involve allegations of sexual abuse.[20]

In criminal proceedings, the standard of proof is the highest—"beyond a reasonable doubt" or "to a reasonable degree of medical certainty." For many physicians, this level of certainty may be a focus of concern because, in this setting, the pediatrician's testimony is part of the information used to ascertain the guilt or innocence of an alleged abuser. Physicians should be aware of the specificity of their findings and their diagnostic significance.[21]

Pediatricians may find themselves involved in civil malpractice litigation. The failure of a physician to recognize and diagnose sexual abuse in a timely manner may lead to liability suits if a child has been brought repeatedly to the physician and/or a flagrant case has been misdiagnosed. With approximately 50% of American children in some form of out-of-home care, the risk of sexual abuse outside the family is substantial (about half that of intrafamilial abuse)[3]and increases the importance of making the diagnosis in a timely manner. The possibility of a suit being filed for "false reports" by physicians exists. Statutes generally provide immunity as long as the report is done in good faith. We are unaware of any successful suits as of this writing.

Civil litigation suits may be filed by parents against institutions or individuals who may have sexually abused their children. The physician may be asked to testify in these cases. In the civil litigation cases, the standard of proof is "a preponderance of the evidence."

CONCLUSION

The evaluation of sexually abused children is increasingly a part of general pediatric practice. The pediatrician will be part of a multidisciplinary approach to the problem and will need to be competent in the basic skills of history taking, physical examination, selection of laboratory tests, and differential diagnosis. An expanding clinical consultation network is available to assist the primary care physician with the assessment of difficult cases.

COMMITTEE ON CHILD ABUSE AND NEGLECT, 1990-1991

Richard D. Krugman, M.D., Chairman
Judith Ann Bays, M.D.
David L. Chadwick, M.D.
Carolyn J. Levitt, M.D.
Margaret T. McHugh, M.D.
J. M. Whitworth, M.D.

Liaison Representatives
Thomas Halversen, M.D., American Academy of Child and Adolescent Psychiatry
Marshall D. Rosman, Ph.D., American Medical Association

Section Liaison
Robert H. Kirschner, M.D., Section on Pathology

REFERENCES

1. Kempe, C. H. Sexual abuse, another hidden pediatric problem: the 1977 C. Anderson Aldrich lecture. *Pediatrics*, 1978; 62:382-389.

2. *National Study on The Incidence of Child Abuse and Neglect.* Washington, D.C.: U.S. Dept. of Health and Human Services; 1988.

3. Finkelhor, D.; Williams, L. M. *Nursery Crimes: Sexual Abuse in Daycare.* Newbury Park, Calif.: Sage Publications; 1988.

4. American Academy of Pediatrics, Committee on Adolescence. Rape and the adolescent. *Pediatrics.* 1988; 81:595-597.

5. Krugman, R. D. Recognition of sexual abuse in children. *Pediatr Rev.* 1986; 8:25-30.

6. Hibbard, R. A.; Roghmann, K.; Hoekelman, R. A. Genitalia in children's drawings: an association with sexual abuse. *Pediatrics.* 1987; 79:129-137.

7. Boat, B. W.; Everson, M. D. *Using Anatomical Dolls: Guidelines for Interviewing Young Children in Sexual Abuse Investigations.* Chapel Hill, N.C.: Dept. of Psychiatry, University of North Carolina; 1986.

8. Jones, D. P. H.; McQuiston, M. *Interviewing the Sexually Abused Child.* 2nd ed. Denver CO: C. Henry Kempe National Center for the Prevention and Treatment of Child Abuse and Neglect; 1986.

9. Guidelines for the clinical evaluation of child and adolescent sexual abuse: position statement of the American Academy of Child and Adolescent Psychiatry. *J Am Acad Child Adolesc Psychiatry.* 1988; 27:655-657.

10. McCann, J.; Voris, J.; Simon, M.; Wells, R. Perianal findings in prepubertal children selected for nonabuse: a descriptive study. *Child Abuse Negl.* 1989; 13:179-193.

11. Muram, D. Child sexual abuse: relationship between sexual acts and genital findings. *Child Abuse Negl.* 1989; 13:211-216.

12. White, S. T.; Ingram, D. L.; Lyna, P. R.. Vaginal introital diameter in the evaluation of sexual abuse. *Child Abuse Negl.* 1989; 13:217-224.

13. Hobbs, C. H.; Wynne, J. M. Sexual abuse of English boys and girls: the importance of anal examination. *Child Abuse Negl.* 1989; 13:195-210.

14. Heger, A.; Emans, S. J. Introital diameter as the criterion for sexual abuse. *Pediatrics.* 1990; 85:222-223.

15. Krugman, R. D. The more we learn the less we know 'with reasonable medical certainty'? *Child Abuse Negl.* 1989; 13:165-166.

16. McCann, J.; Voris, J.; Simon, M.; Wells, R. Comparison of genital examination techniques in prepubertal girls. *Pediatrics.* 1990; 85:182-187.

17. Centers for Disease Control. 1989 sexually transmitted diseases treatment guidelines. *MMWR.* September 1, 1989; 38 (suppl S-8):1-43.

18. American Academy of Pediatrics, Committee on Infectious Diseases. Sexually transmitted diseases. In: *Report of the Committee on Infectious Diseases, 1988.* 21st ed. Elk Grove Village, IL: American Academy of Pediatrics; 1988:79-89.

19. Chadwick, D. L.; Berkowitz, C. A.; Kems, D. A., et al. *Color Atlas of Child Sexual Abuse.* Chicago, IL: Year Book Medical Publishers, Inc; 1989.

20. Nicholson, E. B.; Bulkley, J., eds. *Sexual Abuse Allegations in Custody and Visitation Cases: A Resource Book for Judges and Court Personnel.* Washington, DC: American Bar Association, National Legal Resource Center for Child Advocacy and Protection; 1988.

21. Paradise, J. E. Predictive accuracy and the diagnosis of sexual abuse: a big issue about a little tissue. *Child Abuse Negl.* 1989; 13:169-176.

7-2 APPENDIX

DESCRIPTIVE TERMINOLOGY IN CHILD SEXUAL ABUSE MEDICAL EVALUATIONS

INTRODUCTION

The forensic medical evaluation of suspected child sexual abuse victims has developed into a specialized field of practice in the last ten years. Pediatricians, gynecologists, nurse practitioners, and physician assistants may all be called upon to examine children for suspected sexual abuse and describe their findings. The records of such examinations then become medico-legal documents.

Precision in documentation is critical for all who must communicate and understand medical findings. These terminology Guidelines were developed to assist professionals actively involved in the medical diagnosis and treatment of child sexual abuse to establish a shared vocabulary which is clear, precise, and easily communicated. This shared vocabulary will enable those in child protection, law enforcement, and the courts to understand previously confusing and, at times, inconsistent terminology. Consistency in terminology will also assist in the development of a research language.

The terminology presented in these Guidelines emanates primarily from medical dictionary definitions, anatomy texts, and clinicians actively involved in the care of sexually abused children. Unless otherwise noted, definitions are from Stedman's, Ref. 1. As experience and scientific knowledge expand, further revision of these guidelines is expected.

ANATOMICAL STRUCTURES

1. ANAL SKIN TAG—A protrusion of anal verge tissue which interrupts the symmetry of the perianal skin folds.
2. ANAL VERGE—The tissue overlying the subcutaneous external anal sphincter at the most distal portion of the anal canal (anoderm) and extending exteriorly to the margin of the anal skin.
3. ANTERIOR COMMISSURE—The union of the two labia minora anteriorly (toward the clitoris).
4. ANUS—The anal orifice, which is the lower opening of the digestive tract, lying in the fold between the buttocks, through which feces are extruded (Ref. 9).
5. CLITORIS—A small cylindrical, erectile body situated at the anterior (superior) portion of the vulva, covered by a sheath of skin called the clitoral hood; homologous with the penis in the male (Ref. 9).
6. FOSSA NAVICULARIS/POSTERIOR FOSSA—Concavity on the lower part of the vestibule situated posteriorly (inferiorly) to the vaginal orifice and extending to the posterior fourchette (posterior commissure).
7. GLANS PENIS—The cap-shaped expansion of the corpus spongiosum at the end of the penis; also called balanus (Ref. 9). It is covered by a mucous membrane and sheathed by the prepuce (foreskin) in uncircumcised males (see Figure 1).
8. GENITALIA (External)—The external sexual organs. In males, includes the penis and scrotum (see Figure 1). In females, includes the contents of the vulva (see Figure 2).
9. HYMEN—This membrane (external vaginal plate or urogenital septum) partially or rarely completely covers the vaginal orifice. This membrane is located at the junction of the vestibular floor and the vaginal canal.
10. LABIA MAJORA—("outer lips") Rounded folds of skin forming the lateral boundaries of the vulva (see Figure 2).
11. LABIA MINORA—("inner lips") Longitudinal thin folds of tissue enclosed within the labia majora. In the pubertal child, these folds extend from the clitoral hood to approximately the mid point on the

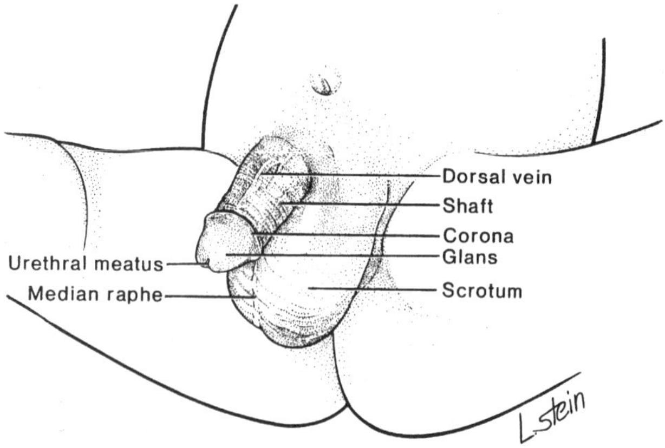

Figure 1 PREPUBERTAL MALE GENITALIA (CIRCUMCISED)

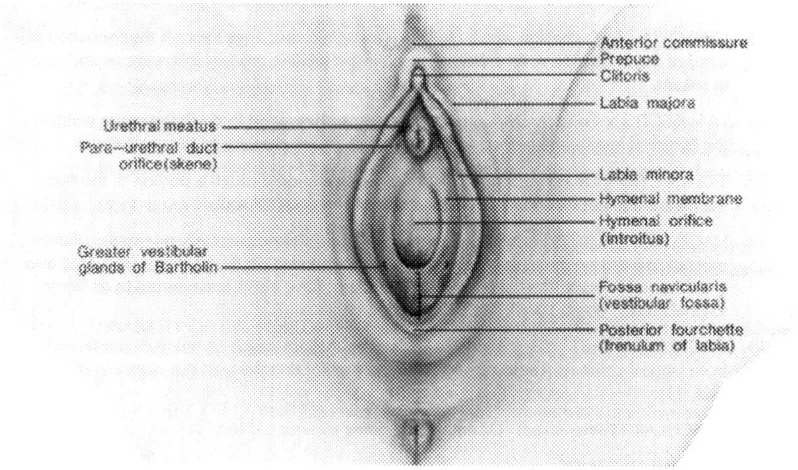

Figure 2 ANATOMIC STRUCTURES IN PREPUBERTAL GIRL

lateral wall of the vestibule. In the adult, they enclose the structures of the vestibule.

12. MEDIAN RAPHE—A ridge or furrow that marks the line of union of the two halves of the perineum (Ref. 9).
13. MONS PUBIS—The rounded, fleshy prominence, created by the underlying fat pad which lies over the symphysis pubis (pubic bone) in the female.

14. PECTINATE/DENTATE LINE—The saw-toothed line of demarcation between the distal (lower) portion of the anal valves and the pectin, the smooth zone of stratified epithelium which extends to the anal verge (Ref. 9). This line is apparent when the external and internal anal sphincters relax and the anus dilates (see Figure 3).
15. PENIS—Male sex organ composed of erectile tissue through which the urethra passes (homologous with the clitoris in the female) (Ref. 9).
16. PERIANAL FOLDS—Wrinkles or folds of the anal verge skin radiating from the anus, which are created by contraction of the external anal sphincter. (Definition not found in Stedman's.)
17. PERINEAL BODY—The central tendon of the perineum located between the vulva and the anus in the female and between the scrotum and anus in the male.
18. PERINEUM—The external surface or base of the perineal body, lying between the vulva and the anus in the female, and the scrotum and the anus in the male (Ref. 1). Underlying the external surface of the perineum in the pelvic floor and its associated structures occupying the pelvic outlet, which is bounded anteriorly by the pubic symphysis (pubic bone), laterally by the ischial tuberosity (pelvic bone) and posteriorly by the coccyx (tail bone).
19. POSTERIOR COMMISSURE—The union of the two labia majora posteriorly (toward the anus).
20. POSTERIOR FOURCHETTE—The junction of two labia minora posteriorly (inferiorly). This area is referred to as a posterior commis-

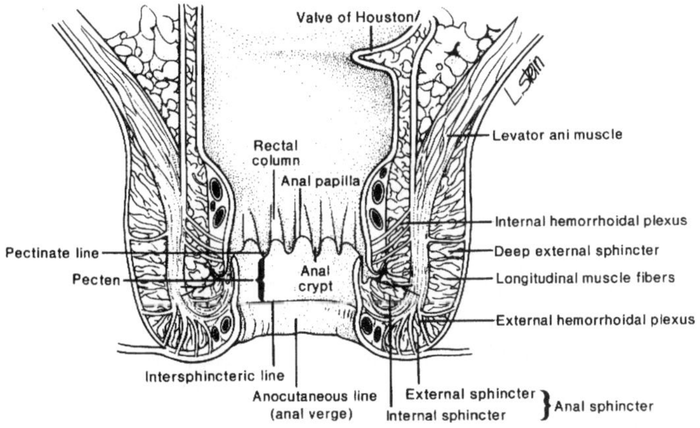

Figure 3 CROSS-SECTIONAL VIEW OF THE ANUS

sure in the prepubertal child, as the labia minora are not completely developed to connect inferiorly until puberty, when it is referred to as the fourchette.

21. SCROTUM—The pouch which contains the testicles and their accessory organs (Ref. 9).
22. URETHRAL ORIFICE—External opening of the canal (urethra) from the bladder.
23. VAGINA—The uterovaginal canal in the female. This internal structure extends from the uterine cervix to the inner aspect of the hymen.
24. VAGINAL VESTIBULE—An anatomic cavity containing the opening of the vagina, the urethra and the ducts of Bartholin's glands. Bordered by the clitoris anteriorly, the labia laterally and the posterior commissure (fourchette) posteriorly (inferiorly). The vestibule encompasses the fossa navicularis immediately posterior (inferior) to the vaginal introitus.
25. VULVA—The external genitalia or pudendum of the female includes the clitoris, labia majora, labia minora, vaginal vestibule, urethral orifice, vaginal orifice, hymen, and posterior fourchette (or commissure) (Ref. 9).

HYMENAL MORPHOLOGY (DEFINITIONS FROM REFERENCE 2.)

1. ANNULAR—Circumferential. Hymenal membrane tissue extends completely around the circumference of the entire vaginal orifice.
2. CRIBRIFORM—Hymen with multiple small openings.
3. CRESCENTIC—Hymen with attachments at approximately the 11 and 1 o'clock positions without tissue being present between the two attachments.
4. IMPERFORATE—A hymenal membrane with no opening.
5. SEPTATE—The appearance of the hymenal orifice when it is bisected by a band of hymenal tissue creating two or more orifices.

DESCRIPTIVE TERMS RELATING TO THE HYMEN

1. ESTROGENIZED—Effect of influence by the female sex hormone estrogen resulting in changes to the genitalia. The hymen takes on as a result a thickened, redundant, pale appearance. These changes are observed in neonates, with the onset of puberty and the result of exogenous estrogen.
2. FIMBRIATED/DENTICULAR—Hymen with multiple projections and indentations along the edge, creating a ruffled appearance.

3. NARROW/WIDE HYMENAL RIM—The width of the hymenal membrane as viewed in the coronal plane, i.e., from the edge of the hymen to the muscular portion of the vaginal introitus (see Figure 4).
4. REDUNDANT—Abundant hymenal tissue which tends to fold back on itself or protrude.
5. MEMBRANE THICKNESS—The relative amount of tissue between the internal and external surfaces of the hymenal membrane (see Figure 4).

STRUCTURES/FINDINGS

1. ACUTE LACERATION—A tear through the full thickness of the skin or other tissue. Examples of lacerations are in Reference 6, page 89 (fourchette); page 113 (hymen); and page 65 (peri-anal tissues).
2. ATTENUATED—This term has been used to describe areas where the hymen is narrow. However, the term should be restricted to indicate a documented change in the width of the posterior portion of the hymen following an injury.
3. DIASTASIS ANI—A congenital midline smooth depression which may be V-shaped or wedge shaped, located either anterior or posterior to the anus, that is due to a failure of fusion of the underlying of the corrugator external and sphincter muscle (Ref. 5).
4. ERYTHEMA—Redness of tissues.

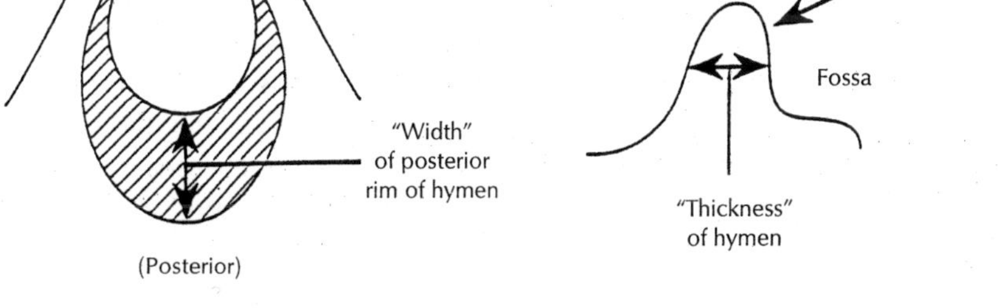

Figure 4 FRONTAL AND CROSS-SECTIONAL VIEWS OF HYMEN, PATIENT SUPINE

5. EXTERNAL HYMENAL RIDGE—A midline longitudinal ridge of tissue on the external surface of the hymen. May be either anterior or posterior. Usually extends to the edge of the membrane (Ref. 2).
6. FRIABILITY OF THE POSTERIOR FOURCHETTE/COMMISSURE—A superficial breakdown of the skin in the posterior fourchette (commissure) when gentle traction is applied, causing slight bleeding (Ref. 11).
7. HYMENAL CYST—A fluid-filled elevation of tissue, confined within the hymenal tissue (Ref. 2).
8. HYMENAL CLEFT—An angular or V-shaped indentation on the edge of the hymenal membrane (Ref. 9). When curved, it creates a hollowed or U-shaped depression on the edge of the membrane which has been referred to as a "concavity" (Refs. 10 & 11).
9. LABIAL AGGLUTINATION (labial adhesion)—The result of adherence (fusion) of the adjacent edges of the mucosal surfaces of the labia minora. This may occur at any point along the length of the vestibule although it most commonly occurs posteriorly (inferiorly) (Ref. 6).
10. LINEA VESTIBULARIS—A vertical pale/avascular line across the posterior fourchette and/or fossa, which may be accentuated by putting lateral traction on the labia major (Refs. 4, 11, & 12).
11. O'CLOCK DESIGNATION—A method by which the location of structures or findings may be designated by using the numerals on the face of a clock. The 12 o'clock position is always superior (up). The 6 o'clock position is always inferior (down). The position of a patient must be indicated when using this designation (see Figure 4).
12. PERINEAL GROOVE—Developmental anomaly, also called "Failure of Midline Fusion" (Ref. 7). The skin and mucosal defect may be located anywhere from the fossa to anus (Ref. 11).
13. PROJECTIONS—
    a. Mound/bump—A solid elevation of hymenal tissue which is wider or as wide as it is long, located on the edge of the hymenal membrane. This structure may be seen at the site where an intravaginal column attaches to the hymen. (Refs. 2, 3, & 11).
    b. Hymenal Tag—An elongated projection of tissue rising from any location on the hymenal rim. Commonly found in the midline and may be an extension of a posterior vaginal column (Refs. 6 & 11).
14. SCAR—Fibrous tissue which replaces normal tissue after the healing of a wound (Ref. 6).
15. SYNECHIA—Any adhesion which binds two anatomic structures through the formation of a band of tissue (Ref. 1). A synechia can result in the healing process following an abrasion of tissues.

16. TRANSECTION OF HYMEN (Complete)—A tear or laceration through the entire width of the hymenal membrane extending to (or through its attachment) to the vaginal wall.
17. TRANSECTION OF HYMEN (Partial)—A tear or laceration through a portion of the hymenal membrane not extending to its attachment to the vaginal wall.
18. VAGINAL COLUMNS (columnae rugarum vaginae)—Raised (sagittally oriented) columns most prominent on the anterior wall with less prominence on the posterior wall. May also be observed laterally (Refs. 2 & 3).
19. VAGINAL RUGAE (rugae vaginales)—Folds of epithelium (rugae) running circumferentially from vaginal columns. These rugae account in part for the ability of the vagina to distend (Ref. 11).
20. VASCULARITY (increased)—Dilatation of existing superficial blood vessels.
21. VESTIBULAR BANDS
    a. Periurethral bands—Small bands lateral to the urethra that connect the periurethral tissues to the anterior lateral wall of the vestibule. These bands are usually symmetrical and frequently create a semilunar shaped space between the bands on either side of the urethral means. Also called urethral supporting ligaments (Ref. 11).
    b. Perihymenal bands (pubo vaginal)—Bands lateral to the hymen connecting to the vestibular wall.

DESCRIPTIVE TERMS FOR VARIATIONS IN PERI-ANAL ANATOMY

1. ANAL DILATATION—Opening of the external and internal anal sphincters with minimal traction on the buttocks (Refs. 5 & 6).
2. ANAL FISSURE—A superficial break (split) in the perianal skin which radiates out from the anal orifice (Refs. 6 & 11).
3. FLATTENED ANAL FOLDS—A reduction or absence of the perianal folds or wrinkles, noted when the external anal sphincter is partially or completely relaxed.
4. VENOUS CONGESTION—Pooling of venous blood in the perianal tissues resulting in a purple discoloration which may be localized or diffuse (Ref. 6).

REFERENCES

1. *Stedman's Medical Dictionary, 22nd Edition*, Williams & Wilkins Co., Baltimore, 1972.

2. Berenson, A.; Heger, A.; Andrews, S. Appearance of the hymen in newborns. *Pediatrics*, 1991; 87:458-465.

3. Berneson, A. B.; Heger, A. H.; Hayes, J. M.; Bailey, R. K.; Emans, S. J. Appearance of the hymen in prepubertal girls. *Pediatrics*, 1992: 89:387-394.
4. McCann J.; Wells R.; Simon M.; Voris J. Genital findings in prepubertal children selected for non-abuse: A descriptive study. *Pediatrics*, 1990; 86:428-439.
5. McCann, J.; Voris, J.; Simon, M.; Wells, R. Perianal findings in prepubertal children selected for non-abuse: A descriptive study. *Child Abuse & Neglect*, 1989; 12:179-193.
6. Chadwick, D.; Berkowitz, C. D.; Kerns, D.; McCann, J.; Reinhart, M. A.; Strickland, S. *Color Atlas of Child Sexual Abuse*, 1989. Yearbook Medical Publishers, Chicago.
7. McCann, J. Use of the colposcope in childhood sexual abuse examination. *Ped Clin N Amer*, 1990; 37:863-880.
8. Adams, J. A.; Phillips, P.; Ahmad, M. The usefulness of colposcopic photographs in the evaluation of suspected child abuse. *Adol Pediatr Gynecol*, 1990; 3:75-82.
9. *Dorland's Illustrated Medical Dictionary, 27th Edition*, W. B. Saunders Co., Philadelphia, 1988.
10. Kerns, D. L.; Ritter, M. L.; Thomas, R. G. Concave hymenal variations in suspected child sexual abuse. *Pediatrics*, 1992; 90:265-272.
11. Heger, A.; Emans, S. J. *Evaluation of the Sexually Abused Child, A Medical Textbook and Photographic Atlas.* Oxford University Press, 1992.
12. Kellog, N. D.; Parra, J. M. Linea vestibularis: A previously underscribed normal genital structure in female neonates. *Pediatrics*, 1991; 87:926-929.
13. Giardino, A. P.; Finkel, M.; Giardino, E. R.; Seidl, T.; Ludwig, S. *A Practical Guide to the Evaluation of Sexual Abuse in the Prepubertal Child.* Sage Publications, Newbury Park, CA, 1992.
14. Finkel, M.; DeJong, A. R. Medical findings in child sexual abuse. In: Reece, R. M. *Child Abuse, Medical Diagnosis and Management.* Lea & Febiger, Philadelphia, 1994.

ACKNOWLEDGMENTS

These guidelines were produced by the Terminology Subcommittee of the APSAC Task Force on Medical Evaluation of Suspected Child Abuse. The Terminology Subcommittee is chaired by Joyce Adams, M.D. The Terminology Subcommittee held open meetings at the San Diego Conference on Responding to Child Maltreatment in January of 1991, 1992, 1993, and 1995 to review and reach consensus on the terms listed. Active members of the subcommittee include Martin Finkel, D.O; Mary Gibbons, M.D; Marcia Herman-Giddens, P.A., Dr.P.H.; Susan Horowitz, M.D.; John McCann, M.D.; Margaret Moody, M.D.; David Muram, M.D.; Sue Perdew, R.N., Ph.D.; _____ Ross, R.N., P.N.P.; Sara Schuh, M.D.; Rizwan Shah, M.D.; and Elizabeth Young, M.D. Valuable contributions were also made by Carol Berkowitz, M.D.; S. Jean Emans, M.D.; Dirk Huyer, M.D.; Carole Jenny, M.D., M.B.A.; and Susan Pokorny, M.D.

8 Representing the Protective Parent or Intervenor

The Forum

Representing the protective parent or intervening party is particularly difficult where that parent is the accuser and the forum is a custody or visitation case.[1] The accuser, statistically most likely to be the mother, often faces a disbelieving court. In part this is because domestic-relations judges typically hear litigants exaggerate minor incidents in an effort to win custody cases. This makes them more skeptical than most judges who routinely hear child-abuse and neglect cases. Further, there is much about child abuse that is counter-intuitive. The public at large is generally surprised to find that even badly abused children may love their abusive parents, may act lovingly toward their parents, and may not exhibit fear toward their parents. Abusers may look like model members of the community. They may have sexual relationships with other adults. They may have never molested a child until the breakdown of the marriage or separation.

1. For a discussion of the special circumstances involved in such cases, see Chapter 2.

A protection case offers a less skeptical forum because judges who hear protection cases are more used to seeing abusive parents. The judge is more likely to be familiar with the dynamics of child sexual abuse. Their goal is to offer services designed to enhance a protective parent's ability to effectively protect the child from abuse. However, even juvenile judges and Child Protective Services workers are likely to be more skeptical of abuse allegations raised when a domestic-relations custody or visitation action is pending. Because many judges and expert witnesses believe that there is an epidemic of false allegations in such circumstances, the lawyer attempting to prove sexual abuse must address that concern.

TAKING THE CASE

If the lawyer does take the case, the first obligation is to investigate whether the allegations are justified by the evidence, because it would be abusive to the child and unethical to pursue such allegations without there being a basis in fact. This involves appropriately qualified experts rather than highly polarized expert witnesses who always find abuse.

Experts should have specialized and up-to-date training in the dynamics of intrafamilial child sexual abuse, including attendance at conferences and regular review of the peer-reviewed literature in the field. The expert may also belong to such organizations as the American Professional Society on the Abuse of Children or the International Society on the Prevention of Child Abuse and Neglect. Often such experts are affiliated with teaching hospitals or are consultants to child-protective-services agencies, thereby seeing enough cases to develop good clinical judgment.

If the allegations do not appear to be true, then the lawyer must determine whether they were deliberately fabricated or merely good-faith misinterpretations. If they were misinterpretations, the expert should explain to the parent why the indicators—typical of childhood depression or anxiety as well as sexual abuse—reveal another problem which needs to be dealt with. It would be unfair to label the child as abused incorrectly and to interfere with the child's relationship with the other parent. The accusing parent will need to be reassured that the child is safe.

If the allegations constitute inappropriate conduct not constituting molestation, such as sleeping or bathing with an older child (the experts differ on the cut-off ages) or failing to give a developing child adequate privacy, the expert should suggest a strategy of educating or sensitizing the other parent.

EDUCATING THE JUDGE

The lawyer must make a special effort to educate the judge about intrafamilial child sexual abuse. There are psychodynamic explanations for why a child may first be molested during the parents' separation or a change in visitation or why a child may first disclose abuse under those circumstances.[2] The timing appears to be too convenient, but a good expert can explain to the judge the underlying reasons for the timing. Some judges resist this education, but the expert evidence is proper and necessary to a fair adjudication of the claims.

It is essential to present effective expert testimony. This may require calling a witness who is not directly involved in the case in addition to any professionals who may have evaluated or treated the parents or children. In addition to being a qualified professional (for example, social worker, psychologist, or physician), the expert must have a good theoretical background and practical experience in this particular facet of child abuse. Many cases are lost because the family physician or counselor doing family therapy did not have sufficient expertise in intrafamilial child sexual abuse. These cases are difficult enough for experienced specialists. Otherwise competent professionals who lack this specialized training and experience may often miss or misinterpret important data.[3]

It is important to establish the expert's *particular* specialized knowledge and not to accept a stipulation to the expert's qualifications. Ask questions specifically directed to training and experience with intrafamilial child sexual abuse, not just child abuse in general.

---

2. *See generally*, Kee MacFarlane, *Child Sexual Abuse Allegations in Divorce Proceedings*, in SEXUAL ABUSE OF YOUNG CHILDREN 121 (Kee MacFarlane & Jill Waterman, eds. 1986).

3. See Chapters 6 and 7 and the appendices to those chapters for further information on the relevant medical and psychological expertise and resources.

Have the expert explain what he or she does to keep up with the rapid expansion of knowledge in the area, such as attendance at seminars and conferences, subscription to abuse-specific journals, and membership in professional organizations dealing with abuse issues. It is also important to establish that the expert has determined *both* that some children have and that others have not been molested. That fact will go a long way to showing the witness' objectivity and fairness.

Have the expert detail any writing or speaking experience in the particular area and identify the audience. Was the expert speaking to members of his or her own profession? A multidisciplinary group? Was the speaking part of a required training program for professionals whose job it is to detect and/or treat that type of abuse? For example, many times local experts provide part of required training for Child Protective Services investigators. Even if a CPS worker was unable to substantiate abuse, a person who *trains* CPS workers may be able to give the judge enough information to override the CPS worker's opinion.

CROSS-EXAMINING THE OPPOSING EXPERT

In addition to presenting one's own expert, the lawyer must demonstrate, if true, that the opposing expert really is not trained in the specific area in question. This is a good type of cross-examination, because it does not impugn the integrity or general competence of the expert, but merely shows that intrafamilial child sexual abuse is a highly specialized area and that this expert just is not well-trained in that narrow subspecialty. The process of that cross-examination is the reverse of the direct examination of the specialized expert, establishing lack of specific training in the field, lack of attendance at specialized conferences and seminars, lack of reading in specialized journals, absence of membership in specialized organizations, and absence of speaking or writing in the specialized area.

Of course, we all know that there are witnesses who purport to be specialized in child sexual abuse and testify widely to the effect that any given child was not molested. The pattern of their testimony is often easy to establish: The witness may never have found a child to be molested. That type of bias undercuts the value of the testimony. Some of these professional experts have little or no clinical training or experience in child sexual abuse. Theoretical knowledge without the practical application of that knowledge provides a much weaker base from which to testify.

Prosecutors, lawyers representing CPS, and various resource organizations, such as the National Association of Counsel for Children,[4] the ABA Center on Children and the Law,[5] or the National Center for Prosecution of Child Abuse,[6] may have helpful information about these professional witnesses, such as citations to court cases discrediting them, transcripts of prior testimony, or critiques of their credentials.[7]

PHYSICAL EVIDENCE

There is a great deal of judicial misunderstanding about physical evidence in child sexual abuse cases.[8] While the presence of physical (medical) evidence is probative of sexual abuse, negative findings *are not* probative. Most acts of child molestation involve fondling, exhibitionism, or oral-genital contact; these would not be expected to leave physical evidence. Most children are not physically injured during the molestation, and even rubbing that leaves skin irritation generally does not leave marks that remain for very long. Even lacerations that may cause bleeding often heal completely in just a few *days*, without leaving a scar or any other evidence.

On the other hand, positive findings can be extremely powerful. A child who has a venereal disease of the same strain as the accused is very likely to have been molested by that person. A particularly useful tool for the physician is the colposcope, which provides a greatly magnified view during a genital examination. Colposcopic photographs can show minute fissures and scars not visible to the unaided eye. It is important to make sure that a physician whose tes-

4. 1205 Oneida Street, Denver, Colorado 80220, (303) 322-2260.
5. 1800 M Street, N.W., Washington, D.C. 20036, (202) 331-2250.
6. 1033 N. Fairfax Street, Suite 200, Alexandria, Virginia 22314, (703) 739-0321.
7. *See also*, ANNA SALTER, ACCURACY OF EXPERT TESTIMONY IN CHILD SEXUAL ABUSE CASES: A CASE STUDY OF RALPH UNDERWAGER AND HOLINDA WAKEFIELD (1991), available through the National Center for Prosecution of Child Abuse. *See also* LEONARD KARP & CHERYL L. KARP, DOMESTIC TORTS: FAMILY VIOLENCE, CONFLICT AND SEXUAL ABUSE ch. 4 (West Supp. 1998).
8. See Chapter 7 for a detailed discussion concerning medical and physical evaluations and evidence.

timony is based on colposcopic examination is properly trained, however. Not many pediatricians have extensive experience in interpreting findings to distinguish between normal variations, congenital abnormalities, and evidence of trauma. It is also important to be aware that negative colposcopic evidence is not inconsistent with molestation even where there was originally some physical damage.

DEALING WITH DIFFICULT FACTS

Cases with difficult facts create proof problems. Most people do not litigate custody where one parent has just been convicted by a jury of molesting the child. It is most likely where the facts are in dispute that parties litigate issues. Child sexual abuse allegations in custody or visitation cases usually involve difficult facts.

Young children often reveal abuse to a parent in private, bringing that parent's credibility into play. Many times young children are unwilling to repeat what they have told the parent, even to trained investigators. Further, often there are "windows of disclosure" in sexual-abuse cases, and there is always a significant chance that investigators and evaluators will never see the child during one of those windows. If the parent tapes the child's conversations in order to prove that the child has really said what the parent has reported, the parent may be accused of coaching the child.

Having a good expert, as discussed above, is the first step towards attempting to prove the facts. Without such an expert, it is virtually impossible to win a case with close facts. The expert must be given sufficient opportunity to spend time with the child, over time, to develop a good rapport and see the child during one of the windows of disclosure, when the child is willing to repeat what happened. Further, the expert should use all appropriate evaluative tools, including play therapy, use of drawings and dolls, and so on, as part of the evaluation. The expert should have full access to the child's records and should discuss the child's behaviors with babysitters, day-care workers, teachers, and other people who have seen the child on a regular basis.

There are cases where despite the use of good experts, sexual abuse cannot be proven. Because the party alleging abuse bears the burden of proving that abuse, the child may not be able to be protected. It is essential that the lawyer for the parent who is attempting to protect the child weigh the risks of going forward with allegations that may be true but cannot be proven.[9] Some judges may be willing to take precautionary steps to protect the child in the face of inconclusive proof, but others may penalize a parent perceived to be vindictive or hysterical. Such a parent may not only be unsuccessful in attempting to limit visitation, but may even lose custody altogether.[10] While a protective parent who has been unsuccessful in convincing the court of the need for protection may be tempted to go underground as a matter of self-help, there are serious drawbacks to such a strategy.[11] The odds of eventually losing custody are greatly enhanced where the parent has absconded with the child, even for the noblest of reasons.

RESULTS OF CPS AND POLICE INVESTIGATIONS

In many contested cases, CPS and/or the police have already investigated the allegations and elected not to proceed. The implication of those decisions in the domestic-relations case is often to substantially weaken the case of the parent attempting to prove the abuse. Therefore, one of the major tasks is to neutralize the power of that negative evidence. The purposes and criteria for proceeding with CPS and criminal cases are different than those applied to custody cases between parents. While judges realize this, they may confuse the agency's decision not to proceed with a factual determination on the truth of the allegations.

Criminal cases must be proven beyond a reasonable doubt to a unanimous jury. Particularly when the parents are estranged, defendants have fertile ground for implanting doubt in the jury by virtue of the relationship between the parents, the nondefendant parent's motive to lie for revenge or in order to get an advantage in the domestic-relations cases. This is particularly true in cases involving

---

9. An excellent resource for protective parents and their lawyers is JOHN E. B. MYERS, A MOTHER'S NIGHTMARE—INCEST: A PRACTICAL LEGAL GUIDE FOR PARENTS AND PROFESSIONALS (1997).

10. *Id.*

11. These issues are dealt with more fully in Chapter 2.

the sexual abuse of young children whose first report was to the nonabusing parent. Prosecutors may decide not to prosecute cases even if they are convinced the abuse occurred because they do not feel they will be able to put on sufficient evidence to convince a jury beyond a reasonable doubt. In addition, some prosecutors believe that child abuse should not be dealt with in the criminal-justice system and, as a matter of policy, do not prosecute those cases unless the abuse is severe. One study found that prosecutors were less likely to prosecute if the abuse was not recent or the offender was accused of abusing only one child.[12] Cases are less likely to be prosecuted where the victim is very young.[13] Cases with male victims may be more likely to be prosecuted than those with female victims.[14] Most importantly for intrafamilial sexual abuse cases, cases are less likely to be prosecuted where the abuser is a parent,[15] in part because family members are less willing to cooperate with prosecution and because criminal-justice personnel assume that the victim will not complete the process.

If CPS investigated but did not substantiate the abuse, the CPS worker involved, any CPS worker or administrator, or an expert with a history of training or working with CPS may be able to testify about the triage procedures of CPS. What is considered insufficient abuse to file a dependency and neglect petition may nevertheless constitute grounds on which to decide custody between parents or even to restrict one parent's visitation to supervised only. Further, CPS often forgoes filing a petition if one parent appears willing and

---

12. *See* Kathleen D. Brewer, Daryl M. Rowe & Devon D. Brewer, *Factors Related to Prosecution of Child Sexual Abuse Cases*, 6/1 J. CHILD SEXUAL ABUSE 91 (1997) (reviewing 200 closed cases during 1989-1990).

13. *See, e.g.*, T. P. Cross, E. De Vos & D. Whitcomb, *Prosecution of Child Sexual Abuse: Which Cases Are Accepted?*, 18/8 CHILD ABUSE & NEGLECT 663 (1994); ELLEN GRAY, UNEQUAL JUSTICE: THE PROSECUTION OF CHILD SEXUAL ABUSE (1993); B. K. MacMurray, *Criminal Determination for Child Sexual Abuse: Prosecutor Case-Screening Judgments*, 4 J. INTERPERSONAL VIOLENCE 233 (1989). *Cf.* David Finkelhor, *Removing the Child—Prosecuting the Offender in Cases of Sexual Abuse: Evidence from the National Reporting System for Child Abuse and Neglect*, 7 CHILD ABUSE & NEGLECT 195 (1983) (cases with 7- to 12-year-old victims most likely to be prosecuted). *But see*, T. L. Bradshaw & A. E. Marks, *Beyond a Reasonable Doubt: Factors that Influence the Legal Disposition of Child Sexual Abuse Cases*, 36 CRIME & DELINQUENCY 276 (1990) (no significant difference in prosecution based on the victim's age).

14. *See, e.g.*, B. K. MacMurray, *Criminal Determination for Child Sexual Abuse: Prosecutor Case-Screening Judgments*, 4 J. INTERPERSONAL VIOLENCE 233 (1989). *But see*, T. P. Cross, E. De Vos & D. Whitcomb, *Prosecution of Child Sexual Abuse: Which Cases Are Accepted?*, 18/8 CHILD ABUSE & NEGLECT 663 (1994) (no significant difference in prosecution based on the victim's gender).

15. *See, e.g.*, J. R. Chapman & B. Smith, *Response of Social Service and Criminal Justice Agencies to Child Sexual Abuse Complaints*, 10/3 RESPONSE TO THE VICTIMIZATION OF WOMEN AND CHILDREN (1987); David Finkelhor, *Removing the Child—Prosecuting the Offender in Cases of Sexual Abuse: Evidence from the National Reporting System for Child Abuse and Neglect*, 7 CHILD ABUSE & NEGLECT 195 (1983).

able to protect the child. If the parents are separated or divorcing, or if the nonabusing parent is willing to seek court protection for the child, the case may be closed even though the agency believes that the abuse occurred. The judge needs to be aware of these considerations.

There is often misunderstanding about what the terms "substantiated," "valid," "founded," and "unsubstantiated," "invalid," and "unfounded," mean. Researchers have had a hard time accurately determining rates of true abuse because of the imprecision of the terms and idiosyncratic ways in which the terms are applied. In the domestic-relations forum, the "un-" terms are frequently construed to mean "false," "untrue," or "fabricated." Many CPS agencies do not even have a category that would cover "I don't know." Even if the abuse did not occur, for custody purposes there is a big difference between a parent vindictively fabricating allegations and a good-faith, but erroneous belief that the abuse occurred. After all, society has a great public-policy interest in having parents who believe their children have been abused taking some action in response. A parent should not be penalized for seeking to protect a child.

It is essential to have the CPS worker or other expert explain what the phrase in question does and does not mean and to clarify whether the negative finding implies bad faith. Even if the CPS worker testifies that the agency determined that the abuse never took place, the worker may have been unaware of additional information that has come to light subsequent to that worker's investigation. Had all of that information been available to the worker, the findings might have been very different.

In addition, the protective parent's expert might be someone whom CPS regularly uses and relies on in determining whether abuse took place. If so, the worker may be willing to back down on his or her opinion if the witness knows that the expert found that there was abuse. Sometimes workers are put off by a hostile parent who accuses the other of abusing the child. The abuser may be quite charming and explain away the allegations as being the by-product of a bitter custody case. There are workers who investigate cases much less thoroughly when there is a custody case in progress, either because they believe that the allegations are inherently less reliable or because they feel that the child will be protected in another forum.

In such cases it is important to expose those preconceptions. For workers who believe that the allegations are inherently unreliable, it is very effective to ask the worker something like: "Isn't it true that many of the petitions CPS files state that the mother does not believe the allegations and is therefore unable or unwilling to protect the child?" "Don't you routinely advise mothers whose children are being abused to leave the abusive spouse or to file for divorce?" "Is it your belief that a mother who believes the abuse and leaves her husband and files for divorce before CPS tells her to must therefore be lying?" Regardless of the witness' answers, the point is made to the court.

BIFURCATING THE ABUSE FROM THE ABUSER

The relevance of abuse allegations really involves two separate questions: 1) was the child abused? and 2) if, so, who abused the child or allowed the abuse? One technique recommended by lawyer Sandra J. Morris of San Diego is to ask the court to bifurcate the two issues, first allowing evidence that would show that the child was abused, and then, only after the judge rules that the abuse took place, trying the issue of whether the other parent was the one who did the abuse.[16]

This is really a brilliant strategy for two reasons. First, the initial inquiry involves no blame. Maybe it wasn't the other parent who abused the child. Maybe it was a relative, acquaintance, or a stranger. Therefore, the other parent has an equal interest in determining whether the child has been abused. If the other parent does not seem to care about finding out, that indifference is a major blow to his or her custody chances. The whole "vindictive spouse" argument, the most frequent defense employed, is irrelevant in the first phase of the trial. If the judge determines that abuse has not been proven, the parent does not need to alienate the judge further by

16. Sandra J. Morris, *Allegations of Sex Abuse in Custody Cases* in ABA SECTION OF FAMILY LAW 1989 ANNUAL MEETING COMPENDIUM 166 (1989).

pointing the finger at the other parent, risking a retaliatory custody award to the "innocent" accused abuser.

On the other hand, if the judge determines that the child *has* been abused, the other parent loses the ability to argue that the allegations are fabricated. The defense then becomes one of mistaken identity. Because the judge has already determined that abuse has occurred, he or she will be less likely to view the accusing parent negatively. At least the judge will know that the child in fact has been abused. Unless there is evidence that the accusing parent did the abuse personally, good faith has likely been established.

EMPHASIZING THE STANDARD OF PROOF

Even though the standard of proof in custody cases is preponderance of the evidence, many judges, in fact, require more to prove sexual abuse allegations. The lawyer must, therefore, reiterate that the proof need only be more likely that the abuse occurred than that it did not.

In the notorious Morgan/Foretich case, the trial judge stated that the proof of whether Dr. Foretich molested his daughter Hillary or not was "in equipoise." It is hard to imagine that there is exact equality of proof in most abuse cases. While a trial judge might feel more comfortable about finding abuse by clear and convincing evidence, the law does not require it. Even if the facts are "in equipoise," it seems reasonable to provide some measure of protection for the child until such time as more information is known. Such strategies are discussed below.

FOCUSING THE CASE ON THE CHILD

The primary focus of the case should always remain on the child: what happened to the child, what the effect on the child was, what special needs the child may now have, and what the ramifications for custody and visitation are. It is a mistake to focus the case on how bad the other parent is or how good your client is. Further, even if the parent is responding badly to the allegations (interrogating the child, coaching the child to elaborate on what really happened, and so on), the child must still be protected. The critical inquiry is what custody/visitation scheme best protects the child's interests. That may involve deciding between two parents who both have problems. Too many extraneous factors enter the case when anything other than the child is at the heart of the case, with every vein of inquiry leading directly to that heart.

Lawyers often argue that the judge should not lightly brand a parent an abuser. But, by the same token, the court should not lightly place a child, ill-equipped to protect himself or herself, in a position of jeopardy. This is particularly true because of the deep and far-reaching effects of sexual abuse on a child. It is important to have the expert testify clearly about both the short- and long-term effects of abuse. Many judges do not realize how pervasive are the consequences of abuse to a child. They do not understand the powerlessness a child feels when he or she is not believed or not protected. The expert must make the judge aware of just how crucial the decision is to the *child's* well-being, and how necessary it is to give protection of the child a high priority.

DEALING WITH THE CLIENT

Many parents of abused children make terrible witnesses in their custody cases. They are angry, frustrated, and may be vindictive. The goal is to differentiate between cause and effect. Did the allegations arise out of the client's anger and vindictiveness or is the client's anger and vindictiveness his or her response to the abuse? The problem of the difficult client may infect the entire case, from how the professionals evaluate the allegations to how the judge adjudicates them. I believe that many valid cases are lost by the failure of the lawyer to analyze the role that the client's "difficulty" plays in the case.[17]

Most parents of abused children in custody cases are angry with the abuser. What good parent would not be? CPS files dependency and neglect petitions for failure to protect when the nonabusing parent of an abused child is nonchalant about the abuse. The "mother bear" traditionally fights to the death anyone who would threaten

---

17. A helpful resource for parents is JOHN E. B. MYERS, MOTHER'S NIGHTMARE—INCEST: A PRACTICAL LEGAL GUIDE FOR PARENTS AND PROFESSIONALS (1997). This book can answer many of the protective parent's questions and explain the need for strategies that otherwise might seem inappropriate to the client.

her offspring. It is not difficult to understand anger, hatred, and even vindictiveness towards a parent who has hurt one's child. The lawyer must convince the judge that this response to abuse is perfectly natural, and even desirable.

Nonetheless, the lawyer must also work with the client to get the client to be circumspect in the expression of the anger. It is safe to express anger to the lawyer or a therapist who is treating the client and who understands the basis for the anger. It is not wise to express anger with abandon to evaluators and the court. This does not mean that the client should deny the anger. It is a matter of how much emotional energy the client allows to come through the expression.

Most parents of sexually abused children who are involved in custody litigation should have at least supportive short-term therapy to help them through the process. It is important, however, that the therapist understand the stress parents in that particular situation are going through. Sometimes the therapist is a good person to explain the parent's anger and hostility to the judge.

A more difficult situation is presented by the client whose anger predates the allegations. If the parent was already angry, it is easier to assume that the allegations are a product of the anger. But this is not necessarily the case. Under such circumstances, it is especially important to have a well-qualified mental-health professional evaluate the client and analyze the content and timing of the anger as well as the parent's motivation to fabricate abuse. Further, the parent's problems should not impair the evaluator's thorough review of the independent evidence in the case.

Friends and relatives may have information that will distinguish the anger from the allegations. For example, the client may be very angry with the other parent but may have an overriding need to protect the child, even from the process of the investigation into the allegations. The client may have told somebody that he or she wondered whether or not to make a report because the child would be hurt by the investigation or because the other parent might retaliate. Such an expression of ambivalence about reporting would undermine the position that the parent fabricated the allegations out of vindictiveness.

The client's anger may be related to a continued pattern of abuse that is consistent with an extension of the abuse to the child. It may be a part of the dysfunction in the family that set up the conditions that allowed the abuse to occur. In any event, the client's anger is an issue that must be thoroughly investigated and discussed at trial in order to prevent the judge from assuming that because the client appears so angry, he or she must be fabricating, or at least greatly exaggerating, the allegations.

When the "protecting parent" has emotional or mental problems, it is easy for a court to conclude that the allegations are a fabrication or exaggeration arising out of the emotional or mental problem. Such clients frequently make very poor witnesses. They may not be able to tell a coherent story or otherwise present themselves as credible. Those same problems may in fact be part of the family dynamic that allowed the abuse to occur.

Again, it is essential to have a mental-health professional educate the judge. One of my most difficult sexual-molestation custody cases taught me how to effectively turn the client's liabilities into assets. I had taken the case over from another lawyer fairly soon before trial and after several pendente lite hearings. On the first day of trial, before any witnesses had been called, the judge announced to me, "I don't believe anything your client says." I knew that the psychologist's report had some pretty negative things to say about my client, and the independent psychiatrist who had evaluated the case felt the evidence for molestation was "very weak."

One of the reasons I ended up winning that case was the way I drew the sting with the psychologist, whom I called in my case-in-chief, knowing that he was a key witness for the father. The psychologist had told me that "in his gut" he felt the father had molested the girls (whom he had not seen), but that he couldn't testify to that. Based on my preparatory conversations with this witness, I started out by asking him to describe some general characteristics that might be seen in the spouse of an incestuous molester. We were careful to clarify the limitation on profiles, but the psychologist listed several common characteristics. I then asked him to identify any of those characteristics revealed in his evaluation of my client. In that context he testified about all of the bad things he had found. Now the judge saw them in a context that helped explain the abusive environment rather than undermining my client's credibility. I am convinced that putting the cart before the horse worked much better than having the psychologist testify about the damaging facts surrounding my client first and then trying to explain their role in setting up the abusive situation.

Careful preparation cannot be overemphasized in getting the court to see through the superficial liabilities of the client to the hard factual issues.

INTERROGATION AND COACHING

A frequent charge against the nonabusing parent is that the parent has influenced the child by coercive or leading interrogation or has coached the child in what to say. This sometimes does happen. But sometimes the parent's comments to the child are misconstrued, even by otherwise careful evaluators.

It is unreasonable to expect a parent not to talk to a child about sexual abuse. If a child is hit on the playground and tells his mother, the mother often asks for elaboration about what happened, whether the child is hurt, whether the other person has hit the child before, and so forth. Certainly if a stranger abused or molested a child, the parent would ask many questions and might comfort the child by saying that it was not the child's fault or that the abuser would be caught by the police and put in jail. However, such typical and expected conversations with children are often viewed in a sinister light when the abuser is the other parent, and domestic-relations litigation is pending between them. The lawyer needs to emphasize through testimony and argument the "real world" context of parents talking to their children about something that has hurt the child.

When a parent takes an abused child to be interviewed by the police, CPS, or an evaluator, the parent generally explains *something* to the child about where he or she is being taken and why. The parent might say to the child "Be sure to tell Dr. Smith everything you told me about what happened. That's the only way she can help you." There is nothing wrong with such a statement. However, after the child has related what happened, Dr. Smith might say, "Did anyone tell you to say those things to me?" The child will say that the mother told him or her to say them. The mother did, but not in the way that Dr. Smith might interpret it. Therefore, it is crucial to have the investigator or evaluator distinguish whether the child is telling something that did not happen because the parent told him to say it, or whether the child was simply told to tell the investigator what had happened.

In my experience, *most* of the time when a child says the parent has told him or her to say something, the evaluator or investigator never clarifies what the child means, even though the expert may have enough child-development knowledge that he or she should realize how concretely the child is answering the question. If the investigator or evaluator did not clarify the issue with the child, the possibility of misunderstanding should be raised while examining the expert witness. Unfortunately, the valid inquiry into coaching is sometimes not as thorough as it should be, and investigations are dropped as soon as the child says that a parent "told me to say that."

Sometimes a parent asks very leading questions while trying to ascertain what has been done to the child. This can contaminate the investigation, but it does not invalidate the fact that the child may have been molested. Research psychologist Gail Goodman and her colleagues have demonstrated that children's disclosures to their mothers can be more accurate than disclosures to people they do not know. They conducted a study[18] to look at the issues of whether interviewer status (the child's mother or a stranger, who was also a mother) or a preconceived bias (based on having been given incorrect information about what actually happened to the child during a videotaped play session) would affect forty preschool children's memory and suggestibility or the interviewers' descriptions of the children's reports. The most inaccurate (commission errors) and least accurate (omission errors) reports by children were those given to the biased stranger interviewers during free recall. Whether or not the mothers had been given the biasing information had no affect on the children's free-recall accuracy. Stranger interviewers' supportive comments were associated with less accuracy during direct questions. Whether or not the mothers made supportive comments had no effect on the children's accuracy during direct questioning. Children were more accurate in answering misleading abuse questions when interviewed by their mothers than by strangers.

---

18. Gail S. Goodman, A. Sharma, S. F. Thomas & M. G. Considine, *Mother Knows Best: Effects of Relationship Status and Interviewer Bias on Children's Memory*, 60 J. EXPERIMENTAL CHILD PSYCHOLOGY 195 (1995).

Mother interviewers reported more correct information than stranger interviewers and children were, at times, less suggestible when being interviewed by their own mothers. These findings appear to support the intuitive hypothesis that children will tell their mothers more things than they will tell strangers. This would seem natural, because children are used to confiding in their parents but not in strangers. This research may help evaluators to realize that abused children may reveal things to their parents that they will not repeat to interviewers. It may also lend support for having a parent in the room during interviews or having the parent ask questions prepared by the expert, while the expert is present in the room.

However, even assuming that parents may obtain more and better information from the child than the evaluator, a major role for the lawyer is to assist the evaluator in having the client not continue to ask the child questions, except as specifically authorized by the evaluator. This is good trial strategy for the client, because the client must realize that the child's allegations are less likely to be believed the more the parent talks to the child. Until the standard of investigation changes, the parent should leave the interviewing to properly trained experts.

JUDICIAL BIAS

Judicial bias is often a problem in these cases. In overcoming judicial bias, the accuser's lawyer should prepare an extensive trial memorandum and must present empirical evidence to back up the expert's opinion. Sometimes the mere mention of an allegation is enough to convince a domestic-relations judge to interrupt the relationship between the child and the accused parent. However, the pendulum has now swung to the point that it is more likely that allegations of molestation will subject the accusing parent to great skepticism and even retaliation. More than one judge has awarded custody of a child to the alleged abuser as punishment for the other parent's "scandalous allegations." Expert witnesses with good reputations and good training are necessary to sway a biased judge.

Where local practice permits peremptorily striking a judge without cause, judges who have known negative biases towards molestation cases should be stricken. However, sometimes the case must be tried to a skeptical judge. A good resource to make available to the judge, typically by trial memorandum or testimony by an expert, is an article which appeared in the ABA publication for judges, *Judges Journal*.[19] That article reported the results of a study by the Association of Family and Conciliation Courts of allegations of child sexual abuse in contested custody litigation. The study showed that, contrary to the hysteria about witch hunts and an epidemic of false allegations in custody cases, the rate of allegations in custody cases is no higher than in the general population. In 169 contested custody cases in twelve states, less than 2 percent involved allegations of molestation. 50 percent were validated, in 33 percent no abuse was felt to have occurred, and in 17 percent the experts were unsure about the abuse. In the 33 percent where no abuse was felt to have occurred, only 25 percent (8 percent of the total number of cases involving sexual abuse allegations) involved any question about whether the allegation was made in good faith. This study remains the largest of its kind to date and is particularly useful because the researchers reviewed cases from a number of different sites, reducing sample bias.

REQUESTING A LAWYER FOR THE CHILD

Next to having a good expert evaluator, having a well-trained lawyer for the child is the most important tool in protecting a molested child from a court order that facilitates further abuse. The child's lawyer or guardian ad litem can rise above the charges of vindictiveness leveled against the other parent. In fact, a well-trained lawyer for the child should take the lead in proving the allegations, with the protecting parent's lawyer playing a secondary role. Such a strategy can enhance the objective presentation of evidence and erode the judge's preconceptions about parents who raise abuse allegations in custody cases.

The most likely pool of well-trained lawyers to represent children in these cases is found in the lawyers who are appointed by the

19. Thoennes, *Child Sexual Abuse: Whom Should a Judge Believe? What Should a Judge Believe?*, 27 JUDGES J. 14 (Summer 1988). *See also* Thoennes & Tjaden, *The Extent, Nature, and Validity of Sexual Abuse Allegations in Custody/Visitation Disputes*, 14 CHILD ABUSE & NEGLECT 151 (1990).

juvenile court in child-abuse cases filed by the state or county. They are more likely than divorce lawyers to have experience in abuse cases and to know how to deal with child clients. The accuser's lawyer should request that the court appoint a lawyer *with experience in intrafamilial child sexual abuse cases* to represent the child's interests at the earliest possible stage of the proceedings. The accuser's lawyer should cooperate fully with the child's lawyer and instruct the client to cooperate fully.

DEALING WITH ALLEGATIONS THAT CANNOT BE PROVEN

There are a number of reasons why allegations cannot be proven, the most common being that the allegations are not true or that the evidence is lacking. If the allegations are not true because they have been fabricated by the client, the client needs mental-health counseling to discover why he or she would make such accusations, knowing them to be false, and to help the parent appreciate that telling a child that he or she has been abused when there was no abuse is in itself *emotional abuse* of the child. Parents who fabricate allegations of sexual molestation may be so filled with hate for the other parent that they do not even think about the effect of the allegations on the child. It is clearly unethical for a lawyer to continue to press allegations of molestation known to be false.

The largest category of allegations that are not true involve misinterpretations of the facts. In the last fifteen years there has been a massive public-awareness campaign seeking to discover and prevent child sexual abuse. Many "red flags" and "warning signs" have been discussed. Unfortunately, with a few exceptions, these warning signs are general indications of childhood depression or anxiety, which may be caused by something other than sexual molestation. The child's depression or anxiety may be caused by the marital disharmony or separation itself.

Accusers who have merely misinterpreted the child's symptoms have acted as *good* parents in recognizing the signs of distress and seeking help. They should not be punished for their vigilance. The accused parent should understand that he or she may just have easily jumped to the wrong conclusion given the signs observed. What is essential is for a well-trained evaluator to determine that the child has not been molested and to reassure the accusing parent that there has not been a molestation. Many of my clients in this category have felt very relieved to know that their children had not been abused. The experts have been able to assure those parents that they acted appropriately, that the children's problems will be addressed, and that there is help available should other troubling symptoms emerge. Handled sensitively by the expert and lawyer, *both* parents can end up feeling that the child's needs have been attended to and that the child is safe.

A more difficult situation involves the lack of evidence. This most frequently involves pre-verbal children or preschoolers who cannot or will not elaborate on what may have happened to them. There may be indications that the child has been abused, but there simply is not enough evidence to prove it or to prove who the perpetrator of the abuse was.

Since most state reporting laws require professionals, and many require parents, to report *suspected* abuse, there is likely to be an obligation to report the accuser's concerns to Child Protective Services. The accuser's lawyer should advise the parent to be as objective as possible in making the report. For example, the parent can say "my child is showing some signs that I have heard are indicative of abuse, but the child cannot (or will not) tell me if anything bad has happened. I don't want to accuse anybody unfairly, but above all, I want to protect my child." If CPS is unable to substantiate abuse, at least the accuser did not appear to be vindictive or, on the other hand, nonprotecting.

When the parent has tried to have well-qualified experts determine if there has been abuse, and abuse has not been ruled out—but there is not enough evidence to prove abuse by a preponderance of the evidence—a strategic decision must be made. The expert should really take the lead in determining how likely it is that further evaluation will reveal the existence of abuse and how much the child is in need of protection. There is a well-conceived model of therapeutic intervention in such cases, which the parents or a court may be willing to adopt.[20] This model involves individual sessions with the

---

20. *See* Sandra K. Hewitt, *Therapeutic Management of Preschool Cases of Alleged But Unsubstantiated Sexual Abuse*, 70 CHILD WELFARE 59 (1991).

child, individual sessions with each parent, and sessions with each parent and the child, during which that parent and child agree on lists of appropriate and inappropriate touching and give the child permission to reveal any abuse to the therapist, with continued monitoring for at least one year. The accused should realize that if there has been no abuse, utilization of this model is more likely to result in everyone's accepting a positive finding of "no abuse," rather than the more ambiguous finding of "we don't know one way or the other." Further, the child will be learning useful self-protection skills, thereby becoming less likely to be abused and less likely to fail to report any abuse that does occur, even at the hands of a third party. Finally, the accusing parent should realize that his or her concerns are being taken seriously, and that the child is being protected.

CONCLUSION

Representing the accuser in a child sexual abuse case in the domestic-relations forum is not for the fainthearted. The ramifications of an incorrect judicial finding in either direction are enormous. The lawyer must be willing to find and use the best available experts, to prepare the case carefully, to preclude or impeach evidence of dubious scientific value, and to keep the case centered squarely where it should be: on the best interests of the child, who depends on the adults in the case for his or her protection.

On the other hand, representing the protective parent in a protection case allows the lawyer to form a productive coalition with the state agency, if any, and the child's lawyer or guardian ad litem. While the same distrust may be expressed about the protective parent's motives, the other independent parties are not subject to the same assumptions. The primary task in the protection case will be to show that the protective parent is supportive of the child and able to provide a safe environment.

Representing the Nonabusing, Nonprotecting Parent

9

Introduction

In some cases both parents or parent-figures are actively engaged in molesting the child. More frequently, however, only one person molests the child. The other, whether out of ignorance, impotence, or complicity, simply fails to protect the child from the abuse.[1]

If a parent is unwilling or unable to protect the child from the sexual abuse, that parent contributes to the child's risk. Child protective services (CPS) workers often remove children from their homes when the

1. *See generally*, Patricia A. Joyce, *Mothers of Sexually Abused Children and the Concept of Collusion: A Literature Review*, 6/2 J. Child Sexual Abuse 75 (1997); J. T. Johnson, Mothers of Incest Survivors: Another Side of the Story (1992); Ila J. Schonberg, *The Distortion of the Role of Mother in Child Sexual Abuse*, 1/3 J. Child Sexual Abuse 47 (1992); M. Elbow & J. Mayfield, *Mothers of Incest Victims: Villains, Victims, or Protectors?*, 72/2 Families in Society: J. of Contemporary Human Services 78 (1991); B. Gomes-Schwartz, J. M. Horowitz, A. P. Cardarelli, P. Salt, M. Myer, L. Coleman & M. Sauzier, *The Myth of the Mother as "Accomplice" to Child Sexual Abuse*, in Child Sexual Abuse: The Initial Effects (B. Gomes-Schwartz et al., eds. 1990); J. L. Jacobs, *Reassessing Mother Blame in Incest*, 15/3 Signs: J. Women in Culture & Society 500 (1990); Kathleen Coulborn Faller, *The Myth of the "Collusive Mother:" Variability in the Functioning of Mothers of Victims of Intrafamilial Sexual Abuse*, 3/2 J. Interpersonal Violence 190 (1988).

nonabusing parent does not protect the child.[2] A great deal of effort has been directed toward community awareness of child sexual abuse over the past fifteen years. One goal of that effort has been to appeal to nonabusing parents to be aware of abuse and to protect their children from that abuse. Ironically, protective parents often have found themselves in a dilemma as a result of their response to those awareness efforts. When protective parents have noticed symptoms and believed their young children's disclosures of abuse, they have often been branded as vindictive fabricators.[3] In reality some CPS workers appear to want an initially unbelieving parent, who is then *convinced* by the worker to be protective and supportive. If those parents give the desired response before being convinced by the worker, they are viewed with suspicion.

THE CHILD'S NEED FOR A PROTECTIVE PARENT

It is crucially important to a child's recovery from child sexual abuse to have a protective, supportive parent.[4] Children look to their parents to keep them safe from outside dangers. When the danger the child faces is from someone in his or her own home, especially someone who exercises power and control over the child, it is especially important to know that there is a protective parent. Otherwise, the already vulnerable child is totally without protection.

It is difficult to learn to trust when one's parents are not trustworthy. Incest victims often blame nonoffending mothers for not protecting them.[5] When the child turns to a parent for protection and is not believed or is not safeguarded, the child is in a particularly precarious position. When the child and the protective parent are not believed by CPS or the court, the child may be left without hope as well as without protection.

---

2. See Chapter 3.
3. See Chapter 8.
4. *See, e.g.*, K. A. Kendall-Tackett, L. M. Williams & D. Finkelhor, *Impact of Sexual Abuse on Children: A Review and Synthesis of Recent Empirical Studies*, 113 PSYCHOLOGICAL BULLETIN 164 (1993); Mark D. Everson, Wanda M. Hunter, Desmond K. Runyon, Gail A. Edelsohn & Martha L. Coulter, *Maternal Support Following Disclosure of Incest*, 59/2 AM. J. ORTHOPSYCHIATRY 197 (1989); Gail Elizabeth Wyatt & M. Ray Mickey, *Ameliorating the Effects of Child Sexual Abuse: An Exploratory Study of Support by Parents and Others*, 2/4 J. INTERPERSONAL VIOLENCE 403 (1987).
5. *See, e.g.*, J. L. Jacobs, *Reassessing Mother Blame in Incest*, 15/3 SIGNS: J. WOMEN IN CULTURE & SOCIETY 500 (1990); J. HERMAN, FATHER-DAUGHTER INCEST (1982).

In some cases clients do not understand why their children were removed from their care if they were not the ones committing the abuse. This is especially true if they were not even aware of the abuse. The client must understand why a protective parent is necessary for the child and why he or she must become a protective parent. Finkelhor and Daro point out that parents "need to know how to make themselves trustworthy to children so that children will be comfortable disclosing to them" and that they need "guidelines to help them deal with children's disclosures and their aftermath."[6] The lawyer's role in this process is to explain to the client why the best legal strategy is to be able to prove that the client is now able and willing to be protective, and to refer the client to an appropriate therapist who can explain the emotional ramifications to the child of not being protected.

DETERMINING WHY THE CLIENT WAS NOT PROTECTIVE

The primary strategy for the lawyer for a nonabusing nonprotective parent is to turn the parent into a protective one. This strategy usually involves both education and supportive therapy for the parent. There are many reasons why a parent may have been nonprotective, and appropriate remediation depends on understanding the individual family's dynamics and addressing them. Therefore, the first step is an individual psychological and psychosocial evaluation. If a child-welfare agency has filed a protection case, the agency is likely to do its own evaluation. The parent's lawyer may want to obtain an independent evaluation if there is a question of bias or completeness in the agency's evaluation. This can be done on a consultation basis, which may shield the results under the lawyer's work product privilege.[7] If the evaluator will submit a report or testify, however, the

6. *See* David Finkelhor & Deborah Daro, *Prevention of Child Sexual Abuse*, in THE BATTERED CHILD 615, 622 (Mary Edna Helfer, Ruth S. Kempe & Richard D. Krugman, eds., 5th ed. 1997).

7. *See, e.g.*, Rule 26(b)(3), FED. R. CIV. P.; Granviel v. Estelle, 655 F.2d 673 (5th Cir. 1981), *cert. denied* 455 U.S. 1003 (1982); United States v. Alvarez, 519 F.2d 1036 (3d Cir. 1975); United States *ex rel.* Edney v. Smith, 425 F. Supp. 1038; People v. Stritzinger, 34 Cal. 3d 505, 668 P.2d 738, 194 Cal. Rptr. 431 (1983); B.B. v. People, 785 P.2d 132 (Colo. 1990); Fields v. State, 379 So.2d 408 (Fla. Dist. Ct. App. 1980). *See generally*, DANIEL W. SHUMAN, PSYCHIATRIC AND PSYCHOLOGICAL EVIDENCE §§ 10.06, 18.01 (1994); 1 SCOTT N. STONE & ROBERT K. TAYLOR, TESTIMONIAL PRIVILEGES ch. 2 (2d ed., 1993); 1 MARC J. ACKERMAN & ANDREW KANE, PSYCHOLOGICAL EXPERTS IN DIVORCE, PERSONAL INJURY, AND OTHER CIVIL ACTIONS § 1.10 (1993).

privilege will be deemed waived.[8] Because the lawyer can always elect to turn the consultant into a witness, having the independent evaluation performed in consultation with the lawyer affords the client the most protection, especially if the evaluation is very negative. However, a consultant-turned-witness may be subject to cross-examination on the issue of bias on the basis of the clear original alliance with the lawyer. For this reason, among others, it is preferable to use only consultants who have a reputation for objectivity and the willingness to deliver bad news about one's client.

MOVING FROM BLAME TO RESPONSIBILITY

Traditionally mothers were blamed as being "collusive" when their children were molested by nonstrangers. They were blamed for their part of the family dynamics leading to intrafamilial sexual abuse and for their denial and lack of supportiveness following the disclosure of abuse.[9] The assumption that maternal collusion is typical has been called a constructed myth based on "scarce documentation and ill-defined concepts" within a patriarchal system blaming mothers for the male offender's abuse.[10] This has been seen as part of a larger trend of holding female victims "accountable for all sorts of sexual assaults."[11]

---

8. *See, e.g.*, Beverage Marketing Corp. v. Ogilvy & Mather Direct Response, Inc., 563 F. Supp. 1013 (S.D.N.Y. 1983); Fitzgibbon v. Fitzgibbon, 197 N.J. 63, 484 A.2d 46 (1984); DeRusse v. State, 579 S.W.2d 224 (Tex. Crim. App. 1979). *See generally*, 1 SCOTT N. STONE & ROBERT K. TAYLOR, TESTIMONIAL PRIVILEGES § 2.12 (2d ed., 1993).

9. *See, e.g.*, D.J. Gelinas, *Family Therapy: Characteristic Family Constellation and Basic Therapeutic Stance*, in VULNERABLE POPULATIONS: EVALUATION AND TREATMENT OF SEXUALLY ABUSED CHILDREN AND ADULT SURVIVORS (Suzanne Sgroi, ed., 1987); B. J. VANDER MEY & R. L. NEFF, INCEST AS CHILD ABUSE: RESEARCH AND APPLICATIONS (1986); M. B. Zuelzner & R. E. Reposa, *Mothers in Incestuous Families*, 5/2 INTL. J. FAMILY THERAPY 98 (1983); C. A. Dietz & J. L. Craft, *Family Dynamics of Incest: A New Perspective*, 61 SOCIAL CASEWORK 602 (1980); B. JUSTICE & R. JUSTICE, THE BROKEN TABOO: SEX IN THE FAMILY (1979); SUSAN FORWARD & CRAIG BUCK, BETRAYAL OF INNOCENCE: INCEST AND ITS DEVASTATION (1978); Henry Giaretto, *Humanistic Treatment of Father-Daughter Incest*, in CHILD ABUSE AND NEGLECT: THE FAMILY AND THE COMMUNITY (Ray E. Helfer & C. Henry Kempe, eds. 1976); Maisch (1973); Tormes (1968); P. Matchotka, P. Pittman & S. Flomenshaft, *Incest As a Family Affair*, 6/1 FAMILY PROCESS 98 (1967); N. Lustig, J. Dresser, S. Spellman & T. Jurray, *Incest: A Family Group Survival Pattern*, 14 ARCHIVES OF GENERAL PSYCHIATRY 31 (1966); B.M. Cormier, M. Kennedy & J. Sangowicz, *Psychodynamics of Father-Daughter Incest*, 7 CANADIAN PSYCHIATRIC ASSOC. J. 207 (1962). *See generally*, Sharon L. Crawford, *Intrafamilial Sexual Abuse: What We Think We Know About Mothers, and Implications for Intervention*, 7/3 J. CHILD SEXUAL ABUSE 55 (1999); Patricia A. Joyce, *Mothers of Sexually Abused Children and the Concept of Collusion: A Literature Review*, 6/2 J. CHILD SEXUAL ABUSE 75 (1997); Ila J. Schonberg, *The Distortion of the Role of Mother in Child Sexual Abuse*, 1/3 J. CHILD SEXUAL ABUSE 47 (1992).

10. *See* E. Wattenberg, *In a Different Light: A Feminist Perspective on the Role of Mothers in Father-Daughter Incest*, 64/3 CHILD WELFARE 203, 204 (1985).

11. *See* Ila J. Schonberg, *The Distortion of the Role of Mother in Child Sexual Abuse*, 1/3 J. CHILD SEXUAL ABUSE 47, 50 (1992). *See also* DIANA E. H. RUSSELL, THE SECRET TRAUMA: INCEST IN THE LIVES OF GIRLS AND WOMEN (1986); K. McIntyre, *Role of Mothers in Father-Daughter Incest: A Feminist Analysis*, 26 SOCIAL WORK 462 (1981).

Clearly there are parents, usually mothers, who fail to protect their children from sexual abuse and who fail to respond supportively upon disclosure. While the pervasiveness of this response has been unfairly assumed, there often remains in law-enforcement officers, CPS investigators, lawyers, judges, and other professionals involved in child sexual abuse cases a great deal of blame directed against these nonprotective parents.

Some nonprotective parents have themselves been victims of child sexual abuse. Some are victims of domestic violence. Some are so economically and emotionally dependent on the abuser that they see no possibility of intervening to prevent further abuse. For parents who may themselves be victims of abuse or who otherwise were not protective because of their own sense of powerlessness, blaming them does little to ameliorate the underlying problems. Nonprotective parents do need to take responsibility for their inability or unwillingness to protect their children. It is important, however, for the lawyer to focus on the responsibility and the necessary changes rather than on adding to the blame.

If any of the other professionals involved in the case appear to be focused on blaming the nonprotective parent, the lawyer should attempt to persuade them to take a more positive approach to help the nonprotective parent become protective. In addition, the lawyer needs to assist the client in the process of becoming protective.

HELPING THE CLIENT TO BECOME PROTECTIVE

Until they deal with their own issues, it is unlikely that nonprotective parents will be able to establish their ability to protect a child. In many cases, this will require a permanent separation from the abuser. If the abuser is the nonprotective parent's spouse, the lawyer should consider recommending that the client file for divorce, or at the very least, separate from the abuser. The sooner the parent is able to establish a home independent from the abuser, the more likely it is that the court will permit placing the child with that parent.

Where the nonabusing parent is economically dependent upon the abuser, it is often important to file an immediate application for temporary child support and/or spousal maintenance, and orders granting exclusive use of the family home by the nonabuser and payment of designated debts by the abuser. Many communities have career counseling or other programs available to assist economically dependent adults find appropriate employment, job training, or education. Sometimes these programs are offered through community colleges or special organizations dealing with displaced homemakers. Information and referral hotlines and social-services agencies also generally can refer clients to programs designed to secure the client's long-term economic independence. Social-services agencies can assist clients with short-term economic assistance, including cash-assistance payments, food stamps, low-cost health care, and low-cost housing.

The lawyer should assist the client in becoming economically independent in the short- and long-term. Sometimes that means encouraging the client to consider living with the client's parents or other relatives. It is important that if the client is shifting economic dependence from the abuser to someone else, the other person or persons are appropriate. The other person should not undermine the client's therapy or pose an independent risk to the child. Unfortunately, some nonprotective parents move from living arrangements with one abusive person to another. The client should be encouraged to live with a stable citizen of reputable moral character if he or she is not in a position to live alone.

A separating or divorcing parent must emotionally separate as well as physically separate from the abuser. Further, that parent must deal with any underlying psychological issues to assure the court that he or she will not merely establish another unsafe relationship. Individual therapy will be necessary to address the client's underlying emotional needs. The lawyer should discuss with the client, and perhaps with the therapist, whether or not such counseling will be deemed confidential. All states have a psychotherapist-patient privilege,[12] and the U.S. Supreme Court recently has recognized the public-policy importance of that privilege to appropriate psycholog-

---

12. *See, e.g.*, ALA. CODE § 34-26-2 (1975); ALASKA RULE EVID. 504; ARIZ. REV. STAT. ANN. § 32-2085 (1992); ARK. RULE EVID. 503; CAL. EVID. CODE ANN. §§ 1010, 1012, 1014 (1995); COLO. REV. STAT. § 13-90-107(g)(1) (1987); CONN. GEN. STAT. ANN. § 52-146c (1995); DEL. UNIFORM RULE EVID. 503; D.C. CODE ANN. § 14-307 (1995); FLA. STAT. ANN. § 90.503 (Supp.1992); GA. CODE ANN. § 24-9-21 (1995); HAW. RULES EVID. 504, 504.1; IDAHO RULE EVID. 503; 225 ILL. COMP. STAT. ANN. § 15/5 (1994); IND. CODE ANN. § 25-33-1-17 (1993); IOWA CODE ANN. § 622.10 (1987); KAN. STAT. ANN. § 74-5323 (1985); KY. RULE EVID. 507; LA. CODE EVID. Ann., Art. 510 (West 1995); ME. RULE EVID. 503; MD. CTS. & JUD. PROC. § 9-109 (1995); MASS. GEN. LAWS § 233:20B (1995); MICH. COMP. LAWS ANN. § 333.18237 (Supp.1996); MINN. STAT. ANN. § 595.02 (1988 and Supp.1996); MISS. RULE EVID. 503; MO. ANN. STAT. § 491.060 (1994); MONT. CODE ANN. § 26-1-807 (1995); NEB. REV. STAT. § 27-504 (1995); NEV. REV. STAT. ANN. § 49.209 (Supp.1995); N.H. RULE EVID. 503;

ical treatment.[13] However, sometimes the peer counseling available from support groups and group therapy is not deemed confidential because of the presence of other people, even if the group is led by a professional whose therapeutic relationships are generally afforded a privilege.[14]

Once the therapist testifies, any privilege that did exist will be waived to some extent. If the nonprotective parent is able to become more aware and protective through the therapeutic process, the loss of privilege is justified by the need to prove that the parent has become an appropriate custodian for the child. On the other hand, if the parent refuses to change or is unable to change within a developmentally appropriate period (taking into consideration the child's sense of time), the therapist may become the most potent witness against the client, even laying the foundation for termination of the parent's rights.[15] It is important, therefore, to discuss the risks and benefits with the client. Child-centered representation, aimed at making the client a better parent, and thereby achieving the client's goal of reunification with the child, is likely to recommend therapy despite the risk.

N.J. STAT. ANN. § 45:14B-28 (West 1995); N.M. RULE EVID. 11-504; N.Y. CIV. PRAC. LAW § 4507 (McKinney 1992); N.C. GEN. STAT. § 8-53.3 (Supp.1995); N.D. RULE EVID. § 503; OHIO REV. CODE ANN. § 2317.02 (1995); OKLA. STAT. ANN. tit. 12 § 2503 (1991); ORE. RULES EVID. 504, 504.1; 42 PA. CONS. STAT. ANN. § 5944 (1982); R.I. GEN. LAWS §§ 5-37.3-3, 5-37.3-4 (1995); S.C. CODE ANN. § 19-11-95 (Supp.1995); S.D. CODIFIED LAWS ANN. §§ 19-13-6 to 19-13-11 (1995); TENN. CODE ANN. § 24-1-207 (1980); TEX. RULES CIV. EVID. 509, 510; UTAH RULE EVID. 506; VT. RULE EVID. 503; VA. CODE ANN. § 8.01-400.2 (1992); WASH. REV. CODE ANN. § 18.83.110 (1994); W. VA. CODE § 27-3-1 (1992); WIS. STAT. ANN. § 905.04 (1993- 1994); WYO. STAT. § 33-27-123 (Supp.1995).

13. *See* Jaffee v. Redmond, 116 S.Ct. 1923, 518 U.S. 1, 135 L.Ed.2d 337 (1996).

14. *See, e.g.*, State v. Boobar, 637 A.2d 1162 (Me. 1994). *But see* Farrell v. Superior Court, 203 Cal. App. 3d 521, 250 Cal. Rptr. 25 (1988) (communication with participants in group therapy fall within psychotherapist-patient privilege); State v. Andring, 342 N.W.2d 128 (Minn. 1984) (physician-patient privilege extends to communications in group-therapy sessions that are part of the patient's diagnosis and treatment, noting that the purpose of the child abuse reporting statutes is to protect children, not to punish those who mistreat them; therefore, the report does not entirely abrogate the patient's right to confidential treatment). *Cf.* Sims v. State, 251 Ga. 877, 311 S.E.2d 161 (1984) (privilege applies in marital therapy); Daymude v. State, 540 N.E.2d 1263 (Ind. Ct. App. 1989) (privilege applies in court-ordered family therapy sessions). Some states specifically include group therapy within their privilege rules and statutes. *See, e.g.*, Colo. Rev. Stat. § 13-90-107(1)(g) (1997); Kan. Stat. Ann. § 65-5602(a) (1992). *See generally*, Thomas J. Reed, *The Futile Fifth Step: Compulsory Disclosure of Confidential Communications Among Alcoholics Anonymous Members*, 70 ST. JOHN'S L. REV. 693 (1996); Jessica G. Weiner, *"And the Wisdom to Know the Difference": Confidentiality vs. Privilege in the Self-Help Setting*, 144 U. PA. L. REV. 243 (1995); Paul S. Appelbaum & Alexander Greer, *Confidentiality in Group Therapy*, 44 HOSP. & COMMUNITY PSYCHIATRY 311 (1993); Howard R. Roback et al., *Guarding Confidentiality in Clinical Groups: The Therapist's Dilemma*, 42 INT'L. J. GROUP PSYCHOTHERAPY 81 (1992); Robert Weinstock, Gregory B. Leong & J. Arturo Silva, *Confidentiality and Privilege*, 1 REV. CLINICAL PSYCHIATRY & L. 83 (1990); Steven R. Smith, *Medical and Psychotherapy Privileges and Confidentiality: On Giving with One Hand and Removing with the Other*, 75 KY. L.J. 473 (1987); Ralph Slovenko, *Group Psychotherapy: Privileged Communication and Confidentiality*, 5 J. PSYCHIATRY & L. 405 (1977); Wayne Cross, *Privileged Communications Between Participants in Group Psychotherapy*, 1970 L. & SOC. ORDER 191 (1970).

15. See Chapter 4.

DEMONSTRATING CHANGE TO THE COURT

Depending on the factual circumstances of the case, some of the existing judicial biases can actually be used positively for the nonprotective parent, especially in the domestic-relations context. For example, the lawyer can point out that unlike a parent willing to immediately assume the worst about her spouse or jump to conclusions in an effort to gain an advantage in the custody case, this mother assumed that the person she married could not have molested her child. However, after becoming more educated on the subject, generally by being presented with an evaluation that diagnosed molestation, she now believes that the child was abused and is ready, willing, and able to protect the child. Further, the parent may now have a better understanding of the consequences of child sexual abuse, which has motivated him or her to become more vigilant and protective.

Where the nonprotective parent had underlying economic-dependency issues, the lawyer can point out the steps the parent has taken to become financially independent of the abuser. The more quickly the parent sought out such alternatives, the stronger the inference that he or she will continue the independence. Even if the client is receiving welfare or assistance from friends or family, it is nevertheless important to show that maintaining a relationship with the abuser is no longer necessary.

Where the client had underlying psychological or emotional problems, the lawyer should present expert testimony that those problems have been dealt with to the extent that the parent is now willing and able to protect the child. The client's compliance with directives of the therapist, including attendance at sessions and ability to articulate plans for protecting the child, should be emphasized. If there was an underlying biochemical basis for the problems, such as biochemically based depression or bipolar disorder, the effects of medication and the client's compliance with the prescribed drug regime should be emphasized.

Cooperation and compliance with recommendations of the social workers and mental-health professionals are extremely important in protection cases. The judge is more likely to return a child to a nonabusing nonprotecting parent if that parent has complied with all aspects of the case plan. Further, caseworkers are more likely to recommend return to parents who have been cooperative. Even if the parent was initially resistant, there is hope for a successful outcome if the parent is able to conform to the requests of the professionals in charge of the case.

Change must be demonstrated concretely and with reference to the purpose for the change. Therefore, it is necessary but not sufficient to show that the parent has attended certain sessions or participated in certain evaluations. It is important to be able to demonstrate that the client has learned something through such attendance and can apply what has been learned. For protection cases it can be useful to have the caseworker provide behavioral objectives in the case plan. Rather than having a vague goal such as "demonstrate sensitivity to the child's needs and provide a protective environment," the case plan should be specific enough to put the client and court on notice of what result should be achieved and, most importantly, what measure will be used to demonstrate achievement. The caseworker should be able to articulate, preferably in the case plan itself, who will make the determination and how the determination will be made that an objective has or has not been met. Some caseworkers resist such specificity, in which case the lawyer can propound interrogatories designed to elicit measurable behavioral objectives. With such specifics articulated, the lawyer can better present evidence that the client has achieved the objectives and is now ready to resume care of the child.

Case plans are rarely involved in domestic-relations cases; however, evaluators may be asked to give recommendations in their reports. The lawyer should request that the evaluator provide recommendations for remediation of the parents' problems. If possible, the evaluator should be asked to provide specific behavioral objectives. If the report does not address remediation specifically, the lawyer can depose the expert and attempt to elicit such objectives. If the expert has opined that the nonprotective parent cannot adequately parent the child at the time of the evaluation, the lawyer should ask what the parent would have to change in order to demonstrate the ability to safely parent. The expert should also be asked what resources are available to assist the parent in acquiring the necessary skills. Even if the evaluator is not familiar with particular programs, he or she can describe the characteristics of what would be helpful. The client should be encouraged to pursue such resources, and the lawyer should present evidence that tracks the evaluator's recommendations. It may be helpful to request an updated evaluation to demonstrate that the client has now remediated the underlying problems and is able to safely parent the child.

In addition to proving that the client has become a protective parent, the lawyer should present evidence concerning changes in the environment and the other parties. For example, if the abuser is in jail or prison or has moved far away from the child, the environment may be safer merely by virtue of that fact. If the abuser is on probation or parole, there may be another layer of authority monitoring him or her, adding an independent layer of protection for the child. If the abuser has successfully completed a program for child sexual abusers, especially if he or she is continuing in individual or group therapy, the risk to the child may be greatly reduced. Finally, if the child has been involved in a prevention program to enhance awareness and assist in reporting, the child may be better able to resist abuse and report any improper contact. It is totally inappropriate to place on the child the responsibility for protection; however, the child's increased ability to self-protect is one factor that may convince a judge that a nonprotective parent will be a safe custodian. This is particularly true where the child had not told the nonprotective parent directly about the abuse, and that parent had not picked up the more subtle clues. Improved parent-child communication and the assurance that the parent is willing to listen and protect may diminish the likelihood of further molestation.

REPRESENTING THE PARENT WHO WILL NOT OR CANNOT CHANGE

If the lawyer is unable to assist the client in becoming protective, he or she must frankly discuss with the client available options. Where one parent is a child molester and the other is not able to protect that child, termination of parental rights of both parents is a very real possibility.[16] Sometimes understanding this likely consequence is enough to motivate a nonprotective parent to become protective. Where it is not, the parent may be able to identify potential adop-

16. See Chapter 4.

tive parents in order to avoid the child being placed with strangers. Sometimes family members or friends are willing to adopt the child. The child's relationship with such potential adoptive parents and those persons' willingness to demonstrate to the court that they will not allow unsafe contact (or even any contact) with the parents are crucial. Close friends and relatives are sometimes rejected as placements because the court does not believe that they will be vigilant in protecting the child from the parent. Therefore, it is important to establish that the chosen third parties place their first loyalty to the child and to complying with all court orders than to the parents. In some cases the third parties will need to sever all ties with the parents.

As was discussed in Chapter 3, children generally feel more comfortable living with people they know than with strangers. Courts often are willing to accommodate children's desires to salvage at least some continuity in their lives. The earlier such third parties are identified, the more likely the child will be placed permanently with them. If the child was placed temporarily with such a family, the lawyer will have an easier time arguing that the child remain permanently in the same place.

If the child is already in a foster home, the lawyer should determine whether that home is a prospective adoptive placement. If not, the lawyer can argue that the child will have to be moved in any event. However, if the foster family is willing to adopt, and the child is comfortable in that home, the court is likely to reject the parent's suggestion that the placement be changed.

The most frustrating parents to represent are those who recognize that the abuse was wrong but whose loyalty to the abuser or anger against "the system" cause them to choose the abuser over the child's interest. I often ask the client, "Do you love your child more than you hate the system?" The client needs to understand his or her priorities, and that if the goal is reunification with the child, and the eventual end of "the system's" involvement, time and energy cannot be spent on an unproductive effort to find vindication against unwarranted governmental intervention.

Sometimes no amount of reasoning or pleading will cause these parents to change their position. The lawyer's only solace is to realize that although the case will almost inevitably be lost, the outcome will be better for the child. Lawyers are not therapists and cannot always impress upon parents the importance of putting their children first. Further, they cannot help clients who refuse to make changes necessary to provide safety for the child. However, the lawyer should document in writing the advice given, including the possible ramifications of not following that advice.

REPRESENTATION IN SUBSEQUENT CASES

The nonabusing nonprotecting parent may require representation in more than one case, especially if the first case was a protection case, and the parent was not successful in regaining custody of the child. A subsequent termination of parental rights action may be filed, and it seems to make sense for the lawyer who represented the parent in the protection case to continue that representation in the termination case. The lawyer is already familiar with the underlying facts and history of the case, the positions of the parties, any defects in state services, and how the witnesses appear in court.

I generally recommend against representation in the subsequent case for several reasons. First, a new lawyer will bring a fresh perspective and approach to the case that may be more successful. If the lawyer was not able to effectuate sufficient change in the client during the protection case, the client may have lost confidence in the lawyer and be less willing to follow that lawyer's advice in the termination case. Both the client and the other parties may be more receptive to a new lawyer's suggestions.

Second, termination cases filed by child-welfare agencies after the case has already been in the juvenile system are usually successful. Sometimes this is because agencies are typically quite conservative about the decision to file a termination case. Sometimes it is because of the growing trend towards speeding up the process of "permanency planning" and moving children out of the "limbo of foster care" and into permanent homes.[17] A parent whose rights have been terminated may be eager to file a disciplinary grievance or malpractice action against the twice unsuccessful lawyer. From a risk-management perspective, it is prudent to allow another, unaffiliated lawyer to handle the termination case.

---

17. The Adoption and Safe Families Act of 1997, P.L. 105-89, is a reflection of this policy on the federal level.

There is certainly no blanket prohibition against continued representation. Some court-appointed counsel have no option to decline appointment in the termination case. Others have good relationships with their clients and viable defenses. However, the decision to continue representation should be made thoughtfully, after weighing the risks and benefits both to the client and to the lawyer.

Representing the Accused Abuser

10

Introduction

The most effective defense of child sexual abuse allegations in protection and domestic-relations cases is to remain child-oriented. The judge is mandated to enter an order in the child's best interests. Therefore, the case should be presented in a way that focuses on those interests, rather than on the wrong being done to the accused parent. Especially if the client did not molest the child, it may be difficult to get beyond the emotional outrage. However, it is important to keep the client focused on the child's circumstances and needs.

Determining the Facts

It is necessary for the lawyer representing a party accused of child sexual abuse to determine, if possible, what the facts are. The defense will be different depending on such issues as whether the client did molest the child, whether somebody else molested the child, whether the allegations represent a good faith but erroneous misinterpretation of behaviors, or whether the allegations are deliberately fabricated. The lawyer for the accused should not rely solely on the child's recantation of the allegation as a determination that no abuse occurred, because false recantations can occur with real abuse.[1] A third-party reporter may also recant allegations for fear of losing economic support, based on family pressure, or based on other considerations. Therefore, even where there is a recantation, the lawyer should be careful to gather affirmative evidence concerning whether or not the client molested the child.

The first place to start is with the client interview. It is important for the client to have permission to tell the truth about what happened. Some people find sexual abuse to be so repugnant, a feeling communicated directly or subtly to the client, that they cannot represent a person accused of molestation unless absolutely convinced of the client's innocence. The client of such a lawyer may never be free to tell the lawyer the truth. Having the client feel free to tell the truth is one of the best ways to determine what happened. The client must be assured that the lawyer is willing to hear the truth and still help the client. The lawyer can begin by stating that knowing the truth will put the lawyer in the best position to advocate for the client's position in court, and that even if the client did molest the child, there are steps the lawyer can take to assure a more favorable outcome than if the lawyer bases his or her trial strategy on a lie.

It is important to realize that the process of disclosure may be just as gradual for the abuser as it was for the molested child. Therefore, it is likely that if the client did molest the child, the story will come out in bits and pieces over time, usually with the most detrimental information coming out later in the process, as the client tests the lawyer's reaction to less damaging admissions.

One way of facilitating honest disclosure is to focus on the child and the child's needs. For example, the lawyer can say, "Children really need two loving parents with whom they can be safe. A parent who has molested a child can still be an important part of that child's life." The lawyer should explain the availability of therapy to help parents who have molested their children and even to help rehabilitate the parent-child relationship when no abuse has occurred but the child or the other parent thinks it has. The lawyer should emphasize that a child who is afraid of a parent—even based on

---

1. *See generally* Chapter 1.

deliberate fabrication and "coaching" by the other parent—is nevertheless really afraid, and that some therapeutic work will be needed to ensure a safe and supportive environment *from the child's perspective* for future contact. It is not sufficient merely to force a visit and demonstrate to the child that he or she does not actually get molested during the visit.

The fact that such allegations have been made has necessarily created turmoil for everybody in the family. By focusing on the child's needs, the accused parent can react in a healthy way for both parent and child. It can help a parent who feels wrongly accused to feel altruistic in responding to the child's needs. Rather than focusing on the anger against the accusing parent and feelings of righteous indignation, the parent can address the needs of the child, who is suffering (either from the abuse, if it occurred, or the turmoil of the accusation, if no abuse occurred).

By getting the parent out of a defensive stance and into a child-oriented stance early in the case, the lawyer can maximize not only true disclosure, but also the ability to have the client demonstrate genuine concern for the child and willingness to cooperate with a plan that will maximize the child's interests. Judges are more likely to respond favorably to such an approach than to one that focuses solely on the parents.

One caveat: if the client admits molestation, the lawyer should strongly consider consulting with or having the client retain a criminal defense lawyer. What may be most beneficial for a domestic-relations or child-protective-services case may be directly contrary to the client's penal interests. If criminal prosecution is likely, and the client did molest the child, the most prudent course may be to forgo contesting the domestic-relations action.

Although I do not believe that polygraphs, sodium amytol, or penile plethysmograph interviews are helpful in determining whether a person molested a child, I do often ask clients if they are *willing* to undergo such procedures. Their response often tells me as much as the questionable results of the tests would have.

The expert evidence from professionals who evaluate the child and the various other parties will be important evidence to use or discredit during negotiations and at trial. Unfortunately, there is no magic bullet to definitively determine what happened and who did what, and except in the most extreme cases, there is always likely to be some degree of uncertainty. There is no battery of tests that can prove a person molested a child or that can exonerate a wrongly accused person. There is also a certain amount of distrust among experts from different "camps," each distrusting the other's methods and conclusions. People with limited credentials or experience in the highly specialized field of child sexual abuse often hold out themselves, or are accepted by courts, as having far more knowledge and clinical judgment than they have. Some experts sell themselves as expert witnesses for a case, taking extreme positions based on shaky evidence, always finding that a child has been abused or never finding that a child has been abused. It is essential that the lawyer find well-qualified, reputable experts who have both clinical experience and knowledge of the current empirical literature in the field.[2]

RISK ASSESSMENTS AND OTHER EVALUATION PROCEDURES

The lawyer for the accused abuser must determine whether or not to obtain a "risk assessment." It is always difficult to prove a negative, and sexual abuse "risk assessments" or evaluations are no exception.[3] The fact that a person has normal adult sexual relationships does not preclude that person's having molested a child.[4] Not all child molesters are pedophiles in the sense that they are sexually aroused primarily or solely by children. They have no definitive psychological characteristics, and do not necessarily show evidence of psychopathology on standard tests. There is not yet consensus in the field that would support expert testimony that a person did not molest a child or did not fit "the profile" of a child molester. For that reason, risk assessments are not particularly useful with parents who deny the allegations. They may be more useful with people who have molested in the past to measure progress in therapy.

Some instruments and procedures widely used with admitted sex offenders, such as penile plethysmography (which physically mea-

2. For a more complete discussion of how to evaluate mental health and physical examinations, *see generally* Chapters 6 and 7.

3. *See generally* Chapter 6.

4. The DSM-IV classifies pedophilia, 302.2, as either Exclusive Type, where the sexual attraction is only towards children, or Nonexclusive Type, where the sexual attraction may also be to adults. AMERICAN PSYCHIATRIC ASSOCIATION, DIAGNOSTIC AND STATISTICAL MANUAL OF MENTAL DISORDERS 527-528 (4th ed. 1994).

sures arousal to certain sexual stimuli) and the Multiphasic Sex Inventory II[5] (a pencil and paper test), are not capable of diagnosing a sex offender. Some risk assessments also use polygraph examinations. These may be particularly unreliable when used with sex offenders, who often do not believe that they did anything wrong, and therefore, do not produce the assumed indicia of lying.

Psychological evaluations by clinicians with experience in the child sexual abuse field are probably more helpful than specific risk assessments, but they still cannot definitively disprove the allegations. Except perhaps in the case of a confession, no psychological evaluation can determine whether any person did or did not commit a particular act. However, an evaluation can look at whether the client has impulse control or judgment problems (often seen in people who molest their children), whether the client has age-appropriate expectations of the child, or whether the client has appropriate boundaries and sensitivities to the child's bodily privacy. Further, the expert can evaluate the client's level of stress, degree of isolation, and emotional support system, all of which are relevant to the circumstances that may create an environment in which an opportunistic molestation may occur. Even though the evaluation cannot rule out molestation, the expert can at least indicate the absence of any indicators that the client is likely to have molested the child. Further, the evaluation may be able to document the client's empathy for the child, knowledge of appropriate boundaries, and ability to self-monitor and control inappropriate impulses.

WHEN THE CLIENT MOLESTED THE CHILD

Where criminal prosecution is a real possibility, the client may not be able to take the most therapeutically appropriate posture in the domestic-relations case (usually, to admit responsibility and seek therapy). However, in some cases prosecutors are willing to agree not to use any statements made in therapy or as part of the protection or custody/visitation case, other than admissions to new incidents. Such agreements reduce the criminal exposure. It is important, however, that any such agreement be in writing, and that the

5. NICHOLS & MOLINDER, MULTIPHASIC SEX INVENTORY II (1990).

client be instructed to reveal admissions only in such a manner as to be protected by the agreement.

Where there is no problem with criminal exposure, the lawyer must decide whether to fight the allegations, putting the other parent to the proof, or trying to settle. My own preference is usually for the latter course. It is less expensive financially and emotionally for the parties and the child.

If the client admits to the molestation, it may be worthwhile to have the client meet with a child psychologist or other expert for advice on what is appropriate for the child. If the child is in therapy or has been evaluated, that professional may be the best person with whom to talk. Psychologists are ethically prohibited from engaging in "dual relationships," so the child's therapist cannot do therapy with the abuser. However, the child's therapist may be able to provide *information* to the abuser or to the abuser's therapist. The goal is to rehabilitate the parent and repair the damage in the parent-child relationship. In the long term this will best serve the client's interests in an on-going relationship with the child. If the other parent sees that the molester is serious about remedying the problem, the entire family may be able to work together toward making the situation better for the child.

WHEN THE CLIENT ENGAGED IN INAPPROPRIATE CONDUCT NOT AMOUNTING TO MOLESTATION

Many times the client's conduct might not rise to the level of molestation, but might still have been inappropriate. Sleeping or bathing with a child of the opposite sex past a certain age (experts differ on what age the cutoff should be), laxness in allowing children to observe sexual conduct between adults or to watch sexually explicit videos, and amorous embraces and kisses that fall short of being overtly sexual are examples of such inappropriate conduct.

In one case of "inappropriate contact," the trial court made the following findings concerning the 61-year-old father's conduct with his four-year-old daughter:

1. Respondent continued to bathe nude with his daughter after the child's mother asked him not to and a counselor advised

him not to, and although his daughter touched his penis and his foot rubbed against his daughter's vagina in the bath;

2. Respondent continued to sleep nude with his daughter after the two were found asleep with the child's hand on his penis and her face in the area of his crotch;
3. Respondent had his daughter sit on his nude belly in the bath;
4. Respondent caused his daughter to have an inordinate amount of viewing of his nude body, including his penis;
5. He encouraged his daughter to touch her tongue to his tongue when kissing;
6. He urinated in his daughter's presence when the child was three years old;
7. He described his daughter as "sexy" in her presence;
8. He questioned his daughter about whether her stepfather sees her naked in the bathtub.[6]

The trial court found that such conduct did not constitute sexual abuse but did constitute neglect.[7] The appellate court found that the father's

> failure to exercise a minimum degree of care in providing proper supervision is demonstrated by the nature of respondent's conduct. Respondent's behavior was more than "unconventional" or "non-traditional." He is not just a parent who subscribed to a belief in the benefits of nudism. His conduct went well beyond the mere casual display

6. *See In re* A.G., 1999 WL 111151, *4–5 (N.Y. App. Div. 1999).

7. *Id.* at 4. It should be noted that the trial court rejected the testimony of the father's former employee concerning witnessed incidents of abuse and discounted the testimony of the investigating detective concerning the child's statements. Further, the corroborating comments of the child's mother and stepfather concerning the child's statements about incidents of sexual abuse were discounted because the "comments were made after a number of investigators had repeatedly asked her direct questions about such conduct." *Id.* The appellate court characterized the evidence that was left as "a reflection of the extent to which the respondent overexposed his child to excessive nudity and overemphasized awareness of their bodies when he was with her." *Id.* at *5. The appellate court also stated that "when the challenged conduct is the touching of a child by a parent, the consideration of whether the contact was for sexual gratification must take into account the nature and circumstances of the act, since the same conduct which constitutes an act of sexual abuse by a stranger could be a mere expression of affection on the part of a parent." *Id.*

> of the body. Rather, as reflected in the findings of the Family Court, he actively encouraged his daughter to inordinately focus on his and her own genitalia and sexuality. As the Family Court noted, there was "an absence of appropriate physical boundaries in the respondent's behavior with [the child]."[8]

The appellate court held that "it was an improvident exercise of discretion for the Family Court to fail to direct any measures to ensure that the child would be protected against any repetition of the misconduct."[9] The court ordered that the trial court modify its order "to the extent of (1) directing continued supervision of respondent by [the child protection agency] for a period of one year, (2) providing that respondent's visitation with the child be supervised pending further court order, and (3) adding an order of protection" that would prohibit the father "from bathing nude with or sleeping nude with the child, or engaging in any other nudity in the child's presence."[10]

This type of conduct might be a prelude to molestation or might just be poor judgment or lack of awareness of appropriate boundaries. For example, a parent might not realize the child's growing sense of body awareness and privacy. What was a warm series of pats on a two-year-old's bottom might be viewed as an unwanted invasion of a nine-year-old's privacy. A child-development expert with experience in the child sexual abuse field is a good resource to educate the client about more appropriate conduct. The goal is to teach the client appropriate boundaries, increase the client's insight into the child's perspective and response to the conduct, and obtain a voluntary commitment to refrain from such inappropriate conduct in the future. If the child has expressed discomfort with the inappropriate conduct, it is helpful to have the expert facilitate preparation of a joint list describing appropriate boundaries. The child and parent then both know what is acceptable, and the child is given permission to report any transgressions.

8. *Id.*
9. *Id.* at *6.
10. *Id.* at *7.

If the case still goes to trial, it is important for the lawyer to convince the court that it is not in the best interests of the child or the accused parent for inappropriate conduct to be labeled sexual abuse, especially if the conduct was the result of poor judgment rather than the grooming phase of a molestation. Obviously the parent does not want to be labeled a child molester. The child's self-esteem is directly affected by interpreting insensitive conduct as sexual abuse. It is not psychologically healthy for a child to be placed in the category of abuse victim (or "survivor") when in fact that is not what happened. The sense of violation and betrayal that accompanies molestation has long-lasting negative effects. The lawyer should consider having a child psychologist testify about these effects. The court is more likely to be persuaded by a child-oriented defense than by a focus on the accused parent's interests.

WHEN THE ALLEGATIONS ARE ERRONEOUS BUT IN GOOD FAITH

The largest group of "false allegations" appear to fall into this category, especially in domestic-relations cases.[11] With the growing public awareness and school prevention programs has come a more acute sensitivity to symptoms of child sexual abuse. Unfortunately, with the possible exception of overt sexual behavior by young children, the warning signs of child sexual abuse are the general symptoms of childhood depression and anxiety. While sexual abuse may certainly result in depression and anxiety, other situations, including marital discord, separation, and divorce, may also produce such symptoms. A well-intentioned parent who is trying to protect his or her child may have legitimate concern based on the child's behavior that warrants further investigation.

There is nothing unusual or sinister about a parent following up on a child's statement or unusual behaviors. In fact, it would be bizarre for a parent confronted with a child's statement of molestation to adopt the posture, "Don't say anything else; I don't want to contaminate the interview; wait until a neutral party talks to you." Parents do not respond in that matter in other circumstances when

11. *See generally* Chapter 2.

their children reveal disturbing or frightening incidents, and it would be an unfortunate perversion of the parent-child relationship to interpose such a requirement in the sole case of allegations of sexual molestation.

One of the greatest errors lawyers make with respect to this category of accused clients is to treat the case as one of deliberate fabrication. That response polarizes the parties, makes meaningful cooperation impossible, and places the client in the position of trying to prove an extreme case, usually unsuccessfully. Further, bridges are burned that may permanently scar the child's relationship with both parents. Even in a heated custody case, to assume malevolent motives on the part of a parent who may only be seeking to protect a child may backfire badly, portraying the accused parent as a self-centered fighter, concerned only with his or her damaged reputation, showing little or no concern for the child.

It is helpful to ask the client how he or she would feel if the child told the client what the child told the other parent. What actions would the client take? Wouldn't the client be angry toward the person the client believed had molested the child? Might not the client hate the parent who had presumably molested the child? This inquiry helps the client to understand the emotion and intensity behind the accusing parent's language and actions. Rather than responding in kind, it is to the benefit of the innocent client to assume a child-centered posture.

The child may in fact have been molested by somebody even if the client is not the molester, or the child may be in distress over some other life circumstances. In such situations *both* parents share an interest in discovering the truth and protecting the child. A thorough evaluation is important to determine whether or not the child was molested and to identify the perpetrator. If the child was not molested, the child may still need therapeutic intervention to deal with the disturbing life circumstances. The accused parent should remain child-focused, rather than self-righteously defensive.

Further, if the child was not molested, the accusing parent needs expert reassurance from a well-qualified professional who has seriously considered, but ruled out, the possibility of molestation. If the child believes that he or she has been molested, the child will also need such reassurance, and there may need to be a period of therapeutic work with the child and the accused parent to re-establish a normal relationship. Again, the accused parent's willingness to understand that an erroneous accusation may nonetheless be made in good faith, and to address the child's needs will be more likely to result in an agreement with the accusing parent or a successful defense at trial.

WHEN THE ALLEGATIONS ARE FABRICATED

Statistically, deliberate fabrication is the least likely factual scenario, even though most defenses appear to be based on the assumption that the allegations are fabricated. Fabricated allegations appear to be more common in divorce and post-divorce litigation than in other contexts, but they are still relatively infrequent. Objective professionals who are experienced in sexual abuse cases consider the possibility of fabrication when they evaluate allegations of sexual abuse.

There are not, however, any scales, instruments, or batteries of tests that can "diagnose" fabrications. One of the most widespread measures, Richard Gardner's Sexual Abuse Legitimacy (SAL) Scale, is deliberately skewed towards finding fabrication, and even Dr. Gardner has now repudiated the scale. Lawyers should not present evidence based on such measures, because they are easily attacked by lawyers and mental-health experts who are properly prepared.

A more effective strategy is to use a well-qualified mental-health professional to do a thorough evaluation. The person should not be a hired gun, who always finds that the allegations were fabricated. The expert should have clinical experience with children who have been molested, as well as broad and current knowledge of the literature in the field. The person should approach the evaluation objectively, considering the possibility that the child was molested, as well as the possibility of fabrication. The expert, or a team of experts, should evaluate the child and, if possible, both parents.

Especially with allegations involving young children, a skilled clinician should be able to uncover the fabrication. Often the children will be willing to reveal that they had merely been told to say certain things, but that they were not true. Further, such "brainwashed" children will be unlikely to be able to maintain the fabrication over time, or will only be able to use the same words, in the same order, with no ability to provide any details or to respond to questions asked out of sequence or with other words the child knows. In some cases children or other reporters have a motive to lie about abuse. Sometimes the fabricating party continues the lie, which makes proving the lie more difficult. Where the only proffered evidence of abuse is the report, it is easier to defend based on attacking the credibility of the report.

Fabrication of abuse allegations is in itself a form of child abuse. Not only do false allegations unfairly disrupt the relationship between the child and the wrongly accused parent, but in the case of young children (who may be led to actually believe that they have been molested), they also unfairly stigmatize the children, whose self-esteem may well reflect the sense of violation and betrayal that may be the most damaging part of molestation. The expert should provide testimony concerning this abusive effect of the allegations, pointing out why under these circumstances it is not appropriate to enter an order as if the allegations were true just to "be safe."

CONCLUSION

Regardless of the truth of the allegations, once they have been made, they inevitably affect the relationship between the accused parent and the child. The child may be afraid of the accused parent, even without a real reason. The fear is real whether or not it is based in fact. While it may be particularly difficult for a wrongly accused parent to be willing to accept anything less than unrestricted contact with the child, it is almost always in best interests of the parent and the child to have therapeutic assistance in re-establishing a safe relationship. An outcome that merely provides unrestricted conduct may be a pyrrhic victory if the child is apprehensive during that contact. In addressing the immediate issue of the allegations, it is important for the lawyer to maintain the broader, long-term perspective.

Representing the Child

11

Benefits of Trained, Independent Representation for Children

It is particularly useful to have a lawyer *who is experienced in sexual-abuse cases* appointed to represent the child where there are allegations of child sexual abuse, especially in domestic-relations cases. This lawyer is in the best position to present unbiased evidence to the court, free from the charge that he or she is manipulating the child one way or another. This is most important in intrafamilial sexual abuse cases.

One of the things that makes litigating such child sexual abuse cases so difficult is that the argument too often becomes a mud-slinging battle between the parents, with the child's interest getting lost in the process. For example, the accusing parent's dysfunction and anger may serve as justification for dismissing the allegation. But children of dysfunctional, angry, and even delusional parents may nonetheless be abused by the other parent. Questions about the protective parent's credibility should not obscure the child's need for protection.

The child's lawyer can be more objective in obtaining and presenting a credible evaluation of the allegations. If the child was really molested, his or her lawyer is not saddled with the credibility problems of the nonabusing parent. On the other hand, if the child was not molested, the child's lawyer can give a more accurate context to the court's desire to protect a child who does not need protecting (or at least does not need protecting from the accused parent).

The court is more likely to be persuaded by the evidence and arguments presented by a properly trained lawyer for the child than by either parent's lawyer. It is the author's strong belief that *every* child in a case involving sexual abuse allegations must have independent *and properly trained counsel.* The ability for the court to determine the truth and act appropriately is seriously jeopardized if the child is not independently represented by counsel who has the training and experience to deal with the case or who is given access to experts who can provide that training. Further, the child's lawyer is in the best position to help guide the child through the process of litigation and, if necessary, the task of testifying.[1]

On the other hand, a child's lawyer who is not properly trained can do immense damage to the child by providing merely an illusion of protection. Even a well-meaning lawyer for the child who is not familiar with the various dynamics and presentations of intrafamilial child sexual abuse can easily believe that a molested child has not in fact been molested and join forces with the abuser against the protective parent. Similarly, untrained lawyers may assume that the allegations are true and inappropriately interfere with a healthy parent-child relationship.

WHO SHOULD BE APPOINTED

A properly qualified lawyer for the child can be of great assistance to the child. However, an unqualified lawyer can be a "loose cannon," damaging the child's case and contributing to an unjust result for all parties. In domestic-relations cases there is a particular need for qualified counsel for the child because there is less likely to be an

1. For an in-depth discussion of the various roles the child's lawyer might play and a guide to representing children in such circumstances, *see*, ANN M. HARALAMBIE, THE CHILD'S ATTORNEY: A GUIDE TO REPRESENTING CHILDREN IN CUSTODY, ADOPTION, AND PROTECTION CASES (American Bar Association 1993). For a comprehensive, state-of-the art model of child representation, *see* JEAN KOH PETERS, REPRESENTING CHILDREN IN CHILD PROTECTIVE PROCEEDINGS: ETHICAL AND PRACTICAL DIMENSIONS (1997).

independent, trained third party involved in the case. Not many domestic-relations lawyers have skill and experience in representing molested children. The court is more likely to find appropriately qualified lawyers among those practicing in child-protective-services cases. Ideally, a lawyer representing the child in a domestic-relations case should have training and experience in child abuse cases as well as in the dynamics of divorce cases. However, if such persons are not available, it is probably most important to have a lawyer with experience in child abuse cases.

The American Bar Association has recommended that judges appointing lawyers for children should, unless impractical, "determine that the lawyer has been trained in representation of children and skilled in litigation (or is working under the supervision of a lawyer who is skilled in litigation). Whenever possible, the trial judge should ensure that the child's lawyer has had sufficient training in child advocacy and is familiar with [the AMERICAN BAR ASSOCIATION STANDARDS OF PRACTICE FOR LAWYERS WHO REPRESENT CHILDREN IN ABUSE AND NEGLECT CASES]."[2] Minimal training should include:

(1) Information about relevant federal and state laws and agency regulations;
(2) Information about relevant court decisions and court rules;
(3) Overview of the court process and key personnel in child-related litigation;
(4) Description of applicable guidelines and standards for representation;
(5) Focus on child development, needs, and abilities;
(6) Information on the multidisciplinary input required in child-related cases, including information on local experts who can provide consultation and testimony on the reasonableness and appropriateness of efforts made to safely maintain the child in his or her home;

2. AMERICAN BAR ASSOCIATION STANDARDS OF PRACTICE FOR LAWYERS WHO REPRESENT CHILDREN IN ABUSE AND NEGLECT CASES Standard H-4 (1996).

(7) Information concerning family dynamics and dysfunction including substance abuse, and use of kinship care;

(8) Information on accessible child welfare, family preservation, medical, educational, and mental-health resources for child clients and their families, including placement, evaluation/diagnostic, and treatment services; the structure of agencies providing such services as well as provisions and constraints related to agency payment for services; and

(9) Provision of written material (for example, representation manuals, checklists, sample forms), including listings of useful material available from other sources.[3]

The Fordham Conference on Ethical Issues in the Legal Representation of Children recommended that children's lawyers have training in at least the following areas:

a. Interviewing, counseling, negotiation.
b. Cultural competence (directed at client population).
c. Role of the lawyer and guardian ad litem (ethical issues).
d. Child development and psychology.
e. The impact on children of the abuse and neglect system.
f. The merits of a professional team approach.
g. Substantive law and procedure (as necessary for effective interviewing and counseling).[4]

Lawyers who are interested enough in child advocacy to become trained may subscribe to relevant child-abuse journals and newsletters[5] and may be members of organizations such as the National

---

3. *Id.*, Standard I-2.

4. *See Recommendations of the Conference on Ethical Issues in the Legal Representation of Children*, 64/4 FORDHAM L. REV. 1306 (1996).

5. For example, the ABA Center on Children and the Law publishes a monthly newsletter, *ChildLaw Practice*, which includes articles, case digests, and legislative news. For subscription information or a sample issue, contact the Center at 740 15th Street, N.W., 9th Floor, Washington, D.C. 20005-1022.

Association of Counsel for Children (NACC),[6] the International Society on the Prevention of Child Abuse and Neglect (ISPCAN), or the American Professional Society on the Abuse of Children (APSAC). These ongoing resources help lawyers to keep abreast of the rapidly advancing state of the art of child advocacy and new empirical data concerning child sexual abuse.

DEVELOPING RESOURCES FOR CHILD ADVOCATES

In domestic-relations cases, unlike child-protection cases, most states do not provide funding to pay for children's lawyers, let alone to provide them with access to independent multidisciplinary resources. Therefore, the child's lawyer is practically limited to using the experts whom the other parties have already involved in the case. Sometimes these experts are not well qualified, have misinterpreted or overinterpreted the data, or are otherwise biased advocates for one party or the other. In such cases, it would be extremely beneficial for the child's lawyer to have access to independent experts for consultation, review, and evaluation.

The author created a program in Pima County, Ariz., to address this need. The program can be easily replicated elsewhere. With the assistance of then Presiding Domestic Relations Judge Margaret M. Houghton, the Arizona Association of Counsel for Children, and the Pima County Bar Association, in 1992 the court created a training program for lawyers who wanted to represent children in domestic-relations cases. Only lawyers who completed the training would be eligible to be appointed to represent children. Allegations of sexual abuse constituted one category of case warranting appointment of such a lawyer for a child. Lawyers agreed to take cases on a sliding scale, including pro bono appointments. If the parents' lawyers were charging their standard hourly rates, the court would generally order that the child's lawyer be permitted to charge standard rates. However, if the parents were unrepresented or repre-

6. The NACC is the country's largest bar association for children's lawyers. The organization can provide referrals to members throughout the United States. For information on local affiliates, membership, referrals, or child advocacy resources, contact the NACC at 1825 Marion Street, Denver, Colo. 80218, telephone (303) 864-5320, fax (303) 864-5351.

sented by pro bono counsel, the child's lawyer would generally be expected to serve pro bono as well. Initial appointment orders state the hourly rate to be charged, allocate payment for the fees between the parties, and provide for an advance retainer. The lawyers billed the parties as directed by the order, and a judgment for any unpaid fees and costs was entered at the end of the case, facilitating collection if necessary.

Once the panel of lawyers was created, a panel of experts was also recruited to serve on a sliding-fee scale.[7] These experts included pediatricians, psychologists, psychiatrists, and social workers. The experts agreed to act as consultants or evaluators for court-appointed lawyers for children. The lawyer would submit a request to the court, and the court would enter an order appointing the expert. The appointment order would be similar to that for the child's lawyer, indicating the hourly rate to be charged (if any), an initial retainer amount, and allocation of payment. The experts billed the parties as directed by the order, and a judgment for any unpaid fees and costs was entered at the end of the case. Experts serving as consultants to the child's lawyer would be covered by the attorney–work-product privilege.[8] Experts conducting evaluations would be subject to the same rules as other testifying experts.

Having such a panel of experts assists the child's lawyer in many ways. For example, the lawyer can ask an expert to review the reports, recommendations, and raw data of the other experts involved to determine whether or not those evaluations were flawed in any way. The expert might assist the child's lawyer in reviewing or developing discovery directed to other experts in the case or to point out areas where further information should be sought. If necessary, an independent evaluation can be performed by the child's expert. Especially where the parties are unrepresented and the court does not have independent evaluators available to it, this may be the only

7. The author, as coordinator of the program, personally telephoned the experts to invite them to participate. Every professional contacted, except for one who no longer practiced in the area, agreed to be on the panel. Some experts who had stopped providing forensic evaluations in abuse cases agreed to do so on behalf of the child's lawyer. The experts appreciated the opportunity to serve as experts directly for the child, to be paid on the same basis as the child's lawyer, including their willingness to serve pro bono where appropriate, to have the liability protection of the court appointment, and to have a judgment without the need to file suit in the event that their fees were not paid in full. The experts were assured that they could decline specific cases and that cases would be distributed so as not to over-work particular experts.

8. *See, e.g.*, Rule 26(b)(3), FED. R. CIV. P. and the state rules patterned thereafter.

evaluation to provide information to the court. Where such resources are not available, lawyers may be able to arrange such services by motion on a case-by-case basis or establish a similar program to the one in Pima County in their own communities.

THE ROLE OF THE CHILD'S ATTORNEY

The role of the lawyer for the child has been debated for decades, generally focusing on whether the lawyer is a guardian ad litem, representing the best interests of the child, or a traditional lawyer, representing the expressed position of the child.[9] The national trend in the 1990s has been towards greater autonomy for child clients and greater recognition of their right to have their positions represented. Some lawyers for children have little understanding of their role and may attempt to act primarily as facilitators and mediators between the parents or between the parents and child protective services. While a child's lawyer who is effective often serves as a catalyst for settlement with the cooperation of the parents' lawyers, he or she should not seek settlement merely for settlement's sake. The lawyer should not sabotage the child's position merely to achieve an agreement. Indeed, one of the major reasons why children need independent counsel is to protect them from having their interests bargained away.

In February 1996 the ABA House of Delegates adopted standards of practice [hereafter Standards] for lawyers representing children in abuse and neglect cases.[10] The Standards are not binding on lawyers but represent the aspirational recommendations of the largest bar association in the world. State and local bar associations and courts may choose to hold children's lawyers to the Standards, and the Standards may become the de facto standard of practice in the field. The Standards were developed by a committee within the ABA's Family Law Section in an attempt to provide the guidance

---

9. *See generally*, ANN M. HARALAMBIE, THE CHILD'S ATTORNEY: A GUIDE TO REPRESENTING CHILDREN IN CUSTODY, ADOPTION, AND PROTECTION CASES ch. 1 (American Bar Association 1993). *See also* Ann M. Haralambie, *In Whose Best Interests?*, 34/6 TRIAL 42 (1998).

10. AMERICAN BAR ASSOCIATION STANDARDS OF PRACTICE FOR LAWYERS WHO REPRESENT CHILDREN IN ABUSE AND NEGLECT CASES (1996).

that Model Rule of Professional Conduct ER 1.14 lacked. The Standards emphasize the need for the child's lawyer to be specially trained and to make use of multidisciplinary resources, particularly regarding issues of child development.

The Standards provide that the child's lawyer owes the same duties of undivided loyalty, confidentiality, and competent representation to the child as is due an adult client, including the duty to advocate the child's articulated wishes. In all but the exceptional case, such as with a preverbal child, the child's lawyer is to maintain this traditional relationship with the client. It is important to understand that the traditional role of a lawyer includes the duty to counsel the client. This is no less true with a child client. Therefore, the lawyer does not merely parrot the child's uninformed position. If the lawyer takes the time to develop a relationship with the child, to understand what Yale Professor Jean Koh Peters refers to as "the child-in-context,"[11] and to advise the child about the available options and their ramifications, most children will authorize the lawyer to advocate reasonable positions on their behalf.

While the Standards express a clear preference for lawyers being appointed in this traditional role, they do recognize the guardian ad litem role, in which case the lawyer is not bound by the child's articulated preference, irrespective of exceptions provided with respect to lawyers acting as traditional lawyer.

The Commentary to the Standards rejects the concepts that children of certain ages are "impaired," "disabled," "incompetent," or lack capacity to determine their position in litigation and that disability must be globally determined.[12] The Comment to Standard B-3 provides: "Rather, disability is contextual, incremental, and may be intermittent. The child's ability to contribute to a determination of his or her position is functional, depending upon the particular position and the circumstances prevailing at the time the position must be determined. Therefore, a child may be able to determine some

---

11. *See, e.g.*, JEAN KOH PETERS, REPRESENTING CHILDREN IN CHILD PROTECTIVE PROCEEDINGS: ETHICAL AND PRACTICAL DIMENSIONS §§ 1-3, 1-4 (1997); Jean Koh Peters, *The Roles and Content of Best Interests in Client-Directed Lawyering for Children in Child Protective Proceedings*, 64/4 FORDHAM L. REV. 1505 (1996).

12. *See also* Ann M. Haralambie & Deborah L. Glaser, *Practical and Theoretical Problems with the AAML Standards for Representing "Impaired" Children*, 13/1 J. AM. ACAD. MATRIM. LAWYERS 57 (1995). The ABA Standards commentary referred to was based primarily on this article.

positions in the case but not others. Similarly, a child may be able to direct the lawyer with respect to a particular issue at one time but not at another. This Standard relies on empirical knowledge about competencies with respect to both adults and children." While this view of child representation provides a great deal of flexibility, it also requires that the child's lawyer be adequately trained and make appropriate use of professionals in other disciplines to determine when the lawyer is and is not directed by the child client.

In December 1995 a symposium was held at the Fordham Law School to discuss the ethical issues involved in representing children in maltreatment cases. During the three days of the symposium, invited participants tackled some of the practical problems raised by the ABA Standards. Individual working groups made recommendations, which were then voted on by the group as a whole on the last day, [hereafter Recommendations].[13] An extraordinary degree of consensus was achieved despite the different perspectives represented by the participants, many of whom were the leading scholars and practitioners on both sides of the traditional child's wishes/best-interest debate.

The symposium participants rejected the entire category of lawyer guardians ad litem to the extent that the role "includes responsibilities inconsistent with those of a lawyer for the child."[14] Participants recommended that laws currently allowing lawyers to be appointed as guardians ad litem be amended to authorize instead appointment of a lawyer to represent the child.[15] Recommendations were made, however, to guide lawyers appointed as traditional guardians ad litem pending changes in state law.[16]

The Recommendations for practice guidelines encompass legal representation of even nonverbal children. The lawyer is advised to "make extensive use of experts (e.g., social workers, psychologists) as well as other interested persons (e.g., family members) in assessing the child's circumstances."[17] Recommendation V(A)(1) provides that

13. *See Recommendations of the Conference on Ethical Issues in the Legal Representation of Children*, 64/4 FORDHAM L. REV. 1301-23 (1996).
14. *See Recommendations of the Conference on Ethical Issues in the Legal Representation of Children*, 64/4 FORDHAM L. REV. 1301 (1996).
15. *Id.*
16. *Id.* at 1314-16.
17. *Id.* at 1304.

where there is evidence that "the child is unable to express a reasoned choice," the lawyer "must engage in additional fact finding to determine whether the child has or may develop the capacity to direct the lawyer's action."[18] This factual determination may be aided by information from various professionals and other concerned parties, with consideration of culture, race, ethnicity, and class, as well as of the child's individual life experiences, family background, and medical history.[19]

However, in construing the flexibility accorded by Model Rule of Professional Conduct Rule ER 1.14 and the ABA Standards, the Recommendations did provide for the lawyer to determine the child's best interests under certain circumstances.[20] Of particular assistance were the recommendations concerning how to make an *objective* determination of the child's best interests, which are set forth here in their entirety. Recommendation IV(B)(3) provides:

> 3. Lawyers for children who must identify, determine, and advocate for their client's interests at any given moment in the representation should employ the following process. This process is intended to assist the child's lawyer in identifying the legal interest or interests to be pursued. The process by which a lawyer acquires understanding of a child's interests and needs is not linear but should be dynamic and evolving over the course of the case or relationship. This process of inquiry always begins and ends with the child-in-context. It is critical to note that, at almost any point in the analysis, this process may leave only one legal interest, at which point the lawyer is constrained to pursue that legal interest.
>
> a. The child client has a universe of possible needs and interests, as defined by any and all persons involved in the child's life. The lawyer must first narrow the area of inquiry by determining the *legal* interests of the child. A legal interest is any interest that the legal proceeding has authority to address. Even when many

18. *Id.* at 1312.
19. *Id.* at 1313.
20. *Id.* at 1308-13.

statutes and decisions require the lawyer to address a child client's best interests, these guidelines require a lawyer in those circumstances to address something that can be more appropriately characterized as a child's legal interests. In other contexts, a child's legal interests could include, for instance, a child's right to "appropriate education," "least restrictive alternative," "least detrimental alternative," as well as children's interests in procedural rights.

b. The process must then focus on the child in her context. It is the lawyer's responsibility to carry out a full, efficient, and speedy factual investigation with the goal of achieving a detailed understanding of the child client's unique personality, her family system, history, and daily life. This process should include the client's own words, stories, and desires at every possible point. Even where the lawyer has determined that the child cannot fully understand or express desires about the legal issues of the case, there will be very few verbal children who cannot express some views about their own lives. As the lawyer gathers information from her client and other sources, the lawyer should organize those facts using devices such as genograms, chronologies, and daily schedules to ensure that the lawyer is working from a thickly detailed view of the child client as a unique individual.

c. Essential to the process is also a snapshot of the child at the moment of the determination. How is the child developing? How is the child behaving? How is the child benefitting or suffering from her current living arrangement? A lawyer should generally obtain this snapshot in part through ongoing current contact with the client.

d. The lawyer must go further and consider the actual alternative options available to the child. The lawyer should understand these options concretely and understand as specifically as possible how that option will be experienced by the child.

i. These options must include all legally available options, including good faith options for seeking modification of the law. The lawyer must continually reevaluate, however, whether these options for law reform are actually attainable given the current legal climate.

ii. These options must also include all options available in the community to the child. These options should be realistically available or obtainable through advocacy, however, and not based on speculation of what the system might some day be able to make available.

e. In considering the actually available options that the lawyer and client have identified, the lawyer should examine each option in light of important paradigms that directly related non-legal disciplines are considering. These paradigms should be determined through interdisciplinary research identified in the Recommendations for Further Study.

f. There will be some cases in which the analysis becomes too complex and lawyers should consult experts for guidance. Lawyers may need to retain experts to aid them in deciding which of the remaining legal interests to pursue. Since much of the data upon which the decision is based will be confidential lawyer-client information, the retained consultant is sometimes the optimal, and only ethically acceptable, guide. When lack of resources or other factors make such a consultant impractical, the lawyer may look to experts already involved with the client, experts retained by other parties, or occasionally court-appointed experts. These latter experts, however, do not share the lawyer's duty of advocacy with respect to the child client's wishes and perspectives, often have other institutional loyalties, may have important ongoing relationships with the child that must not be damaged, or may not offer opinions to the lawyer in a timely fashion.

g. At this point in the process of determining which legal interest to pursue, there still may be no definitively preferable option for the child.

i. At this point the lawyer should return to the thickly detailed understanding of the child, with reference to the child's needs and interests as outlined in the proposed *ABA Standards of Practice for Lawyers Who Represent Children in Abuse and Neglect Cases*, Section B-5 and its Commentary. The lawyer again should seek any information or opinions the child can offer about the options remaining.

ii. The lawyer then should ensure that evidence is presented on the remaining options to the court, and in opposition to all options that were actually available but that have been eliminated from the child's legal interest through the preceding analysis.[21]

By far the most sophisticated and thoughtful model of child representation is that formulated by Professor Jean Koh Peters.[22] She takes the ABA Standards and Fordham Recommendations one step further, finally resolving the wishes versus best interests dichotomy that has plagued the debate on what lawyers for children are supposed to do. Peters was the intellectual architect of the Fordham Symposium's Working Group on Determining the Best Interests of the Child, whose recommendations were adopted unanimously and without change by all members of the Symposium.

As one of the drafters of the ABA Standards and the Fordham Recommendations, I am of the opinion that the model of representation presented by Peters would have been adopted by both groups and is consistent with the ethical guidelines provided by those documents. But her model is more refined and workable, providing a continuum and context that allows the lawyer to fully act as a lawyer while recognizing those areas where the child cannot provide guidance. The Peters model posits "three defaults, three umbrella principles, and seven questions to keep us honest," all of which restrict the child's lawyer's subjective discretion and require development of a "thickly detailed" understanding of the "child-in-context." As a result, the representation is more objective and principled.

The defaults represent a starting place from which the child's lawyer must individualize the representation to maximize the child's participation, reflecting the client's uniqueness. The "relationship default" requires the lawyer to meet and get to know the child unless there is "weighty independent evidence that the meeting would serve the client no purpose or would yield such a minimal benefit to the client that it is outweighed by the costs to the client of planning such a visit."[23] The competency default views the child's competency

21. *Id.* at 1309-11.
22. *See* JEAN KOH PETERS, REPRESENTING CHILDREN IN CHILD PROTECTIVE PROCEEDINGS: ETHICAL AND PRACTICAL DIMENSIONS (1997).
23. *Id.* at § 3-2(b)(1).

along a spectrum within which the child can contribute as much as possible to the representation.[24] The advocacy default requires the lawyer to represent the child's expressed preferences about issues in the case unless the child cannot adequately do so in his or her own interest.[25] An alternative to the advocacy default is provided to cover situations where the lawyer is functioning as a traditional guardian ad litem, required to represent the child's best interests. Under the alternate default, the lawyer is still required to make the child's voice, not the lawyer's, a major focus.[26]

The principles are designed to keep the lawyer focused on the child's perspective and to reduce the likelihood that the lawyer's subjective views will overshadow the child's interests. Principle One is to "revolve one's actions around one's developing view of both the child-in-context and the theory of the case."[27] Principle Two is to "respect one's client, whether present or absent."[28] Principle Three is to "cultivate right relationships with other people in the child's world, keeping in mind the ways in which the child values each of these relationships."[29]

The questions serve as a checklist to keep the representation true to the client:

1. In making decisions about the representation, am I making the best effort to [see] the case, from my client's subjective point of view, rather than from an adult's point of view?
2. Does the child understand as much as I can explain about what is happening in his case?
3. If my client were an adult, would I be taking the same actions, making the same decisions, and treating her in the same way?
4. If I decide to treat my client differently from the way I would treat an adult in a similar situation, in what ways will my client concretely benefit from that deviation? Is that benefit one which I can explain to my client?

---

24. *Id.* at § 3-2(b)(2).
25. *Id.* at § 3-2(b)(3)(i).
26. *Id.* at § 3-2(b)(ii).
27. *Id.* at § 3-2(c)(1).
28. *Id.* at § 3-2(c)(2).
29. *Id.* at § 3-2(c)(3).

5. Is it possible that I am making decisions in the case for the gratification of the adults in the case and not for the child?
6. Is it possible that I am making decisions in the case for my own gratification, and not for that of my client?
7. Does the representation, seen as a whole, reflect what is unique and idiosyncratically characteristic of this child?[30]

The Peters model allows lawyers to exercise an objective type of discretion in determining the child's position under limited circumstances. The reader is referred to Peters' book for a more detailed explanation of how to implement her model.

It is essential that the lawyer, all parties and their counsel, and the judge understand what the role of the child's lawyer is in a given case. Therefore, the lawyer is well advised to seek clarification from the judge on the case unless there is clear local law or a clear description of the role in the order appointing the lawyer. Child sexual abuse cases have spawned an increasing number of tort actions against a variety of defendants,[31] including malpractice actions against children's lawyers. Clarification of the lawyer's role should be considered a major risk-management issue.

THE ETHICAL DILEMMA

One of the most often cited examples of a dilemma for children's lawyers involves the representation of a molested child who does not want the molestation revealed or wants to be in the custody of or allowed unfettered visitation with a molester. The ABA Standards specifically address this issue in Standard B-4(3) and its commentary:

> (3) If the child's attorney determines that the child's expressed preference would be seriously injurious to the child (as opposed to merely being contrary to the lawyer's opinion of what would be in the child's interests), the lawyer may request appointment of a separate guardian ad litem and continue to represent the child's expressed preference, unless the child's position is prohibited by law or without any factual

30. *Id.* at § 3-2(d).
31. See Chapter 5.

foundation. The child's attorney shall not reveal the basis of the request for appointment of a guardian ad litem which would compromise the child's position.

Commentary—

One of the most difficult ethical issues for lawyers representing children occurs when the child is able to express a position and does so, but the lawyer believes that the position chosen is wholly inappropriate or could result in serious injury to the child. This is particularly likely to happen with respect to an abused child whose home is unsafe, but who desires to remain or return home. A child may desire to live in a dangerous situation because it is all he or she knows, because of a feeling of blame or of responsibility to take care of the parents, or because of threats. The child may choose to deal with a known situation rather than risk the unknown world of a foster home or other out-of-home placement.

In most cases the ethical conflict involved in asserting a position which would seriously endanger the child, especially by disclosure of privileged information, can be resolved through the lawyer's counseling function. If the lawyer has taken the time to establish rapport with the child and gain that child's trust, it is likely that the lawyer will be able to persuade the child to abandon a dangerous position or at least identify an alternate course.

If the child cannot be persuaded, the lawyer has a duty to safeguard the child's interests by requesting appointment of a guardian ad litem, who will be charged with advocating the child's best interests without being bound by the child's direction. As a practical matter, this may not adequately protect the child if the danger to the child was revealed only in a confidential disclosure to the lawyer, because the guardian ad litem may never learn of the disclosed danger.

Confidentiality is abrogated for various professionals by mandatory child abuse reporting laws. Some states abrogate lawyer-client privilege by mandating reports. States which do not abrogate the privilege may permit reports notwithstanding professional privileges. The policy considerations underlying abrogation apply to lawyers where there is a substantial danger of serious injury or death. Under such circumstances, the lawyer must take the minimum steps which would be necessary to ensure the child's safety, respecting and following the child's direction to the greatest extent possible consistent with the child's safety and ethical rules.

The lawyer may never counsel a client or assist a client in conduct the lawyer knows is criminal or fraudulent. See ER 1.2(d), Model

> Rules of Professional Conduct, DR 7-102(A)(7), Model Code of Professional Responsibility. Further, existing ethical rules require the lawyer to disclose confidential information to the extent necessary to prevent the client from committing a criminal act likely to result in death or substantial bodily harm, see ER 1.6(b), Model Rules of Professional Conduct, and permits the lawyer to reveal the intention of the client to commit a crime. See ER 1.6(c), Model Rules of Professional Conduct, DR 4-101(C)(3), Model Code of Professional Responsibility. While child abuse, including sexual abuse, is a crime, the child is presumably the victim, rather than the perpetrator of that crime. Therefore, disclosure of confidences is designed to protect the client, rather than to protect a third party from the client. Where the child is in grave danger of serious injury or death, the child's safety must be the paramount concern.
>
> The lawyer is not bound to pursue the client's objectives through means not permitted by law and ethical rules. See DR-7-101(A)(1), Model Code of Professional Responsibility. Further, lawyers may be subject personally to sanctions for taking positions that are not well-grounded in fact and warranted by existing law or a good faith argument for the extension, modification, or reversal of existing law.[32]

The Fordham Symposium's working group on confidentiality also identified the ethical dilemma in representing a child who may be at risk of harm but who refuses to authorize disclosure of confidential information concerning the risk, recognizing that the current ethical rules would prohibit a lawyer from breaching the client's confidences.[33] The working group proposed that Rule 1.6, Model Rules of Professional Conduct, be amended to permit some minimal disclosure of confidential information when necessary to protect the child.[34] The members of the working group did not agree on the level of risked harm necessary to permit disclosure.[35] The recommendations from that working group that were ultimately adopted by the symposium members recommended further study on whether Rule 1.6 "should be amended to permit the lawyer for a child to dis-

---

32. See Standard B-4(3), AMERICAN BAR ASSOCIATION STANDARDS OF PRACTICE FOR LAWYERS WHO REPRESENT CHILDREN IN ABUSE AND NEGLECT CASES (1996).
33. *See Report of the Working Group on Confidentiality*, 64/4 FORDHAM L. REV. 1367 (1996).
34. *Id.* at 1371.
35. *Id.*

close confidences to the limited extent necessary to prevent the child from engaging in conduct likely to result in imminent death or substantial bodily harm to the client."[36]

CONCLUSION

A lawyer who undertakes the representation of an allegedly molested child has a duty to be competent, to become qualified, or to associate with a qualified lawyer. It is an enormous responsibility and a difficult task to be the lawyer for such a child. While the ethical guidelines involved in representing abused children are not yet clear, the emerging national consensus, reflected in the ABA Standards, Fordham Recommendations, and Peters' book, does provide guidance.

36. *See Recommendations of the Conference on Ethical Issues in the Legal Representation of Children*, 64/4 FORDHAM L. REV. 1308 (1996).

12 Children's Memory and Suggestibility

Why Knowing About Memory Is Important

The issue of children's memory has received a great deal of attention from researchers recently, in part because the credibility of children in child abuse, particularly sexual abuse, cases has been attacked in the courtroom. For example, where a preschooler has made allegations of intrafamilial child sexual abuse, the lawyer defending the accused parent typically charges that the child has been coached or brainwashed, usually by the other parent, or that the child's statements have been tainted by the questions of a therapist or investigator. Two issues are really involved in the impeachment of children's accounts of abuse: memory and suggestibility (which is a part of the tainting of memory, whether intentionally or inadvertently).

Many adults assume that children have poor memories and are easily led to believe that things actually happened that did not. A related assumption is that children are unable to separate fact from fantasy. If a trial is really to be a quest for the truth, rather than an elaborate competition or game with the child's future as the prize, then it becomes imperative to know whether children's testimony can be trusted. The question of whether the particular child witness's testimony (or the child's statements made to an adult witness) should be accorded much evidentiary weight has a great deal to do with the judge's general beliefs about children's memory and suggestibility.

Another issue in which memory is relevant to testimony is the effect of the act of testifying on memory. It has been suggested that testifying in a courtroom in itself impairs a child's memory.[1] Lawyers who have been involved with child witnesses have certainly seen children who seemed to be articulate during interviews become uncommunicative in a courtroom setting, especially under even mildly hostile cross-examination. One study involved having eight- to ten-year-old children watch a staged event involving teaching them about body parts and functions, with half of the children questioned about it in a courtroom setting and the other half questioned at their schools.[2] The study found that the children at school recalled significantly more during free recall than did those interviewed in the courtroom. The children interviewed in the courtroom also gave significantly more incorrect answers to direct questions and were more likely to acquiesce to misleading questions. Because of this, some accommodations may need to be made to the courtroom environment to make it more conducive for children to testify accurately and completely.

HOW MEMORY WORKS

Memory involves various tasks.[3] Generally, the first task is to perceive that which will be remembered. If the person cannot perceive

---

1. *See*, Melton, G. & Thompson, R., *Getting Out of a Rut: Detours to Less Traveled Paths in Child-Witness Research*, in CHILDREN'S EYEWITNESS MEMORY 209 (S. Ceci, M. Toglia & D. Ross, eds. 1987).

2. *See*, Karen Saywitz & Rebecca Nathanson, *Children's Testimony and Their Perceptions of Stress in and Out of the Courtroom*, 17 CHILD ABUSE & NEGLECT 613 (1993).

3. There are a number of worthwhile books discussing children's memory in general and how it relates to children's testimony. *See, e.g.*, TRAUMA AND MEMORY (Linda Meyer Williams & Victoria L. Banyard, eds., 1998); MEMORY DEVELOPMENT IN CHILDREN (N. Cowan, ed., 1997); INTERNATIONAL PERSPECTIVES ON CHILD ABUSE AND CHILDREN'S TESTIMONY (Bette L. Bottoms & Gail S. Goodman, eds. 1996); MEMORY AND TESTIMONY IN THE CHILD WITNESS (Maria S. Zaragoza, John R. Graham, Gordon C.N. Hall, Richard Hirschman & Yossef S. Ben-Porath, eds. 1995); CHILD VICTIMS, CHILD WITNESSES (Gail S. Goodman & Bette L. Bottoms, eds., 1993); THE SUGGESTIBILITY OF CHILDREN'S RECOLLECTIONS: IMPLICATIONS FOR EYEWITNESS TESTIMONY (John Doris, ed., 1991); Knowing and Remembering in Children (R. Fivush & J. Hudson, eds., 1990); PERSPECTIVES ON CHILDREN'S TESTIMONY (Stephen Ceci, D. Ross & M. Toglia, eds., 1989); CHILDREN'S EYEWITNESS MEMORY (S. Ceci, D. Ross & M. Toglia, eds., 1987). *Cf.* JOHN R. SPENCER & RHONA FLIN, THE EVIDENCE OF CHILDREN: THE LAW AND THE PSYCHOLOGY (2d ed. 1993) (with reference to the English legal system). The American Professional Society of the Abuse of Children devoted an entire issue of its publication, THE ADVISOR, (volume 5, number 3, summer 1992) to the subject of memory (both children's and adult's memory). The issue is even-handed in its discussion of the controversy and is an excellent resource for lawyers, judges, and mental health professionals. *See also* Karen J. Saywitz, *Children in Court: Principles of*

something, he cannot remember it. Next, the perceived information must be coded and stored. That stored memory must then be retained. Finally, the stored memory must be recalled.

The accuracy of the memory may be affected at any stage in the process. A person's understanding and prior experience are very relevant to the entire process of memory, from how an event is perceived to how it is recalled. More problems with memory occur with how the memory is stored than with how it is recalled.[4]

Some memories are stored deliberately. For example, a child learning spelling words, multiplication tables, or a name and address makes a deliberate effort to store the information. Other memories are not stored deliberately. Most things about which the child witnesses testify involve the latter types of memory. For example, a child who is asked to describe being abused or who is asked which parent performs various care-taking duties usually has not made a deliberate effort to store that information.

Children often misattribute cause and effect. A basic logical fallacy is the post hoc fallacy.[5] Because something happened after something else, children may assume that the first event caused the second. This particularly happens with blame. A child is naughty, the parents later divorce, and the child believes that he or she caused the divorce by being naughty.

Because young children do not understand many human limitations, parents are often regarded as omnipotent. This erroneous worldview allows children to attribute great causative powers to their parents. The parent yelled loudly and then it thundered, so the parent's anger must be able to cause thunder. When the child remembers the event as the parent causing the thunder by yelling, the inaccuracy is caused by the child's imperfect understanding of the parent's power, the mechanism of thunder, and the noncausative coincidence in the sequence of events. It does not mean that the child is lying about the parent causing the thunder, and in such a cir-

---

Child Development for Judicial Application, in A JUDICIAL PRIMER ON CHILD SEXUAL ABUSE 15 (Josephine Bulkley & Claire Sandt, eds. 1993).

4. *See, e.g.*, Charles Brainerd & Peter A. Ornstein, *Children's Memory for Witnessed Events: A Developmental Backdrop*, in THE SUGGESTIBILITY OF CHILDREN'S RECOLLECTIONS: IMPLICATIONS FOR EYEWITNESS TESTIMONY 15 (John Doris, ed., 1991).

5. *Post hoc ergo propter hoc*, the fallacy that confuses sequence with causation. A literal translation of the Latin is "after that, therefore, because of that."

cumstance, nobody would accuse the child of lying, only of misunderstanding. A listener might well believe that the parent had yelled and that shortly thereafter it had thundered. The information remembered was accurate; only the interpretation of the information was inaccurate.

Similar inaccuracies in a child's report of abuse are often used to impeach the child's testimony and infer that the abuse itself never happened. The lawyer presenting the child's testimony (or an adult's testimony about the child's report) should use a child-development expert to explain the developmental basis for the child's error, pointing out that the accuracy of the facts reported is not necessarily compromised by the inaccuracy of the child's interpretation of the facts.

If the event is complex, young children may have more difficulty in conceptualizing it than do adults.[6] Similarly, they may have more difficulty than adults in identifying relationships and feelings and in attributing intentions.[7] Difficulties in coding the memory in the first instance affects the accuracy of the memory when it is stored and recalled. It has been stated that children do not develop into an adult skill level in ordering and interpreting perceptions until about age twelve.[8] However, even three-year-old children can relate autobiographical events from memory.[9] As may be expected, children's memory for central details is better than their memory for peripheral details.[10] Once the memory is successfully perceived, coded, and stored, there is some support in the research that a preschooler can then remember it as well as an adult.[11] However, the child may have

6. *See, e.g.*, Nancy Perry & Teply, L., *Interviewing, Counseling, and In-Court Examination of Children: Practical Approaches for Attorneys*, 18 CREIGHTON L. REV. 1369 (1984-85).

7. *Id.*

8. *See, e.g.*, Nancy Perry, *How Children Remember and Why They Forget*, 5/3 THE ADVISOR 1 (Summer 1992); Collins, W., Wellman, H., Keniston, A. & Westby, S. *Age-related Aspects of Comprehension and Inferences from a Televised Dramatic Narrative*, 49 CHILD DEVELOPMENT 389 (1978); D. FLAPAN, CHILDREN'S UNDERSTANDING OF SOCIAL INTERACTION (1968).

9. *See, e.g.*, Nelson, K., Fivush, R., Hudson, J. & Lucariello, J., *Scripts and the Development of Memory*, in CURRENT TRENDS IN MEMORY DEVELOPMENT 52 (M. Chi, ed. 1983); Nelson, K. & Gruendel, J., *Generalized event representations: Basic Building Blocks of Cognitive Development*, in 1 ADVANCES IN COGNITIVE DEVELOPMENT 131 (M. Lamb & A. Brown, eds. 1981); Todd, C. & Perlmutter, M., *Reality Recalled by Preschoolers*, in CHILDREN'S MEMORY: NEW DIRECTIONS IN CHILD DEVELOPMENT 69 (M. Perlmutter, ed. 1980); Nelson, K., *How Children Represent Their World In and Out of Language: A Preliminary Report*, in CHILDREN'S THINKING: WHAT DEVELOPS? 255 (R. Siegler, ed. 1979).

10. *See, e.g.*, Gail Goodman & Reed, R., *Age Differences in Eyewitness Testimony*, 10 LAW & HUMAN BEHAVIOR 317 (1986).

11. *See, e.g.*, Werber, J. & Perlmutter, M., *Development of Visual Memory in Infants*, in ADVANCES IN CHILD DEVELOPMENT AND BEHAVIOR (H. W. Reese & L. P. Lipsett, eds. 1979) (vol. 14, p. 1).

difficulty in expressing the content of the memory, which is why child psychologists often use play therapy and picture drawing to help unlock what the child cannot express verbally.

Over time memories may be significantly altered. People often romanticize the past or vilify the past or portions of the past. One parent may only remember the child's faults, while the other may only remember the good times. Puzzling events may be reconstructed to conform with what the person knows and understands. People may remember as they wish to remember: a casual glance may be remembered as a fervent communication. Apart from deliberate lying, the memory can be substantially affected based on the significance of the memory to the person's self-esteem. For example, people may alter their memories to make themselves look better: the marginal athlete remembering "the big play" that saved the game, the fisherman describing "the one that got away," the child retelling the conversation she had with the Disney World character.

When a person is repeatedly exposed to particular pattern, such as a routine, memory of that routine may not clearly distinguish between particular occurrences of the pattern. For example, if a person habitually takes a morning shower, that person may have a generic "memory" of the routine. If asked to describe everything about the morning shower two weeks ago, the person might include features that are usually a part of the routine whether or not on that particular day the activity conformed in all respects to the standard pattern. Even young children generally have no difficulty in developing "scripts," a type of summarized knowledge based on having encountered repeated events, such as going to the dentist, going to church, or going to school.[12] Eisen and Goodman explain:

> In general, young children can have a difficult time reporting a specific instance of an episode that does not significantly deviate from what usually happens in their day-to-day life. In addition, young children have more difficulty than older children in separating out repeated instances of similar life events and tend to confuse the details of these

---

12. *See, e.g.*, Bauer, P. & Mandler, J., *Remembering What Happened Next: Very Young Children's Recall of Event Sequences*, in KNOWING AND REMEMBERING IN YOUNG CHILDREN 9 (R. Fivush & J. Hudson, eds. 1990).

experiences. Children develop scripts for these repeated events. Children living in chronically stressful environments will likely develop generalized scripts that contain the gist of their typical abusive experiences.[13]

It may become important for the child to be able to recall deviations from the standard. In order to do this, the child first has to be able distinguish between what are the standard elements and what components are not standard; otherwise, nonstandard elements might be erroneously remembered as part of the standard activity.[14] Failure to differentiate between general script elements and unique features of a repeated event may, for example, make it more difficult for children to testify accurately about specific episodes of molestation when asked to do so in court. Younger children may have more difficulty distinguishing the deviating features from the standard features than older children do.[15] Eisen and Goodman state:

> Although it is generally accepted that omissions and confusions will occur when multiple similar traumatic (or nontraumatic) events are being reported, the presence of omitted details and minor source confusions does not necessarily make the memory report inaccurate or invalid. Skeptics of young children's ability to report the details of their life experiences point to source confusions as an important factor in understanding how memory reports are corrupted through the process of reconstruction. Nevertheless, the reconstructed account of a single episode from a series of similar life experiences will usually include the core elements that are shared across the events, but omit or confuse some unique aspects of any given experience.[16]

---

13. *See* Mitchell L. Eisen & Gail S. Goodman, *Trauma, Memory, and Suggestibility in Children*, 10 DEVELOPMENT & PSYCHOPATHOLOGY 717, 729 (1998).

14. *See, e.g.*, Farrar, M. & Goodman, G., *Developmental Changes in Event Memory*, 63 CHILD DEVELOPMENT 173 (1992).

15. *See* Farrar, M. & Goodman, G., *Developmental Changes in Event Memory*, 63 CHILD DEVELOPMENT 173 (1992) (comparing four-year-olds, who remembered a more generalized event representation, being confused about the details of a specific experience, and seven-year-olds, who were better able to recall distinct memories of separate events). Farra and Goodman's experiment also indicated that "increased standard visit experiences tended to produce poorer overall memory for the deviation visit, as the memory for the standard visit became the primary representation of the event. . . . However, once a deviation visit was encountered, only those children who had additional experience were able to learn the basic event structure." *Id.* at 185. *See also* Fivush, *Developmental Perspectives on Autobiographical Recall*, in CHILD VICTIMS, CHILD WITNESSES 1 at 19-20 (Gail S. Goodman & Bette L. Bottoms, eds., 1993).

16. *See* Mitchell L. Eisen & Gail S. Goodman, *Trauma, Memory, and Suggestibility in Children*, 10 DEVELOPMENT & PSYCHOPATHOLOGY 717, 729–730 (1998).

Some things can refresh the accurate recall of remembered events, while others can distort the real memory. Repeated retelling of the event can help the person not to forget, as can re-experiencing the event.[17] But repeated interrogation may be stressful for the witness and impair memory performance.[18] Where a person is uncertain about some aspect of the memory, "exposure to other accounts of it can lead to an alteration of the memory for the episode."[19] When there is a deliberate effort to mislead, further questions about the event may distort the memory.[20] Finally, even where there is no deliberate effort to mislead, an authoritative questioner may unknowingly cause the child to distort his or her memory.[21]

Recently there has been increased attention among researchers to the issues of children's memory and suggestibility. It is important for lawyers and expert witnesses seeking to use this emerging body of research to scrutinize the methodology of the study and recognize limitations of the various models. For example, research on memory for observed peripheral events, such as asking about the color of the hat on a "robber" in a staged crime, may not be particularly relevant to the issue at hand, such as a child's identification of her mother's long-time boyfriend as the person who has molested her repeatedly. Similarly, memory for real-world events may be different than memory for more artificial staged events in an experimental setting. It is also important to remember that "the mere fact that children's testimony is influenced by suggestion does not necessarily imply that their ability to remember the witnessed event is impaired."[22]

All recollection does not use the same skills, and children who can recall some types of memories may not be able to recall more

---

17. *See*, Charles Brainerd & Peter A. Ornstein, *Children's Memory for Witnessed Events: A Developmental Backdrop*, in THE SUGGESTIBILITY OF CHILDREN'S RECOLLECTIONS: IMPLICATIONS FOR EYEWITNESS TESTIMONY 15 (John Doris, ed., 1991).

18. *See*, Rhona Flin, *Commentary: A Grand Memory for Forgetting*, in THE SUGGESTIBILITY OF CHILDREN'S RECOLLECTIONS: IMPLICATIONS FOR EYEWITNESS TESTIMONY 22 (John Doris, ed., 1991).

19. *See*, Charles Brainerd & Peter A. Ornstein, *Children's Memory for Witnessed Events: A Developmental Backdrop*, in THE SUGGESTIBILITY OF CHILDREN'S RECOLLECTIONS: IMPLICATIONS FOR EYEWITNESS TESTIMONY 15 (John Doris, ed., 1991).

20. *See*, Charles Brainerd & Peter A. Ornstein, *Children's Memory for Witnessed Events: A Developmental Backdrop*, in THE SUGGESTIBILITY OF CHILDREN'S RECOLLECTIONS: IMPLICATIONS FOR EYEWITNESS TESTIMONY 18 (John Doris, ed., 1991).

21. *See*, Charles Brainerd & Peter A. Ornstein, *Children's Memory for Witnessed Events: A Developmental Backdrop*, in THE SUGGESTIBILITY OF CHILDREN'S RECOLLECTIONS: IMPLICATIONS FOR EYEWITNESS TESTIMONY 18 (John Doris, ed., 1991).

22. *See*, Zaragoza, M., *Preschool Children's Susceptibility to Memory Impairment*, in THE SUGGESTIBILITY OF CHILDREN'S RECOLLECTIONS: IMPLICATIONS FOR EYEWITNESS TESTIMONY 28 (John Doris, ed., 1991).

complex types of memory. The most basic type of recall is recognition. Even infants, for example, can recognize their primary caretakers.[23] More complex is reconstruction. Lawyers frequently ask witnesses to reconstruct a scene or an event. An interviewing technique called "context reinstatement" asks the person to reconstruct various elements of the scene or event in an effort to help the person reconstruct the entire event and, thereby, recall more details than they would otherwise.[24] Even young children can benefit from this technique.[25] It is common experience for all of us to remember more about events when given contextual cues.

The most complex type of memory is free recall. Recalling quotations may be difficult for young children. Preschoolers especially have trouble talking about talking and thinking.[26] Fewer errors are likely to occur during free recall than during responses to specific questions.[27] It is free recall that lawyers seek to elicit during direct examination. The witness should not be prompted with leading or suggestive questions in order that the witness' free recall of the event may be tapped without influence. It is this type of recall that is most difficult for children. However, while young children may remember less about an event and may be able to supply fewer details, the research suggests that what they are able to recall is as accurate as what adults recall.[28]

Even if children can accurately remember and relate information, various emotional and situational factors may make it more difficult for them to be *willing* to disclose the information, particularly

---

23. *See, e.g.*, Myers, N. & Perlmutter, M., *Memory in the Years from Two to Five*, in MEMORY DEVELOPMENT IN CHILDREN 191 (P. A. Ornstein ed. 1978); JEAN PIAGET & B. INHELDER, MEMORY AND INTELLIGENCE (1973). Two interesting studies showed that recognition of faces improves from ages six to ten, declines from eleven to twelve, and improves after the age of thirteen. *See*, Gail Goodman & Reed, R., *Age Differences in Eyewitness Testimony*, 10 LAW & HUMAN BEHAVIOR 317 (1986); Carey, S., *A Case Study: Face Recognition*, in EXPLORATIONS IN THE BIOLOGY OF LANGUAGE 175 (E. Walker, ed., 1978).

24. *See, e.g.*, Fisher, R., Amador, M. & Geiselman, R., *Field Test of the Cognitive Interview: Enhancing the Recollection of Actual Victims and Witnesses of Crime*, 74 J. APPLIED PSYCHOLOGY 722 (1989); Geiselman, R., Fisher, R., MacKinnon, D. & Holland, H. *Eyewitness Memory Enhancement in the Police Interview: Cognitive Retrieval Mnemonics Versus Hypnosis*, 70 J. APPLIED PSYCHOLOGY 401 (1985).

25. *See, e.g.*, Perry, N., Nielsen, D., Burns, D., Cunningham, E. & Jenkins, S. *Young Children's Ability to Provide Accurate Testimony Following a Witnessed Event*, paper presented at the spring meeting of the Nebraska Psychological Association, Lincoln, Nebraska (1987).

26. *See, e.g.*, Flavell, J., *Cognitive Monitoring*, in CHILDREN'S ORAL COMMUNICATIONS SKILLS (W. P. Dickson, ed., 1981).

27. *See, e.g.*, Dent, H. & Stephenson, G., *An Experimental Study of the Effectiveness of Different Techniques of Questioning Child Witnesses*, 18/1 BRITISH J. OF SOCIAL & CLINICAL PSYCHOLOGY 41 (1979).

28. *See, e.g.*, Lepore, S., *Child Witness: Cognitive and Social Factors Related to Memory and Testimony*, 3 ISSUES IN CHILD ABUSE ACCUSATIONS 65 (1991); Gail Goodman & Reed, R. *Age Differences in Eyewitness Testimony*, 10 LAW AND HUMAN BEHAVIOR 317 (1986).

concerning such sensitive topics as abuse, particularly sexual abuse.[29] For example, a child who has been threatened or fears punishment for disclosing abuse may be very well able to tell what happened but will choose not to tell.[30] Further, it may be difficult for children to talk about embarrassing or shameful incidents, especially to people they do not know or with whom they do not feel comfortable. It has been shown that young children are more suggestible when questioned in an intimidating atmosphere.[31] The lawyer, as well as anyone who interviews the child, has the responsibility of reassuring the child about the consequences of disclosure, warning the child about possible misleading questions, and of creating an environment most conducive to disclosure.[32]

MEMORY FOR PERSONALLY SIGNIFICANT DETAILS

Common sense indicates that people can remember more about personally significant details than about peripheral details. In this case, common sense is right. For example, most people know their spouse's eye color but not the next-door neighbor's, even if they have observed both people's eyes. Children, too, have more accurate and complete memories about familiar[33] and meaningful[34] events.

Further, young children have better memory for things they have experienced, as opposed to things they have merely observed.[35]

---

29. *See, e.g.*, Batterman-Faunce & Goodman, *Effects of Context on the Accuracy and Suggestibility of Child Witnesses*, in CHILD VICTIMS, CHILD WITNESSES 301 (Gail S. Goodman & Bette L. Bottoms, eds., 1993).

30. *See, e.g.*, Bussey, Lee & Grimbeek, *Lies and Secrets: Implications for Children's Reporting of Sexual Abuse*, in CHILD VICTIMS, CHILD WITNESSES 147 (Gail S. Goodman & Bette L. Bottoms, eds., 1993).

31. *See, e.g.*, Goodman, Bottoms, Schwartz-Kenney & Rudy, *Children's Testimony About a Stressful Event: Improving Children's Reports*, 7 J. OF NARRATIVE & LIFE HISTORY 69 (1991).

32. *See, e.g.*, Geiselman, Saywitz & Bronstein, *Effects of Cognitive Questioning Techniques on Children's Recall Performance*, in CHILD VICTIMS, CHILD WITNESSES 71 (Gail S. Goodman & Bette L. Bottoms, eds., 1993); Karen Saywitz & Snyder, *Improving Children's Testimony with Preparation*, in CHILD VICTIMS, CHILD WITNESSES 117 (Gail S. Goodman & Bette L. Bottoms, eds., 1993); Batterman-Faunce & Goodman, *Effects of Context on the Accuracy and Suggestibility of Child Witnesses*, in CHILD VICTIMS, CHILD WITNESSES 301 (Gail S. Goodman & Bette L. Bottoms, eds., 1993).

33. *See, e.g.*, Baker-Ward, Hess & Flannagan, *The Effects of Involvement on Child Memory for Events*, 5 CHILD DEVELOPMENT 55 (1990); Gail S. Goodman, Rudy, Bette L. Bottoms & Aman, *Children's Concerns and Memory: Ecological Issues in the Study of Children's Eyewitness Testimony*, in KNOWING AND REMEMBERING IN CHILDREN 249 (Robyn Fivush & J. Hudson, eds., 1990).

34. *See, e.g.*, Bjorklund, D. & Muir, J., CHILDREN'S DEVELOPMENT OF FREE RECALL MEMORY: REMEMBERING ON THEIR OWN IN ANNALS OF CHILD DEVELOPMENT (R. Vasta, ed., vol 5 1988); Lindberg, M., *The Role of Knowledge Structures in the Otogeny of Learning*, 30 J. EXPERIMENTAL CHILD PSYCHOLOGY 401 (1980); M. PERLMUTTER, CHILDREN'S MEMORY: NEW DIRECTIONS IN CHILD DEVELOPMENT (No. 10 1980).

35. *See, e.g.*, Tobey & Goodman, *Children's Eyewitness Memory: Effects of Participation and Forensic Content*, 16 CHILD ABUSE & NEGLECT 779 (1992); Baker-Ward, Hess & Flannagan, *The Effects of Involvement on Child Memory for Events*, 5 CHILD DEVELOPMENT 55 (1990); Slackman, Hudson & Fivush, *Actions, Actors, Lins, and Goals: The Structure of Children's Event Representations*, in EVENT KNOWLEDGE (K. Nelson, ed., 1986).

There is research evidence that even children as young as three years of age can accurately report personally significant events.[36] Young children may be able to recall fewer details, but what they do recall can be accurate.[37] The more time passes since the event, the fewer details will be able to be recalled, but what is recalled may still be accurate.[38] However, when the event is repeated and there are similar intervening events, children may confuse details about specific events with details from similar events.[39]

It is important to keep in mind that what is personally significant for children may be different than what is personally significant for adults.[40] Further, children are less skilled than adults in accurately estimating such things as age, height, and weight.[41]

MEMORY FOR TRAUMATIC EVENTS

The most current research indicates that, contrary to previous research,[42] "core features of highly emotional events are remembered especially well, although memory for peripheral details may at times be adversely affected."[43] Therefore, children who testify about

36. *See, e.g.*, Goodman, G., Aman, C. & Hirschman, J., *Child Sexual and Physical Abuse: Children's Testimony*, in CHILDREN'S EYEWITNESS MEMORY 1 (S. Ceci, M. Toglia & D. Ross, eds. 1987).

37. *See, e.g.*, Lepore, S., *Child Witness: Cognitive and Social Factors Related to Memory and Testimony*, 3 ISSUES IN CHILD ABUSE ACCUSATIONS 65 (1991); Goodman, G., Aman, C. & J. Hirschman, *Child Sexual and Physical Abuse: Children's Testimony*, in CHILDREN'S EYEWITNESS MEMORY (S. Ceci, M. Toglia & D. Ross, eds. 1987); Goodman, G. & Reed, R., *Age Differences in Eyewitness Testimony*, 10 LAW AND HUMAN BEHAVIOR 317 (1986).

38. *See, e.g.*, Fivush, R., Hudson, J. & Nelson, K., *Children's Long-Term Memory for a Novel Event: An Exploratory Study*, 30 MERRILL-PALMER QUARTERLY 303 (1984).

39. *See, e.g.*, Myles-Worsley, M., Cromer, C. & Dodd D., *Children's Preschool Script Reconstruction: Reliance on General Knowledge as Memory Fades*, 22 DEVELOPMENTAL PSYCHOLOGY 22 (1986).

40. *See, e.g.*, Mitchell L. Eisen & Gail S. Goodman, *Trauma, Memory, and Suggestibility in Children*, 10 DEVELOPMENT & PSYCHOPATHOLOGY 717 (1998). King & Yuille, *Suggestibility and the Child Witness*, in CHILDREN'S EYEWITNESS MEMORY 24 (S. Ceci, M. Toglia & D. Ross, eds., 1987).

41. *See, e.g.*, Goodman, G. & Lloyd, D., *The Child Witness: Evaluation and Preparation*, in THE NEW CHILD PROTECTION TEAM HANDBOOK 418 (D. Bross, R. Krugman, D. A. Rosenberg & B. D. Schmitt, eds. 1988).

42. *See, e.g.*, ELIZABETH LOFTUS, EYEWITNESS TESTIMONY (1979).

43. *See*, Batterman-Faunce & Goodman, *Effects of Context on the Accuracy and Suggestibility of Child Witnesses*, in CHILD VICTIMS, CHILD WITNESSES 301, at 309 (Gail S. Goodman & Bette L. Bottoms, eds., 1993). *See also*, TRAUMA AND MEMORY (Linda Meyer Williams & Victoria L. Banyard, eds., 1998); Bessel A. van der Kolk, *Trauma and Memory*, in TRAUMATIC STRESS: THE EFFECTS OF OVERWHELMING EXPERIENCE ON MIND, BODY, AND SOCIETY 279 (Bessel A. van der Kolk, Alexander C. MacFarlane & Lars Weisaeth, eds., 1996); Warren & Startwood, *Developmental Issues in Flashbulb Memory Research: Children Recall the Challenger Event*, in AFFECT AND ACCURACY IN RECALL: THE PROBLEM OF FLASHBULB MEMORIES (E. Winograd & U. Neisser, eds. (in press); Christianson, *Emotional Stress and Eyewitness Memory: A Critical Review*, 112 PSYCHOLOGY BULLETIN 284 (1992); Steward, *Preliminary Findings from the University of California-Davis, Child Memory Study*, 5 THE ADVISOR 11 (1992); Goodman, Hirschman, Hepps & Rudy, *Children's Memory for Stressful Events*, 37 MERRILL-PALMER QUARTERLY 109 (1991); Goodman, Hepps & Reed, *The Child Victim's Testimony*, in NEW ISSUES FOR CHILD ADVOCATES 167 (Ann Haralambie, ed., 1986).

traumatic abuse may be particularly reliable when they describe the abusive events. In addition, children may be less suggestible with respect to making commission errors with regard to abuse.[44] It may be that stress improves memory up to a certain point, after which memory is adversely affected.[45]

It is important to remember that a particular child's memory of abuse is individual to that child. The accuracy or completeness of the memory cannot be measured by reference to research studies. Four researchers have summarized the current state of knowledge as follows:

> [A] clear understanding of the relation between stress and memory eludes researchers, perhaps in part because they fail to take individual-difference factors into account. Coping mechanisms associated with experiences of abuse and other forms of victimization may create individual differences in the processing of stressful or traumatic events, with implications for memory. For instance, maltreated children who developed the coping mechanism of dissociation may "tune out" during traumatic experiences, and their memory may thus be adversely affected. Alternatively, abused children may be hypervigilant to threatening events and remember such events with particular clarity.[46]

One interesting study of forty-six children, ages three to ten, involved children's memory for an invasive medical procedure that involved painful, forced genital contact (catheterization through the urethra and infusion of liquid into the bladder), called Voiding Cystourethrogram Fluoroscopy.[47] Some of the children were unable to provide any relevant information during free recall, and some

---

44. *See, e.g.*, Tobey & Goodman, *Children's Eyewitness Memory: Effects of Participation and Forensic Content*, 16/4 CHILD ABUSE & NEGLECT 779 (1992); Rudy & Goodman, *Effects of Participation on Children's Reports: Implications for Children's Testimony*, 27 DEVELOPMENTAL PSYCHOLOGY 527 (1991); Saywitz, Goodman, Nicholas & Moan, *Children's Memories of a Physical Examination Involving Genital Touch: Implications for Reports of Child Sexual Abuse*, 59 J. CONSULTING & CLINICAL PSYCHOLOGY 682 (1991).

45. *See generally*, J. Qin, J.A. Quas, A. Redlich & G.S. Goodman, *Children's Eyewitness Memory*, in MEMORY DEVELOPMENT IN CHILDREN 301 (N. Cowan, ed., 1997).

46. *See* Mitchell L. Eisen, Gail S. Goodman, Jianjian Qin, Suzanne L. David, *Memory and Suggestibility in Maltreated Children: New Research Relevant to Evaluating Allegations of Abuse*, in TRUTH IN MEMORY 163, 173 (Steven Jay Lynn & Kevin M. McConkey, eds. 1998).

47. *See* G. Goodman, J. Quas, J. Batterman-Faunce, M. Riddlesberger & J. Kuhn, *Predictors of Accurate and Inaccurate Memories of Traumatic Events Experienced in Childhood*, 3 CONSCIOUSNESS & COGNITION 269 (1994).

denied the entire experience.[48] The younger children (three- and four-year-olds) recalled less, answered fewer questions correctly, and made more errors.[49] Lack of maternal communication about the test and emotional support after the test was associated with inaccuracies in the children's memories, especially their free-recall responses and suggestibility.[50] The researchers summarized: "Comprehension of the event, maternal attention and compassion, parent-child communication, and children's specific emotional reactions appear to be related to children's memory of a stressful event, at least one involving painful and invasive genital contact."[51] This study points out the variety of influences on children's memory. The researchers caution against automatically generalizing the findings to child sexual abuse, which unlike the medical procedure, is not socially acceptable, may not always be painful, may occur far more frequently, may not be questioned until longer after the incidents, and may involve multiple interviews.

One adaptive behavior to trauma is to forget the traumatic event.[52] This phenomenon is reflected in the current trend to allow tort litigation by adult incest survivors for actions that occurred long before the statute of limitations ran out, based on the "delayed discovery" of forgotten traumatic events.[53] Related to this phenomenon is the charge of false memory.

SUGGESTIBILITY

One of the most popular forms of attack against child-witness testimony involves the charge that children are very suggestible and can be made to say anything. This is particularly true in cases involving

48. *Id.* 288.
49. *Id.* 287.
50. *Id.* 288.
51. *Id.* 290.
52. *See, e.g.*, Linda Williams, *Adult Memories of Childhood Abuse: Preliminary Findings from a Longitudinal Study*, 5 THE ADVISOR 19 (1992); John Briere & Jon Conte, *Self-Reported Amnesia for Abuse in Adults Molested as Children*, 6/1 J. OF TRAUMATIC STRESS 21 (1993).
53. *See, e.g.*, Meiers-Post v. Schafer, 427 N.W.2d 606 (Mich. App. 1988) (statute of limitations does not begin to run until sexual-abuse victim remembers repressed memory of abuse; facts, not just feelings, must have been repressed, and there must be corroboration of the repressed memories); VT. STAT. ANN. tit. 12, § 522 (statute of limitations for child sexual abuse tort begins to run from the time the victim discovered that the injury was caused by the abuse); *see generally*, L. KARP & C. KARP, DOMESTIC TORTS § 4.23 (Clark Boardman Callaghan 1989, West Group 1998).

child sexual abuse in the context of domestic-relations litigation. Therefore, it is important to look at the increasing research involving suggestibility.[54] Researcher Karen Saywitz has stated that "[s]uggestibility depends on cognitive, social, and situational factors. Suggestibility research often produces inconsistent results. For example, multiple interviews and repetition of questions can have both detrimental and beneficial effects.[55] Results vary depending on level of interest, salience of the event, as well as on the emotional state and knowledge base of the witness, and the type of test.[56]

Children are likely to be less suggestible with respect to personally significant events than with respect to peripheral details and unimportant events.[57] The relevant information that arises in the course of litigation, especially in abuse-related litigation, is almost always going to be central information about personally relevant events that they have experienced.

An interesting study looked at the issues of whether interviewer status (the child's mother or a stranger, who was also a mother) or a preconceived bias (based on having been given incorrect informa-

54. For a good general description of the research *see, e.g.* Mitchell L. Eisen, Gail S. Goodman, Jianjian Qin & Suzanne L. Davis, *Memory and Suggestibility in Maltreated Children: New Research Relevant to Evaluating Allegations of Abuse* in TRUTH IN MEMORY 163 (Steven Jay Lynn & Kevin M. McConkey, eds., 1998); J. Qin, J. A. Quas, A. Redlich & G. S. Goodman, *Children's Eyewitness Memory*, in MEMORY DEVELOPMENT IN CHILDREN (N. Cowan, ed., 1997); THE SUGGESTIBILITY OF CHILDREN'S RECOLLECTIONS (John Doris, ed. 1991).

55. *See, e.g.*, W. S. Cassel & D. F. Bjorklund, *Developmental Patterns of Eyewitness Memory and Suggestibility: An Ecologically Based Short-Term Longitudinal Study*, 19 LAW & HUMAN BEHAVIOR 507 (1995); R. Fivush & J. R. Shukat, *Content, Consistency, and Coherence of Early Autobiographical Recall in Memory and Testimony*, in THE CHILD WITNESS 5 (M. S. Zaragoza, J. R. Graham, C. G. N. Hall, R. Hirschmand & Y. S. Ben-Porath, eds. 1995); C. Lewis, R. Wilkins, L. Baker & A. Woobey, *"Is This Man Your Daddy?" Suggestibility in Children's Eyewitness Identification of a Family Member*, 19/6 CHILD ABUSE & NEGLECT 739 (1995); M. D. Leichtman & S. J. Ceci, *The Effects of Stereotypes and Suggestions on Preschoolers' Reports*, 31 DEVELOPMENTAL PSYCHOLOGY 568 (1995); D. A. Poole & D. S. Lindsay, *Interviewing Preschoolers: Effects of Nonsuggestive Techniques, Parental Coaching and Leading Questions of Reports of Nonexperienced Events*, 60 J. EXPERIMENTAL CHILD PSYCHOLOGY 129 (1995); D. A. Poole & L. T. White, *Tell Me Again and Again: Stability and Change in the Repeated Testimonies of Children and Adults in Memory and Testimony*, in THE CHILD WITNESS 24 (M. S. Zaragoza, J. R. Graham, C. G. N. Hall, R. Hirschmand & Y. S. Ben-Porath, eds. 1995); A. R. Warren & P. Lane, *Effects of Timing and Type of Questioning on Eyewitness Accuracy and Suggestibility, in Memory and Testimony* in THE CHILD WITNESS 44 (M. S. Zaragoza, J. R. Graham, C. G. N. Hall, R. Hirschmand & Y. S. Ben-Porath, eds. 1995); C. Brainerd & P. A. Ornstein, *Children's Memory for Witnessed Events: The Developmental Backdrop*, in THE SUGGESTIBILITY OF CHILDREN'S RECOLLECTIONS (J. Doris ed 1991); A. Warren, K. Hulse-Trotter & E. C. Tubbs, *Inducing Resistance to Suggestibility in Children*, 15 LAW & HUMAN BEHAVIOR 273 (1991). *See generally*, J. Qin, J. A. Quas, A. Redlich & G. S. Goodman, *Children's Eyewitness Memory*, in MEMORY DEVELOPMENT IN CHILDREN (N. Cowan, ed., 1997).

56. Karen Saywitz, *The Child as Witness: Experimental and Clinical Considerations*, in CHILDHOOD ASSESSMENT: THROUGH THE EYES OF A CHILD 334 (A. LaGrecca, ed. 1990). For a comprehensive review of the current state of the psychological literature relevant to forensic interviews and children's testimony, *see* John E. B. Myers, Karen J. Saywitz & Gail S. Goodman, *Psychological Research on Children as Witnesses: Practical Implications for Forensic Interviews and Courtroom Testimony*, 28/1 PACIFIC L. J. 3 (1996).

57. *See, e.g.*, Fivush, *Developmental Perspectives on Autobiographical Recall*, in CHILD VICTIMS, CHILD WITNESSES 1, at 20 (Gail S. Goodman & Bette L. Bottoms, eds., 1993).

tion about what actually happened to the child during a videotaped play session) would affect forty preschool children's memory and suggestibility or the interviewers' descriptions of the children's reports.[58] The most inaccurate (commission errors) and least accurate (omission errors) reports by children were those given to the biased stranger interviewers during free recall. Whether or not the mothers had been given the biasing information had no effect on the children's free-recall accuracy. Stranger interviewers' supportive comments were associated with less accuracy during direct questions. Whether or not the mothers made supportive comments had no effect on the children's accuracy during direct questioning. Children were more accurate in answering misleading abuse questions when interviewed by their mothers than by strangers. Mother interviewers reported more correct information than stranger interviewers and children were, at times, less suggestible when being interviewed by their own mothers. These findings appear to support the intuitive hypothesis that children will tell their mothers more things than they will tell strangers. It also raises interesting questions about children's increased resistance to being misled by their mothers than by strangers. Children may be less suggestible when interviewed by warm, supportive interviewers than by more detached, cold interviewers.[59]

In one interesting research study children who had been given an external genital exam during a doctor's visit did not include the genital and anal touches in their descriptions of the examination.[60] It was not until they were asked specific questions such as "Did the doctor touch you there?" that they revealed the information. The allegation that the interviewers' questions implant the idea of abuse in children's memories has caused many lawyers to impeach any information about abuse received, other than in response to open-ended questions. This study demonstrates that sometimes direct

---

58. *See* G. S. Goodman, A. Sharma, S. F. Thomas & M. G. Considine, *Mother Knows Best: Effects of Relationship Status and Interviewer Bias on Children's Memory*, 60 J. EXPERIMENTAL CHILD PSYCHOLOGY 195 (1995).

59. *See, e.g.*, J. Qin, J. A. Quas, A. Redlich & G. S. Goodman, *Children's Eyewitness Memory*, in MEMORY DEVELOPMENT IN CHILDREN (N. Cowan, ed., 1997); C. A. Carter, B. L. Bottoms & M. Levine, *Linguistic and Socio-Emotional Influences on the Accuracy of Children's Reports*, LAW & HUMAN BEHAVIOR (in press).

60. Karen Saywitz, Gail Goodman, Nicholas & Moan, *Children's Memories of a Physical Examination Involving Genital Touch: Implications for Reports of Child Sexual Abuse*, 59 J. CONSULTING & CLINICAL PSYCHOLOGY 682 (1991).

questions are necessary to elicit information about embarrassing information such as might be involved in child sexual abuse cases.

It is important to remember that a particular child's suggestibility is individual to that child under the particular circumstances of the interview. Eisen, Goodman, Qin, and Davis state:

> It is also vital to note the influence of situational variables. Some children are suggestible in certain situations and not others, whereas other children appear to be quite resistant to misleading suggestions in most situations. These same patterns are repeatedly found in adults. Unfortunately, it appears that politics has entered the child-witness debate, with some scientists implying that virtually all children are highly suggestible and can be subject to memory distortion about any aspect of any event, and others implying that children's memory can never be corrupted in any significant way and that children are incapable of lying. As the data mount, it is becoming increasingly clear that neither implication is true and that the answers to these crucial questions fall somewhere in between these extremes.[61]

Lawyers should present expert evidence concerning suggestibility whenever there is an allegation that the child's report was tainted in some way. It would be unfortunate for children who need protection to abandon evidence of abuse merely because it was elicited in response to direct questions. Eisen and Goodman have recently published an excellent, well-researched, and balanced article that should be of great assistance in understanding what is knowledge, what is theory, and what is conjecture concerning children's memory and suggestibility.[62] This article is essential reading for judges, lawyers, interviewers, and expert witnesses who must deal with the real and junk science that abounds in this area.

TESTIMONIAL RELEVANCE OF CHILDREN'S MEMORY

Children's testimony may be greatly affected by their developmental level, emotional status at the time of testimony, and experience with

61. *See* Mitchell L. Eisen, Gail S. Goodman, Jianjian Qin, Suzanne L. Davis, *Memory and Suggestibility in Maltreated Children: New Research Relevant to Evaluating Allegations of Abuse*, in TRUTH IN MEMORY 163, 182 (Steven Jay Lynn & Kevin M. McConkey, eds., 1998) (citation omitted).

62. *See* Mitchell L. Eisen & Gail S. Goodman, *Trauma, Memory, and Suggestibility in Children*, 10 DEVELOPMENT & PSYCHOPATHOLOGY 717 (1998).

the skills necessary to testify effectively. A lawyer familiar with the basic research on children's memory is in a better position to prepare the child to testify, to ask appropriate questions during direct examination, to insist upon age-appropriate cross-examination questions, to seek courtroom accommodations most conducive to complete and accurate testimony, and to present expert evidence to help bolster the child's testimony by explaining what is known about children's memory and how to express that memory.[63]

For example, younger children may need specific questions, memory cues, prompts, and support in order to be able to express the entire event about which they are being asked because they do not yet possess the ability to recount the past in a narrative manner, rather than because they do not remember the information sought.[64] Young children's inconsistent answers given in response to different questions may not reflect inaccurate information, because young children depend on the specific question asked in order to guide their recall.[65] With instruction children's testimony will improve, and with training, they will improve much more.[66]

Because young children can testify more fully with various cues, the lawyer should either learn how to provide the appropriate, non-objectional cues during the child's testimony (and any pretrial interviews) and instruct the child to use the cues, or engage the assistance of a knowledgeable child-development expert who can interview and prepare the child with appropriate cues. Psychologists have found that the technique of "context reinstatement" may best improve the child's recall, especially when it uses actual objects instead of only environmental context cues or model props.[67] The technique asks the person to reconstruct various elements of the scene or event in

63. For a current review of the relevant psychological knowledge *see generally* J. Qin, J. A. Quas, A. Redlich & G. S. Goodman, *Children's Eyewitness Memory*, in MEMORY DEVELOPMENT IN CHILDREN (N. Cowan, ed., 1997).

64. *See, e.g.*, Robyn Fivush, *Developmental Perspectives on Autobiographical Recall*, in CHILD VICTIMS, CHILD WITNESSES 1, at 4-7 (Gail S. Goodman & Bette L. Bottoms, eds., 1993).

65. *Id.*

66. *See* Karen J. Saywitz, Lynn Snyder & Rebecca Nathanson, *Facilitating the Communicative Competence of the Child Witness*, 3/1 APPLIED DEVELOPMENTAL SCIENCE 58 (1999).

67. *See, e.g.*, Pipe, Gee & Wilson, *Cues, Props, and Context: Do They Facilitate Children's Event Reports?*, in CHILD VICTIMS, CHILD WITNESSES 25 (Gail S. Goodman & Bette L. Bottoms, eds., 1993); Saywitz & Snyder, *Improving Children's Testimony with Preparation*, in CHILD VICTIMS, CHILD WITNESSES 117, at 125 (Gail S. Goodman & Bette L. Bottoms, eds., 1993); Saywitz, Goodman, Nicholas & Moan, *Children's Memories of Physical Examinations Involving Genital Touch: Implications for Reports of Child Sexual Abuse*, 59 J. CONSULTING & CLINICAL PSYCHOLOGY 682 (1991).

an effort to help the person reconstruct the entire event. "Cognitive interviewing" may provide additional assistance in helping children to organize and express their memories.[68] The technique involves "mentally restructuring the environmental and personal context that existed at the time [of the event], . . . reporting everything (being complete), even partial information, regardless of the perceived *importance* of the information, . . . recounting the events in a variety of orders, . . . and reporting the events from a variety of perspectives," with additional specific suggestions being given to facilitate recall.[69] It is felt that children should practice cognitive interviews before being interviewed with the technique for anything legally important.[70] The Enhanced Cognitive Interview sequences the primary sections of the interview.[71] A particular type of cognitive interview is called the Step-Wise Interview, which is organized into steps beginning with the most open, nonleading forms of questioning, proceeding to more specific forms as circumstances require.[72] Another procedure to help children remember is called "narrative elaboration."[73] This technique involves training to increase the completeness of children's reports. The children are told that a good way of recounting a past event is to tell about the parts of what happened based on certain categories, such as setting, participants, conversa-

---

68. *See, e.g.*, Karen J. Saywitz & R. Edward Geiselman, *Interviewing the Child Witness: Maximizing Completeness and Minimizing Error* in TRUTH IN MEMORY 190 (Steven Jay Lynn & Kevin M. McConkey, eds., 1998); M. R. McCauley & Robyn P. Fisher, *Facilitating Children's Eyewitness Recall with the Revised Cognitive Interview*, 80 J. APPLIED PSYCHOLOGY 510 (1995); A. Memon, O. Cronin, R. Eaves & R. Bull, *The Cognitive Interview and Child Witnesses in 20 Children*, EVIDENCE AND PROCEDURE: ISSUES IN CRIMINOLOGICAL AND LEGAL PSYCHOLOGY 3 (N. K. Clark & G. M. Stephenson, eds. 1993); R. Edward Geiselman, Karen J. Saywitz & Gail K. Bornstein, *Effects of Cognitive Questioning Techniques on Children's Recall Performance*, in CHILD VICTIMS, CHILD WITNESSES: Understanding and Improving Children's Testimony 71 (Gail S. Goodman & Bette L. Bottoms, eds. 1993).

69. *Id.* at 73 (emphasis in original).

70. *Id.* at 89-90.

71. *See, e.g.*, Karen J. Saywitz & R. Edward Geiselman, *Interviewing the Child Witness: Maximizing Completeness and Minimizing Error* in TRUTH IN MEMORY 190 (Steven Jay Lynn & Kevin M. McConkey, eds., 1998); R. P. Fisher, M. R. McCauley & R. E. Geiselman, *Improving Eyewitness Testimony with the Cognitive Interview* in ADULT EYEWITNESS TESTIMONY AND CURRENT TRENDS AND DEVELOPMENTS 245 (D. Ross, J. D. Read & M. Toglia, eds. 1994); R. P. FISHER & R. E. GEISELMAN, MEMORY ENHANCING TECHNIQUES FOR INVESTIGATIVE INTERVIEWING (1992).

72. *See, e.g.*, J. C. Yuille, R. Hunter, R. Joffe & J. Zaparniuk, *Interviewing Children in Sexual Abuse Cases*, in CHILD VICTIMS, CHILD WITNESSES: Understanding and Improving Children's Testimony 95 (G. S. Goodman & B. L. Bottoms, eds., 1993).

73. *See, e.g.*, Karen J. Saywitz & R. Edward Geiselman, *Interviewing the Child Witness: Maximizing Completeness and Minimizing Error* in TRUTH IN MEMORY 190 (Steven Jay Lynn & Kevin M. McConkey, eds., 1998); Karen J. Saywitz & Lynn Snyder, *Narrative Elaboration: Test of a New Procedure for Questioning Children*, J. CONSULTING & CLINICAL PSYCHOLOGY (in press); Karen J. Saywitz, Lynn Snyder & Vivian Lamphear, *Helping Children Tell What Happened: A Follow-Up Study of the Narrative Elaboration Procedure*, 1/3 CHILD MALTREATMENT 200 (1996).

tions, emotional states, actions, and consequences. Because of their developmental limitations, the cognitive interview (CI) may not be helpful with very young children.[74] Children can also be trained about, and practice, various techniques to enhance the elaboration of the information they are providing.[75] Saywitz and Snyder distinguish training in a methodology to enhance provision of complete reports from substantive coaching and the possibility or appearance of contamination.[76]

Most lawyers are not going to use these techniques themselves, but they should be familiar with them and find local experts who are qualified to interview children using the techniques to enhance the children's recall and ability to express what they have recalled. Because research is only currently being conducted with respect to these techniques to enhance testimony, the expert should be someone who stays up to date with the research. The expert can then teach the lawyer how to build on that work in asking the child questions that will provide more accurate and complete testimony. The expert should testify about the techniques used and be prepared to demonstrate (most probably through current published research) that the techniques enhance accuracy and completeness without introducing error into the child's testimony. The charge of "interview contamination" is particularly frequent in child-sexual-abuse cases, and the lawyer should not compromise the child's credibility by failing to ensure competent interviewing that can withstand scrutiny on cross-examination.

In preparing children to testify, lawyers must understand not only the strengths and limitations of the child witness, but also the child's expectations. For example, children generally expect questions to be sincere, usually with the questioner knowing the answer to the question.[77] Such assumptions are clearly not accurate with respect to many cross-examination questions, and children need to

---

74. *See, e.g.*, D. A. Bekerian & J. L. Dennett, *An Introduction to the Cognitive Interview Technique*, in TRUE AND FALSE ALLEGATIONS OF CHILD SEXUAL ABUSE: ASSESSMENT AND CASE MANAGEMENT 192 (T. Ney, ed. 1995); K. J. Saywitz, R. E. Geiselman, & G. K. Bornstein, *Effects of Cognitive Interviewing and Practice on Children's Recall Performance*, 77 J. APPLIED PSYCHOLOGY 744 (1992).

75. *See, e.g.*, Saywitz & Snyder, *Improving Children's Testimony with Preparation*, in CHILD VICTIMS, CHILD WITNESSES 117, at 126-129 (Gail S. Goodman & Bette L. Bottoms, eds., 1993).

76. *Id.* at 124.

77. *See, e.g.*, Saywitz & Snyder, *Improving Children's Testimony with Preparation*, in CHILD VICTIMS, CHILD WITNESSES 117, at 130-131 (Gail S. Goodman & Bette L. Bottoms, eds., 1993).

be prepared for questions that are intentionally misleading. Children need to practice saying that they do not understand a question or that they do not know the answer. Making the situation even more difficult is the fact that young children may not even realize that they do not understand a question or that their answer has been misunderstood, and so may not make any attempt at clarification.[78]

When the event is repeated and there are similar intervening events, children may confuse details about specific events with details from similar events.[79] This confusion may hamper the testimony of a victim of on-going abuse in distinguishing among specific incidents, making it difficult for the lawyer to lay the proper foundation for the testimony. This evidentiary problem is troubling because it gives more protection to the repeat abuser than to a one-time abuser. Because of this, many trial judges in civil cases allow much broader foundations as to time and place, not requiring young children to give detailed accounts of what happened during specific events.

FALSE MEMORY SYNDROME

An unfortunate addition to the debate about memory involves the term "false memory syndrome," which really is not an accepted syndrome as the behavioral and medical sciences use the term to indicate some diagnostic value to a cluster of symptoms.[80] While it is certainly possible to induce people to believe that they have experienced something that they have not, there is insufficient data to support any finding of widespread false memories of the existence of a false memory syndrome.[81]

---

78. *Id.* at 119.

79. *See, e.g.*, Myles-Worsley, M., Cromer,C. & Dodd, D., *Children's Preschool Script Reconstruction: Reliance on General Knowledge as Memory Fades*, 22 DEVELOPMENTAL PSYCH 22 (1986).

80. For an excellent discussion of syndromes, *see*, John E. B. Myers, *Expert Testimony Describing Psychological Syndromes*, 24/3 PACIFIC L. J. 1449 (1993).

81. For a series of articles that debates the issues of delayed memories, pseudomemories, and false memories, *see*, C. Dalenberg, *Making and Finding Memories: A Commentary on the "Repressed Memory" Controversy*, 3/3 J. CHILD SEXUAL ABUSE 109 (1994); S. Elvik, *Professionals under Fire: Delayed Memories vs. the False Memory Syndrome*, 3/3 J. CHILD SEXUAL ABUSE 123 (1994); Richard Ofshe, *Making Grossly Damaging But Avoidable Errors: The Pitfalls of the Olio/Cornell Thesis*, 3/3 J. CHILD SEXUAL ABUSE 95 (1994); K. Olio & W. Cornell, *Making Meaning Not Monsters: Reflections on the Delayed Memory Syndrome*, 3/3 J. CHILD SEXUAL ABUSE 77 (1994); R. Reece, *Making Meaning: A Pediatrician's View*, 3/3 J. CHILD SEXUAL ABUSE 119 (1994). *See also*, David H. Gleaves, *The Evidence for "Repression": An Examination of Holmes (1990) and the Implications for the Recovered Memory Controversy*, 5/1 J. CHILD SEXUAL ABUSE 1 (1996); American Psychiatric Association *Statement on Memories of Sexual Abuse* (1994); D. Read & D. Lindsay, *Moving Toward a Middle Ground in the "False Memory Debate:" Reply to Commentaries on Lindsay & Read*, 8 APPLIED PSYCHOLOGY 407 (1994); H.G. Pope, *"Recovered Memories": Recent Events and Review of Evidence*, 13/7 CURRENTS IN AFFECTIVE ILLNESS (1994); J. Watkins, *Dealing with the Problem of "False Memory" in Clinic and Court*, J. PSYCHIATRY & LAW 297 (Fall 1993);

The legal issues of delayed discovery of child sexual abuse arise primarily in the context of tort litigation.[82] The false memory syndrome is relevant to cases litigated while the children are still minors because it casts additional doubt on the credibility of child witnesses who have alleged sexual abuse, especially if there was a delay in reporting (which is the rule, rather than the exception) or recantation.[83] Common sense would seem to indicate that something as traumatic and repetitive as intrafamilial child sexual abuse would not be forgotten, only to be recalled later in life. As with many other areas of child abuse, common sense is wrong in this regard. Some sexual abuse victims also make a deliberate attempt to forget the abuse.[84]

CONCLUSION

A lawyer familiar with the current research into memory and suggestibility will be better able to meet unfair cross-examination and judicial skepticism. Because of the importance of the child's statements in or out of court, it is essential that those statements be supported where appropriate.

Expert testimony by a witness familiar with the current research on memory and suggestibility should be presented on the subject of children's memory in general and as applied to the particular child in question. It is helpful to have the witness testify about children's memory in comparison to that of adults, because adults suffer from the same problems of memory and suggestibility as children do. While there may be some differences based on the age and developmental level of the witnesses, it is unfair to paint children's memory as fundamentally more flawed than that of adults.

D. Barstow, *Critical Examination of the "False Memory" Syndrome*, 9/1 FAMILY VIOLENCE & SEXUAL ASSAULT BULL. 21 (1993).

82. *See generally*, LEONARD KARP & CHERYL KARP, DOMESTIC TORTS: FAMILY VIOLENCE, CONFLICT, AND SEXUAL ABUSE § 4.23 (Clark Boardman Callaghan 1989, West Group 1998).

83. For a further discussion of delayed memory, see Chapter 6.

84. *See, e.g.*, D. DiLillo, P. Long & L. Russell, *Childhood Coping Strategies of Intrafamilial and Extrafamilial Female Sexual Abuse Victims*, 3/2 J. CHILD SEXUAL ABUSE 45 (1994) (as compared to extrafamilial abuse victims, intrafamilial abuse victims more often use detachment, trying to forget the whole thing).

13 Children's Statements and Testimony

Introducing the Child's Hearsay Statements

In many cases, especially because physical findings are relatively infrequent,[1] the child's out-of-court statements concerning the abuse are the most crucial evidence in a case.[2] In the great majority of civil child sexual abuse cases the child's statements are admitted through hearsay rather than through direct testimony.[3]

---

1. See Chapter 7.

2. The Ninth Circuit Court of Appeals has noted that in criminal child-sexual-abuse cases, "one of the most difficult to detect and prosecute, a conviction hinges often on the words of children." Swan v. Peterson, 6 F.3d 1373, 1377 (9th Cir. 1993), *cert. denied*, 513 U.S. 985, 115 S. Ct. 479, 130 L.Ed.2d 393 (1994). *See also* McGriff v. State, 672 A.2d 1027,1029 (Del. 1996) ("[a]dmission of hearsay evidence is sometimes essential in these cases. Prosecuting a child sexual abuse case can be difficult not only because of the secretive nature of the offense but because the strongest evidence available to the State is often the victim's out-of-court statements."); Doe v. United States, 976 F.2d 1071, 1074-1075 (7th Cir. 1992), *cert. denied*, 510 U.S. 812, 114 S. Ct. 58, 126 L.Ed.2d 28 (1993) ("the out-of-court statement of the child victim takes on exceptional significance; a youngster's hearsay statements in sex abuse cases often constitute the only proof that a crime has occurred"); *In re* A.S.W., 834 P.2d 801, 804 (Alaska 1992) ("[t]he out-of-court statements of a child in proceedings where abuse is alleged are often quite necessary to the administration of justice"); State v. Jones, 112 Wash.2d 488, 494, 772 P.2d 496, 499 (1989) ("the admissibility of statements children make outside the courtroom, and especially statements made close in time to the acts of abuse they describe, is crucial to the successful prosecution of many child sex offenses").

3. For a comprehensive discussion of the law of hearsay in child abuse cases, *See generally*, 2 John E. B. Myers, Evidence in Child Abuse and Neglect Cases ch. 7 (3rd ed. 1997).

Most often the statements form part of the expert testimony of the Child Protective Services or law-enforcement investigators[4] and the medical or mental-health expert. Sometimes they come in through the testimony of parents, teachers, or other persons to whom the child reported the abuse.

The child's prior hearsay statements describing sexual abuse may be admitted to rebut charges of recent fabrication.[5] However, that use does not permit substantive use of the statements. In a United States Supreme Court case, *Tome v. United States*,[6] a man was convicted of sexually molesting his four-year-old daughter on an Indian reservation. He alleged that the child had lied about the abuse following the parents' divorce so she would not have to live with him. The government offered the child's hearsay statements pursuant to Federal Rule of Evidence 801(d)(1)(B) to rebut the charge of recent fabrication or improper influence or motive. The Court held that the statements should not have been permitted because the government had used the statements substantively on the issue of whether the abuse had occurred, not to rebut the alleged motive to lie. Rule 801(d)(1)(B) permits rebuttal hearsay statements only if the statement was made before the alleged fabrication, influence, or motive occurs. The statements at issue had been made after the motive arose.

Over half of the states have statutes or rules that explicitly permit hearsay evidence of child abuse victims, particularly in civil cases.[7] The child abuse exception does have specific requirements,

---

4. *See, e.g.*, State v. Grego, 648 So.2d 743 (Fla. Dist. Ct. App. 1994), *review denied*, 651 So.2d 1194 (1995) (reversing denial of statements made to social workers and police by two children, ages 9 and 11, 20 months after the alleged sexual abuse; the court goes into detail about why such statements were reliable despite the trial court's finding that they were not); United States v. Cree, 778 F.2d 474 (8th Cir. 1985) (social worker and law-enforcement officer permitted to testify to four-year-old child's statement about physical abuse, where medical evidence substantiated the injuries and statement paralleled prior statements by child).

5. *See, e.g.*, FED. R. EVID. Rule 801(d)(1)(B) and the state rules patterned after it. *See generally*, 2 JOHN E. B. MYERS, EVIDENCE IN CHILD ABUSE AND NEGLECT CASES § 7.24 (3rd ed. 1997).

6. 513 U.S. 150, 130 L. Ed.2d 574, 115 S. Ct. 696 (1995).

7. *See, e.g.*, ALA. CODE § 12-15-65(i) (1997) (admissible in juvenile proceedings under certain circumstances); ALA. CODE § 15-25-31 through 15-25-37 (1997) (admissible in criminal proceedings under certain circumstances); ARIZ. REV. STAT. ANN. § 8-238 (1997) (admissible in adoption, dependency, and termination proceedings under certain circumstances); CAL. EVID. CODE § 1228 (admissible in juvenile proceedings under certain circumstances); CAL. EVID. CODE § 1360 (admissible in criminal proceedings under certain circumstances); COLO. REV. STAT. § 13-25-129 (1997) (admissible in criminal, delinquency, and civil cases where child under certain circumstances); DEL. CODE ANN. tit. 11 § 3513 (1997) (admissible in any judicial proceeding under certain circumstances); FLA. STAT. ANN. § 90.803(23) (1997) (admissible in any civil or criminal proceeding under certain circumstances); GA. CODE ANN. § 24-3-16 (1997) (admissible under certain circumstances); IDAHO CODE § 19-3024 (1997) (admissible in child protection and criminal proceedings under certain circumstances); IND. CODE ANN. § 35-37-4-6 (1997) (applies in criminal cases under certain circumstances); KAN. STAT ANN. § 60-460(dd) (1997) (admissible in criminal, delinquency, and child protec-

including a finding of sufficient indicia of reliability.[8] While these statutes sometimes have been found to be unconstitutional in criminal cases as violating the confrontation clause, they are generally upheld in civil cases. Some courts have also rejected statutory hearsay exceptions as violative of separation of power, ruling that it is for the court, not the legislature, to control evidentiary rules.[9] The California Supreme Court created such an exception in *In re Carmen O.*[10]

Even in states without such specific exceptions, the hearsay statements of children may be admissible pursuant to generally recognized exceptions, particularly where there are allegations of abuse. (Because many states have adopted the Federal Rules of Evidence, citations are made to the federal rule numbers for reference.) All of these exceptions apply regardless of the child's availability to testify. Therefore, the lawyer offering the hearsay evidence does not need to deal with the issue of the child's unavailability because of age or psychological trauma.

---

tion cases under certain circumstances; ME. REV. STAT ANN. tit. 15, § 1205 (1997) (admissible in criminal cases under certain circumstances); MD. CODE ANN., CTS. & JUD. PROC. § 27-755 (1997) (admissible in juvenile and criminal proceedings under certain circumstances); MASS. GEN. LAWS ANN. ch. 233, § 81 (1997) (admissible in criminal proceedings under certain circumstances); MASS. GEN. LAWS ANN. ch. 233, § 82 (1997) (admissible in civil proceedings under certain circumstances); MICH. R. EVID. 803A (admissible in criminal and delinquency proceedings under certain circumstances); MINN. STAT ANN. § 595.02 subd. 3 (1997) (admissible under certain circumstances); MISS. R. EVID. 803(25) (admissible under certain circumstances); MO. ANN. STAT. § 491.075 (1997) (admissible in criminal proceedings under certain circumstances); NEV. REV. STAT ANN. § 51.385 (1985) (admissible in criminal proceedings under certain circumstances); N.J. R. EVID. 803(27) (admissible in criminal, juvenile, and civil proceedings under certain circumstances); N.Y. FAM. CT. ACT § 1046(a) (1998) (admissible in child protection proceedings under certain circumstances); OHIO R. EVID. 807 (admissible under certain circumstances); OKLA. STAT. ANN. tit. 12, § 2803.1 (1997) (admissible in criminal and juvenile proceedings under certain circumstances); OR. REV. STAT. § 40.460(18a) (1997) (admissible under certain circumstances); 42 PA. STAT. ANN. § 5985.1 (1997) (admissible in criminal proceedings under certain circumstances); S.D. CODIFIED LAWS ANN. § 19-16-38 (1997) (admissible in criminal and juvenile proceedings under certain circumstances); TEX. CRIM. P. CODE ANN. § 38.072 (1997) (admissible in criminal proceedings under certain circumstances); TEX. FAM. CODE ANN. § 54.031 (1997) (admissible in delinquency proceedings under certain circumstances); TEX. FAM. CODE ANN. § 104.006 (1997) (admissible in proceedings affecting the parent-child relationship under certain circumstances); TEX. GOV. CODE ANN. § 2001.121 and 2001.122 (1997) (admissible under certain circumstances); UTAH CODE ANN. § 76-5-411 (1997) (admissible in criminal proceedings under certain circumstances); VT. R. EVID. 804a (admissible in civil, criminal, and administrative proceedings under certain circumstances); WASH. REV. CODE ANN. § 9A.44.120 (1997) (admissible in dependency, delinquency, and criminal proceedings under certain circumstances).

8. *See, e.g.*, Matter of Elizabeth G., 680 N.Y.S.2d 32 (App. Div. 1998) (corroboration of child's out-of-court statements may be provided by expert testimony and statements of siblings).

9. *See, e.g.*, State v. Robinson, 153 Ariz. 191, 735 P.2d 801 (1987); Drumm v. Commonwealth, 783 S.W.2d 380 (Ky. 1990); Hall v. State, 539 So.2d 1338 (Miss. 1989). *But see, e.g.*, St. Clair v. State, 301 Ark. 223, 783 S.W.2d 835 (1990).

10. 33 Cal. Rptr. 2d 848, 28 Cal. App. 4th 908 (1994). The Supreme Court later held that courts have the authority to create such exceptions for classes of evidence for which there is substantial need and which possess intrinsic reliability, which the *Carmen O.* exception did. *See In re* Cindy L., 17 Cal. 4th 15, 69 Cal. Rptr. 803, 947 P.2d 1340 (1997).

PRESENT SENSE IMPRESSION, RULE 803(1)

The present-sense impression exception permits admission of a statement "describing or explaining an event or condition made while the declarant was perceiving the event or condition, or immediately thereafter."[11] The event or condition perceived does not have to be disturbing, and the statement does not have to qualify as an "excited utterance." A child's statement of present pain or irritation caused by sexual abuse would be admissible under this exception,[12] as well as under the state of mind exception. Similarly, a child's statement made during the abuse, such as telling the abuser to stop doing some particular act, would be admissible.

EXCITED UTTERANCE, RULE 803(2)

To qualify under the excited-utterance exception, the child must have been under "the stress of excitement" caused by the disturbing event,[13] and the statement must relate to the event. The rationale underlying this exception is that the person making the statement has not had time to reflect upon the event. In general, the statement must be made relatively close in time to the event.[14] For young children, courts frequently extend the time permitted between the event

---

11. *See, e.g.*, In Interest of C.B., 574 So.2d 1369 (Miss. 1990) (statements made days or weeks after the sexual abuse not admissible as present sense impressions because the statements were not made while the child was perceiving the event or immediately thereafter).

12. *See, e.g.*, Guam v. Ignacio, 10 F.3d 608 (9th Cir. 1993) (statement made by three-year-old child while bathing that her vaginal area hurt admissible); Skidmore v. State, 838 S.W.2d 748 (Tex. Ct. App. 1993) (three-year-old child's statement that her father hit her, made within one minute of the incident, admissible as a present sense impression or an excited utterance).

13. *See, e.g.*, *In re* Emilye A., 9 Cal. App. 4th 1695, 12 Cal. Rptr. 2d 294 (1992) (statement made to mother a day or two after the child received her "owie" made spontaneously during play, while she was in pain, indicating that they were made under stress or excitement and while her reflective powers were still in abeyance). An uninterrupted state of excitement is not required so long as the excitement is still dominant over the child at the time of the statement. *See, e.g.*, State v. Shoop, 87 Ohio App. 3d 462, 622 N.E.2d 665 (1993).

14. *Compare* State v. Felix, 109 Nev. 151, 849 P.2d 220 (1993) (statements made one year after the sexual assault and only after substantial prodding and suggestive questioning were not admissible as excited utterances) *with In re* Troy P., 114 N.M. 525, 842 P.2d 741 (1992) (4-year old child's statements to her mother concerning abuse by her babysitter's son which occurred several weeks earlier were admissible; the child had begun screaming in the car when told she was going to go back to her father); State v. Chappell, 97 Ohio App. 3d 515, 646 N.E.2d 1191 (1994) (nine-year-old child's report to her grandmother of her rape 32 hours after the event, when she returned home from an out-of-town visit, admissible as excited utterance); State v. Shoop, 87 Ohio App. 3d 462, 622 N.E.2d 665 (1993) (two-year-old child's statement about sexual abuse made to her babysitter the following day was admissible); Snellen v. State, 923 S.W.2d 238 (Tex. Ct. App. 1996) (thirteen-year-old child's statement to CPS worker made within thirteen hours of sexual assault was admissible). *See generally*, Annotation, *Time Element Affecting Admissibility of Statement or Complaint Made by Victim of Sex Crime as Res Gestae, Spontaneous Exclamation, or Excited Utterance*, 89 A.L.R.3d 102 (1979).

and the statement about the event, in part because of the child's relative naivete and the resulting lack of capacity for fabrication, instead of lack of time for fabrication.[15] Especially where an abuser is a parent or other person of authority within the child's home, courts may permit statements about the abuse that were made at the first safe opportunity,[16] for example, when the abuser moves out of the home or the child is removed from the home.

To qualify as an excited utterance, it is not necessary that the statement be spontaneous in the sense of being volunteered. A response to a question may qualify as an excited utterance so long as the questioning is not unduly leading or is not coercive. In some states the upsetting event may even be something other than the abuse reported if it recreated the stress, triggering the excited utterance.[17]

THEN-EXISTING MENTAL, EMOTIONAL, OR PHYSICAL CONDITION, RULE 803(3)

The "state of mind" exception is a frequently used hearsay exception to admit statements of children in domestic or juvenile cases of all

15. *See, e.g.*, People in Interest of O.E.P., 654 P.2d 312 (Colo. 1982); State v. Plant, 236 Neb. 317, 461 N.W.2d 253 (1990).

16. *See, e.g.*, Morgan v. Foretich, 846 F.2d 941 (4th Cir. 1988) (four-year-old child's statements within three hours of her first opportunity to speak to mother admissible); Dezarn v. State, 832 P.2d 589 (Alaska Ct. App. 1992) (two-year-old child's statement at first opportunity to tell an adult about sexual abuse occurring four hours earlier); People in Interest of O.E.P., 654 P.2d 312 (Colo. 1982) (three-year-old child's statements to foster mother and social worker made the day after the sexual abuse, at the first opportunity to discuss the events with someone other than the mother and her boyfriend, admissible); People v. Nevitt, 135 Ill.2d 423, 553 N.E.2d 368 (1990); Commonwealth v. Crawford, 417 Mass. 358, 629 N.E.2d 1332 (1994); State v. Plant, 236 Neb. 317, 461 N.W.2d 253 (1990) (four-year-old child's statement to police two days after her infant stepbrother was murdered admissible); People v. Kornowski, 178 A.D.2d 984, 579 N.Y.S.2d 258 (1991) (sixteen-year-old's statements to counselor the day after she left home, but two or three weeks after the most recent incident of sexual abuse admissible); State v. Chappell, 97 Ohio App. 3d 515, 646 N.E.2d 1191 (1994) (nine-year-old child's report to her grandmother of her rape thirty-two hours after the event, when she returned home from an out-of-town visit, admissible). *Cf.* State v. Kay, 129 Idaho 507, 927 P.2d 897 (Ct. App. 1996) (four-year-old child's statements to her mother and police officer the night she was returned from being abducted and molested admissible); Commonwealth v. Sanford, 397 Pa. Super. 581, 580 A.2d 784 (1990) (three-year old child's statement to mother thirty minutes after she returned home from attempted rape and assault at babysitter's house admissible).

17. *See, e.g.*, George v State, 306 Ark. 360, 813 SW2d 792 (Ark. 1991) (three-year-old child's statement late at night following a nightmare admissible as excited utterance); People in the Interest of O.E.P., 654 P.2d 312 (Colo. 1982) (four-year-old child's statement several days after the abuse but following viewing photographs of the abusers admissible as excited utterance); Bayne v. State, 98 Md. App. 149, 632 A.2d 476 (1993); State v. Owens, 78 Wash. App. 897, 899 P.2d 833 (1995) (intrusive medical examination and pointed questions from family members about whether he had been molested recreated the original stress caused by the acts of abuse, making statements the child over ten years of age made immediately thereafter admissible).

types. A child's statements concerning current fear of the abuser or statements concerning current pain or discomfort, for example, may be admitted under this exception.[18] Where placement, custody, or visitation is at issue, the child's state of mind is centrally important. Therefore, the child's fear of or discomfort with a parent is relevant even if it is not rationally based.[19]

STATEMENTS FOR PURPOSES OF MEDICAL DIAGNOSIS OR TREATMENT, RULE 803(4)

Another frequent exception used in abuse cases is the medical-diagnosis or treatment exception. Many times molested children are examined by physicians, even though physical findings are relatively rare. Physicians may testify to the child's statements made for purposes of diagnosis and treatment.[20] The child's description of the

18. *See, e.g., In re* Kailee B., 18 Cal. App. 4th 719, 22 Cal. Rptr. 2d 485 (1993) (statements to aunt and pediatrician concerning vaginal soreness admissible); *In re* Emilye A., 9 Cal. App. 4th 1695, 12 Cal. Rptr. 2d 294 (1992) (statement about child's "owie" made during play when the irritated area was accidentally touched and caused her pain admissible); People v. Mindibles, 199 Cal. App. 3d 1277, 245 Cal. Rptr. 2d 553 (1988) (child's statement that she was bleeding and had bled before because her common law stepfather had touched her admissible as statement of present physical condition and her view of the cause); Chance v. Chance, 911 S.W.2d 40 (Tex. Ct. App. 1995) (two- to three-year-old child's statements indicating abuse by father and stepmother admissible as related to his mental and emotional condition). *See also* Posner v. Dallas County Child Welfare Unit of Texas Dept. of Human Services, 784 S.W.2d 585 (Tex. Ct. App. 1990), *writ denied* (1990) (child's statement asking another child to "give me your doll, and I'll show you with mine how daddies sex their little girls" was admissible as a statement of the child's then existing emotional condition and state of mind).

19. *See, e.g.,* Crabtree v. Crabtree, 716 S.W.2d 923 (Tenn. Ct. App. 1986); *In re* Kailee B., 18 Cal. App. 4th 719, 22 Cal. Rptr. 2d 485 (1993).

20. *See* Fed. R. Evid. 803(4) and the state rules patterned after it; United States v. Renville, 779 F.2d 430 (8th Cir. 1985) (physician permitted to testify to child's identification of family member who abused her because identity pertinent to psychological injuries); State v. Kay, 129 Idaho 507, 927 P.2d 897 (Ct. App. 1996) (statements made to emergency-room physician and pediatrician during the course of medical examinations admissible); Drumm v. Commonwealth, 783 S.W.2d 380 (Ky. 1990) (physician need not be treating physician in order to testify about abused child's statements); Doe v. Doe, 644 So.2d 1199 (Miss. 1994) (three-year-old child's statements to social worker admissible as statement made for diagnosis or treatment because the statements were reasonably pertinent to treatment and reasonably relied on by physicians for diagnosis and treatment); State v. Mayer, 146 Or. App. 86, 932 P.2d 570 (1997) (child's statements concerning sexual abuse made to physician admissible); *In re* M.P., 76 Wash. App. 87, 882 P.2d 1180 (1994) (four-year-old child's statements to her non-medical therapist admissible as statement made for diagnosis or treatment); State v. Florczak, 79 Wash. App. 55, 882 P.2d 199 (1994), *review denied*, 126 Wash.2d 1010, 892 P.2d 1089 (1995) (social worker permitted to testify concerning the three-year-old child's statements under the medical diagnosis or treatment exception, even though child did not understand that her statements were necessary for diagnosis or treatment if there is corroboration). *But see, e.g.* United States v. White, 11 F.3d 1446 (8th Cir. 1993) (social worker not permitted to testify because there was no evidence that child understood the social worker's role, that he was talking to a medical professional, or that he believed it was in his best interests not to lie); Webb v. Lewis, 44 F.3d 1387 (9th Cir. 1994) (victim witness social worker's videotaped interview with two-year-old child not admitted because it was not for purposes of treatment or diagnosis and child lacked capacity to seek medical help).

abuse, and even the identity of a family member as the abuser, are pertinent to the diagnosis and treatment of the child.[21] For example, an incestuously molested child is treated differently than a stranger-molested child, because the psychological ("psychiatric" if the state construes the term "medical" strictly) effect of the abuse is different, and the need to remove a perpetrator from the child's environment is different. The entire evaluation, including interview responses and diagnostic procedures, may be admissible under this exception.[22] Most states permit statements made to nurses, psychologists, social workers, or other similar professionals to qualify under this exception.[23] Sometimes statements to a parent or teacher are also admissible if made as a prelude to medical diagnosis or treatment.

---

21. *See, e.g.*, United States v. Balfany, 965 F.2d 575 (8th Cir. 1992) (eight-year-old child's statements as part of medical history given to physician who performed a second medical examination on her, which statements described sexual abuse and identified the abuser, were admissible in a criminal trial as pertaining to diagnosis and treatment; the identity of the abuser was relevant to the physician's recommendations for counseling); State v. Lowe, 140 N.H. 271, 665 A.2d 740 (1995) (four-year-old child's statements about the defendant's role in her injury were reasonably pertinent to the possible diagnosis and treatment of physical child abuse).

22. *See, e.g.*, State v. Barkley, 315 Or. 420, 846 P.2d 390 (1993) (ten-year-old child's videotaped interview at hospital, including demonstration with anatomically complete dolls and identification of father as perpetrator, were admissible in father's criminal trial as pertaining to diagnosis and treatment; child testified and was cross-examined at trial). Some cases have addressed the issue of whether the evaluation is viewed as investigatory rather than diagnostic. *Compare* State v. Felix, 109 Nev. 151, 849 P.2d 220 (1993) (statements made to psychologist at interview requested by prosecutor were not made for purposes of treatment or diagnosis, but rather, were more in the nature of investigatory sessions with the purposes of confirming that sexual abuse had occurred) *with* State v. Jones, 89 N.C. App. 584, 367 S.E.2d 139 (1988) (child's statements to social worker from child protection team were made for purposes of diagnosis and treatment, not for purposes of gathering evidence for the State, despite the fact that the mother was referred to the team by the prosecutor and the child psychologist to whom the prosecutor referred the mother).

23. *See, e.g.*, United States v DeNoyer, 811 F.2d 436 (8th Cir. 1987) (social worker permitted to testify to child's identification because identification necessary to treat psychological problems of child molested by family member); Morgan v. Foretich, 846 F.2d 941 (4th Cir. 1988) (child's statements to mother and psychologist admissible); Doe v. Doe, 644 So.2d 1199 (Miss. 1994) (three-year-old child's statements to social worker admissible as statement made for diagnosis or treatment because the statements were reasonably pertinent to treatment and reasonably relied on by physicians for diagnosis and treatment); State v. Mayer, 146 Or. App. 86, 932 P.2d 570 (1997) (child's statements concerning sexual abuse made to child abuse worker at hospital, to whom the pediatrician had referred the child, admitted as a statement made for diagnosis or treatment); *In re* M.P., 76 Wash. App. 87, 882 P.2d 1180 (1994) (four-year-old child's statements to her non-medical therapist admissible as statement made for diagnosis or treatment); State v. Florczak, 79 Wash. App. 55, 882 P.2d 199 (1994), *review denied*, 126 Wash.2d 1010, 892 P.2d 1089 (1995) (social worker permitted to testify concerning the three-year-old child's statements under the medical diagnosis or treatment exception, even though child did not understand that her statements were necessary for diagnosis or treatment if there is corroboration). *But see, e.g.*, United States v. White, 11 F.3d 1446 (8th Cir. 1993) (social worker not permitted to testify because there was no evidence that child understood the social worker's role, that he was talking to a medical professional, or that he believed it was in his best interests not to lie); Webb v. Lewis, 44 F.3d 1387 (9th Cir. 1994) (victim witness social worker's videotaped interview with two-year-old child not admitted because it was not for purposes of treatment or diagnosis and child lacked capacity to seek medical help); Allison v. State, 661 So.2d 889 (Fla. Dist. Ct. App. 1995) (four-year-old child's statement to psychologist about her father's murder of her mother not admissible because the child being treated was not the victim of the offense).

PAST RECOLLECTION RECORDED, RULE 803(5)

Statements that are recorded when events about which he or she had first-hand information are fresh in the mind of the person recording them may be admitted where the witness no longer recalls the underlying facts or details, despite an attempt to refresh the witness' recollection. Some children keep diaries or journals, and in some cases their entries may include information about sexual molestation. In such cases, the diary or journal entries may be admissible to fill in information which the child no longer remembers. However, the need for such evidence must be weighed against the intrusion into the victim's privacy. For some children, revealing their private diary entries would be further revictimization. The notes of police officers, social workers, and other professionals who investigated the case, as well as more informal contemporaneous notes made by people with whom the child discussed the molestation, may also qualify as past recollections recorded so long as the proper foundation is laid.[24]

BUSINESS RECORDS, RULE 803(6)

Abuse-victims' statements contained in records kept in the regular course of business may be admitted. The most frequent application of this exception is the medical and psychological records of the child. The statement must be a type that would ordinarily be recorded in the business records.[25] For example, the records of a school nurse who regularly writes down the child's complaint and explanation of how an injury was received, may be used to admit the child's statement about being molested. Similarly, a school counselor's regularly kept notes about the child's statements concerning

24. *See, e.g.*, State v. Alatorre, 191 Ariz. App. 208, 953 P.2d 1261 (1998) (eight-year-old child's statements to police detective admissible where child no longer remembered the details by testified that she had truthfully told them to the officer during a tape recorded interview); State v. Guradado, 40 Cal. App. 4th 757, 47 Cal. Rptr. 2d 81 (19) (12-year-old child's statements to police officer, contained in a supplemental report prepared when the events were fresh in the officer's mind, admissible); State v. Locke, 139 N.H. 741, 663 A.2d 602 (1995) (12-year-old child's videotaped statement made to the prosecutor's agent shortly after the abuse was reported admissible). The recorded statement, however, must be based on personal knowledge. *See, e.g.*, State v. Veluzat, 578 A.2d 93 R.I. 1990) (mandatory child-abuse reporting form completed by doctor who examined the child not admissible as past recollection recorded because the report contained statements made to the child concerning events of which he had no personal knowledge).

25. However, the business-records exception may not apply to records created at the request of the court for use in the pending proceeding. *See, e.g.*, *In re* M.A., 832 P.2d 437 (Okla. Ct. App. 1992).

visitation-related stress may be admitted pursuant to this exception. However, the Kentucky Supreme Court has ruled that the business-record exception is unavailable as a basis to permit a child's hearsay statement to a social worker because, unlike the social worker, the *child* was not under a business duty to report her information to the social work agency.[26]

PUBLIC RECORDS AND REPORTS, RULE 803(8)

Many lawyers attempt to have public records admitted under the business-records exception. Because the public-records exception is so inclusive, it is preferable to cite it as authority to admit police records, child-protective-services records, and other records kept by public entities in the course of their official duties.[27] This exception draws a distinction between civil and criminal cases. In criminal cases matters observed by law-enforcement personnel are not admissible under the exception. However, in civil cases, the exception encompasses any report (in any form) setting forth the activities of the office or agency, or matters observed pursuant to a legal duty to report, or factual findings resulting from a legally authorized investigation, unless the sources of the information or other circumstances indicate a lack of trustworthiness. Police officers and Child Protective Services workers are under a legal duty to investigate, including interviewing witnesses, and to write detailed reports of their investigations. However, this duty may not permit automatic admission of all such hearsay statements contained in public reports, particularly otherwise inadmissible hearsay within hearsay.[28]

Lawyers using this exception, especially before judges who try criminal cases, should have a copy of the exception available to hand

26. *See* Prater v. Cabinet for Human Resources, 954 S.W.2d 954, 959 (Ky. 1997).

27. *See, e.g., In re* Lucas, 29 Ohio App. 3d 165, 504 N.E.2d 472 (1985) (case worker's case notes admissible as public records). *Cf.* State in Interest of W.S., 939 P.2d 196 (Utah Ct. App. 1997) (social worker's predisposition report admissible as a public record, but where the witness has no personal knowledge of the hearsay contained in the report, it may not form the sole basis for disposition). *But see, e.g.*, State v. Jeansonne, 567 So.2d 802 (La. Ct. App. 1990) (medical report made as part of child abuse investigation is not a record falling within the public-records exception).

28. *See, e.g.*, Prater v. Cabinet for Human Resources, 954 S.W.2d 954 (Ky. 1997) (child's hearsay statements to social workers in the course of an abuse or neglect investigation are not admissible merely because they are contained in the agency's report); *In re* Freiburger, 153 Mich. App. 251, 395 N.W.2d 300 (1986) (police reports which contain hearsay within hearsay inadmissible as public records unless the double hearsay also falls within a recognized exception).

the judge. In twenty-one years of practice I have never had a judge allow evidence under this exception without seeing the rule. They are generally surprised to see how extensive the exception is in civil cases.

RESIDUAL EXCEPTION, RULE 803(24)

Especially in states without a special child-abuse hearsay exception, the residual clause is often used in an attempt to admit children's statements that do not appear to fall under any of the other specific exceptions. The residual exception allows hearsay concerning a material fact, which hearsay is more probative than any other evidence reasonably available, if the general purposes of the rules of evidence and the interests of justice will be best served by admitting the hearsay.[29] An important prerequisite to offering hearsay under the residual exception is that the adverse party be notified of the intent to use the hearsay, the particulars of the statement, and the name and address of the declarant. The notice must be made sufficiently far in advance to allow the adverse party "a fair opportunity to meet it."

The U.S. Supreme Court, in a criminal child abuse case, *Idaho v. Wright*,[30] indicated that this exception should be narrowly construed. Further, the Court held that in determining whether the hearsay statement possessed the requisite indicia of reliability, courts may *not* include corroborative evidence, but rather, must be limited to an inquiry of the circumstances surrounding the making of the statement. Because the case was decided on the basis of the Sixth Amendment confrontation clause, which is applicable only to criminal proceedings, and not on the basis of the Fourteenth Amendment due process clause, a plausible argument may be made that *Idaho v.*

---

29. *See, e.g.*, State v. Rojas, 524 N.W.2d 659 (Iowa 1994) (social worker's videotaped interview with ten-year-old sexual abuse victim was admissible under the residual exception because the interview was not leading or suggestive, the child's statements were detailed, beyond her age-expected experience, and consistent throughout the interview; the court noted that the videotape was more reliable than many forms of hearsay because the judge could hear the questions and answers directly and view the child's demeanor); McCafferty v. Leapley, 944 F.2d 445 (8th Cir. 1991) (seven-year-old child's statements to her teacher and psychologist were admissible under the residual exception where the totality of the circumstances demonstrated reliability).

30. 497 U.S. 805, 110 S.Ct. 3139, 111 L.Ed.2d 638 (1990).

Wright need not be applied to domestic-relations or nondelinquency juvenile cases.

PREPARING THE CHILD

It is unrealistic to expect a child to be a good witness without adequate preparation. Some courts have programs for children who will testify, and the lawyer planning to call a child witness should determine whether such a program is available in the local court. However, even if there is such a program available, it is necessary to provide specific preparation as well.

The child should be familiar with the courtroom and should know who the other people in the room will be. The child should visit the empty courtroom, sit in the witness chair (or from wherever the child will testify), and should have an opportunity to answer a few simple questions while the lawyer sits or stands where he or she will be during the trial.

The child should know whether there will be breaks and whether a support person (or object) will be allowed to be present. The child should be told that he or she may tell the judge whenever there is a need to get a drink, go to the bathroom, or take a break. However, the child must understand that the questions need to be answered and that taking a break will not result in an end to the testimony. The child should be told that he or she is not being tested, that there are no right or wrong answers, and that the judge just wants to know what really happened.

It is important to give the child explicit permission to tell the judge that he or she does not understand the question or does not know the answer. It may help to assure the child that many adult witnesses get confused by lawyers' questions and tell that to the judge. It is essential for the child to understand the topics that will be covered during the testimony, because that will assist in keeping the child focused.[31]

31. For a more complete discussion of preparing the child to testify, *see, e.g.*, Julie Lipovsky & Paul Stern, *Preparing Children for Court: An Interdisciplinary View*, 2/2 CHILD MALTREATMENT 150 (1997); Karen Saywitz, *Children in Court: Principles of Child Development for Judicial Application*, in A JUDICIAL PRIMER ON CHILD SEXUAL ABUSE 15 (Josephine Bulkley & Claire Sandt, eds. 1994); ANN M. HARALAMBIE, THE CHILD'S ATTORNEY: A GUIDE TO REPRESENTING CHILDREN IN CUSTODY, ADOPTION, AND PROTECTION CASES (1993).

ACCOMMODATIONS FOR CHILD WITNESSES

In many juvenile and domestic-relations cases, children who testify do so in chambers, often outside the presence of the parties.[32] The judge's chambers are less imposing than a courtroom, and all of the people in the room are on the same level. However, unless explicitly waived, the parent has a due-process right to have the child's testimony recorded.[33] Sometimes, however, children must testify, or prefer to testify, in the courtroom. In some of those circumstances, the public may be excluded from the courtroom during the child's testimony. Most child-protection[34] and adoption cases are already closed by statute or court rule; however, domestic-relations actions are generally open to the public. The court has the discretion to exclude the public, including the press, where the child would be unduly traumatized by their presence.[35]

Some courts have special rooms for child witnesses, with child-size furniture, bright colors on the walls, and a more relaxed environment.[36] Other courts may be rearranged to make them less threatening for child witnesses.[37] For example, the child may be per-

---

32. *See, e.g., In re* Appeal in Maricopa County Juvenile Action No. JD-561, 131 Ariz. 25, 638 P.2d 692 (1981) (in-chambers testimony in absence of father permitted where father's presence would be potentially inhibiting and testimony is traumatic in nature); *In re* Mary S., 186 Cal. App. 3d 414, 230 Cal. Rptr. 726 (1986) (testimony in absence of father permitted after in-chambers interview indicated children's fear of testifying in front of parents, where father's lawyer was present and permitted to cross-examine); *In re* Jo-Nell C., 493 A.2d 1053 (Me. 1985) (removing father permitted where his presence would hinder candid testimony and needlessly subject the child to further embarrassment and trauma).

33. *See, e.g., Ex parte* Wilson, 450 So. 2d 104 (Ala. 1984); *In re* Appeal in Maricopa County Juvenile Action No. JD-561, 131 Ariz. 25, 638 P.2d 692 (1981) (in absence of a stipulation, lawyers and court reporter must be present during in-chambers testimony in dependency trial); Watermeir v. Watermeir, 462 So. 2d 1272 (La. Ct. App. 1985) (lawyers and court reporter must be present during in-chambers competency interview); Fisher v. Fisher, 535 A.2d 1163 (Pa. Super. Ct. 1988) (when judge interviews child in custody case, conversation must be transcribed and transcript must be made part of record).

34. Such presumptive closure has been held to not violate the press's First Amendment rights. *See, e.g.*, San Bernardino County Dept. of Pub. Soc. Servs. v. Superior Court, 232 Cal. App. 3d 1988, 283 Cal. Rptr. 332 (1991); *In re* T.R., 52 Ohio St. 3d 6, 556 N.E.2d 439 (1990); Division of Youth & Family Servs. v. J.B., 120 N.J. 112, 576 A.2d 261 (1990); *In re* J.S., 140 Vt. 458, 438 A.2d 1125 (1981).

35. *See, e.g.*, Press-Enterprise Co. v. Superior Court, 478 U.S. 1, 106 S.Ct. 2735, 92 L.Ed.2d 1 (1986) (exclusion of spectators may be permitted during child sexual abuse victim's testimony in a criminal trial); Globe Newspaper Co. v. Superior Court, 457 U.S. 596, 102 S. Ct. 2613, 73 L.Ed.2d 248 (1982) (exclusion of public and press may be permitted in a case-by-case basis to protect child sexual abuse victims from further trauma and embarrassment, but mandatory closure in all such cases violates the First Amendment).

36. *See, e.g.*, Commonwealth v. Amirault, 404 Mass. 221, 535 N.E.2d 193 (1989) (criminal child sexual abuse case); *In re* C.B., 574 So.2d 1369 (Miss. 1990) (dependency case); *In re* C.M., 595 A.2d 293 (Vt. 1991) (dependency case). *But see*, Duffitt v. State, 525 N.E.2d 607 (Ind. 1988) (inappropriate for judge in criminal trial to decorate the court room with posters in deference to the child witness).

37. California explicitly permits relocation within the court room of "the judge, parties, witnesses, support persons, and court personnel . . . to facilitate a more comfortable and personal environment for the child witness" in criminal cases. *See* Cal. Penal Code § 868.8(c) (Supp. 1999).

mitted to sit in a small chair, with the judge and other lawyers sitting around a table.[38]

It is difficult for many children to testify about abuse with the abuser in the courtroom. In *Coy v. Iowa*[39] the U.S. Supreme Court held violative of the Sixth Amendment confrontation clause a statute permitting all child witnesses to testify behind screens or one-way mirrors, but in *Maryland v. Craig*[40] permitted a child victim's testimony by one-way closed circuit television where there was a particularized showing that testifying in the defendant's presence would cause the child trauma, impairing the child's ability to communicate.

Because the Sixth Amendment is inapplicable in civil cases, courts in civil matters are generally willing to permit the child to testify outside of the presence of the abuser, as well as the public, with a less compelling showing of serious trauma to the child. The lawyer should introduce some evidence that testifying in the presence of the abuser would be traumatic for the child. This evidence can come through expert testimony,[41] testimony from a parent,[42] or even the child's own expressions of fear or discomfort.[43] The inherently sensitive nature of the testimony should be sufficient in itself to warrant exclusion of the public during the child's testimony. Due process requires that the lawyers be present[44] or that the interview be recorded[45] in the absence of a stipulation to allow the judge to speak to the child alone in camera.

---

38. *See generally*, Charles Shudson, *Special Techniques to Assist Child Witnesses in Court: The Judicial Tradition of Flexibility and Innovation*, in A JUDICIAL PRIMER ON CHILD SEXUAL ABUSE (Josephine Bulkley & Claire Sandt, eds. 1994).

39. 487 U.S. 1012, 108 S. Ct. 2798, 101 L.Ed.2d 857 (1988).

40. 497 U.S. 836, 110 S. Ct. 3157, 111 L.Ed.2d 666 (1990).

41. *See, e.g.*, Thomas v. Gunter, 962 F.2d 1477 (10th Cir. 1992); State v. Vincent, 159 Ariz. 418, 768 P.2d 150 (1989); State v. Albert, 13 Kan. App. 2d 671, 778 P.2d 386 (1989); Commonwealth v. Amirault, 404 Mass. 221, 535 N.E.2d 193 (1989); State v. Taylor, 562 A.2d 445 (R.I. 1989).

42. *See, e.g.*, State v. Spigarolo, 210 Conn. 359, 556 A.2d 112 (1989).

43. *See, e.g.*, United States v. Carrier, 9 F.3d 867 (10th Cir. 1993) (permitting testimony by closed circuit television where there was a particularized showing that the child sexual abuse victims were unable to testify in the defendant's presence); Hicks-Bey v. United States, 649 A.2d 569 (D.C. 1994) (permitting testimony by closed circuit television where the six-year-old child had trouble testifying in defendant stepfather's presence at competency hearing, hid behind her hands and under the bench, was hesitant and withdrawn, and was able to testify fully only after the defendant was removed; because there was a particularized showing that the child would be traumatized by testifying in the defendant's presence, closed circuit was available despite the absence of authorizing legislation); State v. Crandall, 120 N.J. 649, 577 A.2d 483 (1990).

44. *See, e.g.*, *In re* Appeal in Maricopa County Juvenile Action No. JD-561, 131 Ariz. 25, 638 P.2d 692 (1981); *In re* Mary S., 186 Cal. App. 3d 414, 230 Cal. Rptr. 726 (1986); Stickler v. Stickler, 57 Ill. App. 2d 286, 206 N.E.2d 720 (1965); Duncan v. Duncan, 528 S.W.2d 806 (Mo. App. 1975); Cook v. Cook, 5 N.C. App. 652, 169 S.E.2d 29 (1969); Watermeir v. Watermeir, 462 So.2d 1272 (La. Ct. App. 1985).

45. *See, e.g.*, *Ex parte* Wilson, 450 So.2d 104 (Ala. 1984); Fisher v. Fisher, 370 Pa. Super. 87, 535 A.2d 1163 (1988).

The judge may permit the child to have a support person nearby during the testimony.[46] The reason for allowing a support person is that it makes the child less afraid, and therefore, better able to talk.[47] Some judges permit the child to have a relative, therapist, social worker, or victim-witness advocate present in the courtroom during the child's testimony.[48] Sometimes the child is permitted to testify from the lap of the support person.[49] The proper inquiry for the court is whether the presence of the support person will allow the child to feel comfortable and safe enough to testify truthfully or whether the presence of the support person will bias the child's testimony. Some states have enacted statutes explicitly providing for one or more support persons to be present in the courtroom, and perhaps even at the witness stand, when a child victim testifies in criminal cases.[50] At least as much flexibility should be permitted in civil cases.

---

46. *See, e.g.*, People v. Lord, 30 Cal. App. 4th 1718, 36 Cal. Rptr. 2d 453 (1994); State v. Menzies, 26 Conn. App. 674, 603 A.2d 419 (1992); Stanger v. State, 545 N.E.2d 1105 (Ind. App. 1989); State v. Rowray, 18 Kan. App. 2d 772, 860 P.2d 40 (1993); Commonwealth v. Amirault, 404 Mass. 221, 535 N.E.2d 193 (1989); State v. Pollard, 719 S.W.2d 38 (Mo. App. 1986); State v. Hoyt, 806 P.2d 204 (Utah Ct. App. 1991). *See generally*, 2 JOHN E. B. MYERS, EVIDENCE IN CHILD ABUSE AND NEGLECT CASES § 6.14 (3rd ed. 1997).

47. Current research supports common sense in demonstrating that sexually abused children are better able to testify in criminal cases with a support person present. *See* Goodman, Taub, Jones, England, Port, Rudy & Prado, *Testifying in Criminal Court: Emotional Effects on Child Sexual Assault Victims*, 57 MONOGRAPHS OF THE SOC. FOR RESEARCH IN CHILD DEVELOPMENT (Serial No. 229, No. 5, 1992). In one military case a young child was permitted to whisper her answers to her mother, who then repeated them loudly enough to be heard. *See*, United States v. Romey, 32 M.J. 180 (C.M.A. 1991).

48. *See, e.g.*, State v. Rowray, 18 Kan. App. 2d 772, 860 P.2d 40 (1993) (mother of sexually abused children permitted to sit near them while they testified).

49. *See, e.g.*, People v. Kabonic, 177 Cal. App. 3d 487, 223 Cal. Rptr. 41 (1986) (six-year-old permitted to sit on mother's lap); State v. Reeves, 337 N.C. 700, 448 S.E.2d 802 (1994) (five-year-old permitted to sit in stepmother's lap); State v. Rogers, 213 Mont. 302, 692 P.2d 2 (1984) (four-year-old's testifying from prosecutor's lap not prejudicial); State v. Johnson, 38 Ohio App. 3d 152, 528 N.E.2d 567 (1986) *cert. denied*, 498 U.S. 826, 111 S.Ct. 81, 112 L.Ed.2d 54 (1990) (eight-year-old permitted to sit on aunt's lap); State v. Dompier, 94 Or. App. 258, 764 P.2d 979 (1988) (seven-year-old permitted to sit on foster mother's lap); Commonwealth v. Pankraz, 382 Pa. Super. 116, 554 A.2d 974 (1989), *allocatur denied*, 522 Pa. 618, 563 A.2d 997 (1989) (six-year-old's testifying from grandmother's lap not prejudicial); Kirchner v. State, 739 S.W.2d 85 (Tex. Ct. App. 1987) (four-year-old permitted to testify from older sister's lap); State v. Jones, 178 W. Va. 519, 362 S.E.2d 330 (1987) (seven-year-old's testifying from foster mother's lap not prejudicial); Sexton v. Howard, 55 F.3d 1557 (11th Cir. 1995) (harmless error for five-year-old to sit on prosecutor's lap while testifying); 18 U.S.C.A. § 3509(i). *Cf.* People v. Cintron, 75 N.Y.2d 249, 551 N.E.2d 561, 552 N.Y.S.2d 68 (1990) (testimony by closed circuit television appropriate where four-year-old would not testify even when sitting on interpreter's lap); State v. Thomas, 150 Wis.2d 374, 442 N.W.2d 10 (placing screen between eight-year-old and defendant appropriate where child had difficulty testifying even when sitting on her mother's lap). *But see, e.g.*, State v. Rulona, 71 Hawaii 127, 785 P.2d 615 (1990) (error to permit eight-year-old to sit on sexual abuse counselor's lap); State v. Michaels, 264 N.J. Super. 579, 625 A.2d 489 (1993) (error for children to sit on judge's lap, play ball with judge, and whisper with the judge when testifying by closed-circuit television from chambers).

50. *See, e.g.*, ARK. CODE ANN. § 16-42-102 (1997); CAL. PENAL CODE § 868.5(a) (1997); CONN. GEN. STAT. ANN. § 54-86g(b) (1994); DEL. CODE ANN. tit. 11, § 5134(b) (1997); HAW. REV. STAT. § 621-28 (1997); IDAHO CODE § 19-3023 (1997); MICH. COMP. LAWS ANN. § 600.2163a(4) (1997); MINN. STAT ANN. § 631.046 (1997); N.Y. EXEC. LAW § 642-a(6) (1996); N.Y. CRIM. PROC. LAW § 190.32(5)(c) (1997); R.I. GEN. LAWS § 12-28-9(2) (1994); WASH. REV. CODE ANN. § 7.69A.030(8) (1997); 18 U.S.C.A. § 3509(i) (1997).

Sometimes all a child needs for security is a "support" object, such as a favorite doll, stuffed animal, or blanket.[51] The child may need something in his or her hand as a distraction while discussing private and emotionally difficult topics. While adults often find it annoying to talk to a child who is repetitively twisting into knots a piece of string or turning a toy car end over end, that distractive action may actually enable the child to be more forthcoming with testimony. The lawyer should ask the child in advance whether he or she would feel more comfortable taking a support object to the witness stand with him or her.

Another typical accommodation for children's testimony is the allowance of some leading questions. Of course, it is better for the lawyer to allow the child to speak as much as possible, but it may be necessary to ask leading questions at some point. This is particularly necessary with young children, who often have difficulty with the vague, general types of questions typical of direct examination.[52] They may be developmentally unable to understand the abstract questions being asked of them even though they are able to accurately recount facts if properly cued.

Children have much shorter attention spans than adults, and if they are not allowed frequent breaks during testifying,[53] they may become silly, nonresponsive, or worse, may give any answers which they think the questioner wants to hear just to get the testimony over with. As much as it may inconvenience the adults, frequent breaks during the child's testimony are necessary to maximize the quality of the testimony. Similarly, children may need snacks or juice

---

51. *See, e.g.*, Commonwealth v. Amirault, 404 Mass. 221, 535 N.E.2d 193 (1989) (child victim permitted to testify in a criminal case while holding a toy).

52. *See, e.g.*, Clark v. State, 315 Ark. 602, 870 S.W.2d 372 (1994) (permitting leading questions because of the youth, ignorance, and timidity of the young witnesses); Begley v. State, 483 So.2d 70 (Fla. Dist. Ct. App. 1986) (permitting leading questions to 5-year-old victim); Altmeyer v. State, 519 N.E.2d 138 (Ind. 1988), *habeas corpus denied* (7th Cir. 1995) (permitting leading questions of fourteen-year-old sexual assault victim who was embarrassed and frightened); State v. Kahey, 436 So.2d 475 (La. 1983) (permitting leading questions of eleven-year-old witness); People v. Garland, 152 Mich. App. 301, 393 N.W.2d 896 (1986) (permitting leading questions of 7-year-old sexual assault victim who was mentally retarded); State v. Leigh, 580 S.W.2d 536 (Mo. Ct. App. 1979) (permitting leading questions of timid or fearful child); Barcus v. State, 92 Nev. 289, 550 P.2d 411 (1976) (permitting leading questions of eight- and nine-year-old sexual abuse victims); State v. Lewis, 4 Ohio App. 3d 275, 488 NE2d 487 (1982) (permitting leading questions of 8- and 10-year-old sexual abuse victims); United States v. Iron Shell, 633 F.2d 77 (8th Cir. 1980), *cert denied*, 450 U.S. 1001 (1981) (permitting leading questions of nine-year-old sexual assault victim who was reluctant to testify). *See generally* 2 JOHN E. B. MYERS, EVIDENCE IN CHILD ABUSE AND NEGLECT CASES § 6.9 (3rd ed. 1997).

53. *See, e.g.*, Cal. Penal Code § 868.8(a) (1998) (explicitly providing for breaks). *See also*, Ellen Matthew & Karen Saywitz, *Child Victim Witness Manual*, 12 CJER JOURNAL § 8 (No. 1, 1992).

as an incentive to remain on track with their testimony when they really would rather be somewhere else doing something else. Judges who permit snacks and breaks for children are not conveying special favor for the child. They are merely recognizing the special needs and limitations of children and creating an environment with the greatest potential to facilitate complete and accurate testimony.

EXPERT TESTIMONY IN PREPARATION FOR CHILD'S TESTIMONY

It may be helpful to present expert testimony prior to the child's testimony, both to provide competency information about the child[54] and to alert the court to any particularized need the child might have for special accommodations in the courtroom or method of testifying.

If the child has an idiosyncratic vocabulary or particular body language that should be interpreted in a particular way, the expert should testify as to those matters prior to the child's testimony. Such preparation will enable the court to better understand and evaluate the child's testimony.

COMPETENCY

Most states do not require special competency hearings for children.[55] However, many judges continue to require proof of competency before allowing child-witness testimony. Some statutes explicitly allow child-abuse victims to testify without any competency finding, which should preclude competency hearings in those jurisdictions.[56] Such statutes have been upheld, even in criminal cases.[57]

---

54. *See generally*, 1 JOHN E. B. MYERS, EVIDENCE IN CHILD ABUSE AND NEGLECT CASES § 3.24 (3rd ed. 1997), for information on psychological evaluations regarding competence.

55. *See, e.g.*, Rule 601, Federal Rules of Evidence, and the state rules patterned thereafter. Rule 601 provides "[e]very person is competent to be a witness except as otherwise provided by these rules or by statute." For a comprehensive discussion of children's competency, *See generally* 1 JOHN E. B. MYERS, EVIDENCE IN CHILD ABUSE AND NEGLECT CASES ch. 3 (3rd ed. 1997).

56. See, e.g., ALA. CODE § 15-25-3(c) (1997); COLO. REV. STAT. § 13-90-106(1)(b)(II) (1997); CONN. GEN. STAT. ANN. § 54-86h (1994); GA. CODE ANN. § 24-9-5(b) (1997); MO. ANN. STAT. § 491.060(2) (1996); UTAH CODE ANN. § 76-5-410 (19977); W. VA. CODE § 61-8B-11(c) (1997).

While some states provide a presumption of incompetency below certain ages, a child of any age may be demonstrated to be competent if he or she understands the difference between truth and untruth, understands the requirement of the oath to tell the truth, and is able to testify reasonably accurately.[58] Even when competency need not be shown, it may be a good tactical move to put on some competency evidence to enhance the child's credibility.

In the context of a criminal child sexual abuse case, the New Jersey Supreme Court held that where there is a substantial likelihood that interviews with the molestation victim had been improperly conducted, the court must hold a "taint" hearing, at which the prosecution must prove by clear and convincing evidence that the child's statements are sufficiently reliable to warrant admission.[59] This decision has been severely criticized.[60] Lawyers may need to be prepared to face objections to child abuse victim testimony on the basis of taint. For example, an expert may evaluate the interview process and the child's ability to resist suggestion. An expert may testify generally concerning the most recent research on suggestibility. Research findings from experiments based on deliberately giving false or misleading information to children may not be generalizable to other interview circumstances, and it is important for the expert to be thoroughly familiar with the methodology employed in research cited in support of a tainting charge.

---

57. *See, e.g.*, Moates v. State, 545 So.2d 224 (Ala. Crim. App. 1989); People v. District Court, 791 P.2d 682 (Colo. 1990); State v. James, 211 Conn. 555, 560 A.2d 426 (1989); State v. Silvey, 894 S.W.2d 662 (Mo. 199); State v. Elredge, 773 P.2d 29 (1989).

58. *See, e.g.*, State v. Schossow, 145 Ariz. 504, 703 P.2d 448 (1985) (seven-year-old competent); Hall v. State, 15 Ark. App. 309, 692 S.W.2d 769 (1985) (six-year-old competent); People v. Mincey, 2 Cal. 4th 408, 827 P2d 388, 6 Cal. Rptr. 2d 822 (1992) (five-year-old competent); Galindo v. United States, 630 A.2d 202 (D.C. 1993); People v. Born, 156 Ill. App. 3d 584, 509 N.E.2d 125 (1987) (four-year-old competent); Watson v. State, 512 N.E.2d 885 (Ind. Ct. App. 1987) (five-year-old competent); Maynard v. State, 513 N.E.2d 641 (Ind. 1987) (eight-year-old competent); State v. Hussey, 521 A.2d 278 (Me. 1987) (three-year-old competent); Commonwealth v. Lamontagne, 42 Mass. App. 213, 675 N.E.2d 1169 (1997) (four-year-old competent); People v. Draper, 150 Mich. App. 481, 389 N.W.2d 89 (1986) (three-year-old competent); State v. Earl, 252 Neb. 127, 560 N.W.2d 491 (1997) (six-year-old competent); State v. Briere, 138 N.H. 617, 644 A.2d 551 (1994) (five-year-old competent); State v. Taylor, 103 N.M. 189, 704 P.2d 443 (Ct. App. 1985): State v. Eason, 402 S.E.2d 809 (N.C. 1991) (eight-year-old competent); State v. Kelly, 93 Ohio App. 3d 257, 638 N.E.2d 153 (1994) (four-year-old competent); State v. Howard, 926 S.W.2d 579 (Tenn. Ct. App. 1996) (seven-year-old competent); Reya v. State, 797 S.W.2d 189 (Tex. Ct. App. 1990) (four-year-old competent); State v. Hunsaker, 39 Wash. App. 489, 693 P.2d 724 (1984) (two-year-old competent).

59. *See* State v. Michaels, 136 N.J. 299, 642 A.2d 1372 (1994).

60. *See, e.g.*, John E. B. Myers, *Taint Hearings to Attack Investigative Interviews: A Further Assault on Children's Credibility*, 1/2 CHILD MALTREATMENT 213 (1996); John E. B. Myers, *Taint Hearings for Child Witnesses? A Step in the Wrong Direction*, 46 BAYLOR L. REV. 873 (Fall 1994).

One element of a competency examination is to establish that the child can understand an oath. It is not necessary that the oath given be identical to the oath an adult takes.[61] For example, a child may "promise" to tell the truth.[62] Even very young children generally understand what it is to tell the truth and what it is to lie,[63] even if they cannot understand the concept of "the difference between."[64] The child may be asked whether certain things are "the truth" or a "lie." For example, if the lawyer is wearing a blue jacket, and the lawyer knows that the child can identify colors, the lawyer may ask "if I said my jacket is red, would that be the truth or a lie?" "If I said my jacket is blue, would that be the truth or a lie?" The lawyer should then ask what happens if the child tells a lie. Usually the child will say "I get in trouble" or describe some punishment. The child can then be asked if he or she promises to tell the truth.

The lawyer should demonstrate that the child is able to observe and describe what was observed accurately. For example, the child can list the equipment on the playground. Children, as well as

---

61. *See, e.g.*, Rule 603, Federal Rules of Evidence, and the state rules patterned thereafter. Rule 603 requires only that the oath "be administered in a form calculated to awaken the witness' conscience and impress the witness' mind with the duty to do so." *See also*, 27 CHARLES A. WRIGHT & VICTOR J. GOLD, FEDERAL PRACTICE AND PROCEDURE: EVIDENCE § 6044 (1990); 6 JOHN H. WIGMORE, EVIDENCE IN TRIALS AT COMMON LAW § 1818 (Chadborne rev. 1978); Spigarolo v. Meachum, 934 F.2d 19 (2d Cir.1991) (court may fashion any oath meaningful to the witness). In some states children may be permitted to testify without the need to take any type of oath. *See, e.g.*, FLA. STAT. ANN. § 90.605(2) (1998); N.Y. CRIM. PROC. LAW § 60.20(2) (1992).

62. *See, e.g.*, Cal. Evid. Code § 710; Colo. Rev. Stat. § 13-90-117.5 (1997); Burkett v. State, 439 So.2d 737 (Ala. Crim. App. 1983); Walls v. State, 166 Ga. App. 503 (1983); State v. Busch, 515 So.2d 605 (La. App. 1987); State v. Davis, 66 Wis.2d 636 (1974).

63. *See, e.g.*, *In re* R.R., 79 N.J. 97, 398 A.2d 76 (1979) (four-year-old said that to tell the truth "means to be good" and if he told a lie "I would be bad" and "get a beating"); Heckathorne v. State, 697 S.W.2d 8 (Tex. App. 1985) (five-year-old said that the truth was "what really happened" and a lie was "what didn't really happen"). *See also*, Bussey, *Lying and Truthfulness: Children's Definitions, Standards, and Evaluative Reactions*, 63 CHILD DEVELOPMENT 129 (1992); Haugaard, Reppucci, Laird & Nauful, *Children's Definitions of the Truth and Their Competency as Witnesses in Legal Proceedings*, 15 L. & HUM. BEHAVIOR 253 (1991); Strichartz & Burton, *Lies and Truth: A Study of the Development of the Concept*, 61 CHILD DEVELOPMENT 211 (1990); KEE MACFARLANE & JILL WATERMAN, SEXUAL ABUSE OF YOUNG CHILDREN 27 (1986).

64. *See, e.g.*, Ellen Matthew & Karen Saywitz, *Child Victim Witness Manual*, 12 CJER JOURNAL 40 (No. 1, 1992); People v. Norfleet, 142 Mich. App. 745, 371 N.W.2d 438 (1985) (trial court should have conducted further inquiry to determine if seven-year-old child in fact understood the distinction despite the child's statement that she did not know the difference between the truth and a lie); Commonwealth v. Knapp, 374 Pa. Super. 160, 542 A.2d 546 (1988) (twelve-year-old competent despite his inability to articulate the difference between the truth and a lie or to define the word "truth"); State v. Pettis, 488 A.2d 704 (R.I. 1985) (retarded fourteen-year-old competent despite her inability to explain the difference between the truth and a lie where she had otherwise demonstrated her understanding of the necessity to tell the truth); State v. Dwyer, 149 Wis.2d 850, 440 N.W.2d 344 (1989) (trial court should have conducted further inquiry to determine if four-year-old child in fact understood the distinction despite the child's inability to articulate the difference between the truth and a lie).

adults, may be able to remember and relate certain facts without being accurate about all of the facts.[65]

Even if a child is deemed competent to testify, a court may determine that the child should not testify, especially if the court believes that the experience of testifying will put the child in an awkward situation or be traumatic to the child. Courts are split on whether a parent has an absolute right to call a competent child witness with relevant information to testify, or whether the court can preclude relevant testimony based on the risk of serious emotional harm to the child.[66] If the lawyer believes that the child's testimony is important, a mental-health professional should assess the child and testify concerning the expected impact of testifying on the child.

HOW TO ASK CHILDREN QUESTIONS THEY CAN UNDERSTAND

Lawyers need to understand that young children cannot be questioned in the same manner as older children and adults. The child-witness's credibility is related in part to the ability of the lawyer to ask questions in a way the child can understand in light of his or her language and cognitive development.[67] Children who erroneously think they understand a question or a word and answer incorrectly lose credibility, so lawyers must ensure that their questions are clearly and correctly understood. Karen Saywitz warns that "[a]ccuracy and credibility deteriorate as communication breaks down, not necessarily because children are fabricating their responses or reporting fantasies but because of adult insensitivity to norms of

65. *See, e.g.*, Adamson v. Dept. of Social Servs., 207 Cal. App. 3d 14, 254 Cal. Rptr. 667 (1988) (witness competent despite inconsistent and exaggerated statements); People v. Pike, 183 Cal. App. 2d 729, 7 Cal. Rptr. 188 (1960) (five-year-old child competent despite her inability to tell her address, how long she had lived there, the name of her church, or the names of her classmates); People v. Lamb, 121 Cal. App. 2d 838, 264 P.2d 126 (1953) (four-year-old sexual abuse victim competent despite her insistence that she was five months old because her testimony was otherwise coherent and plausible).

66. *See, e.g.*, Oregon *ex rel* Tillamook Cty. Juvenile Dept. v. Beasley, 314 Or. 444, 840 P.2d 78 (1992) (affirming trial court's denial of father's right to call his thirteen-year-old son to testify in termination of parental rights case; the court stated that unless the probative value of the child's testimony is substantially outweighed by the risk of severe emotional or psychological harm to the child from testifying, the court has no discretion and must allow the testimony).

67. *See, e.g.*, Karen Saywitz & Lorinda Comparo, *Interviewing Child Witnesses: A Developmental Perspective*, 22/8 CHILD ABUSE & NEGLECT 825 (1998); Karen J. Saywitz, *Children in Court: Principles of Child Development for Judicial Application*, in A JUDICIAL PRIMER ON CHILD SEXUAL ABUSE 15 (Josephine Bulkley & Claire Sandt eds. 1994); ANNE GRAFFAM WALKER, HANDBOOK ON QUESTIONING CHILDREN: A LINGUISTIC PERSPECTIVE (1994); Karen J. Saywitz, Rebecca Nathanson, & Lynn Snyder, *Credibility of Child Witnesses: The Role of Communicative Competence*, in 13/4 TOPICS IN LANGUAGE DISORDER (1993).

development."[68] The appropriate procedures and techniques for questioning young children are simply not compatible with traditional courtroom procedures and practices.

For example, children under the age of about seven interpret questions by relying upon concrete circumstances and objects rather than upon verbal language per se. They are much more likely to respond to directions such as to "show me what happened" (using props such as pictures, dolls, objects, and so on), rather than to instructions to "tell me what happened." Young children are also apt to respond to questions with answers that correspond to what they think the questioner wants to hear rather than to tell what actually happened.

Given these considerations, it is not likely that children below the age of six or seven will be able to serve as credible witnesses in courtroom settings because the environment and the nature of legalistic requirements are not conducive to eliciting complete or valid responses from them. It is usually not wise to expect children below the age of six or seven to provide reliable testimony in a courtroom setting.

Exceptions to this general rule may occur. Because children's cognitive, social, and/or emotional functioning level may differ from their chronological age, there are children who may be only five, six, or seven years of age chronologically, but who are developmentally quite advanced and can perform quite effectively in a courtroom. There are also children who may be seven, eight, or nine or even older, but who are delayed in their development, and who cannot perform in a courtroom setting. Therefore, it is often necessary to obtain the services of a child psychologist to determine the child's level of functioning and ability to testify in court.

Children below the age of six or seven can be interviewed, and valid, comprehensive information may be obtained when the appropriate environment and interviewing techniques are utilized, and the appropriate mental-health professional conducts the interview. The information obtained from such an interview may be admissible

---

68. *See* Karen J. Saywitz, Rebecca Nathanson & Lynn Snyder, *Credibility of Child Witnesses: The Role of Communicative Competence*, 13/4 *Topics in Language* 59, 63 (1993).

through the expert testimony of the mental-health professional or by introducing a videotape of the interview as evidence. Some trial judges may permit the child to testify, preferably in chambers, with the mental-health professional asking the questions. All lawyers could submit questions or lines of inquiry for the mental-health professional to use, perhaps in a more developmentally appropriate phrasing.

It is important for lawyers to realize that it is not until the age of ten or eleven that most children may be willing to acknowledge that they do not understand a question or that they do not know the answer or cannot remember. Children under this age may fabricate rather than admit that they do not understand the question or do not remember. Therefore, lawyers may need to carefully explain to the child witness in advance that it is acceptable to answer questions in court by saying that they do not know, do not understand the question, or cannot remember what happened.

In general, children do not respond well to repeated questions on the same topic or to continuing probing. They are likely to become resistant or superficial in such situations. Also, children are extremely reluctant to answer questions to which the answers appear obvious or to which they know the adult questioning them knows the answer. Again, the lawyer should prepare the child in advance for the likelihood of such questions and explain the necessity for the child to answer them.

Another significant issue for children's lawyers to be aware of is the difficulty children experience when they have to face an abuser in the courtroom in a child-abuse case or face a parent in a custody case. Such situations may provoke considerable anxiety or fear in the child and these emotions may interfere with the child's ability to concentrate or to comprehend the questions that are being asked.

ENSURING FAIR CROSS-EXAMINATION

Children are more likely to testify completely and accurately when they are not intimidated[69] or deliberately misled. Opposing counsel

---

69. *See, e.g.*, Goodman, Bottoms, Schwartz-Kenney & Rudy, *Children's Testimony About a Stressful Event: Improving Children's Reports*, 7 J. OF NARRATIVE & LIFE HISTORY 69 (1991).

may attempt to intimidate a child witness during cross-examination. Some judges intervene sua sponte to restrict the manner of examination, but the lawyer offering the child's testimony should be quick to object to any intimidating or unfair questions. It may be helpful to have a trial memorandum prepared in advance citing various research studies that indicate that such tactics *decrease* the accuracy and reliability of the child's testimony, the proper goal of questions.

Because children generally assume that adults ask sincere questions,[70] they must be warned that during cross-examination, the lawyer may attempt to trick or confuse the child. Warning the child about such questions and teaching him or her techniques for responding to misleading questions may significantly enhance the completeness, accuracy, and credibility of the child's testimony.[71]

As mentioned earlier, there is also research support that young children are able to testify more fully and accurately, and with greater credibility, when they are permitted to have a support person in the room with them.[72]

70. *See, e.g.*, Karen Saywitz & Snyder, *Improving Children's Testimony with Preparation*, in CHILD VICTIMS, CHILD WITNESSES 117, at 130-131 (Gail S. Goodman & Bette L. Bottoms, eds., 1993).

71. *See, e.g.*, Karen Saywitz & Snyder, *Improving Children's Testimony with Preparation*, in CHILD VICTIMS, CHILD WITNESSES 117 (Gail S. Goodman & Bette L. Bottoms, eds., 1993).

72. *See, e.g.*, Batterman-Faunce & Goodman, *Effects of Context on the Accuracy and Suggestibility of Child Witnesses*, in CHILD VICTIMS, CHILD WITNESSES 301, at 319-322 (Gail S. Goodman & Bette L. Bottoms, eds., 1993); Gail Goodman, Taub, Jones, England, Port, Rudy & Prado, *Testifying in Criminal Court: Emotional Effects on Child Sexual Assault Victims*, 57 MONOGRAPHS OF THE SOC. FOR RESEARCH IN CHILD DEVELOPMENT (Serial No. 229, No. 5, 1992).

Custody and Visitation Orders

14

Introduction

Courts and lawyers are provided little assistance in crafting appropriate custody and visitation orders where sexual abuse has been alleged. It is difficult to draw conclusions about what evidence warrants imposition of restriction on or denial of visitation in reviewing the cases dealing with the appropriateness of such orders; however, it appears that the reported decisions tend to emphasize parental rights at the expense of the child's rights and interests.[1]

Allegations of molestation elicit strong emotional reactions that often color judicial orders. I once tried a case where the accused father's lawyer was permitted, over my continuing objections, to pose questions to the expert witnesses in terms of "suppose His Honor's child said. . . ." While such explicit invitations to have the judge assume the perspective of an accused parent are rare, implicit in many defense strategies is the desire to have the evaluator, investigator, or court imagine how hard it would be to fight an allegation of molestation. Such tactics evoke a formerly articulated view of rape:

1. *See generally*, Annotation, *Denial or Restriction of Visitation Rights to Parent Charged with Sexually Abusing a Child*, 1 A.L.R. 5th 776.

that it is an easy charge to make, but difficult to prove, thereby warranting extra corroboration and care lest a man be falsely accused. On the other hand, the extreme child-advocacy perspective urges the judge to protect the child at all costs, emphasizing the potential damage to the child. "What if this were your child or grandchild? Wouldn't you want to make absolutely sure the child were safe before permitting contact?"

What makes sense for one family may be inappropriate for another. It is essential that individualized and sensitive attention be given to fact-finding and creating solutions in child sexual abuse cases.

TEMPORARY ORDERS

Restrictive custody and visitation orders are often sought when allegations of sexual abuse are made and prior to their being a full evidentiary hearing on the issue of whether the child was molested, and if so, by whom. A major problem, particularly with young children, is that the first indication that the child *might have been* molested may be fairly weak, and it may take an extended time for a thorough evaluation to assess all of the relevant evidence. Some judges decide to err on the side of restricting contact pendente lite, while others are loathe to interfere with the parent-child relationship in the absence of a showing of abuse. Some courts suspend contact entirely pendente lite.[2]

It would make sense to enter at least an immediate restrictive order, even on an ex parte basis, where the allegations on their face appear to have some reasonable basis. A hearing should be held as soon as practical to determine what kind of evaluation should take place and by whom, and to make interim orders unless the allegations appear to be wholly without merit. After an evidentiary hearing, the court will be in a better position to tailor the restriction, if any, to the facts of the case.[3] At the least, steps should be taken to facilitate disclosure and protect the child from pressure to tell a par-

---

2. *See, e.g., Ex parte* Harris, 506 So.2d 1003 (Ala. App. 1987).

3. For cases upholding restrictions on the accused parent's visitation pendente lite, *see, e.g.*, Cronier v. Cronier, 540 So.2d 1160 (La. App. 1989); S.H. v. B.L.H., 392 Pa. Super. 137, 572 A.2d 730 (1990).

ticular story or to recant true allegations. It is not unusual for children to be threatened, bribed, or otherwise pressured when allegations of sexual abuse have been made.[4] Even supervised visitation may not adequately protect a child from such attempts at coercion or intimidation.[5] Appointment of a qualified lawyer for the child should be made at the earliest possible time, preferably before the temporary hearing, or if that is not possible, at the temporary hearing.

ORDERS WHERE ABUSE HAS BEEN PROVEN

For many parents and their lawyers, the major issue in protection and domestic-relations custody or visitation cases is proving whether or not the sexual abuse occurred. It would be a mistake not to prepare carefully for the second issue that arises after success: What difference does it make to the custody or visitation order? A parent may assume that proving the abuse can result in only one order, sole custody to the nonabuser and no visitation (or at the most, supervised visitation) for the molester or parent who allowed the abuse. But that result is by no means automatic.

New Jersey has enacted a statute denying to a person convicted of sexual assault, custody or visitation with the child born as a result of the assault or who was the victim of the assault, except upon a showing by clear and convincing evidence that it would be in the child's best interests.[6] This statute addresses only the most egregious cases, where there has been a criminal conviction. However, it appropriately recognizes the parent's forfeiture of custody and visitation rights while allowing such rights if they would serve the child's best interests. The statute further provides that denial of custody or visitation shall not by itself terminate the parental rights of the molester.

The Louisiana legislature had enacted a statute that provided that where abuse is proven by a preponderance of the evidence, there be no contact between the child and abusive parent until the abusive parent successfully completes therapy, is not abusing alcohol or psy-

4. See Chapter 1.
5. *See, e.g.*, Beckham v. O'Brien, 176 Ga. App. 518, 336 S.E.2d 375 (1985).
6. *See* N.J. STAT. ANN. § 9:2-4.1 (1998).

choactive drugs, and the court finds that the parent poses no danger to the child and that supervised visitation would be in the child's best interests. However, the Louisiana Supreme Court held that statute to be unconstitutional,[7] holding that because of the disparity in consequences, sexual abuse must be proven by clear and convincing evidence as a matter of procedural due process. This decision fails to adequately consider the child's rights. By requiring proof by clear and convincing evidence, it discounts the child's interest in not being forced to have contact with his or her molester. There is no basis for imposing a heightened burden of proof solely with respect to allegations of sexual abuse. While many states require a showing of significant harm prior to restricting visitation, they do not require proof of such harm by clear and convincing evidence.

However, the Louisiana statute was flawed by lacking an individualized finding concerning therapy and the other prerequisites to contact. As a matter of policy, if the statute were viewed entirely as a rebuttable presumption of no contact under the circumstances described, it would represent a good start in the court's analysis of the individualized factors involved in the case.

Washington has an extensive statute dealing with restrictions in temporary or permanent parenting plans where there has been sexual abuse.[8] This statute avoids the flaws of the Louisiana statute by providing a series of rebuttable presumptions against contact between the molester and the child. This flexibility should avoid the procedural due process problems noted by the Louisiana Supreme Court.

For some judges sexual abuse is so inherently indicative of parental unfitness that the fact of molestation outweighs all other factors.[9] However, some judges will view the abuse as only one among many other factors relevant to a determination of custodial fitness, particularly where misconduct has been found with respect to both parents. How should a judge compare a parent who fondles a child to a parent who fails to supervise the child because of substance abuse? Is it worse for a generally "loving" parent to sexually

---

7. *See* Louisiana *in re* A.C., 643 So.2d 743 (La. 1994).
8. WASH. REV. CODE ANN. § 26.09.191 (1997).
9. *See, e.g.*, Dominick C. v. Rosina C., 230 A.D.2d 760, 646 N.Y.S.2d 696 (1996) (permanent order of protection for father to stay away from his son affirmed where the father had sexually abused his son).

abuse the child or for a "harsh" parent to physically abuse the child? Does it matter that the child wants to live with the molester and is angry with the nonmolester? These are difficult questions that require sensitivity and a broad understanding of the relationships among all of the parties, including most importantly, the child.

In most cases, the court will not award physical custody to a person who has been found to have molested the child. In my opinion, a person who has molested a child should not be awarded joint legal custody, either, because he or she has been shown to place his or her own needs ahead of a parent's fiduciary obligation to care for a child without abusing that child.

In most cases a person found to have molested a child will be given some amount of supervised visitation.[10] In some cases family members or friends provide the supervision. Such supervision is almost always more comfortable for the accused parent; however, friends and relatives may not be appropriately vigilant or supportive to the child, particularly where they do not believe that the parent did in fact molest the child. In many cases it is more appropriate to have a professional, or at least a disinterested lay third party, provide the supervision.[11]

Sometimes courts require that the abuser seek or successfully complete therapy prior to resumption of visitation,[12] sometimes also requiring the abuser to admit the abuse.[13] There has been some debate about whether reunification of sexual abuse perpetrators with their victims is a desirable social goal and whether there is empirical support of the safety of reunification plans.[14] In some cases it is appropriate to suspend or terminate visitation upon a finding of sex-

---

10. *See, e.g.*, Miller v. Hawkins, 549 So.2d 102 (Ala. App. 1989); Mallory v. Mallory, 207 Conn. 48, 539 A.2d 995 (1988); Arnold v. Naughton, 61 Md. App. 427, 486 A.2d 1204, *cert. denied*, 303 Md. 295, 493 A.2d 349 (1985); S.G.K. v. K.S.K., 374 N.W.2d 525 (Minn. App. 1985).

11. For cases involving supervision by a professional, *see, e.g.*, Rester v. Manuel, 619 So.2d 655 (La. App. 1993).

12. *See, e.g.*, S.G.K. v. K.S.K., 374 N.W.2d 525 (Minn. App. 1985).

13. *See, e.g.*, Nelson v. Jones, 781 P.2d 964 (Alaska 1989), *cert. denied* 498 U.S. 810, 111 S.Ct. 44, 112 L.Ed.2d 20 (1990). *But see, e.g.*, Mullin v. Phelps, 647 A.2d 714 (Vt. 1994) (order requiring father to admit molesting child as a condition of future visitation stricken as violative of his privilege against self-incrimination).

14. *See, e.g.* Donna M. Pence, *Family Preservation and Reunification in Intrafamilial Sexual Abuse Cases: A Law Enforcement Perspective*, 2/2 J. CHILD SEXUAL ABUSE 103 (1993); Charles Arnold, II, *Family Preservation and Reunification in Intrafamilial Sexual Abuse Cases: A CPS Attorney's Perspective*, 2/2 J. CHILD SEXUAL ABUSE 109 (1993); Charles P. Ewing, *Family Preservation and Reunification in Intrafamilial Sexual Abuse Cases: A Justice Perspective*, 2/2 J. CHILD SEXUAL ABUSE 113 (1993).

ual abuse.[15] The final decision should not be based on a desire to be fair to the parent who has molested the child, but rather, on the sole desire to be fair to the child who has been molested.

ORDERS WHERE ABUSE HAS BEEN DISPROVED

It is difficult to prove the null hypothesis, that something did not happen. Sometimes judges merely make a finding that the accuser has failed to carry his or her burden of proof. In other cases the judge makes an affirmative finding that the court is convinced that no abuse occurred. Sometimes courts change custody to the accused parent as a reaction to what they have found to be false allegations.[16]

Where abuse has been affirmatively disproved, the context of the allegation becomes crucial. Deliberate fabrications constitute a form of emotional child abuse. Although the single factor of a deliberate fabrication should not in itself determine that parent's right to custody or visitation, it certainly should be a significant negative factor to be weighed among all other factors.

However, good-faith but erroneous allegations may not warrant any negative consequences against the proponent of the allegations. Public policy favors parents taking preemptive action to protect their children from suspected harm, even when it turns out that there was no real risk. For example, few would fault a parent for removing an ostensibly unloaded gun from the vicinity of a child. Parents are daily required to weigh risks and assess danger in making decisions concerning their children. Parents who fail to follow up on suspicions that their children are being abused are labeled neglectful. When courts admonish parents for taking protective action, or in severe cases of overreaction award custody to the accused solely because the allegation was found to be untrue, courts are providing a disincentive for trying to be a good, protective parent.

15. *See, e.g.*, Nelson v. Jones, 781 P.2d 964 (Alaska 1989), *cert. denied* 498 U.S. 810, 111 S.Ct. 44, 112 L.Ed.2d 20 (1990); Freeburg v. Freeburg, 596 So.2d 794 (Fla. App. 1992); *In re* Marriage of Ashby, 193 Ill. App. 3d 366, 549 N.E.2d 923 (1990); D.A.H. v. G.A.H., 371 N.W.2d 1 (Minn. App. 1985); *In re* Shaun "X.," 228 A.D.2d 730, 643 N.Y.S.2d 703 (1996); Seravo v. Seravo, 525 A.2d 922 (R.I. 1985); Stephen L.H. v. Sherry L.H., 195 W.Va. 384, 465 S.E.2d 841 (1995). *But see, e.g.*, Doe v. Doe, 644 So.2d 1199 (Miss. 1994) (court should have restricted, rather than terminated, visitation).

16. *See, e.g.*, B.L.E. v. V.A.E., 791 S.W.2d 427 (Mo. App. 1990).

Where the good-faith allegations are a product of mental illness, the court must determine the impact on the child of the underlying mental illness. For example, the parent may be delusional or paranoid about the allegations and about other issues. The court must see if there is a nexus between the parent's mental illness and the parent's ability and willingness to provide proper care for the child.[17]

Even where the allegations have not been proven, there may be parent-child problems which warrant restrictions on visitation or a therapeutic reestablishment of the relationship.[18] The fact that the allegations were made at all constitute a significant disruption in the family, and the child may be afraid of the accused parent or believe that he or she has been molested even if that is not correct. Under such circumstances, the best course is often to involve a mental-health professional to repair the relationship in a way and at a pace that are comfortable for the child. While an unfairly accused parent may resent having to endure such restrictions, his or her long-term relationship with the child will be better served if the child is not forced into having upsetting contact.

ORDERS WHERE AN AGREEMENT LEAVES THE ISSUE OF CULPABILITY UNANSWERED

It is sometimes tempting for parents to enter into agreements that do not require a finding either that the abuse did or did not occur. This is particularly likely in protection cases when criminal charges are pending. The accused is advised by counsel in the criminal case to say nothing and to have no contact with the alleged victim. The proponent of the accusation wants to protect the child from contact. Therefore, the parties may stipulate to a dependency adjudication based on the facts that the allegation was made, the accused denies the allegations, and the resulting impasse between parent and child renders it unworkable for the child to be in the accused parent's custody. In some cases the court accepts testimony and makes a finding

17. *See, e.g.*, 1 A. HARALAMBIE, HANDLING CHILD CUSTODY, ABUSE, AND ADOPTION CASES §§ 8.23-8.25 (2nd ed, Clark Boardman Callaghan 1993, West Group 1998).

18. *See, e.g.*, Jane P. v. John P., 135 Misc.2d 400, 515 N.Y.S.2d 365 (1987) (overnight visitation suspended temporarily).

that the abuse has occurred. In others the judge assumes that the abuse occurred and makes custody and visitation orders accordingly.

The problem with cases proceeding with a lack of findings is likely to arise at review hearings when the accused seeks to resume or increase contact with the child or even to seek custody. The Maryland Court of Special Appeals addressed this procedural scenario in *In re Iris*.[19] In that case the state filed a protection action, in which the parties entered an agreement lacking a finding concerning whether the child had been molested, and the father entered a nolo contendere plea to the related criminal charge, accepting a sentence of probation before judgment. The trial court in the protection action foresaw a problem with the stipulated no contact order if the accused father later sought to have it lifted without there having been a finding a sexual abuse because there would be no basis for the order.[20] Nevertheless the court accepted the agreement, and at all future review hearings the no contact order was continued, despite the father's requests to reinitiate contact. The appellate court described the case as "an example of a terrible family tragedy that has been exacerbated by those entrusted to give aid and support. A father and stepmother have been totally separated from their daughter by the power of the State for three years, without any tangible efforts at reconciliation."[21] The appellate court noted that although "there had been no finding of sexual abuse, the [trial] court proceeded as though there had been such a finding."[22] Although the child, by then fifteen years old, did not wish to have any contact with her father, the appellate court found that her wishes were not controlling.[23] The court stated that the "greatest restriction that should have been placed upon the father was supervised visitation until the issue of sexual abuse had been determined."[24] Therefore, the court struck the no-contact order and directed that the father be given liberal supervised visitation, with a reasonable effort being made towards reconciliation.[25]

19. 118 Md. App. 636, 703 A.2d 1279 (1998).
20. 703 A.2d at 1281.
21. *Id.* at 1282.
22. *Id.* at 1284.
23. *Id.* at 1285.
24. *Id.* at 1286.
25. *Id.*

While *In re Iris* illustrates the problems that can occur in the absence of a finding one way or the other, and while the court acknowledged that it did not know whether the father had in fact molested the child,[26] the appellate court's remedy is troubling for several reasons. First, the court appears to have elevated the father's rights above the child's rights, particularly if the truth is that the father did molest the child.[27] Second, it assumed that reconciliation and contact are always appropriate until sexual abuse is proven. Most surprising, especially in light of the court's continual references to the lack of a trial court determination of whether Iris was molested, is that the appellate court did not direct that there be a hearing to determine whether or not the child had been molested. The resulting visitation order should flow from such a finding. If, as the father's psychologist indicated, "there is a strong possibility that the charges were fabricated,"[28] the protection case should address the issues underlying the fabrication. If, on the other hand, the father molested the child, a determination to require contact, whether or not supervised, should be based on the child's needs and wishes.

THE CHALLENGE WHERE THE EVIDENCE IS AMBIGUOUS

A most difficult situation is presented where there is reason to believe that the child has been molested, but the proponent of the allegation cannot prove the allegation by a preponderance of the evidence. The best known case of facts being "in equipoise," with equal probative evidence to suggest that the child was and was not molested, is *Morgan v. Foretich*.[29] The trial judge granted Dr. Foretich (the father, who was alleged to have molested his child) a two-week period of summer visitation, over the objection of the mother and the child's guardian ad litem. Rather than exposing her daughter to that unsupervised block of time, Dr. Morgan sent the child "underground" with her parents. She was ultimately jailed for contempt for refusing to produce the child, and she was jailed until

26. *Id.*
27. See Chapter 15 for a discussion of the balancing of rights between parents and children.
28. *Id.*
29. 546 A.2d 407 (D.C. App. 1988), *cert. denied* 488 U.S. 1007, 109 S.Ct. 790, 102 L.Ed.2d 781.

Congress passed special legislation designed to free her. She joined the child in New Zealand; the courts there granted her the custody order she requested, with no visitation for Dr. Foretich.

The *Morgan v. Foretich* case is disturbing in part because there was significant evidence of molestation, but not the "feather on the scale" to tip the balance by a preponderance of the evidence. If it was just as likely that Dr. Foretich had molested the child as it was that he did not, public policy would be served by adopting a more conservative approach to visitation. Judges should take a middle-ground approach that can provide at least some monitoring or other protection for the child under such circumstances. One such approach is described by Sandra K. Hewitt and is reproduced at the end of this chapter.[30] The model involves developing an agreed-upon list of appropriate and inappropriate touches, absolving the child of blame for any inappropriate touches, giving the child permission to object to touches, and to tell the therapist about any inappropriate touches. Both parents endorse the lists and the permission to disclose. The therapist works with the child and each parent and may initiate therapeutically supervised visits, other supervised visits, or unsupervised visits as appropriate during the course of the process. Hewitt recommends using the model for at least one year.

CONCLUSION

There are competing public-policy concerns involved in rendering custody and visitation orders where sexual abuse has been alleged. Parents have rights to the care and companionship of their children, and children have rights to affiliation with their parents. Children also have the right to be protected from abuse and neglect and emotionally harmfully interactions, including with their parents. We want to encourage parents to be sensitive to the needs of the children and to act quickly to protect them from perceived danger. But we do not want parents to invent allegations against each other as a tactic to gain an advantage in a custody or visitation case.

---

30. *See* Sandra K. Hewitt, *Therapeutic Management of Preschool Cases of Alleged but Unsubstantiated Sexual Abuse*, 70/1 CHILD WELFARE 59, at 61-64 (1991), reprinted at Appendix 14-1.

The obvious fact is that we need to know the whole truth. Unfortunately, there are limitations in the ability to definitively determine whether a child has been abused, and if so, by whom. There are limitations in our ability to predict whether abusers have been rehabilitated or whether they pose any continued risks to their children. Therefore, legal decision-makers often must make decisions in the absence of adequate evidence. We must learn to tolerate ambiguity, the doubt which exists in either direction in many child sexual abuse cases. It is that doubt that keeps us honest in the face of the emotional desire to convince ourselves completely that the abuse did nor did not exist, justifying through our certainty whatever decisions we have made.

While we await the magic bullet that will conclusively diagnose sexual abuse, we must make custody and visitation orders rationally, in a child-centered way, devoid of emotionalism and personalization. Custody and visitation decisions were never intended to punish or reward parents. When the desire to do so drives the decision, it is really the child who is punished.

14-1 Appendix

Therapeutic Management of Preschool Cases of Alleged but Unsubstantiated Sexual Abuse

The Therapeutic Process

The procedure outlined in this article has been in use at Midwest Children's Resource Center (MCRC) to manage therapeutically cases of alleged child sexual abuse when visiting has been restored following an abuse investigation, but where there was a clear sense of risk to the children according to the information gathered. Most commonly, the reunion is of children and accused parents, but it also applies to accused stepparents, relatives, and so on. The age of the child for whom this process is suitable can be as young as two and a half, depending on verbal ability. The therapeutic management process follows, in the form of instructions to practitioners.

1. After all investigations have been completed and the reports cannot be substantiated, meet first with these children and let them know that there is a clear change of agenda. Explain that you are not going to ask questions about who did what, but you do want to

understand from them what kind of touching they do and do not like. Your task is to understand what they like and dislike. Often using a figure of a boy or girl such as is found in the coloring book, *Red Flag Green Flag People* [Williams 1980], can help by letting the children focus on various parts of the body where they like to be touched and places they do not like to be touched. No names are elicited and no accusations are made. Simply document their statements in writing so that they can see what their preferences are.

Often a child will be afraid to talk about this question after the investigation; it can be helpful to get "permission" from a parent, or even from the alleged offender, that it is okay for the child to talk to the therapist about the different kinds of touching the child likes and does not like. This helps particularly to free the child from a censorship that the alleged offender may have imposed earlier, because the child is not asked to name a person. At the same time, the alleged abuser is put in a double bind in that no abuser can legitimately, in the eyes of authorities, forbid a child to discuss these matters, and yet, the abuser's permission to talk can help free a censored child. This permission can be obtained in writing from the alleged offender or a tape can be made.

2. Next meet with the nonoffending parents of these children and ask for their own list of appropriate and inappropriate touching. Get a sense of their background and the history of touching norms, privacy, nudity, and so on, that they grew up with. Let the parents know you are aware of the details of the investigation and your focus is now on what will protect the child in the present *and* the future. Affirm appropriate touches and set clear rules for any inappropriate suggested touches.

3. In contested custody cases, if the nonoffending parent is anxious, upset, or obsessive about the nonsubstantiation and about the child's reunion with the alleged offender, listen supportively. Let the parent know that you understand how hard this is for them, and that it would be difficult for you as a parent or professional to return a child to a situation in which you believe abuse had clearly occurred. Let the nonabusing parent know that you would like to support him or her in this, and that you want to offer a referral for individual therapy. If the parent is talking to a professional, it is less likely that the parent's feelings will be channeled to the child, and the parent

will be better able to help the child. This allows you to concentrate on the child, while the nonaccused parent has someone with whom he or she can talk. We ask that a Minnesota Multiphasic Personality Inventory (MMPI) be taken at the onset of therapy for the nonaccused parent so we can better understand his or her therapy needs.

4. Meet together with nonaccused parents and the children to share their lists of appropriate and inappropriate touching, settling on a jointly agreed upon list, with the children's wishes leading. Try to enhance the bond between the parents and children, and repeat often that it is okay for the children to tell the parents if the children don't like what is happening. Have the parents make clear that they would not consider this the children's fault and that the parents would not be angry at the children or stop loving them. This latter point is very important.

5. If the nonoffending parents have a history of putting leading questions or lack credibility in reporting, then have them practice listening techniques with you. Have them listen nondirectly to a hypothetical child's report, and have them write down the information as reported. Instruct them that in the future if there are any statements by the child, they should follow this procedure and turn the information over to you for followup or to a police officer or child protection worker to investigate.

6. Interview the alleged abuser along the same lines as the nonaccused parents in paragraph 2 above.

7. Meet with the children to review the list of appropriate and inappropriate touching, and discuss sharing this with the alleged abuser. At this point, some children have made new or clearer allegations of abuse. New information may surface due to the education the children have been receiving, or the fear associated with an upcoming meeting with the alleged offender. Carefully monitor their level of fear and help them talk about the things that make each afraid. Report any new information to authorities and let them document it.

If there are no new statements, set parameters for an upcoming meeting (e.g., no hugs if the child doesn't want them; safe topics for discussion), and draft the rules the children want (e.g., no hitting). *Do not* leave the child and the alleged offender in the waiting room together. Plan their arrival and departure. Attend to the children's feelings about not having their warring parents in close proximity.

8. Have a meeting with the child and the alleged abuser. Go through the lists. Have the alleged offender reaffirm the child's boundaries by affirming the list of the child's touches; have the alleged offender tell the child what is inappropriate touching. Have the alleged offender sign the child's lists as the rules he or she promises to follow with the child. Have the alleged offender tell the child that it's all right to tell about inappropriate touching. (This may need more than one session).

9. Follow up with other supervised visits of the child and alleged offender as often as the sessions are feasible. Allow a meeting or so individually with the child between joint meetings to deal with feelings and needs.

10. Hold onto the case (even if later on you are not doing the supervised visits yourself) to monitor the child's status and keep in touch with the child. If the visiting is later being monitored by someone else, still try to see the child at least monthly for several following months. Contact then can be made less frequently—once every other month to once in three or four months. Telephone contact may also be used.

Obviously, if the visiting remains with you, you can schedule as needed. In some cases, you might move gradually toward having the visits out of your office, then with someone outside your office for your monitoring, and then to public parent/child outings, depending on the comfort level of the child. Outside supervision can be done by child protection workers, ministers, trusted family friends, and so on. These supervisors have to be persons the children feel comfortable with as well as persons the children feel can protect them. Visits can take place in public places such as shopping malls and restaurants and then in increasingly private places such as visits to the home of the alleged offender. This transition must be done over time and with care, always monitoring the children's sense of security and comfort. It is important that you remain the consultant for the visiting supervisor in high-risk cases. In a few cases, we have recommended no contact outside of a supervised hour because of detrimental behavior observed and documented during this reunion process.

The additional time required for follow-up in an already overloaded system can seem pressing, but few contacts may actually be required, and the continuing affiliation of the child with a therapist monitor may inhibit a potential abuser. Periodic contact can alert a professional to additional problems with the child that can be dealt with then, rather than requiring lengthier treatment later. At least one year for contact is recommended. With clear boundaries, learned ways of reporting, regular contact to monitor status, and increased external inhibitors against abuse, the probability of renewed abuse will be lessened, one hopes, and as these children get older, they can better report and defend themselves.

POLICY CONSIDERATIONS 15

THE CHILD'S VOICE UNDER CIVIL LAW

The party alleging sexual abuse always has the burden of proving that it has occurred. Where the case is between the criminal justice system and an accused defendant, this burden elevates the importance of not convicting an innocent person above the interest of the child victim to be protected. This is an appropriate result because of the importance the United States places on individual liberty.

Several states have enacted "sexually violent predator commitment" laws that permit the civil commitment of certain still-dangerous convicted sexual offenders after their criminal sentence has been completed.[1] These statutes have generally been held to be constitu-

1. *See, e.g.*, ARIZ. REV. STAT. ANN. §§ 13-4601 through -4606 (1997); CAL. WELF. & INST. CODE § 6600 (1997); CONN. GEN. STAT. ANN. §§ 17a-573, 17a-520 (1992); D.C. CODE ANN. §§ 22-3503 through -3511 (1981); 725 ILL. COMP. STAT. ANN. §§ 207/1 through 207/40 (1997); IOWA CODE ANN. §§ 901A.1 (1997); KAN. STAT. ANN. §§ 59-29a01 through -29a17 (1994); MASS. GEN. LAWS ANN. ch. 123A §§ 1 though 9 (1986); MINN. STAT. ANN. § 253B.185 (1997); N.J. STAT. ANN. § 30:4-82.4 (1997); TENN. CODE ANN. §§ 33-6-305 (1997); WASH. REV. CODE ANN. §§ 71.09.010 through 71.09.230 (1997); WIS. STAT. ANN. §§ 980.01 though 980.13 (1997). *See generally*, John Kip Cornwell, *Protection and Treatment: The Permissible Civil Detention of Sexual Predators*, 53 WASH. & LEE L. REV. 1293 (1996); Claudine M. Leone, *New Jersey Assembly Bill 155—A Bill Allowing the Civil Commitment of Violent Sex Offenders After the Completion of a Criminal Sentence*, 18 SETON HALL LEGIS. J. 890 (1994).

tional.[2] In *Kansas v. Hendricks*[3] the U.S. Supreme Court recently reversed the ruling by the Kansas Supreme Court[4] that its state's sexually violent predator civil-commitment act was unconstitutional. Justice Thomas, writing for the Court, found that the statute's prerequisites for commitment—that the person had been convicted of or charged with a sexually violent offense and that the person suffers from a mental abnormality or personality disorder that makes the person likely to engage in the predatory acts of sexual violence—were sufficient to justify civil deprivation of the person's liberty and does not constitute double punishment.[5] These special sexual-predator-commitment laws, as well as special sexual-offender registration and public-notification laws, represent an expression of the public-policy trend towards giving priority to protecting victims and potential victims of sexual offenses.

However, in most cases it is left to the civil justice system to provide protection for the child victim, largely because relatively few intrafamilial sexual abuse cases are criminally prosecuted. It is crucial that the civil courts sensitively balance the rights of the child against those of the parents and the state to ensure that the child is protected. Allegations of sexual abuse, like other allegations of parental unfitness in custody, visitation, and dependency cases, must be proved only by a preponderance of the evidence.[6] A higher burden of proof, as advocated by some, would be inappropriate. There is no public-policy reason justifying a higher standard merely because the allegations involve sexual, rather than physical or emotional, abuse. It would be inappropriate to let the child bear the burden of an erroneous and nonprotective judicial decision merely because a parent's reputation is at stake.

One way that this balancing can be accomplished is to appoint an appropriately qualified and trained lawyer for the child in *every*

---

2. *See, e.g.*, Kansas v. Hendricks, 117 S.Ct. 2072, 138 L.Ed.2d 501 (1997); People v. Hedge, 65 Cal. Rptr. 2d 693, 56 Cal. App. 4th 773 (1997), *review granted*, 945 P.2d 780, 68 Cal. Rptr. 2d 475 (1997); *In re* Gagnon, 425 Mass. 1015, 681 N.E.2d 812 (1997); Caprice v. Gomez, 552 N.W.2d 753 (Minn. Ct. App. 1996); Matter of Paschke, 80 Wash. App. 439, 909 P.2d 1328 (1996); State v. Post, 197 Wis.2d 279, 541 N.W.2d 115 (1995), *cert. denied* 117 S.Ct. 2507, 138 L.Ed.2d 1011. *But see, e.g.*, Young v. Weston, 898 F. Supp. 744 (W.D. Wash. 1995).
3. 117 S.Ct. 2072, 138 L.Ed.2d 501 (1997).
4. Matter of Care and Treatment of Hendricks, 259 Kan. 246, 912 P.2d 129 (1996).
5. *Id.*, 117 S.Ct. at 2080-2086.
6. *See, e.g.*, Mallory v. Mallory, 539 A.2d 995 (Conn. 1988).

civil case in which child sexual abuse is alleged. Whether or not the allegations are true, the fact that they are made places the child at risk for an erroneous determination in either direction. The adult or governmental parties may have biases and motives that hinder a determination of the truth. Custody of and visitation with the child may be used as rewards and punishments, without the child's unique perspective ever being presented to the court. This is particularly true in domestic-relations cases, where lawyers for children are rare.

The specialty of child advocacy, sometimes called pediatric law, is maturing, with its own bar association,[7] standards of practice,[8] jurisprudence,[9] periodicals,[10] legal-resource center,[11] annual advanced training,[12] and integrated three-year law-school program in child advocacy.[13] These trained lawyers for children can make a difference in the quality of evidence presented to the court and the creative solutions offered to the parties in the interests of the child. It is time to recognize that the "best interests of children" and serving children as "our greatest national resource" will not be achieved without providing a voice for the individual child at the center of the controversy. It is time for judges and legislators to mandate the appointment of trained counsel for children in civil child sexual abuse cases. Otherwise, the risk of an erroneous legal determination falls disproportionately on the child, who is the least able to guard his or her own rights and interests.

---

7. The National Association of Counsel for Children, 1825 Marion Street, Suite 340, Denver, Colo. 80218, telephone (303) 864-5320, fax (303) 864-5351, e-mail Advocate@NACCchildlaw.org, web site http://www.NACCchildlaw.org.

8. *See, e.g.*, AMERICAN BAR ASSOCIATION STANDARDS OF PRACTICE FOR LAWYERS WHO REPRESENT CHILDREN IN ABUSE AND NEGLECT CASES (1996); *Recommendations of the Conference on Ethical Issues in the Legal Representation of Children*, 64/4 FORDHAM L. REV. 1301 (1996).

9. *See, e.g.*, JEAN KOH PETERS, REPRESENTING CHILDREN IN CHILD PROTECTIVE PROCEEDINGS: ETHICAL AND PRACTICAL DIMENSIONS (1997); ANN M. HARALAMBIE, THE CHILD'S ATTORNEY: A GUIDE TO REPRESENTING CHILDREN IN CUSTODY, ADOPTION, AND PROTECTION CASES (1993); N. DONALD DUQUETTE, ADVOCATING FOR THE CHILD IN PROTECTION PROCEEDINGS: A HANDBOOK FOR LAWYERS AND COURT APPOINTED SPECIAL ADVOCATES (1990).

10. *See, e.g.*, CHILD LAW PRACTICE; CHILDREN'S RIGHTS JOURNAL; LAW GUARDIAN REPORTER.

11. The American Bar Association Center on Children and the Law, 740 15th Street, N.W., 9th Floor, Washington, D.C. 20005-1022, telephone (202) 662-1720, fax (202) 662-1755, e-mail ctrchildlaw@abanet.org, web site http://www.abanet.org/child.

12. *See, e.g.*, Rocky Mountain Child Advocacy Training Institute (University of Denver College of Law, in cooperation with National Institute for Trial Advocacy); NACC annual convention (National Association of Counsel for Children).

13. Civitas ChildLaw Center, Loyola University Chicago School of Law, 16 E. Pearson Street, Chicago, Ill. 60611, telephone, (312) 915-6481, fax (312) 915-6485.

STANDARDIZED EVALUATION PROCEDURES AND TERMINOLOGY

Expert evaluators often do not use the same terms and do not mean the same things when they do use the same terms, creating confusion for subsequent evaluators and for the courts. This is often true when the expert expresses the ultimate opinion about whether or not the child was molested. Jones and Seig have proposed a very helpful continuum for determining whether or not abuse has occurred. Instead of having the traditional three choices (which are described by various terms, but generally constitute findings that the abuse occurred, did not occur, or that it cannot be determined), they proposed a continuum using the following descriptions: definitely true, probably true, possibly true, possibly false, probably false, definitely false.[14] This approach may seem to muddy the waters, but actually it only reflects the imprecision in current evaluative techniques, keeping the experts honest. While the law prefers clear expert conclusions "to a reasonable professional certainty," the court itself renders decisions based on a continuum of probabilities, whether a preponderance, clear and convincing, or beyond a reasonable doubt. A finding is not worthless merely because it is not definitive. The degrees of doubt expressed should go to the weight, not the admissibility, of the expert evidence. When experts feel compelled to state their opinions with more certainty than the underlying data support, they compromise their professional integrity and do a disservice to the litigants and the court.

Jones and McGraw proposed an organized process for validation,[15] which is used at the C. Henry Kempe Center for the Prevention and Treatment of Child Abuse and Neglect. The American Academy of Child and Adolescent Psychiatry,[16] American Academy

---

14. *See* D. Jones & A. Seig, *Child Sexual Abuse Allegations in Custody or Visitation Disputes*, in SEXUAL ABUSE ALLEGATIONS IN CUSTODY AND VISITATION CASES 22 (E. Nicholson & J. Bulkley eds., 1988).

15. *See*, David Jones & J. Melbourne McGraw, *Reliable and Fictitious Accounts of Sexual Abuse to Children*, 2/1 J. INTERPERSONAL VIOLENCE 27 (1987).

16. American Academy of Child and Adolescent Psychiatry, *Practice Parameters for the Forensic Evaluation of Children and Adolescents Who May Have Been Physically or Sexually Abused*, 36/3 J. AM. ACAD. CHILD. ADOLESC. PSYCHIATRY 423 (1997), reprinted at Appendix 6-1.

of Pediatrics,[17] American Medical Association,[18] and American Professional Society on the Abuse of Children (APSAC)[19] have all promulgated guidelines for evaluating child sexual abuse, and APSAC has promulgated guidelines for descriptive terminology in medical evaluations of child sexual abuse.[20] This greater attention by researchers and professional organizations to standardization is a welcome addition to the field of child sexual abuse. Ad hoc practices and conclusions drawn only from anecdotal experience have helped to create the problems of proof in sexual abuse cases. While failure to follow a particular set of guidelines does not, it itself, indicate poor practice, experts should be required to explain any deviations from professional standards.

THE PROBLEM OF FAILURE OF PROOF

A major problem in many domestic-relations cases is trying to prove sexual molestation when child protective services (CPS) or law-enforcement investigations have been closed without making or clearly articulating affirmative findings of abuse. Lawyers for the accused almost always point to the failure of CPS to pursue the case or the failure of the state to prosecute a criminal case as evidence that the allegations are false. However, CPS and law-enforcement have different criteria and goals in evaluating a case, and the court must be reminded of these differences.

For example, most CPS offices are underfunded and understaffed. As a result, they must triage their cases, with time and attention being given first to those cases in which the child has no other source of protection. Where one parent is willing to protect the

17. American Academy of Pediatrics, Committee on Child Abuse and Neglect, *Guidelines for the Evaluation of Sexual Abuse of Children*, 87 PEDIATRICS 254 (1991), reprinted at Appendix 7-1.

18. American Medical Association Diagnostic and Treatment Guidelines on Child Sexual Abuse (1992), reprinted at 2 ANN M. HARALAMBIE, HANDLING CHILD CUSTODY, ABUSE AND ADOPTION CASES app. 16-1 (2d ed., Clark Boardman Callaghan, 1993).

19. American Professional Society on the Abuse of Children, *Guidelines for Psychosocial Evaluation of Suspected Sexual Abuse in Young Children* (2nd ed. 1990), reprinted at Appendix 6-2; American Professional Society on the Abuse of Children, *Practice Guidelines for Use of Anatomical Dolls in Child Sexual Abuse Assessments* (1995), reprinted at Appendix 6-3.

20. American Professional Society on the Abuse of Children, *Practice Guidelines for Descriptive Terminology in Child Sexual Abuse Medical Evaluations* (1995), reprinted at Appendix 7-2.

child, CPS often leaves it to that parent to pursue his or her domestic-relations options to protect the child. Unfortunately, many CPS workers and their evaluators are very skeptical of allegations brought when there is any custody or visitation case in the offing, and they may fail to adequately evaluate these cases.[21] This fact is particularly disturbing because the protecting parent is often doing exactly what CPS workers criticize reluctant or unbelieving spouses for not doing, often filing dependency petitions impugning the nonabusing parent for "failure to protect." It seems as if many CPS workers want to be the ones to convince the nonabusing parent to support and believe the child and forsake the spouse, failing to appreciate the effect of the massive community awareness and prevention programs which have sought to convey that message to parents without direct CPS persuasion at the time of a report.

The skepticism of CPS workers in this context is also disturbing because it is generally agreed, even by those often found in the forefront of the charge of epidemic false allegations, that the divorce process can *precipitate* disclosure of previous or on-going abuse that had not been previously disclosed, and that the divorce process can *precipitate* sexual molestation even where there was no previous molestation.

Some law-enforcement officers and prosecutors suffer from the same bias as CPS workers do in having preconceived notions that allegations made in the context of a custody or visitation dispute are not likely to be true. Therefore, the criminal investigation may not be as thorough as when a stranger is the alleged perpetrator. Some law-enforcement officers may believe that intrafamilial sexual abuse cases are best dealt with in a social-services setting, rather than in the criminal justice arena, especially if there is at least one parent who appears willing to protect the child.

Law-enforcement officers must assess cases with an eye toward criminal convictions. If a case is not likely to be provable beyond a reasonable doubt to a unanimous jury, the prosecutor's office is unlikely to issue the case. The very existence of a custody or visitation dispute between the parents is often seen as creating reasonable

21. *See, e.g.*, J. Melbourne McGraw & Holly A. Smith, *Child Sexual Abuse Allegations Amidst Divorce and Custody Proceedings: Refining the Validation Process*, 1/1 J. CHILD SEXUAL ABUSE 49 (1992).

doubt in itself, making prosecutors reluctant to pursue cases in that context. In addition, young children may not be able to testify or to testify effectively, further deterring prosecution. Finally, criminal prosecutions are designed to punish or deter the defendant. They do not focus on the needs of the victim, except perhaps in the terms of the defendant's release or sentence. Therefore, the criminal case attempts to achieve different objections and plays by different rules. Even a jury acquittal in a criminal case is not an indication that the defendant did not molest the child or that the child does not need protection. There has been an enormous effort to convince the public in general and professionals dealing with sexual abuse cases that there is an epidemic of false allegations of intrafamilial child sexual abuse, whether made by vindictive spouses and ex-spouses or by incompetent and man-hating evaluators and therapists.[22] This climate has affected the ability of litigants to have a fair hearing on the merits of their cases. Not only may the professional participants have their own assumptions and biases, but professional witnesses with their own agendas may offer "junk science" testimony to show that bona fide cases of abuse are deliberately fabricated.

Mental-health, social-work, and medical professionals must begin to hold one another accountable for the professionalism of their evaluations, therapy, and testimony. Lawyers must learn to critically evaluate the evaluators and challenge questionable evidence. Judges must take more seriously their obligation to require proper foundation for scientific testimony, including determining whether there is empirical support for that evidence, without eliminating the appropriate testimony based on clinical judgment and experience.

No decision can be better than the data upon which it is based. That maxim holds true for judicial decisions as well as for forensic evaluations. Until the parties, experts, and courts require quality evidence, failures of proof will occur with some regularity.

---

22. *See generally*, John E. B. Myers, A MOTHER'S NIGHTMARE—INCEST: A PRACTICAL GUIDE FOR PARENTS AND PROFESSIONALS (1997); THE BACKLASH: CHILD PROTECTION UNDER FIRE (John E. B. Myers, ed. 1994); ELLEN GRAY: UNEQUAL JUSTICE: THE PROSECUTION OF CHILD SEXUAL ABUSE (1993); BILLIE WRIGHT DZIECH & CHARLES B. SCHUDSON, ON TRIAL: AMERICA'S COURTS AND THEIR TREATMENT OF SEXUALLY ABUSED CHILDREN (1989); DAVID HECHLER, THE BATTLE AND THE BACKLASH (1988).

Clearly there are cases, particularly with very young children and infants, where it is impossible to provide sufficient evidence to sustain the burden of proving the allegations. In most civil cases that means that the proponent loses the cases. But particularly in domestic-relations cases, where the dispute is usually between two parents with equal legal claims to the child, it is poor public policy to treat a close failure of proof the same as a finding that no abuse occurred. Domestic-relations cases do not involve merely the technical parties, the parents. They also involve the child, who is typically not a party and typically not represented by counsel. Further, intrafamilial sexual abuse generally occurs in secret, with only the abuser and the child having knowledge of the abuse, making these cases particularly difficult to prove.

If the best available evaluators believe that there is reason for concern, it is irresponsible to say that because the abuse or identification of the abuser was not proven by a preponderance of the evidence, custody and visitation should be ordered as if the child were not at risk. This is true because the allegations in the context of a custody case do not involve merely the adjudication of a claim between the two parties, but also involve the interests of the child, a person who may not be a party to the action, but in relation to whom the court has a parens patriae duty. In some cases supervised or therapeutically supervised visitation is appropriate. Sometimes the evaluator simply needs more time and does not have an answer by the date of the court hearing. If the evaluator believes that limitation or suspension of contact between the child and the alleged perpetrator is necessary for a more accurate evaluation, the court should make such an interim order.

Judges should take a middle-ground approach which can provide at least some monitoring or other protection for the child where there is reason to believe that the child has been molested, but the proponent of the allegation cannot prove the allegation by a preponderance of the evidence. One such approach is described by Sandra K. Hewitt and is reproduced in the previous chapter.[23] The model

---

23. *See* Sandra K. Hewitt, *Therapeutic Management of Preschool Cases of Alleged but Unsubstantiated Sexual Abuse*, 70/1 CHILD WELFARE 59, at 61-64 (1991), reprinted at Appendix 14-1.

involves developing an agreed-upon list of appropriate and inappropriate touches, absolving the child of blame for any inappropriate touches, and giving the child permission to object to touches, and to tell the therapist about any inappropriate touches. Both parents endorse the lists and the permission to disclose. The therapist works with the child and each parent and may initiate therapeutically supervised visits, other supervised visits, or unsupervised visits as appropriate during the course of the process. Hewitt recommends using the model for at least one year.

As a matter of public policy, it is important to encourage parents to act responsibly and protectively toward their children. If there are warning signs that a child may have been abused, those signs must be taken seriously and investigated. Parents should not fear punitive actions by a domestic-relations court (contempt findings, monetary sanctions, and even changes of custody) based on their reasonable actions to investigate reasonable suspicions.

It is often very difficult to determine whether a young child has been molested. If these cases are difficult for the skilled clinicians who evaluate them, they are obviously difficult for courts. Courts should endeavor to find a middle ground, which has as its primary goal the adequate protection of the child and creation of an environment that maximizes the likelihood of being able to ascertain the truth. The consequences of a wrong decision in either direction are too great to allow preconceptions and the distaste of dealing with charges of sexual abuse to interfere with the fact-finding process. Providing some kind of monitoring has several advantages, including protecting the child from future molestation, reassuring a protective parent, and providing clear boundaries for the accused parent. In addition, if there has been no abuse, the accused parent has some protection against future charges of abuse. Done well, a middle-ground approach can educate the parents and the child, clarifying appropriate and inappropriate behavior and providing a safe place to report any abuse or discomfort.

WHAT PROTECTION FOR A MOLESTED CHILD REALLY MEANS

Lawyers and judges must understand that it is not enough merely to protect the child from a repetition of the sexual abuse during visitation. In fact, the severest trauma of child sexual abuse is not the physical act, but rather the emotional repercussions of the abuse, including the abuse of power, betrayal of trust, intimidation, threats, shame, and guilt. The child is not protected from those aspects of the abuse merely because a third party is able to ensure that the physical act is not repeated. A child who maintains contact with the alleged abuser during the evaluation process may *feel* unprotected and may be exposed to very subtle threats and manipulations that impair the child's ability and willingness to disclose the abuse to the evaluator.

To translate the situation into an adult context, no one would consider requiring a victim of date rape to continue an on-going relationship with the rapist merely because they once had a relationship with each other. Sometimes our respect for the rights of parents leads us to assume that all parent-child relationships should be repaired. That assumption leads some judges to order counseling in all cases of child sexual abuse. A better public policy would be to weigh the child's immediate needs most heavily in the decision about ordering therapy in which the child must participate.

On the other hand, it is very important for some children to be allowed to have contact, even during the assessment process. Legal professionals are not qualified to determine what factors will facilitate disclosure for a particular child. A properly qualified expert should be relied on to assist the court in fashioning an interim order that will maximize the likelihood of getting to the truth—what the court proceeding should be about. Ascertaining the truth serves all parties' legitimate interests, including those of a parent who has been unjustly accused.

Even if the court determines that the child has been molested, that child may wish to continue a relationship with the molester. The child may be eager to forgive the molester, especially if he or she has taken responsibility for the abuse. The child may view the abuse as a small negative in comparison with the rest of the parent-child relationship. The child may also feel responsible for the molester or may have been persuaded that the sexual relationship was special and important, desiring to continue in that role. On-going contact may or may not be psychologically healthy for a particular child. The court must make an individualized determination based on the all of the dynamics involved. What is essential is that the legal system use its resources in service of holding adults fully accountable for their actions and taking reasonable steps to minimize further trauma to the child.

In August 1996 the American Bar Association (ABA) passed the following resolutions:

> Treatment in Cases of Child Abuse and Domestic Violence
>
> RESOLVED, that the American Bar Association encourages courts to ensure that counseling, treatment, advocacy and other assistance are made available to child victims of abuse and domestic violence through all available means including the imposition of fines, restitution, and court orders;
>
> FURTHER RESOLVED, that the American Bar Association encourages courts, in appropriate circumstances, to require the perpetrators of child abuse and domestic violence to undergo counseling and other treatment;
>
> FURTHER RESOLVED, that in those jurisdictions where courts do not presently have adequate authority to implement the foregoing recommendations, the American Bar Association encourages state and territorial legislatures to enact enabling legislation.
>
> Children's Waiting Rooms in Courthouses
>
> RESOLVED, that the American Bar Association encourages state, local, and territorial governing bodies and court systems, in conjunction with bar associations, to support and assist in the organization and implementation of waiting rooms for children in every appropriate courthouse.

The ABA has taken significant steps to support victims of child abuse, not only through these resolutions, but also by its formation of the Steering Committee on the Unmet Legal Needs of Children, its support of the ABA Center on Children and the Law, and the programs of its various sections, including the Litigation Section's Task Force on Children. We need to make the protection of children in the legal system a major priority, not only of the organized bar and bench, but also in our daily practices.

THE NONOFFENDING PARENT

Chapters 8 and 9 dealt in more detail with representation of both protective and nonprotective nonoffending parents. With respect to both categories, Sally Cooper is critical of the practice of blaming the nonoffending parent: "In incest cases, the best outcome for the child is not to be torn from family and home, but to remain with his or her nonoffending parent and siblings, if the home can be made safe. If the caseworker judges and blames the nonoffending parent, how can they engage in mutual and collaborative change?"[24]

The same question can be posed to the courts hearing child sexual abuse cases. However much we may want to blame parents for failing to protect their children, if those parents are able to become protective, the legal system needs to give them support in providing homes for their own children. On the other hand, if they cannot provide safe homes, then we must seek alternate permanent homes for the children, preferable with safe adults whom they already know.

There are nonoffending parents whose children were not abused, even though they believe they were. These parents often suffer the greatest blame, accused of deliberately fabricating false allegations. To punish these parents, some judges change custody. If the judge is wrong, the new custodial parent is the molester, a terrifying but real possibility. Not only has the child lost a protector, but he or she has been judicially committed to the exclusive control of the abuser.

It is essential that evaluators and judges consider the origin of allegations deemed not to be true. If they were made in good faith, public policy demands that the parent who tried to do the right thing by seeking help to protect the child not be punished for the attempt. If parents perceive too great a risk in coming forward to report suspected abuse, then a great deal of abuse will go unreported and unstopped. A good, objective, thorough evaluator who finds that the child was not abused can often explain to the reporting parent why certain signs or symptoms were misinterpreted.

If the allegation was not made in good faith, a more difficult clash of policies comes into play. The law does not want to reward perjury or the attempt to disrupt a child's relationship with a

24. *See* Sally Cooper, *The Tyranny of the Urgent: Child Welfare Casework in the 90s*, 6/1 J. CHILD SEXUAL ABUSE 85, 87 (1997).

nonabusing parent, especially when the allegations result in negative consequences to the innocent accused. On the other hand, the custody of a child is not a matter of reward or punishment. A deliberately false allegation of sexual abuse is a terrible thing, but it is still only one factor to be weighed in the final analysis against the other pros and cons which each parent offers. What is necessary is that those who make the evaluations and the decisions distance themselves from the emotional reaction to the allegations and view each case in the totality of the circumstances, understanding what life will look like from the perspective of the child who will have to live with whatever decision is made.

THE NATURE OF THE PARENT-CHILD RELATIONSHIP

At the core of the policy considerations discussed in this chapter are certain assumptions about the parent-child relationship. We have moved beyond the notion that children are the chattel of their parents, but we do not always make decisions based on an understanding of children's independent rights. In fact, there is no consensus about what rights children should have.[25]

Don Bross writes:

> I contend that our power to govern children in democracies (to nurture, train, and educate them—in other words, to "raise" them) is strongly dependent on parents' power to exercise responsible parental oversight (in effect, "use it or lose it"—use responsible parental authority or lose control of our children). Accordingly, I argue that parents' right to privacy should be yielded only to the degree that particular information is needed to establish that each child is safe and receiving minimally adequate care.[26]

As between the state and the parent, the child is entitled only to "minimally adequate care," not to a "good parent." As between parents who bring a custody dispute before the courts, the child is enti-

---

25. *See, e.g.*, Katherine Hunt Federle, *Looking for Rights in All the Wrong Places: Resolving Custody Disputes in Divorce Proceedings*, 15/5 CARDOZO L. REV. 1523 (1994).

26. Donald C. Bross, *The Legal Context of Child Abuse and Neglect: Balancing the Rights of Children and Parents in a Democratic Society*, in THE BATTERED CHILD 61, 62 (Mary Edna Helfer & Ruth S. Kempe, eds., 5th ed. 1997).

tled to have his or her "best interests" served as best they can be given the parents' abilities and desires. Of course, determining what is in the child's "best interests" is based on other assumptions and perspectives. In most cases "best interests" is the label attached to whatever it is that the evaluator or judge wants to see happen. Professor Katherine Hunt Federle identifies the "best interests" standard in divorce cases as "one example of the way an impoverished account of rights disadvantages children."[27] This is so because "[w]e seem to be unable to give any determinate meaning to the term best interests, thus making it extremely difficult to identify the rights and duties flowing from those interests and, when we do provide some substantive content, we do so by reference to the rights of parents and the incapacities and needs of children."[28] Therefore, Federle argues that the best interests standard "fails to provide judges with a rule of decision."[29] Her solution is to view children as having "empowerment rights."[30] Under such a system, the child-welfare system would emphasize "the vindication of children's rights rather than . . . their vulnerabilities and dependence."[31] Under an empowerment-rights perspective, children would have the right to participate in legal proceedings as represented parties, people who had a meaningful voice in the process.[32]

In child sexual abuse cases, the parents appear to be more visible in the process. We are concerned with how they act and what will happen to them as a result of the decisions made in the case. While the rhetoric of most of the professionals involved is couched in child-related terms, in fact we are usually viewing the competing rights of the parents, assuming that the child is somehow the beneficiary of the rights of at least one of the parents. This is particularly true where the child does not have a strong, independent advocate representing that child's voice, the child's perspective as seen through the child's own eyes. This advocacy is to be distinguished

---

27. Katherine Hunt Federle, *Looking for Rights in All the Wrong Places: Resolving Custody Disputes in Divorce Proceedings*, 15/5 CARDOZO L. REV. at 1533 (1994).
28. *Id.*
29. *Id.* at 1540.
30. *See, e.g.*, Katherine Hunt Federle, *Looking Ahead: An Empowerment Perspective on the Rights of Children*, 68/4 TEMPLE L. REV. 1585 (1995).
31. *Id.* at 1603.
32. *Id.* at 1604.

from a view that advocates what it thinks will be best for the child, what the child would want if only the child had good, mature judgment and understood all of the ramifications.

Jean Koh Peters emphasizes the uniqueness of each child's voice and that child's right to representation that is respectful of that uniqueness.[33] In particular, she reminds the professionals involved in children's lives that they are a small part of the child's world, and that the child's life will continue after the legal process is complete.[34] The child will live with what is left of his or her relationships among family members, neighbors, friends, and others. Peters cautions children's lawyers about their "propensity to substitute our own personal and professional needs for our client's needs."[35] These same concerns apply to all of the professionals involved in a child sexual abuse case. We tend to view our role as terribly important, forgetting that we are an ephemeral intervention in the child's world. The actions we take and the decisions we make may have an enormous, long-term effect on the life of the entire family. By failing to recognize the child as an independent-right holder, we find it much easier to simply substitute our own concerns or those of the parent.

Regardless of the standard that we apply to children's rights or interests, the child clearly is entitled to be free from such treatment by the parents that falls below some imprecise floor of societal acceptance. Sexual abuse by a parent should clearly be considered below that floor. "Inappropriate contact" is a more difficult issue, based on how inappropriate the contact was, what motivated it, where it was heading, and whether it is likely to stop. Sexual abuse by a third party under circumstances implying a parent's neglect or failure to protect is also likely to be below the floor of acceptability unless the circumstances have changed, for example, by the nonoffending parent's discontinuation of a relationship with the abuser and others at risk to abuse.

There are things that a parent can do, and molesting his or her child is one of those things, which should forfeit that parent's right to have his or her interests considered in determining the appropri-

33. *See, e.g.*, JEAN KOH PETERS, REPRESENTING CHILDREN IN CHILD PROTECTIVE PROCEEDINGS: ETHICAL AND PRACTICAL DIMENSIONS (1997).
34. *Id.* at 61-64.
35. *Id.* at 18.

ate outcome of a child-protection or domestic-relations case. Dispositional orders should be tailored strictly to serve the child's need for protection—whether that is protection from further abuse of any kind, or protection from being cut off entirely from a parent with whom the child wishes to remain in contact—and wishes for his or her future immediate environment.

Drawing from the United Nations CONVENTION ON THE RIGHTS OF THE CHILD,[36] the U.S. Advisory Board on Child Abuse and Neglect declared in 1991 that:

> Children have a right to protection from all forms of physical or mental violence, injury or abuse, neglect or negligent treatment, maltreatment or exploitation including sexual abuse, while in the care of parent(s), legal guardian(s), or any other person who has the care of the child, including children residing in group homes and institutions.
>
> Children have the right to be provided the opportunity to be heard in any judicial and administrative proceedings affecting them, with ample opportunity for representation and for provision of procedures that comport with the child's sense of dignity.[37]

As a matter of public policy we cannot separate the right of the child to be heard, from the right of the child to be free from sexual abuse and its aftermath. So long as courts continue to decide cases between parents or between parents and the state—with the child as the object of discussion and perhaps as the prize, but without a meaningful independent voice—the quality of judicial decisions will be diminished. Once the legal system is involved, my position is that the child should be a more-equal participant in the balancing of rights. Parents have the right to make certain decisions affecting their children, but just as the rights of the parents are weighed against each other, so too should the independent rights of the child be weighed in the balance.

---

36. It is to the shame of this nation that the United States of America stands nearly alone among industrialized countries in failing to ratify this convention.

37. U.S. Advisory Board on Child Abuse and Neglect, Creating Caring Communities: Blueprint for an Effective Federal Policy on Child Abuse and Neglect (1991), as excerpted in Richard D. Krugman, *Child Protection Policy*, in THE BATTERED CHILD 627, 637 (Mary Edna Helfer & Ruth S. Kempe, eds., 5th ed. 1997).

Table of Cases

Table of Statutes

D.C. Code Ann. § 16-2323(a) (1997), 65
D.C. Code Ann. § 12-302 (1996), 82
D.C. Code Ann. § 14-307 (1995), 258
D.C. Code Ann. § 16-2301(23) and (25), 48
D.C. Code Ann. §§ 22-3503 through -3511 (1981), 355

Fla. Stat. Ann. § 39.01(2), 48
Fla. Stat. Ann. § 90.503 (Supp. 1992), 258
Fla. Stat. Ann. § 39.453(3) (19) (1988), 65
Fla. Stat. Ann. § 90.605(2) (1998), 334
Fla. Stat. Ann. § 90.803(23) (1997), 59, 318
Fla. Stat. Ann. § 95.051 (1997), 84

Ga. Code Ann. § 9-3-90 (1997), 82
Ga. Code Ann. § 15-11-81(b)(4)(B)(iii) (1998), 70
Ga. Code Ann. § 15-11-81(b)(4)(B)(iv) (1997), 69
Ga. Code Ann. § 15-11-81(b)(4)(c), 70
Ga. Code Ann. § 24-3-16 (1997), 318
Ga. Code Ann. § 24-3-16 (1998), 59
Ga. Code Ann. § 24-9-5(b) (1997), 332
Ga. Code Ann. § 24-9-21 (1995), 258
Ga. Code Ann. § 15-11-41(j) (1997), 65

Haw. Rev. Stat. § 587-2, 48
Haw. Rev. Stat. § 621-28 (1997), 330
Haw. Rev. Stat. § 657-13 (1997), 82
Haw. Rev. Stat. Ann. § 587-71(m)(2) (1997), 65
Haw. Rule Evid. 504, 504.1, 258

Idaho Code § 5-230 (1997), 84
Idaho Code § 16-1602(a)(2), 48
Idaho Code § 16-1623(i) (1997), 65
Idaho Code § 19-3023 (1997), 330
Idaho Code § 19-3024 (1997), 59
Idaho Code § 19-3024 (1997), 318
Idaho Rule Evid. 503, 258
Idaho Stat. § 16-2005(i)(1) (1997), 71
Idaho Stat. § 16-2005(j)(1) (1997), 71

225 Ill. Comp. Stat. Ann. § 15/5 (1994), 258
705 Ill. Comp. Stat. Ann. § 405/2-28.01(c) (1997), 65

N.D. Cent. Code § 28-01-25 (1997), 83
N.D. Rule Evid. § 503, 259

Ohio Rev. Code Ann. § 2151.031(A), 48
Ohio Rev. Code Ann. § 2151.416(A) (1997), 65
Ohio Rev. Code Ann. § 2305.16 (1997), 83
Ohio Rev. Code Ann. § 2317.02 (1995), 259
Ohio Rev. Code Ann. § 3107.07(F) (1997), 71
Ohio Rule Evid. 807, 59, 319

Okla. Stat. Ann. tit. 10, § 7006-1.1(A)(6) and (7) (1998), 70
Okla. Stat. Ann. tit. 12, § 2503 (1991), 259
Okla. Stat. Ann. §§ 7003-5.4(A) and 7303-5.6(A) (1997), 65
Okla. Stat. Ann. tit. 12, § 96 (1988), 84
Okla. Stat. Ann. tit. 12, § 2803.1 (1993), 59
Okla. Stat. Ann. tit. 12, § 2803.1 (1997), 319

Or. Rev. Stat. § 12.117 (1996), 83, 84
Or. Rev. Stat. § 12.160 (1996), 83
Or. Rev. Stat. § 40.460 (1997), 59
Or. Rev. Stat. § 40.460(18a) (1997), 319
Or. Rev. Stat. § 419B.502(1) (1997), 69
Or. Rev. Stat. § 419B.504(2) (1997), 69
Or. Rule Evid. 504, 504.1, 259

23 Pa. Cons. Stat. Ann. § 20-7-1734(C) (1997), 71
23 Pa. Cons. Stat. Ann. § 2511(a)(5) and (8), 70
42 Pa. Cons. Stat. Ann. § 5533 (1984), 86
42 Pa. Cons. Stat. Ann. § 5944 (1982), 259
42 Pa. Cons. Stat. Ann. § 6351(e) (1997), 65
23 Pa. Cons. Stat. Ann. § 5303(b) and (c) (1998), 14
42 Pa. Cons. Stat. Ann. § 5533 (1981), 83
Pa. Stat. Ann. tit. 42, § 5985.1 (1998), 59
42 Pa. Stat. Ann. § 5985.1 (1997), 319

R.I. Gen. Laws §§ 5-37.3-3, 5-37.3-4 (1995), 259
R.I. Gen. Laws § 9-1-19 (1997), 83
R.I. Gen. Laws § 12-28-9(2) (1994), 330
R.I. Gen. Laws § 15-7-7(1)(b)(iii) and (c), 70
R.I. Gen. Laws § 40-11-6.1 (1990), 96

TABLE OF AUTHORITIES

American Academy of Child and Adolescent Psychiatry, "Practice Parameters for the Forensic Evaluation of Children and Adolescents Who May Have Been Physically or Sexually Abused," 36/3 *Journal of the American Academy of Child and Adolescent Psychiatry* 423 (1997), 358

American Academy of Pediatrics, Committee on Child Abuse and Neglect, "Guidelines for the Evaluation of Sexual Abuse of Children," 87 *Pediatrics* 254 (1991), 200, 203, 359

American Bar Association, "Standards of Practice for Lawyers Who Represent Children in Abuse and Neglect Cases" (1996), 43, 281, 285, 295, 357

American Medical Association Diagnostic and Treatment Guidelines on Child Sexual Abuse (1992), 359

American Professional Society on the Abuse of Children, "Guidelines for Psychosocial Evaluation of Suspected Sexual Abuse in Young Children" (2nd ed. 1990), 359

American Professional Society on the Abuse of Children, "Practice Guidelines for Descriptive Terminology in Child Sexual Abuse Medical Evaluations" (1995), 359

American Professional Society on the Abuse of Children, "Practice Guidelines for the Use of Anatomical Dolls in Child Sexual Abuse Assessments" (1995), 113, 359

American Professional Society on the Abuse of Children, *The Advisor* (volume 5, number 3, summer 1992), 298

American Psychiatric Association, *Diagnostic and Statistical Manual of Mental Disorders* (4th ed. 1994), 3, 4, 5, 6, 10, 11, 110, 270

American Psychiatric Association *Statement on Memories of Sexual Abuse* (1994), 315

Anderson, J., Martin, J., Mullen, P., Romans, S., and Herbison, P., "Prevalence of Childhood Sexual Abuse Experiences in a Community Sample of Women," 32 *Journal of the American Academy of Child and Adolescent Psychiatry* 911 (1993), 2

Annotation, "Civil Liability of Physician for Failure to Diagnose or Report Child Abuse," 73 ALR 4th 782 (1989 and Supp 1997), 96, 97

Annotation, "Denial or Restriction of Visitation Rights to Parent Charged with Sexually Abusing a Child," 1 A.L.R. 5th 776, 339

Annotation, "Emotional or Psychological 'Blocking' or Repression As Tolling Running of Statute of Limitations," 11 A.L.R. 5th 588 (1993), 84

Annotation, "Posttraumatic Syndrome As Tolling Running of Statute of Limitations," 12 A.L.R. 5th 546 (1993), 84

Annotation, "Running of Limitations Against Action for Civil Damages for Sexual Abuse of Child," 9 ALR 5th 321 (1993), 84

Bussey, "Lying and Truthfulness: Children's Definitions, Standards, and Evaluative Reactions," 63 *Child Development* 129 (1992), 334

Bussey, Lee, and Grimbeek, "Lies and Secrets: Implications for Children's Reporting of Sexual Abuse," in *Child Victims, Child Witnesses* 147 (G. Goodman and B. Bottoms, eds., 1993), 305

Cantwell, H., "Update on Vaginal Inspection as it Relates to Child Sexual Abuse in Girls Under Thirteen," 11/4 *Child Abuse and Neglect* (1987), 202

Carey, S., "A Case Study: Face Recognition," in *Explorations in the Biology of Language* 175 (E. Walker, ed., 1978), 304

Carpenter, M., "Children of the Underground," series in *Pittsburgh Post-Gazette* (December 14-18, 1997), 44

Carter, C., Bottoms, B., and Levine, M., "Linguistic and Socio-Emotional Influences on the Accuracy of Children's Reports," *Law and Human Behavior* (in press), 310

Cassel, W., and Bjorklund, D., "Developmental Patterns of Eyewitness Memory and Suggestibility; An Ecologically Based Short-Term Longitudinal Study," 19 *Law and Human Behavior* 507 (1995), 309

Chadwick, D., "Commentary: The Medical Examination in Child Sexual Abuse: A Balance Between History and Exam," 1/4 *Journal of Child Sexual Abuse* 123 (1992), 200

Chadwick, D., Berkowitz, C., Kerns, D., McCann, J., Reinhart, M., and Strickland, S., *Color Atlas of Child Sexual Abuse* (1989), 200, 202, 203, 204, 205

Chandy, J., Blum, R., and Resnick, M., "Gender-Specific Outcomes for Sexually Abused Adolescents," 20/12 *Child Abuse and Neglect* 1219 (1996), 9

Chandy, J., Blum, R., and Resnick, M., "Sexually Abused Male Adolescents: How Vulnerable Are They?," 6/2 *Journal of Child Sexual Abuse* 1 (1997), 8, 9

Chapman, J., and Smith, B., "Response of Social Service and Criminal Justice Agencies to Child Sexual Abuse Complaints," 10/3 *Response to the Victimization of Women and Children* (1987), 54, 238

Child Victims, Child Witnesses (G. Goodman and B. Bottoms, eds., 1993), 298

Childhood Antecedents of Multiple Personality (R. Kluft, ed., 1985), 11, 111

Children's Eyewitness Memory (S. Ceci, D. Ross, and M. Toglia, eds., 1987), 298

Chou, "Renewing the Good Intentions of Foster Care: Enforcement of the Adoption Assistance and Child Welfare Act of 1980 and the

Substantive Due Process Rights to Safety," 46 *Vanderbilt Law Review* 683 (1993), 100
Christianson, "Emotional Stress and Eyewitness Memory: A Critical Review," 112 *Psychology Bulletin* 284 (1992), 306
Chu, J., and Dill, D., "Dissociative Symptoms in Relation to Childhood Physical and Sexual Abuse," 147 *Journal of Psychiatry* 887 (1990), 11, 111
Coffey, P., Leitenberg, H., Henning, K., Turner, T., and Bennett, R., "Mediators of the Long-Term Impact of Child Sexual Abuse: Perceived Stigma, Betrayal, Powerlessness, and Self-Blame," 20/5 *Child Abuse and Neglect* 447 (1996), 10
Collins, W., Wellman, H., Keniston, A., and Westby, S., "Age-related Aspects of Comprehension and Inferences from a Televised Dramatic Narrative," 49 *Child Development* 389 (1978), 300
Comment, "Adult Survivors of Childhood Sexual Abuse and the Statute of Limitations: The Need for Consistent Application of the Delayed Discovery Rule," 20 *Pepperdine Law Review* 1359 (1993), 84
Conte, J., "Child Sexual Abuse: Awareness and Backlash," 4/2 *The Future of Children* 224 (1994), 38
Conte, J., "Clinical Dimensions of Adult Sexual Abuse of Children," 3 *Behavioral Sciences and the Law* 341 (1985), 108
Conte, J., and Berliner, L., "The Impact of Sexual Abuse on Children: Empirical Findings," in *Handbook on Sexual Abuse of Children* 72 (L. Walker, ed. 1988), 124-125
Cooper, S., "The Tyranny of the Urgent: Child Welfare Casework in the 90s," 6/1 *Journal of Child Sexual Abuse* 85, 87 (1997), 366
Cormier, B., Kennedy, M., and Sangowicz, J., "Psychodynamics of Father-Daughter Incest," 7 *Canadian Psychiatric Association Journal* 207 (1962), 256
Cornwell, J., "Protection and Treatment: The Permissible Civil Detention of Sexual Predators," 53 *Washington and Lee Law Review* 1293 (1996), 355
Corwin, D., Berliner, L., Goodman, G., Goodwin, J., and White, S., "Child Sexual Abuse and Custody Disputes," 2/1 *Journal of Interpersonal Violence* 91 (1987), 36, 125
Courtois, C., "The Memory Retrieval Process in Incest Survivor Therapy," 1/1 *Journal of Child Sexual Abuse* 15 at 18 (1992), 122
Crawford, S., "Intrafamilial Sexual Abuse: What We Think We Know About Mothers, and Implications for Intervention," 7/3 *Journal of Child Sexual Abuse* 55 (1999), 256
Cross, T., and Saxe, L., "A Critique of the Validity of Polygraph Testing in Child Sexual Abuses Cases," 1/4 *Journal of Child Sexual Abuse* 19 (1992), 107

Dziech, B., and Schudson, C., *On Trial: America's Courts and Their Treatment of Sexually Abused Children* (1989), 33, 38, 361

Egeland, B., *et al.*, *MMPI-2 Profiles of Women at Risk (1991), 106*

Eisen, M., and Goodman, G., "Trauma, Memory, and Suggestibility in Children," 10 *Development and Psychopathology* (1998), 302, 306, 311

Eisen, M., Goodman, G., Qin, J., and Davis, S., "Memory and Suggestibility in Maltreated Children: New Research Relevant to Evaluating Allegations of Abuse," in *Truth in Memory* 163, 182 (S. Lynn and K. McConkey, eds., 1998), 307, 309, 311

Elbow, M., and Mayfield, J., "Mothers of Incest Victims: Villains, Victims, or Protectors?," 72/2 *Families in Society: Journal of Contemporary Human Services* 78 (1991), 253

Elliot, D., "Traumatic Events: Prevalence and Delayed Recall in the General Population," 65 *Journal of Consulting and Clinical Psychology* 810 (1997), 122

Elliot, D., and Briere, J., "Posttraumatic Stress Associated with Delayed Recall of Sexual Abuse: A General Population Study," 8/4 *Journal of Traumatic Stress* 629 (1995), 110

Elstein, S., and Davis, N., *Sexual Relationships Between Adult Males and Young Teen Girls: Exploring the Legal and Social Response* (1997), 11

Elvik, S., "Professionals under Fire: Delayed Memories versus the False Memory Syndrome," 3/3 *Journal of Child Sexual Abuse* 123 (1994), 88, 121, 315

Emans, S., "Physical Examination of the Child and Adolescent," in *Evaluation of the Sexually Abused Child: A Medical Textbook and Photographic Atlas* (A. Heger and S. Emans, eds., 1992), 199, 201, 202

Emans, S., Woods, E., Flagg, N., and Freeman, A., "Genital Findings in Sexually Abused, Symptomatic, and Asymptomatic Girls," 79 *Pediatrics* 778 (1987), 201

Ernsdorff, G., and Loftus, E., "Let the Sleeping Memories Lie? Words of Caution About Tolling the Statute of Limitations," 84 *Journal of Criminal Law and Criminology* 129 (1993), 121

Evaluation of the Sexually Abused Child: A Medical Textbook and Photographic Atlas (A. Heger and S. Emans, eds., 1992), 208

Everson, M., and Boat, B., "Putting the Anatomical Doll Controversy in Perspective: An Examination of the Major Uses and Criticisms of the Dolls in Child Sexual Abuse Evaluations," 18/2 *Child Abuse and Neglect* 113 (1994), 112

Everson, M., and Boat, B., "Sexualized Play Among Young Children: Implications for the Use of Anatomical Dolls in Sexual Abuse

Evaluations," 29 *Journal of Acad. Child and Adolescent Psychiatry* 736 (1990), 113
Everson, M., Hunter, W., Runyon, D., Edelsohn, G., and Coulter, M., "Maternal Support Following Disclosure of Incest," 59/2 *American Journal of Orthopsychiatry* 197 (1989), 254
Ewing, C., "Family Preservation and Reunification in Intrafamilial Sexual Abuse Cases: A Judicial Perspective," 2/2 *Journal of Child Sexual Abuse* 113 (1993), 343

Faller, K., "A Clinical Sample of Women Who Have Sexually Abused Children," 4/3 *Journal of Child Sexual Abuse* 13 (1995), 6, 7
Faller, K., *Child Sexual Abuse: An Interdisciplinary Manual for Diagnosis, Case Management, and Treatment* (1988), 104
Faller, K., "The Myth of the 'Collusive Mother': Variability in the Functioning of Mothers of Victims of Intrafamilial Sexual Abuse," 3/2 *Journal of Interpersonal Violence* 190 (1988), 253
Faller, K., "The Parental Alienation Syndrome: What Is It and What Data Support It?," 3/2 *Child Maltreatment* 100 (1998), 32, 115
Faller, K., *Understanding Child Sexual Mistreatment* (1990), 36
Faller, K., "Women Who Sexually Abuse Children," 2 *Violence and Victims* 263 (1987), 6
Famularo, R., Kinscherff, R., and Fenton, T., "Parental Substance Abuse and the Nature of Child Maltreatment," 16/4 *Child Abuse and Neglect* 475 (1992), 14
Farrar, M., and Goodman, G., "Developmental Changes in Event Memory," 63 *Child Development* (1992), 302
Federle, K., "Looking Ahead: An Enpowerment Perspective on the Rights of Children," 68/4 *Temple Law Review* 1585 (1995), 368
Federle, K., "Looking for Rights in All the Wrong Places: Resolving Custody Disputes in Divorce Proceedings," 15/5 *Cardozo Law Review* (1994), 367, 368
Fehrenbach, P., and Monastersky, C., "Characteristics of Female Adolescent Sexual Offenders," 58/1 *American Journal of Orthopsychiatry* 148 (1988), 6, 7
Feiring, C., Taska, L., and Lewis, M., "The Role of Shame and Attributional Style in Children's and Adolescents' Adaptation to Sexual Abuse," 3/2 *Child Maltreatment* 129 (1998), 11
Feldman, W., Feldman, E., Goodman, J., McGrath, P., Pless, R., Corsini, L., and Bennett, S., "Is Childhood Sexual Abuse Really Increasing in Prevalence?: An Analysis of the Evidence," 88/1 *Pediatrics* 29 (1991), 1, 34

Female Sexual Abuse of Children (M. Elliott, ed., 1993), 6
Fergusson, D., Horwood, L., and Lynskey, M., "Childhood Sexual Abuse, Adolescent Sexual Behaviors and Sexual Revictimization," 21/8 *Child Abuse and Neglect* 789 (1997), 9
Finkel, M., "Anogenital Trauma in Sexually Abused Children," 84 *Pediatrics* 117 (1989), 200
Finkel, M., and DeJong, A., "Medical Findings in Child Sexual Abuse," in *Child Abuse: Medical Diagnosis and Management* 185 (R. Reece, ed. 1994), 202
Finkelhor, D., *A Sourcebook on Child Sexual Abuse* (1986), 207
Finkelhor, D., "Current Information on the Scope and Nature of Child Sexual Abuse,"4 *The Future of Children* 31 (1994), 1, 2, 124
Finkelhor, D., "Removing the Child - Prosecuting the Offender in Cases of Sexual Abuse: Evidence from the National Reporting System for Child Abuse and Neglect," 7/2 *Child Abuse and Neglect* 195 (1983), 54, 238
Finkelhor, D., "Sexual Abuse of Boys," in *Rape and Sexual Assault* 97 (A. Burgess, ed. 1985), 6
Finkelhor, D., and Daro, D., "Prevention of Child Sexual Abuse," in *The Battered Child* 615, 622 (M. Helfer, R. Kempe, and R. Krugman, eds., 5th ed. 1997), 255
Finkelhor, D., and Russell, D., "Women as Perpetrators: Review of the Evidence," in D. Finkelhor, *Child Sexual Abuse: New Theory and Research* 171 (1984), 7
Fisher, R., Amador, M., and Geiselman, R., "Field Test of the Cognitive Interview: Enhancing the Recollection of Actual Victims and Witnesses of Crime," 74 *Journal of Applied Psychology* 722 (1989), 304
Fisher, R., and Geiselman, R., *Memory Enhancing Techniques for Investigative Interviewing* (1992), 313
Fisher, R., and McCauley, M., "Improving Eyewitness Testimony With the Cognitive Interview," in *Memory and Testimony in the Child Witness* 141 (M. Zaragoza, J. Graham, G. Hall, R. Hirschman and Y. Ben-Porath, eds., 1995), 17
Fisher, R., McCauley, M., and Geiselman, R., "Improving Eyewitness Testimony with the Cognitive Interview," in *Adult Eyewitness Testimony and Current Trends and Developments* 245 (D. Ross, J. Read, and M. Toglia, eds. 1994), 313
Fivush, R., "Developmental Perspectives on Autobiographical Recall," in *Child Victims, Child Witnesses* (G. Goodman and B. Bottoms, eds., 1993), 302, 309, 312

Fivush, R., and Shukat, J., "Content, Consistency, and Coherence of Early Autobiographical Recall in Memory and Testimony," in *The Child Witness* 5 (M. Zaragoza, J. Graham, C. Hall, R. Hirschmand, and Y. Ben-Porath, eds. 1995), 309

Fivush, R., Hudson, J., and Nelson, K., "Children's Long-Term Memory for a Novel Event: An Exploratory Study," 30 *Merrill-Palmer Quarterly* 303 (1984), 306

Flapan, D., *Children's Understanding of Social Interaction* (1968), 300

Flavell, J., "Cognitive Monitoring," in *Children's Oral Communications Skills* (W. Dickson, ed., 1981), 304

Flin, R., "Commentary: A Grand Memory for Forgetting," in *The Suggestibility of Children's Recollections: Implications for Eyewitness Testimony* 22 (J. Doris, ed., 1991), 303

Forward, S., and Buck, C., *Betrayal of Innocence: Incest and Its Devastation* (1978), 256

Fossey, R., and Demitchell, T., "'Let the Master Answer': Holding Schools Vicariously Liable When Employees Sexually Abuse Children," 25 *Journal of Law and Education* 575 (1996), 102

Freund, K., Watson, R., and Rienzo, D., "Signs of Feigning in the Phallometric Test," 26 *Behavioral Research and Therapy* 105 (1988), 207

Freyd, J., "Personal Perspectives on the Delayed Memory Debate," 9/3 *Family Violence and Sexual Assault Bulletin* 28 (1993), 119

Friedrich, W., "Sexual Victimization and Sexual Behavior in Children: A Review of Recent Literature," 17/1 *Child Abuse and Neglect* 59 (1993), 9, 10, 104, 110

Friedrich, W., "The Clinical Use of the Child Sexual Behavior Inventory: Commonly Asked Questions," 8/1 *APSAC Advisor* 1 (1995), 106

Gardner, J., "Descriptive Study of Genital Variation in Healthy, Non-abused Premenarchal Girls," 120 *Journal of Pediatrics* 251 (1992), 205

Gardner, R., *Psychotherapy with Sex-Abuse Victims: True, False, and Hysterical* (1996), 32

Gardner, R., *Sex Abuse Hysteria: Salem Witch Trials Revisited* (1991), 32

Gardner, R., *The Parental Alienation Syndrome and the Differentiation Between Fabricated and Genuine Sex Abuse* (Creative Therapeutics 1987), 33, 114, 115, 116

Gardner, R., *True and False Accusations of Child Sexual Abuse* (1992), 114

Geiselman, R., Fisher, R., MacKinnon, D., and Holland, H., "Eyewitness Memory Enhancement in the Police Interview: Cognitive Retrieval Mnemonics Versus Hypnosis," 70 *Journal of Applied Psychology* 401 (1985), 304

Geiselman, R., Saywitz, K., and Bornstein, G., "Effects of Cognitive Questioning Techniques on Children's Recall Performance," in *Child Victims, Child Witnesses: Understanding and Improving Testimony* (G. Goodman and B. Bottoms, eds., 1993), 17, 305, 313

Gelinas, D., "Family Therapy: Characteristic Family Constellation and Basic Therapeutic Stance," in *Vulnerable Populations: Evaluation and Treatment of Sexually Abused Children and Adult Survivors* (S. Sgroi, ed., 1987), 256

Geraci, J., "Hollida Wakefield and Ralph Underwager," 3/2 *Paidika, Journal of Paedophilia* 2 (Winter 1993), 90, 119, 126, 127

Giaretto, H., "Humanistic Treatment of Father-Daughter Incest," in *Child Abuse and Neglect: The Family and the Community* (R. Helfer and C. Kempe, eds. 1976), 256

Glaser and Collins, "The Response of Young, Non-Sexually Abused Children to Anatomically Correct Dolls," 30 *Journal of Child Psychology and Psychiatry* 547 (1989), 111

Gleaves, D., "The Evidence for 'Repression': An Examination of Holmes (1990) and the Implications for the Recovered Memory Controversy," 5/1 *Journal of Child Sexual Abuse* 1 (1996), 88, 315

Gomes-Schwartz, B., Horowitz, J., Cardarelli, A., Salt, P., Myer, M., Coleman, L., and Sauzier, M., "The Myth of the Mother as 'Accomplice' to Child Sexual Abuse," in *Child Sexual Abuse: The Initial Effects* (B. Gomes-Schwartz et al., eds. 1990), 253

Goodman, Bottoms, Schwartz-Kenney, and Rudy, "Children's Testimony About a Stressful Event: Improving Children's Reports," 7 *Journal of Narrative and Life History* 69 (1991), 305, 337

Goodman, Hepps, and Reed, "The Child Victim's Testimony," in *New Issues for Child Advocates* 167 (A. Haralambie, ed., 1986), 306

Goodman, Hirschman, Hepps, and Rudy, "Children's Memory for Stressful Events," 37 *Merrill-Palmer Quarterly* 109 (1991), 306

Goodman, Rudy, Bottoms, and Aman, "Children's Concerns and Memory: Issues of Ecological Validity in the Study of Children's Eyewitness Testimony," in *Knowing and Remembering in Young Children* 249 (R. Fivush and J. Hudson eds. 1990), 111, 305

Goodman, Taub, Jones, England, Port, Rudy, and Prado, "Testifying in Criminal Court: Emotional Effects on Child Sexual Assault Victims," 57 *Monographs of the Society for Research in Child Development* (Serial No. 229, No. 5, 1992), 330, 338

Goodman, G., and Aman, C., "Children's Use of Anatomically Detailed Dolls to Recount an Event in Child Development," 61 *Child Development* 1859 (1990), 104, 111

Goodman, G., Aman, C., and Hirschman, J., "Child Sexual and Physical Abuse: Children's Testimony," in *Children's Eyewitness Memory* 1 (S. Ceci, M. Toglia, and D. Ross, eds. 1987), 306
Goodman, G., and Lloyd, D., "The Child Witness: Evaluation and Preparation," in *The New Child Protection Team Handbook* 418 (D. Bross, R. Krugman, D. Rosenberg, and B. Schmitt, eds., 1988), 306
Goodman, G., Quas, J., Batterman-Faunce, J., Riddlesberger, M., and Kuhn, J., "Predictors of Accurate and Inaccurate Memories of Traumatic Events Experienced in Childhood," 3 *Consciousness and Cognition* 269 (1994), 307, 308
Goodman, G., and Reed, R., "Age Differences in Eyewitness Testimony," 10 *Law and Human Behavior* 317 (1986), 300, 304, 306
Goodman, G., and Schwartz-Kenney, B., "Why Knowing a Child's Age Is Not Enough: Influences of Cognitive, Social, and Emotional Factors on Children's Testimony," in *Children as Witnesses* (H. Dent and R. Flin, eds. 1992), 4
Goodman, G., Sharma, A., Thomas, S., and Considine, M., "Mother Knows Best: Effects of Relationship Status and Interviewer Bias on Children's Memory," 60 *Journal of Experimental Child Psychology* 195 (1995), 246, 310
Goodwin, J., Sahd, D., and Rada, R., "False Accusations and False Denials of Incest: Clinical Myths and Clinical Realities," in *Sexual Abuse: Incest Victims and Their Families* (J. Goodwin, ed. 1982), 39
Goodwin, J., Sahd, D., and Rada, R., "Incest Hoax: False Accusations, False Denials," 6 *Bulletin of the American Academy of Psychiatry and Law* 269 (1979), 39
Gray, E., *Unequal Justice: The Prosecution of Child Sexual Abuse* (1993), 238, 361
Green, A., and Schetky, D., "True and False Allegations of Child Sexual Abuse," in D. Schetky and A. Green, *Child Sexual Abuse: A Handbook for Health Care and Legal Professionals* (1988), 33
Greenberg, D., Bradford, J., and Curry, S., "Infantophilia - A New Subcategory of Pedophilia?: A Preliminary Study," 23 *Bulletin of American Academy of Psychiatry and Law* 63 (1995), 2
Guidelines for a Model System of Protective Services for Abused and Neglected Children and Their Families (National Association of Public Child Welfare Administrators, ed. 1988), 51

Hagen, A., "Tolling the Statute of Limitations for Adult Survivors of Childhood Sexual Abuse," 76 *Iowa Law Review* 355 (1991), 84
Hall, G., et al., "The Utility of the MMPI with Men Who Have Sexually Assaulted Children," 54 *Journal of Consulting and Clinical Psychology* 493 (1986), 106

Hammerschlag, M., and Rawstron, S., "Sexually Transmitted Diseases," in *Child Abuse: A Medical Reference* 249-63 (S. Ludwig and A. Kornberg, eds. 1992), 203

Handler, "Civil Claims of Adults Molested as Children: Maturation of Harm and the Statute of Limitations Hurdle," 15 *Fordham Urban Law Journal* 722 (1987), 84

Hanson, R., "The Development of a Brief Actuarial Risk Scale for Sexual Offense Recidivism," *User Report No. 1997-04, Department of the Solicitor General of Canada* (1997), 108

Hanson, R., and Bussiere, M., "Predicting Relapse: A Meta-Analysis of Sexual Offender Recidivism Studies," 66/2 *Journal of Consulting and Clinical Psychology* 348 (1998), 72, 108

Hanson, R., and Bussiere, M., "Predictors of Sexual Offender Recidivism: A Meta-Analysis," User Report No. 1996-04, Department of the Solicitor General of Canada (1996), 104

Haralambie, A., *Handling Child Custody, Abuse and Adoption Cases* (2nd ed. Clark Boardman Callaghan 1993, West Group 1998), 45, 47, 58, 59, 60, 69, 73, 93, 96, 345, 359

Haralambie, A., "In Whose Best Interests?," 34/6 Trial 42 (1998), 285

Haralambie, A., *The Child's Attorney: A Guide to Representing Children in Custody, Adoption, and Protection Cases* (American Bar Association 1993), 15, 43, 280, 285, 327, 357

Haralambie, A., and Glaser, D., "Practical and Theoretical Problems with the AAML Standards for Representing 'Impaired' Children," 13/1 *Journal of American Academy of Matrimonial Lawyers* 57 (1995), 286

Harrison, P., Fulkerson, J., and Beebe, T., "Multiple Substance Abuse Among Adolescent Physical and Sexual Abuse Victims," 21/6 *Child Abuse and Neglect* 529 (1997), 9

Hathaway, S., and McKinley, J., *Minnesota Multiphasic Personality Inventory-2* (1989), 106

Haugaard, J., and Reppucci, N., *The Sexual Abuse of Children* (1988), 103

Haugaard, Reppucci, Laird, and Nauful, "Children's Definitions of the Truth and Their Competency as Witnesses in Legal Proceedings," 15 *Law and Human Behavior* 253 (1991), 334

Haywood, T., and Grossman, L., "Denial of Deviant Sexual Arousal and Psychopathology in Child Molesters," 25 *Behavior Therapy* 327 (1994), 108

Hazzard, A., Celano, M., Gould, J., Lawry, S., and Webb, C., "Predicting Symptomatology and Self-Blame Among Child Sex Abuse Victims," 19/6 *Child Abuse and Neglect* 707 (1995), 10

Hechler, D., *The Battle and the Backlash: The Child Sexual Abuse War* (1988), 33, 361

Heger, A., "Helping the Medical Professional Make the Diagnosis of Sexual Abuse," in *Evaluation of the Sexually Abused Child: A Medical Textbook and Photographic Atlas* 3 (A. Heger and S. Emans, eds., 1992), 208
Heger, A., and Emans, S., "Introital Diameter as the Criterion for Sexual Abuse," 85 *Pediatrics* 222 (1990), 202
Hepburn, J., "The Implications of Contemporary Feminist Theories of Development for the Treatment of Male Victims of Sexual Abuse," 3/4 *Journal of Child Sexual Abuse* 1 (1994), 8, 9
Herman, J., *Father-Daughter Incest* (1982), 104, 108, 254
Herman, J., and Schatzow, E., "Recovery and Verification of Memories of Childhood Sexual Trauma," 4 *Psychoanalytic Psychology* 1 (1987), 122
Hewitt, S., "Therapeutic Management of Preschool Cases of Alleged But Unsubstantiated Sexual Abuse," *Child Welfare* (1991), 250, 348, 362
Holmes, K., Mardh, P., Sparling, P., Wiesner, P., Cates, W., Jr., Lemon, S., and Stamm, W., *Sexually Transmitted Diseases* (2d ed. 1990), 203
Honts, C., "Assessing Children's Credibility: Scientific and Legal Issues in 1994," 70 *North Dakota Law Review* 879 (1994), 114
Horowitz, M., *Stress Response Syndromes* (2 ed. 1986), 121
Howes, R., "A Survey of Plethysmographic Assessment in North America," 7/1 *Sexual Abuse: A Journal of Research and Treatment* 9 (1995), 207
Hunter, J., Jr., Childers, S., Gerald, R., and Esmalaili, H., "An Examination of Variables Differentiating Clinical Subtypes of Incestuous Child Molesters," 34/2 *International Journal of Offender Therapy and Comparative Criminology* 95 (1990), 106

Inderbitzen-Pisaruk, H., Shawchuck, C., and Hoier, T., "Behavioral Characteristics of Child Victims of Sexual Abuse: A Comparison Study," 21 *Journal of Clinical Child Psychology* 14 (1992), 10
Indiana State Bar Association, Legal Ethics Committee, Op. 1-1986 (1986), 97
International Perspectives on Child Abuse and Children's Testimony (B. Bottoms and G. Goodman, eds. 1996), 298
Investigation and Prosecution of Child Abuse (P. Toth and M. Whalen, eds. 1987), 125
Irueste-Montes, A., and Montes, F., "Court-Ordered versus Voluntary Treatment of Abusive and Neglectful Parents," 12/1 *Child Abuse and Neglect* 33 (1988), 16

Jacobs, J., "Reassessing Mother Blame in Incest," 15/3 *Signs: Journal of Women in Culture and Society* 500 (1990), 253, 254
Jacobs, T., *Children and The Law: Rights and Obligations* (Clark Boardman Callaghan 1995, West Group 1997), 47, 59, 69, 73

Jacobson and Herald, "The Relevance of Childhood Sexual Abuse to Adult Psychiatric Inpatient Care," 41 *Hospital and Community Psychiatry* 154 (1990), 103

Jenny, C., "Forensic Examination: The Role of the Physician as 'Medical Detective,'" in *Evaluation of the Sexually Abused Child: A Medical Textbook and Photographic Atlas* (A. Heger and S. Emans, eds., 1992), 199, 208

Jenny, C., *Medical Evaluation of Physically and Sexually Abused Children* (1996), 200, 202, 203, 208, 209

Johnson, C., "Use of an M.D.-Social Worker Team in the Evaluation of Child Sexual Abuse: A Response," 2/2 *Journal of Child Sexual Abuse* 99, 100 (1993), 203

Johnson, J., *Mothers of Incest Survivors: Another Side of the Story* (1992), 253

Jones, B., *The Indian Child Welfare Act Handbook: A Legal Guide to the Custody and Adoption of Native American Children* (American Bar Association 1995), 59, 73

Jones, D., "Assessment of Suspected Child Sexual Abuse," in *The Battered Child* (M. Helfer, R. Kempe, and R. Krugman, eds., 5th ed. 1997), 3, 50-51

Jones, D., "The Untreatable Family," 11/3 *Child Abuse and Neglect* (1987), 76, 77

Jones, D., and McGraw, C., "Reliable and Fictitious Accounts of Sexual Abuse to Children," 2 *Journal of Interpersonal Violence* 27 (1986), 35, 358

Jones, D., and Seig, A., "Child Sexual Abuse Allegations in Custody or Visitation Disputes," in *Sexual Abuse Allegations in Custody and Visitation Cases* 22 (E. Nicholson and J. Bulkley eds., 1988), 358

Joyce, P., "Mothers of Sexually Abused Children and the Concept of Collusion: A Literature Review," 6/2 *Journal of Child Sexual Abuse* 75 (1997), 253, 256

Jumper, S., "A Meta-Analysis of the Relationship of Child Sexual Abuse to Adult Psychological Adjustment," 19/6 *Child Abuse and Neglect* 715 (1995), 10

Justice, B., and Justice, R., *The Broken Taboo: Sex in the Family* (1979), 256

Kalichman, S., *Mandated Reporting of Suspected Child Abuse: Ethics Law and Policy* (1993), 96

Karp, L., and Karp, C., *Domestic Torts: Family Violence, Conflict, and Sexual Abuse* (Clark Boardman Callaghan 1989, West Group 1998), 79, 84, 88, 93, 96, 106, 110, 125, 235, 308, 316

Kaufman, K., Wallace, A., Johnson, C., and Reeder, M., "Comparing Female and Male Perpetrators' Modus Operandi: Victims' Reports of Sexual Abuse," 10/3 *Journal of Interpersonal Violence* 322 (1995), 7

Leifer, M., and Shapiro, J., "Longitudinal Study of the Psychological Effects of Sexual Abuse in African American Girls in Foster Care and Those Who Remain Home," 4/4 *Journal of Child Sexual Abuse* 27 (1995), 10

Leone, C., "New Jersey Assembly Bill 155 - A Bill Allowing the Civil Commitment of Violent Sex Offenders After the Completion of a Criminal Sentence," 18 *Seton Hall Legislative Journal* 890 (1994), 355

Lepore, S., "Child Witness: Cognitive and Social Factors Related to Memory and Testimony," 3 *Issues in Child Abuse Accusations* 65 (1991), 304, 306

Leventhal, Hamilton, Rekedal, Tebano-Micci, and Eyster, "Anatomically Correct Dolls Used in Interviews of Young Children Suspected of Having Been Sexually Abused," 84 *Pediatrics* 900 (1989), 111

Levitt, C., "The Medical Examination in Child Sexual Abuse: A Balance Between History and Exam," 1/4 *Journal of Child Sexual Abuse* (1992), 128, 200, 202, 203, 205

Lewin, S., and Stava, L., "Personality Characteristics of Re-Offenders: A Review," 16 *Archives of Sexual Behavior* 57 (1987), 106

Lewis, C., Wilkins, R., Baker, L., and Woobey, A., "'Is This Man Your Daddy?' Suggestibility in Children's Eyewitness Identification of a Family Member," 19/6 *Child Abuse and Neglect* 739 (1995), 309

Lindberg, F., and Distad, L., "Post-Traumatic Stress Disorders in Women Who Experienced Childhood Incest," 9 *Child Abuse and Neglect* 521 (1985), 122

Lindberg, M., "The Role of Knowledge Structures in the Otogeny of Learning," 30 *Journal of Experimental Child Psychology* 401 (1980), 305

Lindsay, D., and Read, J., "Psychotherapy and Memories of Childhood Sexual Abuse: A Cognitive Perspective," *Applied Cognitive Psychology* 281 (1994), 121

Lipovsky, J., and Stern, P., "Preparing Children for Court: An Interdisciplinary View," 2/2 *Child Maltreatment* 150 (1997), 17, 327

Loftus, E., *Eyewitness Testimony* (1979), 306

Loftus, E., and Ketchum, K., *The Myth of Memory Repression*, (1994), 121

Looman, J., Abracen, J., Maillet, G., and Difazio, R., "Phallometric Nonresponding in Sexual Offenders," 10/4 *Sexual Abuse: A Journal of Research and Treatment* 325 (1998), 207

Lopez, S., "Hide and Seek," *Time* (May 11, 1998, page 56), 44

Lustig, N., Dresser, J., Spellman, S., and Jurray, T., "Incest: A Family Group Survival Pattern" 14 *Archives of General Psychiatry* 31 (1966), 256

Lykken, D., *A Tremor in the Blood: Uses and Abuses of the Lie Detector* (1981), 107

Lyon, T., "The Effect of Threats on Children's Disclosure of Sexual Abuse," 9 *The APSAC Advisor* 9 (1996), 4

MacFarlane, K., "Child Sexual Abuse Allegations in Divorce Proceedings," in *Sexual Abuse of Young Children: Evaluation and Treatment* 121 (K. MacFarlane and J. Waterman, eds. 1986), 36, 233

MacFarlane, K., and Waterman, J., *Sexual Abuse of Young Children* 27 (1986), 334

MacMurray, B., "Criminal Determination for Child Sexual Abuse: Prosecutor Case-Screening Judgments," 4 *Journal of Interpersonal Violence* 233 (1989), 238

Making Reasonable Efforts: Steps for Keeping Families Together (L. Lange, ed., n.d.), 75

Mannarino, A., and Cohen, J., "A Follow-Up Study of Factors That Mediate the Development of Psychological Symptomatology in Sexually Abused Girls," 1/3 *Child Maltreatment* 246 (1996), 51

Mannarino, A., Cohen, J., and Berman, S., "The Relationship Between Preabuse Factors and Psychological Symptomatology" in *Sexually Abused Girls* 63 (1994), 103

Marks, R., "Should We Believe the People Who Believe the Children? The Need for a New Sexual Abuse Tender Years Hearsay Exception Statute," 32 *Harvard Journal of Legislation* 207 (1995), 59

Masson, G., *Assault on the Truth: Freud's Suppression of the Seduction Theory* (1984), 104

Matchotka, P., Pittman, P., and Flomenshaft, S., "Incest As a Family Affair," 6/1 *Family Process* 98 (1967), 256

Mathews, R., Mathews, J., and Speltz, K., *Female Sexual Offenders: An Exploratory Study* (1989), 7

Matthew, E., and Saywitz, K., "Child Victim Witness Manual," 12 *CJER Journal* (No. 1, 1992), 331, 334

McCann, J., "Use of the Colposcope in Childhood Sexual Abuse Examinations," 37 *Pediatric Clinic, North America* 863 (1990), 204

McCann, J., Voris, J., and Simon, M., "Genital Injuries Resulting from Sexual Abuse: A Longitudinal Study," 89 *Pediatrics* 307 (1989), 200

McCann, J., Voris, J., and Simon, M., "Labial Adhesions and Posterior Fourchette Injuries in Childhood Sexual Abuse," 142 *American Journal of Diseases of Children* 659 (1988), 202, 203

McCann, J., Wells, R., Simon, M., and Voris, J., "Genital Findings in Prepubertal Girls Selected for Nonabuse: A Descriptive Study," 86 *Pediatrics* 428 (1990), 202, 203

McCarty, L., "Mother-Child Incest: Characteristics of the Offender," 65/5 *Child Welfare* 447 (1986), 7

McCauley, M., and Fisher, R., "Facilitating Children's Eyewitness Recall with the Revised Cognitive Interview," 80 *Journal of Applied Psychology* (1995), 17, 313

McClosky, L., Figueredo, A., and Koss, M., "The Effects of Systemic Family Violence on Children's Mental Health," 66 *Child Development 1239 (1995), 12*

McGrath, M., Cann, S., and Konopasky, R., "New Measures of Defensiveness, Empathy and Cognitive Distortions for Sexual Offenders Against Children" 10/1 *Sexual Abuse: A Journal of Research and Treatment* 25 (1998), 108

McGraw, J., and Smith, H., "Child Sexual Abuse Allegations Amidst Divorce and Custody Proceedings: Refining the Validation Process," 1/1 *Journal of Child Sexual Abuse* 49, 53 (1992), 52, 360

McIntosh and Prinz, "The Incidence of Alleged Sexual Abuse in 603 Family Court Cases," 17 *Law and Human Behavior* 95 (Feb 1993), 34

McIntyre, K., "Role of Mothers in Father-Daughter Incest: A Feminist Analysis," 26 *Social Work* 462 (1981), 256

McLeer, S., Deblinger, E., Atkins, M., Foa, E., and Ralphe, D., "Post-Traumatic Stress Disorder in Sexually Abused Children," *Journal of the American Academy of Child and Adolescent Psychiatry* 651 (1988), 10

Meinig, "Profile of Roland Summit," 1 *Violence Update* 6 (May 1991), 118

Melton, G., and Thompson, R., "Getting Out of a Rut: Detours to Less Traveled Paths in Child-Witness Research," in *Children's Eyewitness Memory* 209 (S. Ceci, M. Toglia, and D. Ross, eds. 1987), 298

Memon, A., Cronin, O., Eaves, R., and Bull, R., "The Cognitive Interview and Child Witnesses," in 20 *Children, Evidence and Procedure: Issues in Criminological and Legal Psychology* 3 (N. Clark and G. Stephenson, eds., 1993), 17, 313

Memory and Testimony in the Child Witness (M. Zaragoza, J. Graham, G. Hall, R. Hirschman, and Y. Ben-Porath, eds. 1995), 298

Memory Development in Children (N. Cowan, ed., 1997), 298

Mian, M., Marton, P., and LeBaron, D., "The Effects of Sexual Abuse on 3- to 5-Year-Old Girls," 20/8 *Child Abuse and Neglect* 731 (1996), 9

Miller A., *Thou Shalt Not Be Aware: Society's Betrayal of the Child* (1984), 104

Moeller, T., Bachman, G., and Moeller, J., "The Combined Effects of Physical, Sexual, and Emotional Abuse During Childhood: Long-Term Health Consequences for Women," 17/5 *Child Abuse and Neglect* 623 (1993), 12

Monteleone, J., Brewer, J., and Fete, T., "Physical Examination in Sexual Abuse," in *Child Maltreatment: A Clinical Guide and Reference* 133 (A. Brodeur and J. Monteleone, eds. 1994), 202-203

Myers, J., Saywitz, K., and Goodman, G., "Psychological Research on Children as Witnesses: Practical Implications for Forensic Interviews and Courtroom Testimony," 28/1 *Pacific Law Journal* 3 (1996), 17, 124, 309

Myers, N., and Perlmutter, N., "Memory in the Years from Two to Five," in *Memory Development in Children* 191 (P. Ornstein ed. 1978), 304

Myles-Worsley, M., Cromer, C., and Dodd, D., "Children's Preschool Script Reconstruction: Reliance on General Knowledge as Memory Fades," 22 *Developmental Psychology* 22 (1986), 306, 315

National Center on Child Abuse and Neglect, *Third National Incidence Study of Child Abuse and Neglect* (1996), 1, 34

Nelson, K., "How Children Represent Their World In and Out of Language: A Preliminary Report," in *Children's Thinking: What Develops?* 255 (R. Siegler, ed. 1979), 300

Nelson, K., and Gruendel, J., "Generalized Event Representations: Basic Building Blocks of Cognitive Development," in 1 *Advances in Cognitive Development* 131 (M. Lamb and A. Brown, eds. 1981), 300

Nelson, K., Fivush, R., Hudson, J., and Lucariello, J., "Scripts and the Development of Memory," in *Current Trends in Memory Development* 52 (M. Chi, ed. 1983), 300

New Jersey Supreme Court Advisory Committee on Professional Ethics, Op. 280 Supp., 97 N.J.L.J. (1974), 97

Nichols, E., *False Allegations of Child Sexual Abuse: The Attorney's Desk Reference* (1994), 32

Nichols, H., and Molinder, I., *Multiphasic Sex Inventory Manual* (1984), 105

Nichols, H., and Molinder, I., *Multiphasic Sex Inventory II* (1990), 105, 271

Ofshe, R., "Making Grossly Damaging But Avoidable Errors: The Pitfalls of the Olio/Cornell Thesis," 3/3 *Journal of Child Sexual Abuse* 95 (1994), 88, 121, 315

Olio, K., and Cornell, W., "Making Meaning Not Monsters: Reflections on the Delayed Memory Syndrome," 3/3 *Journal of Child Sexual Abuse* 77 (1994), 88, 121, 315

Paradise, J., "The Medical Evaluation of Sexually Abused Children," 37 *Pediatric Clinics of North America* 839 (1990), 205

Pence, D., "Family Preservation and Reunification in Intrafamilial Sexual Abuse Cases: A Law Enforcement Perspective," 2/2 *Journal of Child Sexual Abuse* 103 (1993), 343

Pence, D., and Wilson, C., *Team Investigation of Child Sexual Abuse: The Uneasy Alliance* ch. 11 (1994), 36

Perlmutter, M., *Children's Memory: New Directions in Child Development* (No. 10 1980), 305

Perry, N., "How Children Remember and Why They Forget," 5/3 *The Advisor* 1 (Summer 1992), 300

Perry, N., and Teply, L., "Interviewing, Counseling, and In-Court Examination of Children: Practical Approaches for Attorneys," 18 *Creighton Law Review* 1369 (1984-85), 300

Perry, N., Nielsen, D., Burns, D., Cunningham, E., and Jenkins, S., "Young Children's Ability to Provide Accurate Testimony Following a Witnessed Event," paper presented at the spring meeting of the Nebraska Psychological Association, Lincoln, Nebraska (1987), 304

Perspectives on Children's Testimony (S. Ceci, D. Ross, and M. Toglia, eds., 1989), 298

Peters, J., *Representing Children in Child Protective Proceedings: Ethical and Practical Dimensions* (1997), 43, 280, 286, 291, 292, 357, 369

Peters, J., "The Roles and Content of Best Interests in Client-Directed Lawyering for Children in Child Protective Proceedings," 64/4 *Fordham Law Review* 1505 (1996), 286

Piaget, J., and Inhelder, B., *Memory and Intelligence* (1973), 304

Pipe, Gee, and Wilson, "Cues, Props, and Context: Do They Facilitate Children's Event Reports?," in *Child Victims, Child Witnesses* 25 (G. Goodman and B. Bottoms, eds., 1993), 312

Poole, D., and Lindsay, D., "Interviewing Preschoolers: Effects of Nonsuggestive Techniques, Parental Coaching and Leading Questions of Reports of Nonexperienced Events," 60 *Journal of Experimental Child Psychology* 129 (1995), 309

Poole, D., and White, L., "Tell Me Again and Again: Stability and Change in the Repeated Testimonies of Children and Adults in Memory and Testimony," in *The Child Witness* 24 (M. Zaragoza, J. Graham, C. Hall, R. Hirschmand, and Y. Ben-Porath, eds. 1995), 309

Pope, H., "'Recovered Memories': Recent Events and Review of Evidence," 13/7 *Currents in Affective Illness* (1994), 88, 315

Porter, E., *Treating the Young Male Victim of Sexual Assault: Issues and Intervention Strategies* (1986), 6

Portwood, S., "Coming to Terms with a Consensual Definition of Child Maltreatment," 4/1 *Child Maltreatment* 56 (1999), 2

Post-Traumatic Stress Disorder in Children (S. Eth and R. Pynoos, eds. 1985), 10, 110

Prentky, R., "Child Sexual Molestation," in *Handbook of Psychological Approaches with Violent Offenders: Contemporary Strategies and Issues* 267 (M. Hersen and V. van Hasselt, eds., 1999), 4, 50

Prentky, R., Knight, R., and Lee, A., *Child Sexual Molestation: Research Issues* (National Institute of Justice 1997), 4, 106, 206, 207
"Preparing Child Witnesses - An Interview with Dr. Karen J. Saywitz," 16/11 *Child Law Practice* 161 (1998), 17
Pribor and Dinwiddie, "Psychiatric Correlates of Incest in Childhood," 149 *American Journal of Psychiatry* 52 (1992), 103
Putnam, F., *Dissociation in Children and Adolescents: A Developmental Perspective* (1997), 111
Putnam, F., "Dissociative Disorders in Children: Behavioral Profiles and Problems," 17/1 *Child Abuse and Neglect* 39 (1993), 11

Qin, J., Quas, J., Redlich, A., and Goodman, G., "Children's Eyewitness Memory," in *Memory Development in Children* (N. Cowan, ed., 1997), 307, 309, 310, 312
Quinsey, V., and Laws, D., "Validity of Physiological Measures of Pedophilic Sexual Arousal in a Sex Offender Population: A Critique of Hall, Proctor and Nelson," 58 *Journal of Consulting and Clinical Psychology* 886 (1990), 207
Quinsey, V., Chaplin, T., and Carrigan, W., "Sexual Preferences Among Incestuous and Non-incestuous Child Molesters," 10 *Behavior Therapy* 562-565 (1979), 207

Raskin, D., and Esplin, P., "Assessment of Children's Statements of Sexual Abuse." in *The Suggestibility of Children's Recollections: Implications for Eyewitness Testimony* 153 (J. Doris, ed., 1991), 113, 114
Raskin, D., and Esplin, P., "Statement Validity Assessment: Interview Procedures and Content Analysis of Children's Statements of Sexual Abuse," 13 *Behavioral Assessment* 265 (1991), 114
Raskin, D., and Steller, M., "Assessing the Credibility of Allegations of Child Sexual Abuse: Polygraph Examinations and Statement Analysis," in *Criminal Behavior and the Justice System* 290 (H. Wegener, F. Loesel and J. Haisch, eds. 1989), 114
Read, J., and Lindsay, D., "Moving Toward a Middle Ground in the 'False Memory' Debate: Reply to Commentaries on Lindsay and Read," 8 *Applied Psychology* 407 (1994), 121, 315
"Recommendations of the Conference on Ethical Issues in the Legal Representation of Children," 64/4 *Fordham Law Review* (1996), 43, 282, 287, 288, 296, 357
Reece, R., "Making Meaning - A Pediatrician's View," 3/3 *Journal of Child Sexual Abuse* 119 (1994), 88, 121, 315

Runyan, D., "Commentary: The Medical Examination in Child Sexual Abuse: A Balance Between History and Exam," 1/4 *Journal of Child Sexual Abuse* (1992), 200, 205

Rush, F., "The Freudian Cover-up," 1 *Chrysalis* 31 (1977), 104

Russell, D., *The Secret Trauma: Incest in the Lives of Girls and Women* (1986), 256

Salter, A., *Accuracy of Expert Testimony in Child Sexual Abuse Cases: A Case Study of Ralph Underwager and Holinda Wakefield* (1991), 90, 119, 235

Salter, A., *Transforming Trauma: A Guide to Understanding and Treating Adult Survivors of Child Sexual Abuse* (1995), 124

Salter, A., *Treating Child Sex Offenders and Their Victims: A Practical Guide* (1988), 108

Saltman, V., and Solomon, R., "Incest and Multiple Personality," 50 *Psychological Reports* 1127 (1982), 11

Sanderson, C., *Counselling Adult Survivors of Child Sexual Abuse* (1990), 6

Sands, "The Attorney's Affirmative Duty to Warn Foreseeable Victims of a Client's Intended Violent Assault," 21/2 *Tort and Insurance Law Journal* 355 (1986), 97

Sarwer, D., and Durlak, J., "Childhood Sexual Abuse as a Predictor of Adult Female Sexual Dysfunction: A Study of Couples Seeking Sex Therapy," 20/10 *Child Abuse and Neglect* 963 (1996), 9

Sarwer, D., Crawford, I., and Durlak, J., "The Relationship Between Childhood Sexual Abuse and Adult Male Sexual Dysfunction," 21/7 *Child Abuse and Neglect* 649 (1997), 9

Saunders, B., Villeponteaux, L., Lipovsky, J., Kilpatrick, D., and Veronen, L., "Child Sexual Assaults as a Risk Factor for Mental Disorders Among Women," 7/2 *Journal of Interpersonal Violence* 189 (1992), 10

Saxe, Dougherty, and Cross, "The Validity of Polygraph Testing: Scientific Analysis and Public Controversy," 40 *American Psychologist* 355 (1985), 107

Saywitz, Goodman, Nicholas, and Moan, "Children's Memories of a Physical Examination Involving Genital Touch: Implications for Reports of Child Sexual Abuse," 59 *Journal of Consulting and Clinical Psychology* 682 (1991), 307, 310, 312

Saywitz, K., "Children in Court: Principles of Child Development for Judicial Application," in *A Judicial Primer on Child Sexual Abuse* 15 (J. Bulkley and C. Sandt, eds. 1993), 298-299, 327, 335

Saywitz, K., "Improving Children's Testimony: The Question, the Answer, and the Environment," in *Memory and Testimony in the Child Witness* 113

Tjaden, P., and Thoennes, N., "Predictors of Legal Intervention in Child Maltreatment Cases," 16/6 *Child Abuse and Neglect* 807 (1992), 15
Tobey and Goodman, "Children's Eyewitness Memory: Effects of Participation and Forensic Content," 16 *Child Abuse and Neglect* 779 (1992), 305, 307
Todd, C., and Perlmutter, M., "Reality Recalled by Preschoolers," in *Children's Memory: New Directions in Child Development* 69 (M. Perlmutter, ed. 1980), 300
Trauma and Memory (L. Williams and V. Banyard, eds., 1998), 298, 306

Undeutsch, U., "The Development of Statement Reality Analysis," in *Credibility Assessment 101 (J. Yuille, ed., 1989), 114*
U.S. Advisory Board on Child Abuse and Neglect, *Creating Caring Communities: Blueprint for an Effective Federal Policy on Child Abuse and Neglect* (1991), 370
Urquiza, A., and Capra, M., "The Impact of Sexual Abuse: Initial and Long-Term Effects" in 1 *The Sexually Abused Male: Prevalence, Impact, and Treatment* (M. Hunter, ed. 1990), 8
Urquiza, A., and Keating, L., "The Prevalence of Sexual Victimization of Males," in 1 *The Sexually Abused Male: Prevalence, Impact, and Treatment* (M. Hunter, ed. 1990), 6
Usick, J., *Young, Poor and Pregnant: The Psychology of Teenage Motherhood* (1993), 11

van der Kolk, B., "Trauma and Memory," in *Traumatic Stress: The Effects of Overwhelming Experience on Mind, Body, and Society* 279 (B. van der Kolk, A. MacFarlane, and L. Weisaeth, eds., 1996), 306
van der Kolk, B., and Fisler, R., "Dissociation and the Fragmentary Nature of Traumatic Memories: Overview and Exploratory Study," 8 *Journal of Traumatic Stress* 505 (1995), 121
van der Kolk, B., and Kadish, W., "Amnesia, Dissociation, and the Return of the Repressed" in B. van der Kolk, *Psychological Trauma* (1987), 87, 119, 121
Van Derbur Atler, M., "The Darkest Secret," 35/2 *People Magazine* 88 (June 10, 1991), 87
Vander Mey, B., and Neff, R., *Incest as Child Abuse: Research and Applications* (1986), 256
Veltkamp, L., and Miller, T., *Clinical Handbook of Child Abuse and Neglect* (1995), 103

Wakefield, H., and Underwager, R., *Accusations of Child Sexual Abuse* (1988), 32, 125
Wakefield, H., and Underwager, R., "Magic, Mischief, and Memories: Remembering Repressed Abuse" (n.d.), 90, 119
Walker, A., *Handbook on Questioning Children: A Linguistic Perspective* (1994), 335
Walker, L., "PTSD and Child Sexual Abuse: Commentary," 2/4 *Journal of Child Sexual Abuse* 129 (1993), 10, 122
Wang, C., and Daro, D. *Current Trends in Child Abuse Reporting and Fatalities: The Results of the 1996 Annual Fifty State Survey* (National Committee to Prevent Child Abuse 1997), 2, 48
Ward, E., *Father-Daughter Rape* (1985), 104
Warren and Startwood, "Developmental Issues in Flashbulb Memory Research: Children Recall the Challenger Event," in *Affect and Accuracy in Recall: The Problem of Flashbulb Memories* (E. Winograd and U. Neisser, eds.) (in press), 306
Warren, A., and Lane, P., "Effects of Timing and Type of Questioning on Eyewitness Accuracy and Suggestibility, in Memory and Testimony," in *The Child Witness* 24 (M. Zaragoza, J. Graham, C. Hall, R. Hirschmand, and Y. Ben-Porath, eds. 1995), 309
Warren, A., Hulse-Trotter, K., and Tubbs, E., "Inducing Resistance to Suggestibility in Children," 15 *Law and Human Behavior* 273 (1991), 309
Watkins, J., "Dealing with the Problem of 'False Memory' in Clinic and Court," 21 *Journal of Psychiatry and Law* 297 (1993), 96, 121, 315
Wattenberg, E., "In a Different Light: A Feminist Perspective on the Role of Mothers in Father-Daughter Incest," 64/3 *Child Welfare* 203, 204 (1985), 256
Weiner, J., "'And the Wisdom to Know the Difference': Confidentiality versus Privilege in the Self-Help Setting," 144 *University of Pennsylvania Law Review* 243 (1995), 259
Weinstock, R., Leong, G., and Silva, J., "Confidentiality and Privilege," 1 *Review of Clinical Psychiatry and Law* 83 (1990), 259
Wells, G., and Loftus, E., "Commentary: Is the Child Fabricating? Reactions to a New Assessment Technique," in *Suggestibility of Children's Recollections* 168 (J. Doris, ed. 1991), 114
Wells, R., McCann, J., Adams, J., Voris, J., and Ensign, J., "Emotional, Behavioral, and Physical Symptoms Reported by Parents of Sexually Abused, Nonabused, and Allegedly Abused Prepubescent Females," 19/2 *Child Abuse and Neglect* 155 (1995), 11

Werber, J., and Perlmutter, M., "Development of Visual Memory in Infants," in *Advances in Child Development and Behavior* (H. Reese and L. Lipsett, eds. 1979) (vol. 14, p. 1), 300

Widom, C., and Kuhns, J., "Childhood Victimization and Subsequent Risk for Promiscuity, Prostitution, and Teenage Pregnancy: A Prospective Study," 86/11 *American Journal of Public Health* 1607 (1996), 10, 11

Widom, C., and Morris, S., "Accuracy of Adult Recollections of Childhood Victimization: Part 2: Childhood Sexual Abuse," 9 *Psychological Assessment* 34 (1997), 122

Wigmore, H., *Evidence in Trials at Common Law* (Chadborne rev. 1978), 334

Williams, L., "Adult Memories of Childhood Abuse: Preliminary Findings from a Longitudinal Study," 5/3 *The Advisor* 19 (Summer 1992), 122, 123, 308

Williams, L., "Recovered Memories of Abuse in Women with Documented Child Sexual Victimization Histories," 8 *Journal of Traumatic Stress* 649 (1995), 123

Wilson, R., "Psychophysiological Signs of Faking in the Phallometric Test," 10/2 *Sexual Abuse: A Journal of Research and Treatment* 113 (1998), 207

Wolf, F., *Twelve Female Sexual Offenders* (1985), 7

Wolfe, D., *et al.*, "Factors Associated with the Development of Posttraumatic Stress Disorder among Child Victims of Sexual Abuse," 18/1 *Child Abuse and Neglect* 37 (1994), 10

Wolfe, D., *et al.*, "The Importance of Adjudication in the Treatment of Child Abusers: Some Preliminary Findings," 4/1 *Child Abuse and Neglect* 127 (1980), 16

Wolfe, D., Sas, L., and Wekerke, C., "Factors Associated with the Development of Posttraumatic Stress Disorder Among Child Victims of Sexual Abuse," 18/1 *Child Abuse and Neglect* 37 (1994), 103

Woodling, B., "The Use of the Colposcope in the Diagnosis of Sexual Abuse in the Pediatric Age Group," 10 *Child Abuse and Neglect* 111 (1986), 205

Wright, C., and Gold, V., *Federal Practice and Procedure: Evidence* (1990), 334

Wyatt, G., and Mickey, M., "Ameliorating the Effects of Child Sexual Abuse: An Exploratory Study of Support by Parents and Others," 2/4 *Journal of Interpersonal Violence* 403 (1987), 254

Wynkoop, T., Capps, S., and Priest, B., "Incidence and Prevalence of Child Sexual Abuse: A Critical Review of Data Collection Procedures," 4/2 *Journal of Child Sexual Abuse* 49 (1995), 2

Index